STRANGERS WITHIN THE REALM

Edited by Bernard Bailyn and Philip D. Morgan

Strangers within the Realm

Cultural Margins of the First British Empire

Published for The Institute of Early American History and Culture, Williamsburg, Virginia, by The University of North Carolina Press, Chapel Hill and London

The Institute of Early American History and Culture
is sponsored jointly by the College of William and Mary
and the Colonial Williamsburg Foundation.

Library of Congress Cataloging-in-Publication Data

Strangers within the realm / cultural margins of the first British Empire / edited by Bernard Bailyn and Philip D. Morgan.
p. cm.
Includes index.
ISBN 0-8078-1952-2 (cloth, alk. paper).—ISBN 0-8078-4311-3 (paper, alk. paper)
1. Great Britain—Colonies—History—18th century. 2. Great Britain—Colonies—History—17th century. 3. United States—History—Colonial period, ca. 1600–1775. 4. Great Britain—Colonies—America. I. Bailyn, Bernard. II. Morgan, Philip D., 1949– . III. Institute of Early American History and Culture (Williamsburg, Va.)
DA16.S92 1991
941.06—dc20 90-40278
CIP

The paper in this book meets the guidelines for permanence and durability of the Committee on Production Guidelines for Book Longevity of the Council on Library Resources.

This volume received indirect support from an unrestricted book publications grant awarded to the Institute by the L. J. Skaggs and Mary C. Skaggs Foundation of Oakland, California.

98 97 96 95 94 6 5 4 3 2

To the memory of Stephen Botein

ACKNOWLEDGMENTS

The genesis of this volume can be traced to a conference, "The Social World of Britain and America, 1600–1820: A Comparison from the Perspective of Social History," held in Williamsburg, Virginia, in September 1985 and sponsored by the Institute of Early American History and Culture, together with the Colonial Williamsburg Foundation and the Institute of Historical Research in England. Stephen Botein, then the visiting Editor of Publications at the Institute, attended the conference, saw the promise of one of its sessions, and suggested that several of the papers serve as the basis for a larger volume of essays. He began the project himself, outlined the topics, suggested the title of the prospective volume, and sent out the first invitations to other contributors. After Stephen Botein's death in 1986 the present editors carried the work forward, and in editing the essays they have tried to develop his ideas fully. The responsibility for the volume, however, including the introductory essay, remains theirs, though they hope Botein would have been pleased with the result.

It is a pleasure to thank Thad W. Tate, director of the Institute when the original conference was held, and Peter A. Clark, a major planner of the conference, for their efforts in organizing that event. The editors are also grateful to the Exxon Educational Foundation, the National Endowment for the Humanities, the Colonial Williamsburg Foundation, the British Academy, and the British Council for funding the conference.

CONTENTS

STRANGERS WITHIN THE REALM

INTRODUCTION

The broad context of this book is the expansion of the European world outward into a number of alien peripheries, or marchlands. There, complex societies emerged, shaped by the engagement of the controlling people with the natives or with other peoples who were imported or who freely migrated to these developing worlds. Marginal with respect to the conquering power, these peripheral worlds acquired distinctive and permanent characteristics, and they eventually formed core worlds of their own that, in many cases, generated margins even more complex than they themselves had been.

This dialectical process, which has shaped much of the modern world, is studied here with respect to the early, preindustrial history of England (and then Britain) as a modern imperial power. The essays concentrate on how the central, or hearth, culture of southeastern England interacted with other cultures, other peoples, on a succession of marchlands—Scotland, Ireland, North America, and the Caribbean. No singular "British" system emerged from this global process. There were many systems, linked to each other indirectly, through a common center of power and an extraordinarily pervasive language / culture, centered in southeastern England, which radiated out into the distant corners of the globe.

Aspects of this process have been explored by others. One task, then, is to situate our study within a broader historiographical context. It is emphatically not our intention to be comprehensive, but rather to identify, in selective fashion, certain key developments; and, in this, we hope to break new ground. But these findings are necessarily incomplete and tentative, and they lead us to explore aspirations and to identify promising lines of further research as well.

I

Just over a century ago Sir John Seeley, then Regius Professor of Modern History at the University of Cambridge, published two courses of lectures, entitled *The Expansion of England*. Seeley is not much read nowadays—and, no doubt, for good reasons. He was too much the public propagandist and pedagogue, seeing the present implicit in the past and summoning history to provide lessons and morals for the future. His certitude that England had an imperial destiny, that empire was the "pregnant" essence of

Thanks are due the other contributors of this volume for their many constructive comments.

her history, now raises a wry smile. His view of empire as one of white settlement and his supporting statements—such as, "The English Empire was throughout of civilised blood, except so far as it had a slave population"—leave a bad taste in the mouth. Although Seeley wished to see colonies viewed less as exploitable possessions and more as outposts of the parent state and, as such, part of one organic unit that he termed a "vast English nation," he ignored the legitimate independent interests of the colonists themselves. Nevertheless, for all his blinkers and myopia, Seeley had a keen eye for high drama. He would not overlook the grandeur of eighteenth-century England by focusing on the "petty domestic occurrences, parliamentary quarrels, party intrigue, and court-gossip" that so preoccupied his fellow historians. Rather, for him, "the extension of the English name into other countries of the globe" and "the foundation of Greater Britain" represented a "mighty phenomenon." Indeed, this was "the great fact of modern English history." The prolonged wars of the eighteenth century were, in Seeley's view, less European conflicts than struggles for colonial possessions, and Hanoverian England was less a European insular state than an American and Asiatic empire.[1]

Seeley's vision of England's imperial destiny helped pioneer the study of imperial history. In the early twentieth century this branch of history came of age, with the establishment of three chairs in that subject at English universities and the inauguration of the *Cambridge History of the British Empire*. Notable practitioners included Vincent T. Harlow, J. Holland Rose, Arthur P. Newton, and James A. Williamson, the last of whom published an influential synthesis, *A Short History of British Expansion*, which went into four editions. Their version of imperial history, like Seeley's, was decidedly Anglocentric. Their concerns were aptly phrased in many of the chapter headings of the first volume of the *Cambridge History*, published in 1929: "National Security and Expansion" or "Sea Power and Expansion," indicating an interest in the forces behind imperial growth; "England and the Opening of the Atlantic" or "The Spirit of Adventure," indicating an interest in the exploratory voyages; "Rivalry for Colonial Power" or "International Relations in the Colonial Sphere," indicating an interest in the diplomacy of empire; and "The Acts of Trade" or "The Government of Empire," indicating an interest in the administrative organization of empire.[2]

1. J. R. Seeley, *The Expansion of England: Two Courses of Lectures* (London, 1883), 9–10, 15, 30, 61, 161. For assessments of Seeley, see Peter Burroughs, "John Robert Seeley and British Imperial History," *Journal of Imperial and Commonwealth History*, I (1973), 191–211; P.B.M. Blaas, *Continuity and Anachronism: Parliamentary and Constitutional Development in Whig Historiography and in the Anti-Whig Reaction between 1890 and 1930* (The Hague, 1978), 36–40; and Deborah Wormell, *Sir John Seeley and the Uses of History* (Cambridge, 1980). Seeley's book did not go out of print until 1956, the year of the Suez War.

2. J. Holland Rose, A. P. Newton, and E. A. Benians, eds., *The Old Empire from*

These last two chapters were, in fact, written by an American, Charles McLean Andrews, the most distinguished member of a generation of North American scholars who gave a new impetus and direction to the writing of their country's colonial history. The standard refrain became that, to understand early America, one first needed to understand the whole field of British colonial endeavor. "The focus of interest," wrote George Louis Beer, "is . . . the British Empire, and not the rise of the American nation." Or, to quote Andrews: "The years from 1607 to 1783 were colonial before they were American or national," and "Colonial history considered without a knowledge of the English outlook and apart from the long and continuous relationship of the colonies to the mother country loses its wider and deeper significance." In many ways, Lawrence Henry Gipson's fifteen-volume *British Empire before the American Revolution* represents the culmination of this approach to American history. Although broadly based in geographical terms, this school's subject matter tended to focus rather narrowly on either the commercial or the administrative dimensions of empire. As Andrews put it, "As for the writing of colonial history, I cannot but feel the first subject to be considered must be largely institutional in character, and that before going on to discuss other aspects of the colonial story, both writer and reader should have an adequate knowledge of the structural framework within which the colonists lived and had their being." Andrews and others writing under his shadow laid bare the skeleton, the structural framework of colonial life, but failed to explore its lifeblood, its social, economic, intellectual, and cultural dimensions.[3]

As historians turned to the noninstitutional dimensions of colonial American life particularly from the 1950s onward, they tended to view them from

---

the Beginnings to 1783 (Cambridge, 1929), vol. I of *The Cambridge History of the British Empire*; James A. Williamson, *A Short History of British Expansion* (London, 1922) (later editions in 1930, 1943, and 1953 saw an enlargement to 2 vols.); David Fieldhouse, "Can Humpty-Dumpty Be Put Together Again? Imperial History in the 1980s," *Jour. Imp. and Comm. Hist.*, XII (1984), 9–23, esp. 9–12.

3. George Louis Beer, *British Colonial Policy, 1754–1765* (New York, 1907), v; Charles M. Andrews, *The Colonial Background of the American Revolution: Four Essays in American Colonial History* (New Haven, Conn., 1924), ix; Andrews, "On the Writing of Colonial History," *William and Mary Quarterly*, 3d Ser., I (1944), 29, 30; Lawrence Henry Gipson, *The British Empire before the American Revolution . . .*, 15 vols. (New York, 1936–1970). See also Wesley Frank Craven, "Historical Study of the British Empire," *Journal of Modern History*, VI (1934), 40–69, esp. 61–62; Lawrence Henry Gipson, "The Imperial Approach to Early American History," in Ray Allen Billington, ed., *The Reinterpretation of Early American History: Essays in Honor of John Edwin Pomfret* (San Marino, Calif., 1966), 185–199; and Richard R. Johnson, "Charles McLean Andrews and the Invention of American Colonial History," *WMQ*, 3d Ser., XLIII (1986), 519–541. Johnson's essay is particularly fine for noting the ways in which Andrews can be differentiated from Beer and Gipson in his approach to American colonial history.

within rather than from without, internally rather than externally. There were distinct gains in this shift of scholarly attention. For one thing, institutionally determined categorizations of colonies gave way to the search for coherent regional units. For another, historians were now able to concentrate on local studies in order to recover the full texture of colonial life. Finally, in a corrective to the view that colonies ought always to be viewed from the vantage point of the mother country, many postwar studies stressed the distinctiveness or exceptionalism of early American life. One such feature that began to receive increasing recognition was the multiethnic and multiracial character of colonial American societies. The presence of native Americans, black slavery, and, to a lesser extent, white ethnic minorities has gradually been seen as central to the early American experience in ways that the imperial school had failed to appreciate. And it gradually dawned on those who wished to write of this mingling and clashing of diverse groups and cultures that this story had in large part to be traced backward to Africa, to continental Europe, and even to Asia, thereby enlarging rather than jettisoning the Atlantic perspective of the imperial school.[4]

Still, this phase of American historiography, however fruitful, was in many ways parochial, though not more so than the historiography of England after the Second World War. The vast proliferation of exciting research in early modern English history in the postwar era constituted a golden age of sophisticated literature, but it became increasingly "self-absorbed and self-enclosed." Thus in the historiography of the English Revolution grand interpretations have given way to an attitude best summed up by J. S. Morrill as: "In scholarship as in everything else, if we look after the pennies, the pounds will look after themselves." Part of the reason for this introspection would seem to reside in the extreme specialization and commitment to scholarly technique in which English historians, among others, have gloried. Furthermore, the hiving off of imperial history and the rise of various nationalist histories—whether in the Celtic fringe or further afield—encouraged historians of Little England to ignore their country's expansive past. Certainly the

4. To document all the historiographic trends mentioned in this paragraph is impossible here; and, in any case, Johnson, "Charles McLean Andrews," *WMQ*, 3d Ser., XLIII (1986), 533–534, has already touched upon some of them. See also Jack P. Greene and J. R. Pole, "Reconstructing British-American Colonial History: An Introduction," in Greene and Pole, eds., *Colonial British America: Essays in the New History of the Early Modern Era* (Baltimore, 1984), 1–17. For review essays that note the importance of the multiracial and multiethnic character of early America, see James Axtell, "The Ethnohistory of Early America: A Review Essay," *WMQ*, 3d Ser., XXXV (1978), 110–144; Peter H. Wood, " 'I Did the Best I Could for My Day': The Study of Early Black History during the Second Reconstruction, 1960 to 1976," *WMQ*, 3d Ser., XXXV (1978), 185–225; T. H. Breen, "Creative Adaptations: Peoples and Cultures," in Greene and Pole, eds., *Colonial British America*, 195–232; and James H. Merrell, "Some Thoughts on Colonial Historians and American Indians," *WMQ*, 3d Ser., XLVI (1989), 94–119.

proliferation of single volumes and whole series aimed at telling the history of England rarely mention, even in passing, English contacts with other peoples. Most glaring is the omission of the Anglo-Celtic story, which in the case of the English Revolution is particularly ironic, for this event can be understood only in an archipelagic context as the War of the Three Kingdoms. But a recent history of England covering the years 1550–1760 states: "My subject is England. The Scots, Irish and Welsh have derived a number of disadvantages and benefits from their proximity to the English, but I am confident that any attempt on my part to write their history would be numbered with the former [that is, a disadvantage]. Their cultures were, and in many ways still are, separate, and so should their history be." The retreat from empire—"Now that England's historical destiny has whimpered to its end," to quote Christopher Hill—has no doubt played a central role in this increasingly isolationist stance. In the early 1970s J. G. A. Pocock discerned a willingness among the English "to declare that neither empire nor commonwealth ever meant much in their consciousness, and that they were at heart Europeans all the time." Pocock's relish in pointing out the absurdity of this last claim would have warmed Seeley's heart. Anthony Low's *Contraction of England* is just one indication of how events have come full circle.[5]

Pocock deserves more than incidental mention, because he has been a

5. David Cannadine, "The State of British History," *Times Literary Supplement*, Oct. 10, 1986, 1139–1140, which was then expanded as "British History: Past, Present—and Future?" *Past and Present*, no. 116 (August 1987), 169–191. (Cannadine can himself be criticized, because he usually interprets the "British" in his title to mean nothing more than "English." See, in particular, the contribution of Neil Evans to "British History: Past, Present—and Future?" *Past and Present*, no. 119 [May 1988], 171–203.) J. S. Morrill, "Proceeding Moderately," *TLS*, Oct. 24, 1980, 1196; J. C. Beckett, *The Making of Modern Ireland, 1603–1923* (New York, 1966), 82; J. A. Sharpe, *Early Modern England: A Social History, 1550–1760* (London, 1987), ix; Christopher Hill, *The Experience of Defeat: Milton and Some Contemporaries* (London, 1984), 328; J.G.A. Pocock, "British History: A Plea for a New Subject," *Jour. Mod. Hist.*, XLVII (1975), 602; and D. A. Low, *The Contraction of England* (Cambridge, 1985), which is the inaugural lecture of the Commonwealth History Professor at Cambridge University. Ironically, many English historians are now emphasizing the similarities between England and Europe in the 17th and 18th centuries—see, for instance, J.C.D. Clark, *English Society, 1688–1832: Ideology, Social Structure, and Political Practice during the Ancien Regime* (Cambridge, 1985). Some of the modern series devoted to English history include the Oxford History of England, Pelican History of England, New History of England, Hutchinson Social History of England, and Pelican Social History of Britain (the volumes by Joyce Youings and Roy Porter in this last series are about England, not Britain). It is also true, of course, that Celtic nationalism, among other forces, has encouraged Welsh, Scottish, and Irish historians to ignore the influence of England upon their respective pasts. For recent attempts to overcome this glaring omission in the Scottish case, see William Ferguson, *Scotland's Relations with England: A Survey to 1707* (Edinburgh, 1977); and Roger A. Mason, ed., *Scotland and England, 1286–1815* (Edinburgh, 1987).

significant and, until recently, a rather solitary voice calling for the investigation of "British history." He has pointed out the paucity of works that encompass the shared histories of the peoples living in the Atlantic archipelago lying off the northwestern coasts of Europe and of those that they spawned in various colonies of settlement. Pocock does not deny the importance "of writing the history of the English as that of a self-contained people, who exist in the relations between themselves and the defining structures of their society." But he points out that the history of the English might with "equal validity" be written "as that of an expanding and imperial people, who exist in relations between themselves and other peoples, whom they encounter and whom (particularly in the case of 'British history') they also engender." To write a history of the interaction of several peoples, of "a diversity of several interacting and varyingly autonomous cultures," Pocock well understands, will prove an exceedingly complicated task. It will be difficult to write such a history in other than English terms, for "the conqueror, after all, sets the rules of the game," yet "in no case has the process of anglicisation been [a] simple one-way imperial success story." This new history must, therefore, be pluralist, multicultural, and above all concerned with "an expanding zone of cultural conflict and creation."[6]

It was left to a freelance historian who, like Pocock, is a native of the periphery, to write the most ambitious account of Greater British history to date. As Angus Calder explained in *Revolutionary Empire*, he aimed to "put together the diverse 'stories' of the areas overrun and governed by English-speakers (together with many Gaels and not a few Welsh-speakers)." "These

6. The essay by Pocock mentioned in the preceding note ("British History: A Plea for a New Subject") was first published in the *New Zealand Journal of History*, VIII (1974), 3–21, and was then reprinted in *Jour. Mod. Hist.*, XLVII (1975), 601–621, with comments by A.J.P. Taylor, Gordon Donaldson, Michael Hechter, and a reply by the author, 622–628. See also by Pocock: "1776: The Revolution against Parliament," in Pocock, *Three British Revolutions: 1641, 1688, 1776* (Princeton, N.J., 1980), 265–288; "The Limits and Divisions of British History: In Search of the Unknown Subject," *American Historical Review*, LXXXVII (1982), 311–336; and *Virtue, Commerce, and History: Essays on Political Thought and History, Chiefly in the Eighteenth Century* (New York, 1985). There are signs that Pocock's urgings are having some effect, particularly in the archipelagic context. See Keith Robbins, "Core and Periphery in Modern British History," British Academy, *Proceedings*, LXX (1984), 275–297; Richard S. Tompson, *The Atlantic Archipelago: A Political History of the British Isles* (Lewiston, N.Y., 1986); R. R. Davies, *The British Isles, 1100–1500: Comparisons, Contrasts, Connections* (Edinburgh, 1988); Steven Ellis, "'Not Mere English': The British Perspective, 1400–1650," *History Today*, XXXVIII (1988), 41–48; J.C.D. Clark, "English History's Forgotten Context: Scotland, Ireland, Wales," *Historical Journal*, XXXII (1989), 211–228; and Hugh Kearney, *The British Isles: A History of Four Nations* (Cambridge, 1989). Also relevant is the 1980s London Weekend Television channel 4 series, "The Making of Britain," and accompanying books, in particular, Lesley M. Smith, *The Making of Britain: The Age of Expansion* (London, 1986).

stories," he wrote, "continually intersect, interact, determine each other, under conditions created or exposed by the 'expansion' of Europe from the fifteenth century onwards." He saw his role as the uncovering of these "links, interactions, dialectics" and interweaving them into a single, large-scale narrative. In this he was not always successful. Many of his individual stories seem to stand alone, disconnected from the whole; too often stories are told for their own sake. Analysis and explanation are generally wanting. Nevertheless, Calder has labored on a heroic scale, incorporating a vast amount of material and taking the story from England, to Wales, Scotland, and Ireland, then out into the Atlantic to encompass North America, the West Indies, and Africa, and then further still to Asia. The book is a treasury of information, but the author provides too few interpretative keys to unlock its riches.[7]

Meanwhile, in America, ambitious attempts to explore a Greater British history, or subsume it within an even larger story, seemed to be devolving to social scientists, interested primarily in the relationship of centers and peripheries. Thus in the mid-1970s Michael Hechter published a study of the incorporation of the Celtic fringe into England, in which he viewed the process as imperial rather than as national. The metropolitan Southeast systematically attacked, dominated, and imposed its values on its Celtic periphery by a process of "internal colonialism." At about the same time as Hechter, Immanuel Wallerstein published the first volume of *The Modern World-System*, which claimed that, from as early as the sixteenth century, Europe had an identifiable core that expanded outward to create a capitalist world economy. Located in the Low Countries, northern France, and England, the core was characterized by strong state machineries and the rise of free wage labor in agriculture and manufacture. It was surrounded by a semiperiphery, less developed and frequently marked by sharecropping forms of agriculture. Beyond that lay the periphery doomed to be poor, producing primary goods for the core by a system of forced labor or slavery, and best evident in Eastern Europe and the plantations of the New World.[8]

Admirable for their sweep and breadth, both Hechter's and Wallerstein's analyses are open to a variety of criticisms. Perhaps the most pertinent for our purposes is the insensitivity to the variations possible in the so-called peripheries or semiperipheries. Thus, the anglicization of the Celtic peripher-

7. Angus Calder, *Revolutionary Empire: The Rise of the English-speaking Empires from the Fifteenth Century to the 1780s* (London, 1981), xviii. This book is about 900 pages long, one indication of its ambitiousness.

8. Michael Hechter, *Internal Colonialism: The Celtic Fringe in British National Development, 1536–1966* (Berkeley, Calif., 1975); Immanuel Wallerstein, *The Modern World-System: Capitalist Agriculture and the Origins of the European World-Economy in the Sixteenth Century* (New York, 1974), and *The Modern World-System*, II, *Mercantilism and the Consolidation of the European World-Economy, 1600–1750* (New York, 1980).

ies (certainly *not* periphery, for differences between Scotland, Ireland, and Wales were immense) was much less complete and much less determined by state action than Hechter allows, and the peripheries and semiperipheries of northwestern Europe were not necessarily consigned to dependency by an omnipotent world-system machine, as Wallerstein tends to assume.[9]

But, recently, early American historians have shown signs that social scientists will not have it all their own way. There has been a resurgence of interest in the Atlantic dimensions of American colonization, evident at many levels—village life, economic development, migration, consumer behavior, interest groups, communications, ethnicity, ideological discourse, religion, popular culture, radicalism, and social change generally. Four works or projects, each broad in conception though exploring quite different subjects, merit particular mention. Stephen Saunders Webb sees England's rulers from the middle of the seventeenth century seeking to impose a coherent policy of "garrison government" and "militant imperialism" upon various outlying provinces, including both Celtic countries and New World colonies. Bernard Bailyn aims to "bring together all the major aspects of life in the American colonies" and place them "within the broadest possible context of Western history," by telling the story of the recruitment, settlement patterns, and developing character of the American population in the preindustrial era. To do so is to enlarge "the perspective of early American history to the broadest possible range," extending "from the jagged, windswept Butt of Lewis on the far northern tip of the Outer Hebrides to the Lunda kingdom deep in equatorial Africa, from Prussia south to the Dan-

9. For criticism of Hechter's work from the perspective of Welsh history, see Philip Jenkins, *The Making of a Ruling Class: The Glamorgan Gentry, 1640–1790* (Cambridge, 1983), esp. 214; and, more generally, E. Page, *Michael Hechter's Internal Colonial Thesis: Some Theoretical and Methodological Problems*, University of Strathclyde Center for the Study of Public Policy, Studies in Public Policy, no. 9 (Glasgow, 1977). There are many critiques of Wallerstein's work, but three written from the perspective of the periphery or semiperiphery are particularly insightful: Sidney W. Mintz, "The So-Called World-System: Local Initiative and Local Response," *Dialectical Anthropology*, II (1977), 253–270; T. C. Smout, "Scotland and England: Is Dependency a Symptom or a Cause of Underdevelopment?" with Wallerstein's comment, *Review*, III (1979–1980), 601–640 (see also Christopher Smout, "Centre and Periphery in History: With Some Thoughts on Scotland as a Case Study," *Journal of Common Market Studies*, XVIII [1979–1980], 256–271); and Steve J. Stern, "Feudalism, Capitalism, and the World-System in the Perspective of Latin America and the Caribbean," with Wallerstein's comments and author's reply, *AHR*, XCIII (1988), 829–897. For other work on centers and peripheries, the interested reader might turn to Edward Shils, "Centre and Periphery," in *The Logic of Personal Knowledge: Essays Presented to Michael Polanyi*... (London, 1961), 117–130; D. Sears, B. Schaffer, and M.-L. Kiljunen, eds., *Under-Developed Europe: Studies in Core-Periphery Relations* (Hassocks, 1979); and Jean Gottmann, ed., *Centre and Periphery: Spatial Variation in Politics* (Beverly Hills, Calif., 1980).

ube, and from the Elbe to the Mississippi." Third, Jack P. Greene's *Pursuits of Happiness* seeks, among other goals, to describe a "generalized process of social formation" in each of the major regions of settlement in the early modern British Empire, based on an understanding of the dominant impulses coursing through English society. Finally, David Hackett Fischer, in a provocative and wide-ranging work, argues that British North America is best understood as the product of four competing regional cultures, all originating in Britain. According to Fischer, "The legacy of four British folkways in early America remains the most powerful determinant of a voluntary society in the United States today."[10]

If this betokens a new form of imperial history, it will be very different from that envisaged by Seeley or Andrews. Its contours have been anticipated by imperial historians and historians of colonial America alike. Rather than a narrow metrocentric approach, imperial history must, according to David Fieldhouse, focus upon the area of interaction among the component parts of imperial systems. Instead of a single, coherent outward thrust by the English, the process should be seen as vastly more complicated, much more double-ended, with the colonies playing as dynamic a role as the metropolis. Similarly, T. H. Breen has suggested that "the new imperial history will focus on the movement of peoples and the clash of cultures, on common folk rather than on colonial administrators, on processes rather than on institutions, on aspects of daily life that one would not regard as narrowly political. It will be an integrated story, neither American nor English, but an investiga-

10. Steven Saunders Webb, *The Governors-General: The English Army and the Definition of the Empire, 1569–1681* (Chapel Hill, N.C., 1979); and Webb, *1676: The End of American Independence* (New York, 1984); but see Richard R. Johnson, "The Imperial Webb: The Thesis of Garrison Government in Early America Considered," *WMQ*, 3d Ser., XLIII (1986), 408–430; and Webb, "The Data and Theory of Restoration Empire," *WMQ*, 3d Ser., XLIII (1986), 431–459; Bernard Bailyn, *The Peopling of British North America: An Introduction* (New York, 1986); and Bailyn, *Voyagers to the West: A Passage in the Peopling of America on the Eve of the Revolution* (New York, 1986); Jack P. Greene, *Pursuits of Happiness: The Social Development of Early Modern British Colonies and the Formation of American Culture* (Chapel Hill, N.C., 1988); David Hackett Fischer, *Albion's Seed: Four British Folkways in America* (New York, 1989), esp. 7. For modern scholarship that adopts an Atlantic perspective (too extensive to cite by titles), see the diverse writings of David Grayson Allen (village life); John J. McCusker and Russell R. Menard (economic development); David Cressy, Roger Ekirch, and James P. P. Horn (migration); T. H. Breen (consumer society); Alison Gilbert Olson (interest groups); Ian K. Steele (communications); Jon Butler and Ned Landsman (ethnicity); Bernard Bailyn and J.G.A. Pocock (ideology); Marilyn Westerkamp (religion); Jean-Christophe Agnew (popular culture); the contributors to a volume edited by Margaret Jacob and James Jacob (*The Origins of Anglo-American Radicalism* [London, 1984]) (radicalism); and John Murrin (social change). See also Johnson, "Charles McLean Andrews," *WMQ*, 3d Ser., XLIII (1986), 535–541.

tion of the many links that connected men and women living on both sides of the Atlantic Ocean."[11]

II

There are precursors and clarion calls, then, for the sort of venture upon which we have embarked. Nevertheless, in large part our enterprise is novel. A multicultural, pluralist approach to British history that Pocock has advocated is hardly in sight; a comprehensive and subtle analysis of the relations of European core to Old World and New World peripheries that will withstand the criticisms of specialists is not in view; the story of English emigration and transatlantic immigration is under way, but still unfinished. Given the pioneering nature of our undertaking, it is bound to be partial, tentative, and incomplete. Much is left out.

The omission of an essay devoted solely to England, focusing on the sources of English expansion and linkages between internal and external developments, may seem strange. Part of the explanation lies in the desire to avoid the narrowly metrocentric approach so evident in the older imperial history, although a reasonable retort might be that peripheries without a center are equally deficient. A further, more obvious justification is that the history of England has been well, though contentiously, told by many hands. Another attempt at synthesis might seem unnecessary. But, in fact, the more realistic problem is the reverse: so much information is now available about early modern England, and the interpretations are so conflicting, that the roots of English expansion and the linkages between metropolis and dependencies need much more extensive treatment than is possible here. The possibilities are richly evident in Kenneth R. Andrews's reinterpretation of the origins of the British Empire, in which he argues that maritime enterprise, moving forward in spurts and with many sluggish intervals, yet became of central importance to the development of England itself between 1480 and 1630. The critical backers of England's overseas activities, Andrews argues, were the merchant communities of London, the West Country, and lesser ports; and changes in their economic circumstances largely determined the surges and slumps in England's extra-European enterprise. In short, developments at home were closely linked with activities abroad. As England's empire grew from its sickly infancy, as outlined by Andrews, into

11. Fieldhouse, "Can Humpty-Dumpty Be Put Together Again?" *Jour. Imp. and Comm. Hist.*, XII (1984), 10, 16, 19, 22; T. H. Breen, "An Empire of Goods: The Anglicization of Colonial America, 1690–1776," *Journal of British Studies*, XXV (1986), 473.

sturdy maturity during the seventeenth and eighteenth centuries, other linkages will need to be explored.[12]

For instance, the precocious national unity of England and the rise of a more assertive national sentiment could profitably be connected to developments in the dependencies. Although there were important regional contrasts—between Southeast and Northwest, coast and interior, upland and lowland—the nation was highly integrated by continental standards and became more so during the seventeenth and eighteenth centuries. It possessed a strong royal authority, a powerful state apparatus based on the involvement of local ruling elites, a uniform legal system, a centralized economy, and one dominant language (Cornish became extinct in the eighteenth century). The late seventeenth and the eighteenth centuries saw further consolidation and what John Brewer terms "the fiscal-military state." Moreover, its capital was the realm's nerve center, acting as the powerhouse of politics, center of commerce and finance, and arbiter of fashion. London dominated England in ways that no other capital in Europe could match. Indeed, at a time when most European cities grew slowly, London's population rose by leaps and bounds. By the end of the seventeenth century, it was the largest city in Europe, and perhaps one adult in six in England had direct experience of metropolitan life. This fact alone, E. A. Wrigley has speculated, "acted as a powerful solvent of the customs, prejudices and modes of action of traditional, rural England." Moreover, in the eighteenth century, general urban growth (outpacing even metropolitan growth), together with a vastly improved transport and communication system, an expanding press network, and an increase in the level of literacy, further eroded localism. In addition, of course, early modern England became a predominantly Protestant country, as did Scotland and Wales. Without this shared religion there would have been little unity against Catholic powers; without the concept of an "elect nation," enjoying God's special favor, national self-consciousness may have taken longer to arise; and without the Protestant Bible, A. G. Dickens notes, "we can hardly imagine . . . English imperial expansion." Just as the development of hostilities between England and Spain was crucial to the broadening of England's maritime horizons in the late sixteenth and seventeenth centuries, so the aggrandizement of England in the eighteenth century can be attributed in large part to Anglo-French rivalry. In fact, as Pocock has pointed out, "each major step in the consolidation of the archi-

12. Kenneth R. Andrews, *Trade, Plunder, and Settlement: Maritime Enterprise and the Genesis of the British Empire, 1480–1630* (Cambridge, 1984). For work that takes up the story in less systematic fashion, see, for example, Derek Massarella, " 'A World Elsewhere': Aspects of the Overseas Expansionist Mood of the 1650s," in Colin Jones *et al.*, eds., *Politics and People in Revolutionary England: Essays in Honor of Ivan Roots* (Oxford, 1986), 141–161.

pelago under a single parliamentary monarchy—1689, 1707, 1745, and 1801—was undertaken in the context of one or other of the wars with France," as, of course, was the assertion of British power overseas.[13]

All of this—but not only this—helped encourage British national sentiment at home. In addition, the role of outsiders in the invention of Great Britain was also powerful. Referring to the so-called Union of Wales with England in 1536–1543, Gwyn A. Williams states, "If the Welsh were admitted as junior partners to the new state, . . . it was as senior partners that they helped create that new and imperial *British* identity by which the state lived." The notion that "Britain" owed its name to Brutus, the Trojan and first king of the Britons, was one to which Welsh intellectuals clung fondly. The expression "British Empire" was coined by a Welsh astrologer, Dr. John Dee, in the late sixteenth century. In succeeding centuries many of the more prominent people preaching the importance of a more developed British national consciousness were Irish or Scottish. Witness James Burgh, Oliver Goldsmith, and Tobias Smollett. Or consider that in 1739 a Scottish poet, James Thompson, wrote "Rule Brittania" and that, in the same century, an Irishman whose father was a Protestant and mother a Catholic, Edmund Burke, became the greatest spokesman of Britain's imperial role. The first Welsh society founded in 1715 was named the Society of Ancient Britons, some Welshmen referred to themselves as "Cambro-Britons," and many Scotsmen described their country as North Britain. When George III claimed to "glory in the name of Briton," he found himself accused of saying that he was a Scot.[14]

Involvement in successive global wars was a primary crucible in forging

13. Keith Thomas, "The United Kingdom," in Raymond Grew, ed., *Crises of Political Development in Europe and the United States* (Princeton, N.J., 1978), 41–97, esp. 44–56, 75; Roy Porter, *English Society in the Eighteenth Century* (Harmondsworth, 1982), 51–57; John Brewer, *The Sinews of Power: War, Money, and the English State, 1688–1783* (London, 1989), 7; E. A. Wrigley, "A Simple Model of London's Importance in Changing English Society and Economy, 1650–1750," *Past and Present*, no. 37 (July 1967), 44–70 (quotation at 50); and, for the broader context, E. Anthony Wrigley, "Urban Growth and Agricultural Change: England and the Continent in the Early Modern Period," *Journal of Interdisciplinary History*, XV (1984–1985), 683–728; A. G. Dickens, *The English Reformation* (London, 1967), 193, 264; Pocock, "The Limits and Divisions of British History," *AHR*, LXXXVII (1982), 329.

14. Gwyn A. Williams, *When Was Wales? A History of the Welsh* (London, 1985), 123–124; A. H. Dodd, in A. J. Roderick, ed., *Wales through the Ages* (Llandybie, 1959–1960), I, 2, 54; and Richard Koebner, *Empire* (Cambridge, 1961), 62, as quoted in Calder, *Revolutionary Empire*, 41; Hugh A. MacDougall, *Racial Myth in English History: Trojans, Teutons, and Anglo-Saxons* (Montreal, 1982), 7–8; Linda Colley, review, *TLS*, Nov. 5, 1987, 1186; Arthur H. Williamson, "Scotland, Antichrist, and the Invention of Great Britain," in John Dwyer *et al.*, eds., *New Perspectives on the Politics and Culture of Early Modern Scotland* (Edinburgh, 1982), 34–58 (quotation at 34).

British national sentiment. It led many colonial Americans to offer "frequent, emotional, intense, and eloquent" expressions of loyalty to Britain. The sundering of this loyalty may also have followed similar courses. Thus J. G. A. Pocock has noted the paradox of how "Ireland became more nationalist and more revolutionary as it was increasingly assimilated to English-derived political and cultural norms." The same process may have occurred in parts of North America for the same reasons: "Revolutionary nationalism is less a means of resisting acculturation than a method of asserting one's own power over the process."[15]

Structural developments at home might also be profitably linked to overseas activity. The late seventeenth and the eighteenth centuries saw England's magnates become, in Roy Porter's words, "the most confident, powerful, and resilient aristocracy in Europe." Their strength and self-assurance stemmed from the amalgam they forged between traditional means of authority and progressive modes of commercial activity. From the late seventeenth century onward, it has been rightly argued, England entered an era of "gentlemanly capitalism." And, in the first phase, which lasted well into the nineteenth century, the dominant element was the landed interest, deriving its power primarily from agriculture, specifically from improvements in productivity and increased rental income. Thanks to the financial revolution of the late seventeenth century, particularly the ever-growing importance of the national debt, the main challenge to aristocratic dominance could have come from moneyed circles, but during the eighteenth century, financial, commercial, and industrial interests in fact normally found it prudent to work *with* the landed powers. This cooperation may well help explain what Ian R. Christie has termed the "extraordinary responsiveness of Parliament to the representations of commercial and industrial pressure groups throughout the eighteenth century." By acquiring the trappings of gentlemen—country estates and titles—some City financiers and their associates, the merchant

15. John M. Murrin, "A Roof without Walls: The Dilemma of American National Identity," in Richard Beeman, Stephen Botein, and Edward C. Carter II, eds., *Beyond Confederation: Origins of the Constitution and American National Identity* (Chapel Hill, N.C., 1987), 338; Pocock, "British History," *Jour. Mod. Hist.*, XLVII (1975), 610. On English or British national sentiment, see Hans Kohn, "The Genesis and Character of English Nationalism," *Journal of the History of Ideas*, I (1940), 69–94; Linda Colley, "The Apotheosis of George III: Loyalty, Royalty, and the British Nation, 1760–1820," *Past and Present*, no. 102 (February 1984), 94–129, and "Whose Nation? Class and National Consciousness in Britain 1750–1830," *Past and Present*, no. 113 (November 1986), 97–117; G. R. Elton, "English National Self-consciousness and the Parliament in the Sixteenth Century," in Otto Dann, ed., *Nationalismus in vorindustrieller Zeit* (Munich, 1986), 73–82; Philip Corrigan and Derek Sayer, *The Great Arch: English State Formation as Cultural Revolution* (Oxford, 1985); Gerald Newman, *The Rise of English Nationalism: A Cultural History, 1740–1830* (New York, 1987); and Raphael Samuel, ed., *Patriotism: The Making and Unmaking of British National Identity*, 3 vols. (London, 1989).

princes of London, gained entry into the gentlemanly hierarchy. The dominance of the landed interest at home is evident abroad, where it was replicated and represented by planters in the West Indies and gentry in the mainland colonies, the two most important growth areas for British trade, as well as gentry in Ireland and landholders in India. It is also evident in the pursuit of imperial policies designed to safeguard landed power—namely low land taxes and high tariffs to service the national debt and to finance patronage—policies also amenable to the City. Imperialism, in short, can be seen as an expression of the structure of British society.[16]

English society may have been oligarchic, but it was not inert and immobile. Although much modern research has qualified the supposed permeability of the English elite—an "open aristocracy," as Harold Perkin once described it—England still seems distinctive by continental standards for the ease with which men of new wealth could enter the parish gentry, if not the more exclusive county elite. There was, for instance, a burgeoning of the professions, a 70 percent increase in their numbers at a time of stagnating population, from 1680 to 1730. As channels of social mobility and sources of material influence, they provided powerful structures making for stability, openness, and growth. More generally, "English society was given a basic fluidity of status," Lawrence and Jeanne C. Fawtier Stone have observed, "by the vigour, wealth, and numerical strength of the 'middling sort,' mostly rural but also urban, whose emergence between 1660 and 1800 is perhaps the most important social feature of the age." Those who exercised influence and acquired wealth by personal merit, rather than hereditary rank, were recruited into the gentry. In England the nouveaux riches, particularly professionals and officeholders, turned gentlemen with relative ease. Conversely, the minimal status privileges enjoyed by the English aristocracy ensured a downward movement of individuals within, and even out of, the group. People moved not only up and down the social scale but also from place to place. Most migration was local, with people moving by short steps rather than by long jumps, but a steady turnover of population appears to be one of the more distinctive features of English society. In short, although the traditional features of early modern England should not be underestimated, its dynamism and fluidity, its movement, its competitive and individualistic impulses seem even more notable. This vitality will need to be connected more closely to overseas expansion: emigration has already been seen as an

16. Porter, *English Society*, 70; P.G.M. Dickson, *The Financial Revolution in England: A Study in the Development of Public Credit, 1688–1756* (London, 1967); Ian R. Christie, *Stress and Stability in Late Eighteenth-Century Britain: Reflections on the British Avoidance of Revolution* (Oxford, 1984), 69. The main thrust of this paragraph is indebted to an important essay by P. J. Cain and A. G. Hopkins, "Gentlemanly Capitalism and British Expansion Overseas, I, The Old Colonial System, 1688–1850," *Economic History Review*, 2d Ser., XXXIX (1986), 501–525.

extension of internal population movements, and colonizing ventures an outgrowth of domestic social mobility.[17]

An excellent survey of the economy of British America acknowledged that, in a sense, the concept of a colonial economy is anachronistic. John Stuart Mill argued long ago that colonial trade in some ways should not be considered external trade at all; rather, it "more resembles the traffic between town and country, and is amenable to the principles of home trade." If so, historians of the periphery may need to look more closely at developments at the center. In the main, the burden of recent investigations has been to move the English economy, particularly in its eighteenth-century incarnation, away from a preindustrial, slow-moving, predominantly agricultural stereotype. Even in the seventeenth century, the market was clearly important to most cultivators, even though the country retained pockets of simple subsistence farming. Commercial activity, including active land, labor, and commodity markets, was widespread. For the eighteenth century, some historians have wondered whether "proto-industrialization" best fits this economy's character. Certainly, England had a strikingly large manufacturing sector by contemporary European standards. Moreover, an unusually large proportion of English trade crossed national boundaries. England had shifted from being an importer of manufactured goods and an exporter of unprocessed and semiprocessed goods to being an importer chiefly of raw materials and an exporter of colonially produced raw materials and domestic manufactures. Standards of material comfort and prosperity began to rise to a degree that was wholly without precedent. The society became more comfort- and amenity-conscious, more cultivated and commercialized, than at any pre-

17. On the elite, see Harold Perkin, *The Origins of Modern English Society, 1780–1880* (London, 1969), 17; but now revised by J. K. Powis, *Aristocracy* (Oxford, 1984); M. L. Bush, *The English Aristocracy: A Comparative Synthesis* (Manchester, 1984); John Cannon, *Aristocratic Century: The Peerage of Eighteenth-Century England* (Cambridge, 1984); Lawrence Stone and Jeanne C. Fawtier Stone, *An Open Elite? England, 1540–1880* (Oxford, 1984) (quotation at 408); and J. V. Beckett, *The Aristocracy in England, 1660–1914* (Oxford, 1986). For a perceptive sketch of this aristocratic world, see David Cecil, *Melbourne* (London, 1939), 15–25. On the professions, see Geoffrey Holmes, *Augustan England: Professions, State and Society, 1680–1730* (London, 1982). On the society in general, see Keith Wrightson, *English Society, 1580–1680* (London, 1982); Alan Macfarlane, *The Origins of English Individualism: The Family, Property, and Social Transition* (New York, 1978); and Porter, *English Society*. A number of review essays are useful in keeping abreast of the ferment that is particularly evident in studies of 18th-century England: Frank O'Gorman, "The Recent Historiography of the Hanoverian Regime," *Hist. Jour.*, XXIX (1986), 1005–1020; special issue, entitled *Re-Viewing the Eighteenth Century*, of *Jour. Brit. Stud.*, XXV, no. 4 (October 1986); and Joanna Innes, "Jonathan Clark, Social History, and England's 'Ancien Regime,'" *Past and Present*, no. 115 (May 1987), 165–200. On emigration as an extension of internal population movements, see Bailyn, *Peopling of British North America*, 20–43; and on the importance of domestic social mobility, see Greene, *Pursuits of Happiness*, 30–52.

vious stage. The role of the peripheries in these developments and the impact upon them of these developments require much further elucidation.[18]

Finally, another linkage that might be explored brings us closest to the concerns of our essayists. It has been pointed out that "the British are clearly among the most ethnically composite of the Europeans." English society has always been mixed and has always experienced infusions of outsiders. Indeed, as V. G. Kiernan has noted, "the fact that England was fast evolving into a nation [in the sixteenth and seventeenth centuries] enabled it to assimilate new arrivals, generation by generation." These outsiders were never numerous (although 100,000 Huguenots were said to have immigrated in one decade in the late seventeenth century), but they were varied. They included (in addition to French Protestants) Gypsies, Jews, Germans, Swiss, Flemings, and Walloons. If one of the defining features of overseas expansion (in which, incidentally, many of the outsider groups played important roles) was the close encounter between the English and a host of strangers, persons of different ethnic backgrounds and cultures, it ought not to be forgotten that such an encounter, albeit on a lesser scale, had already taken place, and continued to take place, in England itself.[19]

But, rather than focus on the sources of English expansion or a range of possible linkages between internal and external developments, what this book explores is the centrifugal thrust of metropolitan England into a number of peripheries. But, even here, there is much that is left out. We devote no attention to Wales or to the North Country, for instance. Our sense is that, although the local history of both regions is quite rich, their territorial

18. John Stuart Mill, *Principles of Political Economy, with Some of Their Applications to Social Philosophy* (1848), ed. W. J. Ashley (London, [1940]), 685–686, as quoted in John J. McCusker and Russell R. Menard, *The Economy of British America, 1607–1789* (Chapel Hill, N.C., 1985), 8, and see 39–45 for a discussion of the colonial contribution to the English economy. Just citing some of the more important work on the British economy, see C.G.A. Clay, *Economic Expansion and Social Change: England, 1500–1700*, 2 vols. (Cambridge, 1984); N.F.R. Crafts, *British Economic Growth during the Industrial Revolution* (Oxford, 1985); Roderick Floud and Donald McCloskey, eds., *The Economic History of Britain since 1700*, 2 vols. (Cambridge, 1981); Joan Thirsk, *Economic Policy and Projects: The Development of a Consumer Society in Early Modern England* (Oxford, 1978); Neil McKendrick *et al.*, *The Birth of a Consumer Society: The Commercialization of Eighteenth-Century England* (London, 1982). Particularly helpful here are comments and further references contained in Innes, "Jonathan Clark," *Past and Present*, no. 115 (May 1987), 178–179, 195–196. For one historian who sees the influence of an aspect of these English developments for the colonies, see Breen, "An Empire of Goods," *Jour. Brit. Stud.*, XXV (1986), 467–499, and " 'Baubles of Britain': The American and Consumer Revolutions of the Eighteenth Century," *Past and Present*, no. 119 (May 1988), 73–104.

19. John Geipel, *The Europeans: An Ethnohistorical Survey* (London, 1969), 163–164; V. G. Kiernan, "Britons Old and New," in Colin Holmes, ed., *Immigrants and Minorities in British Society* (London, 1978), 23–59 (quotation at 30).

relationship to the Southeast has been largely ignored. Nor have we included essays on India or the specific geographical regions of North America, though we do include papers on Canada and the West Indies. Rather, we focus on the Atlantic world, isolating key areas of racial and ethnic interaction, without attempting to enlarge the huge outpouring of recent scholarship devoted to New England, the Chesapeake, and the lower South.

III

The volume contains essentially two kinds of essays. First, four contributors focus upon particular ethnic groups—native Americans, African-Americans, Scotch-Irish, and Dutch and Germans. We encouraged these authors to range widely in tracing the relations between these groups and the British and not to be circumscribed by particular regional boundaries. Second, four others explore distinct regions of empire—Ireland, Scotland, Canada, and the West Indies—that have generated quite extensive historiographies but that have rarely been integrated into a larger British history. We encouraged these authors to explore the social and cultural configurations, often multiple ones, that the expansion of England engendered and encountered within their allotted regions. Finally, as a capstone, Jacob M. Price traces some of the influences of the margins on the center itself. What did it mean to Britain that its peripheries were extended into the Western Hemisphere?

The contrasts in the types of encounters between the English and various alien peoples may seem so striking as to render the notion of a shared undertaking impossible. There are obvious differences, for instance, between England's relationship to Scotland and Ireland on the one hand and her relationship to distant overseas colonies on the other, not to mention major distinctions in the experiences of all the so-called dependencies. In the eighteenth century, Scotland, or at least part of it, was less a conquered province than an integral part of the English core state. Indeed, in T. C. Smout's words, "the former semiperiphery was exerting a pull on the core, the tail beginning ever so slightly to wag the dog." Samuel Johnson, in characteristically exaggerated fashion, described the Anglo-Scottish relation as one of exploitation—of the English by the Scots. Ireland had long been subject to English penetration, indeed contained a population that was English by descent, known as the Old English, as well as a native population that, however much likened to Indians, was more densely settled, Christian, and (to English eyes) more culturally advanced than New World natives. Ireland may have been described as "this famous island in the Virginian sea," but proximity to England made it much easier to settle than the New World. There are also obvious differences in the experiences of ethnic groups in the New World itself. Indians were not newcomers, and they experienced an unparalleled demographic disaster. Almost all blacks came to the New World as slaves, a fact that clearly put their experiences on a totally different plane from that of voluntary migrants.[20]

In spite of these, and other, marked differences, English encounters with alien peoples had a number of common characteristics. One pervasive trait was English hostility to, or at least disdain for, the people they encountered and engendered. The English generally thought of the Gaelic Irish as barbarous and uncivilized ("wood-born savages" and "dung-hill gnats," according to one seventeenth-century poem), and they tended to extend these attributes to all inhabitants of the country, even those who were British and Protestant in origin. The image of Highlanders, as Eric Richards points out, was largely that of a wild, primitive people, almost a different race. One contemporary even compared the African slave in the West Indies to the Celtic scallag in the Western Hebrides. If the Welsh had been included in our survey, no doubt we would have learned about their supposed shortcomings, as in the jingle, "Taffy was a Welshman, Taffy was a thief." Frontier antagonists of all stripes, Margaret Hodgen observes, tended to look more or less alike to the English. "Whether Irishmen or Pequots, Scots or Iroquois, they were enemies, they were ignorant, and they were animal-like." The most animallike to English eyes were, of course, Africans and their descendants. Even when the English were not downright hostile, they tended to view alien peoples with condescension. Notions of "noble savagery" were applied to Highlanders and to native Americans alike. Even settlers of Anglophone stock in the various Atlantic colonies were held in low and patronizing regard by their metropolitan brethren.[21]

All of the essays in this volume emphasize that the history of English

20. Smout, "Scotland and England," *Review*, III (1979–1980), 614; Fynes Morrison, cited in David Beers Quinn, *The Elizabethans and the Irish*, Folger Monographs on Tudor and Stuart Civilization (Ithaca, N.Y., 1966), 122. On Irish differences with the New World, see Michael McCarthy Morrogh, "The English Presence in Early Seventeenth-Century Munster," in Ciaran Brady and Raymond Gillespie, eds., *Natives and Newcomers: Essays on the Making of Irish Colonial Society, 1534–1641* (Dublin, 1986), 171–190; and Karl S. Bottigheimer, "Kingdom and Colony: Ireland in the Western Enterprise, 1536–1660, in K. R. Andrews *et al.*, eds., *The Westward Enterprise: English Activities in Ireland, the Atlantic, and America, 1480–1650* (Liverpool, 1978), 45–64. On Scotland, see Brian P. Levack, *The Formation of the British State: England, Scotland, and the Union, 1603–1707* (Oxford, 1987), esp. chaps. 6, 7.

21. Quinn, *Elizabethans and the Irish*, 126; Margaret T. Hodgen, *Early Anthropology in the Sixteenth and Seventeenth Centuries* (Philadelphia, 1964), 364. See also P. J. Marshall and Glyndwr Williams, *The Great Map of Mankind: British Perceptions of the World in the Age of Enlightenment* (London, 1982); Winthrop D. Jordan, *White over Black: American Attitudes toward the Negro, 1550–1812* (Chapel Hill, N.C., 1968); Roy Harvey Pearce, *Savagism and Civilization: A Study of the Indian and the American Mind* (Berkeley, Calif., 1988).

expansion was preeminently a history of *shifting* frontiers. There were no firmly set boundaries of any definition. Relationships were in constant motion. Nicholas Canny discerns contrasting levels of anglicization and corresponding variations in native-newcomer relations in different parts of Ireland. Thus, in early seventeenth-century Munster where the English presence was secure and well established, the settlers lived "in relative harmony" with the natives during times of peace and opposed them quite effectively during times of war. At the opposite extreme lay Ulster, where British settlement was tenuous and openly exploitative—more frontierlike, as it were—thereby provoking much resentment from the Irish population and a particularly violent reaction during the 1641 rising. In Scotland, the crucial divide, a true internal frontier, lay between the Lowlands and Highlands. Eric Richards sees the latter as "the most resistant and challenging marchland in Britain, a province so backward that it was often compared with America as a proper zone for colonization," but it experienced a significant measure of pacification and economic penetration during the eighteenth century, which led many of its people to emigrate as a way of displaying their resentment of and resistance to their region's colonial status.

What was true near at home was also true on the borderlands of the West. In assessing the relations of natives and newcomers in North America, far more vital than differences between North and South or between colonies, James H. Merrell explains, were the specific locations of Indians either side of a moving boundary running longitudinally throughout the continent. On one flank native Americans set many of the terms of cultural contact; on the other, colonists did. In contemporary parlance, the distinction was between "Strangers" and "Neighbors." The crucial line of demarcation for understanding encounters between blacks and whites, Philip D. Morgan argues, is that between slaveowning societies and slave societies, a line that was never rigidly fixed. In the former the number of slaves was insignificant, and they could, in a sense, be treated as "neighbors"; in the latter, large numbers of slaves were held in subjection, were feared, and were generally treated worse than "strangers." In many places, the shift from a slaveowning to a slave society, which often amounted to the overcoming of a frontier, saw a deterioration in the status of slaves. Even the small Dutch community in the mid-Atlantic can be divided into a numerically insignificant and assimilationist group in New York and a numerically strong and more autonomous group in less well developed New Jersey. Much the same yardstick of assimilation and autonomy can be applied to the Scotch-Irish, requiring a differentiation between towns like Philadelphia and backcountry areas like western Pennsylvania. In eighteenth-century Canada there were a variety of emergent cultures, but perhaps the most important dividing line was between the world of "woodrunners" and that of settlers. The British Caribbean, Michael Craton explains, developed along two critical axes. One was spatial, involving the creation of a number of core areas, in Barbados, Antigua, and Jamaica successively, each with its own expanding margins; the other took the form of an internal cultural frontier dividing white creoles from black slaves.

In all of this there is little congruence between significant social and national boundaries. In the early modern period, it is more useful to think in terms of regional entities, rather than, say, Ireland as a whole. Likewise, Lowland Scotland probably had more in common with the four northern counties of England than with the Highlands. Until the mid-eighteenth century, according to Hugh Trevor-Roper, "the West of Scotland, cut off by mountains from the East, was always linked rather to Ireland than to the Saxon Lowlands." The border counties straddling the line between England and Wales formed part of one cultural zone. The British West Indies should be analyzed as island systems, each with its own core and margins. Canada, comprising at least three French cultures and a host of others, was undoubtedly the most complex territory. But diverse communities and cultures existed throughout the first British Empire, in England no less than elsewhere.[22]

Encounters between the English and other peoples varied over time as well as across space. All alien groups were subject to a process of anglicization, but never was a blueprint systematically adopted or applied. England's rulers had few comprehensive programs of social engineering for any province, and those that existed were unsuccessful. At the beginning of our period, Canny's characterization of English policy toward the Irish as one of "drift," punctuated by brief flurries of interest whenever native resistance mounted, would be replicated elsewhere. Similarly, at the end of our period, J. M. Bumsted's conclusion, with respect to Canada, that "the British authorities found it difficult to move a common official culture at the top into penetration at the grassroots" seems like a case of déjà vu. Nor were there any straight-line trajectories. The cultural renaissances and flowerings that occurred among the Scots and the Germans, even as they anglicized, point to the complexity of temporal change. Even when the process was most devastating of indige-

22. Hugh Trevor-Roper, "The Invention of Tradition: The Highland Tradition of Scotland," in Eric Hobsbawm and Terence Ranger, eds., *The Invention of Tradition* (Cambridge, 1983), 15; K. E. Wrightson, "Kindred Adjoining Kingdoms: An English Perspective on the Social and Economic History of Early Modern Scotland," in R. A. Houston and I. D. Whyte, eds., *Scottish Society, 1500–1800* (Cambridge, 1989), 245–260, esp. 256–258; R. A. Houston, *Scottish Literacy and the Scottish Identity: Illiteracy and Society in Scotland and Northern England, 1600–1800* (Cambridge, 1985); Mervyn James, *Family, Lineage, and Civil Society: A Study of Society, Politics, and Mentality in the Durham Region, 1500–1640* (Oxford, 1974); James, *Society, Politics, and Culture: Studies in Early Modern England* (Cambridge, 1986); Steven Ellis, *The English Pale in Ireland and the Far North of England* (Dublin, 1988).

nous life and apparently unilinear, as in the case of Indians and African-Americans, the resilience of both peoples, their ability to reconstruct new societies and cultures, stitching together shreds of the old with fragments borrowed from the new, cannot be underestimated.

Frontiers not only shifted across space and over time but moved according to the status of the people on either side of the divide. A highly skilled settler group in Munster made for different relations with natives than the much worse-off settler group in Fermanagh. The desperate poverty experienced by most Highlanders was crucial to the great gulf opened up not only between them and Lowlanders but between them and their own anglicizing elite. A. G. Roeber finds much value in the concept of cultural brokers, often merchants and clergy, who acted as bilingual patrons bridging two cultures, although in the Dutch case perhaps a better term might be cultural deserters, people who abandoned the values and culture of their local communities—a process paralleled, for instance, among Glamorgan gentry who aped metropolitan fashions, Irish landowners who quickly adopted English dress, and a Lowland Scottish elite keen to purge their vocabularies and their minds of all Scotticisms. In interpreting Dutch interaction with the English, distinctions clearly must be made between the elite of wealthy landowners, merchants, and clergymen and the rank and file of ordinary farmers and artisans. Roeber, for instance, wonders whether cross-cultural exchange was infrequent and hostile at the lower ends of status and income. Morgan argues for a similar attention to rank and status in evaluating white encounters with blacks.[23]

The demographic context of frontier life was also critical in shaping encounters between natives and newcomers. The work of Canny and others has emphasized the importance of different migration streams to the history of seventeenth-century Ireland. Thus Munster was primarily a southwestern English settlement, which may explain the relatively low participation rate of this region's people in the simultaneous migration to the New World, while the east Ulster counties of Antrim and Down were an extension of southwest Scotland, and Ulster in general relied heavily on migrants from north Wales and the northwest of England as well as from Scotland. The differing economic performances of Munster and Ulster are attributable, in part, to the skills, capital, and agricultural technology available in the two regions of origin. The relative strength of Dutch and German cultures in North America can in large part be traced to the character of their different migrant pools. The widespread presence of families among certain immi-

23. P. R. Roberts, "The Union with England and the Identity of 'Anglican' Wales," Royal Historical Society, *Transactions*, 5th Ser., XXII (1972), 49–70; Jenkins, *The Making of a Ruling Class*, esp. 194; Nicholas Canny, *Kingdom and Colony: Ireland and the Atlantic World, 1560–1800* (Baltimore, 1988), chap. 2.

grants, as was the case in the Scottish, Scotch-Irish, and German migrations to the New World, favored the maintenance of homeland customs. Conversely, the lack of women among white migrants to the British West Indies and the Canadian West had a large bearing on the mixed-blood populations that arose in both regions. The pace at which immigrants arrived—whether, in the words of Maldwyn Jones, it was "one-shot or constant renewal"—was also important. Not that a one-shot immigration necessarily led to a diminished culture, as the New Jersey Dutch and, even more, French experience in Canada, indicate.[24]

If the notion of *shifting* frontiers is valuable for understanding the relations between the English and alien peoples, the essays in this volume also suggest the need to think in terms of *multiple* frontiers. Encounters between peoples varied according to what some contributors term domains of contact or contact arenas, which, while interrelated, require disentangling and separate analysis before they can be fully understood. The same spheres of contact are not always explored by each author; indeed, some spheres are only lightly touched upon. Much then remains to be investigated, but collectively these essays point the way.

Language was one crucial arena. Generally, the relationship of alien languages to English was one of confrontation and prolonged retreat, punctuated by occasional retrenchments and periodic revivals. Such is true of the Celtic languages, though there were major differences between the toleration extended the Welsh language and its association with Anglicanism, as against the attempted eradication of Highland Gaelic and its putative association with Roman Catholicism. Nevertheless, despite variations, the dominant story is one of linguistic imperialism, as is clear from the astonishment of Edmund Spenser that English settlers in Ireland should learn to speak the language of that country, "for it hath been ever the use of the conqueror to despise the language of the conquered, and to force him by all means to learn his." Despite this expectation, the advancement of English was in many cases effected less by political dictate (remembering that the significant move

24. On Munster, in addition to his essay in this volume, see Nicholas Canny, "The Irish Background to Penn's Experiment," in Richard S. Dunn and Mary Maples Dunn, eds., *The World of William Penn* (Philadelphia, 1986), 139–156; and Michael MacCarthy-Morrogh, *The Munster Plantation: English Migration to Southern Ireland, 1583–1641* (Oxford, 1986). On Ulster, see T. W. Moody, *The Londonderry Plantation, 1609–41: The City of London and the Plantation in Ulster* (Belfast, 1939); M. Perceval-Maxwell, *The Scottish Migration to Ulster in the Reign of James I* (London, 1973); Philip S. Robinson, *The Plantation of Ulster: British Settlement in an Irish Landscape, 1600–1670* (Dublin, 1984); Raymond Gillespie, *Colonial Ulster: The Settlement of East Ulster, 1600–1641* (Cork, 1985). More generally, see Nicholas Canny, "Migration and Opportunity: Britain, Ireland, and the New World," *Irish Economic and Social History*, XII (1985), 7–32; and the debate between Canny and Gillespie in *Irish Econ. and Soc. Hist.*, XIII (1986), 90–100.

toward a more standardized English, represented by Dr. Johnson's famous dictionary, was largely a one-man operation, not a state enterprise) than by native perceptions that it was the language of opportunity and advancement. Thus Indians keen to trade soon learned to pepper their discourse with English curses, many black slaves aware of the realities of power spoke the dialects and separate languages (including Virginian, Gaelic, and German) of the groups who owned them, and ambitious Scots employed the Irishman Thomas Sheridan to give them elocution lessons. If linguistic imperialism was not solely or even primarily an arm of the state, it nevertheless served the nation's cultural imperialism. Naming is one small example. From the early sixteenth century onward, the Welsh were forced and encouraged to simplify their kindred naming patterns, most notably the long strings of *ap* (son of), and adopt surnames, often English Christian names. An individual might poke fun at the process, as one eighteenth-century signature indicates: "Sion ap William ap Sion ap William ap Sion ap Dafydd ap Ithel Fychan ap Cynrig ap Robert ap Iorwerth ap Rhyrid ap Iorwerth ap Madoc ap Ednawain Bendew, called after the English fashion, John Jones." But humor could not disguise the fact of incorporation. African slaves suffered a more humiliating incorporation as masters largely ignored their homeland names, supplied them with familial, not formal, names—Jack for John, Sukey for Susanna, and so on—and denied them surnames.

But, just as slaves gradually took over their own naming and created distinctive patterns, linguistic contact was never wholly a one-way process. In many contact situations, new hybrid languages—pidgins, which had a short life among many native Americans, and creoles, which proved far more durable among African-Americans and some Amerindian groups—arose. Furthermore, alien languages continuously invigorated English by providing constant transfusions of new words, whether *bottom* and *bucket* from the Scotch-Irish, *caboose* and *cookie* from the Dutch, *shad* and *shamrock* from Gaelic, *tomahawk* and *totem* from native Americans. Perhaps the greatest asset of English today stems from its openness to new influences, most evident in its teeming vocabulary, 80 percent of which is foreign-born. English literature was also invigorated. Some of the finest writers in English—Jonathan Swift, Oliver Goldsmith, Edmund Burke, Robert Burns, and Thomas Jefferson—came from the peripheries. Scots, Irish, and Americans carved a place for themselves in English letters out of all proportion to their numbers.[25]

25. Edmund Spenser, *A View of the Present State of Ireland* (1596), ed. W. L. Renwick (Oxford, 1970), 67 (citation provided by Nicholas Canny); Victor Edward Durkacz, *The Decline of the Celtic Languages: A Study of Linguistic and Cultural Conflict in Scotland, Wales, and Ireland from the Reformation to the Twentieth Century* (Edinburgh, 1983), esp. v, 3, 52; Charles W. J. Withers, *Gaelic in Scotland, 1698–1901: The Geographical History of a Language* (Edinburgh, 1984); Glanmor

The economic realm was another arena of contact in which the double-ended process connecting metropolitan and dependent worlds was most evident. English expansion was, of course, inextricably bound up with economic exploitation. Appropriation of the most productive farmland by British settlers was the primary grievance of the Irish Rebellion of 1641. Nevertheless, *both* native and foreign landowners engaged with new market forces, many Irish tenants took advantage of new opportunities to enter into new contractual relations with the settler landlords, and after the Cromwellian settlement *all* residents suffered, to some extent at least, from the country's economic weaknesses. In Scotland, the costs and benefits of empire divided most graphically along regional lines, with the Highlands bearing most of the brunt of modernization and the Lowlands largely prospering from the new opportunities. In the New World many native Americans saw their traditional economic practices undermined as a result of the English invasion, and, as a result, many experienced debt peonage, indentured servitude, and outright slavery. Yet Indians were not just victims but eager and discriminating participants in the new economic system that ultimately did so much to destroy their way of life. Even black slaves, unquestionably the most exploited group in the first British Empire, refused to accept the role of pawns and sought niches within the system, whether trading in Sunday markets or growing vegetables and fruits on their garden plots and provision grounds.[26]

In fact, all aspects of material culture saw reciprocal borrowings between the English and strangers. Thus some British settlers in Ireland furnished their residences after the English style, but many more accommodated themselves to Irish-style structures. Similarly, these same settlers helped introduce new arable crops, but usually within the context of an older pastoral economy. Even as they anglicized, the Dutch in the New World influenced those around them through their distinctive architecture, range of vegetables, culinary expertise, and Christmas customs. In Pennsylvania, Germans

---

Williams, *Religion, Language, and Nationality in Wales: Historical Essays* (Cardiff, 1979), esp. chap. 6; Glanville Price, *The Languages of Britain* (London, 1984). On standardization, see John Barrell, *English Literature in History, 1730–80: An Equal, Wide Survey* (New York, 1983), esp. 121–157. On naming, see Williams, *When Was Wales?* 118–119. For the effect of linguistic imperialism on literacy, see Houston, *Scottish Literacy and the Scottish Identity*, esp. 70–83. For a useful popular account, see Robert McCrum *et al.*, *The Story of English* (London, 1986).

26. For interesting thoughts on Scottish and Irish economic development and ties to England, see L. M. Cullen, "Scotland and Ireland, 1600–1800: Their Role in the Evolution of British Society," in Houston and Whyte, eds., *Scottish Society, 1500–1800*, 226–244. See also T. M. Devine and David Dickson, eds., *Ireland and Scotland, 1600–1850: Parallels and Contrasts in Economic and Social Development* (Edinburgh, 1983). Exploitation was not always paramount: see Canny, *Kingdom and Colony*, 13–16.

supplied weapons and wagons to the English. The Scotch-Irish contributed the elongated central square to Pennsylvania town plans and helped diffuse the log cabin throughout Pennsylvania and the trans-Appalachian West. British West Indian planters adapted to the local climate, style of life, and materials as well as to Amerindian, Hispanic, and African cultural influences by building houses with piazzas, high ceilings, and verandas and by concocting distinctive foods and drinks.

In the broader cultural realm there was no more significant sphere of contact than religion. Central to the Southeast's assertion of cultural dominance over the rest of England and Wales and later Ireland and Scotland was the Protestant Reformation, as various counter-reactions such as the Pilgrimage of Grace in 1536, the Western Revolt of 1549, and more dramatically the Irish Rebellion of 1641 make clear. A great driving force of this outward expansion was the attempt to develop unity on the basis of religious conformity, but this proved chimerical. As a result, religious divisiveness became a major feature of the first British Empire in its heyday. In England itself the established church confronted dissenters; in Scotland Presbyterians were in the ascendant but were united only in their hatred of Episcopalianism and Popery. In Ireland the Episcopalians, though fewest, dominated Presbyterians and the Catholic majority. In Wales Calvinistic Methodism, as popular as in America, triumphed over Anglicanism. In many parts of British America, but nowhere more notably than in the Middle Colonies, where Dutch, Germans, Scotch-Irish, English, and others came to share a culture of evangelical pietism, the balance tilted even more heavily toward dissent. And in native Americans and African-Americans the English initially found few converts. As Hugh Kearney has rightly noted, "Over much of the history of the English empire during the eighteenth century there looms the shadow of the Reformation."[27]

One final contact arena touched on by some essayists and well worth further investigation is the public realm. Warfare, for instance, is obviously vital to an understanding of English (and European) expansion. Military superiority, partly in technical capacity (best evident in the construction of naval vessels designed to maximize firepower), but perhaps more in a ruthless philosophy of warfare (fighting "dirty," as Geoffrey Parker puts it), gave the English a major edge in their relations with other groups. Elizabethan expeditions to Ireland were enjoined to proceed as if they "were all in warre." Colonization in the Caribbean, Craton observes, was bound up with sea- and land-based military force. Disordered borderlands, whether situated along outer margins in Wales, Ireland, the Caribbean, or North America, were places where, as in the Scottish marchland of the fifteenth

27. Kearney, *The British Isles*, 106–148 (quotation at 148).

century, "violence [was] . . . a way of life." Precisely because these were peripheries thought to be on the outer boundaries of civilization, ordinary restraints of civility could be abandoned. An all-destructive ferocity and indifference to bloodshed took their place. The Narragansett Indians were one of many alien groups who found the Englishmen's way of making war "too furious," so that "too many men" were slain. But a superior technical expertise and a ruthless philosophy of warfare did not necessarily sweep all before them. Native insurrections such as that of 1622 in Virginia or of 1641 in Ireland proved as much, as did the ability of the natives to learn military skills from the settlers. Moreover, Indians lost far more of their numbers to disease than to British arms. Even then, they did not, according to Merrell, "surrender or disappear overnight," although, as Parker concludes, they and other native peoples in Africa and Southeast Asia lost their independence because they seemed unable to adopt or fully incorporate Western military technology.[28]

Indeed, another vital area of the public domain, the law, may be just as important as warfare for understanding English expansion and English encounters with other groups. Certainly, the law in some contexts, as in its use by Sir John Davies, attorney general for Ireland in the early seventeenth century, could be "an instrument of colonization." Yet, many Irish demonstrated their accommodation to the new legal order, no better illustrated than by an incident in Fermanagh during the 1641 rising when a group of tenants "took away the lease, writings, will and escriptions" to several parcels of land. No doubt, in Merrell's words, the "noose of alien law tightened" around Indians over time. Yet he also provides evidence that some Indians at certain times were able to manipulate the law, albeit within highly circumscribed limits. Likewise, even the most exploited group, African-Americans, learned to use the courts to protect themselves. Other, more advantaged groups, such as the Dutch, plunged headlong into the courts, familiarizing themselves with the required legal terms, producing their own successful lawyers, even as they retained elements of their own legal systems. Englishmen's claims to be the "freest people in the world" could be utilized by those with whom they came into contact.[29]

28. Geoffrey Parker, *The Military Revolution: Military Innovation and the Rise of the West, 1500–1800* (Cambridge, 1988), esp. chaps. 3, 4 (quotation at 118); Nicholas Canny, "The Permissive Frontier: The Problem of Social Control in English Settlements in Ireland and Virginia, 1550–1650," in Andrews *et al.*, eds., *The Westward Enterprise*, 17–44 (quotation at 18); D. Hay, "England, Scotland and Europe: The Problem of the Frontier," Royal Hist. Soc., *Trans.*, 5th Ser., XXV (1975), 77–91 (quotation at 82); Bailyn, *Peopling of British North America*, 112–131; James Axtell, *The European and the Indian: Essays in the Ethnohistory of Colonial North America* (New York, 1981), 140. See also Webb, *Governors-General.*

29. On the use of the law in different contexts, see, for instance, Hans S. Pawlisch, *Sir John Davies and the Conquest of Ireland: A Study in Legal Imperialism* (Cam-

Overall, then, the precise mix of assimilation and autonomy that characterized the response of peoples in the peripheries varied enormously. The combination is not easy to calculate in any mechanical fashion, as Craton demonstrates in his sensitive exploration of the Englishness of that Little England, otherwise known as Barbados. Or consider the Welsh, many of whom willingly adopted English ways, and yet (or perhaps it should be, as a result) maintained, as in the strength of their spoken language, or created, as in the suppositous discovery of Welsh bardic poetry or of a largely bogus Druidic past by Iolo Morganwg and others, a sense of special identity. Somewhat similarly, Scots responded to their cultural assimilation and provincialism by exhibiting a degree of economic vitality and cultural extroversion that enriched their sense of separate identity. The Scottish equivalent to Morganwg, James Macpherson, translated the imagined third-century Celtic poet, Ossian, thereby creating a fake Scottish epic, but one that ensured the survival of elements of national and local culture in the collective consciousness. By contrast with Scotland, Ireland was subject to a much greater degree of assimilation: the country was massively settled, the indigenous landed class rooted out, English legal and religious institutions transplanted. And yet the Irish Protestant community could never gain London's trust, constantly sought it, and, partly as a result, maintained little cultural independence. Canadians resisted assimilation and carved out a large measure of cultural autonomy. So much so that their society, as Bumsted explores, was no simple bicultural province, but a congeries of cultures, in which the cultural force of Britain was far from decisive. Lacking the powerful fusion force either of assimilation to metropolitan mores (which might in turn have provoked a nationalist reaction) or of a national revolution as happened further south, Canada moved only gradually toward a sense of national identity.[30]

---

bridge, 1985); S. J. Connolly, "Albion's Fatal Twigs: Justice and Law in the Eighteenth Century," in Rosalind Mitchison and Peter Roebuck, eds., *Economy and Society in Scotland and Ireland, 1500–1939* (Edinburgh, 1988), 117–125; Douglas Deal, "A Constricted World: Free Blacks on Virginia's Eastern Shore, 1680–1750," in Lois Green Carr, Philip D. Morgan, and Jean B. Russo, eds., *Colonial Chesapeake Society* (Chapel Hill, N.C., 1988), 275–305.

30. On Wales, see P. Jenkins, *The Making of a Ruling Class*; Geraint H. Jenkins, *The Foundations of Modern Wales: Wales, 1642–1780* (Oxford, 1987), esp. 386–426; David W. Howell, *Patriarchs and Parasites: The Gentry of South-West Wales in the Eighteenth Century* (Cardiff, 1986), esp. 192–193, 199–203; Gareth Elwyn Jones, *Modern Wales: A Concise History, c. 1485–1979* (Cambridge, 1985); Prys Morgan, *A New History of Wales: The Eighteenth Century Renaissance* (Llandybie, 1981); and Gwyn A. Williams, "Romanticism in Wales," in Roy Porter and Mikuláš Teich, eds., *Romanticism in National Context* (Cambridge, 1988), 9–36. On Macpherson and the creation of a *Kulturvolk*, see Fiona Stafford, *The Sublime Savage: James Macpherson and the Poems of Ossian* (Edinburgh, 1988). See also Trevor-

Parallels and contrasts, then, can be drawn between England's outlying provinces, but so can more direct links. William Christie Macleod was perhaps the first to expound what may be termed the "laboratory" thesis. He argued somewhat crudely that the lessons the English learned in attempts to subjugate the "wild" Celtic-speaking inhabitants of their peripheries were later applied in America. Noting the similarities in colonizing institutions (the joint stock companies designed for both Highlands and America) and in personnel (Raleigh's involvement in both Ireland and America and John Mason's butchering of both Scottish clansmen and Pequot villagers), Macleod argued for direct connections between England's Old World and New World frontiers. David Quinn and, later, Canny have elaborated Macleod's suggestions in more sophisticated fashion, by exploring the extent to which Ireland was a training ground for American adventures. Methods used in creating an Imperium Anglorum were later applied on a global stage.[31]

Even more complicated connections and bilateral relationships arose among the provinces as the Atlantic empire evolved during the eighteenth century. There were, for instance, the connections involved in the circulation of people (and their social characteristics): Scottish Highlanders became "the shock troops" launched at the frontier; about 200,000 people (the majority the descendants of seventeenth-century British settlers) left Ireland for the New World over the course of the century, Caribbean settlers helped establish the Carolinas, and New Englanders helped people the hinterlands of New York and Pennsylvania. Another nexus is suggested by the gravitation of Scottish Lowlanders into certain professional avenues—most notably medicine and commerce—in the empire. As Richards, following Ronald Syme, notes, it seems to be a rule of empires to place a disproportionate reliance upon provincials in the creation of colonial elites. Similarly, in large part the peripheries both financed and then manned the army. About a half

---

Roper, "The Invention of Tradition," in Hobsbawm and Ranger, eds., *The Invention of Tradition*, 15–41. Gilles Paquet and Jean-Pierre Wallot, "Nouvelle France / Quebec / Canada: A World of Limited Identities," in Nicholas Canny and Anthony Pagden, eds., *Colonial Identity in the Atlantic World, 1500–1800* (Princeton, N.J., 1987), 95–114, is useful for confirming the "limited identities" of Canadians, less useful in arguing for "Canadian dualism."

31. William Christie Macleod, *The American Indian Frontier* (New York, 1928), chap. 13; David B. Quinn, "Ireland and Sixteenth Century European Expansion," in T. Desmond Williams, ed., *Historical Studies*, I, *Papers Read before the Second Irish Conference of Historians* (London, 1958), 22–32; Quinn, *The Elizabethans and the Irish*; Nicholas P. Canny, "The Ideology of English Colonization: From Ireland to America," *WMQ*, 3d Ser., XXX (1973), 575–598; Canny, "Dominant Minorities: English Settlers in Ireland and Virginia, 1550–1650," in A. C. Hepburn, ed., *Minorities in History* . . . (London, 1978), 51–69. For other early links, see David B. Quinn, "Wales and the West," in R. R. Davies *et al.*, eds., *Welsh Society and Nationhood: Historical Essays Presented to Glanmor Williams* (Cardiff, 1984), 90–107.

of the peacetime strength of the eighteenth-century army was carried by the Irish taxpayer, and by the end of the Seven Years' War about half the British army, rank and file, and a higher proportion of the officers, consisted of Irishmen and Scots. As another overlapping provincialism, albeit of a bizarre nature, consider the legend that arose in late-eighteenth-century Wales of the Lost Brothers of the Welsh Nation, a group of Welsh Indians who were allegedly descended from a colony planted on the Gulf of Mexico by the Welsh prince Madoc. This myth was symptomatic of a serious attempt to recreate a sense of nationhood both at home and abroad—extending to Beula, western Pennsylvania, and the banks of the Ohio.[32]

Another set of linkages also needs to be explored: how did the peripheries influence the center? Jacob M. Price, who tackles this question directly, begins by noting the range of issues that could be addressed. Among other things, a full answer would need to encompass new patterns of consumption, as in the rising appeal of coffee, sugar, and tobacco; the impact on literature, ranging from travel narratives to the novels of Defoe; and the stimulus to science, for the New World served as a botanical, geological, and zoological experimental station. Confining himself to the thirteen colonies of North America, Price explores a more limited, but no less important, central question: to what extent did this periphery command the attention and concern of people in Britain? On the whole, high-level, or official, Britain tended to be uninvolved in America, if measured in political patronage or direct experience. To be sure, certain groups of members of Parliament with American interests and experience, particularly army officers and merchants, increased markedly in the third quarter of the eighteenth century, but they were still a tiny minority in the House of Commons. On the other hand, an ingenious use of subscription lists, postwar credit claims, and petitions allows Price to

32. William R. Brock, *Scotus-Americanus: A Survey of the Sources for Links between Scotland and America in the Eighteenth Century* (Edinburgh, 1982), 1–2; Bailyn, *Voyagers to the West*, esp. 25–26. On Scottish infiltration of key sectors of colonial life, see, in addition to Richards's essay in this volume, Richard B. Sheridan, "The Role of the Scots in the Economy and Society of the West Indies," in Vera Rubin and Arthur Tuden, eds., *Comparative Perspectives on Slavery in New World Plantation Societies*, New York Academy of Sciences, *Annals*, CCXCII (New York, 1977), 94–106; and Ned C. Landsmen, *Scotland and Its First American Colony, 1683–1765* (Princeton, N.J., 1985). On the army, see L. M. Cullen, "Britain under Westminster," in Smith, ed., *The Making of Britain*, 162; S.H.F. Johnston, "The Irish Establishment," *Irish Sword*, I (1949–1950), 33–36; F. G. James, *Ireland in the Empire, 1688–1770 . . .* (Cambridge, Mass., 1973), 175–181; John Childs, *The Army of Charles II* (London, 1976), 196–209; H.C.B. Rogers, *The British Army of the Eighteenth Century* (London, 1976); and James Hayes, "Scottish Officers in the Scottish Army, 1714–63," *Scottish Historical Review*, XXXVII (1958), 23–33. On the Welsh, see Gwyn A. Williams, *Madoc: The Making of a Myth* (London, 1980); and Williams, *The Search for Beulah Land: The Welsh and the Atlantic Revolution* (London, 1980).

demonstrate a wide diffusion of interest in the American colonies among commercial groups, located most notably in the bigger ports and in major inland marketing centers for export industries. Alongside this commercial network, Price documents an overlapping web of dissenting religious interests with significant transatlantic connections. As for the British nation as a whole, Price first investigates the effect of emigration, which is perhaps best considered locally and selectively: for example, the relief it brought to unemployment in key urban and regional areas and the solution of the prison problem for fifty thousand felons. Similarly, when investigating the British economy as a whole, the benefits of the growing colonial market were not uniformly felt, but, rather, were limited to certain ports, industries, and sectors of the population. This uneven geographical and social distribution of interest, Price believes, is critical to an explanation of the American Revolution.

IV

British imperial history is unfashionable, seemingly rendered irrelevant by decolonization; where it survives, it is focused on the national stories—Canadian, American, West Indian—that depict how the modern nations became disentangled from the larger, original British context. And while former colonial societies study their own separate history and, in this narrowly focused way, their imperial past, rarely do they study the parallel internal developments of other linked dependencies that together made up the whole. It seems doubtful, for example, that historians of British Canada regularly read histories of the British West Indies. "It is easy to see," Pocock notes, "how a derivative society may fall into this highly insular mode of treating its own derivation." At the same time, with the sun setting over the British Empire, historians of England have become even more inward-looking. Indeed, loss of world influence has contributed to a crisis of confidence about the very significance of English history as such. "What virtue," G. R. Elton has asked, "can there be in studying the muddled history of a small offshore island whose supposed achievements have turned out illusory?" At the center and the margins, then, there has been a turning inward and a narrowing of focus, introversion and *dis*integration.[33]

This volume represents a stepping-stone in the opposite direction. It is transnational in spirit, pluralist and multicultural in approach. It attempts to embrace some, at least, of the diverse ethnic experiences of the first British Empire. It links England's Celtic borderlands to colonies overseas. It sees

33. Pocock, "British History," *Jour. Mod. Hist.*, XLVII (1975), 619–620; G. R. Elton, *The History of England* (Cambridge, 1984), 13.

British imperial development as a vastly complicated process: the recruitment of a wide variety of peoples, their interaction, their conflicts, their partial absorption, and their creation of new cultures. It offers ways to integrate these experiences, by suggesting different levels on which they can be studied and by exploring the impact of a major group of colonies on the center. It does none of this to celebrate empire or to indulge in Anglophilia. Rather, the volume simply seeks further understanding of Seeley's "mighty phenomenon"—that huge, outwardly expanding peripheral arc sweeping north and west from London and the Home Counties into Scotland, across Ireland, southwest through Newfoundland, and then down the North American coast into the Caribbean. And this was only the beginning, for this entire interactive Atlantic culture system, this vast band of variant marchlands, was in itself only a segment of a global system that ultimately reached Southeast Asia, Australia, New Zealand, and other parts of the Pacific world as well. But that is another story.

I

The Margins of Britain

NICHOLAS CANNY

The Marginal Kingdom
Ireland as a Problem in the First British Empire

Ireland usually springs to mind whenever reference is made to "Dark Corners of the Land" or to the "Cultural Margins of Britain" during the early modern centuries.[1] Although a considerable part of Ireland had been under the jurisdiction of the English crown since the twelfth century, and although an intensive Anglo-Norman settlement had then been established in the more fertile areas of the eastern half of the country, English people still tended to perceive Irish society as one that was culturally different and, indeed, culturally inferior to their own. Their perception was largely the creation of those who had guided the Anglo-Norman settlement, but it became further entrenched and popularized in the sixteenth and seventeenth centuries, when renewed efforts were made to establish English government authority over all parts of the country.[2] Then it became accepted that the Gaelic elements of the population, who had always remained aloof from the anglicizing influence in the country, were an obdurate people and that a comprehensive reform of their society would have to be enforced as a necessary preliminary to effecting the reform of the population through educational and persuasive means.[3]

Reform, from the sixteenth century forward, had come to mean religious as well as social improvement, and it became the stated aim of the English government to bring all elements of the Irish population to an acceptance of the Protestant faith. The logic of what had been decided in relation to the Gaelic Irish meant that a Protestant evangelization drive would have to be deferred, pending a forceful restructuring of their society. There was no such problem in relation to the descendants of the Anglo-Normans, the so-called

1. The first phrase comes from J.E.C. Hill, "Puritans and 'The Dark Corners of the Land,'" Royal Historical Society, *Transactions*, 5th Ser., XIII (1963), 96–97.

2. Giraldus Cambrensis, *Topographia Hibernica*, ed. James F. Dimock, Rolls Series, XXIe (London, 1867); Giraldus Cambrensis, *Expugnatio Hibernica: The Conquest of Ireland*, ed. and trans. A. B. Scott and F. X. Martin (Dublin, 1978).

3. Nicholas Canny, *Kingdom and Colony: Ireland in the Atlantic World, 1560–1800* (Baltimore, 1988), 31–69.

Old English population of Ireland, because they (or most of them) had always been accepted as a civil people and, indeed, had been traditionally recognized as the upholders of the English interest in the country. Efforts were made in the sixteenth century to draw these people to the Protestant faith, and it was also hoped that they, in turn, would serve as the instruments for bringing that religion to the Gaelic population. However, by the 1590s, a variety of factors had combined to divert the Old English from conforming to Protestantism, which had been defined as the religion of the Irish state; and some of their leaders had, in fact, become firmly attached to Catholic Counter-Reformation doctrines. The Old English thus could no longer be regarded as reliable supporters of crown policy, and some analysts who contemplated the religious reform of Ireland concluded that the Old English, who were becoming fully catechized in Catholic doctrine, would prove more difficult to convert than the Gaelic Irish, who, it was contended, were steeped in heathenish barbarism. These analysts argued that the reform effort in Ireland would have to be established on completely new foundations, and they recommended the immediate dismissal of the Old English from positions of trust as the first necessary step toward a fresh beginning.[4]

Such strategies were proposed by English officials, soldiers, and adventurers who had direct experience with Ireland. None of their several proposals was completely consistent one with the other, nor did any individual author remain attached to any single scheme of reform throughout his career in Ireland. There was, however, a telling common agreement on the essential propositions being advanced. Almost every text on the subject included a fulsome description of the resources of the country and arrived at the predictable conclusion that the country's potential to sustain a civil, prosperous, and Protestant society would be realized only when these resources, as well as the government of the country, had been placed in the hands of zealous English Protestants.[5]

The blatant self-interest of this series of schemes for the reform of Ireland as well as the radical character of what was being proposed was sufficient to discredit these proposals in the eyes of the monarchs and senior government officials to whom they were being addressed. They did succeed, however, in further convincing these rulers of the deplorable social condition of Ireland, but the drastic prescriptions being recommended suggested to England's rulers that their energies and resources would best be confined to their domestic and Continental commitments.

Thus, although convinced and even distressed by the accounts presented to them of Ireland's cultural and religious backwardness, English rulers were

4. Nicholas Canny, "Identity Formation in Ireland: The Emergence of the Anglo-Irish," in Canny and Anthony Pagden, eds., *Colonial Identity in the Atlantic World, 1500–1800* (Princeton, N.J., 1987), 159–212, esp. 165–174.

5. *Ibid.*, 173–174.

generally reluctant to take very decisive action to remedy the perceived deficiencies. Instead, they opted for a policy of drift, sometimes approving initiatives that were recommended to them by their English-born appointees in Ireland only to countermand them at the moment when it became apparent that the suggested measures had aroused the hostility of the local population toward the English government. English rulers were also impressed by the lineages of those who came forward as the leaders of the Old English community; and were it not for the Catholicism of these Old English leaders, successive English monarchs would have been more inclined to place trust in their opinions than in those of English-born officials who frequently attained social status and wealth in Ireland that would have been well beyond their reach had they remained at home.[6]

The very existence of this wealth, which was frequently flaunted by successful English settlers in Ireland, aroused a new interest in Ireland at the English court.[7] This interest was particularly active whenever the crown ran into financial or political difficulty, and it gave rise to the belief that the resources of Ireland could be exploited to resolve the short-term difficulties of the crown. This exploitation could take the form, as it did in the 1620s, of accepting money from the Old English community in return for the royal promise that it would not be penalized because of its religion. Once the crown entered into such engagements, it was, in effect, abandoning all pretense of being concerned to achieve the reform of Ireland, and it was openly discarding the advice that had been provided to it by English officials and settlers in Ireland. This development, naturally, enraged these people, but they contended that their very security was threatened when the crown decided, as it did in the 1630s and again in the 1680s, to exploit Ireland militarily by raising fighting men from among the Catholic population.[8] The crown's intention was to train these soldiers in Ireland and then to convey them across the Irish Sea to assist the monarch in upholding his authority within the kingdoms of England and Scotland.

However much the Protestant population in Ireland might object to this policy, they found it less distressing than the crown's other stratagem to exploit the resources of Ireland by promoting a second phase of plantation in the country. Under this scheme it was intended that most Catholic proprietors in the country should be deprived of two-thirds of their landed property. This intention was consistent with the repeated recommendations of the settler population, and they objected to it only because the crown envisaged

6. This theme is detailed in Nicholas Canny, *The Upstart Earl: A Study of the Social and Mental World of Richard Boyle, First Earl of Cork, 1566–1643* (Cambridge, 1982), esp. 1–40.

7. *Ibid.*, 41–76.

8. T. W. Moody *et al.*, eds., *A New History of Ireland*, III, *Early Modern Ireland, 1534–1691* (Oxford, 1976), 233–269, 478–508.

that the confiscated property would be assigned to a fresh wave of settlers from England rather than to those who were already in the country. These latter, it was alleged, were not entitled to further benefits, because they had failed to achieve the reform of the country that they had so persistently advocated. Instead, they were accused of putting private before public interest, and it was suggested that any estates that they had acquired through corrupt means should be wrested from them and granted instead to English or Scottish favorites of the crown.[9]

These repeated threats of plantation and replantation by monarchs and high government officials reveal the extent to which they, at least, considered Ireland to be a cultural margin of Britain and therefore open to exploitation. This attitude was contested by all elements of the population in Ireland, settler and native alike, and the settlers contended that any weakening of their position would expose them to attack from a supposedly hostile native population. This emphasis on the latent hostility of the Irish population toward the settlers was probably exaggerated, and it was their own greed as much as any interference from England that occasioned the grievance that gave rise to armed uprising against them. However, the lack of consistency in English policy toward Ireland did create the conditions under which armed opposition to English rule in Ireland could be mobilized. Such armed challenge was usually justified within the context of loyalty to the crown and was treated seriously by the government in England only when it threatened the security of that kingdom. Whenever this occurred, as it did in the 1590s, the 1640s, and again in the 1690s, the government in England was overtaken by panic and grasped at the only ready-made strategy that was available to it: that which had been devised by the spokesmen of the Protestant settler community in Ireland.[10]

The result was a sequence of frenzied efforts by the government to bring Ireland under comprehensive control. On these occasions, no money was spared to suppress all military opposition to government authority, massive confiscations of the property of those who had been engaged in insurrection were proceeded with, and plans were set afoot for the distribution of this property among English soldiers and officials who had served in Ireland or to English and Scottish favorites. These shifts in the ownership of property were sometimes associated with formal efforts at plantation, whereby the recipients of escheated land were required to develop their estates after a

9. H. F. Kearney, *Strafford in Ireland, 1633–41: A Study in Absolutism* (Manchester, 1959), esp. 69–84, 104–129.

10. On the outbreak of these uprisings and on official reaction to them, see Nicholas Canny, *From Reformation to Restoration: Ireland, 1534–1660* (Dublin, 1987), 108–150, 188–225; Ciaran Brady and Raymond Gillespie, eds., *Natives and Newcomers: Essays on the Making of Irish Colonial Society, 1534–1641* (Dublin, 1986), 191–213; Moody *et al.*, eds., *Early Modern Ireland, 1534–1691*, 478–508.

stated plan. This plan usually involved the introduction of a specified number of British tenants for every thousand acres of land assigned and the provision of property for the support of a Protestant clergy.[11]

These stipulations did spur the recruitment of British tenants for the plantation estates in Ireland, and some newly established proprietors also recruited artisans from abroad with a view to developing nuclear settlements devoted to manufacturing activity based on the natural resources of the country. Even more determined efforts were made by the government to recruit zealous Protestant clergy who would occupy positions in the Irish church, and all posts in the Dublin administration had been placed in Protestant hands by the first decade of the seventeenth century.[12] These dramatic developments were the product of sudden bursts of enthusiasm by the English government, which then quickly lost interest in Ireland once the moment of crisis had passed. Thereafter, the settler community in Ireland was left to its own devices, but was subjected to intermittent surveys whenever rumor of corruption or mismanagement came to the attention of senior government officials. Such investigations frequently revealed evidence of malfeasance, which served to erode whatever confidence the English government may have had in the new social elite that had come to prominence in Ireland as a consequence of the tumultuous changes of the sixteenth and seventeenth centuries. The investigations produced evidence, however, of a very sizable population movement from Britain into Ireland during the course of these centuries, and this was cited by the leaders of the Protestant community in Ireland to show that they had indeed lived up to their responsibility to establish a Protestant and English-like society in Ireland.[13]

Just how accurate this claim was is difficult to establish, but we can go beyond mere numbers of settlers to obtain some understanding of the British community in Ireland and how it interacted with the native population from the thousands of sworn statements that were collected from the Protestant survivors of the 1641 rising.[14] Those who made depositions were primarily concerned to identify those who had attacked them, with a view to having their revenge once government authority was restored. In the course of doing so they sometimes described their previous relationship with their assailants, and the deponents usually presented an inventory of what they had lost as a

11. The details for the Ulster plantation of the early 17th century are detailed in Moody *et al.*, eds., *Early Modern Ireland, 1534–1691*, 197–205. This was the most detailed plantation scheme for Ireland that was devised in the 16th and 17th centuries.

12. Alan Ford, *The Protestant Reformation in Ireland, 1590–1641* (Frankfurt am Main, 1985), esp. 63–97.

13. The most detailed of such surveys was that of 1622, for which see British Library, Add. MSS 4756, fols. 1–155.

14. Aidan Clarke, "The 1641 Depositions," in Peter Fox, eds., *Treasures of the Library of Trinity College, Dublin* (Dublin, 1986), 111–122.

consequence of the rising. Such inventories provide us with details on the skills and activities of the settlers in Ireland, and we gain even more precise information on the composition of this community because the deponents usually categorized themselves according to either social position or occupation.

The most striking conclusion that emerges from an analysis of the thousands of surviving depositions is that the character of British settlement in Ireland varied from one province to the other and even within each of the four provinces. It appears also that relations between natives and newcomers were equally varied and that the character of the uprising in the different parts of the country was in some respects related to the previous relationships between the settler and native communities. A comprehensive analysis of the entire body of evidence would clearly be beyond the scope of this present essay, so we shall advance our conclusions on the basis of a study of the depositions from the province of Munster, from Queen's County in the Irish midlands, and from County Fermanagh in northwest Ulster.[15]

Two studies of the English presence in Munster have arrived at strikingly similar conclusions. One, based primarily on the 1641 depositions for that province, alludes to the very diverse and highly skilled settler population and posits a figure of fifteen thousand persons for the size of the settler community in Munster at the point when the rising burst forth in 1641. The second study, by Michael MacCarthy-Morrogh, based on a wider range of evidence, suggests a possible English presence in Munster of twenty-two thousand people prior to the 1641 rising.[16] There is agreement that the bulk of the settlers were drawn from the counties of the English southwest and were attracted to Munster by the ready availability of good-quality farmland at low rent. Most who went from England to Munster were seemingly invited there by English proprietors who had acquired land either directly or indirectly through government-sponsored plantation. These proprietors were particularly eager to attract skilled agricultural workers who would have been in plentiful supply in southwest England. These workers, once they had arrived in Ireland, did not necessarily remain on the estates where they were initially settled, and there is plentiful evidence to suggest that the implementation of a plantation in the 1580s does not necessarily explain the pattern of English settlement that had emerged fifty years later. English proprietors whose estates lay in the less fertile regions of County Kerry had, for example,

15. An analysis of the depositions relating to the province of Munster has been presented in Nicholas Canny, "The Irish Background to Penn's Experiment," in Richard S. Dunn and Mary Maples Dunn, eds., *The World of William Penn* (Philadelphia, 1986), 139–156; for Queen's County, see MS 815, Trinity College, Dublin; and for County Fermanagh, see MS 835, TCD.

16. Canny, "The Irish Background," in Dunn and Dunn, eds., *World of William Penn*; Michael MacCarthy-Morrogh, *The Munster Plantation: English Migration to Southern Ireland, 1583–1641* (Oxford, 1986), esp. 136–176, 244–284.

to retain Irish-born tenants, because the English settlers they had introduced had proven themselves unwilling to remain with them. On the other hand, Irish-born Catholic landowners in the fertile parts of counties Limerick and Tipperary had accepted many English tenants on their properties. Settlement was most dense, however, where plantation coincided with good-quality land. The result was that virtually all the land in a few concentrated areas of Munster was owned by and rented to English people, and an Irish presence in these areas was only evident at the subtenant level.

The valleys of the Blackwater and Bandon rivers were two such areas, and a third was the zone of fertile land that stretched from east County Limerick into the western part of County Tipperary. Yet another pocket of settlement existed in the borderland of northwest County Cork and southwest County Limerick. Proprietors in each of these four areas had built handsome, defensible houses or had rebuilt or redesigned existing castles and towers. These residences were usually surrounded by landscaped gardens and even deer parks, and the landowners frequently set an example for their social inferiors by developing home farms. These usually were organized around the most advanced methods in tillage and pastoral farming, and the fields were frequently divided by fences or by ditches topped with quick-set hedges after the fashion of the West of England.[17]

The patchwork appearance that derived from this mode of organization was sometimes extended into the properties held by the principal English tenants. They were usually required under the terms of their leases to improve their farms, by which was meant the construction of stone houses and out-offices and the enclosure of some fields and meadows. English tenants in Munster usually earned their main income from sheep and cattle farming, but most produced sufficient grain for domestic consumption and earned a rental income from those portions of their rented properties that they in turn let out to subtenants. Those who did engage in tillage cultivated the full range of cereal crops as well as peas and beans. Gardens, which produced such exotic vegetables as the potato, were frequently kept by English tenants, and the more venturesome maintained orchards and dairies or went in for beekeeping.[18]

Many English tenants lived in isolated farmsteads, but a nuclear appearance was provided to the settlement because many English artisans were also attracted to the province. They were lured by the plentiful supply of raw materials, and the artisans most in evidence were those associated with

17. Canny, "The Irish Background," in Dunn and Dunn, eds., *World of William Penn*; MacCarthy-Morrogh, *The Munster Plantation*, 227–230. For a contemporary estate map, see map no. 12 in J. H. Andrews, *Irish Maps*, Irish Heritage Series, no. 18 (Dublin, 1978).

18. Canny, "The Irish Background," in Dunn and Dunn, eds., *World of William Penn*; MacCarthy-Morrogh, *The Munster Plantation*, 223–243.

leather and wool manufacturing and those skilled in the working of timber and the smelting of iron. Artisans, although resident in towns and villages, also took advantage of the abundance of good farming land and diversified into agriculture. Protestant clergy, merchants, and minor traders also took up residence in towns, and some sizable settlements, such as Bandon-Bridge, Tallow, and Youghal were almost entirely English in their population. Large clusters of English people also took up residence in the established port towns of Cork, Waterford, and Limerick, but they were deliberately confined to particular quarters by the Catholic Old English merchants, who were socially dominant in these towns down to 1641. Besides these coherent communities of settlers in Munster, there were smaller clusters wherever natural resources attracted them. There were, for example, small settler communities in west Kerry that were engaged in iron smelting, and there was a chain of settlements along the south coast of Cork where people devoted themselves to fishing and the curing of fish.[19] All, whether artisans or farmers, derived some portion of their income from land, and all deferred to principal Protestant landowners who had come to dominate political life in the province from the early decades of the seventeenth century forward.

There is, therefore, clear evidence that an English community had been brought into existence in Munster during the first half of the seventeenth century, and it even assumed the appearance of self-sufficiency wherever the settlers were thick on the ground and were linked to the Southeast of England by water. Two such communities were those English who had established themselves in the town of Youghal and its vicinity, and those who had settled in the valley of the Bandon River, which flows into the sea at Kinsale. Elsewhere in the province, the English presence was a minority, and while the settlers were sufficiently numerous to maintain a Protestant church structure, they had generally failed to draw the native population into religious communion with them. Moreover, and despite the Protestant political dominance of the province, their leaders were not sufficiently confident to move against the Continent-trained Catholic clergy who were engaged in missionary work among the native population in Munster. The result was the emergence of two rival communities in the province, which were most sharply defined by their religious allegiances and ethnic origins. The divisions between the two communities were heightened by political and economic rivalries, but while the Catholic sector had lost heavily to the recently arrived Protestants at the outset of the period of settlement, there is evidence that they had learned to compete and to hold their ground once they had absorbed the initial shock. There seems reason to believe, therefore, that, if left to themselves, they could have continued to live in relative harmony; and it was the outbreak of disorder in the other provinces of Ireland, combined

19. *Ibid.*

with the heightening of political tensions in England and Scotland at the midpoint of the seventeenth century, that determined that the existing rivalries between the two communities would erupt into open conflict. This in itself provided evidence to English critics that even this most anglicized province of Ireland still lay at the margins of civility.

Queen's County, like Munster, had been subjected to an official plantation in the sixteenth century. This, however, had resulted only in the establishment of a chain of fortified positions, each of which was provided with some portion of adjacent land for its maintenance. This scheme had led to the permanent settlement in the county of some military families, and coherent communities of English settlers developed in the principal garrison towns. The settlement was, however, disturbed by the frequent and sometimes prolonged revolts that characterized the history of Ireland in the sixteenth century, and those who then settled in the province enjoyed uninterrupted occupancy only when more peaceful conditions came to prevail in the seventeenth century.[20]

Some of the Elizabethan settlers in Queen's County, or their descendants, were still prominent there by 1641, and a few of their number, including some Hovendens and Cosbys, had so come to identify with their locale that they took the part of the insurgents in the rising of that year.[21] The intended role of these Elizabethan settlers as leaders of the Protestant interest had, by the 1640s, been taken over by a fresh group of settlers, most of them officeholders in the Dublin administration. They sought to add to their social prestige by the acquisition of land, and they were attracted to Queen's County because it contained a reasonable proportion of good-quality land and was proximate to Dublin. Some property was acquired by English officeholders through purchase and mortgage transactions, but more was obtained by fraudulent means through a calculated misuse of office.[22]

As a consequence, an English Protestant landed elite had come to dominate Queen's County by the middle of the seventeenth century, and it included some of the most influential people in the Dublin government. The most forceful of these was Sir Charles Coote, whose property lay in the town and barony of Mountrath. Others who emerged as leaders of a new settler community were Thomas Ridgeway, earl of Londonderry, whose property,

20. For the 16th-century settlement, see Dean G. White, "The Tudor Plantations in Ireland before 1571" (Ph.D. diss., University of Dublin, 1968).

21. See the deposition of John Barnard, MS 815, fol. 162, TCD. He had been a soldier in the Elizabethan wars and listed those of English surname who participated in the insurrection.

22. Terence O. Ranger, "Richard Boyle and the Making of an Irish Fortune, 1588–1614," *Irish Historical Studies*, X (1956–1957), 257–297.

the manor of Gallen Ridgeway, lay in the vicinity of Ballinakill; Adam Loftus, Viscount Ely, whose county seat was at Monasterevan; and Charles, Lord Lambert, who held property in the vicinity of Mountmellick. The English-based George, Lord Digby (and son-in-law to the earl of Cork), also held an estate in the county, and substantial properties were also held by George Grymes, Esq., and by Oliver Walshe, an Irish Protestant who occupied a position in the Court of Common Pleas.[23]

Most of these, and others besides, invested heavily in the construction or repair of residential castles and in the development of ornamental grounds and estate towns or villages. The earl of Londonderry, for example, purchased his property at Ballinakill from the Cosby family, the original Elizabethan grantees, "and afterwards planted, built and made a town corporate . . . which cost by estimation £10,000."[24] This figure, if true, was clearly exceptional, but the principal planters did invest heavily in the establishment of manufacturing towns, where artisans from England settled. That promoted at Mountrath by Sir Charles Coote seems to have been the most substantial, and there was a total of forty-five individuals from that town who made depositions in 1642. Many of these were textile workers employed in woolen manufacturing or in the linen and fustian works that Coote established in the town. Philip Sergeant, who identified himself as the overseer of this latter enterprise, placed a value of £716 on Coote's losses in fustians, linen cloth, and cotton yarn while another servant of Coote, named Isaac Sands, provided an inventory of the woolen cloth and weaving equipment that had been lost as a consequence of the rising and valued it at £560. These "broadcloths, broad bays and serges, both coloured and plain," had been "sold (but not delivered) by articles of agreement to merchants at Youghal . . . who were to transport them to Spain and the Low Countries."[25]

Output of the ironworks that had been got underway by Lord Viscount Ely and of the coal mining that had been promoted by George Grymes was transported to the Munster ports, taking advantage of inland waterways. These enterprises also created the need to import skilled workers to Queen's County, and one John Winsmore, who had been employed at Mountmellick, alleged that he could earn fifty pounds a year from his skill as an ironworker. What his precise skill in ironworking was is not specified, but he included among his belongings some "writings of consequence as instructions for the casting of brass and iron ordnance."[26]

Such exceptionally skilled workers would have been invited to Queen's

23. These depositions are as follows: MS 815, fols. 142, 144, 149, 154, 180, 221–224, 335, 358, 371, TCD.

24. *Ibid.*, fol. 358.

25. *Ibid.*, fols. 180, 351.

26. The details are provided in Gerard Boate, *Ireland's Naturall History* . . . (London, 1652), 136–137.

County by the principal English proprietors, who would also have borne most of the cost involved in setting them up in business. Artisans with more commonplace skills associated with leather making, coal mining, and timber processing seem to have been attracted by the availability of raw materials; and it would appear that they themselves bore the principal cost of developing their farms and promoting their crafts. Thus, for example, a smith named William Cooke who had been brought to the county by George Grymes had invested £100 of his own money in acquiring a coal mine and in purchasing "materials for that work." At the same time, he received from Grymes a farm on a long lease (of which fifty-six years were still unexpired in 1641), but for this he had to pay an entry fine of £220 and was obliged to invest £200 "in building and ditching." Similar is the case of Thomas Campion, a tanner who had settled at Mountrath under Sir Charles Coote. He was obliged to lay out £100 in the "planting" of his tanyard, the erection of a residence, and the acquisition of two leases of land. The investment would appear to have generated an immediate income, because Campion claimed to have lost leather to the value of £200 in 1641 besides losses amounting to £60 in cattle, horses, and sheep. What was involved in getting a tanyard under way was spelled out more precisely by Matthew Morris of Maryborough, who described himself as "a great dealer" who had "a great charge in hides." Morris had invested an initial £60 "in planting and building on his tenement, tanhouses, a malt house and a stable." Then he spent a further £40 in "sowing his birch," which provided him with a supply of bark for tanning, and he expended as much as £100 at one time in purchasing "new green hides," which were likely to spoil if they were not immediately treated in his brass pans.[27]

Those English artisans who had settled in Queen's County seemed satisfied that their initial investment was justified by the opportunities that were open to them. Landlords appeared equally satisfied, because they enjoyed an initial cash injection from the entry fines paid by English settlers, while the long-term value of their property was enhanced by the improvements made by their artisan tenants.

Arrangements made by the principal landlords when disposing of their estates in Queen's County seem to have been strikingly similar to those made when leasing their urban properties. On these occasions, large parcels of land, sometimes with castles attached, were assigned to incoming English gentlemen freeholders. Many of these appear to have been drawn from the army, and the rule seems to have been that such gentlemen were assigned large holdings for terms ranging from fifty to ninety-nine years in return for entry fines that could be as high as five hundred pounds, depending on the size and quality of the property. The tenant was then required to pay a small

27. Cooke: MS 815, fols. 144, 154, TCD. Campion: fol. 158. Morris: fol. 236.

annual rent but was also obliged to improve the property. This work could take the form of "enclosing of his whole ground with post and rail," as it did in the case of Edward Benfield, or of "building of several shingled houses of clay, stables and offices."[28]

It was always in the interest of these gentlemen tenants to develop a home farm from which they would generate a regular source of income and provide food for their domestic requirements. No cost was spared in this effort, and the outlay in house building, field division, and the stocking of a home farm could sometimes exceed one thousand pounds.[29] All gentlemen tenants promoted some mixed farming, presumably to meet domestic requirements; most also maintained a garden plot, where vegetables and sometimes potatoes were grown; and a few kept orchards.[30] Thereafter, gentlemen tended to favor either tillage or stock raising on the home farm for commercial purposes, and it is not clear whether choices were dictated by the nature of the soil or by their previous experience with agriculture. Those who opted for stock raising kept cattle, sheep, horses, swine, and poultry, and they specified in their depositions whenever their stock was of English breed.[31] Those who favored tillage farming produced wheat, oats, barley, and rye, and they also cultivated peas and beans in large quantities.

Some of the native proprietors in Queen's County followed the example of their settler counterparts and assigned sizable estates to English gentlemen. The lure of entry fines may have determined their choice of such principal tenants, even when it was certain to provoke resentment among their kinsmen and followers. Barnaby Dunne of Brittas, who had already placed a strain on his kinship connection by converting to Protestantism, was the most active in this respect and claimed that he had settled English tenants on his estate "to the number of upwards of twenty."[32]

Those English Protestants who were assigned principal tenancies were alert for every opportunity to advance themselves socially and economically. Some did this by taking several leases from different proprietors while others expanded their holdings by accepting land as security on loans that they extended to native landowners.[33] All such acquisitions were with a view to

28. For examples of gentlemen's leases in Queen's County, see *ibid.*, fols. 142, 169, 184, 185, 198, 199, 209, 212, 218, 246, 261, 268, 277, 328, 330, 358. Quotations *ibid.*, fols. 169, 199.

29. *Ibid.*, fol. 142.

30. See, for example, *ibid.*, fols. 198, 330.

31. *Ibid.*, fol. 184.

32. *Ibid.*, fols. 190–193, 230, 246; see also Kenneth Nicholls, ed., *The O Doyne (O Duinn) Manuscript* (Dublin, 1983). This manuscript traces the career of Dr. Charles Dunne, the first of his family to become a Protestant, who left his inheritance to his nephew Barnaby Dunne, also a Protestant.

33. See especially the depositions of Job Ward, MS 815, fols. 277–287, and that of Oliver Walshe, fol. 149, TCD.

gaining a regular rental income that would compensate them for their initial outlay. Their preferred tenants were English husbandmen, and some were successful in attracting such tenants. Lieutenant Henry Gilbert, for example, claimed that he and Sir William Gilbert had jointly settled five hundred English people (including wives and children of tenants) on their estate.[34] Settlement on this scale seems to have been highly exceptional, and the depositions for the county suggest rather a thin scatter of English yeomen and husbandmen on the principal holdings held by English settlers in the county.

These English farmers followed the example of their social betters in the agriculture they pursued. Most appear to have been well equipped with iron plows, plow chains, and oxen, but carts with ironbound wheels appear to have been in short supply. These cultivators indicated that they grew the full range of cereal crops while some harvested peas and beans in quantity and grew vegetables, including the potato.[35] Some tenant farmers indicated that they had invested substantially in improving their properties, and a few revealed themselves to be specialist farmers. Richard Queensie of Mountrath, for example, specified that he kept eleven cows for milking, and Rowland Vaughan, who held his farm from Barnaby Dunne, had concentrated on fruit farming, which provided him with an annual income of twenty pounds. He had apparently every intention of expanding his business, because he lost in 1641 "6,000 young trees of pears and apples of choicest sort," which he estimated to be worth forty pounds.[36]

Such individuals were enterprising by any standard, but they were few in Queen's County. Why this was so is nowhere mentioned, but we can take it that the only concentrations of English settlement in the county were in the manufacturing towns and their immediate vicinity. Because they were thinly scattered, the English settlers in Queen's County identified very closely with the proprietors who had brought them there and whom they recognized as their protectors. This is revealed most explicitly in the case of John Fortune, who had settled at Ballinakill on an estate held by Captain Richard Steele, "a gentleman of his Majesty's privy chamber," from the earl of Londonderry. Fortune, in his deposition, revealed that he had been a servant to Captain Steele for thirty years but that he was "by birth an Indian Pethagorian but now a Christian and lately an inhabitant of Ballinakill."[37]

What emerges from this study of English settlement in Queen's County is that the principal resources of the county had been brought effectively into English hands. A substantial amount of the productive land had come into

34. *Ibid.*, fol. 328.
35. *Ibid.*, fols. 167, 212, 227, 239, 292, 302, 321, 323.
36. *Ibid.*, fols. 215, 273.
37. *Ibid.*, fols. 322, 358.

English possession by 1641, and the available raw materials in the county were being exploited by communities of settler artisans. Land occupancy in the vicinity of these settlements had shifted in favor of these recent arrivals in the county, but beyond these limited areas land appears to have been farmed by Irish tenants and subtenants. Everything points to the fact that the settlers were a distinct but a very visible minority in the county, but it was also evident that little had been achieved beyond the imposition of an English appearance upon a county that was still essentially Irish in character. Not only that, but it was also a county that was essentially Catholic, and it was decidedly different from Munster, because the native proprietors who had lost their property to make room for the settlers were in many cases still alive and resentful. So also were the Irish tenants who had been pushed off the better holdings on the estates of the new Protestant landowners, and both groups were watchful for every opportunity to recover what they, and their priests, believed was rightfully theirs. The English community was therefore much less securely based than was its counterpart in Munster, and it was very quickly wiped off the land once political order broke down in Ireland during the closing months of 1641. Therefore, if proof were required, this established the case for Englishmen that the Irish midlands was still an Irish, Catholic, and essentially barbaric region.

An English, or more accurately a British, appearance had also been imposed on County Fermanagh, which was one of the six Ulster counties subjected to systematic plantation in the years after 1609. Land in this county under the plantation scheme was granted to English and Scottish undertakers and to deserving natives, and each occupied distinct areas of the county.[38] Their holdings were interspersed by the property assigned for the endowment of the established church, the free school of the county, and Trinity College, Dublin. Most of this land fell into the hands of Englishmen who enjoyed special favor in these three institutions, and the servitors who received grants of land in County Fermanagh were also usually Englishmen. Servitors, under the conditions of the Ulster Plantation, were those who had served the crown in a civil or military capacity in the years previous to the plantation, and it was the intention of the government that they should be granted estates within the area assigned to the Gaelic Irish population so that they could stand guard against them in the event of any further insurrection. These considerations meant that there was some English settlement in all parts of the county, whereas the Scottish and the Irish proprietors tended to be confined to particular baronies.[39]

38. For the Ulster plantation scheme, see n. 11, above.
39. See the details for the Ulster plantation referred to in n. 11, above.

One study of the progress of the plantation in the county indicates that the settler proprietors quickly made their presence visible architecturally with the construction of fortified positions throughout the county. Of these, the castles built by the Scots proved the more durable, because the Scots built strong, defensible buildings of the type that were still necessary in the turbulent conditions of the Scottish lowlands. Some of the English settlers in Fermanagh adopted some military features of these Scottish castles, but they more frequently favored defensible houses of the type that were prevalent in England.[40]

Scots, in the first instance, proved more enterprising in the matter of drawing tenants to the county, but the English, or at least the English servitors, quickened their activity during the years 1613–1619, when recession conditions were manifest in England. Proprietors from England seemed also more willing to employ agents to manage their properties, and the more dynamic of these managers established ownership to property in the county through purchase or mortgage transactions. Englishmen had also proved themselves the more enterprising in taking advantage of the commercial and manufacturing opportunities in the county, and the towns of Enniskillen, Newtown Butler, and Lowtherstown were the results of their endeavors.[41]

There were, as has been noted, physical reminders of the settler presence scattered throughout the county, but settlement was uneven and was concentrated where the land was most fertile. The muster roll of circa 1630 revealed a total adult male presence of 922. The historian of the settlement has concluded that plantation society was very stratified, with a small number of successful landowners and professionals at one extreme and the vast majority of "more humble folks whose lowly status meant that they hardly differed except in nationality and religion from the natives" occupying the lower ranks of the settler community.[42]

This conclusion is borne out by the 143 settlers who made depositions in the aftermath of the 1641 rebellion. Those at the top of the social pyramid—such as Nicholas Willoughby, Esq., of the barony of Coole; Ann Blennerhassett, the widow of Francis Blennerhassett, Esq., of Hassetsford; and Alice Champion, widow of Arthur Champion, Esq., of Shanoge—revealed that they had succeeded economically as well as almost any settler group in the country.[43] All three revealed that they had held property in several counties, and all estimated their losses in thousands of pounds. Their depositions also

40. John Dennis Johnston, "The Plantation of County Fermanagh, 1610–41: An Archaeological and Historical Survey" (master's thesis, Queen's University, Belfast, 1976), esp. 106–118, 147–189.

41. *Ibid.*, 118–138.

42. *Ibid.*, 77–79.

43. Their depositions, respectively, are as follows: MS 835, fols. 184, 236, 196, TCD.

alluded to the substantial investment that they had made in developing their properties and revealed the means by which they had advanced themselves. Ann Blennerhassett supplied little detail on what had been lost besides mentioning that it included lands, castles, houses, and farms as well as crops and stock on the land and the investment involved in "building improvements" on the lands and farms in counties Fermanagh, Cavan, and Monaghan and on an ironworks. What precise improvements were promoted by the Champions emerges from the deposition of Alice Champion, where she made reference to the castle and mansion at Shanoge together with jewels, plate, and ready money to the value of £820 and household stuff, hangings, carpets, bedding, and linen with other implements and furniture to the value of £500. The Champions had stocked their property in Fermanagh with sheep and cattle "of English breed," and they apparently cultivated spring as well as winter corn. A detailed inventory of his losses in counties Fermanagh and Monaghan was provided by Nicholas Willoughby, and they included large quantities of wheat, barley, and oats, a flock of 240 sheep, a herd of 200 oxen, cows, and younger cattle, and about 40 stud mares as well as other mares, colts, and garrans. Willoughby's house at Carrow in the barony of Coole seems to have been furnished just as luxuriously as that of the Champions at Shanoge, because he estimated his loss in plate, household goods, apparel, and linen at £275.

What is most interesting about these depositions is that they reveal how these particular families advanced themselves. All three had some land in freehold, but more extensive properties were leased from other landowners and were then rented out in large blocks to subtenants on annual terms that allowed for the increase of rents as the properties were improved.[44] They also seem to have been in the business of lending money, and Willoughby divulged that he had lost up to £800 in ready money and that two of his properties were held by him "in mortgage for monies lent," one for fifteen years to come and the other for twenty-six years yet to come. Alice Champion revealed that she and her husband were owed £697 by "bonds, specialities conveyances and assurances for money lent and trusted."[45] Who their creditors were is not specified, and if we can assume that they were mostly belonging to the Gaelic population, it emerges from the deposition that the Champions also made use of their money to promote themselves at the expense of their planter neighbors. Besides the manor and lands at Shanoge that were the basis of their advance, the Champions had acquired the manor and lands of Castle Coole from Captain Roger Atkinson and Edith, his wife, for an annual rent of £20, which was to increase to £100 on the death of

44. See the three depositions as listed *ibid.*
45. Willoughby: MS 835, fol. 184, TCD. Champion: fol. 196.

either one of the Atkinsons. Then, after the death of the surviving partner, the property of Castle Coole was to revert "to Arthur Champion and his heirs for ever."[46]

What this arrangement reveals is how an astute manager in Fermanagh was able to gain possession of a property that produced a rental income of £200 per annum for little more than the payment of a retirement pension to the original owners. Professionals who moved into the county enjoyed similar opportunities to advance themselves, although not to anything like the same level of affluence. Clergymen seem to have been particularly successful in promoting themselves and their children in County Fermanagh. They were able to do so because the church, and its supporting institutions, was particularly well endowed under the terms of the plantation in Ulster, and clergymen were thus able to employ their profits to extend their holdings in the county. How this could be done is evident from the deposition of the Reverend George Fletcher. His parsonage was worth £200 per annum to him, and his stock on his parsonage in 1641 was estimated by him as worth £270 in cattle and £60 in corn. He also owned household goods, books, plate, apparel, and ready money to the value of £150, and he claimed that debts to the amount of £360 were owing to him from British and Irish inhabitants of the county.[47] The size of this sum, and the fact that similar amounts were owing to the other Protestant clergy from County Fermanagh, suggests that extending money on loan to their neighbors was one means by which these clergymen advanced their fortunes.[48] More of the income that came from their church lands must have been used to pay entry fines to landowners who would accept them as tenants. George Fletcher had acquired a long lease on an extensive property from Nicholas Willoughby, another from Christopher Whittendale, yeoman, of which sixteen years were still unexpired in 1641, and a third extensive lease from Mr. John Hamilton for the duration of Hamilton's life.[49]

Other clergymen from the county identified similar arrangements they had transacted with the Protestant proprietors there. One Robert Flack of Mullaghmore, who identified himself as "son and heir to Robert Flack, clerk deceased," claimed gentry status for both himself and his brother Philip Flack. That he considered himself entitled to do so is suggested by his ownership of "freehold lands of inheritance of clear yearly rent of three score pounds whereupon there was built one fair house or castle which cost the building six hundred pounds." He was able to afford this style of living

46. *Ibid.*, fol. 196.
47. *Ibid.*, fol. 105.
48. For other Protestant clergy engaged in moneylending, see *ibid.*, fols. 143, 167, 238.
49. *Ibid.*, fol. 105.

because he also possessed the rents and profits of considerable scopes of church land besides other leases of property, and he had stocked an extensive home farm and engaged in lending money to his neighbors.[50]

These depositions from clergymen and their children reveal that economic and social advancement could be attained by enterprising settlers in County Fermanagh. So also do the depositions from those who held civil offices in the county and those who assumed the description "yeoman."[51] Thereafter, however, there occurs an economic chasm descending toward those who categorized themselves by trade rather than social position. A wide range of artisans—blacksmiths, skinners, tailors, carpenters, and linen and wool weavers—was included, but none of them appears to have acquired any considerable wealth as had their counterparts in Munster and in Queen's County. Neither had those who were engaged in commercial occupations, despite the fact that both artisans and traders seem to have been enterprising. One Ursula Robinson revealed that she and her late husband, John, had stocked wines and spirits as well as clothing in their store when she claimed losses to the value of £9 in "wines as sack, white wine, claret wine and aquavitae," but her total losses in the insurrection still amounted to only £231.[52]

Why the manufacturing and commercial elements among the settler population in Fermanagh endured rather than flourished remains something of a mystery. The remoteness of County Fermanagh from any dynamic markets such as were available to settlers in Munster probably has something to do with this economic sluggishness. So also may the fact that most settlers there came from Scotland and the northwest of England, where exposure to advanced manufacturing and agricultural skills would have been altogether less than that available to settlers in Munster and the Irish midlands, who came usually from the more economically advanced southern half of England. Although not spectacularly successful economically, the artisan settlers in County Fermanagh did establish urban communities, even if the houses they erected corresponded with their wealth. The landed property of the urban settlers in Fermanagh would also appear to have been confined to the towns and their immediate vicinity and did not extend deep into the countryside as was the case in Queen's County and in Munster. This trait is probably accounted for by the fact that relatively poor artisans, such as existed in Fermanagh, would not have commanded sufficient money to pay entry fines that would have appealed to landowners in the county. The promotion of a civil appearance of the county rested, therefore, principally upon landowners, Protestant clergy, and their close associates, and it was

50. *Ibid.*, fol. 201.

51. See the following depositions, *ibid.*, fols. 84, 125, 131, 147, 162, 205, 207, 209.

52. *Ibid.*, fol. 213.

consequently less comprehensive than what has been noted in the other areas that have been considered. More to the point, these successful ones were generally more parasitic and were less active in promoting wealth than were their counterparts in Munster and the Irish midlands. This fact may explain why the assault against the British presence in Fermanagh, and throughout Ulster, was more comprehensive and more bloody than in the other areas of settlement when political authority collapsed in 1641.

This survey of British settlement in three distinct parts of Ireland indicates that a settler presence was evident everywhere in the country and that all landowners who would survive, whether native or foreign, recognized the need to maximize their rents and to make full use of existing raw materials with a view to generating extra income through the promotion of manufacturing. This need meant that traditional communal and kinship obligations were progressively disregarded and that the good landlord had now become identified as the economically successful one. Such landlords, whether natives or newcomers, spoke English and were familiar with English law, and they vied with each other to become involved in the administration of the country at the central and local levels. All of this was regarded positively in England, as was the fact that all parts of Ireland appeared to be under secure English government control. As a consequence, there was no longer any difficulty, as there had been in the sixteenth century, of persuading Englishmen to accept positions in the Dublin administration or in the Irish Protestant church, and frequent keen competition between Englishmen occurred over the senior and more lucrative posts. Some even believed that service in Ireland could lead to career advancement in England, and there was clear evidence that those (whether Scots or English) who had acquired property in Ireland and who had persisted with the development of their estates had attained economic and social advancement far in excess of what would have been within their reach had they remained at home.[53]

This success was symbolized by grand residences, by the ostentatious funeral rites that were favored by all landed families in Ireland, and by the persistent demand for Irish titles that produced an inflation of honors that, proportionally, was far in excess of anything that happened in England at the same time.[54] Those who had emerged as leaders of the Irish Protestant

53. See, for example, the keen competition for the governorship of Ireland at the time of Wentworth's appointment, a thing unthinkable in the 16th century (Kearney, *Strafford in Ireland*, 24–31). On economic chance at home, see Canny, *The Upstart Earl*.

54. C. R. Mayes, "The Early Stuarts and the Irish Peerage," *English Historical Review*, LXXXIII (1959), 227–251; Rolf Loeber, "Sculptured Memorials to the Dead in Early Seventeenth-Century Ireland," Royal Irish Academy, *Proceedings*,

community also had sufficient confidence in themselves to play a direct part in the shaping of English, and even Scottish, politics whenever intervention seemed to be in the interest of their own advancement or self-preservation.[55] Some of those who made their careers in the Irish church also became involved in the formulation of a general Protestant theology, and it seems to have been a matter of great pride to the Protestant community in Ireland that one of their number, Archbishop James Ussher of Armagh, had won international recognition as a formulator of Protestant doctrine. Finally, as the capstone of their success, leaders of the settler community in Ireland could negotiate marriage alliances with English and Scottish noble and gentry families.[56]

All of these developments were noted favorably in England, but they were outweighed by the fact that, despite such evidence of wealth and success, Ireland continued to be a drain upon the English exchequer. Efforts were made by Thomas Wentworth, earl of Strafford, who served as governor in Ireland 1633–1641, to remedy this situation, and he also sought to make Ireland a truly civil and Protestant society by extending plantation into the areas that were hitherto untouched.[57]

The fact that Strafford wished to offer the spoils of this further confiscation to a new wave of settlers from England, and that he would have entrusted the government of the country to such new favorites rather than to the existing Protestants, reflected his (and the English government's) disdain for the altered society that had developed in Ireland. It was also evident to Strafford, as it was to the Irish Protestant community, that their success had been achieved at the expense of a native population that was evidently resentful of the losses that it had sustained and that was clearly cut off from the settler society by religious divisions. The frequency with which the settlers alluded to the existence of plots to achieve their overthrow suggests that they themselves were aware that they lived in an unstable order.[58]

It is strange, in the light of these frequent alarms, that the Protestant

LXXXI, sect. C (1981), 267–293; Terence Francis McCarthy, "Ulster Office, 1552–1800" (master's thesis, Queen's University, Belfast, 1983), esp. 153–184; Raymond Gillespie, "Funerals and Society in Early Seventeenth-Century Ireland," *Journal of the Royal Society of Antiquaries of Ireland*, CXV (1985), 86–91.

55. The politics of the Irish Protestant community in the first half of the 17th century can best be traced in Kearney, *Strafford in Ireland*. See also J. R. MacCormack, "The Irish Adventurers and the English Civil War," *Irish Historical Studies*, X (1956–1957), 21–58; Julia Buckroyd, "Lord Broghill and the Scottish Church, 1655–1656," *Journal of Ecclesiastical History*, XXVII (1976), 359–368.

56. R. Buick Knox, *James Ussher, Archbishop of Armagh* (Cardiff, 1967); Canny, *The Upstart Earl*, esp. 77–123.

57. Kearney, *Strafford in Ireland*, esp. 104–129; Terence Ranger, "Strafford in Ireland: A Revaluation," *Past and Present*, no. 19 (April 1961), 26–45.

58. Raymond Gillespie, *Conspiracy: Ulster Plots and Plotters in 1615* (Belfast, 1987).

settlers in Ireland were caught unawares by the popular insurrection against them that erupted, initially in Ulster and quickly throughout the country at large, in October 1641 and the subsequent winter months of 1641–1642.[59] They (or their spokesmen) quickly concluded that the insurrection had been long in preparation and that it was guided by clearly defined objectives that had been agreed upon between the Catholic landowners in Ireland and their Catholic sponsors in continental Europe. When witnessed from this perspective, what occurred in Ireland was part of an international conspiracy aimed at universal overthrow of Protestantism and particularly in the British dominions that were perceived as the final bastion of Protestantism in Europe. Much of the self-scrutiny that the victims of the assault were encouraged to engage in provided some support for this interpretation, but such generalizations were contradicted by the thousands of more casual admissions that were made by those Protestants who made sworn statements in the aftermath of the revolt.

Those who collected the depositions were concerned to give ample exposure to those witnesses who could present evidence to the effect that the rising was indeed the product of a Catholic conspiracy. One witness who could do so was the Reverend Ricard Bourke, master of the free school in County Fermanagh.[60] Bourke was himself an Irish Protestant, a native of County Galway and a graduate of Trinity College, Dublin. He suffered his principal losses in County Fermanagh, where he had enjoyed his benefices, but he also lost some property that he had inherited in County Galway. He therefore had occasion to report on what he understood of the rising there and in neighboring County Clare as well as in County Fermanagh. In doing so he believed himself better able than most deponents to divine the motivation of the insurgents, because he was conversant in the Irish language and familiar with Gaelic literature. There was no doubt in Bourke's mind as to the priestly origin of the insurrection, and he alluded to the popularization of the prophecies of Irish saints that were "very commonly, confidently, and vehemently urged and justified by their priests for undoubted verities," and "all which prophecies the rebels did conceive to import the extirpation of the English and the settling of the whole kingdom in the Irish." In support of this Bourke cited from one such prophecy in the Irish language and supplied an English translation of what he had cited, and he further testified that he "saw . . . in the hands of one of the rebels . . . an English book printed in the Low Countries importing another prophecy of St. Patrick."

59. Aidan Clarke, "The Genesis of the Ulster Rising of 1641," in Peter Roebuck, ed., *Plantation to Partition* (Belfast, 1981), 29–45; Raymond Gillespie, "The End of an Era: Ulster and the Outbreak of the 1641 Rising," in Ciaran Brady and Gillespie, eds., *Natives and Newcomers: Essays on the Making of Irish Colonial Society, 1534–1641* (Dublin, 1986), 191–213; Canny, *From Reformation to Restoration*, 205–211.

60. MS 835, fol. 258, TCD.

Besides fueling the rebellion by authenticating such prophecies, the priests had, according to Bourke, also incited the Irish to revolt by leading them to believe "that the popish clergy beyond the seas did and would assist them with gunpowder and arms in this war which they call the Holy War of the Confederate Catholics." Bourke professed that he had heard statements to this effect from priests and friars themselves and also to the effect that "the Popish clergy beyond sea [had] publicly preached, applauded and commended" the war in Ireland as "a Catholic war" aimed at "destroying of the Puritans whom they called heretics." Then, when referring to the actual unfolding of the revolt, Bourke had "observed generally and . . . in some instances" that the priests in Ireland "were great incendiaries of cruelties." When Bourke had heard a rebel wish that the English in Ireland were gone to Newfoundland, he had witnessed the same rebel reprimanded by "a priest standing by [who] maliciously answered he would not wish so good a land to be defiled by them." Priestly concern with defilement was again evidenced, according to Bourke, by their refusal to have Protestants buried in their family graves, "as they said heretics must not be buried in hallowed ground," and by their concern to exhume the corpses of Protestants from churches that had come under Catholic control as a consequence of the rising. All such instances, according to Bourke, were proof that Catholic priests wanted to rid the country of Protestants, and he alleged that Ever Mac Mahon, "a priest titulary bishop of Down," was "a prime contriver" of the insurrection. Moreover, Bourke was convinced that priests were the authors of the cruelties associated with the rising, and he reported "as he heard that Hugh McGuire McDeegan a popish priest at Letterstowe stood by as commander and judge while fifteen English Protestants were hanged by rogues by him brought thither for that purpose."[61]

Several other deponents from County Fermanagh presented testimony to the evil actions and evil intention of this particular priest, but the general thrust of the evidence presented was that priests exerted a restraining rather than a provocative influence upon the insurrection.[62] This is not to suggest that Bourke's allegations were completely fanciful, but, rather, that he failed to acknowledge that the Catholic clergy were generally opposed to the wanton slaughter that became associated with the insurrection in Ulster and some other areas of the country. To this end, priests sometimes acted as protectors of Protestants against their would-be assailants, and this was duly acknowledged in several depositions. Priests also seem to have been concerned that Protestants should be given the opportunity to convert to Catholicism before being disturbed by the insurgents, and many deponents

61. *Ibid.*

62. See, for example, the deposition of Robert Flack, *ibid.*, fol. 201, and that of Elizabeth Fletcher, fol. 242.

testified that they had been offered promises of immunity in return for their conversion.[63] On the other hand, there is ample corroborating evidence of the desire of particular priests to clear what they regarded as sanctified ground of the corpses of heretics, and there is supporting evidence from Gaelic as well as Protestant sources that frequent reference was made to prophecy to predict a successful outcome to the insurrection.[64]

It appears, therefore, that the Reverend Mr. Bourke was correct in attributing an active role to the Catholic clergy during the course of the insurrection—what he did not admit was that the Catholic clergy were attempting to direct the insurrection to serve their particular purpose of advancing the position of Catholicism in Ireland and that they stood out against the insurgents whenever they threatened to deviate from this purpose. Such divergences occurred whenever the participants in the insurrections placed immediate material gain over loftier objectives. This conduct could take the form of wanton killing and robbing of the settler population, the seizure of their property, and the destruction of the improvements they had promoted. The efforts of the Catholic clergy to prevent such occurrences proved to be of little purpose as the movement spilled over everywhere to become a popular outburst of resentment against the changes that had been proceeding in Ireland over the previous half-century.

The first reason for this resentment was the fact that the better farms of land had come into Protestant occupancy almost everywhere in the country. Next was the level of indebtedness of the native population, which had accelerated their loss of property to the newcomers, and third was the operation of new market forces, which always seemed to favor the settler over the native. With a view to remedying these grievances, insurgents throughout the country seized control of the lands that they coveted, they systematically destroyed documentary evidences of entitlement to those properties, and they took possession of all movable wealth while also tearing up whatever bills of indebtedness they could find.[65] Some insurgents, appar-

63. Among the depositions for County Fermanagh, for example, there is that of Francis Wyne, who believed he would have been murdered but for one "Turlough O Queely a popish priest who carried him nine miles out of the town to a private place of safety" (*ibid.*, fol. 251). One Morris Middlebrook from County Fermanagh testified that he was compelled to leave or have the house burned over his head "unless he and they would go to Mass and lie in garrison with them" (*ibid.*, fol. 141).

64. From Queen's County alone there are references to exhumation in the following depositions: MS 815, fols. 183, 190, 217, 241, TCD. On prophecy: Cecile O'Rahilly, ed., *Five Seventeenth-Century Political Poems* (Dublin, 1977), 27–28, 29–30, 31.

65. In County Fermanagh one Grace Lovett testified that her assailant "also took away the lease, writings, will and escriptions that this deponent had that contained the estate of the said several parcels of land" (MS 835, fol. 133, TCD). Edward Slack, for example, was deprived of "bonds and bills due from English and Irish" (fol. 170).

ently in their desire to destroy the symbols of the new economic order that had led to their destruction, broke up the various manufacturing works and even the enclosures that had been introduced by the settlers, and many of the mansions of the Protestant landowners were also burned and demolished during the course of the rebellion.[66]

When the insurgents were engaged upon these acts of destruction, atrocities frequently occurred as the settlers either attempted to defend their property or refused to divulge where their money was hidden. Such incidents were general throughout the country; but in Ulster, where, as was noted, the British settlement had assumed a more parasitic aspect, assault against the person was more deliberate and more widespread. The Protestant clergy among the Ulster deponents claimed repeatedly that members of their profession had been specifically identified for extermination, and the truth of this claim would not be surprising when account is taken of their role as moneylenders in the community. Clergy would also have become targets for attack whenever they came forward as leaders of the Protestant community against the assailants and whenever they invited fleeing Protestants to take refuge in their houses and churches. Many besides clergy were, of course, killed in Ulster, and it was the bloody incidents that occurred in that province that gave rise to the notion that a general massacre of the Protestants in Ireland was in prospect.

The argument for a massacre is not sustained by the experience in the Irish midlands, where the purpose of the assailants was clearly to recover lost property through the expulsion, rather than the slaughter, of the settler population. This relative moderation may, of course, be explained by the fact that the settlers in such areas as Queen's County were thin on the ground and were not therefore in a position to resist the assault that had been launched against them. The experience of Munster was closer to that of Queen's County than to what occurred in Ulster. While similar, the experience in Munster was not identical with that in the midlands, because the heavy concentration of settlers in particular areas of Munster enabled them to stand their ground against their assailants until they received military assistance from England.

This summary of what happened in 1641 suggests that there was some correlation between the nature of the assault against the settlers in particular areas of Ireland and the character of the settlement in those areas. The suggestion cannot be pushed too far, however, because the rising did not happen simultaneously in all parts of the country, and both settlers and insurgents outside Ulster would have had an opportunity to learn from what had happened in that province. One factor that was general, however, was

66. The most graphic description of such a destruction comes from County Down in the deposition of Major William Burley (MS 837, fol. 29, TCD).

the opposition of the Catholic clergy to the excesses that occurred and the failure of Protestant leaders to acknowledge this restraining influence. Instead, the publicists on the Protestant side engaged upon a blatant propaganda exercise that asserted that the rising was religious in its motivation and that ignored any grievances the Catholics might have had because of the political or economic policies of the settlers. Such simplification made it easier for the pamphleteers to call upon the government in England to take revenge upon the Irish Catholic population for the alleged massacre that had been perpetrated by their priests.[67] Insofar as an economic dimension entered into their argument, it was that the settlers were credited with creating the conditions that would lead to the enrichment of everybody in Ireland, and those who had engaged upon the insurrection were blamed for a wanton destruction that had returned Ireland to the barbarism from which it had been recently recovered.[68]

This second point, which implied that all Irish Catholics were barbarians, won ready acceptance in England, but not so the further claim that the behavior of the settlers had been exemplary. Instead, the occurrence of the rising was widely attributed in England to the negligence and cupidity of the settlers, and while the primary purpose of government was to take revenge upon those who had been involved in the insurrection, the second ambition became one of establishing a new social and political order as an assurance against a repetition of what had happened. The rapid development of civil tumult in England itself meant that the government of Charles I was never able to come to grips with the Irish problem, and it fell to Oliver Cromwell, who had emerged victorious in the English Civil War, to reestablish English government authority in Ireland. The military actions of Cromwell certainly achieved the revenge that was called for, and he also devised a comprehensive scheme of land confiscation for the entire country. This was designed to bring all ownership of property, and with it all political influence in Ireland, into the hands of ardent English Protestants who had supported the cause of Parliament during the years of civil war. They, it was hoped, would create a secure political order and would establish an environment whereby the entire Irish population would, for the first time, be brought to an acceptance of the Protestant faith.[69]

As it happened, the Cromwellian regime was not sufficiently enduring nor were its spiritual personnel sufficiently numerous to achieve this second

67. Keith J. Lindley, "The Impact of the 1641 Rebellion upon England and Wales, 1641–5," *Irish Historical Studies*, XVIII (1972–1973), 143–173.

68. This point was advanced aggressively in Boate, *Ireland's Naturall History*; see esp. 89.

69. Karl S. Bottigheimer, *English Money and Irish Land: The "Adventurers" in the Cromwellian Settlement of Ireland* (Oxford, 1971); T. C. Barnard, *Cromwellian Ireland: English Government and Reform in Ireland, 1649–1660* (Oxford, 1975).

objective. Many Cromwellians who were granted land in Ireland also proved lukewarm in their commitment to the country and quickly sold out, and the Cromwellian government was forced to come to terms with those Protestant landowners who were already established in Ireland. The result was a country that was indeed under secure Protestant control—albeit old pre-Cromwellian Protestants—but where the bulk of the population still clung to the Catholic religion. This latter factor made Ireland an oddity in European terms as well as within the context of a British empire, and the experience of 1641 and its aftermath also reestablished the notion that Ireland suffered from latent instability.

This view was hotly disputed by the Protestants who were dominant in Irish government, but it was given added authority by the dilution of the Cromwellian land settlement that was countenanced by Charles II after he had been restored to the English crown in 1660. Under this new arrangement some land was returned to those Irish Catholics who had remained true to the loyalist cause during the interregnum.[70] This provided Catholics in Ireland with a new power base, which they extended through the purchase and lease of property from Protestants during the 1660s and 1670s. As a consequence, when in 1685 political circumstances turned unexpectedly in favor of Catholics with the accession of a Catholic monarch, James II, to the English throne, the leaders of the Catholic interest in Ireland grasped at this God-given opportunity to recover that property of which they had been deprived under the Cromwellian settlement.[71]

This ambition to overthrow the Cromwellian land confiscation was not favored by the monarch himself or by his advisers in England, lest it provoke opposition to his rule at home. However, James had no option but to support this scheme once he had been ousted from the crown of England by his son-in-law William of Orange, who was enthroned as William III. Thereafter the only support that was available to James came from his Irish Catholic subjects who were willing to hold out in his favor and, with the support of troops from Louis XIV of France, assist him in his bid to recover the position that he had just lost.

This bid proved futile, but the immediate consequence for Ireland was that most of the country had been placed under Catholic control during 1688 and 1689, and a full recovery of the Protestant position had not been attained until the last embers of resistance to the forces of William had been quenched in 1691. This reversal of the Protestant position did not result, as it did in 1641, in any major onslaught against Protestant settlers in Ireland, but it did arouse fears among Protestants that an attack was in prospect, and

70. Karl S. Bottigheimer, "The Restoration Land Settlement in Ireland: A Structural View," *Irish Historical Studies*, XVIII (1972–1973), 1–21.

71. Moody *et al.*, eds., *Early Modern Ireland, 1534–1691*, 420–453, 478–508.

it established the belief in England as well as in Ireland that the country was destined to experience a major political disturbance once every half-century.[72] This belief, in itself, consolidated the opinion that Ireland lay beyond the margins of civility, and it became accepted that Protestant political leaders in Ireland were fully justified in imposing a draconian authority over the Catholic population of the country to ensure that they would never again have the opportunity to challenge the status quo. The program of legislation, known as the Penal Laws, was ostensibly designed to create the conditions whereby the Catholic church in Ireland would wither away and the population at large would be left with no choice but to conform to the established Protestant religion.[73]

This hope, however, made little sense as long as the repressive measures were not complemented by an evangelization drive, and, in the absence of such, Ireland became unique in Europe as a Protestant state that ruled over a generally Catholic society. The zeal of that state in asserting its dominance over a recalcitrant population sometimes proved embarrassing for the English government in its diplomatic negotiations with Catholic Austria, but for the most part the government in London acquiesced in the cancellation of the civil and political rights of the Irish Catholic population. Government officials were able to do so because popular sentiment against Catholics remained intense in England throughout most of the eighteenth century but also because Ireland had come to be perceived in England as a place where conventional political norms did not apply. This stance was justified on the grounds that Ireland had proved itself an unstable and ungovernable place over the previous two centuries, and even the Protestants who held political sway there had come to be considered in England as undeserving of political respect and patronage.[74]

There were, therefore, good political reasons why Ireland should again have become marginalized in the eyes of English policymakers at the outset of the eighteenth century. These were complemented by economic reasons as the continued efforts of the settler community in the decades after the Cromwellian resettlement of the country failed to produce the desired regeneration of the economy. The model of economic progress that was constantly held before later generations of settlers was that which had been achieved by those who had made their fortunes in the country in the decades before

72. This point was put explicitly in William King, *The State of the Protestants of Ireland under the Late King James's Government* . . . (London, 1691), 147–148.

73. S. J. Connolly, "Religion and History," *Irish Economic and Social History*, X (1983), 66–80; Maureen Wall, *The Penal Laws, 1691–1760: Church and State from the Treaty of Limerick to the Accession of George III* (Dundalk, 1961); Robert E. Burns, "The Irish Popery Laws: A Study of Eighteenth-Century Legislation and Behavior," *Review of Politics*, XXIV (1962), 485–508.

74. This theme runs throughout the essays in Thomas Bartlett and D. W. Hayton, eds., *Penal Era and Golden Age: Essays in Irish History, 1690–1800* (Belfast, 1979).

1641.[75] The efforts of these founding fathers in such matters as house construction, estate management, and the promotion of manufacturing villages were assiduously imitated but failed to produce the desired results in the post-Restoration period. This failure provoked much anguish among the settlers in Ireland, and their spokesmen tended toward attributing failure to restraints placed upon their activities by the Parliament in England rather than to any insufficiency in themselves, and less still to any deficiency in the model that was being applied.[76]

There were, however, major deficiencies in the economic model that are evident to us now but were not evident to contemporaries. First, it is apparent that the economic success of the pre-1641 period was achieved at a time when the indigenous population of the country was extremely low (probably about 750,000 people) in the aftermath of a half-century of war, and when the natural resources of the country had not been subjected to systematic economic exploitation. It was, therefore, possible for the first generation of settlers to acquire large holdings of land and to manage it as they would without encountering any major social resistance. Furthermore, they could and they did finance their initial capital outlay by exploiting the natural resources of the country, notably timber and fish. They also gained quick returns on investment from the export of cattle and sheep in large quantities to England and from the processing of their skins and wool. Finally, to support the efforts of the settler landowners who promoted change, a plentiful supply of highly skilled migrants from England and Scotland was available.[77]

Similar opportunities and resources seemed to be at hand for the benefit of those Protestants who were granted property in Ireland under the Cromwellian settlement. Large estates of land were numerous, and little resistance to the scientific organization of that property could be expected from a population that had been cowed into submision by the war effort of the Cromwellians. Again, in the aftermath of the sequence of wars and disturbances that had beset the country during the years 1641–1652, the population level was low (probably 1,100,000 people after 1652), and farms would have been available in abundance to accommodate foreign Protestant as well as native-born tenants.[78] Furthermore, the devastation that had been wreaked on the organization of the Catholic church in Ireland during the Cromwellian era

75. See Boate, *Ireland's Naturall History*, esp. the preface.

76. T. W. Moody and W. E. Vaughan, eds., *A New History of Ireland*, IV, *Eighteenth-Century Ireland, 1691–1800* (Oxford, 1986), 123–157; L. M. Cullen, "Problems in the Interpretation and Revision of Eighteenth-Century Irish Economic History," Royal Historical Society, *Transactions*, 5th Ser., XVII (1967), 1–22.

77. Canny, *From Reformation to Restoration*, 150–187.

78. L. M. Cullen, "Population Trends in Seventeenth-Century Ireland," *Economic and Social Review*, VI (1975), 149–165.

meant that the one institution that had stood in the way of the conversion of the Irish population to Protestantism had been greatly weakened, and settlers could look forward to the prospect of Ireland's becoming a genuinely Protestant society.[79]

These possibilities were rightly highlighted in the propaganda literature published in support of the Cromwellian settlement, but those who engaged upon that settlement had to confront difficulties that nobody had anticipated. The first and most intractable difficulty was the destruction that had occurred during the war years. This meant that the settlers who had acquired property in Ireland were faced with the requirement for huge cash outlays associated with the construction and repair of buildings and the laying out of their estates. Such problems had also beset the earlier generation of settlers, but now England and Scotland were themselves devastated in the aftermath of the civil wars, and settlers could not hope to draw upon any cash resources from there. Even more serious was the fact that Ireland's natural timber supplies (and particularly those that lay proximate to profitable land) had been largely exhausted by the 1650s, with the result that the new settlers enjoyed but a meager income from such activities as iron smelting and timber exportation that had produced an income for the earlier settlers. Coastal fishing also became a big disappointment for the new generation of settlers, because the pilchard, which had proved so profitable for those who had engaged in the curing of fish in the pre-1641 period, had for some ecological reason deserted Irish waters by the later seventeenth century.[80]

These factors determined that no windfall profits were available to the Cromwellian settlers as they had been to those who went to Ireland during the reign of James I. Thus it was difficult for the Cromwellians to establish themselves as landowners, and their long-term prospects were adversely affected, because the agricultural products that could best be raised in Ireland were no longer in demand in England or in continental Europe. Both areas suffered from population stagnation from the mid-seventeenth century forward to the second half of the eighteenth century, and much of the land employed for tillage when population was increasing was now converted to pastoral farming. This conversion meant that England and continental Europe were sufficiently supplied with meat, and they were also well supplied with wool and animal skins to supply their textile and leather manufacturing. The result was that the very products that had facilitated the enrichment of the Irish settler population during the early seventeenth century served only to glut the market in the subsequent period. Because of this, the Irish economy remained generally stagnant down to the middle of the eighteenth

79. Patrick J. Corish, *The Catholic Community in the Seventeenth and Eighteenth Centuries* (Dublin, 1981), 43–81.

80. Moody *et al.*, eds., *Early Modern Ireland, 1534–1691*, 181, 447.

century, and not even the best efforts of the Protestant landowners to develop ornate mansions, model farms, or manufacturing villages could disguise their own general poverty and that of the society at large.[81]

This economic retardation, which was accentuated by intermittent famines (previous to the famine of 1741 when perhaps 30 percent of the Irish population perished), served to consolidate the impression, already established in England, that Ireland was a marginal society. So also did the general failure of Irish Protestants to bring the Irish population at large to an acceptance of their own faith when the opportunity to do so seemed propitious. Officials in England were no longer convinced by the explanations offered for such failures, and they tended to attribute them to insufficiencies in those who had come to dominate Irish Protestant society. They were not considered equals by their social counterparts in England, nor were they considered worthy to be entrusted with high civil or ecclesiastical functions in Ireland.[82] Posts went instead to Englishmen, who viewed their Protestant subordinates with a disdain different only in degree from that in which they held the Catholic population of the country. Irish Protestant leaders, in turn, greatly resented being thus treated as colonials, but even they themselves admitted that they had failed in their mission of establishing Ireland as a secure Protestant society.

Explanations for this failure are varied and complex. One relevant factor is that the Protestant proprietors in Ireland failed in their efforts to attract desirable settlers from Britain. Particular difficulty was experienced in drawing settlers from the dynamic South of England during the decades after the Restoration, presumably because the expansion of the southern English economy provided the would-be migrants with plenty of employment at home. This lack meant that Protestant landowners in the south of Ireland who had traditionally relied upon this source were left short of Protestant tenants, and they either had to satisfy themselves with Irish Catholic tenants or else seek after Huguenots, Palatinates, and other discontented Protestant groups in continental Europe. Protestant landowners in the northern half of Ireland were more fortunate in their efforts to attract tenants from abroad, and it was during the second half of the seventeenth century that the northeastern section of the province of Ulster became a distinctly Protestant

81. Moody and Vaughan, eds., *Eighteenth-Century Ireland*, 123–157. For the broader picture, see Jan de Vries, *The Economy of Europe in an Age of Crisis, 1600–1750* (Cambridge, 1976). Thomas Dineley, *Observations in a Voyage through the Kingdom of Ireland . . . 1681*, ed. James Graves (Dublin, 1870), describes the developments that had been promoted by the social elite in Ireland.

82. Bartlett and Hayton, eds., *Penal Era and Golden Age*, esp. 32–55, 88–113; on the famine of 1741 and population trends, see D. Dickson *et al.*, "Hearth Tax, Household Size, and Irish Population Change, 1672–1821," Royal Irish Academy, *Proceedings*, LXXXI, sect. C (1982), 125–181.

area. Evidence is available from one barony in County Armagh that the population there increased by a staggering 4.5 percent per annum during the course of the second half of the seventeenth century and that much of this increase resulted from resumed migration from Britain. The migrants to this barony originated principally in the North of England, especially Yorkshire, during the 1660s and 1670s and overwhelmingly in Scotland during the last two decades of the century. Their settlement in Ulster, however, did little to enhance the reputation of that province in the estimation of either the London or Dublin authorities. This was the case, first, because the English settlers in the province included substantial numbers of Baptists, Quakers, and other sectaries who threatened the coherence of the Protestant presence in Ireland, and, second, because the Scottish migrants were considered a challenge to the social no less than the religious order in the province.[83]

These Scottish migrants of the later seventeenth century were quite a distinct element from the Scots who had settled in Ulster during the earlier decades of that century. The earlier settlers were attracted to Ulster by the opportunities that province presented, and some abandoned relatively secure positions in Scotland with a view to advancing themselves socially and economically both within the six Ulster counties where formal plantation occurred and in the two Ulster counties of Antrim and Down, which lay closest to Scotland across the Irish Sea. These Scots remained a distinct element within the province, both because they tended to settle on property that was owned by Scots and because they inclined toward a more Calvinistic version of Protestantism than did their English counterparts and even brought their own ministers with them.[84]

Despite these tendencies, the Scots of the early seventeenth century sought to accommodate themselves within the framework of the Irish Protestant church as it was established by law, some Scots accepted leases from proprietors other than Scots, and some even spread themselves beyond the confines of Ulster into such neighboring counties as Longford.[85] To this extent the existence of a Scottish settler population in Ireland was not a subject of major controversy until Lord Deputy Wentworth made it so by attempting to

83. R. G. Gillespie, ed., *Settlement and Survival on an Ulster Estate: The Brownlow Leasebook, 1667–1711* (Belfast, 1988), xvi–xxv; Marilyn J. Westerkamp, *Triumph of the Laity: Scots-Irish Piety and the Great Awakening, 1625–1760* (Oxford, 1988), esp. 43–73. For an example of the bitterness of the official feeling against Scots in Ulster, see the bishop of Derry's charges against Thomas Wallis, dean of Derry, circa 1695, in T. W. Moody and J. G. Simms, eds., *The Bishopric of Derry and the Irish Society of London, 1602–1705* (Dublin, 1983), 165–166.

84. M. Perceval-Maxwell, *The Scottish Migration to Ulster in the Reign of James I* (London, 1973), esp. 252–273; Raymond Gillespie, *Colonial Ulster: The Settlement of East Ulster, 1600–1641* (Cork, 1985).

85. This is clear from the 1641 depositions for that county, for which see MS 817, fols. 154, 189, 192, 200, 201, 208, TCD.

have the Scottish settlers subscribe to an oath that would have obliged them to sever all connection with their covenanting coreligionists in Scotland. The Scottish migration of the late seventeenth century, which persisted into the 1720s, was controversial from the outset. This was so, first, because those who went to settle in Ulster were fleeing from the famine conditions associated with the collapse of the Scottish agrarian economy and, second, because they were committed Presbyterians who were not only opposed to the Anglican form of worship prescribed by law in Ireland but who threatened through their revivalist conventicles to draw away existing Protestants from the path of orthodoxy.[86]

This second Scottish migration, which totaled about fifty thousand families, was therefore perceived as a threat to the economic as well as the spiritual survival of an Irish Protestant community. Because of this, some upholders of Protestant orthodoxy welcomed the departure for the American colonies throughout the eighteenth century of a continuous stream of these Ulster Scots who had previously existed on the margins of society through farming their small holdings and engaging in linen production.[87] The more perceptive, however, recognized that, while these Scottish Protestants might fall short of the ideal, their departure would weaken what was already a fragile Protestant position in the country. These perceptive ones recognized the importance of the flourishing linen industry to the Irish economy and recognized also that the loss of thousands of settlers would threaten their own positions as landowners in Ulster by reducing competition for farms.[88] Those who argued in this fashion were those Irish Protestant landowners most attuned to English thinking on Ireland. They realized that Ireland was destined to remain a marginal kingdom, at least in English minds, as long as it was predominantly Catholic and as long as its Protestant gentry remained poor. While such conditions obtained, those Irish Protestants who were guided by metropolitan values could see that the country that provided them with an income was still a society in the making rather than a sister kingdom of England.

86. Moody *et al.*, eds., *Early Modern Ireland, 1534–1691*, 267–268; Moody and Vaughan, eds., *Eighteenth-Century Ireland*, 14, 133–134; J. C. Beckett, *Protestant Dissent in Ireland, 1687–1780* (London, 1948); Westerkamp, *Triumph of the Laity*, 63–73.

87. R. J. Dickson, *Ulster Emigration to Colonial America, 1718–1775* (London, 1966), 32–47.

88. Bernard Bailyn, *Voyagers to the West: A Passage in the Peopling of America on the Eve of the Revolution* (New York, 1986), 29–36.

ERIC RICHARDS

Scotland and the Uses of the Atlantic Empire

On this new year day, many happy yeares are wished by me (and I am sure by many Scotsmen) to yow and your family, and (as that which I think Scotland's cheeff politick good) to ane intire union with England,—I doe not mean without provisions and exceptiones—that were ridiculous for both—but in substantials, that both head and body might be one politick body. Unless wee be a part each of other, the union will be as a blood puddin to band a catt, *i.e.*, till one or the other be hungry, and then the puddin flyes. God give all of yow prudence, wisdome, and honesty, and Brittish minds. May wee be Brittains, and down goe the old ignominious names of Scotland, of England. Scot or Scotland are words not known in our native language; England is a dishonorable name, imposed on Brittains by Jutland pirats and mercinaries to Brittains, usurping on their Lords. Brittains is our true, our honorable denomination. But of this more, perhaps, heerafter.—George First Earl of Cromartie to [John Earl of Mar] Edinburgh, 1st January 1706

I. The Loss of Nationality

In 1793 the radical Scottish peer Lord Daer declared that "Scotland has long groaned under the chains of England." Since the Union of 1707 its political development toward democracy had been stunted: Scotland was no more than "a conquered province" of England. To the historian Hume Brown, Scotland was now "a severed and a withered branch and her people knew it."[1] Such Caledonian gloom was a recurrent refrain in contemporary letters; the Union had institutionalized the nation's sense of inferiority toward England. Scotland had been reduced to cultural provinciality, a subordinate outlier of the far greater London metropolis. The royal court had been removed from Edinburgh to the south, the Scottish Parliament was now dissolved, and with it went all executive authority, royal patronage, and the

I wish to thank Ms. Robin Haines for her assistance.

1. Daer quoted in J. M. Bumsted, ed., *The Writings and Papers of Thomas Douglas, Fifth Earl of Selkirk*, I, *The Collected Writings of Lord Selkirk, 1799–1809* (Winnipeg, 1984), 20; Brown quoted in P. H. Scott, *In Bed with an Elephant* (Edinburgh, 1985), 14. (Epigraph from William Fraser, *The Earls of Cromartie* [Edinburgh, 1876], II, 1–2.)

control of foreign policy. And in Scotland's own regions there would be yet more severe upheavals: in the barely assimilated Highlands there would be rebellion, resistance, and military pacification that brought accusations of genocide against the Hanoverian conqueror. Meanwhile, throughout the eighteenth century, Scots found themselves ever further dispersed from their homelands, extruded into their western towns, into England, even to India, America, and Australia.

Yet the colonial yoke fitted poorly about Scottish shoulders. Twenty years after the Union, Daniel Defoe, highly conscious of "northern vanity," was hard-pressed to find evidence of English penetration of its northern neighbor, either for good or for ill. True, the movement of commodities each way across the old frontier had hastened. Oddly, he thought, the flow of people, of ideas, of culture seemed increasingly to be directed south rather than north. The greatest visible impact of the Union was to open "the door to the Scots in our American colonies." The Glasgow merchants had already seized the opportunity. At the same time, the Scots had begun to emigrate in such numbers "that if it goes on for many years more, Virginia may be rather called a Scots than an English plantation."[2] Defoe's remarks indeed presaged a century of economic vitality and cultural extroversion in Scotland achieved primarily within the wider boundaries of the Atlantic empire.

Unquestionably, the Union of 1707 was an unequal connection: Scotland was poorer in virtually everything. Its population and wealth were smaller. Its political condition was less stable and its culture less homogeneous than its greater neighbor's. Its recent history had demonstrated conclusively that it could not enter the imperial world by its own resources. Its lack of markets and its meager capacity to generate capital had consigned Scotland to a peripheral and inferior status in the affairs of Europe and the Atlantic empires. Now, in 1707, it appeared to be swallowed by its much larger neighbor, destined to be assimilated as a province of London, no longer a freestanding polity.

The Union, in the event, had complicated consequences for the Scots, and the balance sheet is still being drawn. The notion that the Scots were reduced, in their economy, society, and culture, to provinciality remains contentious. Far from becoming a mere satellite of England, a provincial dependency and a dormant partner in subsequent imperialism, Scotland seemed to use America (and the later empire) for the release and exercise of its revealed talents and capital, and the Scots grew well on the arrangement. There emerged a sense of new and creative intersections of the Scottish world with the worlds of England and America. Novel permutations and opportunities, at the center and on the shifting margins, were now realizable—in London,

2. Daniel Defoe, *A Tour through the Whole Island of Great Britain* (1724–1726), ed. Pat Rogers (Harmondsworth, 1971), 559–561, 606–609.

in Edinburgh, in the Highlands and islands, and, most of all, across the Atlantic. In the end the nominal dominance of London was, perhaps, less vital than the space created for Scottish expansion.

Access to England and to the Atlantic empire opened new horizons to the Scots in the eighteenth century. They seemed, in both spheres, to make a considerable success of their opportunities. The Scots seemed to belie their secondary status in the Union. By 1775, in trade, industry, education, politics, religion, and literature, the Scots had generated admiration and envy on both sides of the Atlantic. On the other hand the very fear of provincialization, the danger of cultural assimilation, may have been the goad that generated Scotland's extraordinarily vigorous response. It was expressed most favorably in the development of Scottish trade and industry, in the northern version of the Enlightenment, and in the preservation of the Scottish identity, attenuated and redefined though it was.[3]

The source of this expansive mentality resided in obscure processes hardly yet explored. But for some Scots the activating circumstances were clear enough. Hunger and local pessimism could cause Scots, like others, to flee their homelands. Commercial profit could light the eyes of a commercial minority on the Clyde. A tradition of mobility and military service, now reinforced by colonial success as well as recognition by the imperial rulers, further primed the migrant psychology. Yet the variegated mass of emigrant decisions seems to defy any coherence, resisting the notion of a primum mobile in that Atlantic system. Some historians, however, have sought to detect certain structural pressures in Scotland's condition in the eighteenth century—of being a poor promontory of a rich imperial island ruled from London rather than from Edinburgh, Glasgow, or Inverness. There was a cultural tension at its center that caused the smaller country to turn outward and to emerge, ultimately, with its nationality enriched and intact.

Nevertheless, there may have been common elements in the outreach of the Scots toward North America (as well as to other opportunities within the Atlantic world now opened to them). There may have been a denominator that expressed the relationship between the north of Britain and its new imperial core. Scotland indeed was generally poorer than its southern neighbor and poorer than much of the western part of Europe. Its poverty and its inferiority—in economic, political, and military possibilities—pressed its attention and energies westward and southward. The colonial drive of the Scots may have expressed a special variety of provincialism, a positive response to a challenge that, at most times, would be expected to defeat societies and turn them inward. Instead, by the mid-eighteenth century,

3. The best introduction to the cultural and economic achievements of Georgian Scotland is found in T. C. Smout, *A History of the Scottish People, 1560–1830* (London, 1969), chap. 19 and postscript.

many Scots opted for the widest opportunities—in America, in India, in England itself—in a dynamic response in part to their provincial status in the British imperium.

II. The Necessity of Union

Before the Union of 1707 Scotland's expansive inclinations were painfully constricted. Even its migration was constrained. Scots were formally barred from both the English and the Dutch colonial possessions, and there was an accumulation of domestic political pressure to establish an independent Scottish empire. The Scottish economy, probably less developed even than Ireland's, had been battered by bad harvests and declining markets in the 1690s. The urgency of Scotland for colonies was demonstrated in the aggression of its merchants for access to the Atlantic markets and in the frustration of its aristocrats (especially its younger sons) for places abroad. The rancorous failure of the Darien scheme between 1695 and 1700—when Scotland "made one last bid for a foothold in the New World and the golden treasure of colonial trade" in an attempt to create a dynamic outpost of Scotland in the swamps of Panama—caused Scots to blame London for their humiliation.[4] Initially it jeopardized the idea of Union; eventually it emphasized the necessity of an arrangement that gave Scots access to the imperial fold. The age of colonial frustration ended in 1707, though the benefits were far from instantaneous.

The notion that Scotland was not big enough for the Scots was not new. Scots had traditionally migrated, or sought military employment, within northern Europe, most notably in Poland and Scandinavia. Much greater numbers, from the south and east of Scotland, had taken up opportunities for settlement in the Ulster Plantations between 1688 and 1715. The exodus to Ulster, totaling perhaps fifty thousand families, may have signaled a profound land hunger, especially in the 1690s, when it was said that

4. On harvests and markets, see Rosalind Mitchison, "Ireland and Scotland: The Seventeenth-Century Legacies Compared," in T. M. Devine and David Dickson, eds., *Ireland and Scotland, 1600–1850: Parallels and Contrasts in Economic and Social Development* (Edinburgh, 1983), 4. On merchants, see, for example, the spirited activities of Clydeside traders in defiance of imperial impediments, as documented in D. R. Hainesworth, ed., *The Correspondence of Sir John Lowther of Whitehaven, 1693–1698: A Provincial Community in Wartime*, British Academy, Records of Social and Economic History, n.s., VII (London, 1982). On aristocrats, see, for instance, the remarks of Lord Tarbat quoted by Bruce Lenman, "The Highland Aristocracy and North America, 1603–1784," in L. Maclean, ed., *The Seventeenth Century in the Highlands* (Inverness, 1986), 178–179. On the Darien scheme, see Rosalind Mitchison, *A History of Scotland* (London, 1970), 301–302.

"troupes of the poor [were] deserting [their] native country for Ireland." Fletcher of Saltoun, in 1698, estimated that there were 200,000 beggars in Scotland. There was a general perception, even in a period of demographic recession, that the country was overpopulated—"Scotland, by reason of her populousnesse being constrained to disburden her selfe (like the painfull bees), did every year send forth swarmes."[5] For the Atlantic world the Scotch-Ulster phenomenon was the first of a two-phase process, since the descendants of the Scottish planters and their kinfolk in Ulster itself, in the following century, became a prime source of emigrants to America. Land hunger had propelled them first across the Irish Sea and then the Atlantic.

Before the Union, Scots entered America only by unofficial or untoward avenues. They could not enter even as indentured labor except by extraordinary arrangements, as for instance to the West Indies between 1665 and 1685, and to East New Jersey in 1685. South Carolina gave refuge to small numbers of Scottish covenanters, and other English colonies encouraged the plantation of Scots and the recruitment of Scottish convicts. But these exceptions to the rule merely demonstrated the priority of American needs over the official policy of exclusion. They were, in any case, only the narrowest of conduits for the Scots and hardly presaged the much greater flows that eventually developed under the Union. In key matters between Scotland and England, the Scots were treated as foreigners: for example, the English Navigation Act of 1660 was a great impediment to Scottish trade, and the Alien Act of March 1705 was a threat to tighten the trade noose completely while also preventing Scots from inheriting property in England.[6]

Scotland entered the Union of 1707 in the full knowledge of the danger of being overwhelmed and comprehensively absorbed by her richer and more powerful neighbor. The anti-Union riots observed by Daniel Defoe in Edinburgh in 1706–1707 were clear evidence of popular opposition.[7] The great debate that swirled about Scotland at the time was directed ultimately to the judgment that balanced the risks of Union with England against the countervailing benefits anticipated. It was a measure of the desperation of the Scots (and of the efficacy of the complex political management that achieved the fusion) that the risks to nationhood and autonomy were accepted.

5. Michael W. Flinn, ed., *Scottish Population History: From the Seventeenth Century to the 1930s* (Cambridge, 1977), 7–8. Fletcher is quoted in David Daiches, *The Paradox of Scottish Culture: The Eighteenth-Century Experience* (London, 1964), 5.

6. On limits to immigration, see Ian Charles Cargill Graham, *Colonists from Scotland: Emigration to North America, 1707–1783* (Ithaca, N.Y., 1956), 43–44; Mitchison, *History of Scotland*, 266. On the restrictive acts, see T. C. Smout, "Union of the Parliaments," in Gordon Menzies, ed., *The Scottish Nation* (London, 1972), 155–156; Smout, *Scottish People*, esp. chap. 5; Mitchison, *History of Scotland*, 307.

7. G. H. Healey, ed., *The Letters of Daniel Defoe* (Oxford, 1955), 132–143.

Although Scotland, until 1707, was "a sovereign and independent kingdom," it was already entwined in the embrace of England.[8] The court had moved from Edinburgh to London in 1603, and the partnership had already created awkward dependencies. But the danger of upsetting prevailing arrangements alarmed many Scots, especially when England employed the threat of the Navigation Acts and Settlement Laws over them. Fears of further political instability, and the insecurity of the royal succession for both kingdoms, added to the difficulties surrounding the construction of the Treaty of Union. Within Scotland there were critical problems that made such a radical solution seem imperative and irresistible. Some observers, including the penetrating Clerk of Penicuik, believed that Scottish independence had long been a fiction and that the Scottish exchequer was virtually bankrupt: only the Union could cure the fundamental faults of Scotland's finances.[9]

It is still sometimes argued that the pressures of party management and political corruption determined the outcome and shape of the Union, but it is more probable that the Scots took the opportunity of political circumstances to gain respite from the accelerating economic crisis of the time. Nicholas Phillipson, for instance, contends that Scotland precipitated the Union crisis with England and succeeded in resolving it to her own satisfaction on the assumption that access to England (and her markets) was the solution to her increasingly painful and obvious backwardness. The Scots' ruling oligarchy calculated their own, and the nation's, loss of autonomy against their resolve to galvanize the nation into economic improvement. And it seems true that England herself had few direct ambitions in the north and was somewhat apathetic about the negotiations. But the English economist Charles Davenant could see the advantage to both sides. As he wrote in 1704, "We can give Scotland no Equivalent for joining in our Settlement of the Succession, but a free Communication of our Trade, which among them must be popular."[10]

Scotland's willingness to seek these benefits, at the cost of her own sovereignty, was a clear symptom of her economic weakness. Union with England

8. William Ferguson, "Recent Interpretations of the Making of the Treaty of Union of 1707," *Scottish Tradition*, VII (1977–1978), 110.

9. Athol L. Murray, "Administration and Law," in T. I. Rae, ed., *The Union of 1707: Its Impact on Scotland* (Glasgow, 1974), 31. This view is confirmed by Rosalind Mitchison, "Patriotism and National Identity in Eighteenth Century Scotland," in T. W. Moody, ed., *Nationality and the Pursuit of National Independence* (Belfast, 1978), 75.

10. Nicholas Phillipson, "Towards a Definition of the Scottish Enlightenment," in Paul Fritz and David Williams, eds., *City and Society in the Eighteenth Century* (Toronto, 1973), 128. Davenant quoted in David A. G. Waddell, "An English Economist's View of the Union, 1705," *Scottish Historical Review*, XXXV (1956), 144–149.

was, in the extreme view, the only exit from national despair. "At the end of the seventeenth century," according to H. R. Trevor-Roper, "Scotland was a by-word for irredeemable poverty, social backwardness, political factions. The Universities were the unreformed seminaries of a fanatical clergy."[11] If Scotland dwelt in such decayed circumstances, its subsequent rise, of course, was the more phoenixlike. In essence, the Scottish oligarchy—its landed elite—had chosen to forgo present power and prestige, even its own identity and Parliament, in the cause of eventual economic development. The recent frustrations in Darien and the progressive constriction of trade by mercantilist competitors had focused their minds. Moreover, the secular reshaping of Scottish commercial exchanges, away from France, Holland, and the Baltic and toward England, now its greatest trading partner, reinforced their thoughts. The Scots had had enough of colonization, and it was undoubtedly the English market that dominated their aspirations, the Atlantic horizon being relatively a remote possibility in 1707. And though ministerial opportunism and rank corruption helped propel Scotland toward Union, it was her dire economic state that forced her into the arms of a complacent England. Scotland had hardly survived the economic crisis of the 1690s, and remained at the mercy of adverse English legislation. The Union, therefore, was "the only practical solution to a deepening political and economic crisis. The Scots did not go into Union simply because they were poor and saw no other way of riches, but because they were poor and rapidly getting poorer."[12]

In the outcome, after long and complex negotiations, the terms of the Union were less total, less obliterating of Scottishness, than expected. The settlement left room for maneuver and for a markedly Scottish response to the redefined world as it emerged in the following half-century. Ostensibly, Scotland lost its political heart, its Parliament, in return for modest representation in the London Parliament, relinquishing the central levers of power to the metropolis. The fact that the larger part of the Scottish ruling class could not afford even the cost of attending the political and social season in London appeared to underline Scotland's reduced status in the now-united nations. (Scottish members of Parliament were given secret subsidies to ensure their attendance at Westminster.) It was further emphasized by the

11. Repeatedly cited, e.g., Andrew S. Skinner, introduction, in R. H. Campbell and Skinner, eds., *The Origins and Nature of the Scottish Enlightenment* (Edinburgh, 1982), 4 (see also 26).

12. On landed elite and economic development, see N. T. Phillipson, "Culture and Society in the Eighteenth Century Province: The Case of Edinburgh and the Scottish Enlightenment," in Lawrence Stone, ed., *The University in Society* (London, 1975), II, 413. On English markets, see William Ferguson, *Scotland's Relations with England: A Survey to 1707* (Edinburgh, 1977), 114 n. 42; T. C. Smout, "The Road to Union," in Geoffrey Holmes, ed., *Britain after the Glorious Revolution, 1689–1714* (London, 1969), 186. Quotation is from Mitchison, *History of Scotland*, 311.

small amount of legislation devoted to her problems in the first fifty years of the Union: Scotland was frequently ignored by her larger partner.

In practice, some of the negative aspects of the Union redounded, in the long run, to Scotland's advantage and may have encouraged her vigorous grasp of opportunities when they arose. Some of Scotland's key institutions remained unaffected by the Union. Scotland retained control of its educational system, its church government, and its legal system. The law, the courts, the burghs, the electoral system, the schools, the universities, and the church remained intact. Scottish law had developed into an enclosed system before 1707 that was "peculiarly well adapted to resist English influence." Its survival ensured that Edinburgh would not be reduced to a provincial backwater. The law became the magnet for the employment of the gentry's sons, and lawyers formed the nucleus on which was ultimately built the cultural and intellectual strengths of mid-eighteenth-century Edinburgh.[13]

More surprisingly, it rapidly became apparent that London found it convenient to leave most political business in Scotland in the hands of a northern "manager." Scottish political affairs were left in Scottish hands partly because they were too difficult and convoluted for London to understand.[14] As Rosalind Mitchison says, "The political system ensured stability without subservience," and its local complexities effectively prevented carpetbaggers from England from taking control of the northern arena. The Scottish political system allowed home-based patronage to lubricate its own wheels, so that, eventually, the Scots exerted greater political influence in the south than could otherwise have been anticipated. And, precisely because so large a part of the old elite could not afford to attend London (until about 1760), it continued to regard Edinburgh as its natural focus, provincial or not. Thus Edinburgh remained an important political and social capital, despite the loss of the Scottish Parliament: it continued to exist as the second largest city in the Union, a smaller rival pole to London in its social and political magnetism. In the long run it was possible to regard the Union, even in Scottish eyes, as an extraordinarily sensible arrangement, "not as the absorption of one nation by another, but as a unique balance of assimilation and autonomy." In effect the arrangement, as it worked in practice, created a framework that allowed a quasi-independent Scottish response to the stimuli and opportunities that emerged in the Atlantic world. As Christopher Harvie suggests:

> The Union allowed Scottish nationalism to survive, accompanied by a distinctive pattern of government and society, and the consequences of this relationship were sanctioned by an intelligentsia whose own charac-

13. On law, see Murray, "Administration and Law," in Rae, ed., *Union of 1707*, 44. On lawyers, see Mitchison, *History of Scotland*, 312.

14. Murray, "Administration and Law," in Rae, ed., *Union of 1707*, 37.

ter was pervaded by a parallel dualism between the cosmopolitan and the native.[15]

The role of the intelligentsia in the newly defined Scottish province over the long run may indeed have been critical. But neither it nor anyone else could counter the initial disappointment and disillusion with the Union. Certainly the immediate economic consequences were inauspicious. In 1707 the earl of Stair warned England of the dangers of rebellion in Scotland, and the imminent destruction of the Union itself, if England continued to ignore her northern partner and if the harsh economic effects of the Union were not mitigated.[16] The dangers of Scottish rebellion became reality in the Jacobitism of 1715 and 1745, though the prompt suppression is usually interpreted as measures of the strength rather than the weakness of the Union. Certainly the economic benefits of Union had been agonizingly slow to emerge. An entire generation passed without visible gain, and until 1727 Scottish affairs were strained by economic depression and political nervousness. Opposition to the Union continued to reverberate: in 1719 a Swedish visitor to Scotland said that the Union had simply exacerbated the "natural jealousie betwixt the two nations." "Nobility is obliged to go up to London to search for prefferments" to such a degree that Edinburgh was impoverished and depopulated. It was natural, at the time, to blame Scotland's continuing poverty on the supposed ill effects of the Union, but the more intelligent observers realized that national poverty predated the Union and that nothing could have been worse than the condition of pre-Union Scotland. It was the essential purpose of such men to dampen the inevitable anti-Union eruptions that occurred during these decades.[17]

In the short run the Union was clearly no panacea. Yet the gloom was exaggerated—for instance, even in the worst phase, Edinburgh had continued to grow in population, and there were signs, both there and in the rest of the country, that the spirit of enterprise and intellect was regenerating. Ultimately, by the late 1740s, it was not incredible to speak of a Scottish renaissance, that everlasting puzzle in modern Scottish history by which Scotland emerged from its provincial chrysalis into the golden age of the Enlightenment, the startling growth of an exciting provincial culture out of the shadow of England. The great question of the time was, How could such

15. Christopher Harvie, *Scotland and Nationalism: Scottish Society and Politics, 1707–1977* (London, 1977), 16; Mitchison, *History of Scotland*, 354.

16. J. G. Shaw, *The Management of Scottish Society, 1707–1764* (Edinburgh, 1983), 43.

17. T. C. Smout, ed., "Journal of Henry Kalmeter's Travels in Scotland, 1719–1720," in R. H. Campbell, ed., *Scottish Industrial History: A Miscellany* (Edinburgh, 1978), 9–11. For an intelligent observer, see Clerk of Penicuik, quoted in David Daiches, *Scotland and the Union* (London, 1977), 136.

"a small nation, so poor and rude, survive in such a world"? Here, indeed, was one of the central intellectual questions that engaged the best minds of the Scottish Enlightenment itself—the problem of the relationship between rich and poor countries, and how small countries could be incorporated into larger entities without also becoming venal.[18]

The cultural and economic revitalization of Scotland in the eighteenth century (in company with that of certain colonies) was a practical enactment of a certain sort of solution to that puzzle. For, within that century, Scotland redefined its relationship with England and with the Atlantic empire. It was a solution in which the Enlightenment itself was a part, and a solution that the Enlightenment literati found as difficult as subsequent historians to explain. The Union of 1707, which converted Scotland into a species of province, may have been the "great hinge upon which the domestic history of Scotland turns," but the precise nature of the mechanism has remained obscure.[19]

The Scottish experience as a British province in the eighteenth century gives every appearance of a success story. Its greatest marks were its unheralded economic growth and its extraordinarily vigorous contributions to the Enlightenment. Scotland's status in the world shifted dramatically. By mid-century its traders had penetrated the entire Atlantic system; its industries and agriculture would soon form part of the cutting blade of the British economic revolution. Scotland's professional classes would invade the higher reaches of government and public services, and while its population multiplied, its migrants would be found everywhere across the British world, especially in the metropolis itself. And, most spectacularly, its literati would become intellectual leaders casting an influence across the whole Atlantic world, Europe not excluded. None of this was predictable in 1707; little of it could have been anticipated in 1740. Eventually, however, Scotland was left with a crisis of identity: was it "a nation, a province, a lost kingdom, a culture, a history, a body of tradition, a bundle of sentiments, a state of mind, was it North Britain or Caledonia?"[20] Whatever it was, it had transcended the provincial backwater of 1707, but its transcendence was peculiarly difficult to account for.

18. See G. E. Davie, *The Scottish Enlightenment* (London, 1981), 21–22; and Istvan Hont, "The 'Rich Country–Poor Country' Debate in Scottish Classical Political Economy," in Hont and Michael Ignatieff, eds., *Wealth and Virtue: The Shaping of Political Economy in the Scottish Enlightenment* (Cambridge, 1983), 317–344.

19. Smout, "Road to Union," in Holmes, ed., *Britain after the Glorious Revolution*, 176.

20. Janet Adam Smith, "Some Eighteenth-Century Ideas of Scotland," in N. T. Phillipson and Rosalind Mitchison, eds., *Scotland in the Age of Improvement: Essays on Scottish History in the Eighteenth Century* (Edinburgh, 1970), 107.

III. Scottish Receptivity

The revival of Scotland's cultural vigor and identity in the mid-eighteenth century, complex though the process was, ultimately depended on Scotland's place in the British archipelago and its interactions with the evolving Atlantic world. The secondary status ascribed to and largely accepted by the Scots created myriad stresses and compulsions through which the country reshaped its purpose in the course of a century. And as the Scots elbowed their way into these new spheres, they set up recurrent tensions with England and the colonies, some abrasive, some undoubtedly creative. But Scotland's response to the opportunities of the Atlantic empire and also the character of the ensuing encounters between Scots and English (on both sides of the Atlantic) were conditioned by forces already at work in Scotland at the time of the Union.

History, like nature, abhors discontinuities. The roots of the mid-eighteenth-century Scottish renaissance are now being dug deep in the previous century. The notion of a backward, introverted, and uncultured outpost of the British archipelago is dissolving, derided as an absurd caricature. For instance, the Scots had long experience of migration and foreign involvement: there were said to be ten thousand Scots in Europe in the seventeenth century, often in mercenary employment. Scotland had developed already before 1707 "an emigration ideology" containing values and techniques appropriate to overseas settlement, and a lessened attachment to the native soil.[21] Centrifugal forces were at work among the Scots long before Scotland became one of the greatest suppliers of emigrants to the Atlantic world in the eighteenth century.

There have emerged also powerful arguments that both economic development and cultural resurgence were already in train before 1707. A crucial transition had been effected before the Union. The view expressed many years ago, that a revaluation of Scottish cultural history between 1670 and 1707 was required, has been answered and has indeed confirmed the suggestion that the church, the bar, and the universities in Scotland demonstrated that "a spirit of increasing tolerance and ever-broadening intellectual and cultural interests had by then invaded all three of those institutions to a considerable degree." The universities had been reanimated by 1660, and science had awoken by 1680. Some historians find the long-distance origins of the Scottish Enlightenment in these developments.[22] One of the beset-

21. On the caricature, see, for instance, Ferguson, "Recent Interpretations," *Scot. Trad.*, VII (1977–1978), 97. On emigration, see Harvie, *Scotland and Nationalism*, 95–96.

22. John Clive and Bernard Bailyn, "England's Cultural Provinces: Scotland and America," *William and Mary Quarterly*, 3d Ser., XI (1954), 202 n. 4. On origins, see

ting faults of Scottish historiography, the failure to recognize the constructive aspects of the late seventeenth century, has been corrected. In particular, there were basic transformations at work, gradual to be sure, in the economy. They were to be seen in important changes in agricultural organization and productivity, in the new patterns of trade, and in the encouragement of economic improvement offered by the Edinburgh government. Already the landed oligarchy of Scotland had developed an increasingly self-conscious mentality of improvement.

Consequently, therefore, the indisputable economic and demographic horrors of the 1690s have been redrawn as a temporary dislocation along a decidedly positive trend toward economic and cultural advance. No one doubts that there was desperate famine in the 1690s, but now its significance rests on the fact that it was the last national famine in Scottish history. Thereafter, most of Scotland fed itself and produced increasing food surpluses. Agriculture, therefore, was in the midst of a critical transition, during which an indigenous tradition of dynamic improvement was established, much reinforced by the Scottish Parliament and a governing class already receptive to improvement thinking before 1707. The increasing commitment of landed society to improvement, especially on questions of tenure, was matched by a growing maturity in the Scottish business classes. The impact of the Union was overarched, therefore, by longer trends already in operation. For instance, even before 1707 the crust of custom was cracking: "The more vigorous official constraints on recruitment to the merchant rank were beginning to break down," and new blood was already entering the Glasgow mercantile corps. In the half-century after 1680, Scottish merchants from Glasgow, Ayr, Irvine, Aberdeen, and Edinburgh were entering the Atlantic trade, fructifying enterprise, and stimulating social mobility within Scotland itself.[23] The benefits were slow to accrue and hardly pervasive before 1740, but it is not hard to see a precocious receptivity to opportunity among the Scottish mercantile community, the basis of a large reputation for entrepreneurial energy by the midcentury.

The Scots in the Atlantic seem to have cut their teeth on the Caribbean trade. For instance, when Saint Kitts was ceded by France in 1713, half the land grants went to Scots. Long before the midcentury the Scots were dominant in Tobago and were grossly overrepresented in the settlement of Ja-

---

Skinner, introduction, in Campbell and Skinner, eds., *Scottish Enlightenment*, 4 (see also 26).

23. T. M. Devine, "The Scottish Merchant Community, 1680–1740," in Campbell and Skinner, eds., *Scottish Enlightenment*, 26–41; Devine, "The Union of 1707 and Scottish Development," *Scottish Economic and Social History*, V (1985), 23–40; A. Fenton, "Scottish Agriculture and the Union: An Example of Indigenous Development," in Rae, ed., *Union of 1707*, 75–93.

maica. Meanwhile, in Scotland the western parts, most obviously in Glasgow, grew disproportionately on the basis of the Atlantic trade, outstripping Leith and Edinburgh in the process. Yet the Scots had no special advantage in oceanic trade, and their general poverty would suggest the opposite. They became noted for creative improvisation in trade and developed great efficiencies in the use of scarce capital resources in trade, credit, and general commercial transactions. In the 1720s the Scots had created enough confidence to enable them to attract capital support from England for their ventures. Their manipulation of credit sources overcame basic capital deficiencies. T. M. Devine offers the example of an enterprising Scottish trader in 1728 who was able to finance a voyage taking in Leith, Newfoundland, and Barcelona with a personal capital of five pounds sterling. Such local improvisations complemented the strengths of the Scottish banking system, often regarded as more flexible and inventive than its English counterpart.[24]

Scottish merchants, assisted by creative methods of mobilizing capital, reconnoitered their way about the Atlantic trading basin and displayed a mercantile sophistication that may have been derived from their training.[25] Many of these overseas merchants had received classical educations in the town grammar schools or university and displayed extraordinary "cultural cosmopolitanism." For instance, a Glasgow merchant in the tobacco trade in the early part of the century, George Bogle, was a cultivated man possessing a library of intellectual tastes that included Pufendorf and Grotius, and he was not alone in such cultural refinement. Moreover, in the Scottish social ethos, there was no divide between merchants and the landed elite, but rather a genuine interpenetration of the two worlds. As Devine suggests:

> The ease with which sons of the laird class could become merchants and merchants could buy land points to a significant fluidity in the social structure of the Scottish élite which enabled commercial attitudes to be widely held and accepted. . . . The business classes possessed the sophistication crucial to later advance.

More succinctly, R. G. Cant remarks that there was less "brittle elitism" in Scotland than elsewhere.[26]

The search for the secrets of Scotland's receptivity to opportunities in the Atlantic empire of the eighteenth century, therefore, has tended to diminish the historical significance of the Union. Origins are now found "in the

24. Devine, "Union of 1707," *Scot. Econ. and Soc. Hist.*, V (1985), 39 n. 28; G. E. Davie, "Anglophobe and Anglophil," *Scottish Journal of Political Economy*, XIV (1967), 296.

25. See Alexander Carlyle, quoted in Smout, *Scottish People*, 383.

26. Devine, "Scottish Merchant Community," 34–37; Ronald G. Cant, "Origins of the Enlightenment in Scotland: The Universities," 59—both in Campbell and Skinner, eds., *Scottish Enlightenment.*

gradual transformation of Scottish culture which began long before 1707." There is, nevertheless, still a central role ascribed to cultural preparation, to a collective psychology of improvement adapted wholeheartedly by its social leaders, its merchants, literati, landowners, and aristocrats—in a long transition of which the Union itself was part.[27]

The transition was least effective and most resisted in the Highlands, which were beyond an internal frontier and were a profound challenge to the capabilities of the Hanoverian state machine. The Highlanders seemed almost a different race, a people from an altogether more primitive and barbaric state of society. Defoe, in 1706, had drawn a picture of a Highland gentleman out of his element in the streets of the Scottish capital: "a man in the mountain habit with a broad sword, targett, pistol or perhaps two at his girdle, a dagger and staff, walking down the street as upright and haughty as he were a lord—and withall driving a cow." The Highlands in the Georgian age remained a frontier society, riddled with contradictions. Here was the last home in the British Isles of witchcraft and witch burning, of intercommunal violence and barbarism, of absolute patriarchal autonomy, of a persisting Gaelic civilization, of a local culture enriched by its own isolation. Here coexisted a claret-drinking, cosmopolitan elite, some of them educated at the university and in France, living beside a painfully poor peasantry existing on the edge of famine for much of their lives, with local loyalties of extraordinary tenacity.[28] To some the apparent juxtaposition of culture and barbarity, of medieval pride and honor with mysticism, cattle raiding, and ritual executions, was a beguiling combination. Mostly, however, the Highlanders were regarded with derision, as unchristian barbarians, "a belief which justified barbaric proceedings against them." Even the Kirk experienced the greatest difficulties in maintaining discipline, and the lowest stratum of Highland society lived in extreme poverty and dependency. The Reverend John Lane Buchanan, writing in the 1780s, drew a comparison between "the African in the West Indies and the Celtic slave or scallag in the Western Hebrides" and concluded that the Highlanders worked longer hours and received worse treatment. The arbitrary heriditary power over life and death exercised by the chiefs was regarded by southerners as a continuing outrage against civilization. As late as 1748 a report of the Scottish Society for the Propagation of Christian Knowledge described the Highlanders as "not quite civilised" and how many of them were "wild and barba-

27. Skinner, introduction, *ibid.*, 1–5.

28. Defoe is quoted in Peter Earle, *The World of Defoe* (Newton Abbot, 1977), 18; see also Eric Richards, *A History of the Highland Clearances*, I, *Agrarian Transformation and the Evictions of 1746–1886* (London, 1982), 112–113; John E. Donaldson, *Caithness in the Eighteenth Century* (Edinburgh, 1938), esp. 11–12, 50–57; and Donaldson, ed., *The Mey Letters . . .* (Sydney, 1986).

rous."[29] Here indeed was the last rough edge of vestigial feudalism in the British Isles.

It was an image that became reality and scarifying in the Jacobite Uprising of 1745, an image to frighten and quell children during the rest of the century.[30] Highlanders were not popular in Edinburgh, just as Scots in general were not popular in London. Even as late as 1775, and even in the eyes of an enlightened English agriculturalist, the northern Scots remained a barbarous extremity of British civilization. Matthew Culley wrote:

> Before I was acquainted with North Britain, I durst not have ventured to travel in these parts alone, such was the notion I had conceived of the rapacity of the natives, but now that I have actually traversed different parts of their country, I have so perfect a confidence in the integrity and discretion of these Northern inhabitants, that I could step in the poorest hutts amongst them without apprehension of ill consequences, excepting perhaps their want of cleanliness.[31]

Although the Highlands were increasingly penetrated by commercial forces and even though tribalism was diminishing in power by the time of the Union, the great divide remained and was, perhaps, widened by the military suppression of Jacobitism. The Highlands represented the most resistant and challenging marchland in Britain, a province so backward that it was often compared with America as a proper zone for colonization. The benefits of the Enlightenment and economic growth hardly reached the Highlands in the eighteenth century.

By contrast, Lowland Scotland, itself trapped in economic adversity and provincialism for several decades after the Union, emerged with astonishing vigor by 1750. It was expressed, characteristically, in two forms: in its cultural distinction, created primarily in Edinburgh, and in its economic improvement, which affected both rural and urban life across the Lowlands. Both forces eventually spanned the Atlantic. But the connection between the two processes is problematic. Adam Smith hinted that such phenomena operated together:

29. See Mitchison, *History of Scotland*, 347; John Lane Buchanan, *Travel in the Western Hebrides: From 1782 to 1790* (London, 1793), 4–5. Report quoted by Annette M. Smith, "Annexed Estates in the Eighteenth Century Highlands," *Northern Scotland*, III (1977–1978), 25.

30. Smith, "Annexed Estates," *Northern Scotland*, III (1977–1978), 26.

31. Culley Papers ZCU43, p. 122, Northumberland County Record Office. Intolerance of the Highlanders was a continuous theme in Lowland history. In the 1590s the Master of Stair typified this attitude: "It shocked his orderly mind that one half of Scotland should be as barbarous as the wilds of America" (John Buchan, *The Massacre of Glencoe* [London, 1934], 71).

> The same age which produces great philosophers and politicians, renowned generals and poets, usually abounds with skilful weavers and ship carpenters. . . . The spirit of this age affects all the arts; and the minds of men, being once roused from their lethargy, and put into a fermentation, turn themselves on all sides, and carry improvements into every art and science.[32]

Such fermentation describes well the intellectual and entrepreneurial climate of Scotland by the 1760s. Moreover, there were direct links between the Enlightenment and the economy. The life of Lord Kames in law, letters, and agricultural improvement was a fine example of the practical application of the intellectual values associated with some elements in the Enlightenment. It was a climate in which, for example, the great traditions of medicine and engineering, direct agencies of human improvement, were powerfully encouraged. The Edinburgh intellectuals demonstrated a practical bent that helped to inculcate "a much-needed empirical scientific method" for the solution of industrial problems as well as its application to the broader problems of the scientific explanation of society itself. Most of all, the Enlightenment created an ethos of improvement and rationality that fired the movement for agricultural progress among the landowning class. Yet, granting these beneficial intellectual influences deriving from the Enlightenment, the receptivity of Scottish society remains unexplained. Moreover, it has been further argued that "improvement" as an ideology in Scotland predated "the florescence of the Enlightenment," thereby casting doubt on the causal sequence.[33]

There were, in eighteenth-century Scotland, certain general circumstances that facilitated both intellectual and economic progress. Political stability, greater religious toleration, and the benefits of a national system of education have been given much credit in Scotland's transformation. Macaulay himself had argued the case. Although civil peace was dislocated by the Jacobite eruptions and by recurrent bouts of food riots, anti-Catholic riots, and varieties of internecine bitterness, nevertheless Scotland had, in the eighteenth century, become a more reasonable country. Some thought, indeed, that the loosening of the iron grip of Calvinism, and the lessening of the barren disputes that had racked the church in the previous century, had left a blessed quiet and stability in which the nation would again prosper and think. The secular rationalism of the Enlightenment, offering an optimism

32. Quoted by R. H. Campbell, "The Enlightenment and the Economy," in Campbell and Skinner, eds., *Scottish Enlightenment*, 8.

33. *Ibid.*, 8–11, 23; see also Campbell, "The Union and Economic Growth," in Rae, ed., *Union of 1707*, 58–74.

for human betterment, was able to blossom as the great Calvinist tradition weakened, leading to a more open, liberal, and progressively democratic context for thought and action.[34] That the Scottish church had rendered the country insecure and intellectually inert in the previous century is not a proposition that passes uncontested, and it is still argued that Scottish Calvinism was a positive force that urged the individual into various forms of social and political action.[35] Calvinism was an activating religion that gave a training in argumentation, itself a positive influence against conservative frames of mind. But the fact that less intellectual energy was channeled exclusively into the sands of theological dispute perhaps saved more for liberal cogitation, giving release to the intellects of Edinburgh.

The provincial fermentation was already a complex brew. The education system has been the social variable most widely invoked in the search for the causes of Scottish success; and, indeed, the greatest names of the Scottish Enlightenment were products of a system that provided a cheap and obligatory education in most Lowland parishes and offered a ladder of social mobility into the Scottish universities. Although the Scottish Act of 1696 prescribed a school in every parish, it was not comprehensively operational; yet it is said to have provided an unrivaled system, and one especially "geared to the filling of the professions"—enabling Scotland to respond disproportionately to the opportunities of the new century.[36]

Research has been destructive of these orthodoxies. Employing a rigorous comparative method and various forms of statistical testing, R. A. Houston rejects emphatically the entire notion that the eighteenth-century Scots were either more literate or more democratically educated than their contemporaries. He demolishes the assumption of Scottish educational superiority on the evidence of simple literacy throughout the population. He totally denies the idea that this was a uniquely literate society with open and equal access to education for all classes. He asserts that the assumptions about the demo-

34. The religious tranquillity of Scotland in the 18th century was, of course, strictly relative. It was, equally with New England, subject to religious awakenings, endless splits, and extremism, as in the 1740s. See, for example, Harold P. Simonson, "Jonathan Edwards and his Scottish Connections," *Journal of American Studies*, XXI (1987), 353–376. On the general context of Scottish religion, see Smout, *Scottish People*, 509–513.

On the rationalism: as Smout puts it, "A tradition was built up after Hutcheson which involved academics in philosophical disquisition without the possibility of interference from theologians," but this was not to deny that the moral and social forms of Scottish philosophy were derived, in part, from Calvinism (*Scottish People*, 481).

35. See Campbell, "Enlightenment," in Campbell and Skinner, eds., *Scottish Enlightenment*, 12–15.

36. Mitchison, *History of Scotland*, 350; and see, for instance, Smout, *Scottish People*, 476–479.

cratic nature of Scottish schooling were simply the romanticization of the Scottish past by later nationalists.[37] And he contends, consequently, that the education factor has been absurdly overstressed as a cause of Scottish economic and intellectual advance.

Houston is prepared to concede that in some specific sectors, among tradesmen and craftsmen, levels of literacy were somewhat higher than in England. But the Scots in general had little edge over contemporary Holland, Sweden, or even northern England, in either the range or the quality of their basic education. Even the role of the Scottish university education is questioned, at least in terms of its availability. The provision of university places had difficulty keeping pace with Scottish population growth in the eighteenth century, and participation rates were not high by current European standards: "There is nothing remarkable about the percentage of the eligible population entering university in eighteenth century Scotland." With another sweep of his claymore, Houston concludes, "The further we go into the subject of Scottish education the more its much vaunted achievements fade into a range of mythology."[38] Such robust iconoclasm leaves the central elements of the Scottish renaissance bare of explanation. Contemporary observation of the forms and style of Scottish behavior, in business and social life, may contain better clues to their success, both at home and abroad.

IV. The Mentality of Emulation

There was something inordinately deliberate about the way Scots confronted the world of the Atlantic empire in the eighteenth century. For all their pride in their education and their universities (well founded or not), the Scots displayed a compulsion to adapt, to change, to improve. They were conscious to a painful degree of their backwardness, their poverty, their lack of polish, their provinciality. They adopted a mentality of emulation, a catching-up ideology of imitation and self-improvement that, though it may have predated the Union, became more urgent by the 1720s. There was, therefore, a candid acceptance of inferiority in economic life, in cultural attainment, and in manners. The consequence was, not a stolid stoicism, but a concerted effort, almost a collective mission, to reach forward toward the standards set

37. R. A. Houston, *Scottish Literacy and Scottish Identity: Illiteracy and Society in Scotland and Northern England, 1600–1800* (Cambridge, 1985), esp. 244–247; and Houston, "The Literacy Myth? Illiteracy in Scotland, 1630–1760," *Past and Present*, no. 96 (August 1982), 81–102.

38. Houston, *Scottish Literacy*, 244, 247. His views do not pass uncontested; see D. J. Withrington, "A Half-Educated Nation?" *Scot. Econ. and Soc. Hist.*, VII (1987), 72–74.

by London and by England. It announced itself in myriad ways: most painfully in the conscious aping of English ways, most productively in the import of agricultural and industrial methods into Scotland, most abrasively in the outward thrust of Scots bent on taking advantage of the world of opportunity beyond Scotland. It was a distinctive mentality that pervaded their entire exploration of the Atlantic world. Increasingly, Scots came face-to-face with the English, cast in the role of inferiors, as provincials on the make. For a time it made some of them figures of derision; eventually they outgrew their reputation and developed several types of status far beyond earlier expectations.[39]

Encounters with the English in the early and mid-eighteenth century were less than edifying for the maintenance of a sense of Scottish nationality. The redefinition of Scotland after the Union entailed a deliberate contraction of its language, identity, and pride. The process was led by the landed classes in Scotland in a self-anglicization and voluntary assimilation toward London. It was seen in the great popularity of London periodicals in Scotland, notably the *Tatler* and the *Spectator*, which were cheaply reprinted in Edinburgh and much imitated in the quest for social improvement, virtù, and acceptance in the wider world. The Scots language was eroded in favor of a universal English usage, which led to the spectacle of the finest figures of the Enlightenment devoting their energies to the expurgation of embarrassing Scotticisms from their discourse.[40] Scots anglicized their names and attended elocution lessons to eradicate traces of their objectionable accents. English was thereby accepted as the necessary language of civilization. It required the suppression of Scottish provincialisms "to enable the provincial Scots to engage with the culture of England on that culture's own ground." Partly also it was an effort to mask origins when anti-Scottish feeling in England became virulent in the 1760s, at a time when Hume himself was anxious that his nationality would damage the sales of his *History*. When Hume's friend Gilbert Elliot was snubbed by the English, Elliot rejected his friend's indigna-

39. It has been suggested that such inferiority had pervaded the cultural life of both the Scots and the Americans, but the Scots, being closer to English standards, were able to "mediate metropolitan culture to America and that in various ways." Bruce Lenman, *Integration, Enlightenment, and Industrialization: Scotland, 1746–1832* (London, 1981), 44–45.

40. On periodicals, see Phillipson, "Culture and Society," in Stone, ed., *University in Society*, II, 429. Sir John Clerk of Penicuik remarked that "the English language . . . since the Union wou'd always be necessary for a Scotsman in whatever station of life he might be in, but especially in any publick character" (quoted by Murray, "Administration and Law," in Rae, ed., *Union of 1707*, 31). See also, David Daiches, *James Boswell and His World* (London, 1976), 7–8, 22; H. J. Hanham, *Scottish Nationalism* (Cambridge, Mass., 1969), chap. 2; and on the deliberate anglicization of the young earl of Elgin in the 1770s, Sydney Checkland, *The Elgins, 1766–1917: A Tale of Aristocrats, Proconsuls, and Their Wives* (Aberdeen, 1988), 5–7.

tion, turned the other cheek, and, in true provincial style, counted his blessings: "We are both Englishmen; that is, true British subjects, entitled to every emolument and advantage that our happy constitution can bestow."[41]

There was a distinct "cultural cringe" in the postures adopted by the "Londonized Scots," in the effort to "out-English the English."[42] It was mirrored in political style also, among the Scottish representatives at Westminster, who, by reputation, were generally despised for their endless compliance, even obeisance, to figures of power, in the hope of receiving patronage. Demeaning or not, the overwhelming desire to pass as English and to transcend Scottish origins was symbolic of the more pervasive fertilization of Scottish life with external influences. It eventually facilitated the vital universalization of Scottish scholarship, which was the hallmark of the Enlightenment and the outreach of its own culture. It displayed itself across the Atlantic, where Scottish teaching, textbooks, and book learning were built into a regular and permanent nexus between the two cultural provinces. It enabled Scots to penetrate the frontiers of the Atlantic world, even into the heartland itself: such indeed was the essence of its intellectual, economic, and medical efforts. In some instances, emulation produced superiority, as, for instance, in the progress of Scottish agriculture by the end of the century, by which time Scottish methods, farmers, and managers were invading England itself.

Scottish progress eventually proceeded with such vigor that it created its own tensions and reactions. Among the English a general attitude of condescension began to give way to expressions that combined resentment with growing respect. When the flower of the English aristocracy began to journey north in the 1790s for "Scotch knowledge," it was evident that a certain reversal had occurred. In Scotland itself there were parallel fears that assimilation, and the dissolution of Scotland into England, had gone too far. Bruce Lenman suggests that the completeness of her assimilation was demonstrated by Scottish loyalty to London during the Jacobite uprisings and in the

41. Robert Crawford, review, *London Review of Books*, Jan. 21, 1988, 16; Daiches, *Paradox of Scottish Culture*, 20–23, 71; John Brewer, "The Misfortunes of Lord Bute: A Case-Study in Eighteenth-Century Political Argument and Public Opinion," *Historical Journal*, XVI (1973), 22; J.Y.T. Greig, ed., *The Letters of David Hume*, 2 vols. (Oxford, 1932), I, 491–492, 516, 519–521, II, 154, 409. Hume quoted in Mitchison, *History of Scotland*, 356.

42. Janet Adam Smith, "Eighteenth-Century Ideas of Scotland," in Phillipson and Mitchison, eds., *Scotland in Age of Improvement*, 112. See also Andrew Hook, *Scotland and America: A Study of Cultural Relations, 1750–1835* (Glasgow, 1975), 36. "Cultural cringe" is to adopt the derisive phrase often used in association with a later but no less provincial culture, that of Australia in the mid-20th century. It has been defined as "the denigration by Australians of their own culture, and their attitudes of subservience to the culture of overseas countries" (G. A. Wilkes, *A Dictionary of Australian Colloquialisms* [Sydney, 1985], 119).

American Revolution—so much so that Scotland had caused itself to be "the least demanding and subservient of British colonies." Sir Walter Scott was furious about the folly of assimilation, which had reduced Scotland to "a subordinate species of Northumberland" and which threatened the extermination of all Scottish national characteristics.[43] Yet the truth was that, by cleaving toward England with such success, the Scots had redefined themselves and dissolved the normal meaning of the terms "province" and "nation."

V. The Scottish Invasion of England

The obverse of cultural assimilation was the muscular seizure of opportunities by Scots throughout the Atlantic world. It was demonstrated in emigration, trade, politics, colonial service, practically everywhere. In some arenas it caused a certain collision of Scottish energy with entrenched interests. In the first instance, however, it derived from the single-minded pursuit of the opportunities that flowed from the Union and the expansion of the empire, but most obviously of those in the south. As late as 1850 Henry Cockburn was still complaining about the magnetic effect of England upon the most talented Scots of his day: "hungry London" had "drained all my friends," he declared.[44] By then the high road south had been worn smooth by a sesquicentenary of ambitious or adventurous Scots.

There was little counterflow of Englishmen into Scotland, which was itself testimony to the direction of the benefits of the Union and the meaning of provincialism. George Lockhart described the southerners who took employment in Scotland as the "scum and candlia" of England, an exaggeration yet clear enough sign of the outlandishness of Scotland in the eyes of London. When Francis Phillipson arrived in Edinburgh in 1708 to take up the post of deputy auditor of excise, he wrote home to England that it was not as awful as they might think:

> I am come downe into a strange place and amongst a strange set of people, yet I find them more civiller and regular than I expected and much better living than our common notions of the place.

In 1708 Daniel Defoe, ever the propagandist, tried to reeducate his southern compatriots who generally regarded Scotland as

43. Keith Robbins, "Core and Periphery in Modern British History," British Academy, *Proceedings*, LXX (1984), 275–297; N. T. Phillipson, "Scottish Public Opinion and the Union in the Age of the Association," in Phillipson and Mitchison, eds., *Scotland in Age of Improvement*, 144 (quote); Lenman, *Integration*, 42 (quote).

44. Quoted by Sydney Checkland and Olive Checkland, *Industry and Ethos: Scotland, 1832–1914* (London, 1984), 136.

> a desert, a wast howling Wilderness, a Place of wild Folks that live in Mountains, live they know not how, and feed upon they know not what, and not at all like other parts of the World.

These prejudices weakened only slowly, and the northward flow of English people, apart from the regiments, was slight. Nor were the English necessarily welcome, and Boswell "was unusual in wanting more official Englishmen in Scotland to make the Union more complete."[45]

At the time of the Union the fear of Scottish invasions, peaceful or otherwise, was widespread in England. As S. G. E. Lythe puts it, "Zoological metaphor was strained to the limit to describe the ravening hordes of Scotsmen waiting the chance to flood south."[46] In reality the flood was more a selective seepage, slow to develop but widening out toward the end of the eighteenth century. In the earlier phases there was a noticeable infiltration of the imperial employment market by the sons of the landed classes. For them Scottish job opportunities were narrower than for their southern counterparts: for instance, the Scottish church was far less a source of places than the Anglican church, and the chances of medical employment in Scotland were also poorer.[47] Least surprising, discounting the matter of the Jacobite Rebellions, was the great influx of Scots into the Hanoverian regiments of the British army. The Scots, high and low, were poorer than the English, and there was, in any case, a long-standing tradition of military service abroad. The Scottish nobility had greater need of such employment and fewer inhibitions about accepting it. Some of the great Scottish landed families had been committed to military service abroad for generations. In the British army of the mid-eighteenth century they soon came to be overrepresented at all levels. By 1752, Scots were a quarter of all regimental officers, mainly Lowlanders, but there were already specifically Highland companies being regimented as early as 1739, long before Pitt's famous recruitments in the far north. The suspicion of Jacobitism may have constrained some Scottish military careers, but there was no wholesale purging of Scots after either 1715 or 1746. In truth, therefore, the Scots fared well in the British army and were not disadvantaged by their national origins.[48]

45. Phillipson quoted in Shaw, *Management of Scottish Society*, 67. Defoe quoted in Houston, *Scottish Literacy*, 14. Boswell: Clive and Bailyn, "England's Cultural Provinces," *WMQ*, 3d Ser., XI (1954), 208.

46. Quoted by Smout, "Road to Union," in Holmes, ed., *Britain after the Glorious Revolution*, 177. There were reciprocal fears in Scotland of an English invasion "for places"—see Healey, ed., *Letters of Defoe*, 231–232.

47. Consequently, especially after 1760, "hordes of Scottish doctors" settled "in lush English practices," according to Linda Colley, "The Multiple Elites of Eighteenth-Century Britain," *Comparative Studies in Society and History*, XXIX (1987), 410.

48. James Hayes, "Scottish Officers in the British Army, 1714–63," *Scot. Hist. Rev.*, XXXVII (1958), 23–33.

On the other hand, naturally enough, there was audible resentment in England at Scottish success in the British army. There was jealousy of their growing influence. In December 1747 Lieutenant William Dworkin of the Thirty-ninth Regiment complained that if he had been a Scot rather than a Cumbrian he would have gained a company long since: Scots won preferment "at an easier rate." Ten years later, Charles, duke of Richmond, warned his younger brother against growing "so fond" of Scots, both in general and in the regiment:

> Be civil to them as they have been to you. Allow them great merit as good officers. But do not choose among them your friends. It can never do you honour and may be of disservice to you.

But no amount of disdain or distrust prevented the Scottish advancement in the army.[49]

Nor did mere prejudice prevent the Scottish penetration of other spheres of British life, except at the very highest levels of government.[50] A key example was their steady infiltration of the diplomatic service after 1707. By 1770, "Scotsmen had charge of British relations with nearly every major European court," from Paris to Scandinavia, from Prussia to Venice. The entry of Scots from the landed class into the British diplomatic service, as an alternative to domestic poverty or conventional military service, helped to make the Union more palatable to that class. Other English professions, including the law, the church, and much of politics, were for many decades effectively the preserve of the best English families. But the English generally looked upon diplomatic service, especially in the less salubrious capitals of the Continent, with palpable distaste if not aversion. Their poorer Scottish counterparts were less fastidious and were prepared to accept even the least desirable postings. They were also prepared to take low pay and learn the necessary languages of their employment. They demonstrated professional attitudes in a service which itself was becoming increasingly professionalized: the Scots were "eager, ambitious, and on the whole hard-working careerists." Not surprisingly, their success also engendered a degree of resentment that, in its extreme form, began to be regarded as a sinister conspiracy by a phalanx of Scots determined to deprive honest Englishmen of their rights and privileges. One such Englishman in 1773 declared that his countrymen were a "ruined and insulted people" who had lost their honor to "the black whirlpool of the North" that had "borne all before it."[51]

There was no secret in the fact that Scots looked to London (and, to a

49. Quoted *ibid.*, 29–30.

50. See Mitchison, "Patriotism and National Identity," in Moody, ed., *Nationality*, 73.

51. G. J. Bryant, "Scots in India in the Eighteenth Century," *Scot. Hist. Rev.*, LXIV (1985), 22–41.

lesser degree, to the colonies and then to India) for greater scope for the exercise of their financial and social ambitions. Robert Adam was candid: "Scotland is but a narrow place." Boswell had proclaimed that Scotland was too cramping for any Scotsman with a measure of culture. David Hume told Adam Smith, "Scotland is too narrow a place for me," and announced, "London is the Capital of my own Country."[52] The southward trek of talented but constrained Scots had been predicted by the Scottish member of Parliament R. R. Hepburn:

> It is natural for people who can afford it to get near the seat of Government . . . you feel you are in a better country, amongst a richer and happier people. We are only fit to supply England with inhabitants and very few of these that can help it will ever return except on a visit.[53]

The permeation of English political life, and of the growing Hanoverian bureaucracy, by the Scots was a slower process. The political management of Scotland by Archibald Campbell, earl of Islay, and by Henry Dundas undoubtedly gave scope for the manipulation of considerable patronage. When Bute, "the northern Machievel," occupied the citadel of power in London in the 1760s, many Englishmen were prepared to believe that the northern flood was a danger to the entire nation. But the best example of Scottish influence occurred when Dundas took charge of the India Board of Control and made it a great source of patronage for his fellow Scots in the 1780s and after. In reality it had taken the Scots two generations to penetrate the East India Company, to break into the entrenched position of the English. Dundas was subsequently accused of peopling the company with his own countrymen as part of his strategy to manage Scottish politics. As late as 1821 Sir Walter Scott was able to describe India as "the cornchest of Scotland where we poor gentry must send our youngest sons." In fact the trend had been long established. In 1772 Scots in the company represented one in nine of its civil servants, one in eleven of its common soldiers, and, already, one in three of its officers. An Englishman complained to Clive's secretary in 1767, "What has ruined this service is the number of officers admitted into it from North Britain."[54] They included a preponderance of Highlanders from the stratum of the lesser gentry. India, like the army, the navy, and the colonies, was an avenue for the improvement of family finances, and the Scots exhibited less reluctance to serve than their southern counterparts. As

52. Quoted in Janet Adam Smith, "Eighteenth-Century Ideas of Scotland," in Phillipson and Mitchison, eds., *Scotland in Age of Improvement*, 108–109.

53. Quoted in Karl Schweizer, "Scotsmen and the British Diplomatic Service, 1714–1789," *Scot. Trad.*, VIII (1978–1979), 116.

54. Bryant, "Scots in India," *Scot. Hist. Rev.*, LXIV (1985), 21–22. See also J. M. Bourne, *Patronage and Society in Nineteenth-Century England* (London, 1986), 128–130.

Bryant remarks, "That they were successful to some extent seems to have been due to men of higher social standing than the English at first offering themselves for service." To some, like Charles Grant, an Indian career brought great riches; for others, like Count Macleod, it helped rescue their estates from forfeiture and bankruptcy.[55]

VI. Scottish Encounters in America

The position of America in the Scottish exploration of the opening frontiers of the Atlantic empire was more complex. America offered the Scots further lebensraum, an arena in which "the people of a small, poor, but vigorous country sought opportunity to prosper," a country in which "too many competed for too few resources," providing a vital opportunity so that "Scottish enterprise and settlement flourished within the framework of imperial law."[56] The westward reach of the Scots to America was a variant of their penetration of England and demonstrated similar opportunities for advance, similar dynamism, and comparable tensions. But there were key differences: for instance, the transatlantic migrations were more concentrated and caused a fear of wholesale population loss in Scotland. They involved far larger numbers of Highlanders than did the southern drift. Moreover, Scotland developed a varicty of nexuses with the American colonies that suggested overlapping provincialisms and more complex interrelationships as the Atlantic empire evolved during the eighteenth century. By 1800 the economic and cultural matrix of the Atlantic world had become multilateral, and the Scots had become enmeshed in the full confusion of imperial and industrial forces. Influences were now received by and transmitted from several different and semi-independent points in the system—from Boston, Edinburgh, and Glasgow, certainly, as well as from London—and were reciprocated in more complex forms. Lowland Scotland had overcome its provinciality and had become an autonomous source of technological, intellectual, and political ideas, all of which were broadcast across the Atlantic world and within Scotland itself. By then Scotland was transforming and restructuring its economy and society in reaction to widening forces to which Scotland and America had both contributed. The tentacles of economic and

55. Bryant, "Scots in India," *Scot. Hist. Rev.*, LXIV (1985), 29. Lord Macleod and his father, the third earl of Cromartie, had served Charles Edward Stuart in 1745–1746. After his trial and release, Macleod served with distinction in the Swedish army and was made count in the Swedish order. He later returned to Britain and raised a regiment for George III.

56. William R. Brock, *Scotus Americanus: A Survey of the Sources for Links between Scotland and America in the Eighteenth Century* (Edinburgh, 1982), 2, 4, 11, 18, 127.

cultural change eventually reached even into the fastnesses of the northern Highlands and into the remotest islands of the Hebrides.

The movement of Scottish people across the Atlantic mirrored the changed circumstances within Scotland. There is no doubt that the extraordinary commercial energy of the Clyde merchants found its greatest scope for expansion in the American colonies. They built the American connection, which broadened to encompass practically every sector of Scottish life. The growth of trade and the improvement of shipping to America accelerated the possibilities of emigration. By the 1770s the emigrants included growing numbers of mobile and individualistic laborers responding to shifts of opportunity in the commercial economy of the Scottish Lowlands. There were also quasi-cooperative associations of lowland farmers that financed well-articulated migrations to cheap land in the colonies. It is unlikely that such people were the poorest in the farming community, though they may have been near the margin of rural profitability. Some were driven by adversity, but there is a greater sense of free calculation of benefits and the exercise of youthful enterprise in the Lowland outflow. In America most of these Scots had little collective visibility, partly because they were quickly assimilated into the community: they spoke English, and they tended to disperse. Among them were enough artificers and skilled people to excite local alarm for the future of industry in the south of Scotland in the 1770s. In 1819 it was reported that many laborers had gone to America, almost invisibly: "They retire peaceably, and indeed slip away, without their design being generally known in the vicinity."[57]

Emigration from the Highlands was a more desperate phenomenon, which reflected the economic and social turmoil of that part of Scotland that partook scarcely at all in the general Scottish success story of the eighteenth century. Transatlantic migration from the Highlands began earlier than the Lowland exodus, although both reached new heights immediately before and after the War of Independence. The sources of the Highland emigrations were concentrated in various parts of the west coast and caused great anxiety as early as the 1730s, among a landlord class whose possessive attitude toward their tenantry was legendary. In the middle years of the century the Highlands passed through precipitate change—of rebellion, subjugation, modernization, and agrarian transformation. But Highland emigration had long predated both Culloden and the sheep clearances. Poverty, famine, and now rapid population growth all combined to create increasing pressure on resources in the region, and the extrusion of people from the west coast was

57. See Graham, *Colonists from Scotland*, 27–28, 93; Abbot Emerson Smith, *Colonists in Bondage: White Servitude and Convict Labor in America, 1607–1776* (Chapel Hill, N.C., 1947), 49; *Farmer's Magazine*, XX (1819), quoted in Malcolm Gray, "Scottish Emigration: The Social Impact of Agrarian Change in the Rural Lowlands, 1775–1875," *Perspectives in American History*, VII (1973), 97.

mainly an expression of increasingly competitive conditions for land in the Highlands. America offered an escape that was strongly countered by internal efforts made by proprietors to retain their people.

Emigrants from the Highlands seem to have journeyed mainly in communal formation. Some, no doubt, moved in dog-leg fashion—first to the Lowlands and then across the ocean as individuals. More commonly, however, they left directly from the northwest coast of Scotland, coordinated by a leader and organized into cohesive groups: there were many examples of this model during the decade of frantic departure just prior to the American Revolution. In similar formation many Highlanders would, after 1783, depart for Canada and sometimes as far as Australia.[58]

As early as the 1760s the main recruiting and mobilization mechanisms of emigration were already developed along the west Highland littoral. Ships' captains and landbrokers knew that the key link was the local minister or tacksman (a major leaseholder and often a subleaser) who could persuade the community to migrate, even across the Atlantic. They manipulated the general psychology of the people. In June 1754 a scheme to take West Highlanders to Carolina hinged upon the influence of a minister, Neill McLeod, who was "a very popular man amongst the Commonality [who] would incourage numbers to leave this County . . . he is a good preacher and full master of the highland tongue and am sure w'd please all partys." Twenty years later Samuel Johnson and James Boswell testified to the ease with which the Highlanders entered into the business of transatlantic migration. It was powerfully reinforced by sophisticated methods of persuasion and enticement at the hands of emigration agents already at work by 1770.[59] By the 1760s the emigrations from the Highlands represented a radical drain of people out of one of the poorest regions of the British archipelago, an escape from adversity rather than an expression of provincial revival.

The communal formations under which many Highlanders crossed the Atlantic, together with the organizing functions of their leaders (notably the

58. See Eric Richards, "Varieties of Scottish Emigration in the Nineteenth Century," *Historical Studies*, XXI (1984–1985), 473–494.

59. McLeod quoted in Brock, *Scotus Americanus*, 81. On the central role of the ministers, see J. L. MacDougall, *History of Inverness County, Nova Scotia* (n.p., 1922), 35. Johnson: "Whole neighbourhoods formed parties for removal, so that their departure from their native country is no longer exile. . . . They change nothing but the place of their abode," quoted in Rosemary E. Ommer, "Highland Scots Migration to Southwestern Newfoundland: A Study of Kinship," in John J. Mannion, ed., *The Peopling of Newfoundland: Essays in Historical Geography* ([Toronto], 1977), 230.

Emigration agents described in George Patterson, *A History of the County of Pictou, Nova Scotia* (Montreal, 1877), 79; Patterson, *Memoir of the Rev. James MacGregor, D.D. . . .* (Edinburgh, 1859), 137. More generally, see Bernard Bailyn, *Voyagers to the West: A Passage in the Peopling of America on the Eve of the Revolution* (New York, 1986).

tacksmen), all favored the replication in America of social systems from the Highlands. The conservative impulse to recreate stability no longer possible in the homeland undoubtedly activated some of these leaders, even as late as the 1840s. Some measures of social cohesion were indeed sustained: unlike the Lowland Scots, the Highlanders were prepared to follow their superiors and settle in identifiable groups—hence the geographical concentrations in Cape Fear Valley, North Carolina, in the Mohawk and Upper Hudson valleys in New York, and the Altamaha Valley in Georgia. The strength of this cohesion was testified to by the post-Revolutionary, second-phase migrations to Pictou in Nova Scotia and Prince Edward Island. Religion combined powerfully with economic adversity to mobilize emigration from the western Highlands. Mostly these people were a conservative peasantry looking for a continuation and preservation of their mental worlds, in which a rigorous and demanding religion provided the fulcrum of their lives. Their ministers provided leadership and cohesion in their oceanic migration and continuity over several generations. The tightly organized migrations from the western Highlands to Nova Scotia in 1786–1787 further exemplified the pattern and were documented in letters sent back to relatives. Such letters were

> caused to be written . . . informing them that they had the gospel here in purity, inviting them to come over, and telling them that a few years would see them free from their difficulties.[60]

Some of the exterior characteristics of these societies were also maintained—for example, in the persistence over several decades of the Highland costume and language. There were well-attested accounts of slaves practically monolingual in Gaelic. From Charleston in 1797 it was repoted, "The *Negroes* were dresst in the Scotch blue bonnet." Moreover, the Highlanders appear to have concentrated their energies in farming, in rural settlement, and settled further upcountry than the Lowlanders, reproducing their old economic strengths in cattle rearing and even fishing.[61] Yet, while it is true that the Highland emigrants created relatively stable communities on arrival in America (in contrast to the dispersing Lowlanders), there was no question of

60. Patterson, *Memoir of MacGregor*, 139. It remains surprising that no clergymen accompanied the Highland migrants to North Carolina (one of their principal destinations) until 1770. See J. D. Beckett, *A Dictionary of Scottish Emigrants into England and Wales* (Manchester, 1984), 143.

61. Quotation from Lady Liston's Diary, 1797, Liston Papers, MS 5696, pp. 12, 19–20, National Library of Scotland. Generally, however, it was difficult to sustain the language over more than two generations, despite concerted efforts. See, for instance, Patterson, *Memoir of MacGregor*, 405. On farming, see Duane Meyer, *The Highland Scots of North Carolina, 1732–1776* (Chapel Hill, N.C., 1961), 58, 120; Graham, *Colonists from Scotland*, 107–108, 114. Johnson thought that some of "the men of considerable means may establish new clans in the other hemisphere" (quoted in Graham, 40).

the replication of old forms of social structure in the host country. Virtually all feudal and patriarchal aspirations were swiftly dissolved in the colonial climate, and clanship and other quasi-feudal structures were not transplanted with any true effect. For instance, a private venture was launched in 1734 by Lachlan Campbell of Islay, who proposed to settle loyal Protestants on a 100,000-acre land grant in New York. In the following three years he undertook, at his own expense, the immigration of five hundred Highlanders. His intention, to replicate a laird-dom in the colonies, was disappointed. He learned a much-repeated lesson, that the transplanted Highlanders were a liberated people and invariably resisted any suggestion of refeudalization.[62] Though they may have been prepared to follow their social superiors and to settle in identifiable groups, even to reemigrate en masse to Nova Scotia and Prince Edward Island, there was no re-creation of clanship in the new world.

In a vivid and suggestive phrase, W. R. Brock has described the Scottish Highlanders in colonial America as "the shock troops" thrown at the frontier. They were the rural settlers and frontier people par excellence, a reservoir of the lowest form of colonizers who could easily be expended on the roughest edge of expansion in the new continent. The Highlanders were relatively poor and less easily assimilated, "rendered desperate in their original homes"; consequently the Highlanders "seemed to be the ideal colonists to endure the hardships of winter and to cultivate a wilderness," and the pioneering efforts of their own kinsfolk provided a channel for waves of others to join them in Highland districts in America. Thus the Scots from the north constituted a special stratum for the peopling of America—"one of the population reserves upon which colonial legislators and land speculators drew to subdue the wilderness and civilise the continent."[63] It suggests that the Highlands was a rich recruiting ground for America precisely because it was peripheral and essentially semicolonial within the internal British world.

By contrast the Lowland Scots tended to merge into the colonial population with less apparent difficulty. The more successful of them performed a disproportionate role in several key sectors of colonial life: in official employment, religion, medicine, and higher education and, most of all, in commerce. They followed channels of trade and became extraordinarily successful in transatlantic commerce, sufficiently dominant in the tobacco trade to generate envy and worse on both sides of the ocean.[64] Clydeside

62. Based on Graham, *Colonists from Scotland*, 76–85.

63. Brock, *Scotus Americanus*, 1–2, 85, 163.

64. On merging, see, for instance, Bernard Bailyn, "1776: A Year of Challenge—A World Transformed," *Journal of Law and Economics*, XIX (1976), 447; T. H. Breen, "Cultural Adaptations: Peoples and Cultures," in Jack P. Greene and J. R. Pole, eds., *Colonial British America: Essays in the New History of the Early Modern Era* (Baltimore, 1984), 223. Brock, *Scotus Americanus*, 14, says that the majority of

merchants had already honed their competitive edge in the European theaters of trade, especially in the Baltic—they had accumulated skills and capital against considerable commercial opposition. They were a lean and hungry mercantile corps, already armed with the instruments of credit, banking, and risk-taking entrepreneurship. It was said that most of the two thousand factors who controlled the Virginia trade on the eve of the Revolution were Scots, and they operated at all levels, often, for instance, acting as traders to the upcountry Highlanders.[65] They were link-men, commercial go-betweens, of the economy from the wilds of America to the domestic sources of industry and people in Scotland, London, and Europe. Compared with the Highlanders, they were urban folk, better educated and connected, people with skills, trades, and wider horizons, people who knew how to organize trade and industry, churches and schools, medical practices and libraries. The outward dynamic of the Glaswegian merchants was in part the reciprocal of their frustrations with their poor markets within Scotland: now they could live and prosper on the periphery of the North Atlantic.

The Lowland Scots included smaller lairds, merchants, farmers, professional men, and younger sons who reveled in the opportunities opened up in America.[66] Several became colonial governors, and they entered colonial service as an identifiable cadre or caste. Ned Landsman has argued that Lowlanders from the upper echelons of their own society found escape and opportunity in American life, an avenue to sustain otherwise frustrated ambitions; such men populated colonial officialdom "in unusual proportion." There were indeed many examples in the ruling elites of colonial America: Scots appear to have been particularly adept at infiltrating the upper reaches of intellectual, mercantile, and administrative life in the colonies as well as in the metropolitan center of the British imperium.[67] It was, naturally, one cause of their unpopularity in some circles. There may indeed have been a certain systematic skewing in the recruitment of colonial elites toward the northern provinces of the British Atlantic world. Wider parallels suggest a recurrent pattern in disproportionate reliance upon provincials in

---

emigrating doctors were Scots. See also William C. Lehmann, *Scottish and Scotch-Irish Contributions to Early American Life and Culture* (Port Washington, N.Y., 1978), 65. On tobacco trade, see, for example, Smout, *Scottish People*, 383.

65. See, for instance, Graham, *Colonists from Scotland*, 124; and Harry Roy Merrens, *Colonial North Carolina in the Eighteenth Century: A Study in Historical Geography* (Chapel Hill, N.C., 1964), 57.

66. Devine says that "The British Empire provided a new range of career opportunities for ambitious Scots in military and administrative service, merchanting and medicine, and much of the resulting income percolated through the Scottish economy in consequence of the adventuerers' habit of returning to their homelands with the profits of their varied enterprises" (Devine and Dickson, eds., *Ireland and Scotland*, 12).

67. Graham, *Colonists from Scotland*, 129.

the creation of colonial elites. The experience of imperial administration in the Roman and the Spanish empires suggests that provincials—notably the "sons of impoverished local gentry and small time bourgeoisie"—could create for themselves status and wealth in the outlying zones of empire. The scions of Scottish aristocratic and gentry families exerted themselves more successfully in America, in Australia, and in the East India Company than did their English counterparts. Employment opportunities for the sons of aristocracy and gentry were too narrow in Scotland, and consequently they turned outward, causing what Linda Colley describes as "a haemorrhage of Scottish *patrician* talent" into England and the colonies. Moreover, this elite Scottish infiltration into the British imperial job market accelerated after the Seven Years' War.[68]

Nor was Scottish success in America restricted to the Lowlanders. Bruce Lenman claims a long continuity of the upper levels of Highland society in colonial enterprise, before 1745 and certainly before 1707. After Culloden, he says, America was vital for the blighted Highland aristocracy, which now used the remnants of the old social system to recruit regiments for service in the British army of the Hanoverians, many of whom served on American soil. It was, however, in essence, a further extension of the age-old military entrepreneurship of the Highland patriarchy. By forming companies and regiments out of the old tradition (now somewhat anachronistically), Highland aristocrats were able to purchase their renewed recognition in Westminster. As Lenman says, "They had finally become part of the British establishment, but they had to go to America to do it."[69] It was also a measure of their poverty and their loss of autonomy in the Highlands, now a distant province of London.

If the Scots were frustrated by their lack of empire in the late seventeenth century, then its availability after 1707 would explain their enthusiasm for the great widening of horizons in America and beyond. It may be that "their role in all of these activities grew out of their position as a provincial elite in Great Britain," that is, that their colonial success was an expression of their essential provinciality.[70] Yet this could never be more than half of the explanation; the Scots could not have grasped this opportunity without reinvigo-

68. See Ronald Syme, *Colonial Elites: Rome, Spain, and America* (London, 1958), 24, 30, 50–51. I wish to thank my colleague Dr. Francis Brooks for this reference. Cf. Linda Colley, "Whose Nation? Class and National Consciousness in Britain, 1750–1830," *Past and Present*, no. 113 (November 1986), 111, especially concerning the "co-option" of parts of the Welsh and Scottish elites "into a truly British ruling class"; and Colley, "Multiple Elites," *Comp. Studies in Soc. and Hist.*, XXIX (1987), 410.

69. Bruce Lenman, *The Jacobite Clans of the Great Glen, 1650–1784* (London, 1984).

70. Ned C. Landsman, *Scotland and Its First American Colony, 1683–1765* (Princeton, N.J., 1985), 10.

rating their own culture and economic dynamic in the eighteenth century. Scotland, and especially, of course, Edinburgh and Glasgow, exerted a quasi-independent influence, a smaller rival pole of economic and cultural pretension, in the Atlantic world of the eighteenth century. The ostensibly provincial character of Scotland's cultural relationship with London may have made it more compatible with colonial America, yielding an affinity, a shared sense of inferiority and aggression vis-à-vis London. As William R. Brock suggests, "This awareness of Scotland as an alternative English-speaking culture was the most significant aspect of the Scottish influence upon America." It may explain the vigorous interchange between the "Atlantic provinces"—symbolized by the fact that, before 1776, more Americans chose to graduate through Edinburgh University than either Oxford or Cambridge.[71] Taking the competitive provinciality argument to its logical limit, it has been suggested that the success of the Scots offered a model for the Americans themselves to emulate and that this was the most lasting consequence of the productive intersection of two provincial cultures.[72]

VII. Reactions against the Scots

The extrovert energy of the Scots caused friction and abrasion in many sectors of the Atlantic world. Though their general contribution in the American colonies was well recognized, the Scots also aroused resentment and unpopularity. The excessive success of the Clydeside merchants in the Atlantic trade had generated animosity for decades. Middlemen, undertakers, and controllers of the hinges of trade, especially in tobacco, not entirely unlike Chinese traders in the twentieth-century Pacific, they were envied and resented by their suppliers, their customers, and their debtors. The Scots in America were unpopular for the same reasons that they were unpopular in England—they were too pushy, too successful, and sometimes too close to government. Their extraordinary success in the Atlantic system caused Samuel Johnson to believe that the Anglo-Scottish relationship was based on exploitation, that of the English by the Scots. It was enough to call into question the very direction of imperialism. Too many Scots, proportionately, sought advancement in government as well as in trade. As I. C. C. Graham

71. Brock, *Scotus Americanus*, 171. Hook suggests that "before the cultural bar of London . . . the Scot and the American appeared as a distant provincial" (*Scotland and America*, 12–16). On universities, see Syme, *Colonial Elites*, 56. On cultural interchange in the age of the Enlightenment, see Hook, *Scotland and America*.

72. On emulation, see Brock, *Scotus Americanus*, 132. For an interesting summary of some of the provinciality arguments, see Lenman, *Integration*, 43–47. On intersection of cultures, see Clive and Bailyn, "England's Cultural Provinces," *WMQ*, 3d Ser., XI (1954), 200–213.

suggests, "More Scottish officials and officers than English went to America, and more Scots of the upper class than English had relatives in America or were intermarried with American families." The Scots came to exert in America an influence "far beyond what might have been expected of her [Scotland's] slender resources and population."[73] They touched colonial sensitivities and nerves much as they did in London. There were even echoes of the Wilkesite vituperation directed at Scots on the fringes of court life:

> In America Scottish merchants shared in the opprobrium when they seemed to seek the favour of royal officials. To this was added the poor reputation that traders and monied men always enjoy in a society dominated by upper-class landowners.[74]

The American Revolution seemed to confirm precisely the anti-Scottish attitude of republican colonists. Though doubt has been properly cast on the notion that all Scots, even all Highlanders, were loyal to the Hanoverian crown in 1776, there was sufficient evidence for the general stigma to adhere. The Scots in North Carolina, mainly Highlanders, became "known chiefly in American revolutionary history for their devotion to the cause of George III." The British crown expected, and indeed to a considerable degree received, the loyalty of its Highland subjects during the War of Independence. The substantial and disproportionate remigration of Scots out of the Union and into Canada was another evident mark of such loyalties. According to Lady Liston, visiting an old Highland settlement in the Carolinas in 1797, those that remained had suffered for their loyalty during the Revolutionary war, but their language and religion had both survived the turmoil.[75]

Resentment against the Scots on both sides of the Atlantic was therefore a rough measure of their successful invasion of the opportunities beyond their homeland. Scotophobia in London could be traced back at least to 1603, but it reached vitriolic levels during the reign of the unpopular royal favorite, Bute, in the 1760s.[76] The public vilification of his political influence became

73. See Graham, *Colonists from Scotland*, 129, 143, 181; Hook, *Scotland and America*, 43.

74. Brock, *Scotus Americanus*, 128, 129. See also Hook, *Scotland and America*, 48–50. There was of course a reciprocal anti-London feeling in Scotland—see, for example, the *Bee*, edited in Edinburgh from 1790.

75. Meyer, *Highland Scots*, 3; Brock, *Scotus Americanus*, 129–130; Lady Liston's Diary, 12. On some of the mechanisms for retaining loyalty at work, see "Letterbook of Captain Alexander McDonald of the Royal Highland Emigrants, 1775–1779," New-York Historical Society, *Collections*, XV (1882 [1883]), 203–498.

76. On resentment, see Graham, *Colonists from Scotland*, 181. On Scots in England, see, for instance, George Rudé, *Wilkes and Liberty: A Social Study of 1763 to 1774* (Oxford, 1962), 21–22. Johnson is quoted in Colley, "Multiple Elites," *Comp. Studies in Soc. and Hist.*, XXIX (1987), 410. On Scotophobia, see Lenman, *Integration*, 40.

thoroughly confused with his Scottishness, certainly in the minds of the London crowds, well encouraged by Wilkes. Bute provided an excellent symbol for anti-Scottish feeling in the capital: he was the Scotch parvenu personified, the toadying immigrant as a threat both to the living standards and to the liberties of the English. Brewer remarks:

> The Scots, especially in London, enjoyed the dubious distinction of being marginally more unpopular than the Jews. To Englishmen of almost every rank the Scot was a contemptible creature. He was poorly fed, as Dr Johnson reminds us, spoke unintelligibly and suffered from that unpleasant but characteristically Scottish disease, the itch. Although thought to be subservient by nature, he was also deemed totally untrustworthy.[77]

In the common caricature of the day the Scot was pro-Stewart, pro-French, and pro-Catholic and supported standing armies. Mostly this was outrageous chauvinism, fanned by Wilkes and by the popular belief that "most places of Trust and Profit in England were engross'd by Scotchmen."[78] At its worst it witnessed the formation of anti-Caledonian clubs in London taverns and the open jeering and taunting of Scots in public places. An Anglican parson devised a plan to dissolve the Union and redefine Scots as foreigners.

The anti-Scots episodes of the 1760s represented the crude confrontation of Scots and English in the metropolis. Feeding on ludicrous national stereotypes, both Wilkes and "Junius" believed they had every right to cast aspersions on Scottish traits, since they were essentially obnoxious. Yet, for all their momentary virulence, the events passed away and made little difference to the continuing penetration of the Scots into the English heartland. In any case, the winds of chauvinism in London were notoriously fickle. Fifteen years later Scots were themselves leading popular rampages against Papist chapels in London during the Gordon Riots.[79]

In reality the Scots were extraordinarily successful at overcoming social ostracism and every other barrier to entry into the diverse sectors of British life. By the end of the eighteenth century the Scots had conquered their sense of provincial inferiority and were vigorously exploring the possibilities of trade and social advance wherever they went. In some degree the effort was itself self-reinforcing, since, the more the Scots cleaved to English standards, the more they were compelled to strive for higher incomes. Seeking status demanded better resources, which, in the early eighteenth century, were

77. Brewer, "Misfortunes of Lord Bute," *Hist. Jour.*, XVI (1973), 19–20.
78. Caleb Whitefoot, quoted *ibid.*, 21 n. 94.
79. *Ibid.*, 23 n. 106. On riots, see George Rudé, *Paris and London in the Eighteenth Century: Studies in Popular Protest* (London, 1970), 314–315, 327.

generally beyond the Scottish gentry. As Montrose said in 1708, "London journeys dont verie well agree with Scots estaites." By 1733 James Erskine of Grange was remarking on the growing exodus from his district: "This country now and for some years past, has lookt on itself as deserted, not only by the courtiers, but by the principale part of the nobility and gentry."[80] It was an exaggeration, but eventually, certainly by the 1760s, the Scots ruling class was indeed learning expensive new standards of consumption and metropolitan ways. Some found the transition too much and fell into bankruptcy and worse. But for many, though we do not know how many, the effort to emulate the English gentry rendered the entire landed class the more suggestible to the idea of making money in trade and industry, in colonial service, in London and the Americas, and on their own estates. As G. J. Bryant hypothesizes, "They may also have been more willing than English gentlemen to work for a merchant company, because their educational background was more egalitarian."[81]

Out of disadvantage, out of provincial inferiority, the Scot emerged well prepared for the world of transatlantic trade, for India and beyond, even for encounters in the metropolitan cultural heartland. No one saw the "strangeness" of this phenomenon with greater clarity and pride than David Hume, as early as 1757:

> Is it not strange that, at a time when we have lost our Princes, our Parliaments, our independent Government, even the Presence of our chief Nobility, are unhappy, in our Accent and Pronunciation, speak a corrupt Dialect of the Tongue which we make use of; is it not strange, I say, that, in these Circumstances, we shou'd really be the People most distinguish'd for Literature in Europe?[82]

VIII. The Irony of Cultural Provincialism

In his poignant consciousness of his nation's provinciality, Hume had undoubtedly spoken for many fellow Scots. It applied simultaneously to a want of culture and polish and to the emotional attachment to Scotland also. It has been argued that there were potent but obscure processes contained within the very condition of cultural provincialism that ultimately yielded a rich harvest of intellectual and economic responses. The energy and cultural

80. Quoted in Devine, "Union of 1707," *Scot. Econ. and Soc. Hist.*, V (1985), 29.
81. Bryant, "Scots in India," *Scot. Hist. Rev.*, LXIV (1985), 29.
82. Quoted in Janet Adam Smith, "Eighteenth-Century Ideas of Scotland," in Phillipson and Mitchison, eds., *Scotland in Age of Improvement*, 110.

extroversion displayed after 1740 have been represented as the collective response to the loss of autonomy since the time of the Union. Edinburgh had emerged in the role of provincial capital, a magnet for the stranded classes upon whom was thrust the task of collective leadership. Among them certain professional cadres, notably the ministers and the lawyers, joined the landed classes to become a social vanguard, acting as cultural go-betweens from London to Edinburgh, forming "self improvement societies of auto-didacts" and "constantly aware that they lived on the periphery of a greater world." The hair shirt of provincialism, the profound feeling of inferiority, caused complex patterns of behavior and response, but in the process shook "the roots of habit and tradition" and liberated the imagination.[83] Rather than cripple enterprise, a mechanism was set working, a spur to emulate the metropolis, helped by the fact that the provincial capital was now less fettered by political imbroglios. In the beginning, however, were the identity crisis and the realization of the role and obligations of the provincial elite.

In these explanations the Scottish renaissance emerges as an essentially provincial phenomenon derived from "an efflorescence of introspection," a specifically Scottish response to the loss of status at the time of the Union. Energies released by this "process of introversion" were reapplied in creative fields such as philosophy, education, religion, and economic development.[84] The Scot's complex sense of inferiority "made demands upon him unlike those felt by the equivalent Englishman."[85] The key agents in the process, argues Phillipson, were members of the Edinburgh elite from whose ranks eventually emerged the literati. Phillipson indeed develops an embryonic theory of provincial elites that allows him to compare the experience of Edinburgh with other provincial capitals such as Boston, Bordeaux, Dublin, Copenhagen, Philadelphia, and Dijon. The exact mechanism in operation is in dispute as is the evolving composition of the elite leadership. But central among them were the lesser landowners, bereft of political function, who turned their talents to a highly self-conscious improvement of themselves and their estates. The "assimilationist pressures" were widely accepted, seen, not as a threat to Scottish life and culture, but as a stimulus. English or London civilization now offered "new and exciting categories in which to think about the problems of progress and the Union provided Scotsmen with

83. See Clive and Bailyn, "England's Cultural Provinces," *WMQ*, 3d Ser., XI (1954), 200–213; John Clive, "The Social Background of the Scottish Renaissance," in Phillipson and Mitchison, eds., *Scotland in Age of Improvement*, 225–240; and Clive, *Scotch Reviewers: The Edinburgh Review, 1802–1815* (London, 1957), esp. 18–19.

84. Campbell, "Enlightenment," in Campbell and Skinner, eds., *Scottish Enlightenment*, 13; Houston, *Scottish Literacy*, 259.

85. Clive and Bailyn, "England's Cultural Provinces," *WMQ*, 3d Ser., XI (1954), 213.

a series of opportunities to be exploited."[86] Many Scots were explicit about the task: for instance, Alexander Wedderburn in 1755, who remarked, "If we are far behind, we ought to follow further." Thus the old fragmented governing class, confined to "the familiar, cheerful and economical pleasures of Edinburgh," cast themselves in the role of rejuvenating Scotland in the model of civilization as defined by London, "a desire to fashion a new Scotland through a systematic and rational improvement in the spheres of both material and cultural life."[87]

The outcome was that, by the 1750s, Edinburgh had developed an identifiable cultural style, a provincial culture eventually able to influence the metropolis and the Atlantic world in general. It was achieved in two stages by way of a provincial elite acting as "the legitimate guardians of provincial liberties and as agents of improvement who would modernize their province by means of energetic, intelligent, and public-spirited leadership and draw it from a state of rudeness to one of cosmopolitan refinement."[88] The first stage saw the stranded lesser nobility absorbing an ideology of improvement as their honorable function in the post-Union era, focusing on the improvement of their estates and economic growth in conjunction with local professional and mercantile groups: the lawyers, ministers, professors, doctors, and merchants. Their preoccupation and sense of committed social purpose was best manifested in the Honourable Society for Improvement in the Knowledge of Agriculture (1723–1745): "They sought to improve themselves and a wider community, and in so doing began to see themselves, as did the literati, as a modern-minded elite whose duty it was to regenerate a backward society."[89] They determined to encourage economic growth along specifically English models. Ambassador Sir Robert Murray Keith com-

86. Phillipson's influential views, which may be juxtaposed with the original thesis of Clive and Bailyn, are developed in several places: "Definition of the Scottish Enlightenment," in Fritz and Williams, eds., *City and Society*, 125–147; "Scottish Public Opinion," in Phillipson and Mitchison, eds., *Scotland in Age of Improvement*, 125–147 [*sic*] (quotation 144–145); "Culture and Society," in Stone, ed., *University in Society*, II, 407–448; and again in "The Scottish Enlightenment," in Roy Porter and Mikuláš Teich, eds., *The Enlightenment in National Context* (Cambridge, 1981), 19–40; and "Politics, Politeness, and the Anglicisation of Early Eighteenth Century Culture," in R. A. Mason, ed., *Scotland and England, 1286–1815* (Edinburgh, 1987), 226–246.

87. Wedderburn quoted by Phillipson, "Scottish Public Opinion," in Phillipson and Mitchison, eds., *Scotland in Age of Improvement*, 143; Phillipson, "Definition of the Scottish Enlightenment," in Fritz and Williams, eds., *City and Society*, 130; Devine, "Union of 1707," *Scot. Econ. and Soc. Hist.*, V (1985), 24. See also Mitchison, "Patriotism and National Identity," in Moody, ed., *Nationalism*, 74–78.

88. Phillipson, "Definition of the Scottish Enlightenment," in Fritz and Williams, eds., *City and Society*, 127, 138–141.

89. *Ibid.*, 132. See also the summary in Jane Rendall, *The Origins of the Scottish Enlightenment* (London, 1978), 12–19.

plained about the excessive agricultural enthusiasm of Scottish lairds who "could talk of nothing but of dung and of bullocks."[90]

Edinburgh, in effect, generated the sort of activity expected of any provincial capital, the typical copyist, polite, provincial culture that could be found in many parts of contemporary Europe. But in the 1740s and 1750s, there was a second age of growth, the true flowering of its philosophical, scientific, and literary talents, with the university at its center. Intellectuals were accorded remarkably high status and a responsibility for social leadership in the general improvement of society: "It was generally understood that the city's reputation rested on the achievements of her philosophers and men of letters." But the literati were themselves a delicate growth: as T. C. Smout puts it, the

> Scottish intellectuals were so emotionally dependent upon the approval and support of the landed classes that it is scarcely conceivable that the cultural golden age could have taken place if the gentry and nobility had been unwilling to become its patrons.

A new generation had emerged with greater confidence and universality of outlook. The literati in particular broke out of the confines of Edinburgh toward the "more expansive London-oriented life," increasingly cosmopolitan and capable of exerting their own intellectual magnetism.[91] In the shift the literati were accorded a very high status in Scottish society, becoming guardians of the virtù of aristocratic society. They were required to satisfy the ideological needs of society, which in the 1750s were invested with a greater sense of urgency and the belief that intellectual inquiry was vital for social progress. Thus the remnants of the old provincial oligarchy and the professional elites of Edinburgh and Glasgow combined "to offer a disoriented society the leadership it lacked." In form the intellectual movement entailed a preoccupation with the study of human behavior in the conscious pursuit of social and economic improvement. So successful did it develop that it became possible to talk of Edinburgh as a northern Athens and a Republic of Letters.[92]

The brilliant achievements of the Scottish Enlightenment, of course, coincided with the attainment of economic growth and the political stability of post-Culloden society in Scotland. With greater confidence, resources, and a growing maturity, the literati outgrew their environment and felt compelled by intellectual ambition to invade London. It may be true that the alliance for improvement persisted and that "the literati and the provincial oligarchy

90. Alexander Carlyle, *Autobiography of the Rev. Dr. Alexander Carlyle* (Edinburgh, 1860), 459.

91. Phillipson, "Definition of the Scottish Enlightenment," in Fritz and Williams, eds., *City and Society*, 134–138; Smout, *Scottish People*, 506.

92. Phillipson, "Culture and Society," in Stone, ed., *University in Society*, II, 435.

of enlightened Edinburgh . . . formed a single extraordinarily complex social unit." But eventually the elite outstripped its more functional role in Scotland, transcended its provincial roots, and adopted what George Davie describes as "the de-nationalised tones" of the Scottish Enlightenment. By the end of the century there was even a sense of alienation that provoked an indentifiable reaction toward a more nativist tradition in Scottish letters. It was as though a critical mass had been achieved, at which point the local scale of Edinburgh dominance began to break up.[93]

Dugald Stewart described Edinburgh's golden age as that "sudden burst of genius which to a foreigner must seem to have sprung up in this country by a sort of enchantment, soon after the rebellion of 1745." The idea of provincialism cannot be expected to carry the entire weight of explanation. Within the mechanism of challenge and response resides enough space for the chance concatenation of genius. Moreover, it may be argued that, in philosophy and science, Scotland had been decidedly unprovincial since the previous century. Scotland's connections with European intellectual discourse predated the Union and were critical in the genesis of further advance—Stewart himself emphasized the vital role of the "constant influx of information and liberality from abroad." Provincialism is perhaps too London-oriented a view to penetrate the Scottish mystery.[94]

Scotland had discovered ways in which a small nation could survive and prosper in a far larger polity and had generated an intellectual movement that reverberated throughout the system, just as its emigrants and merchants penetrated to all corners of the Atlantic world. The success of the Scottish response was measured by its outreach into the rest of the British world, of which it had become part without divesting itself of its culture and identity, despite the growing anxiety of romantic nationalists in Scotland. As Keith Robbins has said, "A commitment to an imperial vision did not imply the erosion of Scottish identity."[95] The space created by empire and by the dissolution of internal frontiers compensated for the loss of independence. In the process new contexts were found for conflict and for national anxiety. If Scotland was one of the marchlands of the Atlantic world, then Edin-

93. *Ibid.*, 447; Davie, "Anglophobe," *Scot. Jour. Pol. Econ.*, XIV (1967), 291; and see Janet Adam Smith, "Eighteenth-Century Ideas of Scotland," in Phillipson and Mitchison, eds., *Scotland in Age of Improvement*, 115–123.

94. Stewart quoted by Gladys Bryson, *Man and Society: The Scottish Inquiry of the Eighteenth Century* (Princeton, N.J., 1945), 5. See also Skinner, introduction, in Campbell and Skinner, eds., *Scottish Enlightenment*; and Anand C. Chitnis, *The Scottish Enlightenment: A Social History* (London, 1976), 246–247. For a lively critique of "explanations" of the Scottish Enlightenment, see Charles Camic, *Experience and Enlightenment: Socialization for Cultural Change in Eighteenth-Century Scotland* (Edinburgh, 1983).

95. Robbins, "Core and Periphery," British Academy, *Proceedings*, LXX (1984), 277.

burgh had effectively created a new status for itself. To the north, however, there were equally far-reaching transformations that pointed in the opposite direction.

IX. The New Map of Provincialism

The success of the well-assimilated, enlightened Lowlands was not reproduced in the Highlands. Here, indeed, the internal frontier of the Atlantic world, the resistant and awkward marchland, had been unable to integrate smoothly into the new world of the improvers. The Highlands in the late eighteenth century witnessed the penetration of powerful economic and political influences in a culture and environment much less receptive than the Lowlands. Consequently, far-reaching and disruptive changes were forced on a region that had not been conditioned or prepared for such a transformation. In the long run the Highlands of Scotland diverged from the general experience of the south and was reaffirmed in its isolation.

Jacobitism in the Highlands died a swift death after 1746. Once its leaders had capitulated, there was scarcely a spark of resistance left. The lairds and their tacksmen generally accepted the terms of the settlement imposed at the end of a bayonet with little obstruction, but change had already crept into the north before Culloden. One contemporary saw the transformation as a matter of taming an uncivilized frontier:

> It is remarkable, that in some districts bordering upon the Highlands, where within memory the inhabitants spoke the Irish Language, wore the Highland dress, and were accustomed to make use of Arms, upon the accidental introduction of industry, the Irish language and Highland dress gave way to a sort of English, and lowland Cloathing; the Inhabitants took to the Plough in place of Weapons; and, tho' disarmed by no Act of Parliament, are as tame as their Low Country neighbours.[96]

The process was heavily reinforced by objective changes in the character of the economy, itself the generator of both emigration and, in the form of regimental service, loyalty to the Hanoverians. The tools of subjugation and modernization—the Commissioners of the Forfeited and Annexed Estates, together with the Society for the Propagation of Christian Knowledge—operated decisively, but not necessarily oppressively, to extend the influence of improvement in this outlying province of London's hegemony.

One of the key instrumentalities of the commercial penetration of the

96. Duncan Forbes (?), "Some Thoughts concerning the State of the Highlands of Scotland" (1746), in *Culloden Papers* . . . (London, 1815), 301.

Highlands was the British Fishery Society, designed to promote fishing, industry, and settlement along the remote west coasts. As its chief spokesman, the eternally enthusiastic George Dempster, remarked in 1787 in a discourse on the discouragement of emigration, "It would seem as if providence had contrived the Society for the purpose of rendering the change in the manners of the Highlands conducive to the strength of the State." Dempster thought the Highlands should be improved into "a *People Warren* for supplying their King with brave soldiers and sailors and the more fertile parts of the kingdom with faithful servants of every description." He said as clearly as he could that the Highlands had as much claim to government financial assistance as any colony in America. It was as though there was no real difference.[97]

Meanwhile, however, many Highland proprietors gave way to the temptations of southern life and became thoroughly anglicized. John Knox observed the transition in 1786: "The value of [the] natural produce, by sea and land, is almost wholly absorbed by the great landholders, and by many of them spent at Edinburgh, London, Bath and elsewhere; and the people are thus left more or less at the mercy of stewards and tacksmen." A new breed of estate managers, factors, was taking over the supervision of Highland estates, men often trained in the south and roundly blamed for "blinding" their employers and squeezing the tenantry with high rents and impossible demands.[98] In this, however, the Highlands were not unique—contemporary Yorkshire, for instance, echoed with similar complaints.

It is, therefore, tempting to think of both the emigration of the Highlanders to America, and their behavior in the American Revolution, as expressions of their inferior, indeed, conquered status within the British Isles. The region became an internal colony that served as a demographic and military reservoir for service in external colonies within the British Atlantic system. The processes of pacification and the compulsory extension of the English language, commercial Smithian economy, and the entire ideology of improvement broke up the northern fastnesses. It demanded the introduction of alien ways and an eradication of feudalism: indeed, there were many who clearly regarded the Highlands as an underdeveloped region that required a transfusion of new blood—southern entrepreneurs, advisers, technicians, and farmers—to inaugurate the process of civilization. An anonymous ob-

97. James Fergusson, ed., *Letters of George Dempster to Sir Adam Fergusson, 1756–1813* (London, 1934), 182, 188; Dempster to William Smith, Oct. 14, 1895, Dempster Letters, MS 4319, National Library of Scotland. See also the *Bee*, Aug. 24, 1791.

98. John Knox, *A Tour through the Highlands of Scotland, and the Hebride Isles . . .* (London, 1787), 39, 176.

server in 1782 described the Highlanders as "a hardy Race of people who only want a spirit of Industry and Commerce to be excited among them to render them useful members of the State."[99] In the outcome many of the people, and more particularly their nervous and embattled middle-level leaders, chose to depart in many directions, but particularly beyond the Atlantic. As in many other parts of Europe the termination of feudalism was a prelude to mobility.[100]

There is considerable evidence that some Highlanders indeed sensed themselves to be colonized and pacified, even to the point of resisting their fate. The act of emigration, in one view, was itself a rejection of the conditions imposed upon the people by their masters, who, ostensibly, were progressively anglicized under the influence of southern values and pressures to conform. The severe increase of rents in the 1770s—the precipitant of much emigration to America and to the south—was partly blamed on landlords who had been intoxicated by southern standards of landlordism. In many cases their demeanor and patterns of conspicuous consumption became increasingly provincial, vying to emulate Edinburgh and London manners. As Thomas Pennant wrote in 1769, "The chieftains, tasting the sweets of advanced rents, and the benefits of industry, dismisses from the table the crowds of retainers, the former instruments of the oppression and freakish tyranny."[101]

In 1775 Matthew Culley, a well-known avant-garde Northumbrian grazier, observed some of the recent Highland emigrations.

> We found . . . good evidence that the chief reason why the poor people migrated to America . . . was entirely owing to the tyranny under which they groaned from Donald Macdonald of the Isles, and other chieftains who oppressed these poor vassals so much by raising their rents as to force them, by a voluntary Banishment, to seek their bread which their native country denied them, in the inhospitable provinces of Canada.[102]

99. On new blood, see, for instance, [Alexander Sutherland], *A Summer Ramble in the North Highlands* (London, 1825), 99; and Veritas, letter, *Scots Magazine*, XXXIV (1772), 697. Quote from "Observations on the Improvement of Highland Estates on the North West Coast of Scotland" (1782), Adv. MS 20.5.5, National Library of Scotland.

100. See F. Thistlethwaite, "Migration from Europe Overseas in the Nineteenth and Twentieth Centuries," Onzième Congrès International des Sciences Historique, *Rapport*, V, *Histoire contemporaine* (Uppsala, 1960), 51–53. For evidence of Highlanders emigrating to escape feudalism, see the *Bee*, May 16, 1792.

101. Thomas Pennant, *A Tour In Scotland, 1769* (Warrington, 1774), 194.

102. Quoted in Richards, *Highland Clearances*, II, *Emigration, Protest, Reasons* (London, 1985), 188.

More than this, however, Culley reported a case of direct action prior to emigration, an instance that may suggest the mentality of many more who emigrated to America. He recorded that a Highland laird had refused to lower his rents or pay compensation to the people as they vacated their lands. By way of reprisal the people, three hundred altogether, had decided collectively to fire their own houses and combustible property, specifically to deny their landlord any gain from their evacuation to America. It was an unpublicized and unrepeated act of arson, of social protest, which suggests more than meek submission to fate in the post-Jacobite Highlands. Similarly, emigration plans were used as a bargaining counter by which to threaten a rack-renting landlord. In April 1774 it was reported from the north of Scotland that "already some of these haughty landlords now find it necessary to court and caress these same poor people, whom they lately dispised and treated as slaves and beasts of burden."[103]

Less isolated were sporadic episodes of resistance to the infiltration of the Highlands by southern sheepfarmers and their agents. There were many cases of conflict and even low-level guerrilla-style resistance, sometimes of riot. Lowland farmers and estate factors were often regarded as agents of an alien set of values, of an adversary commercialism that was causing evictions and poverty in the Highlands. There was a profound conservatism among the peasantry of the Highlands, which expressed itself in several ways, in emigration, in sullen refusal to cooperate with the improvement plans of landlords, and in petty and largely ineffective modes of preindustrial social protest.[104]

An elaborate and detailed investigation of Highland emigration, instigated by northern landlords in 1803, yielded an image of an entire region seething with discontent, the final manifestation of which was emigration. While the Lowlands and the southern agriculture of Scotland had been transformed without massive social dislocation, the Highlands seemed unable to assimilate such change. Highland society was convulsed, perhaps because the new agriculture was introduced precipitately onto a tenaciously peasant structure, perhaps also because its social bonds were differently constructed. There was a sense of outrage and shock in the reports. Thus of the great migrations from Kintail, Reay, Sutherland, and Breadalbane in 1770–1774, it was said that they arose chiefly

> from discontent, at what the people then thought a contemptuous conduct, and treatment from Proprietors; poverty from a series of unfa-

103. See Annette Smith, "Annexed Estates," *Northern Scotland*, III (1977–1978), 75; Lenman, *Jacobite Clans*, 215. The 1774 account is from the *Scots Magazine*, XXXVI (1774), 346.

104. See Richards, *Highland Clearances*, esp. II, parts 2, 3.

vourable years, on the West Coast, which reduced them to low circumstances, at the same time, that a rise of rent was demanded.[105]

There was a general turmoil of shattered expectations and a sense that a local moral economy had been assaulted by alien forces—that the cultural marches had been breached.

Among the antagonizing forces that aroused the collective ire of the people, the most fundamental seems to have been the rationalization of tenure and rent, the great shift out of the remnants of feudalism. The 1803 enquiry noted the effects of the "rash plans of Improvement" in the Highlands, which were "subversive of Customs endeared by innumerable ties, and sanctioned by Ages; disgusting and alienating the People, even to Emigration." The enquiry remarked that

> the Highlanders were accustomed to be caressed and cherished by their Lairds, and used to look up to them for protection and comfort, in all their distresses; the Lairds had an absolute command over them, not coercive but paternal; the people would never offend their Chiefs or Chieftains; they prided themselves in being taken notice of by them, they gloried in the great qualities of their superiors, and themselves possessed an innate spirit incapable of mean and inglorious actions.

There may have been an element of hyperbole in the diagnosis, and the inflation, even tenfold increase, of rent was possibly more instrumental in the emergence of social tensions. The landlords had become "mercenary beings": "avarice and vanity are at the bottom of this, and every dignified feeling yields to the abasement of interested feelings," leading to "a total Alienation of the affection of the Landholders from the People."

The theme of injured pride recurred throughout the decades of Highland emigration, and it seemed to signal the erosion of one of the last surviving frontiers of the British mainland. In 1772 the McLeod properties on the island of Harris had witnessed a remarkable emigration to America. The laird had imposed a new regime of the latest improvement thinking upon this Hebridean outlier, and the people bridled and refused to cooperate and, finally, emigrated. The contemporary explanation was written in the language of resistance, which suggests a combative frame of mind with which such people entered America:

> Disdaining to become possessors of ffarms [sic] in the low Countries and follow the Customs of its inhabitants which they had held in Contempt they launched out into a new World breathing a Spirit of Liberty and a Desire of every individual becoming a Proprietor, where

105. Quotes in this and next paragraph from "Enquiry into Emigration 1803," 26, 29, 77, 81, 166, Adv. MS 35.6.18, National Library of Scotland.

> they imagine they can still obtain land for themselves, and their flocks of Cattle at a triffling Rent, or of conquering it from the Indian with the Sword the most desireable holding of any for a Highlander.[106]

Thirty years later, Highland emigrants were still pictured as resisting "the degradation of their offspring" by heading for "the wilds of America": "The spirit of independence rises, in all its force, he emigrates."[107]

There is also much evidence that the Highlanders were the object, in the late eighteenth century, of an ascribed colonial status. The entire vocabulary of agrarian improvement was colonial and condescending in tone: the native people must be brought forth for the benefits of civilization. The Reverend John Lane Buchanan in 1783 remarked on the attitudes of the incoming agents of agricultural and moral advancement: they were "necessitous strangers who have obtained leases from absent proprietors who treat the natives as if they were a conquered and inferior race." The legislation governing the forfeiture of the Jacobite Estates after 1746 was explicitly designed "for the better civilising and improving the Highlands of Scotland, and preventing disorders there in future."[108] Implicit, indeed sometimes explicit, in such accounts were assumptions about relative stages of history and racial development often underlined by Whig notions of progress. At its most extreme were the Lowland thinkers who believed that the Highlanders were feckless and backward "aborigines" who would do better in America—

106. "Observes or Remarks upon the Lands and Islands Which Compose the Barony Called Harries the Property of Norman McLeod of McLeod Esq 1772," MS 3431, p. 188, National Library of Scotland.

The landlords, by introducing new methods and tenures, did not expect to stimulate emigration—it was "an unintentional by-product; the landlords were more perplexed than pleased, at least until the second decade of the 19th century" (Malcolm Gray, *The Highland Economy, 1750–1850* [Edinburgh, 1957], 63–64; see also Gray, "Scottish Emigration," *Perspectives in Am. Hist.*, VII [1973], 93–174). Some Highland landlords went to great lengths to deter emigration, establishing new enterprises, moderating rents, and promoting the fishing industry. Colin MacDonald of Boisdale, in 1778, was especially commended for his "patriotism and liberality" on South Uist. His policies had the "great merit in inducing the people to desist from emigrating. . . . Such humane treatment has caused a great increase of inhabitants" (David Loch, *Essays on the Trade, Commerce, Manufactures, and Fishing of Scotland . . .*, 3 vols. [Edinburgh, 1778–1779], I, 176). The irony was that such humanity exacerbated the demographic congestion of the Highlands, which became evident to all by 1820.

107. Edward S. Fraser of Relig (?), "On Emigration from the Scottish Highlands and Isles" (circa 1803), MS 9646, p. 77, National Library of Scotland. Matthew Culley (Culley Papers ZCU43, p. 122) spoke of the people about to emigrate as "a refractory race of beings, fond, to a degree of Enthusiasm, of ancient usages and modes of living."

108. Buchanan is quoted in Graham, *Colonists from Scotland*, 69. The legislation (20 Geo. II c. 41) is quoted in Parliamentary Papers, *Report from the Committee on the Funds Arising from the Forfeited Estates of Scotland* (London, 1806).

their ancestral lands paying a better return under sheep.[109] Much of the state-assisted as well as privately sponsored investment in the Highlands in the late eighteenth century was based on the premise that the region needed to be incorporated into the national polity and the national economy, which, of course, contemporaries thought would also reduce emigration. At its most philanthropic and condescending, this colonial mentality expressed itself in the strains of the "noble aborigine"—as a writer in 1803 put it, the Highlanders were splendidly "uncontaminated by the profligacy, sedition and [atheism?] of modern philosophy, conveyed in a language to which they are as yet generally strangers." They had been abandoned by their landlords "and often forced to seek an asylum in America because of their propensity to agricultural life."[110]

The Lowland Scots in America represent the opposite provincial case in the Atlantic system. The Union of 1707, for some, already represented a total absorption of Scotland, but especially of its impecunious aristocracy, into the English political system, and a prelude to anglicization and the evolution of "a common culture."[111] The American colonies (and indeed England) constituted not so much an escape as an opportunity, less a refuge than an avenue of advancement, especially in trade, government, and the professions. In all this they were well equipped to take advantage. Having failed to carve an independent Scottish empire, they elbowed their way into England's. They were prepared to submerge their nationality for the benefits of a liberated market: their participation and complicity in empire brought rich imperial rewards. The vigor of the Scottish response to these opportunities, even if it entailed a quasi-provincial status, worked paradoxically to feed and reinvigorate the culture and economy of Lowland Scotland.

Moreover, the intersection of the two cultures, English and Scottish, was more complex than simply the domination of the first over the second. More energy and influence seemed to radiate out of the Scottish Lowlands—toward London, Birmingham, Boston, the Chesapeake, Calcutta, and Botany Bay—than into Scotland itself. The dynamism of Scottish traders, philosophers, doctors, administrators, political managers, economists, teachers, ideologues, theologians, and more seemed an unbroken wave in the decades about the end of the century. The radiation (which was especially penetrating in the Scottish Highlands) derived greatly from the vigor of commerce,

109. See Eric Richards, "The Mind of Patrick Sellar (1780–1851)," *Scottish Studies*, XV (1971), 1–20. On Lowland contempt toward the "natives" of the north even as late as 1814, see J. H. Clapham, *An Economic History of Modern Britain*, 3 vols. (London, 1926–1938), II, 62.

110. "Enquiry into the State of Emigration 1803," Adv. MS 35.6.18.

111. See Frank O'Gorman, "The Recent Historiography of the Hanoverian Regime," *Hist. Jour.*, XXIX (1986), 1011.

industry, and agriculture in southern Scotland and is clearly difficult to reconcile with notions of unidirectional dominance from London. As Frank O'Gorman says, "At some point in historiographical time, Great Britain must be treated as a multi-state rather than England with a few Celtic projections."[112]

The dual provincialism that marked Scotland's contribution to the North American population was, certainly by the time of the Declaration of Independence, in the course of redefinition. By then there were more profound forces let loose in the British sector of the Atlantic system that transcended the interprovincial relationship of Scotland and the American colonies. Population growth and industrialization in the British Isles were in the process of remolding the relations of the regions. They paralleled the growth of a more broadly based British consciousness and complex changes in Celtic nationalism within the British Isles.[113] Some zones—Clydeside, the West Midlands, Lancashire, much of Yorkshire, and Ulster, for example—now marched ahead in rapid economic transformation. Ultimately they were given the benefits of industrial productivity beyond the dreams of Adam Smith. Other regions—the West of Ireland, West Wales, part of East Anglia, the West Country, the Highlands—were to fall into relative retrogression, retarded by the differential impact of industrialization. There was a new hinge of history, a new set of regions and the provinces, and London itself seemed for a time vulnerable.[114] These mechanisms of provincial change overarched the older identification with nationality; in Scotland it tended to reemphasize the gulf between Highlands and Lowlands. The meaning, however, was of wider significance: for now the provinces were redrawn, and parts of England and Ireland converged with the Highlands as the provincial

112. *Ibid.* For a clarifying discussion of the relations between "regions" in Scotland, Great Britain, Europe, and the Atlantic, see Christopher Smout, "Centre and Periphery in History: With Some Thoughts on Scotland as a Case Study," *Journal of Common Market Studies*, XVIII (1979–1980), 256–271. Further paradoxes of the intra-British world are toyed with by Robbins, "Core and Periphery," British Academy, *Proceedings*, LXX (1984), 175–197. An even longer historical perspective on intra-British colonization that particularly deals with the earlier efforts of the Scottish and English crowns to colonize in the Celtic territories and across the Atlantic is found in John G. Reid, *Acadia, Maine, and New Scotland: Marginal Colonies in the Seventeenth Century* (Toronto, 1981).

113. On the redefinition of regions, cores, peripheries, provinces, and so forth, see Smout, *Scottish People*, 263; and Robbins, "Core and Periphery," British Academy, *Proceedings*, LXX (1984), 283–284. On British consciousness, see Linda Colley, "Whose Nation?" *Past and Present*, no. 113 (November 1986), 97–117.

114. The argument is further developed in Eric Richards, "Regional Imbalance and Poverty in Early Nineteenth-Century Britain," in Rosalind Mitchison and Peter Roebuck, eds., *Economy and Society in Scotland and Ireland, 1500–1939* (Edinburgh, 1988), 193–207.

casualties of industrialization. In a sense the Highlands, while drawn more firmly into the national economy, were increasingly peripheralized, reconfirmed in their marginal status on the outer edge of the Atlantic world.

In some ways, therefore, Scotland's relation with British North America had been precocious. As early as 1760 the dual character of its emigrants was already evident—partly because the Highlands had begun early, under some institutional pressure, a process of massive structural transformation. This released migrants at an early stage. Under the influence of subsequent demographic revolution and industrialization, only the central Lowlands was able to absorb and accommodate the swollen numbers (augmented by migrants from Ireland and the Highlands).[115] The Highlands continued in poverty and adversity, reinforced by the pressures of sheepfarming and deindustrialization. Shifting terms of trade propelled the adverse structural change. Despite concerted efforts between 1770 and 1820 to incorporate the Highlands in the center, more powerful economic forces were released that further reinforced the marginal status of the region. The fate of the Highlands had been perplexing: in its interaction with the Atlantic world it had generated great increases in its people only to lose most of them, it had created new wealth but had remained poor, and it had integrated itself in the great trading system of the Atlantic empire only to become further isolated from its most dynamic industrial development.

The consequence was that the pre-1776 trends in Scottish migration were continued after the War of Independence. Indeed, emigration from the Highlands for several decades accelerated, and the Clydeside merchants concentrated, successfully in the outcome, on repairing their war-damaged trade.[116] The fact that the latter adjusted successfully to the drastically altered conditions was proof, yet again, of their responsiveness to circumstances of the Atlantic system. For the Highlanders, America (now meaning Canada) remained a refuge from rising rents, from rising population, and from the age of improvement. A cultural margin of the Atlantic world continued to fracture and decline.

115. Malcolm Gray has argued cogently that agrarian changes precipitated migration both in the Lowlands and the Highlands and that these dislocations produced reservoirs for emigration. It is clear, however, that the two societies possessed quite different capacities to absorb the consequences of rural disturbance. "Scottish Emigration," *Perspectives in Am. Hist.*, VII (1973), 93–174.

116. See Brock, *Scotus Americanus*, 161, quoting a Catholic tacksman in 1793 advising the common people to migrate to the good lands in America, where "they need not be afraid of being tossed by the avarice of landlords." More generally, see J. M. Bumsted, *The People's Clearance: Highland Emigration to British North America, 1770–1815* (Edinburgh, 1982).

II

Borderlands of the West

JAMES H. MERRELL

"The Customes of Our Countrey"
Indians and Colonists in Early America

It was 1634, Maryland's first year, and already there was trouble on the colony's northern border. At William Claiborne's Chesapeake Bay trading outpost on Kent Island a Susquehannock Indian had injured a Wicomiss while both were doing business there, and some of Claiborne's men thought it funny. Soon five Susquehannocks and three of Claiborne's people lay dead, ambushed by angry Wicomiss warriors. Now, two months later, the Wicomisses sent a messenger to Governor Leonard Calvert with word that they wanted to make amends for the actions of their young men. "What will give you content," the envoy asked Calvert. The governor's answer was simple: turn over the culprits "unto me, to do with them as I shall thinke fit."

There was "a little pause." Then the Wicomiss spokesman tried to set the governor straight. "It is the manner amongst us Indians," he said, "that if any such like accident happen, wee doe redeeme the life of a man that is so slaine, with a 100. armes length of *Roanoke* . . . and since that you are heere strangers, and come into our Countrey, you should rather conforme your selves to the Customes of our Countrey, then impose yours upon us." If Calvert understood, he did not let on. "It seemes you come not sufficiently instructed in the businesse which wee have with the Wicomesses," he replied; "therefore tell them what I have said; and that I expect a speedy answere; and so dismist him."[1]

Calvert's conversation with the Wicomiss was part of a continuing debate in colonial times as native Americans and Anglo-Americans tried to establish whose country this was and whose customs ought to hold sway. Their exchange was more explicit than most, however, because in 1634 both natives and newcomers could at least claim to rule the Chesapeake. Elsewhere the issue was not in doubt, and conformity was not up for debate.

1. "A Relation of Maryland, 1635," in Clayton Colman Hall, ed., *Narratives of Early Maryland, 1633–1684* (New York, 1925), 88–90.

When John Lawson left Charleston, South Carolina, in 1700 to head inland through "a Country inhabited by none but Savages," for example, he was careful to behave in a manner "acceptable to those sort of Creatures." He relied on Indian guides, said nothing when his Keyauwee hosts served such delicacies as "Fawns, taken out of the Doe's Bellies, and boil'd in the same slimy Bags Nature had plac'd them in," and sat patiently through the night in a Waxhaw council house as old men sang and young people danced.[2]

Compare this with Dr. Alexander Hamilton's journey from Maryland to Maine and back again more than forty years later. Hamilton, too, met many native Americans in his travels, enjoyed the hospitality of a local headman, and sat with Indians at a sacred ceremony. Yet here any resemblance to Lawson's journey ends, for Hamilton never left the familiar Anglo-American confines of taverns and clubs, concerts and churches, enthusiastic New Lights and impertinent social upstarts. Along the coast colonists were many, natives few, and it was Indians who had to fit in. Instead of fawns, Hamilton's Indian host (who "lives after the English mode") served him a glass of excellent wine. Instead of joining the "confused Rabble" in the Waxhaw council house, Hamilton took a pew near some Indians during a service in a Boston church.[3]

Between Hamilton's journey and Lawson's lay a barrier that scholars have labeled a frontier, a cultural divide, or a marchland.[4] On one side of this line native Americans set the conditions under which intercultural encounters occurred; on the other, colonists did. Frederick Jackson Turner's Eurocentric version of the American frontier has given the concept a bad name, but there can be no doubt that a frontier existed in colonial times. Certainly English colonists had no doubts. "Wee are here att the end of the world," wrote William Byrd I in 1690 from his plantation at the falls of the James River. And Byrd was right: it was the end of his world, the English world, and

2. John Lawson, *A New Voyage to Carolina*, ed. Hugh Talmage Lefler (Chapel Hill, N.C., 1967), 6, 22, 39, 43–45, 58.

3. Carl Bridenbaugh, ed., *Gentleman's Progress: The Itinerarium of Dr. Alexander Hamilton, 1744* (Chapel Hill, N.C., 1948), 98, 110.

4. See Jack D. Forbes, "Frontiers in American History and the Role of the Frontier Historian," *Ethnohistory*, XV (1968), 203–235; James Axtell, "The Ethnohistory of Early America: A Review Essay," *William and Mary Quarterly*, 3d Ser., XXXV (1978), 110; Robert F. Berkhofer, Jr., "The North American Frontier as Process and Context," in Howard Lamar and Leonard Thompson, eds., *The Frontier in History: North America and Southern Africa Compared* (New Haven, Conn., 1981), 43–75; John T. Juricek, "American Usage of the Word 'Frontier' from Colonial Times to Frederick Jackson Turner," American Philosophical Society, *Proceedings*, CX (1966), 10–34; Alden T. Vaughan and Daniel K. Richter, "Crossing the Cultural Divide: Indians and New Englanders, 1605–1763," American Antiquarian Society, *Proceedings*, XC (1980), 23–99; Bernard Bailyn, "The Challenge of Modern Historiography," *American Historical Review*, LXXXVII (1982), 14–15.

the beginning of another—called "Indian Country"—where different rules applied.[5]

Different sorts of Indian peoples lived on opposite sides of this frontier. The natives Hamilton and other coastal travelers encountered, a common sight even late in the eighteenth century, were variously termed "neighbour-Indians," "little Tribes," "domestic Indians," "resident Indians," "plantation Indians," "Settlement Indians." Those Lawson and other explorers visited were "remoter Indians," "wilder Indians," "Inland Indians," "back nations," "strange Indians," "foreign Indians."[6] Within each category there was considerable variety. "Remoter Indians" ranged from the Santees of South Carolina, "very tractable" because of their heavy involvement in colonial trade, to Tomahittans in the Virginia mountains, who were so unaccustomed to seeing Europeans that they raised a scaffold when the first Englishmen arrived in 1670 so "theire people might stand and gaze at them and not offend them by theire throng." Similarly, the "neighbour-Indians" Hamilton met included not only the Boston churchgoers but also a band of Indian oysterers wading naked through the shallows alongside the road.[7]

5. Marion Tinling, ed., *The Correspondence of the Three William Byrds of Westover, Virginia, 1684–1776* (Charlottesville, Va., 1977), I, 136; *Minutes of the Provincial Council of Pennsylvania, from the Organization to the Termination of the Proprietary Government*, 10 vols. (Philadelphia, Harrisburg, Pa., 1851–1852), V, 119, 122, VII, 6.

6. William P. Cumming, ed., *The Discoveries of John Lederer . . .* (Charlottesville, Va., 1958), 41, 42 ("remoter"). Joseph Ewan and Nesta Ewan, eds., *John Banister and His Natural History of Virginia, 1678–1692* (Urbana, Ill., 1970), 385 ("neighbour"). James Axtell, *The Invasion Within: The Contest of Cultures in Colonial North America* (New York, 1985), 206 ("little Tribes" and "back nations"). Jane Henry, "The Choptank Indians of Maryland under the Proprietary Government," *Maryland Historical Magazine*, LXV (1970), 179; Samuel Cole Williams, ed., *Adair's History of the American Indians* (New York, 1974 [orig. pub. 1930]), 369 ("domestic"). Kathleen Joan Bragdon, "Crime and Punishment among the Indians of Massachusetts, 1675–1750," *Ethnohistory*, XXVIII (1981), 23 ("plantation"), 25 ("strange"). Yasuhide Kawashima, "Indians and Southern Colonial Statutes," *Indian Historian*, VII (1974), 11 ("resident"). Chapman J. Milling, *Red Carolinians* (Columbia, S.C., 1969 [orig. pub. 1940]), 62 ("Settlement"). Robert Maule to Mr. Chamberlaine, Aug. 2, 1711, Great Britain, Society for the Propagation of the Gospel in Foreign Parts, Ser. A, VII, 364 (microfilm, Library of Congress). Edward McM. Larrabee, *Recurrent Themes and Sequences in North American Indian-European Culture Contact*, APS, *Transactions*, n.s., LXVI, pt. 7 (Philadelphia, 1976), 11 ("wilder"). Daniel Gookin, "Historical Collections of the Indians in New England . . . ," Massachusetts Historical Society, *Collections*, 1st Ser., I (Boston, 1806 [orig. pub. 1792]), 156 ("Inland"). Wesley Frank Craven, *White, Red, and Black: The Seventeenth-Century Virginian* (New York, 1977), 60 ("foreign").

7. Lawson, *New Voyage*, ed. Lefler, 23; "Letter of Abraham Wood to John Richards, August 22, 1674," in Clarence Walworth Alvord and Lee Bidgood, eds., *The First Explorations of the Trans-Allegheny Region by the Virginians, 1650–1674* (Cleveland, Ohio, 1912), 213; Bridenbaugh, ed., *Gentleman's Progress*, 34, 172. I derive the insight into the spectrum of possibility portrayed in Hamilton from Angus

Nonetheless, this spectrum of native cultures broke down into two basic types: those inhabiting Byrd's world and those from Indian Country.

The invisible barrier between the Santees and the oysterers was crucial in shaping the life of an Indian people. A tribe's population, its economy, and its political life—indeed, its entire culture—depended less on whether it lived in New England, New York, or North Carolina than on whether it was located among the English. Thus "plantation Indians" in Massachusetts and Virginia had more in common with one another than with some "back nation" nearby. North or south, their numbers were small, their subsistence routine disrupted, their political autonomy compromised, their customs under indirect influence from colonial neighbors if not direct attack from Christian missionaries.[8]

Not the least of the differences between resident and inland groups was the way they interacted with the English. While hardly a precise gauge, laughter helps draw this distinction, because in intercultural contacts whoever made fun of the other generally was in control of the situation. In Indian Country the joke was on the colonist. Lawson's hosts often "laugh'd their Sides sore" at his antics, and he was not alone. Natives made fun of the Anglo-American because his fingernails were too short and his spoons too small. They laughed at his attempts to speak their language, laughed at his prayers, laughed at his beard.[9] Where a man like Hamilton felt at home, on the other hand, Indians tended to be the butt of the jokes. When the "queen" of a local tribe performed a ceremonial dance in Williamsburg in 1702, the audience burst out laughing, and the laughter never stopped. Colonists mocked Indian efforts to speak English or ride a horse, dress in English clothing or understand English law.[10]

Calder, *Revolutionary Empire: The Rise of the English-speaking Empires from the Fifteenth Century to the 1780s* (New York, 1981), 509.

8. D. W. Meinig (*The Shaping of America: A Geographical Perspective on Five Hundred Years of History*, I, *Atlantic America, 1492–1800* [New Haven, Conn., 1986], 208) notes that "the most obvious variations were more longitudinal than latitudinal," though he argues for three zones of interaction.

9. Lawson, *New Voyage*, ed. Lefler, 46, 47, 62, 176; Ewan and Ewan, eds., *Banister and His Natural History*, 382; and Robert Beverley, *The History and Present State of Virginia*, ed. Louis B. Wright (Chapel Hill, N.C., 1947), 182 (spoons); Allen W. Trelease, *Indian Affairs in Colonial New York: The Seventeenth Century* (Ithaca, N.Y., 1960), 169–170 (prayers); William Wood, *Wood's New-England's Prospect*, Burt Franklin, Research and Source Works Series, no. 131 (New York, 1967 [orig. pub. Boston, 1865, Publications of the Prince Society, III]), 72. See also James Smith, *An Account of the Remarkable Occurrences in the Life and Travels of Col. James Smith, during His Captivity with the Indians, in the Years 1755, '56, '57, '58, and '59*, ed. William M. Darlington (Cincinnati, Ohio, 1907), 15, 20, 24, 32, 59, 98–99.

10. William J. Hinke, trans. and ed., "Report of the Journey of Francis Louis Michel from Berne, Switzerland, to Virginia, October 2, 1701–December 1, 1702," *Virginia Magazine of History and Biography*, XXIV (1916), 132–134 (speech and

"Above all things," wrote one colonist of the Massachusett Indians, they "loved not to be laughed at."[11] The Massachusetts—and, eventually, Indians throughout the East—would have to get used to it. When English colonists first arrived in America, virtually all of the land between the Atlantic and the Mississippi was Indian Country; by the end of the colonial era virtually none of it was. The history of Indian-English relations in early America is the story of how this dramatic change in the country and its "Customes" came about. It is no laughing matter, but listening for laughter is one way of retracing the steps that led from "remoter Indians" to "neighbour-Indians," from "wild" to "domestic." To tell that story we must try to grasp what forces turned Tomahittans tractable, pulled Santees across that invisible line, and put clothes on those naked oysterers.

I

The place to begin is with that border between Anglo-America and Indian America, a border as difficult to pinpoint on a map as it was real. Sometimes its location was obvious. In 1524, when Abenakis on the Maine coast refused even to allow Giovanni de Verrazano's exploring party to come ashore, it reached right down to the water's edge. Plotting its position thereafter can be more complicated. For one thing, there was no inexorable advance across the continent; the English push into the interior could quickly reverse itself when Indians fought back. During King Philip's War of 1675–1676, for example, native warriors destroyed thirteen New England towns, and it was 1700 before colonists reoccupied the lands they had held at the war's beginning.[12] Even when the boundary did move west, its progress was uneven. Much depended on when the English arrived in a particular area: Carolinians in 1670 (not to mention Georgians in 1732) were clinging to the beaches at a time when their fellow colonists to the north had con-

---

dress); William Byrd, *The Prose Works of William Byrd of Westover: Narratives of a Colonial Virginian*, ed. Louis B. Wright (Cambridge, Mass., 1966), 316; and Edward Porter Alexander, ed., *The Journal of John Fontaine: An Irish Huguenot Son in Spain and Virginia, 1710–1719* (Williamsburg, Va., 1972), 99 (horses); Bragdon, "Crime and Punishment," *Ethnohistory*, XXVIII (1981), 24; and Francis Jennings, *The Invasion of America: Indians, Colonialism, and the Cant of Conquest* (Chapel Hill, N.C., 1975), 241 (laws).

11. Quoted in Kathleen J. Bragdon, "'Emphaticall Speech and Great Action': An Analysis of Seventeenth-Century Native Speech Events Described in Early Sources," *Man in the Northeast*, no. 33 (Spring 1987), 106.

12. Neal Salisbury, *Manitou and Providence: Indians, Europeans, and the Making of New England, 1500–1643* (New York, 1982), 52; Douglas Edward Leach, *Flintlock and Tomahawk: New England in King Philip's War* (New York, 1966 [orig. pub. 1958]), 243, 247.

quered the entire coastal plain. To complicate matters further, navigable rivers helped some colonists get ahead in the race for land. Thus the Connecticut River valley boasted a thriving English population one hundred miles from the coast at a time when most towns were little more than a day's walk from Boston or Plymouth, and this pattern of settlement was followed later along the Hudson, the Potomac, and the Savannah.

Whatever its twists and turns, its distortions and detours on the way west, the frontier did move across the continent, and the principal forces behind it were warfare, disease, and colonial settlement. Each was crucial in tipping the scales from what John Winthrop called a land "full of Indians" to one dominated by European immigrants. The familiar roster of names representing Indian warfare in colonial times—from Powhatan and Opechancanough in the Chesapeake, to Pequots and King Philip in New England, to Tuscaroras and Yamasees in the Carolinas—testifies to war's prominent role in the conquest of America. In Virginia, battles with colonists during the first half of the seventeenth century reduced the Powhatan Confederacy to a "harmless curiosity." The natives of New England lost some ten thousand people in wars with colonists between 1600 and 1750, and in North Carolina one thousand Tuscaroras were killed or enslaved during a single campaign in 1712. And these were only a fraction of the Indians' combat losses; violence along the edges of the colonial world was endemic, and untold numbers of natives perished in forgotten skirmishes.[13]

The casualties suffered in wars with Anglo-America were certainly appalling; the Indians' losses from exposure to alien diseases—conservatively estimated at 75 percent in New England alone—almost defy comprehension. Yet noting that demographic disaster formed a grim backdrop to all of colonial history is one thing, coming up with reliable population estimates for Indians quite another. A best guess for the number of natives east of the Mississippi River on the eve of permanent English settlement might be close to 1,000,000; a century earlier the total would have been higher still, for by the time the English set foot on these shores, Indians were well acquainted with imported diseases.[14] Whatever the earlier figures, after Anglo-Ameri-

13. Quotations in Jennings, *Invasion of America*, 28; and Craven, *White, Red, and Black*, 65. For warfare, see Sherburne F. Cook, "Interracial Warfare and Population Decline among the New England Indians," *Ethnohistory*, XX (1973), 1–24; Hugh T. Lefler and William S. Powell, *Colonial North Carolina: A History* (New York, 1973), 78.

14. On Indian deaths: Sherburne F. Cook, "The Significance of Disease in the Extinction of the New England Indians," *Human Biology*, XLV (1973), 501. Alden Vaughan places the figure of combat losses at 15–20% of the population (*New England Frontier: Puritans and Indians, 1620–1675*, rev. ed. [New York, 1979], 329). For a general discussion of disease, see Jennings, *Invasion of America*, chap. 2; J. Leitch Wright, Jr., *The Only Land They Knew: The Tragic Story of the American*

cans arrived native numbers plummeted with frightening speed. In 1674, inquiries among New England tribes elicited similar answers: from 4,000 warriors to 300, from 5,000 to 1,000, from 3,000 to 300, from 3,000 to 250, on and on the roll call of death went as memory called forth the world Indians had lost. Some thirty years later another curious colonist took a census of natives in Virginia, and again the response was a litany of loss: "much decreased of late"; "reduc'd to very few Men"; "a small number yet living"; "almost wasted"; "Wasting"; "but three men living, which yet keep up their Kingdom, and retain their Fashion."[15]

Sickness did its terrible work in different ways. It wiped out the Patuxets in a single stroke in 1616–1617 while the nearby Narragansetts, who escaped that particular scourge, watched tuberculosis and pneumonia steadily reduce their numbers during the rest of the seventeenth century. In the Carolina piedmont epidemics came once a generation—in 1698, 1718, 1738, and 1759—cutting the Catawbas' population from perhaps 5,000 to a mere 500.[16] Whether disease struck in one fatal blow or over several generations,

---

Indians in the Old South (New York, 1981), 22–26; James Axtell, "The English Colonial Impact on Indian Culture," in Axtell, *The European and the Indian: Essays in the Ethnohistory of Colonial North America* (New York, 1981), 248–253; Alfred W. Crosby, "Virgin Soil Epidemics as a Factor in the Aboriginal Depopulation in America," *WMQ*, 3d Ser., XXXIII (1976), 289–299.

When recent population estimates for Virginia on the eve of English settlement range from 14,000 to 170,000 and for New England from 70,000 to more than 125,000, no total for the East can be more than conjecture. I base this conjecture on what I consider the more reliable revisions of James Mooney's figures, many of which seem to fall around a total three times greater than his estimate of 300,000 for Indians east of the Mississippi River in what is now the United States. For example, Mooney estimated the Conoys (Piscataways) of Maryland at 2,000; careful study of archeological and historical evidence suggests 7,000. Mooney's figure for New England is 55,600; Neal Salisbury offers a range from 126,000 to 144,000. For the East as a whole, Ubelaker's small collection of revised estimates allowed him to project a tentative total of 900,000. See Douglas H. Ubelaker, "The Sources and Methodology for Mooney's Estimates of North American Indian Populations," in William M. Denevan, ed., *The Native Population of the Americas in 1492* (Madison, Wis., 1976), 243–288; Ubelaker, "Prehistoric New World Population Size: Historical Review and Current Appraisal of North American Estimates," *American Journal of Physical Anthropology*, XLV (1976), 661–665. For Virginia, see Christian F. Feest, "Seventeenth Century Virginia Algonquian Population Estimates," Archeological Society of Virginia, *Quarterly Bulletin*, XXVIII (1973–1974), 66–79; and Wright, *Only Land They Knew*, 24. For New England, see S. F. Cook, *The Indian Population of New England in the Seventeenth Century*, University of California Publications in Anthropology, no. 12 (Berkeley, Calif., 1976); and Salisbury, *Manitou and Providence*, 22–30.

15. Jennings, *Invasion of America*, 26; Beverley, *History*, ed. Wright, 232–233.

16. Salisbury, *Manitou and Providence*, 103; Paul A. Robinson *et al.*, "Preliminary Biocultural Interpretations from a Seventeenth-Century Narragansett Indian Ceme-

the end result was the same. At the close of the colonial period there were only 150,000 Indians left in the East. Survivors of the devastation understood neither its cause nor its cure, but they knew who was to blame. "They have a superstition," wrote one Pennsylvania colonist, "that as many Indians must die each year, as the number of Europeans that newly arrive."[17]

English colonists considered the Indians' catastrophic losses a sign of God's favor. It was, wrote one colonial governor, "as if Heaven designed by the Diminuition of these Indian Neighbours, to make room for our growing Settlements," and indeed disease often did clear the way for colonial farmers.[18] But the farmers helped. Natives still around when the English moved into an area found that their new neighbors were "like pidgeons": "where one of those people settled, . . . a thousand more would settle." A generation or so after the first pioneers arrived, the colonial population would reach a critical mass, the pressure on Indians would increase, and many tribes would retreat.[19] Within twenty years of Pennsylvania's founding, Indians near Philadelphia talked of heading into the hinterlands, and near Charleston in 1710 local native groups had "gone further up in the Country Thro' badd usage they received from some of Our People." In 1755 Edmond Atkin, soon to be the crown's superintendent of Indian affairs for the Southern Department, blamed it less on "badd usage" than a simple "difference of manners and way of life" between Indian and English. Whatever the reason, history taught him that "the Indians generally chuse to withdraw, as white People draw near to them." "Will not it be impossible for Indians and White people

---

tery in Rhode Island," in William W. Fitzhugh, ed., *Cultures in Contact: The Impact of European Contacts on Native American Cultural Institutions, A.D. 1000–1800*, Anthropological Society of Washington Series (Washington, D.C., 1985), 108, 118; James H. Merrell, "The Indians' New World: The Catawba Experience," *WMQ*, 3d Ser., XLI (1984), 542.

17. J. Leitch Wright, Jr., *Britain and the American Frontier, 1783–1815* (Athens, Ga., 1975), 3; Francis Daniel Pastorius, "Circumstantial Geographical Description of Pennsylvania" (1700), in Albert Cook Myers, ed., *Narratives of Early Pennsylvania, West New Jersey, and Delaware, 1630–1707* (New York, 1912), 410–411.

18. Alexander Spotswood to the Board of Trade, Dec. 22, 1718, PRO, CO 5/1318, 590–591 (Lib. of Cong. transcripts, 488). See also Vaughan, *New England Frontier*, 22; "A New Description of That Fertile and Pleasant Province of Carolina, by John Archdale, 1707," in Alexander S. Salley, Jr., ed., *Narratives of Early Carolina, 1650–1708* (New York, 1911), 285.

19. Samuel Hazard, comp., *Pennsylvania Archives: Selected and Arranged from Original Documents in the Office of the Secretary of the Commonwealth*, 1st Ser., 12 vols. (Philadelphia, 1852–1856), III, 548. I estimate the timing from my own work (James H. Merrell, *The Indians' New World: Catawbas and Their Neighbors from European Contact through the Era of Removal* [Chapel Hill, N.C., 1989], chaps. 2–4); and from Peter A. Thomas, "Cultural Change on the Southern New England Frontier, 1630–1665," in Fitzhugh, ed., *Cultures in Contact*, 131–161.

to live together?" wondered a Pennsylvanian. "Will not there be . . . a perpetual Scene of quarreling?" The answer, throughout England's mainland provinces, was often yes.[20]

War, disease, settlement—these three horsemen of the Indian apocalypse are essential to an understanding of English contacts with native America. But they are more the story's beginning than its end, for they cannot capture the substance and subtlety of the American encounter. The conquest of the continent was not as swift as the emphasis on depopulation and displacement implies; Indians did not surrender or disappear overnight. Without belittling the devastation wrought by smallpox, militias, or settlers, we need to remember that Indians survived. While some abandoned traditional burial rituals in the aftermath of an epidemic, most continued to inter their dead in customary fashion.[21] While warfare or sickness utterly destroyed some groups, others constructed new societies from fragments of the old. While many did retreat when faced with the prospect of being hemmed in by farms and fences, many others did not.

To understand how the Indians lost America and the English won it, we must look past the grand events—warfare, epidemics, the frontier's advance—to examine the less celebrated but no less important meetings between peoples. The real (and still largely untold) story is less dramatic than invasions and battles, less drastic than sickness and settlement; more intimate, more human in scale, it is also harder to uncover. These long-forgotten encounters lie in scraps of evidence, mere snatches of conversations that took place in several different contact arenas—linguistic, economic, diplomatic, legal, and religious—where Indian met colonist. The conversations, taken together, speak of a shift in patterns of interaction as face-to-face contacts slowly became more Anglo-American than native American, more like Alexander Hamilton's journey than John Lawson's. If that shift, that frontier, is often hard to pin down precisely, the overall trend is unmistakable: Indians slowly gave way and colonists slowly took over, until the line

20. Pastorius, "Geographical Description," in Myers, ed., *Narratives of Pennsylvania*, 410; Frank J. Klingberg, ed., *The Carolina Chronicle of Dr. Francis Le Jau, 1706–1717*, University of California Publications in History, no. 53 (Berkeley, Calif., 1956), 78; Wilbur R. Jacobs, ed., *Indians of the Southern Colonial Frontier: The Edmond Atkin Report and Plan of 1755* (Columbia, S.C., 1954), 47; Hazard, comp., *Penn. Arch.*, 1st Ser., II, 214. For general discussions of settlers, see William Cronon, *Changes in the Land: Indians, Colonists, and the Ecology of New England* (New York, 1983); Merrell, *Indians' New World*, chaps. 5–6.

21. Salisbury, *Manitou and Providence*, 106; James Axtell, "Last Rights: The Acculturation of Native Funerals in Colonial North America," in Axtell, *European and Indian*, 110–128; James H. Merrell, "Cultural Continuity among the Piscataway Indians of Colonial Maryland," *WMQ*, 3d Ser., XXXVI (1979), 561; Robinson *et al.*, "Narragansett Cemetery," in Fitzhugh, ed., *Cultures in Contact*, 108–109, 122–124.

between one world and another was not Verrazano's shore or Byrd's plantation but the Appalachians and then beyond.[22]

II

American Indians and English colonists brought to their encounter considerable experience with exotic peoples. For native Americans the English were only the latest in a series of European intruders, while those English colonists had a fund of knowledge about alien cultures derived from books about America and contacts with Ireland.[23] Yet if neither were novices in dealing with foreigners, they had a hard time making sense of one another once sustained interaction began at the end of the sixteenth century. Indians in New England called "every thing which they cannot comprehend" *Manitóo*, and they used the term frequently when talking among themselves about the English. Indians, whose cultures emphasized personal restraint, were appalled by the colonists' "excited chattering, . . . the haste and rashness to do something," and some wondered aloud why, if "the *Europeans* are always rangling and uneasy, . . . they do not go out of this World, since they are so uneasy and discontented in it."[24] Colonists were no better at comprehending natives. "Uncivil and stupid as garden poles," noted one. "A very strange kind of People," wrote another. "An odd sort of People," agreed a third. "Their way of Living is so contrary to ours," concluded John Lawson in 1709, after studying Carolina Indians for eight years, "that neither we nor they can fathom one anothers Designs and Methods."[25]

True understanding of the other would remain elusive. But the quest for that elusive goal started immediately, with a search for some way to cross the linguistic barrier. Thus began a tug-of-war between English and Indian as each tried to impose its modes of communication on the other. Natives expected colonists to follow local custom, which dictated that "the most

22. See T. H. Breen, "Creative Adaptations: Peoples and Cultures," in Jack P. Greene and J. R. Pole, eds., *Colonial British America: Essays in the New History of the Early Modern Era* (Baltimore, 1984), 196–197; Berkhofer, "North American Frontier," in Lamar and Thompson, eds., *Frontier in History*, 67–72.

23. For Ireland, see Nicholas P. Canny, "The Ideology of Colonization: From Ireland to America," *WMQ*, 3d Ser., XXX (1973), 575–595.

24. Roger Williams, *A Key into the Language of America; or, An Help to the Language of the Natives in That Part of America Called New-England . . .*, Rhode Island Historical Society, *Collections*, I (Providence, R.I., 1827), 95, 111; Charles T. Gehring and Robert S. Grumet, eds., "Observations of the Indians from Jasper Danckaerts's Journal, 1679–1680," *WMQ*, 3d Ser., XLIV (1987), 109; Lawson, *New Voyage*, ed. Lefler, 184.

25. Quoted in Trelease, *Indian Affairs*, 39; Robert Maule to Mr. Chamberlaine, Aug. 2, 1711, SPG, Ser. A, VII, 363 (microfilm, Lib. of Cong.); Lawson, *New Voyage*, ed. Lefler, 239, 240.

powerful Nation of these Savages scorns to treat or trade with any others (of fewer Numbers and less Power) in any other Tongue but their own." The English agreed in principle, but insisted that they, not Indians, had the numbers and the power. Moreover, colonists felt that the English language should prevail not only because England *should* rule; it would actually *help* England rule, because "changing of the language of a barbarous people, into the speech of a more civil and potent nation" was a way "to reduce such a people unto the civility and religion of the prevailing nation."[26]

Colonists expecting Indians to welcome the chance to learn "the treasure of our tongue" were disappointed.[27] The intruders did eventually win the war of words, but it was a long struggle, waged against stiff opposition. At first an elaborate pantomime was probably the most common means of conversing, no doubt accompanied by wild swinging of arms, exaggerated facial expressions, and whatever sounds might help get the gist of the message across. Crude, perhaps, but it worked. It was not hard to guess that Indians waving furs on the end of a stick at a passing ship were interested in trade or that an Englishman piling beads into an Indian's canoe wanted to make friends. Nor was it easy to mistake the meaning behind "stern-look'd Countenances" or a "scornefull posture."[28]

In the early stages of contact, aboriginal symbol systems expanded the mime's repertoire, and colonists had to read a foreign text. Seventeenth-century Virginians learned when to head west into Indian Country by counting the pebbles, knots in a string, or kernels of corn sent from native traders in the interior. Those same colonists could tell the tribe of the Indian bringing the message by a glance at his tattoo or paint: a serpent meant Occaneechi, a terrapin Susquehannock, three arrows Nahyssan. Crown officials went along with the traders: South Carolina sent knotted strings as messages to distant Indians, and New York authorities demanded that the Iroquois not only receive but give belts of wampum beads. Even colonists who still used pen and paper might go out of their way to accommodate Indians. One Albany trader recorded his transactions with natives by drawing in an account book "crude sketches of each beaver so that at a future date the

26. Lawson, *New Voyage*, ed. Lefler, 233; Gookin, "Historical Collections," MHS, *Colls.*, 1st Ser., I (1792), 221–222.

27. Quoted in Stephen J. Greenblatt, "Learning to Curse: Aspects of Linguistic Colonialism in the Sixteenth Century," in Fredi Chiappelli, ed., *First Images of America: The Impact of the New World on the Old* (Berkeley, Calif., 1976), II, 561. My thinking here owes a great debt to Greenblatt's article; to Lois M. Feister ("Linguistic Communication between the Dutch and Indians in New Netherland, 1609–1664," *Ethnohistory*, XX [1973], 25–38); and to James Axtell ("The Indian Impact on English Colonial Culture," in Axtell, *European and Indian*, 286–287).

28. See Salisbury, *Manitou and Providence*, 53; and J. Frederick Fausz, "Present at the 'Creation': The Chesapeake World That Greeted the Maryland Colonists," *MHM*, LXXIX (1984), 17; "The Discovery of New Brittaine, 1650," in Salley, ed., *Narratives of Carolina*, 9; "Relation of Hilton," in Salley, 41, 51.

customer would be able to look in the book and see for himself the amount owed."[29]

Useful as they were, pictographs and pantomime had their limits, and attempts to talk to one another followed close on the heels of contact. The conversations that ensued were easy prey to misinterpretation, however. Philip Amadas and Arthur Barlowe returned from their 1584 voyage to the Carolina coast certain that the Indian name for the area was "Wingandacoia." Sir Walter Raleigh, their sponsor, was equally certain that they were wrong: the word actually meant "you wear good clothes, or gay clothes." Modern linguists have suggested that both were mistaken, that in fact the Indians were talking about some trees in which they thought the visitors were interested. Those more fluent in the local language could also be fooled. On one occasion when the Virginia colonist William Strachey informed his native companion that he was hungry and the Indian replied "I will give you food," Strachey thought he was being called a beggar.[30]

Despite the pitfalls, the need to discuss more complex matters encouraged the two cultures to break through the language barrier. The first halting steps were probably secondary to the sign language in common currency: a verbal exchange between the explorer William Hilton and a tribe of Carolina Indians, for example, consisted of many gestures but only two words, "Bonny" and "Skerry." Far more useful were pidgin languages—English as well as several different Indian versions—that developed. Impatient colonists, who called these inventions "a broken language," "a made-up, childish language," were always trying to learn more, but Indians held back.[31] In

29. Ewan and Ewan, eds., *Banister and His Natural History*, 384; Beverley, *History*, ed. Wright, 160–161, 190; Cumming, ed., *Discoveries of Lederer*, 13; Lawson, *New Voyage*, ed. Lefler, 48; Mary A. Druke, "Iroquois Treaties: Common Forms, Varying Interpretations," in Francis Jennings *et al.*, eds., *The History and Culture of Iroquois Diplomacy: An Interdisciplinary Guide to the Treaties of the Six Nations and Their League* (Syracuse, N.Y., 1985), 89; Thomas Elliott Norton, *The Fur Trade in Colonial New York, 1686–1776* (Madison, Wis., 1974), 29–30.

30. Karen Ordahl Kupperman, *Roanoke: The Abandoned Colony* (Totowa, N.J., 1984), 17; Frank T. Siebert, Jr., "Resurrecting Virginia Algonquian from the Dead: The Reconstituted and Historical Phonology of Powhatan," in James M. Crawford, ed., *Studies in Southeastern Indian Languages* (Athens, Ga., 1975), 292.

31. "Relation of Hilton," in Salley, ed., *Narratives of Carolina*, 50–51. See Gerald Sider, "When Parrots Learn to Talk, and Why They Can't: Domination, Deception, and Self-Deception in Indian-White Relations," *Comparative Studies in Society and History*, XXIX (1987), 11–13. Colonists quoted in Feister, "Linguistic Communication," *Ethnohistory*, XX (1973), 31–32. For studies of pidgins, see James M. Crawford, *The Mobilian Trade Language* (Knoxville, Tenn., 1978); Ives Goddard, "The Ethnohistorical Implications of Early Delaware Linguistic Materials," *Man in the Northeast*, no. 1 (March 1971), 14–26; Goddard, "The Delaware Language, Past and Present," in Herbert C. Kraft, ed., *A Delaware Indian Symposium*, Anthropological Series, no. 4 (Harrisburg, Pa., 1974), 103–110; Goddard, "Some Early Exam-

New Netherland, where the linguistic battle has been studied most thoroughly, natives clearly sought to establish and then maintain the upper hand. One frustrated colonial student claimed "that they rather try to conceal their language from us than to properly communicate it, except in things that have to do with everyday trade, saying that it is sufficient for us to understand them to this extent." The Indians' purpose was obvious: "Even those [colonists] who can best of all speak with the savages, and get along well in trade, are nevertheless altogether in the dark and as bewildered, when they hear the savages talking among themselves." Another "Indian grammarian" trying to crack this code became hopelessly confused by the different tenses and pronunciations: "I stand oftentimes and look, but do not know how to put it down." His efforts to sort out the confusion failed, for Indians, he concluded, were "very stupid" and his fellow colonists ignorant. One supposed expert, consulted about variable pronunciations, explained the mystery by claiming that local tribes altered their entire language every few years.[32]

The "Indian grammarians" did not give up easily. Their persistence, coupled with the growing need to communicate as contacts became more frequent, overcame the Indians' reluctance to train capable linguists. Most early interpreters were colonists who mastered a native language, not Indians speaking English, for despite claims that some natives were delighted to learn and then show off their English, most colonists agreed that the local tribe's speech "is the first thing to be employed with them."[33] Over time, however, Indians were the ones expected to learn a foreign language. Not surprisingly, neighboring groups were the first to face this language requirement; indeed, a pledge to learn English could be part of formal submission to colonial rule. In Maryland, the Piscataway tayac (chief) began English lessons at the same time that he gave up polygamy, began dressing in English clothes, and converted to Christianity. Across the Potomac River in Virginia, colonial authorities during the 1670s encouraged the shift to English by insisting that tributary Indians provide their own interpreter at official meetings. More often, Settlement Indians simply picked up the language by imitating the English around them. In 1710, only forty years after South

---

ples of American Indian Pidgin English from New England," *International Journal of American Linguistics*, XLIII (1977), 37–41; Emanuel J. Drechsel, "Towards an Ethnohistory of Speaking: The Case of Mobilian Jargon, an American Indian Pidgin of the Lower Mississippi Valley," *Ethnohistory*, XXX (1983), 165–176.

32. Quoted in Feister, "Linguistic Communication," *Ethnohistory*, XX (1973), 32–33.

33. *Ibid.*, 33–37; J. Frederick Fausz, "Middlemen in Peace and War: Virginia's Earliest Indian Interpreters, 1608–1632," *VMHB*, XCV (1987), 41–64; Wood, *New-England's Prospect*, 103; quoted in Feister, "Linguistic Communication," *Ethnohistory*, XX (1973), 31.

Carolina's founding, a colonist noticed that "the Young Indians born since we inhabited these parts and that converse with us . . . speak good English."[34]

Even as they lost linguistic predominance, Indians resisted by refusing whenever possible to speak an alien tongue. "If you ask them a question," one Virginian complained of the tributary Indians in the 1680s, "unlesse they be made three parts drunk they will not answer, tho they can speake English." "Notwithstanding some of them could speak good English," reported another visitor to the colony's tributaries three decades later, "yet when they treat of any thing that concerns their nation, they will not treat but in their own language, . . . nor will not answer to any question made to them without it be in their own tongue." Such stubbornness only slowed the spread of linguistic imperialism, however. In 1734, "seeing the tributary Indians understand and can speak the English language very well," Virginia removed the natives' facade of superiority by discharging its official interpreters.[35]

A similar shift from Indian to English occurred in nonverbal modes of discourse. Not content to deal solely in wampum and tattoos, Anglo-Americans introduced competing symbols that eventually supplanted those devised by Indians. During the seventeenth century the Virginia assembly, impressed by the native custom of tribal identification, "took up the humour" and began issuing medals to friendly Indians. But there was an important difference: with medals, colonists no longer had to decipher tribal markings, or even tell one tribe from another, since from the English point of view the only important distinction was medal or no medal, friend or foe. In the eighteenth century, New Jersey made the same distinction by using red ribbons that the colony's Indians were to wear at all times.[36]

Along with their ribbons, New Jersey's native friends carried another mark of their loyalty, a "Registration Certificate," and ultimately it was pieces of paper like these that replaced the pictographs and pebbles. Natives themselves helped hasten the spread of writing. Awed by this new means of

34. Merrell, "Cultural Continuity," *WMQ*, 3d Ser., XXXVI (1979), 557; "Virginia Colonial Records: Commissions, Bacon's Rebellion, etc.," *VMHB*, XIV (1906–1907), 294; Klingberg, ed., *Carolina Chronicle*, 68. See also Hinke, trans. and ed., "Journey of Michel," *VMHB*, XXIV (1916), 134; Durand of Dauphiné, *A Huguenot Exile in Virginia . . .*, ed. Gilbert Chinard (New York, 1934), 154; Maule to Chamberlaine, Aug. 2, 1711, SPG, Ser. A, VII, 364 (microfilm, Lib. of Cong.).

35. Edmund Berkeley and Dorothy S. Berkeley, eds., "Another 'Account of Virginia,' by the Reverend John Clayton," *VMHB*, LXXVI (1968), 434; Alexander, ed., *Journal of Fontaine*, 93; William Waller Hening, ed., *The Statutes at Large: Being a Collection of the Laws of Virginia . . .*, IV (Richmond, Va., 1820), 461.

36. Beverley, *History*, ed. Wright, 190; Larrabee, *Recurrent Themes*, APS, *Trans.*, n.s., XVI, pt. 7, 7.

conversing and eager to capture its power, Indians copied the figures John Lawson jotted down, asked that their initials be carved into a tree alongside those of colonial explorers in order to "be an Englishman," and pestered Roger Williams, "Make me a paper."[37] Even native diplomats who protested against "that Pen and Ink work" began demanding copies of the treaties to take home.[38]

Indian and English forms coexisted well into the eighteenth century. In 1758, messengers sent from Philadelphia to the Ohio country carried belts of wampum that were keyed to a written speech, so that the talk could be read and the belts delivered simultaneously. To Indians this marked a real improvement, for it "was like two tongues": the letter "confirmed what the Messenger said to them" through the belts. Even so, the direction—from the rattle of wampum beads to the scratch of pen on paper—was clear. A few Indians learned to read and write, either in English or in their own language.[39] But the vast majority remained illiterate, inhabitants of a symbolic universe they were unable to decipher.

III

Much of the impetus for communication between peoples—that march from gesture through jargon to fluency—came from a shared eagerness for trade. It was trade that prompted Indians to hoist furs on sticks, trade that gave birth to the pidgin languages, trade that trained most interpreters. The lists of Indian words colonists compiled reveal how closely talking was tied to trading. Each phrase book had Indian equivalents for all sorts of merchandise, numbers for counting these items, and handy phrases every enterprising

37. Lawson, *New Voyage*, ed. Lefler, 57; "John Clayton's Transcript of the Journal of Robert Fallam," in Alvord and Bidgood, eds., *First Explorations*, 191; Williams, *Key into the Language*, 66. For other examples see Larrabee, *Recurrent Themes*, APS, *Trans.*, n.s., XVI, pt. 7, 7; John Phillip Reid, *A Better Kind of Hatchet: Law, Trade, and Diplomacy in the Cherokee Nation during the Early Years of European Contact* (University Park, Pa., 1976), 136–137; Merrell, *Indians' New World*, 150–151. An excellent introduction to the Indians' reaction is James Axtell, "The Power of Print in the Eastern Woodlands," *WMQ*, 3d Ser., XLIV (1987), 300–309.

38. *Penn. Ccl. Minutes*, IV, 708; William N. Fenton, "Structure, Continuity, and Change in the Process of Iroquois Treaty Making," in Jennings *et al.*, eds., *Iroquois Diplomacy*, 26; Druke, "Iroquois Treaties," in Jennings *et al.*, 86–88.

39. *Penn. Ccl. Minutes*, III, 189, VIII, 212; Gookin, "Historical Collections," MHS, *Colls.*, 1st Ser., I (1792), 197–198; Laurie Weinstein, "'We're Still Living on Our Traditional Homeland': The Wampanoag Legacy in New England," in Frank W. Porter III, ed., *Strategies for Survival: American Indians in the Eastern United States*, Contributions in Ethnic Studies, no. 15 (Westport, Conn., 1986), 92; Bragdon, "Native Speech Events," *Man in the Northeast*, no. 33 (Spring 1987), 107–108.

salesman should know, like "How d'ye do," "Have you got anything to eat," "Englishman is thirsty," "What price," "I will sell you Goods very cheap," "I will pay you well," "My money is very good," and "It is worth it."[40]

The colonists' concern with price serves as a reminder that, while Indian and English were both experienced traders and each had products the other wanted, they were schooled in different classrooms. Hence handing over one object in return for another was not as simple or as easy as it looked. Among Indians, exchange was embedded in a ceremonial code designed to cement relations between peoples; in these rituals the giving itself was as important as the gift. Colonists, on the other hand, tended to think more of prices and profits. Intercultural trade in colonial America combined both traditions at first; eventually, however, commerce went the way of speech, and natives ended up living by the economic rules of the Atlantic world.

Indians unacquainted with European ways were a colonial trader's favorite customers. These people, still operating within the context of aboriginal exchange, cared little about sampling the entire range of trade goods and less about prices. They sought wares that fitted established norms—glass instead of shell beads, for instance, or mirrors that substituted for crystal—and in return they gave whatever the colonist considered fair. It did not take Indians long to catch on, however. In New England they had "already" in 1634 "learned much subtiltie and cunning by bargaining with the *English*," and Roger Williams agreed that "they are marvellous subtle in their Bargaines." Experience made natives discriminating consumers: instead of accepting whatever was offered, they began to shop more carefully. "The Indians wilbe very long and teadeous in viewing" a trader's merchandise, complained one colonist, "and doe tumble it and tosse it and mingle it a hundred times over."[41] They were looking not just for beads or mirrors but cloth, tools, and weapons. Moreover, that cloth had to be "a sad colour," that iron hoe a

40. Lawson, *New Voyage*, ed. Lefler, 233–239; Edward P. Alexander, "An Indian Vocabulary from Fort Christanna, 1716," *VMHB*, LXXIX (1971), 309–310; Wood, *New-England's Prospect*, 111–116; Williams, *Key into the Language*, esp. chap. 25. The following analysis of trade is indebted to Axtell, "English Colonial Impact," in Axtell, *European and Indian*, 253–265; Jennings, *Invasion of America*, chap. 6; Salisbury, *Manitou and Providence*, chaps. 2, 5; Cronon, *Changes in the Land*, chap. 5; Richard White, *The Roots of Dependency: Subsistence, Environment, and Social Change among the Choctaws, Pawnees, and Navajos* (Lincoln, Nebr., 1983), pt. 1; Christopher L. Miller and George R. Hamell, "A New Perspective on Indian-White Contact: Cultural Symbols and Colonial Trade," *Journal of American History*, LXXIII (1986–1987), 311–328.

41. Salisbury, *Manitou and Providence*, 52–53; Cronon, *Changes in the Land*, 83; Cumming, ed., *Discoveries of Lederer*, 42; Miller and Hamell, "Cultural Symbols," *JAH*, LXXIII (1986–1987), 315–318. Quotations from Wood, *New-England's Prospect*, 88; Williams, *Key into the Language*, 135; Albright G. Zimmerman, "European Trade Relations in the Seventeenth and Eighteenth Centuries," in Kraft, ed., *Delaware Indian Symposium*, 66.

certain weight, that gun a light flintlock instead of a cumbersome matchlock.[42] And all—cloth, hoe, gun—had to be for sale at a fair price, for the more Indians traded with colonists, the fewer qualms they had about haggling over rates of exchange.[43]

Indians, though soon enough "wise in trade and traffic" with colonists, did not immediately become slaves to European habits of exchange or pawns in the Atlantic economic system. In fact, during the early years of intercultural trade the colonist who hoped to succeed tried to meet his customers' needs and obey their rules. In putting together a cargo he selected the right color, the right weight, and the right price. Upon arriving in a village he gave gifts to the proper people and accepted their offer of adoption, even marriage, into a kinship network. Once the bargaining began, he said nothing about the Indians' preference for bartering, "not by any certeyne measure or by our English waightes and measures," but by an arm's length instead of a yard and a mouthful instead of a pint. He went along because competition for Indian customers was fierce—not only between England and France but between Pennsylvania and New York, Albany and Schenectady, even within (especially within) Albany itself—and Indians could afford to be selective. "If any traders will not suffer the Indians soe to doe [examine the goods for sale]," one colonist lamented, "they wilbe distasted with the said traders and fall out with them and refuse to have any trade."[44]

As time went on, however, few Indians could simply refuse to trade. While natives did not become dependent on European wares overnight, within a generation or two of their entry into regular trade relations they did become dependent. The early shift from comity to competition and from passive acceptance to active haggling was only the beginning. The next stage removed the production of goods from its traditional context. Deer once put to many different uses were now left to rot as the hunter stripped the skin

42. Williams, *Key into the Language*, 134; Merrell, "Indians' New World," *WMQ*, 3d Ser., XLI (1984), 549; Norton, *Fur Trade in New York*, 31; Trelease, *Indian Affairs*, 49; Axtell, "English Colonial Impact," in Axtell, *European and Indian*, 254–255; Ted J. Brasser, *Riding on the Frontier's Crest: Mahican Indian Culture and Culture Change*, National Museum of Man, Mercury Series, Ethnology Division, paper no. 13 (Ottawa, 1974), 16; Vaughan, *New England Frontier*, 220; Reid, *Better Hatchet*, 38, 84; Patrick M. Malone, "Changing Military Technology among the Indians of Southern New England, 1600–1677," *American Quarterly*, XXV (1973), 52.

43. Salisbury, *Manitou and Providence*, 52–54; Cronon, *Changes in the Land*, 83; Cumming, ed., *Discoveries of Lederer*, 42.

44. Quoted in Zimmerman, "European Trade Relations," in Kraft, ed., *Delaware Indian Symposium*, 62, 66. This summary of traders' behavior is drawn from Merrell, *Indians' New World*, 29–32. See also Lawson, *New Voyage*, ed. Lefler, 210. For the competition, see Norton, *Fur Trade in New York*, chaps. 4–5; Francis Jennings, "The Indian Trade of the Susquehanna Valley," APS, *Procs.*, CX (1966), 406–424; Trelease, *Indian Affairs*, chap. 5.

from the carcass and moved on. Prisoners of war once adopted to replace dead kinfolk or tortured to assuage a mourner's grief were now sold. Wampum once restricted to persons of high status was now mass-produced by coastal communities that interrupted their seasonal subsistence routine to concentrate on the shells.[45] The final step was more obvious, as people less able to remember and to replicate traditional craft skills found they simply could not get along without European commodities.

Settlement Indians were the first to pass through these three stages. But even peoples well removed from colonial settlements found that a generation or so of colonial trade had taken its toll and "they cannot live without the assistance of the English." "What are we red People?" a Cherokee asked in 1753. "The Cloaths we wear, we cannot make ourselves, they are made to us. . . . We cannot make our Guns, they are made to us. Every necessary Thing in Life we must have from the white People." Lest any Indians forget this harsh truth, colonists reminded them: "We can live without you, but you cannot live without us." "'Tis in vain for you to stand out [against us]," a South Carolinian informed the Creeks in 1728. "What can you do without the English?"[46]

If trade could reach beyond the frontier to control distant natives, its effect on those living amid colonists can be imagined. Among neighbor Indians the appetite for English goods remained; the accepted means of acquiring them did not. The spread of colonial farms accelerated the depletion of game begun by the fur trade, and colonists frowned on native hunters traipsing across fenced fields in pursuit of what animals were left. Other ways of earning a living would have to be found.

Many put old skills to new uses. Indian priests cured a Maryland planter, and they ended the drought ruining William Byrd's crops. Indian warriors defended a colony against other Indians, fought the French or Spanish, and captured runaway slaves. Indian farmers found a ready market for their

45. John Brickell, *The Natural History of North-Carolina* (Dublin, 1737; rpt. 1911), 119–120; Hinke, trans. and ed., "Journey of Michel," *VMHB*, XXIV (1916), 42 (deer). Theda Perdue, *Slavery and the Evolution of Cherokee Society, 1540–1866* (Knoxville, Tenn., 1979), chaps. 1–2; Wright, *Only Land They Knew*, chap. 6, and 221 (slaves). Cronon, *Changes in the Land*, 95–97, 102–103; Salisbury, *Manitou and Providence*, 147–152 (wampum).

46. Quoted in Merrell, "Indians' New World," *WMQ*, 3d Ser., XLI (1984), 553; William L. McDowell, Jr., ed., *Documents Relating to Indian Affairs, May 21, 1750–August 7, 1754* (Columbia, S.C., 1958), 453; Cadwallader Colden, *The History of the Five Indian Nations Depending on the Province of New-York in America* (Ithaca, N.Y., 1958), 66; W. Noel Sainsbury, comp., Records in the British Public Record Office Relating to South Carolina, 1663–1782, 36 vols. (microfilm, Columbia, S.C., 1955), XXIII, 125. See also Reid, *Better Hatchet*, 194. My estimate of the timing of dependence is based on my own research (*Indians' New World*, chap. 2), and Thomas, "Cultural Change," in Fitzhugh, ed., *Cultures in Contact*, 144–149.

produce in the cities and among colonists recently arrived in an area. And Indian hunters were still at work, despite colonial resistance. When, in 1759, Pamunkeys paddled off into the Virginia marshes to hunt birds that were then peddled to local planters, they followed a routine common all along the eastern seaboard for generations.[47] Indians generally sold the same kinds of game they had always eaten themselves; but if deer and turkey were scarce, enterprising hunters still found a way to make a sale. On Long Island they killed colonists' livestock, advertised it as venison, and vended it to unsuspecting customers in New York City; another hunter in New England sold beef as moose meat to the president of Harvard.[48]

Aboriginal craft skills proved equally adaptable. Indian woodworkers, from the obscure Virginia native John the Bowlmaker to the celebrated Mohegan preacher Samson Occom, carved not only the traditional bowls and spoons but also a flat-bottomed vessel specifically designed for Anglo-American tables. Potters, too, catered to consumer tastes, developing shapes aimed at the colonial market.[49] Among those who made containers out of fiber rather than wood or clay, the step from aboriginal practices to production for Anglo-America may have been bigger. Indians managed to sell their

47. Priests: Lawson, *New Voyage*, ed. Lefler, 227–228; Beverley, *History*, ed. Wright, 204–205. See also Ted J. Brasser, *A Basketful of Indian Culture Change*, National Museum of Man, Canadian Ethnology Service, Mercury Series, paper no. 22 (Ottawa, 1975), 15; Brasser, *Frontier's Crest*, 40.

Warriors: Richard R. Johnson, "The Search for a Usable Indian: An Aspect of the Defense of Colonial New England," *JAH*, LXIV (1977–1978), 623–651; Wright, *Only Land They Knew*, 87–88, 124, 166. For runaways, see Wright, 168–169; Jacobs, ed., *Atkin Plan*, 45; Williams, ed., *Adair's History*, 370.

Farmers: Hinke, trans. and ed., "Journey of Michel," *VMHB*, XXIV (1916), 122; Peter A. Thomas, "The Fur Trade, Indian Land, and the Need to Define Adequate 'Environmental' Parameters," *Ethnohistory*, XXVIII (1981), 359–379; Trelease, *Indian Affairs*, 44, 68, 189.

Hunters: Andrew Burnaby, *Travels through the Middle Settlements of North America, in the Years 1759 and 1760*, 3d ed. (London, 1798), in Rufus Rockwell Wilson, ed., *Burnaby's Travels through North America* (New York, 1904), 62–63. See also Burnaby, 157–158; Wright, *Only Land They Knew*, 159–160; Cronon, *Changes in the Land*, 99–100; Frank W. Porter III, "Behind the Frontier: Indian Survivals in Maryland," *MHM*, LXXV (1980), 47, 49, 50. For other contemporary accounts, see Brickell, *Natural History*, 42; "Carolina; or, A Description of the Present State of That Country, by Thomas Ashe," in Salley, ed., *Narratives of Carolina*, 150; "An Account of the Province of Carolina, by Samuel Wilson, 1682," in Salley, 170; Archdale, "New Description," in Salley, 289; Jacobs, ed., *Atkin Plan*, 45.

48. Trelease, *Indian Affairs*, 89–90; Vaughan, *New England Frontier*, 199–200.

49. See Brasser, *Basketful of Change*, 15–16, 21; Brasser, *Frontier's Crest*, 40; Porter, "Behind the Frontier," *MHM*, LXXV (1980), 46. For Samson Occom, see Axtell, *Invasion Within*, 204. John the Bowlmaker is mentioned in Wright, *Only Land They Knew*, 98, 162. Wright identified this Indian as a potter, but since potters were commonly women and woodworkers men, it seems more likely he was skilled in woodworking. On potters: Wright, *Only Land They Knew*, 162, 240–241.

aboriginal cane or hemp baskets at first, but at the end of the seventeenth century they apparently began to adopt from colonists not only new styles but new materials, fashioning woodsplint basketry modeled after patterns Swedish and German emigrants brought to the Delaware Valley.[50]

The line between fitting old skills to new circumstances and developing wholly new abilities is blurred. Were the Cherokees making woodsplint baskets the same ones who knew split-cane weaving? Was Edward Gunstocker merely trying his hand at a different form? Were the New England Indians who fashioned shingles and clapboards for sale in Boston already accomplished woodworkers? The answers are unclear. But often the boundary between old and new was more obvious, for many plantation Indians learned to work at novel tasks. They became wheelwrights and tailors, blacksmiths and shoemakers, experts at building stone walls and adepts at chasing the whale on the open sea.[51]

The work resident Indians took up to make a living in the Anglo-American world lends credence to colonial claims that they could "soon learne any mechanicall trades, having quicke wits, understanding apprehensions, strong memories, with nimble inventions, and a quicke hand."[52] Their "apprehensions" enabled them to discern the best means of earning an income using what they already knew; their "inventions" facilitated imitation of alien forms when that became necessary. But while the skills and the products were much the same for all natives living among the English colonists, the terms on which they worked were not. Some were more fortunate than others. The luckiest were those like the Pamunkeys or the "venison" merchants in New York and Boston, peddlers hawking their merchandise from place to place. Next came those who hired themselves out to a colonist or local government for a task or a season, whether it be to help a farmer in North Carolina plant his crops or a Dutchman along the Hudson harvest

50. See Brasser, *Basketful of Change*. For the trade in aboriginal basketry, see Brasser, 22; Ewan and Ewan, eds., *Banister and His History*, 384; Mark Catesby, *The Natural History of Carolina, Florida, and the Bahama Islands . . .*, 3d ed. (London, 1771), I, 11. Recently some doubt has been cast on the view that this craft tradition is derived solely from European roots (Kathryn Bardwell, "The Case for an Aboriginal Origin of Northeast Indian Woodsplint Basketry," *Man in the Northeast*, no. 31 [Spring 1986], 49–67), though all authorities agree that there was considerable European influence.

51. Wright, *Only Land They Knew*, 167 (for other gunstockers, see Lawson, *New Voyage*, ed. Lefler, 175; and Brickell, *Natural History*, 281–282); Gookin, "Historical Collections," MHS, *Colls.*, 1st Ser., I (1792), 184; Vaughan and Richter, "Crossing the Cultural Divide," AAS, *Procs.*, XC (1980), 36; John A. Sainsbury, "Indian Labor in Early Rhode Island," *New England Quarterly*, XLVIII (1975), 380–381; Trelease, *Indian Affairs*, 179, 199–200; Daniel Vickers, "The First Whalemen of Nantucket," *WMQ*, 3d Ser., XL (1983), 560–583.

52. Wood, *New-England's Prospect*, 88. For similar assessments in the Southeast, see Lawson, *New Voyage*, ed. Lefler, 175, 243; Brickell, *Natural History*, 281–282.

his, to build a stone wall for a town in Rhode Island or to hunt wolves for a county in Virginia.[53]

Many Indians could only dream of such freedom, for they were trapped in one form of bound labor or another, from debt peonage to indentured servitude to outright enslavement. Among Settlement Indians the road from free to forced labor was wide, slippery, and all downhill, with colonists often pushing from behind. Indian debtors, Indian criminals, Indian paupers, even Indian students who received poor marks—all might wind up in servitude. War captives might also be made servants, but the more common fate for them was enslavement. In 1708, South Carolina planters held no fewer than fourteen hundred Indians in bondage, and countless other natives ended their days on a Chesapeake tobacco quarter, a West Indian sugar plantation, or a New England farm. Whether slave or servant, in Rhode Island unfree Indian labor was so common that, when Dr. Alexander Hamilton rode through in 1744, children fled at the sight of his black slave, "for here negroe slaves are not so much in use as with us, their servants being chiefly bound or indentured Indians."[54] There might seem to be little resemblance between remote Indians admiring a trader's glass beads and the native workers Hamilton saw. But all occupied a single spectrum of economic activity; they were at once participants in and victims of a world market.

IV

Following the native Americans' entry into an alien economic system obscures how far trade remained what it had been in aboriginal America, an arm of diplomacy. Certainly Indians and colonists were aware that swapping merchandise was more than a way to make a living. Natives often spoke of peace and trade as one and the same thing, and colonists were quick to agree. In 1736, after giving some of the credit to God and the king, the South

53. Brasser, *Frontier's Crest*, 33; Sainsbury, "Indian Labor," *NEQ*, XLVIII (1975), 380–381; Wright, *Only Land They Knew*, 157–158; Trelease, *Indian Affairs*, 179.

54. Vickers, "First Whalemen," *WMQ*, 3d Ser., XL (1983), 570–583; Sainsbury, "Indian Labor," *NEQ*, XLVIII (1975), 381–385; Yasuhide Kawashima, *Puritan Justice and the Indian: White Man's Law in Massachusetts, 1630–1763* (Middletown, Conn., 1986), 24, 143; Wright, *Only Land They Knew*, 154–170; Axtell, *Invasion Within*, 160.

On war captives: Sainsbury, "Indian Labor," *NEQ*, XLVIII (1975), 385–388; Wright, *Only Land They Knew*, chap. 6; Almon Wheeler Lauber, *Indian Slavery in Colonial Times within the Present Limits of the United States*, Columbia University Studies in History, Economics, and Public Law, LIV, no. 3 (New York, 1913).

Hamilton: Bridenbaugh, ed., *Gentleman's Progress*, 167–168. See also William S. Simmons, "Red Yankees: Narragansett Conversion in the Great Awakening," *American Ethnologist*, X (1983), 258.

Carolina legislature asserted that the colony's "Security and Welfare . . . hath been owing to nothing more than the Regulations . . . with regard to the Trade and Commerce carryed on from hence with the several Nations of Indians almost surrounding us. . . . [I]t is by these means alone that We have been able to preserve a general Peace and Friendship with them."[55] For trade to serve as a vital cog in any diplomatic machine, however, that machine had to be built; learning to communicate and working out rules of exchange were essential to successful diplomacy, but without a mutually agreed-upon body of protocol for conducting a formal conversation they were just talking and trading.

Confusion reigned at first, in part because many early colonial leaders—Ralph Lane at Roanoke, John Smith in Virginia, Miles Standish of Plymouth—were by training and temperament about as far from diplomats as they could be. The conquistador was their model, and they came to America fresh from service among alien peoples where the sword was the first rather than the last resort. But even colonists who put more stock in negotiation often fared little better. Faced with a political world that bore little resemblance to their own, they tried to conjure up emperors, kings, and nations that were not there.[56] However comfortably the word "Emperor" may have fitted Powhatan, it was ill suited to a Piscataway tayac or a Tuscarora headman, who were also awarded the title.[57] In fact, most eastern Indian chiefs led by persuasion and example, custom and council. Whatever authority a headman did wield generally was limited to a narrow sphere of face-to-face relations; few ruled an extensive territory. Nonetheless, Anglo-Americans looked for, and thought they found, not only emperors but also vast nations of Tuscaroras, Cherokees, Creeks, and Iroquois, when what they actually saw were independent villages linked (if at all) by kinship, language, ethnicity, or crisis. Reality inevitably intruded, leaving many English diplomats feeling as Carolina authorities did in 1682 as they cast about

55. Merrell, "Indians' New World," *WMQ*, 3d Ser., XLI (1984), 553; Peter Wraxall, *An Abridgement of the Indian Affairs . . . Transacted in the Colony of New York, from the Year 1678 to the Year 1751*, ed. Charles Howard McIlwain (Cambridge, Mass., 1915), 195; Sainsbury, comp., BPRO Recs. Relating to So. Car., XVIII, 85–86 (see also VII, 77–78; and Hazard, comp., *Penn. Arch.*, 1st Ser., III, 486).

56. Kupperman, *Roanoke*; Philip L. Barbour, *The Three Worlds of Captain John Smith* (Boston, 1964); Salisbury, *Manitou and Providence*, chap. 4. Some scholars argue that colonists were more aware of Indian political culture than I give them credit for here. See Jennings, *Invasion of America*, 114–115; Karen Ordahl Kupperman, *Settling with the Indians: The Meeting of English and Indian Cultures in America, 1580–1640* (Totowa, N.J., 1980), chap. 3; Wright, *Only Land They Knew*, 16; Salisbury, *Manitou and Providence*, 42–43.

57. Merrell, "Cultural Continuity," *WMQ*, 3d Ser., XXXVI (1979), 550; Cumming, ed., *Discoveries of Lederer*, 33. See also Hinke, trans. and ed., "Journey of Michel," *VMHB*, XXIV (1916), 129.

for an alliance with a people "whose Government is lesse Anarchicall" than the colony's current friends.[58]

Experience taught colonists the limitations of kingly power and the narrow definition of nationhood in native America. With time came more invitations to the king *and* headmen, stricter insistence on speaking with representatives of every town in a nation, and greater concern that each of those villages receive gifts. In 1755 Edmond Atkin knew enough to write of "the Cherokee Nations," and he went on to explain that these entities were not only politically independent but different in character. "The Indians . . . have no such titles or persons, as emperors, or kings," wrote the trader James Adair at the close of the colonial era. "The power of their chiefs, is an empty sound. . . . Every town is independent of another."[59]

Colonists sorting out Indian political reality also had to undergo a crash course in native diplomacy, for, once diplomatic relations opened, Indian rules prevailed. The Covenant Chain, forged in the late seventeenth century to connect the Iroquois and other Indians with New York and other colonies, was only the most famous example of how native diplomacy shaped formal intercultural contacts. From Creeks and Cherokees to Delawares and Shawnees, natives set the tempo and tenor of diplomatic encounters. They came when they pleased, and in delegations larger than cost-conscious crown officials liked. They insisted on preliminary rituals ("the usual Salutation of Shaking of hands" in the Southeast, "the usual Compliments of Condolence" in Iroquoia) and punctuated their talks with wampum belts and gifts. The talks themselves sounded strange to colonial ears, for native ambassadors spoke in a rich, metaphorical language of elder brothers and nephews, paths clear or bloody, hatchets taken up or thrown down, a language that invested kinship terms and everyday objects with deeper meaning.[60]

58. T.J.C. Brasser, "The Coastal Algonkians: People of the First Frontiers," in Eleanor Burke Leacock and Nancy Oestreich Lurie, eds., *North American Indians in Historical Perspective* (New York, 1971), 65; Jennings, *Invasion of America*, 115; Salisbury, *Manitou and Providence*, 42–47; Cronon, *Changes in the Land*, 59–60; John Phillip Reid, *A Law of Blood: The Primitive Law of the Cherokee Nation* (New York, 1970), chaps. 1–7; Douglas W. Boyce, "Did a Tuscarora Confederacy Exist?" in Charles M. Hudson, ed., *Four Centuries of Southern Indians* (Athens, Ga., 1975), 28–45. Quotation from A. S. Salley, Jr., indexer, *Records in the British Public Record Office Relating to South Carolina*, 5 vols. (Atlanta, Columbia, S.C., 1928–1947), I, 117.

59. H. R. McIlwaine *et al.*, eds., *Executive Journals of the Council of Colonial Virginia*, 6 vols. (Richmond, Va., 1925–1966), III, 412, 422; Lawson, *New Voyage*, ed. Lefler, 48–49; William L. McDowell, Jr., ed., *Documents Relating to Indian Affairs, 1754–1765* (Columbia, S.C., 1970), 35; Jacobs, ed., *Atkin Plan*, 49, 53; Williams, ed., *Adair's History*, 459–460.

60. Fenton, "Iroquois Treaty Making," in Jennings *et al.*, eds., *Iroquois Diplomacy*, 6; Francis Jennings, *The Ambiguous Iroquois Empire: The Covenant Chain Confederation of Indian Tribes with English Colonies from Its Beginning to the*

"Indian Business" often tested the colonists' patience. First they had to sit through "a long and tedious Relation using all the Indian Ceremonies and Phrases." Then, knowing from experience that "the manner of saying things to Indians depends . . . on Forms and a narrow Observation of them," they had to respond in the same fashion, even while "thinking it most proper to deliver it according to our own way of speech than to conform ourselves to the Indian dialect." A colonial official might consider wampum only shells and presents mere bribes, but before starting negotiations with native leaders, he made sure he had both on hand and that all proceeded "according to the custum of the Indians."[61]

Anglo-American diplomats went along initially because they had to: their pretensions to conquest aside, the English simply lacked the power to dictate forms, much less terms. But they continued to play the diplomatic game by Indian rules, because treaty protocol became a tool for exerting influence. Wherever the fall in native numbers and the Indians' dependence on trade tipped the balance of power toward the English, native diplomatic formulas became a means of wielding that power. Skillfully employed, diplomacy was a vehicle not only for contracting alliances and settling differences but also for issuing threats, acquiring land, and, as one governor phrased it, putting "a Bridle in the Mouths of our Indians." It is true that for the Five Nations treaty councils were "a species of drama in which the Iroquois were the playwrights, the directors and the teaching actors"; but with Indians along the coast in the seventeenth century, Anglo-Americans had begun to direct the play themselves, and, before 1800, more distant groups also found that the path between peoples was becoming a one-way street, the chain was becoming fetters.[62]

Once the fetters were in place, colonial officials demonstrated the depth of their commitment to native treaty forms by abandoning them. For Catawbas, the shock came shortly after the smallpox epidemic of 1759 cut to one hundred the number of warriors they could muster and threats from

---

Lancaster Treaty of 1744 (New York, 1984); Druke, "Iroquois Treaties," in Jennings *et al.*, eds., *Iroquois Diplomacy*, 85–98; Fenton, "Iroquois Treaty Making," in Jennings *et al.*, 3–36; Michael K. Foster, "Another Look at the Function of Wampum in Iroquois-White Councils," in Jennings *et al.*, 99–114; Reid, *Better Hatchet*, 135; Merrell, *Indians' New World*, 145–150. Quotations are from Merrell, 147; *Penn. Ccl. Minutes*, VI, 275.

61. *Penn Ccl. Minutes*, II, 606, VI, 284, VII, 48, 53, 226; South Carolina Upper House Journal, Feb. 3, 1722, in William Sumner Jenkins, comp., Records of the States of the United States (microfilm, Washington, D.C., 1949), S.C. A.1a, reel 1, unit 1, 166.

62. Sainsbury, comp., BPRO Recs. Relating to So. Car., XXIV, 74; Fenton, "Iroquois Treaty Making," in Jennings *et al.*, eds., *Iroquois Diplomacy*, 7; Jennings, *Ambiguous Empire*, chap. 17. Dorothy V. Jones, *License for Empire: Colonialism by Treaty in Early America* (Chicago, 1982), dates this shift to the years after 1763.

Cherokees and the French subsided. South Carolina saw little point in placating its old allies any longer, and a Catawba delegation visiting Charleston in September 1761 found its efforts to follow "the usual" rituals brusquely turned aside. Officials complained that the Indians had come, complained about the size of the delegation, complained about the presents requested, and bluntly informed the Indians not to return unless summoned. The chill in the air was perceptible, and later delegations found it still colder. By the end of the American Revolution Catawbas rarely approached the South Carolina capital, and even the once-mighty Iroquois faced diplomats who believed that "instead of conforming to Indian political behavior We should force them to adopt ours—dispense with belts, etc."[63]

Anglo-America could afford to treat Catawbas and Iroquois so casually because they were joining Pamunkeys, Narragansetts, and the many other tribes that long since had been surrounded by settlers.[64] Among some of these neighboring peoples the diplomatic niceties might still be observed for a time—negotiations continued, treaties were signed—but they were now at best a mere shadow of their former grandeur, at worst a caricature. Native delegations accustomed to arriving when it suited them now came once a year at a time set by the colony. The ceremonial exchange of gifts turned into a public display of subjection, with Indians handing over a few pelts or arrows as token tribute and officials responding with a present or two that was more charity than bribery. In such encounters it is safe to assume that native formal expression went the way of large delegations, elaborate presents, and official interpreters, forcing headmen to conform to English speech and English practice.

With even the pretense of equality stripped away, function followed form; diplomatic relations became less negotiation than protection and, finally, less protection than subjection. The time devoted to hearing a tributary's complaints and the energy spent redressing grievances dwindled with the years, and enforcement of treaty rights, never very rigorous, fell still lower on the public agenda. In the end, diplomacy was a way to build a paper prison. Treaties stipulated that the selection of headmen be supervised, contacts

63. Merrell, *Indians' New World*, 202–209; quotation in Anthony F. C. Wallace, *The Death and Rebirth of the Seneca . . .* (New York, 1970), 197.

64. This analysis of tributary peoples draws upon Paul R. Campbell and Glenn W. LaFantasie, "'Scattered to the Winds of Heaven'—Narragansett Indians, 1676–1880," *Rhode Island History*, XLVII (1978), 66–83; Henry, "Choptank Indians," *MHM*, LXV (1970), 171–180; Merrell, "Cultural Continuity," *WMQ*, 3d Ser., XXXVI (1979), 548–570; Porter, "Behind the Frontier," *MHM*, LXXV (1980), 42–54; Porter, "A Century of Accommodation: The Nanticoke Indians in Colonial Maryland," *MHM*, LXXIV (1979), 175–192; W. Stitt Robinson, "Tributary Indians in Colonial Virginia," *VMHB*, LXVII (1959), 49–64; Trelease, *Indian Affairs*, chap. 6; Gene Waddell, *Indians of the South Carolina Lowcountry, 1562–1751* (Spartanburg, S.C., 1980).

with other native groups curtailed, and the tribe confined to certain lands. Some of these clauses were difficult to enforce in the backwaters where Settlement Indians commonly lived, and old habits proved hard to break.[65] Nonetheless, even where traditional chiefs still held sway and people still slipped off to fight old enemies or visit old friends, they did so knowing that they could be called to account through the same diplomatic channels that once had brought English crown and Indian tribe together as equals on a stage arranged according to native custom.

V

For most native Americans, judges took up where diplomats left off, and the courtroom, not the council chamber, regulated intercultural relations. Unlike diplomacy, trade, or language, however, when it came to questions of law English colonists never considered submitting to native forms. The reason was simple: by English standards Indians had no law to speak of. There was no written code, no institution to interpret and enforce that code, in short nothing recognizable in English terms. Indian law consisted of rules upheld by ostracism, shaming, compensation, and—between clans or tribes—retaliation.[66] Colonists, who missed the power of ridicule and looked upon revenge as savagery, had no misgivings about imposing their own legal framework upon the native. From the very outset they promised to punish any colonist committing a crime against an Indian but insisted that, if the situation were reversed, the Indian must submit to English law.[67]

English assertions of legal imperialism had little impact on tribes far from colonial capitals. As Leonard Calvert had learned from the Wicomisses in 1634, claiming jurisdiction was one thing, exercising it quite another. Some distant Indians might sign a treaty in which they agreed to surrender a native suspected of committing a crime against Anglo-America. But, treaty or no

65. See Merrell, "Cultural Continuity," *WMQ*, 3d Ser., XXXVI (1979), 559–567; Elise M. Brenner, "To Pray or to Be Prey: That Is the Question: Strategies for Cultural Autonomy of Massachusetts Praying Town Indians," *Ethnohistory*, XXVII (1980), 135–152; Bragdon, "Crime and Punishment," *Ethnohistory*, XXVIII (1981), 25; Susan MacCulloch, "A Tripartite Political System among the Christian Indians of Early Massachusetts," *Kroeber Anthropological Society Papers*, no. 34 (1966), 63–73.

66. Kawashima, *Puritan Justice*, 5–8, 15; Reid, *Law of Blood*, esp. chap. 21; Jennings, *Invasion of America*, 111; James P. Ronda, "Red and White at the Bench: Indians and the Law in Plymouth Colony, 1620–1691," Essex Institute, *Historical Collections*, CX (1974), 201; Wallace, *Death and Rebirth of the Seneca*, 25–26.

67. Ronda, "Red and White at the Bench," Essex Inst., *Hist. Colls.*, CX (1974), 201–202; Salisbury, *Manitou and Providence*, 115, 186–187; Vaughan, *New England Frontier*, 186–187; Kawashima, *Puritan Justice*, chap. 1.

treaty, natives beyond the frontier commonly dealt with an unruly colonist in their own way and ignored pleas to give up any Indians wanted for trial.[68] The best that Anglo-Americans could hope for was that diplomatic pressure might persuade these Indians to do the job themselves. In 1748, South Carolina informed the Cherokees that, if they executed an Indian who had killed a colonist, the province would build a long-promised fort in the Cherokee country; if not, the colony's traders would withdraw. After the Cherokees complied, Governor James Glen proclaimed it "a great step towards civilizing savage and barbarous Nations when they can be brought to doe Publick acts of Justice upon their Criminals."[69] Certainly the Cherokees' acquiescence testified to the power of trade, but it was still a long way from getting the wrongdoer into a colonial court. That would have to wait until distant Indians became neighbors.

Once that change had taken place, an Indian committing a crime was far more likely to wind up in court. Civil disputes still might be handled by negotiation and provincial magistrates might overlook crimes among Indians, but a native who killed, robbed, or otherwise harmed a colonist was going to come before the bench.[70] In many colonies the accused stood at least a chance of receiving equitable treatment, especially in the early years, when the English felt most vulnerable to native retaliation. The form of an Indian's arrest, confinement, and trial followed English patterns, and if the suspect was found guilty, the sentence handed down often was comparable to that given to a colonist convicted of the same offense. Moreover, colonists guilty of a crime against an Indian might be punished. In 1638, for example, Plymouth magistrates tried, sentenced, and executed Arthur Peach and two others for killing a Narragansett, despite grumbling among the populace that no Englishman should hang for killing an Indian.[71]

68. Ronda, "Red and White at the Bench," Essex Inst., *Hist. Colls.*, CX (1974), 205; Kawashima, *Puritan Justice*, 21–23, 228–229; Trelease, *Indian Affairs*, 186.

69. Sainsbury, comp., BPRO Recs. Relating to So. Car., XXIII, 110, 170–171. For other examples, see Salley, indexer, *BPRO Recs. Relating to So. Car.*, III, 109–110; *South-Carolina Gazette*, July 7, 1739.

70. For civil disputes settled, see Kawashima, *Puritan Justice*, 25, though many of these cases between Indian and English did come before the court (chap. 7). For Indians' sometimes being left alone to work out their differences among themselves, see "The Journal of Madam Knight," in Perry Miller and Thomas H. Johnson, eds., *The Puritans* (New York, 1938), 437; Merrell, "Cultural Continuity," *WMQ*, 3d Ser., XXXVI (1979), 562. Many crimes among Indians did come before the courts, however. See Kawashima, *Puritan Justice*.

71. Trelease, *Indian Affairs*, 185–186; Vaughan, *New England Frontier*, chap. 7; Kawashima, *Puritan Justice*, chaps. 5–7. Kawashima notes the differential treatment of Indians and colonists without noting any chronological development in those differences. For an exception to this early trend, see Michal J. Rozbicki, "Transplanted Ethos: Indians and the Cultural Identity of English Colonists in Seventeenth-Century Maryland," *Amerikastudien / American Studies*, XXVIII (1983), 425–427.

Natives could improve their chances of seeing justice done by becoming adept practitioners of English law. Some registered their land and wrote a will to ensure that it would pass safely to the next generation. Others took colonists to court for debt, trespassing, attempted enslavement, or other offenses. A few of these Indian plaintiffs hired lawyers, but most served as their own counsel, pursuing their cases through the system so energetically that Anglo-Americans occasionally became alarmed. In 1669 the citizens of Hempstead on Long Island complained that the local Indians were too litigious. Four years later, besieged by natives pressing their claims, the Plymouth General Court voted to ban them from town on most court days.[72]

While some "Indian Attornies" won their cases, it was always an uphill struggle to receive equal treatment under English law.[73] Many were at a disadvantage from the outset, because they were denied the right to testify in court. Many others were too poor or too unfamiliar with the judicial process to prosecute their cases or defend themselves. Those with some knowledge of proper procedure faced other obstacles. In Plymouth, an Indian who wanted satisfaction when a colonist's cattle wrecked his crops first had to catch the offending livestock and drive them to the town pound; only then could he ask for restitution—by laying his case before two colonists.[74]

Difficult as it was for an Indian to be treated fairly at any time, it became harder over the years. During the seventeenth century, provincial legislatures passed separate statutes regarding natives—prohibition of guns and alcohol were the most common—which further set Indians off from the rest of society in the eyes of the law. At the same time, more Indians were falling under the law's purview; even as the native population in New England fell during the seventeenth century, the number brought before the bench increased. The Indians charged were less likely to be handed sentences comparable to those given colonial criminals, for penalties against natives—not always the same as those meted out to colonists in the best of circum-

---

On Peach, see Glenn W. LaFantasie, "Murder of an Indian, 1638," *R.I. Hist.*, XXXVIII (1979), 66–77; Ronda, "Red and White at the Bench," Essex Inst., *Hist. Colls.*, CX (1974), 202–203, 205–206, 210; Kawashima, *Puritan Justice*, 152; Trelease, *Indian Affairs*, 64–65, 186.

72. Laurie L. Weinstein, "Survival Strategies: The Seventeenth-Century Wampanoag and the European Legal System," *Man in the Northeast*, no. 26 (Fall 1983), 81–86; Kawashima, *Puritan Justice*, 145–148, 195–199, and 186 (debt), 190 (trespass), 218 (enslavement). On Hempstead and Plymouth, see Trelease, *Indian Affairs*, 185; Ronda, "Red and White at the Bench," Essex Inst., *Hist. Colls.*, CX (1974), 210; Kawashima, *Puritan Justice*, 209. See also Cronon, *Changes in the Land*, 130–131.

73. Hazard, comp., *Penn. Arch.*, 1st Ser., III, 346. The term denoted five Delawares in New Jersey who in 1758 had been granted power of attorney by their people to deal with that colony in future land transactions.

74. Weinstein, "Survival Strategies," *Man in the Northeast*, no. 26 (Fall 1983), 84.

stances—became more severe over time. Meanwhile, convictions of colonists for any crime against Indians were increasingly hard to obtain, and those convicted got off more easily. Arthur Peach proved to be the exception rather than the rule.[75]

The erosion of native legal rights was most evident in New England, where those rights had been most advanced. During the first decades of colonization some Indians were active participants in the judicial system, sitting on juries, giving testimony, serving as constables, even running their own courts. This was hardly equality: native jurors were balanced if not outnumbered by settlers, and restricted to cases involving Indians; native courts operated under the watchful eye of a supervisor who could overturn decisions. But it was more justice than they had after King Philip's War, when even this limited say in judicial affairs crumbled swiftly. Colonial officials, claiming that natives could not handle the responsibility, dismantled Indian courts and replaced them with "guardians" or "overseers," men appointed by the executive whose powers over their native charges reached beyond the courtroom. During the same period the number of statutes discriminating against Indians expanded dramatically. To the old laws aimed at keeping kegs and muskets out of native hands were added curfews and restrictions on assembly and travel; even carrying a cane could land an Indian in trouble.[76]

The Indians' treatment at the hands of colonial law cannot obscure the more fundamental legal issue at stake here: whose rules were law. While Anglo-American leaders may have sought justice as they construed it, Indians saw things differently. To them, crimes were being defined in alien terms and dealt with in alien ways. The gap between the colonial ideal of justice for all and the native view of proper treatment was evident in Virginia in 1729,

75. Ronda, "Red and White at the Bench," Essex Inst., *Hist. Colls.*, CX (1974), 203–204, 206, 207, 209–212, 214, n. 46; Kawashima, *Puritan Justice*, 79–85, chap. 6. Kawashima (149) finds that the number of Indians before the bar peaked during Queen Anne's War; he also notes (chap. 6) different treatment without considering its chronological dimension.

76. On early colonization: Kawashima, *Puritan Justice*, 28–29, 129, 130–131; Bragdon, "Crime and Punishment," *Ethnohistory*, XXVIII (1981), 23–24; Vaughan, *New England Frontier*, 192–193.

After King Philip's War: Kawashima, *Puritan Justice*, 29–33; Kawashima, "Legal Origins of the Indian Reservation in Colonial Massachusetts," *American Journal of Legal History*, XIII (1969), 46–47, 49, 52–53; Bragdon, "Crime and Punishment," *Ethnohistory*, XXVIII (1981), 24–25. Ronda, "Red and White at the Bench," Essex Inst., *Hist. Colls.*, CX (1974), 211, 214, finds the situation deteriorating in Plymouth before the outbreak of the war. Kawashima accepts the colonists' argument that Indians were incompetent; I do not.

On new statutes: Kawashima, *Puritan Justice*, 82–85, 205–217; Weinstein, "Wampanoag Legacy," in Porter, ed., *Strategies for Survival*, 89–90; Simmons, "Red Yankees," *Am. Ethnologist*, X (1983), 258.

when an intoxicated Saponi headman killed a colonist. The Saponis considered this an unfortunate accident that should be forgotten, since by native custom those under the influence of alcohol were not responsible for their actions.[77] Virginia's governor, William Gooch, thought otherwise, and unlike Leonard Calvert a century earlier he was in a position to do something about it. He sent word to the Indians to give the culprit up and ordered them to Williamsburg to witness the proceedings. During the ensuing trial and execution Gooch took great pains to explain to the assembled natives "that the proceedings in the Court against Him were the same as in the like Case, they would be against a white Man, and indeed as it hap'ned, . . . there was one tryed and executed with him."[78]

Colonist and Indian, swinging side by side from the gallows: what could be more fair? The Saponis, Gooch concluded happily, sat through it all "without any sign of resentment." Appearances were deceiving, however. Even as Gooch closed the books on the case, Saponis were leaving the colony in search of more civilized patrons. Small wonder that as the noose of alien law tightened, many neighboring Indians—in New York, South Carolina, Virginia, and elsewhere—still tried to go through diplomatic channels when disputes arose or crimes were committed, preferring to take their chances with governor and council rather than with judge and jury.[79]

VI

The legal controls that Saponis and other tribes tried to escape went hand in hand with the work of English missionaries. It was a fundamental tenet of the faith English colonists brought to America that belief and behavior were two sides of the same coin, that civilization must accompany—indeed, it must precede—Christianity. The law could not dictate belief, but it could do something about behavior. In 1646, a week after skeptical Indians heckled a Puritan minister during a sermon, Massachusetts Bay passed a law against blasphemy by anyone, Christian or pagan. Six years later, Plymouth legislators forbade Indians from working on the Sabbath, and in 1675 Connecticut went even further, not only insisting that natives honor the Sabbath but

77. Kawashima, *Puritan Justice*, 15–16, 177–179; Lawson, *New Voyage*, ed. Lefler, 210; "Letter from William Penn to the Committee of the Free Society of Traders, 1683," in Myers, ed., *Narratives of Pennsylvania*, 236; Gehring and Grumet, eds., "Danckaerts's Journal," *WMQ*, 3d Ser., XLIV (1987), 115.

78. Gooch to Board of Trade, June 29, 1729, PRO, CO 5/1322, 19–20 (Lib. of Cong. trans., 8–9).

79. *Ibid.* (quotation); Byrd, *Prose Works*, ed. Wright, 315; McIlwaine *et al.*, eds., *Exec. Jnls. Ccl. of Va.*, IV, 209. For a similar clash of legal cultures, which in this instance led to war, see Anthony F. C. Wallace, *King of the Delawares: Teedyuscung, 1700–1763* (Salem, N.H., 1984 [orig. pub. 1949]), 197–200.

requiring their "ready and comely attendance" whenever preachers held services for them.[80] Once the law had stopped Indians from working or heckling and got them to pay attention, it was up to missionaries to do the rest.

The missionary's ability to win an Indian audience for Christ depended largely on where that audience was. Tribes beyond the frontier were for the most part indifferent to the Christian message as translated by the English, in part because English clergymen, unlike the Jesuits operating in New France, rarely visited Indian Country to spread the word.[81] In New England, every minister was tied to a particular congregation and therefore could not venture too far away in search of converts. But even men recruited to do the Lord's work among remote tribes tended to hug the coast. Clergymen sent to South Carolina in the early eighteenth century by the Society for the Propagation of the Gospel in Foreign Parts to "propagate Christianity . . . among the wild Indians in the woods" found some excuse—rumblings of war among those distant peoples, plenty of pagans close at hand among the colonial population—to postpone their mission. Few went beyond asking traders about the best tribes to approach and having the Lord's Prayer translated into Yamasee or Shawnee for future use. In Virginia the story was much the same. "The missionaries that are now sent," reported the Anglican cleric Hugh Jones in 1724, "generally keep among the English, and rarely see an Indian."[82]

Reluctance to head into the interior may have stemmed from a lack of nerve, but it also could have arisen from a sense that Indians there were not

80. Jennings, *Invasion of America*, 241; Ronda, "Red and White at the Bench," Essex Inst., *Hist. Colls.*, CX (1974), 209; Axtell, *Invasion Within*, 221. Entire codes of laws were an early and important part of John Eliot's praying towns. See Neal Salisbury, "Red Puritans: The 'Praying Indians' of Massachusetts Bay and John Eliot," *WMQ*, 3d Ser., XXXI (1974), 33; Kenneth M. Morrison, "'That Art of Coyning Christians': John Eliot and the Praying Indians of Massachusetts," *Ethnohistory*, XXI (1974), 82–83; Axtell, *Invasion Within*, 142, 170, 175.

81. Gary B. Nash, "Notes on the History of Seventeenth-Century Missionization in Colonial America," *American Indian Culture and Research Journal*, II, no. 2 (1978), 3–8; William S. Simmons, "The Great Awakening and Indian Conversion in Southern New England," in William Cowan, ed., *Papers of the Tenth Algonquian Conference* (Ottawa, 1979), 26; Axtell, *Invasion Within*, 138–139, 220–221, 242.

Axtell, *Invasion Within*, offers the best comparison of English and French efforts; see chap. 10 for the few ventures the English did undertake beyond the frontier.

82. "Documents concerning Rev. Samuel Thomas, 1702–1707," *South Carolina Historical and Genealogical Magazine*, V (1904), 43; Hugh Jones, *The Present State of Virginia . . .*, ed. Richard L. Morton (Chapel Hill, N.C., 1956), 62. For missionary endeavors, see Wright, *Only Land They Knew*, 182–183, 188–194; for the Lord's Prayer, see 176, 184, 191, 192. More positive assessments of these efforts can be found in W. Stitt Robinson, Jr., "Indian Education and Missions in Colonial Virginia," *Journal of Southern History*, XVIII (1952), 152–168; Richard Beale Davis, *Intellectual Life in the Colonial South, 1585–1763*, I (Knoxville, Tenn., 1978), 106, 187–196.

very fertile soil for sowing the English version of Christianity. Jesuits with a tolerance for native ways, a gift for languages, and a religion rich in symbol and ritual enjoyed considerable success. English Protestants, on the other hand, usually lacked the delicate touch needed to convert distant Indians. They "know but little how to manage them [Indians]," Jones remarked; "for you may as well talk reason, philosophy, or divinity to a block, as to them, unless you perfectly understand their temper, and know how to humour them." If a missionary did make the effort, he discovered that natives beyond the frontier were uninterested in the gospel according to the English, especially when they found out that conversion entailed political subjection and cultural suicide. Some reacted with open scorn, laughing or going so far as "flatly to say, that our Lord God was not God, since hee suffered us to sustaine much hunger, and also to be killed of the Renapoaks." Others listened politely and walked away. Still others were ready to grant that Christianity was fine for the English but not for Indians, who preferred a different way.[83] "We are Indians," they would say when pressed, "and don't wish to be transformed into white men. . . . As little as we desire the preacher to become Indian, so little ought he to desire the Indians to become preachers."[84]

Settlement Indians were more susceptible to the missionary's message. Confidence in their own cultural traditions had been badly shaken by demographic disaster; who could doubt the power of the Englishman's God when Indians mysteriously died by the score and colonists did not even become ill? The awe an epidemic could inspire was clear from the very beginning of the English colonial venture. At Roanoke, where disease visited every native town that opposed the English beachhead and "the people began to die very fast," colonists reported that survivors were "perswaded that it was the worke of our God through our meanes, and that wee by him might kil and slai whom wee would without weapons and not come neere them." Once the colonists' more conventional weapons had defeated Indians in battle, the newcomers further sapped native commitment to ancient deities and added to the growing evidence of the Christian God's power.[85]

Defeated and surrounded, these internal colonies were reminded of the weakness of their spiritual powers in incidents less dramatic but perhaps no

83. Quotations in Jones, *Present State of Va.*, ed. Morton, 62; and Craven, *White, Red, and Black*, 53. For the Indian response, see James P. Ronda, " 'We Are Well as We Are': An Indian Critique of Seventeenth-Century Missions," *WMQ*, 3d Ser., XXXIV (1977), 66–82; Axtell, *Invasion Within*, 266, 284–285.

84. Quoted in Porter, "A Century of Accommodation," *MHM*, LXXIV (1979), 179. Similar sentiments are in Jones, *Present State of Va.*, ed. Morton, 59.

85. Thomas Harriot, *A Briefe and True Report of the New Found Land of Virginia: The Complete 1590 Theodor De Bry Edition* (New York, 1972), 28. See Axtell, *Invasion Within*, 10; William S. Simmons, *Spirit of the New England Tribes: Indian History and Folklore, 1620–1984* (Hanover, N.H., 1986), 75.

less significant than losses to disease or combat. Take, for example, a confrontation in Stonington, Connecticut, between an English colonist named Thomas Stanton and an Indian shaman from Long Island who had come over to bewitch a local native. When Stanton defended the Indian, the shaman "grew still more high and positive in his language, until he told Mr. Stanton he could immediately tare his house in pieces, and himself flye out at the top of the chimney." Unimpressed, Stanton grabbed the shaman, tied him up, and "whipped him untill he promised to desist and go home." Local Indians who had gathered outside to watch now waited expectantly for the house to be torn apart by the forces the shaman could summon. Nothing happened, and at last they "went away much Surprised."[86] In such surprises lay the seeds of doubt, and they left conquered natives more ready to listen and more likely to be convinced.

But if practically all Christian Indians were Settlement Indians, not all Settlement Indians were Christian. Many lived among colonists for years without being approached and offered the opportunity to convert. In New England, where English missionaries were most active, no more than twenty Congregational clergymen attempted to spread the gospel among the Indians even on a part-time basis. Connecticut was particularly slow to act; its 1675 law requiring polite attention to any minister who visited the natives was a dead letter, for few if any ministers bothered. A traveler passing through the colony in 1704 found "every where in the Towns as I passed, a Number of Indians . . . , the most salvage of all the salvages of that kind [Settlement Indians] that I had ever Seen: little or no care taken (as I heard upon enquiry) to make them otherwise."[87]

Those neighboring Indians who *were* offered the chance to convert sometimes turned it down. Narragansetts, Mohegans, and other groups defeated in King Philip's War wanted nothing to do with the religion of the victors, and well into the eighteenth century they spurned missionary overtures. In South Carolina, clergymen in coastal parishes conversed regularly with "Neighbouring Indians," but found these remnant groups unlikely candidates for conversion. They "are a moving People," one reported, "often changing their place of habitation so that I can give no account of their Number"—much less the state of their souls. Prodding them did no good, for they seemed "wholy addicted to their own barbarous and Sloathful Customs and will only give a laugh w[he]n pleased or a grin w[he]n dis-

86. William S. Simmons, "Southern New England Shamanism: An Ethnographic Reconstruction," in William Cowan, ed., *Papers of the Seventh Algonquian Conference* (Ottawa, 1976), 245–246; Axtell, *Invasion Within*, 229. See also Simmons, *New England Tribes*, 76–77.

87. Henry W. Bowden and James P. Ronda, eds., *John Eliot's Indian Dialogues: A Study in Cultural Interaction*, Contributions in American History, no. 88 (Westport, Conn., 1980), 22–23, 26; "Journal of Knight," in Miller and Johnson, eds., *The Puritans*, 437. See Axtell, *Invasion Within*, 186–187, 220–221.

pleas'd for an Answer." "It must be the work of time and power that must have any happy Influence upon em," one would-be savior concluded glumly.[88]

Some were willing to spend more time and wield more power in the crusade for Christ, but even they found it difficult to exert much influence. The least successful tended to be those who expected the most, who insisted that civility and Christianity go hand in hand. John Eliot's Massachusetts praying towns were the classic example. Here, Eliot predicted, natives seeking Christ would be isolated from the corrupting influence of other Indians or of colonists, here they could be instructed in the finer points of faith and civility, and here carefully watched to ensure that the lessons—from length of hair to cut of coat to knowledge of Christ's teachings—had been learned. In the third quarter of the seventeenth century, Eliot established fourteen of these villages, brought more than one thousand Indians to live in them, and translated the Bible into Algonquian. By his own admission, however, few praying Indians actually mastered his difficult course of instruction well enough to pass the stringent requirements for church membership in Puritan New England. His hopes that the future would yield a more abundant harvest of souls were dashed when many of his charges joined King Philip's war parties and many of the rest ended up imprisoned on an island in Boston Harbor, kept there by a populace convinced that Eliot's experiment was a failure.[89]

Plans to isolate and educate individual Indians rather than whole towns enjoyed still less success. Harvard's Indian College, built in the mid-1650s, housed only a handful of native students (more of whom died at the school than graduated from it) before being torn down four decades later. Its counterpart at William and Mary, the Brafferton building, housed many more pupils, but none lived up to expectations. Upon completing the course of instruction and going home, wrote William Byrd II, "instead of civilizing and converting the rest, they have immediately relapsed into infidelity and

88. For New England, see Simmons, "Awakening and Indian Conversion," in Cowan, ed., *Pprs. Tenth Algonq. Conf.*, 26–27; Simmons, "Red Yankees," *Am. Ethnologist*, X (1983), 260; Bowden and Ronda, eds., *Eliot's Dialogues*, 33, 40; Axtell, *Invasion Within*, 243–247. For South Carolina, see in SPG, Ser. A: Thomas Hasell to the Secretary, Apr. 15, 1724, XVIII, 72; Benjamin Dennis to the Secretary, Mar. 21, 1714, X, 83–84; Richard Ludlam to the Secretary, Mar. 22, 1725, XIX, 62.

89. See Vaughan, *New England Frontier*, chaps. 9–11; Jennings, *Invasion of America*, 232–253; Axtell, *Invasion Within*, chaps. 7, 9; R. Pierce Beaver, "Methods in American Missions to the Indians in the Seventeenth and Eighteenth Centuries: Calvinist Models for Protestant Foreign Missions," *Journal of Presbyterian History*, XLVII (1969), 134–136; Salisbury, "Red Puritans," *WMQ*, 3d Ser., XXXI (1974), 27–54; Salisbury, "Prospero in New England: The Puritan Missionary as Colonist," in William Cowan, ed., *Papers of the Sixth Algonquian Conference, 1974* (Ottawa, 1975), 254–261; Morrison, "Coyning Christians," *Ethnohistory*, XXI (1974), 77–92.

barbarism themselves." Similarly, Eleazar Wheelock's grand schemes for schooling Indians ended up as Dartmouth, a college for colonial boys, after a series of failures that left its founder deeply embittered. "It grieves and breaks my heart," Wheelock wrote in 1768 after fourteen years of trying, "that while I am wearing my life out to do good to the poor Indians, they themselves have no more Desire to help forward the great Design of their Happiness. . . . [There] are so many of them pulling the other way and as fast as they can undoing all I have done." From John Eliot onward, others who adopted a strict approach to Indian conversion felt the same sense of frustration.[90]

A few missionaries took a different tack among Settlement Indians and were better rewarded. The work of the Mayhew family on Martha's Vineyard offers the best contrast in both method and result. The Mayhews were unusually well versed in native culture, and rather than demand immediate, sweeping changes in Indian habits, they were willing to accept slow progress toward English notions of civility. Upon their arrival in the 1640s they encountered a native population still relatively intact but well aware that English colonists had just destroyed the Pequots not far away on the mainland. Added to these promising ingredients were certain fortuitous (Mayhew called them providential) events—diseases spared Christian Indians, lightning struck a sachem who had mocked a convert—that made skeptics into believers. The result was a swift, widespread, and deeply rooted commitment to Christianity, a commitment that Eliot, laboring away on the mainland, could only envy and try to claim for himself.[91]

The Mayhews' formula also worked elsewhere. In 1714 Virginia lieutenant governor Alexander Spotswood set up a mission at a frontier fort that was as promising as it was undemanding. Children of tributary Indians trooped into Charles Griffin's classroom by day and returned to their nearby

90. Vaughan, *New England Frontier*, 281–284; Jennings, *Invasion of America*, 247–248; Axtell, *Invasion Within*, 182–183; Salisbury, "Red Puritans," *WMQ*, 3d Ser., XXXI (1974), 46–47; Beaver, "Methods in American Missions," *Jour. Presb. Hist.*, XLVII (1969), 141 (Harvard). Wright, *Only Land They Knew*, 180, 185–187; Axtell, *Invasion Within*, 190–196; Byrd, *Prose Works*, ed. Wright, 220–221 (quotation on 220); Jones, *Present State of Va.*, ed. Morton, 114; Gregory A. Stiverson and Patrick H. Butler III, eds., "Virginia in 1732: The Travel Journal of William Hugh Grove," *VMHB*, LXXXV (1977), 25 (William and Mary). The Wheelock quotation is in Margaret Connell Szasz, " 'Poor Richard' Meets the Native American: Schooling for Young Indian Women in Eighteenth-Century Connecticut," *Pacific Historical Review*, XLIX (1980), 235. See also Axtell, *Invasion Within*, 206–207.

91. William S. Simmons, "Conversion from Indian to Puritan," *NEQ*, LII (1979), 197–218. See also Vaughan, *New England Frontier*, 242–244, 295–298; Jennings, *Invasion of America*, 230–231, 245–247; Salisbury, "Prospero in New England," in Cowan, ed., *Pprs. Sixth Algonq. Conf.*, 261–266; James P. Ronda, "Generations of Faith: The Christian Indians of Martha's Vineyard," *WMQ*, 3d Ser., XXXVIII (1981), 369–394.

village at night. In school they learned to recite prayers; at home they mastered the war dance, complete with "antic motions, and hideous cries." Whether Griffin could have become another Mayhew will never be known; after a few years, political squabbles in Williamsburg dismantled Spotswood's school. More impressive and more enduring results came during the Great Awakening, when New England Indians long resistant to any strain of the Christian faith changed their minds. These holdouts responded enthusiastically to preachers who had the oratorical skill, the emotional performance, the disdain for doctrinal detail, and the tolerance of congregational participation that corresponded to the natives' own religious traditions.[92]

After more than a century, the missionary campaign had enjoyed mixed results. On the one hand, signs of progress were clear: in New England at one time or another more than a score of Indian churches had been built, nearly one hundred praying towns or reservations organized, and even more natives had become teachers or preachers. On the other hand, however, those bent on wiping out every stain of paganism were disappointed. Too many Indians remained outside the fold, and those within it had entered on their own terms, shaping the new religion to serve their spiritual and cultural needs. Far from making Indians English, the new faith (where natives embraced it) proved to be a powerful revitalizing force, helping people to cope with defeat and dispossession, to rebuild their aboriginal communities on a new foundation.[93]

VII

In the end it proved easier to kill Indians than convert them, easier to make them speak English than make them listen to a sermon, easier to get them into a courtroom than into a church, easier to bring them to acknowledge the English king than the English God. The missionary's failure to see his dreams become reality is a useful reminder that natives were neither the "Indian dust" one early New Englander envisioned nor the "soft Wax, ready to take any Impression" that a Virginian described.[94] Far from crumbling

92. On Virginia: Alexander, ed., *Journal of Fontaine*, 90–98 (quotation on 98); Jones, *Present State of Va.*, ed. Morton, 59. For more pessimistic views of this experiment, see Wright, *Only Land They Knew*, 187–188; Axtell, *Invasion Within*, 192–193.

On Great Awakening: Simmons, "Awakening and Indian Conversions," in Cowan, ed., *Pprs. Tenth Algonq. Conf.*, 27–33; Simmons, "Red Yankees," *Am. Ethnologist*, X (1983), 261–267.

93. Axtell, *Invasion Within*, 273; Axtell, "Some Thoughts on the Ethnohistory of Missions," *Ethnohistory*, XXIX (1982), 35–40.

94. Quoted in Salisbury, *Manitou and Providence*, 153; Beverley, *History*, ed. Wright, 16 (Beverley was imagining the views of earlier colonists). For an analysis of

and being swept aside or passively receiving everything the English handed them, Indians learned to conform to the new "Customes of the Countrey" without surrendering unconditionally to the country's new rulers.

It was not easy. Some tribes fought, some fled. Others stayed behind and protested the invasion of America in their own way, stealing a colonial school's Latin and Greek books or burning a planter's fences, acts some have termed "purely whimsical" but that may have had symbolic significance.[95] Still others made their feelings known by refusing to abide by colonial customs. The problem in the Massachusetts praying town of Natick was as simple as saying "Hello." Waban, the community's first headman and one of John Eliot's converts, won praise for greeting colonists "with English salutations." But some inhabitants of Natick would not follow Waban's lead. In 1680 they were "refusing to take notice of an Englishman if they meet him in the street," and decades later one holdout, Hannah Pittimee, still "past by . . . with a great deal of scorn . . . with her face turned right from us."[96]

Pittimee and every other Settlement Indian had reason to be scornful, for those natives living behind the frontier faced a future of poverty and oppression. As their resources disappeared and their skills eroded, natives searched desperately for ways to put food in their mouths and a roof over their heads. The search sometimes led to an ancestor's grave, which Indians ransacked for the valuable wampum it contained. Not everyone was driven to such lengths, but almost all struggled to scrape together the necessities of life, and they did so amid the insults, the laughter, the abuses spawned by the conquerors' hatred. Sometimes that hatred was disclosed only by a slip of the pen: a clerk in a Massachusetts court referred to an Indian as "it," and a Philadelphia scribe wrote that the spectators at a council consisted of "many other People and Indians."[97] More often the colonists' feelings were easier to detect. Young Indian apprentices discovered that "their fellow Prentices viz.

---

the natives' place in New England at the end of the colonial era, see Cronon, *Changes in the Land*, 162–165.

95. Bragdon, "Crime and Punishment," *Ethnohistory*, XXVIII (1981), 27 (books); Inhabitants of the Waxhaws to Samuel Wyly, Apr. 16, 1759, encl. in Wyly to Gov. William Henry Lyttelton, Apr. 26, 1759, Lyttelton Papers, William Clements Library, Ann Arbor, Mich. (fences). The comment is Bragdon's, on the theft of the books. For the symbolic significance of fences, see Cronon, *Changes in the Land*, esp. chap. 7.

96. Quoted in Morrison, "Coyning Christians," *Ethnohistory*, XXI (1974), 81–82; and in Bragdon, "Crime and Punishment," *Ethnohistory*, XXVIII (1981), 27. For the politics of greeting, see Bragdon, "Native Speech Events," *Man in the Northeast*, no. 33 (Spring 1987), 103.

97. John Witthoft, "Archaeology as a Key to the Colonial Fur Trade," in *Aspects of the Fur Trade: Selected Papers of the 1965 North American Fur Trade Conference* (St. Paul, Minn., 1967), 61; Kawashima, *Puritan Justice*, 109; *Penn. Ccl. Minutes*, III, 167.

English Boys will dispise them and treat them as Slaves." The colonial youths picked up this attitude from their parents, who openly doubted that anything besides "Powder and Ball" would convert the natives, and, acting on that belief, placed only "a Bullet and Flynt" in a missionary's collection plate. Even colonists with good intentions inflicted their own kind of pain. When the evangelist George Whitefield's colleague Benjamin Ingham built a schoolhouse for Indians atop an ancient temple mound near Savannah, Georgia, he dismissed the local Creeks' spiritual attachment to the site and insisted that it now serve a different deity.[98]

But if neighboring Indians did not prosper, they did survive. One secret of their survival was the ability they had to make themselves inconspicuous. When drinking, for example, they aped their English neighbors. "It rent my heart as well as ears," wrote one Virginian in the 1680s, "when once passing by a company of Indians in James City, that drinking in a ring were deplorably drunk . . . one cried to another swear swear, you be Englishman swear, w[i]th that he made a horrid yelling, imperfectly vomited up oaths, whereupon the other cryd, oh! now your [*sic*] be Englishman."[99]

Natives learning to drink and curse like an Englishman were also learning to dress like one, and this camouflage, too, was crucial to their survival. Simply putting on English clothes was not enough; one had to know how to wear them. A century after John Smith, Virginia Indians had not yet mastered the art. "They were ridiculously dressed," a colonist noted in 1702. "One had a shirt on with a crown on his head, another a coat and neither trousers, stockings nor shoes." The Indian "queen" was better dressed, in "nice clothes of a French pattern," but still "they were not put on right. One thing was too large, another too small, hence it did not fit." By the end of the colonial period Virginia Indians had conformed to what colonists considered "right." "They commonly dress like the Virginians," the traveler Andrew Burnaby observed in 1759, and in fact they were so well disguised that Burnaby admitted he had "sometimes mistaken them for the lower sort of that people." Four years later, Indians living near Braintree, Massachusetts, had also perfected their disguise and were said to be "actually very often mistaken for English."[100]

As important as this mimetic talent was the ability to retain a distinctly Indian identity. Natives imitating colonists still stood out in subtle ways in every sphere of contact. For most, English was a second language, imperfectly mastered and used only for talking with colonists and slaves. In the

98. Axtell, *Invasion Within*, 210 (quotation); Wright, *Only Land They Knew*, 208–209.

99. Berkeley and Berkeley, eds., "Another 'Account of Virginia,' by Clayton," *VMHB*, LXXVI (1968), 436.

100. Hinke, trans. and ed., "Journey of Michel," *VMHB*, XXIV (1916), 132–133; Burnaby, *Travels*, 62; Kawashima, *Puritan Justice*, 121 (quotation).

mid-eighteenth century, one Rhode Island native woman's English vocabulary consisted of a single word—"broom"—and in Massachusetts confused colonists learned that the Braintree Indians' English disguise held up only "till you come to converse with them."[101] In material culture and economic pursuits, too, their conversion was less than complete. Many led a peripatetic life modeled on traditional habits of seasonal migration. From Etiwans in South Carolina to Naticks in Massachusetts, they were "strangely disposed and addicted to wander from place to place." If they did come to lead what colonists considered a settled existence, Indians still might depart from colonial norms. One built an English frame house but no chimney, preferring to rely on an open fire; others put brick fireplaces into their wigwams; still others bought tea tables, dressers, chairs, and other articles commonly found in colonial households, then placed the furniture in the domed dwellings they made out of bark and saplings.[102]

The same habit of blending into the landscape of English America without becoming wholly invisible can be seen in diplomacy, law, and religion. Though native enclaves might be "little Tribes," tribes they were, not mere aggregates of individuals or a vaguely defined ethnic group. However unequal the terms of diplomacy had become, Indians with their own corporate identity and cadre of leaders were equipped to deal with colonial politicians on a diplomatic footing. They were also in a position to police themselves, and many continued to settle their own disputes. In 1704, some Settlement Indians in New England were "Govern'd by Law's of their own making." "If the natives committ any crime on their own precincts among themselves, the English takes no Cognezens of it," and the same was true of South Carolina's Indians more than a century later.[103] Finally, and perhaps most important, the Christianity that some remnant groups used as the new foundation for an ancient identity remained distinct from its English progenitor. The sharing of tobacco during services on Martha's Vineyard incorporated old rituals into a new ceremonial context, and in Rhode Island the Narragansetts'

101. Simmons, "Red Yankees," *Am. Ethnologist*, X (1983), 262; Kawashima, *Puritan Justice*, 121. See also Frances Svensson, "Language as Ideology: The American Indian Case," *Am. Indian Cult. and Res. Jour.*, I, no. 3 (1975), 29–35; Brasser, "Coastal Algonkians," in Leacock and Lurie, eds., *North American Indians*, 84; Kathleen J. Bragdon, "Probate Records as a Source for Algonquian Ethnohistory," in Cowan, ed., *Pprs. Tenth Algonq. Conf.*, 140; Bragdon, "Native Speech Events," *Man in the Northeast*, no. 33 (Spring 1987), 108.

102. Bragdon, "Probate Records," in Cowan, ed., *Pprs. Tenth Algonq. Conf.*, 138 (quotation); Simmons, *New England Tribes*, 19; Weinstein, "Wampanoag Legacy," in Porter, ed., *Strategies for Survival*, 91–92; Bragdon, "Probate Records," in Cowan, ed., *Pprs. Tenth Algonq. Conf.*, 137–138; Vaughan and Richter, "Crossing the Cultural Divide," AAS, *Procs.*, XC (1980), 36–37; William C. Sturtevant, "Two 1761 Wigwams at Niantic, Connecticut," *American Antiquity*, XL (1975), 437–444.

103. "Journal of Knight," in Miller and Johnson, eds., *The Puritans*, 437; Merrell, *Indians' New World*, 235–236.

August Meeting—several days of services, feasts, and dances—harked back to a traditional harvest festival.[104] In all of these ways, Indians managed to pacify the powerful without losing all sense of a unique past—and a separate future.

This adaptive talent was present from the first. In 1634—the very year Calvert and the Wicomiss were meeting along the Chesapeake—it was already on display in New England, where William Wood and two companions got lost on the way to Plymouth, "being deluded by a misleading path." It was, the travelers thought, too wide to be an Indian trail, but they were wrong. They had been fooled because "the dayly concourse of *Indians* from the *Naragansets* who traded for shooes, wearing them homewards had made this *Indian* tract like an *English* walke, and had rear'd up great stickes against the trees, and marked the rest with their hatchets in the *English* fashion, which begat in us a security of our wrong way to be right."[105] Like Narragansetts, Indians throughout the East who might look English were in fact following, indeed carving, paths that took them toward another destination. Learning to survive as a conquered people by combining European and aboriginal ways: this was the fate in store for every native group as the English and other migrants from the Old World pushed deeper into the heart of the American continent.

104. Bragdon, "Native Speech Events," *Man in the Northeast*, no. 33 (Spring 1987), 108; Simmons, "Red Yankees," *Am. Ethnologist*, X (1983), 263–264. See also Ronda, "Generations of Faith," *WMQ*, 3d Ser., XXXVIII (1981), 369–394.

105. Wood, *New-England's Prospect*, 79.

PHILIP D. MORGAN

British Encounters with Africans and African-Americans, circa 1600–1780

In 1756 a confused and frightened Ibo boy, aged about eleven, kidnapped in the eastern part of the present Benin province and conveyed to the Bight of Biafra coast, caught his first glimpse of white men. They were British slavers, but the boy knew them only as "white men with horrible looks, red faces, and loose hair." He fainted at the sight. Fearing them as cannibals, the boy grew more anxious as he witnessed their "savage" manner and their "brutal cruelty," which was particularly impressed upon him when they flogged to death one of their own sailors. After the horrors of the middle passage and brief spells in Barbados and Virginia, the young African was purchased by a British naval officer and transported to England. On the journey, he experienced his first "kindly" treatment from whites, when common jack-tars befriended him. For the next seven years the boy enjoyed the camaraderie and even friendship of fellow sailors as he accompanied naval expeditions to both Europe and Canada. In the frequent layoffs in British ports, he found much to inspire his wonder. How was it that the British ate with unwashed hands, how could they touch their dead, why were the women so slender and so much less modest than African women?[1]

I presented this paper at a Williamsburg conference and the Columbia Seminar in Early American History in 1985, a Berkeley seminar in 1986, and a W. E. B. Du Bois Center seminar in 1988. I cannot now recall who said what, but some suggestions were surely helpful. Since this essay is in many ways a distillation of the work of others, I wish to thank all the authors mentioned in my footnotes.

1. Sources for this and the following paragraph are Paul Edwards, ed., *The Life of Olaudah Equiano; or, Gustavus Vassa the African, 1789*, 2 vols. (London, 1969 [orig. publ. London, 1789]), I, 70–71, 72, 75, 95, 98, 106, II, 64 (only quotes). For further information on Equiano, see G. I. Jones, "Olaudah Equiano of the Niger Ibo," in Philip D. Curtin, ed., *Africa Remembered: Narratives by West Africans from*

This African's adventures had only just begun. In the next two-and-a-half decades, he visited almost every corner of Britain's first empire. In 1763 his life took one of its many dramatic turns when he was sold and shipped to Montserrat in the West Indies. There, he observed at close quarters the unspeakable cruelties wrought on the slaves of sugar plantations; he, like many another urban slave, rented out his services for a daily wage; and he sailed to most of the British Caribbean islands as well as to Dutch Saint Eustatius and French Guadeloupe. He visited various mainland seaports like Philadelphia and was the victim of sharp practices when selling his own wares in Charleston (where he also witnessed the jubilant demonstrations celebrating the repeal of the Stamp Act), but by 1766 he had acquired enough money to purchase his own freedom. He suffered a shipwreck in the Bahamas and was tempted to settle with free blacks on New Providence, whose situation was "very happy." He drank punch with white watchmen in Savannah. He set up in business as a barber in London, but, in need of funds, he returned to the sea and visited lands as far-flung as Madeira and Greenland, Turkey and Portugal, even venturing on an Arctic voyage in 1773. He worked as an overseer, helping an English doctor establish a plantation on the Mosquito Shore. He cut mahogany and traded with Miskito Indians. From 1776 to 1785, he alternated work as a sailor and servant. He ended his days as a leader of the black community in Britain, visiting Wales, Scotland, and Ireland, working at first to advance the expedition of Black Poor to Sierra Leone in 1786–1787, but then opposing the way it was organized. To further the antislavery cause, he published his autobiography in 1789. Late in life—in 1792—he married an English woman and fathered two daughters. He died five years later, leaving half the residue of his estate, should his daughters not survive him, for the foundation of schools in Sierra Leone.

The kaleidoscopic story of Olaudah Equiano, or Gustavus Vassa, as he

---

the Era of the Slave Trade (Madison, Wis., 1967), 60–98; Paul Edwards, "Three West African Writers of the 1780s," in Charles T. Davis and Henry Louis Gates, Jr., eds., *The Slave's Narrative* (New York, 1985), 175–198; Edwards, ". . . Written by Himself: A Manuscript Letter of Olaudah Equiano," *Notes and Queries*, n.s., CCXIII (1968), 222–225; Ian Duffield and Paul Edwards, "Equiano's Turks and Christians: An Eighteenth-Century African View of Islam," *Journal of African Studies*, II (1975–1976), 433–444; and Folarin O. Shyllon, *Black People in Britain, 1555–1833* (London, 1977), appendix 1.

A brief word about nomenclature: when I describe a person as *black*, I mean to infer merely that he or she was of African descent, not that he or she was necessarily dark-skinned; essentially, the term replaces *Negro*, used by an older generation of scholars. *Mulatto* is employed in the North American, rather than in the Caribbean, sense to refer to any person of mixed racial origin (more precise gradations were current in some British West Indian islands, with mulatto generally restricted to the offspring of a black and a white). I use the term *colored*, common in the Caribbean, synonymously with mulatto. In none of this, of course, am I assuming that race is an immutable biological fact.

came to be known, is a history in miniature of the sort of encounters that occurred between whites and blacks in every part of Britain's expanding empire. Of course, Equiano was hardly a typical African. Most blacks who came into contact with the British remained slaves throughout their lives. And the experiences of most slaves were far less varied, far less successful, and far more pedestrian than those of Equiano. Nevertheless, Equiano endured the horrors and terrors of slavery and continued to witness them even after securing his own freedom. Moreover, his life links the three key areas of white-black contact in this empire—Britain, Africa, and the New World. A brief review of the white and black populations of these three areas can put his experiences in context and limn the outer dimensions of the great cross-cultural encounter between Britons and Africans and their descendants.

In Britain itself the earliest record of an African presence dates from the days of Roman occupation. But not until the second half of the sixteenth century were black faces more than occasionally seen in England. In seventeenth-century London, the nerve center of a rapidly expanding empire, blacks became everyday sights, and, by the middle of the eighteenth century, the city contained about ten thousand to fifteen thousand blacks, grouped in particular parishes, such as Paddington and St. Giles-in-the-Fields (where resided "St. Giles's Black birds"). Outside of African cities, this number constituted the largest urban concentration of blacks in the British Empire, although they formed only about 2 percent of the capital's total population. At about the same time, another five thousand or so blacks resided in the provinces. There were notable concentrations in the slavetrading seaports of Bristol and Liverpool, but blacks were also scattered throughout the countryside. An African wandered through Grasmere and into Dorothy Wordsworth's journal; another married the landlady of a York tavern; John McRae, a mulatto, "born in Yorkshire, Old England," became a sailor. In Scotland the black "ladye with the mekle lippis [great lips]," immortalized by the poet William Dunbar, was famous in early sixteenth-century Edinburgh society. Samuel Johnson and James Boswell came across an African as they proceeded through the Highlands, and Joseph Knight, destined to be the Scottish equivalent of James Somerset, lived in Perthshire. A number of Africans were apparently brought to Ireland by Vikings as early as the ninth century, a black actor was a famous figure on the eighteenth-century Dublin stage, and Irish links with the slave trade made blacks well known in various parts of the island.[2] So commonplace were blacks in eighteenth-century

2. Peter Fryer, *Staying Power: The History of Black People in Britain* (London, 1984), 1, 58–64, 68; Paul G. Edwards and James Walvin, *Black Personalities in the Era of the Slave Trade* (Baton Rouge, La., 1983), 3–5, 11, 18–19; Shyllon, *Black*

Britain that an author in the *Universal Modern History*, published in 1748, felt it unnecessary to describe them because "every man who has ever stepped beyond the place of his birth, has seen them." Later in the century, an abolitionist appealed to "the personal experience of every man in Britain" in arguing against pejorative stereotypes generated by West Indian slavery.[3]

Although many British people encountered the occasional black person on their home turf, a much smaller group confronted Africans on their native continent. From the middle of the sixteenth century, the British began to undertake sporadic expeditions to West Africa. Not until the early seventeenth century, however, did British traders begin to make real inroads along the African coast, and only in the 1660s and 1670s did they establish secure bases, centering their settlements on the Gold Coast. And yet, over the course of the next century—from 1680 to 1780—no more than 15,000 Britons left their native shores to reside on the African coast. An extraordinarily hostile disease environment deterred effective British settlement. At any one time in the seventeenth and eighteenth centuries, there were probably "more free Africans in Europe than Europeans in the lightly manned trading posts of tropical Africa." Far more numerous than British residents on the coast were the kingdom's seamen involved in the transatlantic slave trade. Their numbers over the course of the seventeenth and eighteenth centuries amounted to approximately 330,000. In all, then, about 350,000 Britons had some measure of direct contact with blacks on the African littoral from 1600 to 1780.[4]

Most Britons and Africans encountered one another, not in either of their respective homelands, but in the New World. Initially, the transatlantic

---

People, 46, 101–102, 104; Paul Edwards and James Walvin, "Africans in Britain, 1500–1800," in Martin L. Kilson and Robert I. Rotberg, eds., *The African Diaspora: Interpretative Essays* (Cambridge, Mass., 1976), 172–173, 184–188; on McRae: Drury Warren, Purdie and Dixon's *Virginia Gazette* (Williamsburg), May 24, 1770; James Kinsley, ed., *The Poems of William Dunbar* (Oxford, 1979), 106; Folarin O. Shyllon, *Black Slaves in Britain* (London, 1974), 6–9, 177–183; James Walvin, *Black and White: The Negro and English Society, 1555–1945* (London, 1973), 10–11, 47, 72. The number of black people in 18th-century Britain can never be known. Most estimates fall between 10,000 and 20,000, with an increase after the American Revolution.

3. Both quoted in Anthony J. Barker, *The African Link: British Attitudes to the Negro in the Era of the Atlantic Slave Trade, 1550–1807* (London, 1978), 25. When Edward Bancroft referred to Negroes, he noted that they "are sufficiently known in *England*" (*An Essay on the Natural History of Guiana, in South America* . . . [London, 1769], 366).

4. Curtin, ed., *Africa Remembered*, 13; the 15,000 figure is an estimate based on known figures presented for the period 1694–1732 in K. G. Davies, "The Living and the Dead: White Mortality in West Africa, 1684–1732," in Stanley L. Engerman and Eugene D. Genovese, eds., *Race and Slavery in the Western Hemisphere: Quantitative Studies* (Princeton, N.J., 1975), 83; Davies, *The Royal African Company* (London, 1957), 193–194.

population flow was heavily British. In the 1630s, about 70,000 whites left their native shores for British America, and a much smaller number of Africans—no more than 5,000—were forced to join them. By the 1660s, however, the number of white emigrants had slowed, amounting to 40,000, while African emigrants had risen to almost that level. By 1680—and this was to remain true for another century—more blacks than whites left their respective homelands for British America. In fact, from 1680 to 1740 the ratio was more than three to one; from 1740 to 1780 it increased to almost six to one. Over the one-and-a-half centuries from 1630 to 1780 about 2,340,000 Africans—almost three times the number of all Europeans—left their native lands for British America (see Table 1). In sheer number of emigrants, British America was actually more black than white.

And yet, of course, the proportion of whites and blacks in the total population of British America was the reverse of the emigration totals. In 1680 and 1780 alike, the white population was more than double that of the black (see Table 1). Setting so many people in motion had tragic consequences, particularly for the Africans. In 1780 the number of blacks in British America was less than half of the total number of African emigrants received in the previous century and a half, whereas the white population exceeded its emigrant group almost three times over. The key to the black disaster lay in their experiences in the Caribbean, where about one in four Africans died within the first three years of residence and where sugar production proved a veritable destroyer of life. In this region as a whole, African slaves and their descendants never produced enough children to offset the staggering number of adult deaths. The Caribbean remained the principal destination of African immigrants and continued to swallow them up at a frightening rate. Conversely, the key to white demographic success was the remarkable fecundity of European immigrants and their descendants in the New England and mid-Atlantic regions of the mainland. Within British America, then, two distinct poles of settlement arose. By the late seventeenth century, white and black majorities were located at the northern and southern extremities, respectively.[5]

The differential migration flows and the survival and fertility rates of whites and blacks, just as much as Equiano's manifold adventures, underline

5. Orlando Patterson, *The Sociology of Slavery: An Analysis of the Origins, Development, and Structure of Negro Slave Society in Jamaica* (London, 1967), 98; Michael Craton, *Sinews of Empire: A Short History of British Slavery* (London, 1974), 194; Craton, "Jamaican Slave Mortality: Fresh Light from Worthy Park, Longville, and the Tharp Estates," *Journal of Caribbean History*, III (1971), 1–27; Kenneth F. Kiple, *The Caribbean Slave: A Biological History* (New York, 1984); and Richard B. Sheridan, *Doctors and Slaves: A Medical and Demographic History of Slavery in the British West Indies, 1680–1834* (New York, 1985), 132, 188. For a recent revisionist view, see J. R. Ward, *British West Indian Slavery, 1750–1834: The Process of Amelioration* (Oxford, 1988), 125–129.

Table 1. Population of and Emigration to British America, 1630–1780

Date		Whites		Blacks	
Population	*Emigrants*	Population	*Emigrants*	Population	*Emigrants*
1630		10,000		1,000	
	1630–1650		*138,000*		*27,000*
1650		97,000		17,000	
	1650–1680		*166,000*		*111,000*
1680		185,000		87,000	
	1680–1700		*73,000*		*210,000*
1700		266,000		146,000	
	1700–1720		*92,000*		*295,000*
1720		432,000		245,000	
	1720–1740		*145,000*		*519,000*
1740		790,000		400,000	
	1740–1760		*63,000*		*446,000*
1760		1,305,000		667,000	
	1760–1780		*136,000*		*731,000*
1780		2,253,000		1,064,000	
Total			*815,000*		*2,339,000*

Sources: Emigrant figures: Henry A. Gemery, "Emigration from the British Isles to the New World, 1630–1700: Inferences from Colonial Populations," *Research in Economic History,* V (1980), 179–231; Gemery, "European Emigration to North America, 1700–1820: Numbers and Quasi-Numbers," *Perspectives in American History,* n.s., I (1984), 282–342; Philip D. Curtin, *The Atlantic Slave Trade: A Census* (Madison, Wis., 1969), 119, but with these 17th-century figures modified in the light of 20% middle passage mortality and figures in table 7.3 of James A. Rawley, *The Transatlantic Slave Trade: A History* (New York, 1981), 167; David Richardson, "The Eighteenth-Century British Slave Trade: Estimates of Its Volume and Coastal Distribution in Africa," *Res. Econ. Hist.,* XII (1989), 151–195, esp. 157, provides perhaps the best estimates for the 18th century, but also see Paul E. Lovejoy, "The Volume of the Atlantic Slave Trade: A Synthesis," *Journal of African History,* XXIII (1982), 473–501.

Population figures: Gemery articles cited above; John J. McCusker and Russell R. Menard, *The Economy of British America, 1607–1789* (Chapel Hill, N.C., 1985), 54, 103, 136, 153, 154, 172, 203.

All figures have been rounded to the nearest thousand.

an obvious, but all too easily overlooked, fact: encounters between whites and blacks varied enormously. They varied most notably across space, over time, by social rank, and according to arena of contact. All of these variations influenced the ways in which Africans and British whites experienced each other.

I

The key distinction in white-black interaction in the first British Empire follows the fault line differentiating a slaveowning society from a slave society. In the former, some slaves exist; in the latter, slavery is *the* determinative institution. A slaveowning society may become a slave society, but only when a significant proportion of its population is enslaved (say, for argument's sake, more than 20 percent) and, more important, when slavery becomes central to the economic functioning of that society.[6] What has not been sufficiently recognized is that most societies in Britain's first empire experienced the slaveowning phase of development, though for varying lengths of time. Britain itself, of course, was an extreme example, but New England and the Middle Colonies on the North American mainland were always slaveowning societies, while southern mainland colonies like Virginia, Maryland, and North Carolina remained so for many decades before becoming slave societies. In Virginia's case, the phase was the longest-lived of any British colony, lasting almost a century. Certain island colonies like Bermuda and the Bahamas functioned for about half a century before becoming slave societies. In yet other island colonies, like Barbados and the Leewards, the slaveowning phase was much shorter. Only in a few plantation societies established by or ceded to the British late in the seventeenth and eighteenth centuries was the slaveowning phase avoided altogether.

Race relations tended to be more flexible in slaveowning than in slave societies. Three features particularly reveal the differences between the two systems. First, the legal status of blacks was often uncertain or ambiguous in societies where bondmen were few, and the slave might pass fairly readily from bondage to freedom or live in some twilight zone between the two. By contrast, whenever slavery became a central institution, elaborate legal codes dispelled any uncertainty concerning the slave's status, and the opportunities for freedom generally narrowed. Second, in societies where slavery

6. Keith Hopkins, *Conquerors and Slaves*, Sociological Studies in Roman History, I (Cambridge, 1978), 99; M. I. Finley, *Ancient Slavery and Modern Ideology* (New York, 1980), 79–80. For others who have made use of this distinction, see Paul E. Lovejoy, *Transformations in Slavery: A History of Slavery in Africa* (New York, 1983), 9–10; and Martin A. Klein, "The Study of Slavery in Africa," *Journal of African History*, XIX (1978), 601.

was economically marginal, the niches for blacks tended to be quite wide-ranging. At least work was not primarily associated with the drudgery of field labor, so prevalent in slave societies. Finally, sexual relations between whites and blacks tended to involve choice as well as coercion in slaveowning, as opposed to slave, societies. Slaveowning societies and slave societies were not, of course, uniform across space and time. Rather, within each type a spectrum existed, with differences in environment, demographic structure, and, in particular, stage of economic development producing significant variations.

With a minute fraction of its population composed of blacks and with slavery a minor feature of its social structure, England represents an extreme case of a slaveowning society. The insignificance of slavery did not, however, deter English slaveowners from asserting their rights to human property. In 1701 one master, referring to his black servant, noted, "I take him to be in the nature of my goods and chattels." Other Englishmen acted on the same assumptions, for blacks were regularly bought and sold throughout the country, and advertisements for runaway slaves dotted local newspapers. Nevertheless, since freedom, not bondage, was the norm in England, slaves were emboldened to throw off the yoke of thralldom. In the words of one contemporary writing in the mid-eighteenth century, blacks ceased "to consider themselves as slaves in this free country," and Sir John Fielding thought that slaves became "intoxicated with Liberty" in England. Certainly the Barbadian slave tailor, sent to England as a servant about the 1760s, was inspired by freedom to give his imagination free rein. After passing as free for about half a century, he strained credulity only when, after a shipwreck and arrival in Jamaica, he petitioned the mayor and corporation of Kingston for support, claiming to be Augustus Frederick Horatio, Prince de Bundo, the grandson of an African high priest, born in England, educated at Eton and Oxford University, ordained in the Anglican church, married to a Polish princess, and on intimate terms with the royal family and "that *worthy Saint*, Mr. Wilberforce," with whom he dined on Tuesdays, Thursdays, and Fridays. That the Jamaican authorities took him seriously even for a minute indicates the openness of the metropolitan world.[7]

7. The Will of Thomas Papillon, 1700–01, V.1015.T.44, Kent Archives, as cited in Paul Edwards, "Black Writers of the Eighteenth and Nineteenth Centuries," in David Dabydeen, ed., *The Black Presence in English Literature* (Manchester, Eng., 1985), 51; *Gentleman's Magazine*, XXXIV (1764), 493; Sir John Fielding, *Penal Laws*, 144, as cited in J. Jean Hecht, *Continental and Colonial Servants in Eighteenth Century England*, Smith College Studies in History, XL (Northampton, Mass., 1954), 43 (see also 37–40); *Royal Gazette* (Kingston, Jamaica), Oct. 26, 1816, and Kingston Vestry and Common Council Minute Book, Jan. 27, 1817, as cited in Edward Brathwaite, *The Development of Creole Society in Jamaica, 1770–1820* (Oxford, 1971), 199–200. Augustus's story suggests a familiarity with the life of Job Ben Solomon, who

Legal uncertainty about their status also encouraged slaves to seek freedom in England. Despite rulings that arrival in England did not free slaves or that, in the words of one magistrate, "they are like stock on a farm," some judges and private citizens subscribed to what may be termed a theory of quasi slavery—the notion that slavery was suspended, though not extinguished, by residence in England. In December 1762, Olaudah Equiano claimed freedom on the grounds that, among other things, "no man has a right to sell" a slave in England, an opinion he had "heard a lawyer and others at different times tell my master." The celebrated Somerset case a decade later was a watershed, for, although it did not secure freedom for blacks in England (as the less famous Knight case of 1778 did in Scotland), many slaveholders and slaves acted as if it did. Lord Mansfield merely outlawed the forcible removal of a black slave from England, but he thereby removed perhaps the most serious threat to slaves. Illegal kidnappings continued to occur, but the observation of the former governor of Massachusetts to Mansfield in 1779 suggests the nature of the change. In recent years, he stated, American masters bringing slaves to Britain had "relinquished their property in them, and rather agreed to give them wages, or suffered them to go free." Some slaves in the farthest corners of the New World heard the news and headed for the metropolis.[8]

By custom, if not law, most of the twenty thousand blacks in mid-eighteenth-century Britain already occupied a position intermediate between chattel slavery and the domestic service of white servants. The vast majority were household servants, working as pages, valets, footmen, coachmen, cooks, and maids. A slave in Britain was, above all, a symbol of prestige, an "Index of Rank," an exotic ornament, a fashionable appendage, decked out in ostentatious livery and metal collar (this last, often made of silver, served neatly as a badge of both servitude and opulence). As exotica, the blacker the slave the better—a reversal of the prevailing color consciousness in Anglo-

---

was reputedly the son of the high priest of Bondu, and perhaps also with the violinist Bridgetower, mentioned later in this essay, for Bridgetower had a Polish connection.

8. Helen T. Catterall, *Judicial Cases Concerning American Slavery and the Negro*, I (Washington, D.C., 1926), 13; Edwards, ed., *Life of Equiano*, I, 177; Peter Orlando Hutchinson, ed., *The Diary and Letters of His Excellency Thomas Hutchinson . . .*, II (Boston, 1886), 277; Seymour Drescher, "Manumission in a Society without Slave Law: Eighteenth Century England," *Slavery and Abolition*, X (1989), 85–101. There has been much discussion of the Somerset case; for an essay that mentions most of the pertinent preceding work, see James Oldham, "New Light on Mansfield and Slavery," *Journal of British Studies*, XXVII (1988), 45–68. For slaves making for England and supposed freedom, see John Austin Finnie, Purdie and Dixon's *Va. Gaz.*, Sept. 30, 1773; Gabriel Jones, *ibid.*, June 30, 1774; and Elsa V. Goveia, *Slave Society in the British Leeward Islands at the End of the Eighteenth Century* (New Haven, Conn., 1965), 256, 334.

American slave societies. Thus, one prospective purchaser in Britain wanted a slave "of a deep black complexion," and a seller touted an African whose color was "an excellent fine Black." Of those blacks who were not servants, many were employed as sailors, some plied a trade, and a few worked as agricultural laborers. Eighteenth-century Britain also gave employment to black circus artists, singers, actors, musicians, boxers, and prostitutes as well as bizarre freaks at traveling shows.[9]

In slaveowning Britain, a marked preponderance of black men (a much more imbalanced sex ratio than existed even among Caribbean blacks) made it inevitable that many would have sex with local white women. Olaudah Equiano was hardly atypical, then, in marrying an English woman. Nor was the fictional Sambo in *The Divorce* (1781) when he stated, "Yes, Massa—me want to marry a pretty white woman." But demographic facts and black wishes cannot fully explain interracial sex and marriage in Britain. Rather, the preferences of white women have to be taken into account. The "local maidens" of Ystumlyn near Criccieth in north Wales "used to dote on [Jack Black] and would compete for his favours." Margaret, a young maidservant, eventually became his wife. Black's biographer found it "difficult to fathom the attraction which this dark boy had for the young ladies of the district," but perhaps he was being deliberately obtuse. According to Samuel Johnson, his black servant Francis Barber "carried the empire of Cupid farther than most men." On one occasion, a female haymaker pursued Barber from Lincolnshire to London. In many an English print, blacks are shown actively participating in the subculture of the lower classes. In William Humphrey's 1772 print, *High Life below Stairs*, the black butler pets the white maid, who responds warmly to his affections. Most notably of all, Hogarth's *Four Times of Day—Noon* juxtaposes a group of reserved, foppishly dressed, wealthy whites and a black man fondling the breast of a white servant maid. Visitors from the New World were shocked by these scenes. Edward Long of Jamaica was incensed at the "lower class of women in *England*, [who] are remarkably fond of the blacks, for reasons too brutal to mention." Benjamin Silliman, from Connecticut, was astonished to see "a well dressed white girl, who was of a ruddy complexion, and even handsome, walking arm in arm, and conversing very sociably, with a negro man, who was as well dressed as she, and so black that his skin had a kind of ebony lustre." The sexual interest in black men could be found high up the social scale. There was scandalized talk of the relations between the duchess of Queensberry and her

9. Fryer, *Staying Power*, 60 (quote), 63, 72–75 (quote on 73); Hecht, *Continental and Colonial Servants*, 35–36, 40–45; Edwards and Walvin, *Black Personalities*, 28, 32, 151, 163–164, 186–187; Shyllon, *Black People*, 76, 78; Edwards and Walvin, "Africans in Britain," in Kilson and Rotberg, eds., *The African Diaspora*, 188–194; Shyllon, *Black Slaves*, 6–9 (quote on 7); Walvin, *Black and White*, 60, 62, 70–73.

black servant, Soubise, who was regarded "as general a lover as Don Juan." In 1794 the *Times* reported the case of a wife of a gentleman at Sheerness who had eloped with a black servant. When the couple were caught, the wife said she would "live with no man but the Black." Many an English woman expressed in word and deed an unequivocal interest in black men.[10]

Within the empire, the colonies that most closely approximated the metropolitan slaveowning model were those of New England. In 1680, New England's blacks numbered fewer than 1,000—not even 1 percent of the total population. A century later, the black population had grown to more than 14,000—still fewer than in Britain—constituting 2 percent of the region's total population. More so than in Britain, however, significant clusters of blacks were to be found in certain areas. Blacks congregated in and around coastal urban centers and along river systems. In 1765, the 811 blacks living in Boston represented one-sixth of all blacks living in Massachusetts. At midcentury certain townships in the Narragansett region of Rhode Island were from one-fifth to one-third black. Nevertheless, in New World terms, New England as a whole contained remarkably few blacks.[11]

As in Britain, slavery's marginality in New England permitted a narrowing of the chasm between bondage and freedom. For instance, in seventeenth-century Massachusetts, "Negroes and whites received essentially equal treatment before the law." Even a slave's word was admissible as evidence against whites, and blacks generally possessed the right of appeal, had the use of

10. [Isaac Jackman], *The Divorce* (London, 1781), 34, as cited in Hecht, *Continental and Colonial Servants*, 47; Edwards and Walvin, *Black Personalities*, esp. 21, 30, 33, 218–219; Hester L. Piozzi, *Anecdotes of the Late Samuel Johnson* (London, 1786), 210, as quoted in Shyllon, *Black People*, 102–103; see also Shyllon, *Black Slaves*, 162–163; David Dabydeen, *Hogarth's Blacks: Images of Blacks in Eighteenth Century English Art* (Kingston upon Thames, 1985), 37, 52, 62–64; [Benjamin Silliman], *A Journal of Travels in England, Holland, and Scotland, and of Two Passages over the Atlantic in the Years 1805 and 1806 . . .*, 3d ed. (New Haven, Conn., 1820), I, 272; Edward Long, *Candid Reflections upon the Judgement Lately Awarded by the Court of King's Bench . . .* (London, 1772), 48, as quoted in Edwards and Walvin, "Africans in Britain," in Kilson and Rotberg, eds., *The African Diaspora*, 185, 193.

11. John J. McCusker and Russell R. Menard, *The Economy of British America, 1607–1789* (Chapel Hill, N.C., 1985), 103; Lorenzo J. Greene, *The Negro in Colonial New England, 1620–1776* (New York, 1942), 72–99; William D. Piersen, *Black Yankees: The Development of an Afro-American Subculture in Eighteenth-Century New England* (Amherst, Mass., 1988), 14–18; Gary B. Nash, "Forging Freedom: The Emancipation Experience in the Northern Seaport Cities, 1775–1820," in Ira Berlin and Ronald Hoffman, eds., *Slavery and Freedom in the Age of the American Revolution* (Charlottesville, Va., 1983), 4–7; Louis P. Masur, "Slavery in Eighteenth-Century Rhode Island: Evidence from the Census of 1774," *Slavery and Abolition*, VI (1985), 139–150; Rhett S. Jones, "Plantation Slavery in the Narragansett Country of Rhode Island, 1690–1790: A Preliminary Study," *Plantation Society*, II (1986), 157–170.

counsel, and received due process. Admittedly, most black servile protest, which grew more widespread as blacks came to dominate the ranks of bound laborers, took the form of unruly behavior and running away rather than recourse to legal remedy. Nevertheless, the legal privileges extended New England blacks encouraged some to seek freedom through the courts. Others took advantage of their right to property to purchase their freedom, as in the case of "Angola the Negro" who was left a legacy of £2 by his master and by dint of industry acquired land. The most impressive rags-to-riches story concerns the family of Cuffe, or Kofi, Slocum, an African who gained his freedom in the mid-1740s and whose son, Paul Cuffe, became perhaps "the wealthiest black in America." Black election day, when blacks voted for their own "governors," a widespread festivity in New England, is another indication of the unusual sociopolitical opportunities available to New England slaves. Most notably, of course, the functional unimportance of slavery to the New England economy facilitated the institution's abolition during the Revolutionary era. By 1790 the overwhelming majority of the seventeen thousand blacks in New England were nominally free.[12]

As in Britain, many slaves in New England were family domestics. New England may have received younger slaves than was normal in the slave trade because the region's masters preferred to groom children for household service. Perhaps the examples of Phillis Wheatley, brought to New England at the age of seven, and of Ruth, bought by a Danvers master at the age of two, were not unusual. Household slavery inevitably led to a measure of familiarity. One visitor expressed disgust at Connecticut farmers who allowed their black servants "to sit at table with them (as they say to save time), and into the dish goes the black hoof as freely as the white hand." Unlike their counterparts in Britain, however, many New England slaves were agricultural laborers, acquainted with all aspects of mixed farming. Indeed, in the Narragansett region, slaves specialized as stockmen and dairy

12. Robert C. Twombly and Robert H. Moore, "Black Puritan: The Negro in Seventeenth-Century Massachusetts," *William and Mary Quarterly*, 3d Ser., XXIV (1967), 224–242 (quote on 227); Lawrence W. Towner, " 'A Fondness for Freedom': Servant Protest in Puritan Society," *WMQ*, 3d Ser., XIX (1962), 214; David Thomas Konig, *Law and Society in Puritan Massachusetts: Essex County, 1629–1692* (Chapel Hill, N.C., 1979), 151; Piersen, *Black Yankees*, 34. For an interesting portrait of a part-Indian, part-black slave, who sued for her freedom, see Charles L. Hill, "Slavery and Its Aftermath in Beverly, Massachusetts: Juno Larcom and Her Family," Essex Institute, *Historical Collections*, CXVI (1980), 111–130. On Cuffe and his family, see Lamont D. Thomas, *Rise to Be a People: A Biography of Paul Cuffe* (Urbana, Ill., 1986), esp. 22. On election day, see Joseph P. Reidy, " 'Negro Election Day' and Black Community Life in New England, 1750–1860," *Marxist Perspectives*, I (1978), 102–117, and Piersen, *Black Yankees*, 117–140. The story of abolition is told in Arthur Zilversmit, *The First Emancipation: The Abolition of Slavery in the North* (Chicago, 1967).

hands. The colonial New England economy put a premium on versatility and diversification, so that many of the region's slaves acquired a wide range of skills.[13]

Legally sanctified interracial marriages were possible in most of New England (being outlawed only in Massachusetts after 1705), thereby making the region atypical of British America. Interracial marriages were "very rare," noted a prominent Boston merchant, and were "oftener between black men and white women than on the contrary." Thus black men in New England enjoyed a sliver of sexual freedom. Lemuel Haynes, the first African-American to preach regularly to a white congregation in America, was the child of an African father and white mother and married a white woman himself. Most interracial sex outside wedlock was undoubtedly between white men and black women, but the inverse combination seems more common in New England than elsewhere in British America. The extensiveness of interracial sex is impossible to gauge. Only one census of a New England colony distinguished between mulattoes and blacks. In 1782 one-eighth of Rhode Island's black population was listed as of mixed racial parentage.[14]

Another colony in which a significant minority of blacks appear to have "enjoyed a measure of freedom and a status similar to that of white laborers" is Bermuda, Britain's first slaveowning society in the New World. From 1616, when blacks were first introduced into the colony (four years after its first settlement), to the mid-1660s, Bermuda's white population far outnumbered its black inhabitants. Not until about 1670 did the slave population reach more than 20 percent of the colony's population, when the colony's white population stood at forty-three hundred and its black population at eleven hundred. During this first half-century, some black immigrants served seven-year indentures, some black children were to be freed when they reached thirty years of age, and some black adults lived and worked independently of whites either as servants or as free people. In 1617 Symon was condemned to be a slave to the colony during the governor's pleasure (a punishment also directed toward a white laborer at the same assize), an indication that this black was either free or a servant before he committed his transgression. An occasional black secured an audience for a complaint against a white master, receiving treatment much like a white servant's. In 1655 a black woman, wife to "James the negro at Herne Bay," complained to the governor and council that four white men had abused her "in a

13. Piersen, *Black Yankees*, 5–6, 28, 31 (quote), and chap. 3; Greene, *Negro in Colonial New England*, 222; Masur, "Slavery in Eighteenth-Century Rhode Island," *Slavery and Abolition*, VI (1985), 143–146.

14. Greene, *Negro in Colonial New England*, 201–202, 206–207, 210; Twombly and Moore, "Black Puritan," *WMQ*, 3d Ser., XXIV (1967), 231.

royetous way." They were fined forty pounds of tobacco for their offense, ten pounds of which went to the woman. Six years later another black woman complained of her mistress's cruelty. Should the cruelty continue, the council determined, the black woman would be assigned to another master. In 1669 several black Bermudians petitioned for their liberty "alledgeing, the Gospel allowes noe bondmen."[15]

For the first half-century, the Bermudian economy was not heavily reliant on black labor, and the roles played by blacks were quite varied, though certainly not to the same extent as in Britain. The first black men sought by Bermudian whites were pearl-divers. Others were valued for their specialized agricultural skills. A "neger whose name is Francisco" was apparently employed to teach Robert Rich's tenants how to cure tobacco; another of Rich's most prized possessions was a black man especially skilled in the "planting of west endy plants." Yet others were employed in maritime work, the activity for which this colony's black population would become famous. In 1622, for example, two black indentured servants received wages for salvage operations on a shipwreck. Thirty-seven years later, seven Bermudian blacks deserted their ship in Plymouth, England.[16]

Bermuda was unusual for British America in having a rough balance of the sexes early in its existence. In 1622 there were 413 men and 393 women and children among its white population. At some point in the seventeenth century, both white and black populations had female majorities, for by the end of the century the adult sex ratio was 76 men per 100 women among whites and 87 among blacks. An availability of black females, however, did not curb sexual relations between black men and white women. In 1661, for example, the wife of John Sanders was found to have committed adultery with a male slave, and Amy Swan willingly admitted that the father of her child was a black slave. In 1670 Judith Porter, a white female servant, was whipped for giving birth to a "Blacke Childe." Nor did the availability of white women halt some white men from entering into marriages with black or mulatto women. In 1660 John Davis, a mariner, gained permission to marry Penelope Strange, a mulatto. Perhaps such marriages were not rare,

15. Cyril Outerbridge Packwood, *Chained on the Rock: Slavery in Bermuda* (New York, 1975), 5, 73, 85, 130, 163; James E. Smith, *Slavery in Bermuda* (New York, 1976), 16–17; Virginia Bernhard, "Beyond the Chesapeake: The Contrasting Status of Blacks in Bermuda, 1616–1663," *Journal of Southern History*, LIV (1988), 545–564, esp. 549 and 557; John Henry Lefroy, ed., *Memorials of the Discovery and Early Settlement of the Bermudas or Somers Islands, 1511–1687*, 2 vols. (London, 1877–1879), I, 127, 526, II, 61, 150–151, 293. Still the best general history of early Bermuda is Wesley Frank Craven, "An Introduction to the History of Bermuda," *WMQ*, 2d Ser., XVII (1937), 176–215, 317–362, 437–465, XVIII (1938), 13–63.

16. Packwood, *Chained on the Rock*, 2–3, 5–6; Smith, *Slavery in Bermuda*, 17; Lefroy, *Memorials*, II, 126–127.

for three years later a law was passed in which a free person could be banished for marrying "any negroes, molattoes, or musteses."[17]

The history of Virginia was closely linked to that of Bermuda. Virginia received its first blacks only a few years after its sister colony, but remained a slaveowning society for much longer. Only by the end of the seventeenth century did slaves come to play a central role in the Chesapeake's productive activities, and not until 1710 in Virginia and 1720 in Maryland did slaves come to represent 20 percent of the total population. During this slave-owning phase of Virginia's history, access to freedom was greater for blacks than it ever would be again until the Civil War. Some slaves were allowed to earn money; some even bought, sold, and raised cattle; and some used the proceeds to purchase their own freedom. Two blacks who showed an unwillingness to work received an indenture guaranteeing their freedom in return for four years' labor and seventeen hundred pounds of tobacco. Some seventeenth-century Chesapeake slaves sued for their freedom in their local courts.[18]

Since the Chesapeake's labor requirements were overwhelmingly agricultural, most of the region's early blacks worked alongside white servants in the tobacco fields. Of the slaveowning societies explored, the Chesapeake provided the least variety to its black population. Nevertheless, black slaves were important to the diversification of Chesapeake agriculture that occurred in the second half of the seventeenth century. In late-seventeenth-century Charles County, Maryland, there were more cattle in the all-black or mixed-race quarters than in those composed solely of whites. Whether this was coincidental, represented a recognition of black skills in caring for livestock, or, conversely, signified their marginality to the key economic activity of the region is an open question. What it undoubtedly means,

17. Virginia Bernhard, "Bermuda and Virginia in the Seventeenth Century: A Comparative View," *Journal of Social History*, XIX (1985–1986), 66; Lefroy, *Memorials*, II, 141; Smith, *Slavery in Bermuda*, 29–31, 47; Packwood, *Chained on the Rock*, 56, 86, 132.

18. Russell Menard, "From Servants to Slaves: The Transformation of the Chesapeake Labor System," *Southern Studies*, XVI (1977), 360–362; Carville V. Earle, *The Evolution of a Tidewater Settlement System: All Hallow's Parish, Maryland, 1650–1785*, University of Chicago, Department of Geography, Research Paper no. 170 (Chicago, 1975), 47; Edmund S. Morgan, *American Slavery, American Freedom: The Ordeal of Colonial Virginia* (New York, 1975), 155; T. H. Breen and Stephen Innes, *"Myne Owne Ground": Race and Freedom on Virginia's Eastern Shore, 1640–1676* (New York, 1980), esp. 72–79; Warren M. Billings, ed., *The Old Dominion in the Seventeenth Century: A Documentary History of Virginia, 1606–1689* (Chapel Hill, N.C., 1975), 165–171; Billings, "The Cases of Fernando and Elizabeth Key: A Note on the Status of Blacks in Seventeenth-Century Virginia," *WMQ*, 3d Ser., XXX (1973), 467–474; Ross M. Kimmel, "Slave Freedom Petitions in the Courts of Colonial Maryland" (MS).

however, is that a significant number of slaves escaped field labor. In 1697, for instance, at an all-black quarter in Charles County, one old black man and two elderly black women, together with four children, managed a herd of fifty cattle and forty-eight hogs. In 1673, when Edward Lister of Northumberland County, Virginia, thought of taking advantage of the ranching opportunities provided by the nascent colony of South Carolina, he had enough confidence in his slaves to send them on ahead to "settle them upon a Plantacon, together with Some Cattle."[19]

As in other slaveowning societies, interracial sex in the early Chesapeake was often between black men and white women. A number of white female servants gave birth to mulatto children. The only realistic conclusion to be drawn from this evidence—and Virginia's ruling establishment was not slow to see it—was that "black men were competing all too successfully for white women." In addition, there were a number of marriages between free black men and white women in the early Chesapeake. Occasionally, even a male slave was able to engage the affections of white women. The most celebrated example concerns Lord Baltimore's Irish maidservant, Nell Butler, who fell in love with Major Boarman's "saltwater" Negro slave, Charles. When, in 1681, she informed Lord Baltimore of her intention to marry Charles, he attempted to dissuade her by pointing out that she would thereby enslave herself and her children. For his pains, he was reportedly told, "She had rather Marry the Negro under them circumstances than to marry his Lordship with his Country." Nell Butler was not alone in the annals of the early Chesapeake, nor in other slaveowning societies, in preferring a black partner.[20]

In full-fledged slave systems, as opposed to slaveowning societies, race relations were much more rigid, particularly in the earliest years, as ruling

19. Lorena Seebach Walsh, "Charles County, Maryland, 1658–1705: A Study of Chesapeake Social and Political Structure" (Ph.D. diss., Michigan State University, 1977), 205–207; Peter H. Wood, *Black Majority: Negroes in Colonial South Carolina from 1670 through the Stono Rebellion* (New York, 1974), 30–31.

20. E. Morgan, *American Slavery, American Freedom*, 155–156, 333–336 (quote on 336); Philip Alexander Bruce, *Economic History of Virginia in the Seventeenth Century: An Inquiry into the Material Condition of the People* (New York, 1895), II, 110–112; Billings, ed., *The Old Dominion*, 157–158, 160–163; Ross M. Kimmel, "Free Blacks in Seventeenth-Century Maryland," *Maryland Historical Magazine*, LXXI (1976), 20; Kimmel, "Slave Freedom Petitions," 19–22, 31–33; Benjamin B. Weisiger III, comp., *Charles City County, Virginia, Court Orders, 1687–1695 . . .* (Richmond, Va., 1980), 54, 96, 200; George M. Fredrickson, *White Supremacy: A Comparative Study in American and South African History* (New York, 1981), 102–103; Joseph Douglas Deal III, "Race and Class in Colonial Virginia: Indians, Englishmen, and Africans on the Eastern Shore during the Seventeenth Century" (Ph.D. diss., University of Rochester, 1981), esp. 214–215; deposition of Samuel Abell, Jr., *Mary Butler* v. *Adam Craig*, General Court of the Western Shore, Court of Appeals, Judgments no. 3, June 1791, Maryland Hall of Records, Annapolis.

elites grappled with the consequences of importing large numbers of alien Africans. Variations among slave societies occurred, of course, depending very largely on their particular demographic and economic structures: the types of crops grown, the average size of estate, the mix of Africans and creoles, the sex ratios of both whites and blacks, and the incidence of absenteeism were important in structuring the circumstances of black-white contact in slave societies. Space will not allow a detailed investigation of the way these and other variables shaped encounters between whites and blacks. Instead, three slave societies will be briefly explored in order to illustrate a range of inflexible race relations.

If one discounts Providence Island, a short-lived British colony but one that was half black as early as 1637, Barbados was Britain's first slave society. It became one in the mid-1640s, less than two decades after initial British settlement. By 1650 its black population numbered thirteen thousand people, one-third of the colony's total. In another decade, this number had more than doubled, representing more than half of the total population of the island and three-quarters of all the blacks in British America. As Richard Dunn has pointed out, what is remarkable about Barbadian planters is their unreserved, headlong plunge into slaveholding. The consequences of this precipitous descent into slavery were not edifying. Bryan Edwards put his finger on the most elemental effect when he declared, "In countries where slavery is established, the leading principle on which government is supported, is *fear*." One year after Providence Island became 50 percent black, a serious slave rebellion, the first in the Anglo-American world, occurred (in 1638). It was put down only with the greatest of difficulty. The writing was on the wall, and Barbadians had no trouble reading it. Although Barbados waited a quarter-century after achieving a black majority before experiencing its first serious slave conspiracy (in 1675), its masters had much earlier responded to the portents by creating one of the most nakedly racial and ruthlessly exploitative societies in Western history.[21]

A striking characteristic of early Barbadian slavery, Dunn has emphasized, was the planters' determination to keep their blacks at arm's length. Very few

21. Arthur Percival Newton, *The Colonizing Activities of the English Puritans: The Last Phase of the Elizabethan Struggle with Spain*, Yale Historical Publications, Miscellany, I (New Haven, Conn., 1914), 258, 261; Richard S. Dunn, *Sugar and Slaves: The Rise of the Planter Class in the English West Indies, 1624–1713* (Chapel Hill, N.C., 1972), esp. 224, 226; Bryan Edwards, *The History, Civil and Commercial, of the British Colonies in the West Indies*, 3 vols. (London, 1807 [orig. publ. London, 1793–1801]), III, 13; Jerome S. Handler, "Slave Revolts and Conspiracies in Seventeenth-Century Barbados," *Nieuwe West-Indische Gids*, LVI (1982), 5–42 (esp. 13–19); and Handler, "The Barbados Slave Conspiracies of 1675 and 1692," *Journal of the Barbados Museum and Historical Society*, XXXVI (1982), 312–333. There was no rebellion in 1675—compare Gary A. Puckrein, *Little England: Plantation Society and Anglo-Barbadian Politics, 1627–1700* (New York, 1984), 163.

blacks were permitted inside their masters' homes; indeed, the fortified designs of many seventeenth-century structures, referred to as "castles" by one observer, stand as testaments to white fears. Segregation extended to minds as well as to houses. Barbadians were the first coherent group within the Anglo-American world to portray blacks as beasts or as beastlike. Even Richard Ligon, resident on the island in the late 1640s and prepared to find good in blacks, referred to them "as neer beasts"; a few years later, Henry Whistler described them as "apes whou [the planters] command as they pleas . . . sel[ling] them from one to the other as we doue shepe." The 1661 comprehensive slave code characterized Negroes as "an heathenish, brutish and an uncertaine, dangerous kinde of people" who had to be governed by special laws, and in the 1670s Morgan Godwyn was told by one Barbadian that a minister "might as well baptize a puppy" as a black and by another that Negroes were "beasts, and had no more souls than beasts." Harsh actions matched hostile attitudes. For suspected black criminals, no punishment was too brutal: they were burned alive, beheaded, and starved to death. After a slave conspiracy was discovered in 1692, the colony paid ten guineas to Alice Mills for castrating forty-two blacks, "an episode," remarks Winthrop Jordan dryly, "which says a good deal about Barbados and something about Alice Mills." In the next century, a slave convicted of raping a white woman was chained to the stake, had his "privy members . . . cut off and burned before his face," and was then burnt alive.[22]

Jamaica became a slave society a few decades later than Barbados, but its planters soon made up for lost time. As early as 1690, blacks outnumbered whites in Jamaica by four to one, as high a proportion as was ever reached in Barbados during the slavery era. Yet in Jamaica the ratio quickly climbed much higher: six to one in 1710, ten to one in 1740, and twelve to one by 1780. For most of the eighteenth century, Jamaica was British America's most heavily black slave colony (in the 1770s it was surpassed by Antigua, Dominica, Grenada, and Tobago). Moreover, by 1780, there were almost a quarter of a million slaves in Jamaica, making it Britain's largest and densest slave society. More than one in four of all the blacks in British America

22. Jerome S. Handler and Lon Shelby, eds., "A Seventeenth-Century Commentary on Labor and Military Problems in Barbados," *Jour. Barbados Museum and Hist. Soc.*, XXXIV (1973), 118; Richard Ligon, *A True and Exact History of the Island of Barbados* (London, 1657), 47; "Extracts from Henry Whistler's Journal of the West India Expedition," in C. H. Firth, ed., *The Narrative of General Venables . . .* (London, 1900), 146; Barbados Act for the Better Ordering and Governing of Negroes, Sept. 27, 1661, as cited in Dunn, *Sugar and Slaves*, 239; Morgan Godwyn, *The Negro's and Indians Advocate . . .* (London, 1680), 38–39; Handler, "Slave Revolts and Conspiracies," *Nieuwe West-Indische Gids*, LVI (1982), 14, 20, 23–24; Winthrop D. Jordan, *White over Black: American Attitudes toward the Negro, 1550–1812* (Chapel Hill, N.C., 1968), 156; Letters Written in Governor Pinfold's Administration, Aug. 10, 1764, Pinfold Manuscripts, Library of Congress.

resided on Jamaica's forty-five hundred square miles, a land mass about the size of the English county of Yorkshire or the American colony of Connecticut.[23]

Since black slaves so heavily outnumbered whites, one might realistically predict that race relations in Jamaica would be the most brutal in all of British America. This expectation seems to have been met. Jamaica's penal code was nothing short of savage. A 1664 act concerning slave crime denied bondmen even the most elementary due process. "No other English statute of the century," Richard Dunn points out, "stated quite so nakedly the white man's arbitrary determination of black crime." Although this act was soon superseded and although there was occasional benign legislation, such as the 1696 statute calling for masters to instruct their bondmen in Christianity, Jamaica's black code was notoriously severe. Nor was savagery confined to formal legislation. Masters concocted exquisite punishments within the confines of their own plantations. Thomas Thistlewood, an overseer and later a small planter, flogged his slaves unmercifully, applied face brandings, shackled slaves in bilboes, put cart chains around their necks, and rubbed salt, lime juice, and urine into their wounds. For eating sugar cane, he devised "Derby's dose," whereby the slave Derby would defecate into a culprit's mouth, which would then be gagged shut for some hours. Nor should it be surprising that two of the most virulently racist thinkers in British America, Edward Long and Philip Thicknesse, were one-time residents of Jamaica.[24]

The one society on the mainland that approximated the rigidity of a Caribbean slave society was, of course, South Carolina. It was the one British colony in North America where black slavery was introduced at the outset of settlement. Before the society even came into existence, slaves were considered essential to its success. In its first few years, the colony was already one-fourth to one-third black. In short, South Carolina was a slave

23. Population estimates for Jamaica were derived from a number of sources, but John Jay McCusker, Jr., "The Rum Trade and the Balance of Payments of the Thirteen Continental Colonies, 1650–1775" (Ph.D. diss., University of Pittsburgh, 1970), 609, is the most comprehensive.

24. Dunn, *Sugar and Slaves*, esp. 243; Douglas Hall, *In Miserable Slavery: Thomas Thistlewood in Jamaica, 1750–86* (London, 1989), 72–73; Philip D. Morgan, "Three Planters and Their Slaves: Perspectives on Slavery in Virginia, South Carolina, and Jamaica, 1750–1790," in Winthrop D. Jordan and Sheila L. Skemp, eds., *Race and Family in the Colonial South* (Jackson, Miss., 1987), 74; Edward Long, *Candid Reflections*, as cited in Edwards and Walvin, "Africans in Britain," in Kilson and Rotberg, eds., *The African Diaspora*; Long, *The History of Jamaica . . .*, 3 vols. (London, 1774); Philip Thicknesse, *A Year's Journey through France, and Part of Spain*, 2 vols. (London, 1778 [orig. publ. Bath, 1777]); Thicknesse, *Memoirs and Anecdotes . . .*, 2 vols. (London, 1778). See also Patterson, *Sociology of Slavery*; Brathwaite, *Development of Creole Society*; Michael Craton, "Jamaican Slavery," in Engerman and Genovese, eds., *Race and Slavery*, 249–284; Craton, *Searching for the Invisible Man: Slaves and Plantation Life in Jamaica* (Cambridge, Mass., 1978).

society from the first. Naturally, there were many parallels between Carolinian and Caribbean slavery. South Carolina's slave code, modeled on that of Barbados, was the most severe on the continent. Carolinian planters gained a deserved reputation for their brutality. Early in the eighteenth century a missionary saw a slave woman burned to death on one lowcountry plantation. Another master employed "a hellish machine contrived in the shape of a coffin" to torture his slaves. The famous scene, so movingly rendered by Crèvecoeur, of a slave, barely alive, suspended in a cage and preyed upon by birds and insects, derived from South Carolina. No less telling an indictment was Crèvecoeur's observation that Carolinians looked on their slaves "with half the kindness and affection with which they consider their dogs and horses." According to Benjamin West, a South Carolinian planter would "shoot a Negro with as little emotion as he shoots a hare." The most significant slave revolt to take place on the mainland in the eighteenth century occurred in the lowcountry.[25]

Race relations, then, were more fraught with tensions, more brutal, and more potentially explosive in slave, as opposed to slaveowning, societies. Yet, as slave societies matured, as their reliance on blacks deepened, relations between master and bondman became somewhat less polarized. Masters still committed chilling acts of savagery, and undercurrents of fear and brutality always lurked close to the surface, but, as masters and slaves became more familiar with one another, they found ways to live together. Economic roles, sexual relations, and access to freedom illustrate this development.

As New World masters turned to slaves for all their laboring needs, they gradually began to place their bondpeople not just in the fields but in supervisory, domestic, and skilled positions. The vast majority of slaves remained field hands, but over the course of the eighteenth century a growing minority escaped field labor. Nowhere was this development more evident than in the factory-in-a-field of the sugar plantation system, which wedded brute manual labor and skilled work par excellence. By the late eighteenth century, about a quarter to a third of adult slaves in the sugar islands worked primarily *outside* the fields. For men, the proportion was much higher, for they monopolized privileged positions. Conversely, few women escaped field labor, and increasingly they dominated field gangs. In less industrial plantation regimes, occupational opportunities tended to be more limited. On rice-growing plantations in the lower South, only about one in four slave men and one in twenty slave women escaped the drudgery

25. Francis Le Jau to the Society for the Propagation of the Gospel (SPG), Mar. 22, 1709, A4/142, Feb. 20, 1712, A7/395–398, and Feb. 23, 1713, A8/346–348, SPG Archives, London; [M. G. St. J. de Crèvecoeur], *Letters from an American Farmer* . . . (London, 1782), 242–245; James S. Schoff, ed., *Life in the South, 1778–1779: The Letters of Benjamin West* (Ann Arbor, Mich., 1963), 33; Wood, *Black Majority*, 308–326.

of field labor. The proportions were even lower on tobacco plantations in the upper South. But, if the absolute level of skills was highest in the most specialized plantation regimes (sugar being the exemplar), the range of skills was widest in the most diversified plantation regimes (in the Chesapeake, for example, slaves were employed as shoemakers, tailors, spinners, and weavers). The same contrast can be extended to slave occupations in slave, as opposed to slaveowning, societies. In slaveowning societies the range of economic niches for slaves was extremely wide, but the proportion of slaves in skilled and supervisory positions was greatest in full-fledged slave societies.[26]

No matter how large the proportion of non–field hands, the emergence of a significant minority of skilled or semiskilled slaves introduced a new element into master-slave relations. Clement Caines pinpointed the change in outlining how to deal with slave boilers: a judicious planter, he noted, "had better superintend and inspect his boilers, than dictate to them," for they were "more perfect in their business, than any white man can pretend to be." The allocation of extra allowances, particularly for tradesmen—"the flower of the slave population" in one Jamaican's evaluation—arose from the value masters placed on such slaves. Certainly, as the chaplain to the Codrington plantations in Barbados put it in 1789, "the principal negroes . . . have a surprising influence over their inferiors, and enjoy several privileges and advantages above them." Drivers, domestics, and tradesmen received extra food, additional clothing, sometimes had more elaborate houses and household furnishings, and even received monetary payments or re-

26. The most useful occupational profiles of slaves on sugar plantations at the end of the 18th century can be found in Craton, *Searching for the Invisible Man*, 141, 180–181; Richard S. Dunn, "A Tale of Two Plantations: Slave Life at Mesopotamia in Jamaica and Mount Airy in Virginia, 1799 to 1828," *WMQ*, 3d Ser., XXXIV (1977), 52; Dunn, "'Dreadful Idlers' in the Cane Fields: The Slave Labor Pattern on a Jamaican Sugar Estate, 1762–1831," in Barbara L. Solow and Stanley L. Engerman, eds., *British Capitalism and Caribbean Slavery: The Legacy of Eric Williams* (Cambridge, 1987), 174. For the early 19th century, see B. W. Higman, *Slave Population and Economy in Jamaica, 1807–1834* (Cambridge, 1976), 36–42, 187–211; and Higman, *Slave Populations of the British Caribbean, 1807–1834* (Baltimore, 1984), 158–204. There is incidental information scattered in other works: Dunn, *Sugar and Slaves*, 319; Richard B. Sheridan, *Sugar and Slavery: An Economic History of the British West Indies, 1623–1775* (Baltimore, 1974), 257–258; Sheridan, *Doctors and Slaves*, 91–93, 240; David Barry Gaspar, *Bondmen and Rebels: A Study of Master-Slave Relations in Antigua, with Implications for Colonial British America* (Baltimore, 1985), 105–107; Ward, *British West Indian Slavery*, 191; and Goveia, *Slave Society*, 146, where she reports a 1788 estimate that nearly *half* of all adult slaves at Montserrat were employed outside the field. For the lower and upper South, see my *Slave Counterpoint: Black Culture in the Eighteenth-Century Chesapeake and Lowcountry* (forthcoming); and Allan Kulikoff, *Tobacco and Slaves: The Development of Southern Cultures in the Chesapeake, 1680–1800* (Chapel Hill, N.C., 1986), 384–385, 400.

wards. Plantation artisans in particular were often allowed to hire out their labor in their spare time and to pocket part of their earnings. But the most important privilege of all—and it was an opportunity that widened over the course of the eighteenth century, at least so far as creole men were concerned—was simply to escape from field labor and to hold a specialized post.[27]

Throughout British American slave societies, but most notably in the West Indies, colored slaves were prominently represented among the ranks of the skilled and semiskilled. The existence of this group raises the question of the extent and nature of interracial sexual relations in slave societies. Where there was a marked imbalance of white to black, a scarcity of white women, a high rate of planter absenteeism, and a consequent widespread employment of lowly whites—best evident in Jamaica and the Leewards—concubinage became an integral, customarily accepted aspect of everyday life. Open liaisons between white men and black women were commonplace, whereas sexual relations between black men and white women were strictly proscribed. Unquestionably there was much callous sexual exploitation of black women. The six or so white men living on one Jamaican estate in the early nineteenth century were twice as likely as the ninety black men there to sire a slave baby. None of the slave mistresses on this estate were manumitted (although a fifth of the mulatto children were freed—a proportion that was exactly matched among the more than four thousand colored slave children born in Jamaica between 1829–1832)—but "the power of sex to persuade the planters to free their property," Richard Pares notes, "is illustrated by the fact, reported by the legislature of Nevis in 1789, that there were 5 female slaves to every 4 male slaves, but 9 free negresses to every 4 free negroes." Nor should the informal influence of slave mistresses be underestimated, for white men were said to be "negrofied" by their connections with slave women who, in Pares's words, "led them by the nose." Edward Long thought that a white man became an "abject, passive slave" to his black mistress's "insults, thefts, and infidelities." Furthermore, a modern study of the patterns of miscegenation in early nineteenth-century Jamaica suggests an active role for slave women, because colored births were greater where slave women outnumbered slave men than where white men outnumbered white

27. Clement Caines, *Letters on the Cultivation of the Otaheite Cane* . . . (London, 1801), 98; Thomas Roughley, *The Jamaica Planter's Guide; or, A System for Planting and Managing a Sugar Estate* . . . (London, 1823), 61; J. Harry Bennett, Jr., *Bondsmen and Bishops: Slavery and Apprenticeship on the Codrington Plantations of Barbados, 1710–1838*, University of California Publications in History, LXII (Berkeley, Calif., 1958), 18; Jerome S. Handler and Frederick W. Lange, *Plantation Slavery in Barbados: An Archaeological and Historical Investigation* (Cambridge, Mass., 1978), 75–82; Karl Watson, *The Civilized Island, Barbados: A Social History, 1750–1816* (Barbados, 1979), 74–76; Goveia, *Slave Society*, 139–142, 229–233; Ward, *British West Indian Slavery*, 226–229.

women. In other words, direct physical compulsion cannot explain patterns of miscegenation in any simple way, and sex in such slave systems certainly acted, in part at least, as a racial solvent.[28]

In slave societies where there was no marked imbalance of white to black and where white women were less scarce—most notably, the upper South from the middle of the eighteenth century onward—open, publicly acknowledged liaisons between white men and black women were almost unthinkable. By the late eighteenth century a traveler to the Chesapeake reported that a man's reputation could be ruined by fathering a mulatto child. He "would be scorned, dishonoured; every house would be closed to him; he would be detested." South Carolina, with its black majority, was the one place on the mainland where, in Josiah Quincy's words, "the enjoyment of a negro or mulatto woman is spoken of as quite a common thing." Liaisons between white men and black women were not as common or as open in South Carolina as in the West Indian islands, but the Carolina pattern of miscegenation stood halfway between the Caribbean and the Chesapeake models. Barbados was Carolina's equivalent in the islands. Possessing by far the largest white population of any sugar island, it was the one place in the British West Indies where planters made any concerted effort to prohibit "improper intercourse" between their white employees and slaves. Nevertheless, whatever the public attitude toward miscegenation, interracial sex occurred anyway. Its most obvious result—the proportion of mulattoes among the slave population—cannot be measured with any precision across slave societies. But, as a crude index to the difference between the mainland and the islands (even when making allowances for different lengths of settlement), note that colored slaves formed 8 percent of Maryland's slave population in 1755 and almost twice that proportion among the slaves of Barbados sixty years later. The bridge between the races that sex could represent was thus more evident in the islands than on the mainland.[29]

28. Dunn, "A Tale of Two Plantations," *WMQ*, 3d Ser., XXXIV (1977), 48–49, 54; Dunn, "'Dreadful Idlers' in the Cane Fields," in Solow and Engerman, eds., *British Capitalism and Caribbean Slavery*, 175–176; Higman, *Slave Population and Economy*, 143–147; Richard Pares, *A West-India Fortune* (London, 1950), 134, 354; Long, *History of Jamaica*, II, 327. For conflicting views of the significance of interracial sex, see Patterson, *Sociology of Slavery*, 42, 159–162, and Barbara Bush, "White 'Ladies,' Coloured 'Favourites,' and Black 'Wenches': Some Considerations on Sex, Race, and Class Factors in Social Relations in White Creole Society in the British Caribbean," *Slavery and Abolition*, II (1981), 245–262. For further insights, see Goveia, *Slave Society*, 215–217, 232–233; Watson, *The Civilized Island*, 91–92; and esp. Craton, *Searching for the Invisible Man*, 75–76, 149, 168–169, 235–243, 259, 262–264, 269–270.

29. Ferdinand-M. Bayard, *Travels of a Frenchman in Maryland and Virginia . . .*, trans. and ed., Ben C. McCary (Williamsburg, Va., 1950), 20; Jordan, *White over Black*, 136–178 (quotation on 145); Jordan, "American Chiaroscuro: The Status and Definition of Mulattoes in the British Colonies," *WMQ*, 3d Ser., XIX (1962), 183–

Access to freedom, almost nonexistent in the early years of most full-fledged slave societies, inched wider as time progressed, in large part because some white fathers freed their colored offspring. Manumission was never widely practiced in any of the slave societies of British America. Nevertheless, there were variations, most notably between the islands and the mainland. By the late eighteenth century, for example, the proportion of freedmen in the population of Jamaica was about four times that found in the United States South. Barbados, as always, was something of a halfway house. With the large minority of poor whites on their island, Barbadian masters saw little need for freedmen. Indeed, in 1786 only about 1 percent of Barbados's total population consisted of freedmen (a proportion that was exceeded in the upper South). Jamaican masters, on the other hand, surrounded by a mass of black slaves, found more use for a buffer group of free coloreds. The contrast can be seen in the role freedmen played in the respective island militias. In late-eighteenth-century Jamaica, free colored militiamen outnumbered whites in certain local units (and by 1830 formed a majority of the total militia force). In late-eighteenth-century Barbados, on the other hand, freedmen formed only about 10 percent of the militia (never reaching more than 25 percent during the era of slavery). The status of freedmen was also marginally better in Jamaica and Antigua (in the former, private enabling acts secured some of the privileges of white men for some freedmen; in the latter, free mulattoes were allowed to vote) than in Barbados. Perhaps this is why a "significant few" Barbadian free coloreds threw in their lot with slaves in that island's 1816 slave rebellion, whereas the involvement of free blacks in Jamaica's 1831–1832 slave rebellion was negligible. In general, all island freedmen possessed a few more privileges and rights than their counterparts in the mainland South. But, whatever the variations, everywhere the bipolar structure of slave societies was gradually altered by the emergence of an intermediate racial group, a "third party in a system built for two."[30] In this penumbra can be found the meaning of racial slavery.

200; Evarts B. Greene and Virginia D. Harrington, *American Population before the Federal Census of 1790* (New York, 1932), 126; Higman, *Slave Populations*, 116, 150.

30. David W. Cohen and Jack P. Greene, eds., *Neither Slave nor Free: The Freedmen of African Descent in the Slave Societies of the New World* (Baltimore, 1972), 1–18, 193–277; Jerome S. Handler, *The Unappropriated People: Freedmen in the Slave Society of Barbados* (Baltimore, 1974); Handler, "Joseph Rachell and Rachael Pringle-Polgreen: Petty Entrepreneurs," in David G. Sweet and Gary B. Nash, eds., *Struggle and Survival in Colonial America* (Berkeley, Calif., 1981), 376–391; Handler and John T. Pohlmann, "Slave Manumissions and Freedmen in Seventeenth-Century Barbados," *WMQ*, 3d Ser., XLI (1984), 390–408; Handler, "Freedmen and Slaves in the Barbados Militia," *Jour. Caribbean Hist.*, XIX (1984), 1–25, esp. 4–6; Arnold A. Sio, "Race, Colour, and Miscegenation: The Free Coloured of Jamaica and Barbados," *Caribbean Studies*, XVI (1976), 5–21; Sio, "Marginality and Free Coloured Identity in Caribbean Slave Society," *Slavery and Abolition*, VIII (1987), 166–

II

Focusing only on slave societies, major spatial and temporal variations in race relations can be explored by ringing changes on the concept of frontier. The term does not have to imply a positive march forward, a boundary or line marking the advance of civilization; rather, it is best conceived as a territory or zone of interpenetration on an outer periphery.[31] Viewed in this way, at least three frontiers exemplify this process. First, plantation slavery expanded continually from one frontier zone to another in our period. Barbadian planters helped settle Jamaica and later introduced slavery into the Carolinas; planters from the Leewards helped open up new frontiers in the Windward Islands, Trinidad, and Guiana; South Carolinians established plantations in Georgia and East Florida; Virginia planters were instrumental in the expansion of slavery into the Southwest. Even after a slave society was fully established, frontier zones (as in the Cockpit country of Jamaica, for instance) continued to exist, often for many years. In all these cases, open frontiers eventually closed; the former represented transitional phases of development. Second, in other British settlements, the frontier phase was much longer-lived and general. Dotted about Britain's first empire were settlements like those on the Bay of Honduras, the Mosquito Shore, the Cayman Islands, and, most prominently, large parts of Africa, where frontier conditions prevailed for centuries. Finally, another frontier, urban in character, arose in the very heartland of almost all slave societies. Towns can be considered internal frontiers in two senses: British American slave societies were overwhelmingly rural, and the few towns in them were generally located on the edges of great plantation tracts. Although race relations were

---

182; Samuel J. Hurwitz and Edith F. Hurwitz, "A Token of Freedom: Private Bill Legislation for Free Negroes in Eighteenth-Century Jamaica," *WMQ*, 3d Ser., XXIV (1967), 423–431; Brathwaite, *Development of Creole Society*, 166–175, 186–190, 193–198, 291–292; Gad J. Heuman, *Between Black and White: Race, Politics, and the Free Coloreds in Jamaica, 1792–1865* (Westport, Conn., 1981), 3–32; Goveia, *Slave Society*, 82–83, 96–101, 203–204, 214–229, 232–233, 250–252, 315–317; Ira Berlin, *Slaves without Masters: The Free Negro in the Antebellum South* (New York, 1974), 3–50; Douglas Deal, "A Constricted World: Free Blacks on Virginia's Eastern Shore, 1680–1750," in Lois Green Carr, Philip D. Morgan, and Jean B. Russo, eds., *Colonial Chesapeake Society* (Chapel Hill, N.C., 1988), 275–305; Michael Craton, *Testing the Chains: Resistance to Slavery in the British West Indies* (Ithaca, N.Y., 1982), 256, 260, 316–317; Jordan, *White over Black*, 122–128, 134 (quotation), 406–414, 577–581.

31. Howard Lamar and Leonard Thompson, eds., *The Frontier in History: North America and Southern Africa Compared* (New Haven, Conn., 1981), 7; Bernard Bailyn, "New England and a Wider World: Notes on Some Central Themes of Modern Historiography," in David D. Hall and David G. Allen, eds., *Seventeenth-Century New England*, Publications of the Colonial Society of Massachusetts, LXIII (Boston, 1984), 327–328.

hardly the same in these three frontier settings, each needs to be distinguished from the archetypal plantation slavery characteristic of slave societies.

If Britain represents the extreme in the spectrum of slaveowning societies, then coastal Africa represents another in terms of frontier regions. Within various African societies scattered along the coast from the Senegal to the Congo rivers, various British settlements were no more than small territorial enclaves (in a way similar to the black enclaves in the port cities of London, Liverpool, and Bristol). Moreover, just as blacks in Britain were so few as to be accorded a measure of tolerance, the British in Africa enjoyed—or, more appropriately, suffered—a similar fate. A brief look at settlement patterns on the Gold Coast, far the most important region of British interest, will illustrate the weakness of their position. In 1700 there were slightly more than two hundred British residents on the Gold Coast. The size of Cape Coast Castle, the major garrison, was one hundred whites at best. By comparison, black forest and hinterland towns were generally five thousand to twenty thousand strong. Even the coastal towns, which were the least populous, held about two thousand to four thousand people. British settlements were inevitably considered insignificant when compared to such centers. Furthermore, British settlements involved no alienation of land; they existed only in return for regular payments of rent, tribute, or taxes. As the Board of Trade noted in 1752, "In Africa we were only tenants of the soil which we held at the goodwill of the natives." Britons on the African coast came under the protection of an African landlord. Under these circumstances, the British obviously remained heavily dependent on the cooperation of African rulers and middlemen for their trade. Without the landlords' role as intermediary, the British could get no slaves, for they never ventured far outside the walls of their forts. The modes, if not always the terms, of their bargaining were drawn more often from African than from European culture. Yet, even if the British ultimately gained the most in financial terms from this collaboration, payments to natives on the Gold Coast made up more than half the annual expenses of fort services. British buyers had thus entered into a partnership with African sellers. Together they exploited the African masses.[32]

32. Davies, *Royal African Company*, 4; Ray A. Kea, *Settlements, Trade, and Polities in the Seventeenth-Century Gold Coast* (Baltimore, 1982), 34–39. For the later Gold Coast, see Eveline C. Martin, "The English Establishments on the Gold Coast in the Second Half of the Eighteenth Century," Royal Historical Society, *Transactions*, 4th Ser., V (1922), 167–189; Journal of the Board of Trade and Plantations, Feb. 14, 1752, C.O. 391/59, as quoted in Eveline C. Martin, *The British West African Settlements, 1750–1821: A Study in Local Administration* (London, 1927), 48; Walter Rodney, *A History of the Upper Guinea Coast, 1545–1800* (Oxford, 1970), 77, 82–87, 89, 180, 189–192, 195–199; V. R. Dorjahn and Christopher Fyfe, "Landlord and Stranger: Change in Tenancy Relations in Sierra Leone," *Jour. African Hist.*, III (1962), 391–397; Philip D. Curtin, *Economic Change in*

Confined to the coastal perimeter, British settlements became part of societies that were either slaveowning or, more often, in the process of becoming large-scale slave systems. In fact, many West African societies retained more of their new slaves, generally obtained as war captives, than they exported. British settlements relied on local slaves for their lifeblood, even though the number of slaves was always small. In the late seventeenth and early eighteenth centuries, for instance, the British enclaves contained no more than 350 white men and around 200 castle slaves, known as *grumetes*. At James Fort on the Gambia, where the population was usually not greater than 100 or so, there were 32 company slaves in 1730 and 43 in 1763. These slaves operated the local stations. They fulfilled the same roles—domestics, agricultural workers, craftsmen, sailors, and common laborers—that were common throughout British America, though the range of their activities and, more particularly, the opportunities available to them were unusual. Most, for instance, were wage earners. *Grumetes* and their descendants sometimes invested successfully on their own account. One small insight into the unusual status of such slaves is provided by the activities of Richard Oswald. In 1774 he proposed to purchase about 100 "Grametas or Island Slaves" from the proprietors of Bance Island and ship them to his plantations in South Carolina. He promised these "Negroes not to expose them to public Sale in the manner of African Cargoes, but if possible and with their liking and good behaviour to keep them together to work on his plantation." Oswald's American factor proposed allowing "those Gramatas who are Water Men . . . to reside in Charles Town on the Salt Water and with their own Consent . . . Sell or hire out all Such."[33]

Since there were extremely few white women among the British in Africa (a situation parallel to the black community in Britain), the settlers had to look toward the natives for partners. Some took slaves as concubines. Most, like the Owen brothers (impoverished Irish gentry reduced to slave brokerage in the Sherbro estuary), became integrated into their host society through intermarriage. They conformed to African norms and reinforced their business connections with ties of kinship. When the Irish trader Richard Brew died on the Gold Coast in 1776, his estate of almost nine thousand pounds was divided between his African wife and their two mulatto daughters, one given the English name Eleanor, the other called, in Fanti fashion,

---

Precolonial Africa: Senegambia in the Era of the Slave Trade (Madison, Wis., 1975), I, 95–100; Curtin, *Cross-Cultural Trade in World History* (New York, 1984), 57–59.

33. Lovejoy, *Transformations in Slavery*, esp. 64–65, 109, 128–129; Davies, *Royal African Company*, 240–290; Rodney, *History of Upper Guinea*, 266–268; Martin, *British West African Settlements*, 52–53; Nicholas Owen, *Journal of a Slave-Dealer . . .*, ed. Eveline Martin (Boston and New York, 1930), 39, 101, 104–105; George C. Rogers, Jr., *et al.*, eds., *The Papers of Henry Laurens*, IX (Columbia, S.C., 1981), 395–396.

Amba. The mulatto children of British fathers in the Sherbro and Sierra Leone peninsula served as middlemen, collecting African produce and slaves at convenient points and in convenient quantities for loading on oceangoing ships. As a subsidiary activity, they engaged in many branches of purely local commerce. The Caulkers, Rogers, and Clevelands in the district immediately south of the Sierra Leone peninsula became important power brokers—"merchant princes" according to one historian—in their own right. These Afro-Europeans straddled two worlds and could identify with each. Of James Cleveland, it was said, "To sum up his character in a few words: with a White Man he is a White Man, with a Black Man a Black Man."[34]

A similar dependence of white upon black, although never approaching the extremes of Africa, characterized race relations in other frontier zones. This dependence best reveals itself in three areas—the workplace, the emergence of a free colored group, and military relations. In some respects, the flexibility of race relations in a slaveowning society was duplicated on the frontiers of slave societies. But there was a difference, for, where the exigencies of frontier life often led whites to rely heavily on blacks, and in turn gave blacks some latitude in their relations with whites, race relations on the peripheries of slave societies could be as harsh as in their heartlands—sometimes even harsher—as urban slavery best indicates.

First, work was often varied and unregimented on the frontier, sometimes bringing slaves into close contact with whites and occasionally according them a measure of autonomy. Among the logwood cutters on the Bay of Honduras, for instance, the slaves, who constituted from one-half to three-quarters of the population throughout much of the eighteenth century, worked in small, isolated camps. Initially, a white man might cut logwood "with a single Negro"; even if successful, the white master would continue to employ a small gang, managed perhaps by a white foreman. Since all the slaves possessed machetes and axes, they possessed the means to elicit a measure of respect. Where mahogany was sought, the gang relied heavily on the skills of the slave "huntsman," who searched the woods alone in order to locate the best stands. This job was highly prestigious and left the incumbent free to roam the woods.[35]

34. Owen, *Journal*, 44, 70, 76, 102; Rodney, *History of Upper Guinea*, 200–222; Christopher Fyfe, *A History of Sierra Leone, 1400–1787* (London, 1962), 10; George E. Brooks, Jr., "The *Signares* of Saint-Louis and Gorée: Women Entrepreneurs in Eighteenth-Century Senegal," in Nancy J. Hafkin and Edna G. Bray, eds., *Women in Africa: Studies in Social and Economic Change* (Stanford, Calif., 1976), 19–44; Margaret Priestly, *West African Trade and Coast Society: A Family Study* (London, 1969); Adam Jones, "White Roots: Written and Oral Testimony on the 'First' Mr Rogers," *History in Africa*, X (1983), 151–162.

35. O. Nigel Bolland, *The Formation of a Colonial Society: Belize, from Conquest to Crown Colony* (Baltimore, 1977), 28–32, 49–51, 54–57; C. H. Grant, *The Making of Modern Belize: Politics, Society, and British Colonialism in Central*

Fishing, whether it was the speciality of the slaves in a frontier zone, as in the Caymans, or whether it was confined to the periphery of settled regions throughout plantation America, was another activity that permitted the slaves a significant measure of independence. Fishing slaves, according to Richard Price, "benefitted from considerable trust and possessed liberties not granted to other" bondmen. Johann David Schoepf, a visitor to the Bahamas, spoke glowingly of the "general contentment" of those island slaves, many of whom made their living from the sea. By "paying a small weekly sum," Schoepf continued, "they are left undisturbed in the enjoyment of what they gain." A Bermudian slaveowner warned her neighbors against paying wages to her slave men for fishing in their boats. William Wylly, a Bahamian slaveowner, thought that slave seamen enjoyed more freedom than other slaves, for they were allowed a percentage of the profits of their fishing and turtling and were treated almost exactly like ordinary white seamen. As a frontier activity, fishing encouraged the transmission of techniques between native Indians, Europeans, and African-Americans.[36]

In pioneer South Carolina, and this must have been true for other slave colonies in the early years of their existence or expansion, the slaves were called upon to serve a variety of needs, such as log cutting and fishing, but much more besides. Frontier existence, as Peter Wood has argued, represented "the high-water mark of diversified Negro involvement in the colony's growth." Many slaves spent most of their lives clearing land, working wood, hunting, cultivating provisions, and raising cattle. More often than not, blacks labored alongside whites and sometimes Indians. Thus the lowcountry estate of John Smyth, who died in 1682, included nine blacks, four Indians, and three whites. Undoubtedly, all sixteen worked shoulder-to-shoulder at least some of the time. The picture of Elias Horry working "many days with a Negro man at the Whip saw" was hardly an isolated incident in late-seventeenth-century South Carolina.[37]

Second, the emergence of a significant free colored group was often a feature of frontier regions. In most frontier zones, men outnumbered women

---

America (Cambridge, 1976), 30–31; Narda Dobson, *A History of Belize* (London, 1973), 67–68, 149–150; Alan K. Craig, "Logwood as a Factor in the Settlement of British Honduras," *Caribbean Studies*, IX (1969), 53–66, esp. 60–61.

36. Richard Price, "Caribbean Fishing and Fishermen: A Historical Sketch," *American Anthropologist*, LXVIII (1966), 1363–1383; Sidney W. Mintz, "Labor Exaction and Cultural Retention in the Antillean Region," in James Schofield Saeger, ed., *Essays on Eighteenth-Century Race Relations in the Americas* (Bethlehem, Pa., 1987), 41–42; Michael Craton and Gail Saunders, "Time Longer Dan Rope: A History of the Bahamian People" (MS); Smith, *Slavery in Bermuda*, 115. On slave fishermen in general, see Higman, *Slave Populations*, 176, 236–237; Neville Williams, *A History of the Cayman Islands* (Grand Cayman, 1970), 20–21.

37. Wood, *Black Majority*, esp. 95 (quote), 97.

heavily, much more so among whites than blacks. Not surprisingly, therefore, whites took black women as wives and concubines. Relatively large free colored groups arose when masters manumitted their mulatto children and the mothers. On the Bay of Honduras in the late eighteenth century, white men outnumbered white women four to one, and one-sixth of the total population comprised free people of color, a majority of whom were women. Among the freedmen, one owned 126 slaves and was the largest slaveowner in the settlement, two possessed more than 30 slaves each, and a number of others owned more than 10 slaves. These men earned the respect of their white neighbors. On the Grand Caymans at the turn of the nineteenth century, about one-third of the total families comprised free blacks. John Faturn of Doddentown commanded 10 slaves. In early South Carolina, access to freedom, although never widespread, appears to have been more extensive than in later times. There was even a report in 1701 that "Malatoes and Negroes were Polled" in assembly elections. At the turn of the eighteenth century, Read Elding, a mulatto, ruled in the pirate-infested Bahamas; he was the first and only nonwhite in such authority for 250 years. A few decades later, Benjamin Sims, a mariner, probably a colored man passing for white, died leaving legacies to both whites and free blacks or mulattos. His two executors were substantial white planters and slaveowners. Sims himself owned 9 slaves, all of whom he freed, perhaps because they were part of his family. Social and racial categories were obviously fluid in the frontier Bahamas.[38]

Finally, the most distinctive feature of race relations in frontier areas was in the military sphere. To conceive of frontier zones is to think of marchlands, of border regions rather than of civil societies. As theaters of war, frontier regions brought blacks and whites together in a military relationship. From the earliest settlement of South Carolina until the conclusion of the Yamasee War in 1718, blacks played a significant role in the defense of the colony, acting not only as messengers, drummers, and pioneers but also as armed militiamen. In a 1680 description of South Carolina, the author referred to a force of "500 fighting English men beside many trusty Negroes." In 1708, when taking stock of the colony's defensive capabilities, a South Carolinian could take comfort in the reliance placed upon the "1000 good Negroes that knows the Swamps and Woods, most of them Cattle Hunters." Two years later, Thomas Nairne added his testimonial, pointing out that "a considerable Number of active, able Negro slaves were enrolled

38. Bolland, *Formation of a Colonial Society*, 41–42, 45–46; Williams, *Cayman Islands*, 34–35; Wood, *Black Majority*, 96; Craton and Saunders, "Time Longer Dan Rope." For a comparable example on another continent, see Richard Elphick and Hermann Giliomee, eds., *The Shaping of South African Society, 1652–1820* (Cape Town, 1979), 383–384.

in the militia." As rice began to dominate the colony's economy in the early eighteenth century, slaves became increasingly relegated to the role of field worker, and were thought of less as useful and loyal servants than as degraded and resentful laborers, too dangerous to be used in military actions.[39]

Yet the eighteenth century did not see the complete disappearance of armed cooperation between black and white in South Carolina. It merely shifted to the frontier. In the 1760s and 1770s, the backcountry region comprised strolling hunters seen as "little more than white Indians," wandering bandit gangs, and restless squatters as well as farmers and prospective planters. The struggle between hunters and farmers was, according to one commentator, "a new species of war." A notable feature of the backcountry bandit gangs was their interracial character. Woodmason thundered against the "Gangs of Rogues . . . composed of Runaway negroes, free mulattoes and other mix'd Blood." On the other side was a man like Gideon Gibson, a mulatto slaveholder and a prominent Regulator. After a violent incident in 1768, Provost Marshall Roger Pinckney sent fifteen militiamen to arrest Gibson, only to be thwarted by a large group of Regulators, who refused to hand over one of their leaders, since, as they said, he "was one of them." Interracial fraternity among both bandits and Regulators was of a very different order from that obtaining in the rigid slave society of the adjoining coastal littoral.[40]

In frontier zones it was almost imperative to arm slaves. In the timber camps on the Bay of Honduras, slaves often possessed muskets for hunting. In 1788, a white resident of the Bay of Honduras stated that "it has always been the Custom with us to allow our Negroes Firearms." Two decades earlier, "Twenty three British Negroes, Armed" had fled to the Spaniards. In 1773, some fifty slaves, "armed with sixteen Musquets, Cutlasses, etc.," succeeded in overrunning five settlements and killing six whites before British naval reinforcements drove them into the woods. At the same time, some of these armed slaves must have sided with their masters; certainly many of the free blacks were prominent in the militia. In 1779, an observer of the Bay settlement noted that two hundred of the five hundred English were able to

39. Maurice Mathews, "A Contemporary View of Carolina in 1680," *South Carolina Historical Magazine*, LV (1954), 158; Thomas Nairne, *A Letter from South Carolina . . .* (London, 1710), 31; *Boston News-Letter*, May 17–24, 1708, as quoted in Clarence L. Ver Steeg, *Origins of a Southern Mosaic: Studies of Early Carolina and Georgia* (Athens, Ga., 1975), 106; Wood, *Black Majority*, 124–130.

40. Rachel N. Klein, "Ordering the Backcountry: The South Carolina Regulation," *WMQ*, 3d Ser., XXXVIII (1981), 668–678; see also Klein, "Frontier Planters and the American Revolution: The South Carolina Backcountry, 1775–1782," in Ronald Hoffman, Thad W. Tate, and Peter J. Albert, eds., *An Uncivil War: The Southern Backcountry during the American Revolution* (Charlottesville, Va., 1985), 56, 60–61.

bear arms while about five hundred of the three thousand slaves could "be depended on." In the late eighteenth century, at least three free blacks commanded divisions of the militia.[41]

The most notable military encounters between whites and blacks in a frontier zone involved colonists and maroons. These incidents occurred along a belt of marches and involved maroon groups from such small and unlikely places as the forested hills of Providence Island and the wooded thicket of Saint Philip's Parish, Barbados, in the early seventeenth century, to the mountain fastnesses of Dominica and Saint Vincent in the late eighteenth century. The earliest encounter occurred in the 1570s, when Francis Drake allied himself with "certaine valiant Negros" who guided him across the Isthmus of Panama in an attack on the Spaniards. The *cabildo* of Panama observed that the "league between the English and the negroes is very detrimental to this kingdom, because, being so thoroughly acquainted with the region and so expert in the bush, the negroes will show them methods and means to accomplish any evil design that they may wish to carry out." Edmund Morgan has claimed that these Englishmen "had cast themselves as liberators and had allied with blacks against whites." More than two hundred years later, five hundred or so maroons waged war against the British in frontier Dominica. The conflict lasted from the mid-1780s to 1814, when the maroons were finally defeated.[42]

41. Bolland, *Formation of a Colonial Society*, 30, 45–46, 74, 84. In "Time Longer Dan Rope," Craton and Saunders write, "Curiously, and in contrast to most other colonies, Bahamian slaves were allowed to carry firearms when it suited their owners—for example, for fowling, hoghunting or protection against Spaniards or pirates—as long as they carried permits to produce on a demand from any freeman. Bahamian slaves were also permitted to serve under arms against foreign enemies in time of war." The frontier nature of the Bahamas, even in the middle of the eighteenth century, accounts for this curiosity.

42. Richard Price, ed., *Maroon Societies: Rebel Slave Communities in the Americas* (Garden City, N.Y., 1973); I. A. Wright, ed., *Documents concerning English Voyages to the Spanish Main, 1569–1580*, Hakluyt Society, 2d Ser., LXXI (London, 1932), 49–50, 109–113, 132–133, 142, 336; Kenneth R. Andrews, *The Spanish Caribbean: Trade and Plunder, 1530–1630* (New Haven, Conn., 1978), 139–145; E. Morgan, *American Slavery, American Freedom*, 13; Bernard A. Marshall, "Maronage in Slave Plantation Societies: A Case Study of Dominica, 1785–1815," *Caribbean Quarterly*, XXII (1976), 26–32, and Marshall, "Slave Resistance and White Reaction in the British Windward Islands, 1763–1833," *Caribbean Qtly.*, XXVIII (1982), 33–46. For a comprehensive treatment of military encounters between British-Americans and slaves, see Peter Michael Voelz, "Slave and Soldier: The Military Impact of Blacks in the Colonial Americas" (Ph.D. diss., University of Michigan, 1978); and Roger Norman Buckley, *Slaves in Red Coats: The British West India Regiments, 1795–1815* (New Haven, Conn., 1979). The military use of slaves both in the American Revolutionary war and in the early 19th-century British Caribbean was a matter of expediency, often dictated by metropolitan needs. It cannot be considered part of the flexibility of race relations on the frontier—at least not in the same way as the above and subsequent examples.

But the most significant internal frontier of this type was undoubtedly the Cockpit Country and Blue Mountains of Jamaica, where in the middle of the eighteenth century about one thousand persons, just under 1 percent of the island slave population, lived under the jurisdiction of two maroon groups. By 1739, when the colonial government of Jamaica recognized their free and separate existence, these bands (the Windward Maroons in the eastern mountains and the Leeward Maroons in the western interior) had been waging war against whites for more than eighty years. Cudjoe, the leader of the Leeward Maroons, divided his people into companies under captains who "exercise[d] their respective men in the Use of the Lance, and small arms after the manner of the Negroes on the Coast of Guinea." Because of their military skills, posttreaty maroons proved effective allies of the whites, tracking down slave runaways and rebels. A 1750 encounter between a white overseer and Cudjoe, now a colonel accompanied by "one of his wives, one of his Sons—a Lieutenant and other attendants," is instructive. Cudjoe shook the white by the hand and asked for a dram of liquor, which he received. A military bearing—a feathered hat, a sword by his side, and gun upon his shoulder—gave Cudjoe "a Majestic look" and reminded his admiring white witness of Robinson Crusoe. In 1795, the maroons of Trelawny Town engaged in one last two-year war with government troops. When they finally surrendered, apparently on the understanding that the government would listen to their grievances, they were transported to Nova Scotia. Descendants of maroons, still living in separate communities on land their ancestors defended (surrounded by place names, such as Land of Look Behind, Quick Step, Me no Sen You no Come, and Dont Come Back, to remind them of an earlier martial past), are proud of their history as guerilla fighters whom the British could not defeat.[43]

43. The best work on the Jamaican maroons is Barbara Klamon Kopytoff, "The Maroons of Jamaica: An Ethnohistorical Study of Incomplete Politics, 1655–1905" (Ph.D. diss., University of Pennsylvania, 1973), and the many articles therefrom, e.g. "The Development of Jamaican Maroon Ethnicity," *Caribbean Qtly.*, XXII (1976), 33–50; "Jamaican Maroon Political Organization: The Effects of the Treaties," *Social and Economic Studies*, XXV (1976), 87–105; "Guerilla Warfare in Eighteenth-Century Jamaica," *Expedition*, XIX (1977), 20–26; "The Early Political Development of Jamaican Maroon Societies," *WMQ*, 3d Ser., XXXV (1978), 287–307; "Colonial Treaty as Sacred Charter of the Jamaican Maroons," *Ethnohistory*, XXVI (1979), 45–64; and "Religious Change among the Jamaican Maroons: The Ascendance of the Christian God within a Traditional Cosmology," *Jour. Soc. Hist.*, XX (1987), 463–484. See also Daniel Lee Schafer, "The Maroons of Jamaica: African Slave Rebels in the Caribbean" (Ph.D. diss., University of Minnesota, 1973); Mavis C. Campbell, *The Maroons of Jamaica, 1655–1796: A History of Resistance, Collaboration, and Betrayal* (South Hadley, Mass., 1988); Orlando Patterson, "Slavery and Slave Revolts: A Socio-historical Analysis of the First Maroon War, Jamaica, 1655–1740," *Soc. and Ec. Stud.*, XIX (1970), 289–325; Rhett S. Jones, "White Settlers, Black Rebels: Jamaica in the Era of the First Maroon War, 1655–1738"

Relations between whites and maroons were akin in some ways to white-Indian relations. In both cases, whites came to recognize, and then violate, the territorial integrity of their opponents, often confining them to reservations. Whites made treaties with both groups, each of which possessed its own political and religious organizations and was to some extent an independent polity, an imperium in imperio. Both maroons and Indians were skillful exponents of guerilla warfare and imposed a strict military discipline on their members. Both groups suffered from interethnic or intertribal rivalries; at times, both fought long wars against white adversaries. Both entered into an uneasy symbiosis with the British, seeking arms, tools, pots, and cloth as well as employment as military allies or as runaway slave–catchers. These dependent relationships ultimately destroyed maroon and Indian ways of life. To bring the parallels even closer, Indians were often employed by the British as the most effective combatants of maroons, and some blacks and Indians joined forces, as with the Black Caribs on Saint Vincent or the blacks and Seminoles in Florida.[44]

On closing frontiers the fluidity of race relations and the latitude extended blacks gave way to increasingly rigid racial orders. As plantation economies took firm hold, the apparatus of social control tightened. Slavery in towns, generally located at the very heart of these settled plantation regions, should reveal this rigidity better than anywhere else. And, in some ways, it does.

The forces of social control were generally greater in town than countryside. Although it is true, for instance, that many towns contained relatively large numbers of slaves in one confined place (and would, therefore, seem to be dangerous places), many towns, even in the most heavily black of slave societies, contained either a majority of whites or relatively equal numbers of whites and blacks. Since most urban slaves worked as domestics and were part of small households under the direct supervision of their masters, they were under constant and immediate scrutiny. Nor were urban whites con-

---

(Ph.D. diss., Brown University, 1976); L. Alan Eyre, "The Maroon Wars in Jamaica—A Geographical Appraisal," *Jamaican Historical Review*, XII (1980), 5–19; Craton, *Testing the Chains*, esp. 61–96; and Hilary M. D. Beckles, "The 200 Years War: Slave Resistance in the British West Indies: An Overview of the Historiography," *Jamaican Hist. Rev.*, XIII (1982), 1–10.

44. For other work on maroons, see Anthony Synnott, "Slave Revolts in the Caribbean" (Ph.D. diss., University of London, 1976); David Barry Gaspar, "Runaways in Seventeenth-Century Antigua, West Indies," *Boletin de estudios latinamericanos y del Caribe*, XXVI (1979), 3–13. Still useful as a study of the Black Caribs is Sir William Young, *An Account of the Black Chairaibs in the Island of St. Vincent's . . .* (London, 1795), but see also Bernard Marshall, "The Black Caribs—Native Resistance to British Penetration into the Windward Side of St. Vincent, 1763–1773," *Pan-African Journal*, VIII (1975), 139–152; Nancie L. Gonzáles, "New Evidence on the Origin of the Black Carib, with Thoughts on the Meaning of Tradition," *Nieuwe West-Indische Gids*, LVII (1983), 143–172.

fronted with a disproportionate share of single, restless male slaves. Black women outnumbered men in Port Royal, Jamaica, by 1680, as they would seventy years later in Charleston, ninety years later in New York City, and, by the early nineteenth century, if not much earlier, in every other British Caribbean town. Towns contained many more visible symbols of public terror, in the guise of workhouses, cages, jails, and stocks, than ever existed in the countryside, and, certainly, urban masters relied heavily on these public agencies for disciplining their slaves. Military force was conspicuous in towns. British troops were often stationed in urban centers, armed watches maintained order during the night when curfews were imposed on slaves, and militia patrols were an additional weapon in the battle to keep urban slaves in order.[45]

Another aspect of this rigid racial order was the heightened hostility faced by urban slaves. Much of this enmity was economic in origin. In towns the threat posed by slaves to the livelihoods of white artisans and laborers was readily apparent. Even in London in 1731 city authorities decreed that no blacks were to be apprenticed to tradesmen or artificers, though this action does not seem to have derived from lower-class white agitation. In colonial towns, the authorities were often bombarded by petitions from white artisans objecting to the unfair competition—as they saw it—presented by slaves. During the course of the eighteenth century, a succession of Charleston artisans complained that slaves were taking their jobs. In 1758 the pressure of Savannah artisans forced the Georgia Assembly to pass an act curtailing "the employing Negroes and other Slaves being handicraft Tradesmen in the said Towns." In 1780 the Antiguan legislature prohibited blacks from acting as "public Cryers" in the town of Saint John in order to protect "White Cryers." In forwarding the act, the governor also mentioned that "the Inferior Artificers . . . were much injured" by the competition that they faced from slave tradesmen. The failure to halt this process was hardly designed to make white manual workers look kindly upon neighboring blacks.[46]

And, yet, there was another side to race relations in towns. A measure of social fluidity, characteristic of frontier regions, did exist. The latitude of urban slavery is perhaps best revealed in the system of "self-hire," as it was known, where slaves were allowed to find their own employers and pay their

45. Dunn, *Sugar and Slaves*, 179; Michael Pawson and David Buisseret, *Port Royal, Jamaica* (Oxford, 1975), 98–99; Philip D. Morgan, "Black Life in Eighteenth-Century Charleston," *Perspectives in American History*, n.s., I (1984), 189; Nash, "Forging Freedom," in Berlin and Hoffman, eds., *Slavery and Freedom*, 12n; Higman, *Slave Populations*, 118, 226–259.

46. Fryer, *Staying Power*, 74–75; P. Morgan, "Black Life in Charleston," *Perspectives*, n.s., I (1984), 204; Betty Wood, *Slavery in Colonial Georgia, 1730–1775* (Athens, Ga., 1984), 132–134; Goveia, *Slave Society*, 164. See also Edgar J. McManus, *Black Bondage in the North* (Syracuse, N.Y., 1973), 44–45.

owners a stipulated sum either weekly or monthly. In major towns like Kingston, Jamaica, Bridgetown, Barbados, and Charleston, South Carolina, perhaps a fifth of the adult slaves engaged in this independent economic behavior. On the eve of the Revolution, even one in ten of the adult blacks of a small town like Savannah, Georgia, worked in this way. In Kingston, Jamaica, there were even slave artisans who hired other slaves to work under them, paying them hourly, daily, or weekly rates. Openings for skilled labor seem to have been at least twice as great in towns as in the countryside. The urban artisan was also more likely to work alongside free craftsmen. Black women often outnumbered black men in towns because of the urban demand for their labor as domestics, washerwomen, seamstresses, and higglers.[47]

Nor were the opportunities presented by the urban environment confined just to the economic realm. For one thing, living arrangements for some urban slaves—their ability to rent separate dwellings, for example—permitted them a considerable measure of independence. Second, as in rural frontier regions, men often outnumbered women among urban whites. Widespread miscegenation was the inevitable result. Many of the resulting children (and their mothers) were eventually freed. Indeed, manumission was predominantly an urban phenomenon in British America, and freedmen congregated in towns. In Barbados in the middle of the eighteenth century, 60 percent of all the island's freedmen lived in Bridgetown. In Saint Kitts toward the end of the century, about 70 percent of the free colored population lived in the two parishes containing large towns. In Jamaica and South Carolina around 1790, a third of the two provinces' free blacks lived in the respective port towns of Kingston and Charleston. Third, in densely settled slave societies, possessing no open frontier, towns provided the major refuges for runaway slaves. In early nineteenth-century Jamaica, for instance, the proportion of fugitives in Kingston was double that elsewhere on the island. Finally, towns possessed a greater cultural mix of blacks than the countryside. Early nineteenth-century West Indian towns contained surprisingly large African populations and many creoles born in other colonies. In these and many other ways, the patina of race relations in towns assumed a remarkably open and fluid character, despite the heightened forces of repression and the tensions of the workplace.[48]

47. P. Morgan, "Black Life in Charleston," *Perspectives*, n.s., I (1984), 191–192; Wilma R. Bailey, "Kingston, 1692–1843: A Colonial City" (Ph.D. diss., University of the West Indies, Mona, 1974), 141; Higman, *Slave Populations*, 244–246.

48. Handler, *The Unappropriated People*, 20; Goveia, *Slave Society*, 228; Colin G. Clarke, *Kingston, Jamaica: Urban Development and Social Change, 1692–1962* (Berkeley, Calif., 1975), 8, 141; P. Morgan, "Black Life in Charleston," *Perspectives*, n.s., I (1984), 212; Higman, *Slave Populations*, 123–126, 135, 388. On social opportunities in towns, see the above and, in addition, Michael Mullin, "British Caribbean and North American Slaves in an Era of War and Revolution, 1775–

These frontier situations were always minority experiences for slaves. True, many black slaves were exposed to frontier conditions, more particularly in the early formation of particular plantation societies than in long-lived frontier settlements like the Bay of Honduras or the Cayman Islands. Nevertheless, the vast majority of slaves lived in long-settled, mature plantation heartlands. Moreover, the first British Empire was predominantly a rural world, the major exception being, of course, London, which in the middle of the eighteenth century had the largest black population of any urban place in the empire. Elsewhere in the empire, towns were much smaller, for the most part containing no more than about 5–10 percent of any colonial society's population. But factors of class and status affected experience, even for the overwhelming number of blacks who lived in an agrarian setting.

III

Race relations not only varied between and within societies but also according to the status of individuals and groups interacting across racial lines. As part of the flexibility and fluidity of race relations in slaveowning societies, frontier regions, and urban settings, fraternization between races in the lower classes occurred. In full-fledged slave societies, as channels of communication routinized, the varying status of slaves affected the nature of their relationships with white masters.

Slaveowning societies, which by definition comprised mostly free people and few slaves, might be expected to exhibit the fewest tensions between poor whites and blacks. A striking example of such cooperation concerns David Spens, a black resident of Fife in Scotland. In 1770 Spens was the subject of a legal action that aimed to return him as a slave to the West Indies. Fortunately for him, the miners and salters of his parish came to his defense. Their action may have owed something to self-interest, for workers in the coal mines and salt pits of Scotland suffered from their own form of bondage. Bound for life to their mineowner, colliers could not move without written permission. Any who disregarded this requirement were likely to be

1807," in Jeffrey J. Crow and Larry E. Tise, eds., *The Southern Experience in the American Revolution* (Chapel Hill, N.C., 1978), 242–244; and N.A.T. Hall, "Slavery in Three West Indian Towns: Christiansted, Fredericksted, and Charlotte Amalie in the Late Eighteenth and Early Nineteenth Century," in B. W. Higman, ed., *Trade, Government, and Society in Caribbean History, 1700–1920: Essays Presented to Douglas Hall* (Kingston, 1983), 17–38. A study of black religious opportunities in towns, ranging from Richard Allen in Philadelphia to George Liesle in Kingston, might be illuminating.

imprisoned as thieves on the grounds that they had "stolen" themselves from their master. Some colliers even bound the labor of their children from birth in return for bounty money. This inheritable serfdom, together with the physical isolation common to all mining communities, led to a measure of isolation, even social ostracism. One authority described Scottish miners as "a separate and avoided tribe." In parts of Fife during the eighteenth century, colliers could not be buried in consecrated ground. These black and grimy men seem to have been associated in the popular mind with the devil. Surely it was not difficult for such men to see parallels between their own situation and that of David Spens. At any rate, the miners and salters raised a large sum of money for Spens's legal defense.[49]

In towns, particularly where blacks posed little economic threat to lower-class whites, close and quite friendly ties between the two groups could develop. Nowhere in the empire was this more true than in London. This is not to say that there were no signs of resentment expressed by white laborers toward blacks. Ignatius Sancho referred to himself as "one of those people whom the vulgar and illiberal call 'Negurs,' " and experienced a measure of public abuse and harassment when out and about the city's streets. Yet many poor whites and blacks shared a cultural environment of poverty, which seems to have fostered cooperative feelings. In 1768, Sir John Fielding noted that the London mob made it difficult for slaveowners to retrieve their runaway black servants. In 1780, when two blacks fought a duel in the city, their seconds were two white footmen. Colonel John Hill's black servant Pompey was popular enough with fellow footmen to consider standing for speaker in their mock Parliament.[50]

Particularly noticeable in the seaports of the British Atlantic world and on shipboard was the lack of antagonism between white and black sailors. Olaudah Equiano referred repeatedly to his being on good terms with British and American seamen. In his novel about a seaman (*Mr. Penrose: The Journal of Penrose, Seaman*), William Williams, who sailed the seas and lived for some years in the Caribbean, has an "old Negro" teach his hero Penrose how to make fishing lines. In the Bahamas Penrose later "had frequent converse" with another "White headed old" Negro man, "who in his younger days had been well acquainted with many of the Buckneers, sail'd with

49. Edwards and Walvin, *Black Personalities*, 159–162; Alan B. Campbell, *The Lanarkshire Miners: A Social History of Their Trade Unions, 1775–1974* (Edinburgh, 1979), 9–15; T. C. Smout, *A History of the Scottish People, 1560–1830* (London, 1969), 168–170; Rab Houston, "Coal, Class and Culture: Labour Relations in a Scottish Mining Community, 1650–1750," *Social History*, VIII (1983), 1–18 (esp. 3–4).

50. Fryer, *Staying Power*, 71–72; *Lloyd's Evening Post*, XLVI (1780), 194; and Jonathan Swift, *Journal to Stella* (London, 1901), 76–77, as quoted in Shyllon, *Black People*, 102.

them, and knew many of their haunts, but had come in by the Queens Act of Grace and then followed Piloting or went out to hunt after wrecks about the coast." In Norfolk, Virginia, in 1771, Tom, a Bermudian-born slave who "went to Sea from that Island when a Boy," was encouraged by "some People" (fellow sailors perhaps) to "lay Claim to his Freedom." One basis for his claim, his master explained, was that in "*Bermuda* Owners of Vessels generally man them with their Slaves, and it is very customary, in War Time, to procure Passes for them as Freemen, in Case they should be taken by the Enemy." Working alongside whites, with papers documenting their freedom, slave sailors not surprisingly thought of themselves as on a par with their white counterparts. Some white sailors protested at this presumption: in 1722, several white seamen petitioned the Antiguan legislature to forbid slaves from working as mariners. But hostility appears not to have been either long-standing or universal. A visitor to Jamaica in the early nineteenth century, for instance, noted that white sailors and black slaves "are ever on the most amicable terms." He spoke of their "mutual confidence and familiarity." In "the presence of the sailor," he proclaimed, "the Negro feels as a man." Similarly, Bryan Edwards related an incident at Old Harbour, where a runaway, hunted by maroons, was defended by a party of sailors. Back in England, white prisoners in a Liverpool jail prevented the removal of black sailors wrongfully detained by their captain.[51]

In the slaveowning societies of the New World, indentured white servants often saw affinities between themselves and slaves. The most dramatic and well known example of cooperation between the two groups is the involvement of about one in ten of Virginia's slaves alongside white servants in Bacon's Rebellion. One of the last rebel groups to surrender was a mixed band of eighty blacks and twenty white servants. Less striking but no less revealing is the action of a Chesapeake servant who fought alongside a slave

51. Edwards, ed., *Life of Equiano*, I, 95, 98–100, 111, 123, 135–136, 138–139, 151, 171–173, 178–179, 184–185, 217, 252; William Williams, *Mr. Penrose: The Journal of Penrose, Seaman*, ed. David Howard Dickason (Bloomington, Ind., 1969), 74, 79; Archibald Campbell, Purdie and Dixon's *Va. Gaz.*, Sept. 17, 1771; another Bermudian sailor claiming to be free was put in the Camden jail (John Hutchins, *South-Carolina and American General Gazette* [Charleston], July 9, 1778); David Barry Gaspar, "A Dangerous Spirit of Liberty: Slave Rebellion in the West Indies during the 1730s," *Cimarrons*, I (1981), 91n; James Kelly, *Voyage to Jamaica . . .* (Belfast, 1838), 29–30; and Bryan Edwards, Add. MSS 12413, BM, as quoted in Brathwaite, *Development of Creole Society*, 301; Shyllon, *Black People*, 102. Significantly, other than the Antiguan seamen, one of the few whites to object to the black presence was a West Indian governor who thought "that the Number of Negroe slaves employed in navigating the Trading Vessels in these seas (particularly from Bermuda) . . . increase so much as to require the attention of the British legislature, as it throws English seamen out of employment" (quoted in Ruth A. Fisher, "Manuscript Materials Bearing on the Negro in British Archives," *Journal of Negro History*, XXVII [1942], 88).

in 1680 when two yeoman whites had begun a quarrel by saying "they were not company for Negroes." Evidence from the slaveowning societies of the British Caribbean also points to the close familiarity and occasional solidarity of servants and slaves. If this were not the case, why would the Montserrat assembly pass an act in 1670 against servants' "Runing away with theire combination with Slaves," or the Antiguan legislature in 1677 recognize that runaway servants often encouraged or forced slaves to leave with them, or the Nevis legislature in 1675 forbid servants and slaves to "company" or drink together?[52]

Irish servants were particularly feared as potential allies of black slaves. In Bermuda in 1661 a conspiracy came to light that was planned jointly by blacks and Irish servants. In early Barbados, the first recorded instance of a maroon group (in 1655) was a multiracial coalition of Irish servants and slaves, numbering about thirty. Indeed, in that year, Barbadian planters complained that their Irish servants were "a profligate race who were in the habit of joining themselves to runaway slaves." Thirty-one years later, rumors circulated in Barbados of a "rising designed by the Negroes" in "combination with the Irish servants . . . to destroy all masters and mistresses." Eighteen Irish servants were arrested but then released for want of sufficient evidence. The 1692 slave conspiracy marked the last time in Barbados that black slaves and Irish servants were suspected of plotting a rebellion. Significantly, in this case, most of the leaders of the conspiracy were creoles, extremely conversant with white ways. They aimed to secure arms from the magazine in Bridgetown and planned to enlist "four or five Irish men" who were to go into the fort, get the guards drunk, and then admit the armed slaves.[53]

52. T. H. Breen, "A Changing Labor Force and Race Relations in Virginia, 1660–1710," in T. H. Breen, *Puritans and Adventurers: Change and Persistence in Early America* (New York, 1980), 127–147 (esp. 137–139); E. Morgan, *American Slavery, American Freedom*, 269; Stephen Saunders Webb, *1676: The End of American Independence* (New York, 1984), 6–7, 16, 66, 110–111, 121–122, 141; Breen and Innes, *"Myne Owne Ground,"* esp. 5–6, 29–30, 80, 98–99, 104–107; Deal, "Race and Class in Colonial Virginia," esp. 401; York County Deeds, Orders, Wills, no. 6, 362, Virginia State Library, Richmond; Gaspar, "Runaways in Seventeenth-Century Antigua," *Boletin de estudios*, XXVI (1979), 5n.; C.S.S. Higham, *The Development of the Leeward Islands under the Restoration, 1660–1688: A Study of the Foundations of the Old Colonial System* (Cambridge, 1921), 175.

53. Smith, *Slavery in Bermuda*, 53–54 (see also 28–29, 48); Packwood, *Chained on the Rock*, 169; Handler, "Slave Revolts and Conspiracies," *Nieuwe West-Indische Gids*, XXXVI (1982), 9, 20–21, 26–27. See also Hilary McD. Beckles, *White Servitude and Black Slavery in Barbados, 1627–1715* (Knoxville, Tenn., 1989), esp. 115–139. For advertisements mentioning Irish men or women, usually servants, and black slaves running away together, see Thomas Bray, Park's *Va. Gaz.*, Feb. 9, 1739; John Chiswell, Hunter's *Va. Gaz.*, Oct. 17, 1751; Anthony Martin, Purdie and Dixon's *Va. Gaz.*, Feb. 7, 1771; George Matthews, Purdie and Dixon's *Va. Gaz.*, June 27, 1771;

This apparent willingness to cooperate does not mean, as one historian has noted, that white laborers regarded blacks as their equals. It does indicate, however, the extent to which racial differences could be overlooked by whites who were exploited almost as ruthlessly as blacks. Indeed, if some West Indian contemporaries are to be believed, slaves were actually better off than servants in the seventeenth century. Certainly the living conditions each group suffered were similar enough to make them believe they were sharing the same predicament. Irishmen, in particular, were viewed with almost as much contempt as Africans. Epithets such as "a bloody people," "perfidious," "wicked," "good for nothing but mischief," and "very Idle," which were bandied about in reference to Irishmen, could just as easily have been applied to slaves. Nor were Scotsmen always uniformly favored. A most extraordinary instance to the contrary appears in a Barbadian newspaper advertisement of 1805. It offered for sale "a European white man," who had been mistaken for a "mulatto of very fair complexion," but who was later identified as being from a poor part of Scotland. The advertiser continued, "It is repugnant to the feeling of his owner that a white man in this island shall be a slave; and . . . will [therefore] part with the said man at half the price given for him, to a person who will put him to no meanly office and treat him with lenity."[54]

No matter how poor whites and blacks viewed one another, their fraternization led to cultural exchanges. In the seventeenth-century British Caribbean, Carl and Roberta Bridenbaugh claim, Irishmen were so numerous and so closely associated with slaves that they bequeathed a pronounced brogue to the slaves' pronunciation. Later in the eighteenth century, when Scotsmen came in large numbers to Jamaica, the creole slaves and free people of color were said to have been heavily influenced by Scottish fiddles, reels, and other dances. Perhaps the Virginia jig, which contemporaries acknowledged owed much to the slaves, was also a fusion of Scottish and African influences. A

Sampson Mathews, *Virginia Gazette; or, The American Advertiser* (Richmond), June 26, 1784; *South-Carolina Gazette* (Charleston), Mar. 22, 1735; Thomas Fuller, *South-Carolina Gazette; And Country Journal*, Aug. 18, 1767.

54. Breen, "Changing Labor Force," in Breen, *Puritans and Adventurers*, 133; Carl Bridenbaugh and Roberta Bridenbaugh, *No Peace beyond the Line: The English in the Caribbean, 1624–1690* (New York, 1972), 106, 300, 302–303. Aversion to the Irish is discussed *ibid.*, 15, 17; Smith, *Slavery in Bermuda*, 28; Higham, *Development of the Leeward Islands*, 169–170; Vincent T. Harlow, *A History of Barbados, 1625–1685* (Oxford, 1926), 308–309; Jill Sheppard, *The "Redlegs" of Barbados: Their Origins and History* (Millwood, N.Y., 1977), 23, 35; *The Impartial Expositor* (Bridgetown, Barbados), June 19, 1805, as quoted in Higman, *Slave Populations*, 156–157. In 1690, the Council of Barbados declared that it wanted no "Irish Rebels . . . for we want not labourers of that Colour to work for us." Presumably, "Colour" can be translated as "stripe," but one wonders.

cultural transfer in the opposite direction stemmed from the way in which West Indian slave mothers carried their children across the hip instead of cradling them in their arms. George Pinckard observed that the "lower class of white women in Barbados have adopted this custom, from the example of the negroes, among whom it seems to be the universal mode of nursing."[55]

The same process that Edmund Morgan has outlined for late-seventeenth-century Virginia—one where cooperation between lower-class whites and blacks began to dissolve—occurred throughout Anglo-America. The same explanations adduced by Morgan adhere elsewhere too. Most elementary, of course, servant numbers declined as black numbers increased. A greater distance between the two groups inevitably arose as the disparity in numbers grew and as more and more black newcomers arrived directly from Africa, unable to speak English and utterly alien in appearance. Finally, ruling establishments everywhere did all they could to foster the contempt of poor whites for blacks. The laws Virginians passed to discriminate in favor of poor whites and against blacks were already on the Bermudian statute books; as early as 1644, the Antiguan legislature had composed a law designed to prevent interracial sex, which stipulated fines for any freeman or freewoman who fornicated with a black and extended the indenture when the culprit was a servant. In the 1670s, Barbadian planters began removing white female servants from their fields. In 1696, it became lawful in Montserrat to shoot at any black who stole from the provision grounds of poor whites. The antipathies fostered between poor whites and blacks were not solely the prerogative of a white skin. As early as the 1660s, the poor whites of Barbados were being "derided by the Negroes and branded with the epithet of white slaves." Slaves coined the term "Po' white buckra" or "walking buckra."[56]

55. Bridenbaugh and Bridenbaugh, *No Peace beyond the Line*, 17, 352; John R. Rickford, "The Insights of the Mesolect," in David DeCamp and Ian F. Hancock, eds., *Pidgins and Creoles: Current Trends and Prospects* (Washington, D.C., 1974), 106–110; and John R. Rickford, "Social Contact and Linguistic Diffusion: Hiberno-English and New World Black English," *Language*, LXII (1986), 245–289; Patterson, *Sociology of Slavery*, 45–46, 236, 238, 240–241; Richard B. Sheridan, "The Role of the Scots in the Economy and Society of the West Indies," in Vera Rubin and Arthur Tuden, eds., *Comparative Perspectives on Slavery in New World Plantation Societies*, New York Academy of Sciences, *Annals*, CCXCII (New York, 1977), 94–106; Rhys Isaac, *The Transformation of Virginia, 1740–1790* (Chapel Hill, N.C., 1982), 84–87; George Pinckard, *Notes on the West Indies . . .*, 3 vols. (London, 1806), I, 215.

56. E. Morgan, *American Slavery, American Freedom*, 311–315, 330–337 (see also Breen, "Changing Labor Force," in Breen, *Puritans and Adventurers*, 127–147); Smith, *Slavery in Bermuda*, 52–54; Packwood, *Chained on the Rock*, 85, 119, 122; Dunn, *Sugar and Slaves*, 228, 242; Bridenbaugh and Bridenbaugh, *No Peace beyond the Line*, 118; Howard A. Fergus, "The Early Laws of Montserrat (1668–1680): The Legal Schema of a Slave Society," *Caribbean Qtly.*, XXIV (1978), 39; Beckles, *White*

As slave societies solidified and as frontiers closed, the relationship between whites and blacks grew more fractured, more divided. Open hostility between poor whites and black slaves certainly became much more commonplace. This trend toward separation should not, however, obscure an equally important development—the emergence of regular channels of communication between whites and blacks, most particularly between masters and slaves. Encounters between owners and bondpeople became more routinized and predictable over time, a development encouraged by the increasing social differentiation among slaves. Just as white society was demarcated into planters, overseers, artisans, and the like, a whole series of gradations existed among slaves. The range of distinction between driver and field hand, for example, was as great as that between attorney and bookkeeper or between manager and overseer. Once elevated to a supervisory position, the slave entered into a qualitatively different relationship with his master, other whites, and his fellow slaves. Encounters between whites and blacks must therefore be differentiated according to a hierarchy within each group.

A fundamental, perhaps the most fundamental, distinction that emerged among slaves was between those born in Africa and those born in the New World. Natives or creoles were generally regarded as more tractable than Africans and certainly as better candidates for specialist tradesmen. Masters valued creoles more highly than Africans in property assessments by as much as 20–25 percent. In describing their creole slaves, masters also employed a battery of flattering adjectives, describing them as sensible, smart, sharp, shrewd, subtle, and the like. On the other hand, Africans were generally seen as "outlandish," "salt-water Negroes," or "Guinea birds," not least because of their ritual scars, filed teeth, and alien customs. They were often overtly rebellious. Many absconded within the first few months of their arrival in the New World. Both *grand marronage* (establishing maroon communities) and *petit marronage* (truancy, or individual or small group flight) were far more widespread when Africans constituted a large proportion of the slave population.

But these standard viewpoints and behaviors were often qualified by experience. Creoles frequently proved as troublesome as Africans, but in different ways. They rarely ran away in large groups or tried to form maroon settlements, as did Africans, but they absented themselves quite frequently, often to visit kin, or to go to towns, and remained at large for lengthy periods. Even without running away, many creoles proved extremely irksome to their masters, who soon began speaking of them in much more

Servitude and Black Slavery, 115–139. For the later history of poor white-black interaction in Barbados, see Sheppard, *"Redlegs,"* 44–49, 119–120. For a marvelous story concerning a slave and a poor white, see Rev. C. Jesse, "Du Tertre and Labat on 17th Century Slave Life in the French Antilles," *Caribbean Qtly.*, VII (1961), 151.

derogatory terms, as audacious, saucy, knavish, deceitful, and the like. Over time, creoles fomented far more dangerous rebellions than their African predecessors, as those of Barbados in 1816, Demerara in 1823, and Jamaica in 1831–1832 reveal. In 1792, a Jamaican absentee reflected on the change: "I remember the great rebellions in Jamaica projected and supported by Guinea negroes alone. Creoles were *then* content with their situation."[57]

Conversely, the extent to which masters and their representatives often struck up intimate relations with supposedly recalcitrant Africans should not be underestimated. A small minority of talented Africans—people like Equiano—impressed whites. In seventeenth-century Barbados Richard Ligon sang the praises of Macow, a "very valiant man" and skilled musician, and Sambo, an "ingenious, . . . honest, and . . . good a natur'd poor soul." In early eighteenth-century Maryland, when the master of Ayuba Suleiman Ibrahima, otherwise known as Job Ben Solomon, found out that his African was a "Mahometan," knew Arabic, and was no "common slave," he "was much kinder to him than before; allowing him a place to pray in." In early nineteenth-century Georgia, Belali Mahomet and Salih Belali, both Moslems who knew Arabic, became respected drivers. In early nineteenth-century Trinidad, Jonas Mohammed Bath, a Susu Moslem priest, was put in charge of a gang constructing Fort George because he was "discovered to be a person of eminence in his own Country," and Mohammedu Sisei, a Mandingo from Gambia, who knew the Koran well and wrote Mandingo in Arabic, enlisted alongside many other Africans in a British West India regiment.[58]

But African field hands could also impress whites. In the early eighteenth century Hans Sloane admired the cleanliness of Africans, who bathed far more frequently than Europeans, and respected African parents, who had "so great a love" for their children that no Jamaican master "dare sell or give away one of their little ones, unless they care not whether their Parents hang themselves or no." A century later a Demerara planter believed that "Africans are physically a strong race of men, and it is frequently found that

57. Almost all studies of New World slavery examine the different relations that whites had with Africans and creoles, but see, in particular, Patterson, *Sociology of Slavery*; Brathwaite, *Development of Creole Society*; Gerald W. Mullin, *Flight and Rebellion: Slave Resistance in Eighteenth-Century Virginia* (New York, 1972); Kulikoff, *Tobacco and Slaves*; Craton, *Testing the Chains*; Ward, *British West Indian Slavery* (quote on 218); and Gaspar, *Bondmen and Rebels*.

58. Ligon, *A True and Exact History*, 47–50; Philip D. Curtin, "Ayuba Suleiman Diallo of Bondu," in Curtin, ed., *Africa Remembered*, 42–43; Ivor Wilks, "Salih Bilali of Massina," *ibid*., 145–151; Allan D. Austin, ed., *African Muslims in Antebellum America: A Sourcebook* (New York, 1984); Carl Campbell, "Mohammedu Sisei of Gambia and Trinidad, c. 1788–1838," *Bulletin of the African Studies Association of the West Indies*, VII (1974), 29–38; Campbell, "John Mohammed Bath and the Free Mandingos in Trinidad: The Question of Their Repatriation to Africa 1831–1838," *Jour. Af. Stud.*, II (1975–1976), 467–495.

imported Africans, in certain descriptions of labour, will perform more than Creoles." Richard Dunn's detailed research into laboring patterns on a Jamaican sugar estate supports such a view. Furthermore, masters came to value certain ethnic groups. In the West Indies, Coromantines were thought to be especially hardy and resourceful. Christopher Codrington of Barbados considered them "not only the best and most faithful" slaves, but "really all born Heroes." His father had observed that "Noe man deserved a Corramante that would not treat him like a Friend rather than a Slave." It has been generally assumed that Caribbean whites preferred creole women as sexual partners, but the first detailed window into the sexual proclivities of a humble white Jamaican reveals that he had a particular eye for Africans.[59]

Another clear division among slaves occurred when masters elevated one or more of their bondpeople to a supervisory position. The person with the most authority and greatest responsibility among slaves—at least in the workplace—was the driver, foreman, or ranger. A slave driver could become the virtual manager of a plantation, and his opinion held great sway. In paying an order for corn, one South Carolina master informed his furnishing merchant that his "driver insists upon it that there is a mistake of no less than 550 bushels in the last year's account." The owner was inclined to think there was a mistake, but had kept no record himself; the driver, however, specified the size of the errors in two specific shipments more than a year apart. Either he kept his own accounts, or his memory was so well attuned to his master's interest that he could recall grain deliveries some fifteen months previous. In Jamaica the white manager was said to perform "his duties through the negro headmen, who know the routine of the business a great deal better than he does." Drivers received many favors not shared by other slaves.[60]

At the apex of slave society, drivers were truly men-in-between, whose allegiances were always equivocal. Some drivers, at certain points, could be the most loyal of slaves. When, in 1831–1832, a massive slave rebellion erupted in western Jamaica, Samuel Williams, a thirty-four-year-old driver who had spent all his life on Mesopotamia estate, helped dissuade his slave gang from joining the rebels. At the behest of Williams and others, the

59. Hans Sloane, *A Voyage to the Islands Madera, Barbados, Nieves, St. Christopher, and Jamaica . . .*, I (London, 1707), liv and lvii; Higman, *Slave Populations*, 197–198; Craton, *Searching for the Invisible Man*, 407. During Thomas Thistlewood's first year in Jamaica, he had 13 sexual partners, 10 of whom were Africans. See also Hall, *In Miserable Slavery*, 89, 221, 283. Plantation records that show whites' having children with light-complexioned women may not tell the whole story.

60. Thomas Pinckney to ?, Mar. 1792, Thomas Pinckney Papers, University of South Carolina, Columbia; Higman, *Slave Populations*, 170. See also Patterson, *Sociology of Slavery*, 62–64.

Mesopotamia slaves even seized rebel agents when the latter ventured onto the plantation and actually started up the sugar mill voluntarily during the absence of the entire white managerial staff. On another Barham estate, the Island, the head driver received a watch for risking his life to stop the rebels from firing the sugar works. At the same time, however, drivers led many of the slave revolts and conspiracies that occurred throughout eighteenth- and early nineteenth-century British America. Indeed, most of the leaders of the great Jamaican rebellion were "head people." John Baillie reported that one of the leaders on his estate was worth many hundreds of pounds, owned cattle, and had been his head driver. No fewer than twenty-seven of the eighty-eight slaves executed for their part in the Antiguan slave conspiracy of 1736 were drivers. Most of the leaders of the Tobago slave conspiracy of 1801 were drivers, such as Roger of Belvedere, described as "a remarkable active and intelligent Creole," and other "principal people," who "were not only in possession of the Comforts, but even the Luxuries of Life." Perhaps the most telling example comes from Demerara, as narrated by Michael Craton. Converted to Christianity, Telemachus, a driver, refused to continue punishing his hands. After much coercion, his master finally relegated his trusted leader to the fields. When the great rebellion broke out in 1823, Telemachus was one of the rebel leaders.[61]

At the bottom of the plantation hierarchy were slave women. In general, planters, particularly those in the Caribbean, preferred to stock their labor gangs with physically strong male laborers. But, because men were almost exclusively put to skilled trades and because women proved the tougher of the two, women gradually came to dominate field gangs, most particularly on sugar plantations. Strenuous, backbreaking labor was the lot of most women on New World slave plantations. If Mesopotamia in Jamaica was typical, women were more sickly than men, even though they demonstrated greater powers of endurance. Female field hands may have interacted with masters differently than their male counterparts. On the basis of the King plantations in Grenada, British Guiana, and Dominica, one historian has argued that women were far more often accused of insolence, quarreling, and "disorderly conduct" than men. Some women faked pregnancies to avoid labor. On the other hand, far fewer women ran away than men. In all the runaway slave populations so far studied, the ratio of men to women ranged from a low of two to one to a high of ten to one. Sedentary, conten-

61. Dunn, "'Dreadful Idlers' in the Cane Fields," in Solow and Engerman, eds., *British Capitalism and Caribbean Slavery*, 189–190; Higman, *Slave Population and Economy*, 227–228; Gaspar, *Bondmen and Rebels*, 30–35; K. O. Laurence, "The Tobago Slave Conspiracy of 1801," *Caribbean Qtly.*, XXVIII (1982), 1–9 (quote on 5); Craton, *Testing the Chains*, 55, 122, 278–279. See also H. McD. Beckles, "Emancipation by Law or War? Wilberforce and the 1816 Barbados Slave Rebellion," in David Richardson, ed., *Abolition and Its Aftermath: The Historical Context, 1790–1916* (London, 1985), 80–104 (esp. 89).

tious, and resilient slave women played vital roles in fashioning black culture and guiding cultural exchanges with whites.[62]

IV

Encounters between blacks and whites were not just meetings of people differentiated by status; they were collisions of cultures that occurred in a variety of arenas—linguistic, musical, economic, even attitudinal, to name just a few. Naturally, European values and institutions held the upper hand. White rulers had the highest status and their culture the greatest prestige. Africans were the ones who had to make the most severe cultural accommodations. Nevertheless, the more heavily black a society, the more reliant it was on slaves for its economic well-being, and the greater the likelihood that blacks would influence whites. Societies like Jamaica or Barbados, which attempted to keep blacks at arm's length, were precisely the ones most profoundly shaped by the overwhelming black presence. Even where blacks were a distinct minority, there were some realms of cross-cultural contact—most notably music and dance—where blacks exerted considerable influence.

Central to cross-cultural exchange is linguistic communication. Between whites and blacks the range was enormous. On the African coast, British residents often learned African languages, though in time many African cultural brokers emerged who spoke an English-based creole, perhaps even Standard English. In the interior of Jamaica in the eighteenth century, the Trelawny maroons, while employing English, also held to a form of their Akan language, making use of their own linguistic brokers. The Black Caribs of Saint Vincent spoke Arawakan and used interpreters. In certain plantation regions, one might hear a variety of African languages, various forms of

62. Higman, *Slave Populations*, 189 (see also Lois Green Carr and Lorena S. Walsh, "Economic Diversification and Labor Organization in the Chesapeake, 1650–1820," in Stephen Innes, ed., *Work and Labor in Early America* [Chapel Hill, N.C., 1988], 176–183); Dunn, "A Tale of Two Plantations," *WMQ*, 3d Ser., XXXIV (1977), 45; Dunn, "'Dreadful Idlers' in the Cane Fields," in Solow and Engerman, eds., *British Capitalism and Caribbean Slavery*, 179–181; Richard S. Dunn, "Sugar Production and Slave Women in Jamaica," in Ira Berlin and Philip D. Morgan, eds., *Cultivation and Culture: Labor and the Shaping of Slave Life in the Americas* (forthcoming); Lucille Mathurin Mair, *Women Field Workers in Jamaica during Slavery*, Elsa Goveia Memorial Lecture (Mona, Jamaica, 1987), 7–8; Barbara Bush, "Towards Emancipation: Slave Women and Resistance to Coercive Labour Regimes in the British West Indian Colonies, 1790–1838," *Slavery and Abolition*, V (1984), 228–229; Michael Mullin, "Women and the Comparative Study of American Negro Slavery," *Slavery and Abolition*, VI (1985), 25–40; Betty Wood, "Some Aspects of Female Resistance to Chattel Slavery in Low Country Georgia, 1763–1815," *Historical Journal*, XXX (1987), 603–622; Philip D. Morgan and Michael L. Nicholls, "Eighteenth-Century Virginia Runaway Slaves in New World Perspective" (MS).

pidgin as well as creole languages, the last being spoken by some whites. In the towns, among some privileged rural slaves (particularly domestics), and in slaveowning societies, most blacks probably spoke a language undergoing rapid decreolization, and some no doubt spoke Standard English.[63]

The norm, however, seems to have been that most blacks in early Anglo-America spoke a creole language, which derived much of its vocabulary from English, but the phonology and syntax of which owed much to a prior West African creole or pidgin and, beyond that, to various African languages. In other words, Africans grafted a European vocabulary onto West African grammatical structures that had much in common. In heavily black societies like Jamaica, Maria Nugent's observation that "the Creole language [was] not confined to the Negroes" is surely apt. As an example of the "broken English," the "indolent drawling out of their words" spoken by Jamaican whites, particularly the women, she mentioned standing next to a lady one night and remarking that the air was much cooler than usual. The reply was pure creole: " 'Yes, ma-am, him rail-ly too fra-ish.' " J. B. Moreton also reported the speech of creole white women: "Tank you sir, *wid* all my *haut* [heart]" or "Do, momma, get me some mauby [mobby, a drink], *mine* head no *'tand* good." Jamaican creole was, then, profoundly influenced by various African languages, most powerfully in pronunciation and grammar, but also in vocabulary. Everyday words, like bush knife (*afini*), basket (*banka*), pot (*yabba*), poke (*juke*), and eat (*nyam*) can be traced to specific African languages, most particularly Twi.[64]

On the mainland and on an island like Barbados (where whites were relatively numerous), the bilingual proficiency of whites and the African influence on the creole language were much reduced. However, they should not be underestimated. In the middle of the eighteenth century, a British

63. Ian Hancock, "The Domestic Hypothesis, Diffusion, and Componentiality: An Account of Atlantic Anglophone Creole Origins," in Pieter Muysken and Norval Smith, eds., *Substrata versus Universals in Creole Genesis: Papers from the Amsterdam Creole Workshop, April 1985* (Amsterdam, 1986), 71–102; David Dalby, "Ashanti Survivals in the Language and Traditions of the Windward Maroons of Jamaica," *African Language Studies*, XII (1971), 31–51; Dell Hymes, ed., *Pidginization and Creolization of Languages* (Cambridge, 1971); a number of essays by William A. Stewart, e.g., "Continuity and Change in American Negro Dialects," in Robert H. Bentley and Samuel D. Crawford, comps., *Black Language Reader* (Glenview, Ill., 1973), 55–69; Albert Valdman, ed., *Pidgin and Creole Linguistics* (Bloomington, Ind., 1977); Albert Valdman and Arnold Highfield, eds., *Theoretical Orientations in Creole Studies* (New York, 1980); Mervyn C. Alleyne, "A Linguistic Perspective on the Caribbean," in Sidney W. Mintz and Sally Price, eds., *Caribbean Contours* (Baltimore, 1985), 155–179.

64. Frank Cundall, ed., *Lady Nugent's Journal . . .* (London, 1907), 132; J. B. Moreton, *Manners and Customs in the West India Islands* (London, 1790), 116, 131; Frederic G. Cassidy, *Jamaica Talk: Three Hundred Years of the English Language in Jamaica* (London, 1961), 22, 31–32, 34, 81, 85, 146, 152, 394.

traveler to the mainland colonies criticized planters in "regard to their Children . . . [for] when young they suffer them too much to prowl amongst the young Negroes, which insensibly causes them to imbibe their Manners and broken Speech." Even on the early nineteenth-century frontier (in this case, Kentucky), a traveler could meet a German immigrant "who had lived long enough in Virginia to pick up some Negro-English." A visitor to Barbados in the early nineteenth century observed that the distinctive island "manner of speaking" was not "confined to the people of colour; it occurs like wise among the whites, particularly those who have not visited Europe, nor resided for some time away from the island." Some African words were introduced into the speech of whites. In early eighteenth-century Virginia visitors noted that the inhabitants talked of "toting" a bag rather than carrying it. Unlike Jamaican creole, however, the direct loan-words were many fewer and generally were more specialized zoological, botanical, or culinary items, such as *cooter* (turtle) from Mandingo; *banana*, *yam*, and *benne* (sesame) from Mandingo and Wolof; *cola* from Temne; and *pindar* and *goober* (both meaning peanut) from Western Bantu languages. Moreover, in almost all the mainland territories and on an island like Barbados, the forces propelling rapid decreolization were powerful. As early as the 1660s, Barbados contained, in the words of one contemporary, "many thousands of slaves that speak English." By the late eighteenth century, most slaves in the Chesapeake region—the largest congregation of slaves on the mainland—probably spoke a nonstandard English dialect.[65]

Only South Carolina and, later, Georgia on the British American mainland seem to have produced a more African-influenced creole, one that

65. Quoted in Allen Walker Read, "British Recognition of American Speech in the Eighteenth Century," *Dialect Notes*, VI (1933), 329; Thomas Ashe, *Travels in America, Performed in the Year 1806 . . .* (London, 1808), 79; Pinckard, *Notes*, I, 294; David Dalby, "The African Element in Negro English," in Thomas Kochman, ed., *Rappin' and Stylin' Out: Communication in Urban Black America* (Urbana, Ill., 1972), 170–186; "Some Observations on the Island Barbadoes," 1667, C.O. 1/21, no. 170, P.R.O., as quoted in Handler and Pohlmann, "Slave Manumissions," *WMQ*, 3d Ser., XLI (1984), 405. See also J. L. Dillard, *Black English: Its History and Usage in the United States* (New York, 1972); John Holm, "African Features in White Bahamian English," *English World-Wide: A Journal of Varieties of English*, I (1980), 45–65. There is a dispute about the extent or even presence of a creole language in Barbados: see Ian F. Hancock, "Gullah and Barbadian—Origins and Relationships," *American Speech*, LV (1980), 17–35; Audrey Burrowes and R. Allsopp, "Barbadian Creole: Its Social History and Structure," in Lawrence D. Carrington *et al.*, eds., *Studies in Caribbean Language* (St. Augustine, Trinidad, 1983), 38–45; and Frederic G. Cassidy, "Barbadian Creole—Possibility and Probability," *Am. Speech*, LXI (1986), 195–205. For a possible description of a creole in Delaware in 1748, see John C. Van Horne, ed., *Religious Philanthropy and Colonial Slavery: The American Correspondence of the Associates of Dr. Bray, 1717–1777* (Urbana, Ill., 1985), 100; and for New York, see Shane White, "A Question of Style: Blacks in and around New York City in the Late 18th Century," *Journal of American Folklore*, CII (1989), 26.

whites more readily spoke. Ebenezer Hazard noted in the late eighteenth century that the "common country people talk very much like Negros." Even a Baptist minister, not particularly sympathetic to the nuances of black speech, must have studied the subject somewhat, for he debated whether to produce an instructional text in Standard English or in "the Negro stile." The creole origins of Gullah are now accepted by most linguists. Not only are a number of its words of African origin, but particular regional influences have been detected. Thus, of Gullah, one linguist has said, "We know of nowhere else in America [the New World] where the influence of Sierra Leone languages can still be traced, to anything like this extent." Actually, of the 251 African words in regular use among Gullah speakers in the 1940s, fully 40 percent were from the Angola region, outdistancing Senegambia and Sierra Leone, which together contributed 38 percent. Further, it has been recently argued that languages from southern Nigeria and the Gold Coast form the central syntactic core of Gullah.[66]

In addition to the deep likenesses of structure, whether syntactic or phonological, underlying Atlantic creole languages, they possess other common elements that owe a particular debt to Africa. The ubiquity of polite modes of address and of elaborate greetings had roots in African forms of etiquette. The artfulness of black speech was widely recognized. Bryan Edwards said of Jamaican slaves that they "convey much strong meaning in a narrow compass," and acknowledged his surprise at the "figurative expressions" and "pointed sentences" of which they were capable. As illustration, he related a story of a slave whose sleep was interrupted: before returning to his slumbers, the bondman exclaimed, "*Sleep hab no Massa*." In South Carolina, St. George Tucker witnessed the return of his brother, Tudor, to his Dorchester plantation, where one slave "expressed himself in a most energetical Metaphor—approaching his Master he accosted him in these words—Aw, Mawser, me hungry for see You!" Tucker was amused at the "droll Idiom he had introduced in our language." In fact, black speech was peppered with proverbs, which were a highly prestigious form of speech in many African

66. H. Roy Merrens, "A View of Coastal South Carolina in 1778: The Journal of Ebenezer Hazard," *SCHM*, LXXIII (1972), 192; Edmund Botsford to Dr. Richard Furman, Oct. 15, 1808, Botsford Papers, Baptist Historical Collection, Furman University, Greenville, S.C.; P.E.H. Hair, "Sierra Leone Items in the Gullah Dialect of American English," *African Language Review*, IV (1965), 79–84; Frederic G. Cassidy, "The Place of Gullah," *Am. Speech*, LV (1980), 3–16; Cassidy, "Sources of the African Element in Gullah," in Carrington *et al.*, eds., *Studies in Caribbean Language*, 75–81. The pioneering work was Lorenzo Dow Turner, *Africanisms in the Gullah Dialect* (Chicago, 1949). See also Frederic G. Cassidy, "Some Similarities between Gullah and Caribbean Creoles," in Michael B. Montgomery and Guy Bailey, eds., *Language Variety in the South: Perspectives in Black and White* (University, Ala., 1986), 30–37; and John Holm, "On the Relationship of Gullah and Bahamian," *Am. Speech*, LVIII (1983), 303–318.

languages. The verbal dexterity of Caribbean and North American blacks, evident in their rapping, rhyming, and playing the dozens (verbal contests, usually insulting), suggest another continuity. Many African exclamations and interjections infiltrated various Atlantic creoles. The word *ki*, or *kie*, an expression of surprise, is a classic example that has been reported in slave speech from places as remote as Demerara and South Carolina. But, significantly perhaps, the most ubiquitous word was *buckra*, from the Efik *mbakara* ("he who surrounds or governs"); it appeared in the speech of every black linguistic community in the eighteenth-century Anglo-American world. It became, of course, synonymous with "white man."[67]

In much the same way as a broad spectrum of linguistic forms existed among blacks brought into contact with the British, stretching from Standard English to, say, Twi, a continuous scale of musical expression, ranging in inspiration from Europe to Africa, also unfolded. At one extreme stood George Augustus Polgreen Bridgetower, the virtuoso violinist for whom Beethoven composed the *Kreutzer* Sonata. Brought to England from the European continent by his African father, the ten-year-old gave recitals in the salons of Brighton, Bath, and London. Of lesser renown, but just as popular, were those blacks who became integral members of European military bands. Some black musicians became street players: Billy Waters, for example, a one-legged, black ex-navy man, claimed to earn "an honest living by the scraping of cat-gut" on London streets. At the other extreme were the slaves at Vineyard livestock pen in Jamaica, who in 1751 made music for their overseer. He marveled at their "tip-top performances," particularly those by slaves who "danced congo," sang, and drummed. Two decades later, Olaudah Equiano wandered out to Spring Path, just outside Kingston,

67. Edwards, *History, Civil and Commercial*, II, 101; St. George Tucker's Journal to Charlestown, Apr. 14, 1777, Tucker-Coleman Papers, typescript, Colonial Williamsburg Foundation, Williamsburg, Va. On proverbs, see Ruth Finnegan, *Oral Literature in Africa* (Oxford, 1970); and Joyce Penfield, *Communicating with Quotes: The Igbo Case*, Contributions in Intercultural and Comparative Studies, no. 8 (Westport, Conn., 1983). The best study of Afro-American eloquence is Roger D. Abrahams, *The Man-of-Words in the West Indies: Performance and the Emergence of Creole Culture* (Baltimore, 1983). For examples of *ki*, see William Moultrie, *Memoirs of the American Revolution, So Far as It Related to the States of North and South Carolina, and Georgia* (New York, 1802), II, 356; Patricia Jones-Jackson, *When Roots Die: Endangered Traditions on the Sea Islands* (Athens, Ga., 1987), 44; Henry Bolingbroke, *A Voyage to Demerary, Account of the Settlements There, and of Those on the Essequibo and Berbice, 1799–1806* (London, 1807), 96, 105; F. G. Cassidy and R. B. Le Page, eds., *Dictionary of Jamaican English*, 2d ed. (Cambridge, 1980), 259. Incidentally, this word does not seem to have formed the basis for that ubiquitous Americanism, *O.K.*, as has been claimed; see Frederic G. Cassidy, "OK—Is It African?," *Am. Speech*, LVI (1981), 269–273. The best study of the similarities among Atlantic creole languages is Mervyn C. Alleyne, *Comparative Afro-American: An Historical-Comparative Study of English-based Afro-American Dialects of the New World* (Ann Arbor, Mich., 1980).

and saw "each different nation of Africa meet and dance after the manner of their own country." A range of African-style instruments has been documented in the eighteenth-century British Caribbean.[68]

At most of these musical levels, there was considerable cultural borrowing by whites from blacks. Among the military bands, the association of blacks with percussive instruments—cymbals, tambourines, triangles, and, most particularly, drums—introduced new sounds into British military music. White Londoners began dancing to black dance music, not in the twentieth, but in the late eighteenth century, when the "black hops" became the latest craze. Many popular sea chanteys bore striking resemblances to Caribbean slave songs. In the plantation world, the penetration of black musical forms was even more extensive. In eighteenth-century Jamaica, an observer of white dances noted the "deafening noise of the drums, which the negro musicians think indispensable, and which the dancers strangely continue to tolerate." Eighteenth-century Virginians danced "everlasting jigs" to "some Negro tune" and to the accompaniment of both banjos and fiddles, symbolizing cultural fusion.[69]

Afro-American music developed in ways akin to the formation of creole languages. A basic musical grammar, as it were, with an emphasis on the importance of music and dance in everyday life and the role of rhythm and percussion in musical style, survived the middle passage. Even complex musical instruments made the crossing, although more notable is how slaves adapted traditional instruments, invented new ones, and borrowed Euramerican ones. These adaptations, inventions, and borrowings, however, were interpreted and reinterpreted according to deep-level aesthetic principles drawn from Africa. Blacks, in the Herskovitses' words, retained "the inner meanings of traditional modes of behavior while adopting new outer institutional forms." In musical terms, the key elements of the inner structure were complex rhythms, percussive qualities, syncopation, and antiphonal

68. Shyllon, *Black People*, 212–221; Edwards and Walvin, eds., *Black Personalities*, 163–167; Henry George Farmer, *Military Music* (London, 1950), 35–37; Thomas Thistlewood diary, July 6–8, 1750, Monson MSS, Lincoln County Record Office, England; Edwards, ed., *Life of Equiano*, II, 101. See also Jerome S. Handler and Charlotte J. Frisbie, "Aspects of Slave Life in Barbados: Music and its Cultural Context," *Caribbean Stud.*, XI (1972), 5–46; and Dena J. Epstein, *Sinful Tunes and Spirituals: Black Folk Music to the Civil War* (Urbana, Ill., 1977), esp. 3–62.

69. Roger D. Abrahams, *Deep the Water, Shallow the Shore: Three Essays on Shantying in the West Indies* (Austin, Tex., 1974); Fryer, *Staying Power*, 81; John Stewart, *A View of the Past and Present State of the Island of Jamaica . . .* (Edinburgh, 1823), 207; *The Journal of Nicholas Cresswell, 1774–1777* (New York, 1924), 30, 53; Isaac, *Transformation of Virginia*, 80–87; Mechal Sobel, *The World They Made Together: Black and White Values in Eighteenth-Century Virginia* (Princeton, N.J., 1987), 167.

patterns. These central features of black music in turn influenced white music.[70]

A more prosaic area of fertilization between whites and blacks occurred in the economic realm. Africans benefited from New World crops, most notably maize and cassava, which helped sustain their populations. Conversely, watermelons, okra, and groundnuts (the last not present in North America, though originally of South American origin) accompanied the slaves and became ubiquitous throughout Anglo-America. There were, however, pockets of deeper penetration, linked, not surprisingly, to areas of heavy black concentration. In the Caribbean, some of the most important domesticated plants introduced into the region—great millet, pearl millet, bananas, plantains, eddoes, the "Guinea" or "Negro" yam, and, of course, akee (which, together with saltfish, now forms Jamaica's national dish)—came from Africa. Even some of the most important weeds in the Caribbean are African in origin. Moreover, about 60 of the 160 species of medicinal plants in Jamaica are known to have been or continue to be used in Africa. Kola, or bissy, nut, for instance, which is used in Jamaica for stomach pains, was brought to the island from the Guinea coast. Quite how these plants were introduced and disseminated throughout the Caribbean is unclear. We know that Guinea grass was introduced into Jamaica in 1744 and that akees followed in 1778 via "a slave ship from the Coast of Africa." How much of a role slaves played in their dispersal is unknown.[71]

On the mainland, South Carolina was the one colony to reveal any comparable level of African crop infiltration, and apparently its slaves were instrumental in cultivating the new plants. In the third decade of the eighteenth century, Mark Catesby observed two African varieties of corn (millet) in the lowcountry, but only among the "Plantations of *Negroes*." When William Bartram visited the lowcountry in the 1770s, he noticed that the tania, or tannier (probably an eddo, a root found in the West Indies and tropical Africa), was "much cultivated and esteemed for food, particularly by the Negroes." Bernard Romans attributed the introduction of the

70. Melville J. Herskovits and Frances S. Herskovits, *Trinidad Village* (New York, 1947), vi. See also Kenneth M. Bilby, "The Caribbean as a Musical Region," in Mintz and Price, eds., *Caribbean Contours*, 181–218.

71. Peter J. Ucko and G. W. Dimbleby, eds., *The Domestication and Exploitation of Plants and Animals* (London, 1969); Jack R. Harlan *et al.*, eds., *Origins of African Plant Domestication* (The Hague, 1976); John H. Parry, "Plantation and Provision Ground: An Historical Sketch of the Introduction of Food Crops into Jamaica," *Revista de historia de America*, XXXIX (1955), 1–20; Sidney W. Mintz, "Reflections on Caribbean Peasantries," *Nieuwe West-Indische Gids*, LVII (1983), 8–9; Mintz, *From Plantations to Peasantries in the Caribbean*, Woodrow Wilson International Center for Scholars (Washington, D.C., 1984), 10; Sheridan, *Doctors and Slaves*, 95. See also Carl Sauer, *Agricultural Origins and Dispersals* (New York, 1952).

"sesamen of oily grain" to lowcountry slaves; they used it, he maintained, "as a food either raw, toasted or boiled in their soups and are very fond of it, they call it *Benni*." Sesame seed cakes are a specialty of the lowcountry to this day.[72]

Crop exchanges were part of a larger trade between whites and blacks. It may seem far-fetched to conceive of trade as an important area of contact between the two groups. Olaudah Equiano, hardly the typical slave, it will be recalled, might have had a keen eye for business and traded with whites throughout Anglo-America, but how could a population that was enslaved, legally propertyless, and largely powerless exchange anything? Yet, as Orlando Patterson has reminded us, in all slaveholding societies the slave was allowed a *peculiam*, that is, the ability "to possess and enjoy a given range of goods," and slaves were "frequently allowed to trade and engage in business" using their possessions.[73]

Perhaps the most extreme case of this phenomenon in the Anglo-American world involved the few hundred slaves who lived on eighteenth-century Barbuda, a sixty-square-mile island in the Leeward chain and a private preserve of the Codrington family. By the late eighteenth century, these few hundred slaves, supervised by only a few whites, enjoyed an abundance of provisions from their own gardens, from hunting game in the forest, and from fishing. In the early nineteenth century, the manager reported that individual provision grounds were as large as ten to eleven acres, "the produce of wch of course is their own Property." The slaves also owned "hundreds of Hogs and Goats . . . plenty of Turkeys, fowls, and Guinea-birds." They habitually sold much of their foodstuffs, firewood, fish, and livestock to passing ships or to neighboring Antiguans, using Codrington's own vessels. A parallel situation emerged on the Rolle estate in Great Exuma, part of the Bahamas, in the early nineteenth century. There, too, slaves gained their own extensive provision grounds, owned flocks of goats and sheep, and spent much of their time fishing. According to Michael Craton, "The transition from 'proto-peasant' to true peasant . . . was probably farther advanced in Exuma and similar Bahamian islands than anywhere else in the British colonies." If this was true, the model already existed in eighteenth-century Barbuda.[74]

72. Philip D. Morgan, "Work and Culture: The Task System and the World of Lowcountry Blacks, 1700 to 1880," *WMQ*, 3d Ser., XXXIX (1982), 573–574.

73. Orlando Patterson, *Slavery and Social Death: A Comparative Study* (Cambridge, Mass., 1982), 182–186.

74. David Lowenthal and Colin G. Clarke, "Slave-Breeding in Barbuda: The Past of a Negro Myth," in Rubin and Tuden, eds., *Comparative Perspectives*, 510–535 (esp. 512–516); Michael Craton, "Hobbesian or Panglossian? The Two Extremes of Slave Conditions in the British Caribbean, 1783 to 1834," *WMQ*, 3d Ser., XXXV (1978), 324–356 (esp. 354–355). For other work on Barbuda, see Riva Berleant-Schiller, "The Social and Economic Role of Cattle in Barbuda," *Geographical Re-*

In more typical Caribbean plantation regions, the slaves also managed to raise provisions and engage in trade, but sugar production left little time or, in some cases, land for the slaves' private enterprise. In the smaller sugar islands, like Barbados and Antigua, slaves were permitted only garden plots. In late-eighteenth-century Antigua, John Luffman observed that adult slaves were allocated patches of ground no more than "twenty five to thirty feet square." The slaves, however, cultivated these plots so intensively that, as Luffman noted, "their produce principally suppl[ied] the 'Sunday market' . . . with vegetables." By this means, Antiguan whites were "prevented from starving." Barbadian slaves also produced remarkably high yields from their plots, if one of the island's planters can be believed, for he claimed that many reaped "annually 1,000 lbs of yams each, besides Guinea and Indian corn, eddoes, potatoes, cassava, ginger, and the more industrious plant arrowroot, which they prepare and sell for a good price." George Pinckard, who visited Barbados around the turn of the eighteenth century, observed that the "markets of the island depend almost wholly upon" the slaves' "private stock."[75]

In the larger sugar islands, like Jamaica, the slaves' access to extensive provision ground in the backlands served as the basis for even more intensive marketing. By the late eighteenth century, if not earlier, slaves had become the most important suppliers of foodstuffs to all Jamaicans, and many of the island's minor exports—everything from gums to arrowroot, from oil nuts to goatskins—were produced on their grounds. Edward Long estimated that one-fifth of the currency circulating on the island was in slave hands. By the early nineteenth century, the provision ground method of feeding slaves had also been generally adopted in the Windward Islands—"second phase" British colonies, in Barry Higman's useful typology. As in Jamaica, a wooded, mountainous, or hilly interior encouraged the allocation of provision grounds. In Saint Vincent, for instance, "great tracts" of interior land were said to be "wholly devoted" to provision ground cultivation. Again, as in Jamaica, the produce of Windward Island grounds (and of the slave yards and yam plots) formed the basis for an expanding local market. Thus the Kingstown markets in Saint Vincent were said to be "almost exclusively supplied by [slaves] with pork, poultry, vegetables and fruit."[76]

---

view, LXVII (1977), 299–309; and Berleant-Schiller, "The Failure of Agricultural Development in Post-emancipation Barbuda: A Study of Social and Economic Continuity in a West Indian Community," *Boletin de estudios*, XXV (1978), 21–36; and on the Bahamas, see Gail Saunders, *Bahamian Loyalists and Their Slaves* (London, 1983), 21–27.

75. John Luffman, *A Brief Account of the Island of Antigua . . .* (London, 1788), 94–95; Joseph William Jordan, *An Account of the Management of Certain Estates in the Island of Barbados* (London, 1824), 3–4; Pinckard, *Notes*, I, 370.

76. Sidney W. Mintz and Douglas Hall, *The Origins of the Jamaican Internal Marketing System*, Yale University Publications in Anthropology, no. 57 (New Ha-

On the mainland, South Carolina slaves, working by task rather than by gang (thereby allowing the more industrious to earn time on a daily basis), were able to raise stock, tend crops, and exchange their relatively extensive produce with whites. The Sunday "Negro market" in Charleston was a more modest equivalent of those markets in Kingston, Bridgetown, and other British Caribbean towns. In the Chesapeake, on the other hand, the slaves had little time to work on their own account. Moreover, since Chesapeake planters accorded a much higher priority to foodstuffs production than did their lowcountry counterparts, Chesapeake slaves were much less encouraged to engage in part-time, private subsistence activities. Their trading opportunities were therefore much more severely circumscribed.[77]

Blacks and whites not only exchanged words, music, and crops; they also shaped their attitudes toward one another. The subject of racial attitudes is extraordinarily complex and has generated a richly provocative literature. At the risk of gross oversimplification, two lines of force frame prevailing interpretations of English attitudes toward blacks. One school emphasizes the fateful association of blackness with evil, danger, and filth in English culture (and other cultures, it might be added) and the acute sense of revulsion that English people displayed for all things African. In this reading, English racial preconceptions provide the key that unlocks the Pandora's box of black debasement and enslavement. The other school may concede that these hostile attitudes existed (though it usually downplays them by pointing to parallels in English attitudes toward the poor and other alien groups), but finds them insufficient to explain why blacks were singled out as slaves. Rather, prejudice is said to have arisen or hardened only when blacks were made into plantation laborers; this process occurred primarily for economic reasons and because Africans were both the most available and most vulnerable source of labor. As with many a historical controversy, the truth probably lies somewhere between the two interpretations. If ingenious attempts to extrude racial identification as important in enslavement are ultimately unpersuasive, the same applies to those who would abstract attitudes from their social context. Racial prejudice, however inchoate, does seem to have been sufficient to single out the African as a potential victim, but the question then remains of how this was done, and this in turn raises issues of power, class, and economic force. Prejudice often existed, but the historian

---

ven, Conn., 1960), 3–25; Woodville Marshall, "Provision Ground and Plantation Labour in Four Windward Islands: Competition for Resources during Slavery?" in Ira Berlin and Philip D. Morgan, eds., *The Slaves' Economy: Independent Production by Slaves in New World Plantation Societies* (forthcoming). Marshall questions the efficacy of the provision ground system, as does Sheridan (*Doctors and Slaves*, 164–169).

77. Philip D. Morgan, "Task and Gang Systems: The Organization of Labor on New World Plantations," in Innes, ed., *Work and Labor*, 189–220.

needs to ask what was made of it. How did it vary across space, within particular social groups as well as over time? Neither school has devoted enough attention to this subject.[78]

In metropolitan society, many educated Britons were probably familiar with at least some of the information to be gleaned from classical and Renaissance authors, much of it distorted and absurd, to be sure, about the societies of black Africa. Overlaid upon this foundation was the literature of geographical exploration. Perhaps Kenneth R. Andrews strains a little too hard when he claims that, for the most part, the Africans' appearance and ways of life were reported in neutral terms, but certainly horror and revulsion were not the overriding responses. Although the English pioneers "carried with them a strong sense of national loyalty and took a predictably ethnocentric view of alien cultures," the explorers were "not equipped with a definite set of ethnic stereotypes," and their approach to "non-Europeans was normally commercial and pragmatic." Much more influential than either of these two bodies of literature in shaping the personal responses of Britons to blacks were their contacts with them and the information that began filtering back from America. In both cases, of course, Englishmen came to know blacks in the context of slavery. If stereotypes about black inferiority became commonplace in British society, it is not so clear that extreme hostility represented any substantial body of opinion. There is even evidence to suggest that blacks were assimilated into the lower class as readily as white servants from the Continent. There were the famous Elizabethan deportation orders, it is true, but these were crisis measures, and other alien groups were equally harassed. Most interesting, when the problems of the Black Poor came to the fore in the late eighteenth century, another time of economic crisis, their fate met with little hostility and much sympathy.[79]

78. On the one side, beginning with the most subtle and magisterial treatment, are Jordan, *White over Black*; Carl N. Degler, "Slavery and the Genesis of American Race Prejudice," *Comparative Studies in Society and History*, XI (1959), 49–67; and, for other cultures, Bernard Lewis, *Race and Color in Islam* (New York, 1971). On the other side, beginning again with the most stimulating work, see E. Morgan, *American Slavery, American Freedom*; J. H. Plumb, *In the Light of History* (London, 1972); George M. Fredrickson, *The Arrogance of Race: Historical Perspectives on Slavery, Racism, and Social Inequality* (Middletown, Conn., 1988); Fredrickson, *White Supremacy*; and Breen and Innes, *"Myne Owne Ground."* For the most extreme statements in this latter genre, see Oscar Handlin and Mary F. Handlin, "Origins of the Southern Labor System," *WMQ*, 3d Ser., VII (1950), 199–222; and Barbara J. Fields, "Ideology and Race in American History," in J. Morgan Kousser and James M. McPherson, eds., *Region, Race, and Reconstruction: Essays in Honor of C. Vann Woodward* (New York, 1982), 143–177. For a penetrating critique of Morgan's book, see J. R. Pole, "Slavery and Revolution: The Conscience of the Rich," *Hist. Jour.*, XX (1977), 503–513.

79. Kenneth R. Andrews, *Trade, Plunder, and Settlement: Maritime Enterprise and the Genesis of the British Empire, 1480–1630* (Cambridge, 1984), 37, 101–115;

English weakness on the African coast inclined the visitors to be respectful. Rarely could the English overawe the natives; alliances and partnerships were the order of the day. As one English trader in the mid-eighteenth century put it, "We . . . always [side] with the great men of the country who defends in case of quarels or any disturbance." Certainly, this dependence could breed mistrust, and the African leaders' willingness to play one European nation against another earned them a reputation for duplicity. Implicit in this criticism, however, is a reluctant recognition that the African leader possessed enough wit and intelligence to match the European at his own game. Indeed, Englishmen came to appreciate particular ethnic groups and their leaders. Of certain Cape Verde people, one reporter said, "These men are more civill than any other." Nicholas Owen discovered a group "more civilized and hospitable to strangers" and spoke of their receiving him "with a great dail of good nature." The marital partnerships into which so many whites entered, particularly on the upper Guinea coast, were often based on a profound appreciation of the qualities of African women. In 1758 the Reverend John Lindsay was almost ecstatic about the chastity, politeness, and cleanliness, not to mention the "fine features," of Senegalese women. According to John Atkins, the governor of Cape Coast Castle "doted" upon his mulatto wife and, in part because of her influence, preferred the fetishes on his wrists to European medicine. And yet, as much as the British intermingled with Africans, they were rarely absorbed. Few lived long enough, of course, but, from the 1620s, when Richard Jobson piously and inaccurately claimed that he came from "a people who did not . . . buy or sell one another," to the 1750s, when Nicholas Owen asserted that he was "surounded by the worst of people, . . . a barbarous people," the British generally maintained their sense of superiority.[80]

The best-developed plantation societies in the New World were the sources of the most virulent comments about blacks. Earlier histories of race relations in British society often failed to recognize that the most hostile words written about blacks came from the pens of expatriate West Indians. It was almost as if writers like Edward Long, Philip Thicknesse, Samuel Estwick, and James Tobin injected into metropolitan society the poisonous venom nurtured in their various slave societies. At the same time, these

---

Barker, *The African Link*, contains the best discussion of the exploration literature. On servants, see Hecht, *Continental and Colonial Servants*. An interesting model for my theme of variation is William B. Cohen, *The French Encounter with Africans: White Responses to Blacks, 1530–1880* (Bloomington, Ind., 1980).

80. Owen, *Journal*, 24, 26, 61–62, 77; Rodney, *History of Upper Guinea*, 83, 125, 199; Brooks, "*Signares* of Saint-Louis," in Hafkin and Bray, eds., *Women in Africa*, 26; John Atkins, *A Voyage to Guinea, Brasil, and the West Indies* . . . (London, 1735), 94–95. See also Philip D. Curtin, *The Image of Africa: British Ideas and Actions, 1780–1850* (Madison, Wis., 1964), I, 3–119.

violent prejudices took time to develop and were almost always stated with a measure of ambivalence (even from Long). Richard Ligon exemplifies the embryonic, ill-formed racial prejudices of seventeenth-century Barbadians. As we have noted earlier, Ligon spoke of blacks as "neer beasts," but he could also admire "handsome Negroes," their fencing, singing, and swimming skills, and the chastity of their women. He could find as "honest, faithfull, and conscionable people amongst [Africans], as amongst those of *Europe*." Even by the late eighteenth century, a man like Bryan Edwards, who equaled Long in his racism, was yet acutely aware of ethnic differences among Africans (describing Mandingoes as notable for "the gentleness of [their] disposition and demeanour") and could present detailed and sympathetic accounts of their culture.[81]

The black response to whites is, of course, very much harder to decipher, but, of one thing we can be sure: it too was hardly homogenous. On the African coast, amusement and ridicule were common black reactions to whites. Senegalese women who bathed twice a day had a "hearty contempt for all white people" because of their uncleanliness. Senegalese men could not "be brought to look upon the prettiest of our [white] women, but with the coldest indifference." Nicholas Owen thought that "the country people are in dread of a white man," but townsmen were generally "saucey and give bad language." Owen also found that Christianity "made no impression in the least otherwise then a matter of redicule or laughter," and Anna Marie Falconbridge quoted the African explanation for mulattoes' going to Europe—they go "to 'Read book, and learn to be *rogue* so well as white man.'" Even when attitudes were respectful, Africans often dictated the terms. Thus, many Cape Lopez residents, as reported by Atkins, "borrowed Names from the *Europeans* that put in here, and are pleased when you will adopt them to wear such a Cognizance of your Remembrance; they do not sollicit this Favour till after several views, that they see something to be admired, or that the Person asked, has a fancied Sympathy of Temper, or likeness with themselves."[82]

In Britain, the greater proximity and frequent contact between blacks and whites no doubt helped reduce such ethnocentric attitudes. However, there is evidence that blacks preferred their own company, thereby passing indirect

81. Fryer, *Staying Power*, esp. 135–163; but compare Barker, *African Link*; Ligon, *True and Exact History*, 43, 47, 50–53; Edwards, *History, Civil and Commercial*, II, 72.

82. Brooks, "*Signares* of Saint-Louis," in Hafkin and Bray, eds., *Women in Africa*, 26; Owen, *Journal*, 62, 71; A. M. Falconbridge, *Narrative of Two Voyages to the River Sierra Leone, during the Years 1791–1793 . . .* (London, 1794), 77, as quoted in Rodney, *History of Upper Guinea*, 221; Atkins, *Voyage*, 198. See also T. H. Breen, "Creative Adaptations: Peoples and Cultures," in Jack P. Greene and J. R. Pole, eds., *Colonial British America: Essays in the New History of the Early Modern Era* (Baltimore, 1984), 202.

judgment on their white neighbors. At one public house in Fleet Street in 1764, black domestics "supped, drank, and entertained themselves with dancing and music, consisting of violins, French horns, and other instruments . . . till four in the morning." Significantly, "no Whites were allowed to be present." Blacks also combined to agitate for their freedom. The number of blacks found in the gallery when Lord Mansfield handed down his ruling in the Somerset case is testimony enough, but consider too Sir John Fielding's complaint that blacks "intoxicated with Liberty" and "grown refractory" were entering "into Societies, and mak[ing] it their Business to corrupt and dissatify the Mind of every fresh black Servant that comes to England."[83]

In the New World, black attitudes toward whites ranged from the ridicule expressed by their African forebears to the assertion of dignity characteristic of their counterparts in Britain. Any comprehensive survey would need to embrace the blind hatred of the rebel and the open hostility to Christianity characteristic of plantation slaves throughout the New World (and thereby paralleling the views of many in their homeland), the ridicule of whites encapsulated in many a slave song, the sullen indifference of the browbeaten field hand, the honest goodwill of many a slave driver, and the private affection of the slave concubine. If New World slaves could not be as contemptuous of whites as their African cousins, nor as assertive in claiming freedom as their metropolitan counterparts, they were not reticent in exhibiting both responses, and many others besides. One of the most pungent observations was one of the earliest. In 1676, a Barbadian slave exclaimed that the "Devil was in the Englishman that he makes everything work; he makes the Negro work, the Horse work, the Ass work, the Wood work, the Water work and the Winde work."[84]

This cursory and, in many ways, highly oversimplified survey of attitudes confirms the central thrust of this essay. Patterns of cultural interaction between whites and blacks, of which attitudinal exchanges and responses were just a part, varied immensely throughout Anglo-America. Attitudes were shaped by social forces, and these forces assumed different configurations in different places. At the same time, however, it is undeniable that even the most privileged black, no matter in what corner of the Anglo-American world he resided, faced at least a measure of hostility suffered by few other ethnic groups. Moreover, racial boundaries hardened rather than softened over time. Even a black person as highly adept at settling into the white man's world as Ignatius Sancho could confess, "I am a lodger—and hardly that."[85]

83. Fryer, *Staying Power*, 69, 71, 204.

84. Anon., *Great Newes from the Barbadoes* . . . (London, 1676), 6–7, as cited in Craton, *Testing the Chains*, 109.

85. Paul Edwards, ed., *Letters of the Late Ignatius Sancho, an African* . . . (London, 1968), 72.

Perhaps a last word can be left to our most inspired informant, Olaudah Equiano. His narrative is riven with ambivalent feelings toward white society. In one family in Guernsey, the woman of the house showed him "great kindness and attention" and taught him "every thing in the same manner as she did her own child." At times Equiano felt "almost an Englishman" and, on his travels, longed to "return to Old England." At the same time, he never ceased to be aware of himself as an African, a former slave, and a member of a despised and maltreated race. Equiano repeatedly recognized that the very people who assisted him were, in fact, playing their part in the system that brutalized and enslaved him and his people. Even his "true and worthy friend," Captain Farmer, who helped secure Equiano's freedom, tried to take advantage of their friendship. Virtually the last word on Equiano is his action opposing the organization of the Sierra Leone expedition. At his instigation, the disenchanted black members boycotted the expedition's religious services, which led the chaplain to complain that the snub was "for no other reason whatever than that I am *white*." For his role as agitator, Equiano found himself accused by an abolitionist of "advancing falsehoods as deeply black as his jetty face." Even Equiano could not bridge the ever-present and widening divide between white and black.[86]

V

Olaudah Equiano, an African born about 1745, experienced a range of contacts with whites as he traversed the farthest reaches of the British Empire before his death in 1797. His story suggests both the omnipresence of blacks in the first British Empire, and the great variations in their interactions with whites depending on where, when, with whom, and how these contacts occurred. Another individual, Billy Blue, was born in the same decade as Equiano, but was a creole rather than an African, and his longevity (he died in 1834) linked him to the death of one empire and to the establishment of another.

Like other blacks before him (those brought into ninth-century Ireland, for instance), Billy Blue seems to have got his name from his particularly black hue, sometimes referred to as blue by contemporaries. He was probably born in British America and, by his own recollection, fought under Wolfe at Quebec and served as a "Spie or Guide" under Cornwallis in the disastrous Virginia campaign. If it seems a little coincidental that Blue avowed an association with two of the more notable British military commanders, blacks certainly were part of the British army in the Seven Years' War and

86. Edwards, ed., *Life of Equiano*, I, xxxviii, 109, 132, 176–177, 250, II, 11, 15–20, 28, 33; and Edwards, "Three West African Writers," in Davis and Gates, eds., *Slave's Narrative*, 191–196.

acted as spies in the Revolutionary war. Olaudah Equiano, for example, served with Wolfe in Canada (indeed Wolfe was on the same ship as Equiano and "saved [him] once a flogging for fighting with a young gentleman") and participated in the siege of Louisburg. If Blue embellished his war record, its outlines could still be true. Moreover, Blue's removal to England after the war, his residence in the parish of Saint Paul's Deptford, and his employment as a dockside "lumper" and chocolate-maker fit plausibly into what is known about the fate of blacks who fought on the losing side. In 1796, Blue was sentenced to transportation for seven years for stealing sugar from a ship. After a number of years in prison, he embarked on the *Minorca* and in 1801 arrived in another New World—Sydney, Australia.

There, he joined hundreds of other British blacks who were transported to New South Wales and Tasmania in the late eighteenth and early nineteenth centuries, while others were sent to the West Indies, Saint Helena, the Cape Colony, and Mauritius. Although a small minority of all transportees, these blacks personify the involvement of their race in all aspects of imperial life. In fact, Billy Blue's story became enmeshed with that of his adopted country. He became a folk hero, a legendary figure, whose escapades epitomized the emergent Australian virtues of independence, hard if not always legitimate work, pugnacious defense of the powerless against the powerful, and loyalty to one's mates. The long and affectionate obituary accorded Blue in the *Sydney Gazette* mentioned a smuggling conviction, Blue's close relationship to Governor Lachlen Macquarie, and his work as ferryman and watchman of the harbor. His cottage became a local landmark, and the land he owned became known as Billy Blue's Point.[87]

If Blue appears to have thoroughly assimilated to, and indeed to have helped form, the values of his new homeland, this accommodation was not at the expense of older ethnic traditions. Of particular interest is Billy Blue's role as outspoken jester. Oral history has Billy Blue bantering with the governor—Blue's nickname, "The Old Commodore," stemmed from his insistence that everyone, high and low, salute him. His method of asserting himself was time-honored among African-American slaves—not overt aggression, as practiced by the likes of a fellow black and First Fleet transportee John Caesar, said to be the "most intransigent convict in the

87. Sources by Ian Duffield for this and the following paragraph are "Billy Blue: A Legend of Early Sydney," *History Today*, XXXVII (1987), 43–48; "Alexander Harris's *The Emigrant Family* and Afro-black People in Colonial Australia," in Dabydeen, *Black Presence*, 68–94; "Martin Beck and Afro-Blacks in Colonial Australia," *Journal of Australian Studies*, XVI (1985), 3–20; "From Slave Colonies to Penal Colonies: The West Indian Convict Transportees to Australia," *Slavery and Abolition*, VII (1986), 25–45. For Equiano and Wolfe, see Edwards, ed., *Life of Equiano*, I, 121.

early colony," but rather a more indirect and subtle attempt to gain the upper hand. Apparently, Billy Blue was a trickster, mocking and mimicking whites, playing out a role performed by countless other Africans and African-Americans. Even in a far-off land, Billy Blue remained true to his cultural heritage.

A. G. ROEBER

"The Origin of Whatever Is Not English among Us"

The Dutch-speaking and the German-speaking Peoples of Colonial British America

English colonizers encountered former inhabitants of the Dutch Republic, the Helvetic Confederation, and the Holy Roman Empire throughout the Americas from the Caribbean to Nova Scotia. Although the shorthand that English-speakers used to identify these diverse peoples implied that the "Low Dutch" and the "High Dutch" were related by language, in fact the geography implicit in the English terminology—proximity to and distance from the North Sea—underscored the variety of speech and culture flourishing within this language family. Religion helped to bind emigrants from the Continent together, for most shared a commitment to Reformed, Lutheran, or free church Christianity, all three traditions generously leavened by the pietist renewal movement that began in the late seventeenth century to transform the international face of European Protestantism.[1]

I thank the participants at the Roundtable Conference on the history of the early modern period, University of Göttingen, May 1988, and the participants at the Philadelphia Seminar in Early American Studies, January 1989, for helpful comments and suggestions. In particular I thank Rudolf Vierhaus, Hermann Wellenreuther, T. H. Breen, Hans Medick, John Brewer, Richard Dunn, John Murrin, Marianne Wokeck, Stephanie Graumann Wolf, John Franz, and the editors of this volume.

1. The English use of "Dutch" for both German- and Dutch-speakers stemmed from a modernization of Middle English *dietsch*, the word identical with the Flemish term meaning "speech of the people." See the literature and discussion in Werner König, *Atlas zur deutschen Sprache: Tafeln und Texte* (Munich, 1978), 59–60, 230–241; see also Wilhelm Breuer, " 'Dietsch' and 'Duutsch' in der mitelniederländischen Literatur," *Rheinische Vierteljahrsblätter*, XXXVII (1973), 328–347. From the 16th century, the English referred to the "high Dutch tongue" in which the *Kanzleisprache* used in official government work was adapted and augmented from Saxon dialect by Luther in his translation of the Bible.

Furthermore, Dutch- and German-speaking communities in North America seemed to observers like Thomas Jefferson to have maintained their distinctiveness in similar ways—by dialects of their respective languages, cultivated particularly at home and in church. One scholar, in probing the distinctiveness of these continental settlers and their interaction with English-speakers, argued that both Dutch and Germans "organized their communities on the basis of relationships which we consider private and personal." Familial, religious, artisanal, and agricultural traditions were communicated and handed down "independently of public cultural institutions."[2]

Yet private and public worlds cannot be divorced entirely, and it is precisely in this interrelationship that the Dutch and the Germans exhibited markedly different histories in British North America. Thus New Netherland was left weak and vulnerable by meager migration into an ethnically diverse colony and the absence of support networks and leaders interested in creating a Dutch culture. After a bloodless English conquest, public life in New York and New Jersey quickly anglicized. Forced from the public into the domestic and spiritual realms, Dutch culture survived for another century essentially in private, before being abandoned. By contrast, the German-speakers arrived in great numbers, never enduring any conquest by the English. Supported by self-conscious leaders and support networks, they established a press in their own language and cultivated an extensive trade and religious communication via London and Holland to the Reich and across colonial boundaries in North America. This mélange of German-speakers eventually enjoyed a more unified experience in North America than they had known in Europe. Marveling, as one Lutheran pastor put it, at the absence of "difficulty, oppression and violence, which is exactly the famous English liberty," German-speakers eventually mastered legal and political life in North America. By the 1760s, they had embraced a political culture they confidently expected would protect their private interests.[3]

That so many diverse peoples eventually committed themselves to "the famous English liberty" makes their story seem almost inevitable and straightforward. Closer analysis of migration patterns, support networks, and the domestic and religious cultures of Dutch- and German-speakers, however, reveals the complexities of their encounter with English-speakers.

2. Alice P. Kenney, "Private Worlds in the Middle Colonies: An Introduction to Human Tradition in American History," *New York History*, LI (1970), 25.

3. Johann Martin Bolzius, *Reliable Answer to Some Submitted Questions . . .*, in Klaus G. Loewald *et al.*, eds. and trans., "Johann Martin Bolzius Answers a Questionnaire on Carolina and Georgia," *William and Mary Quarterly*, 3d Ser., XIV (1957), 226. Boltzius, like many residents of North America, was no constitutional scholar. The German living in America "enjoys all the privileges of the kingdom like the native Englishmen" (255).

I

Migration to New Netherland was an option considered by people on the margins of the spectacular Dutch culture and economy of the seventeenth century. The first colonists were Walloon refugees from the southern part of the Spanish Netherlands, and they mingled with West Frieslanders and others with a minimal stake in the mainstream of Netherlands society. Most came from economically depressed areas such as Utrecht, whose earlier glory had been eclipsed by the rise of Gouda, Delft, and Haarlem. Amsterdam, the cultural center of the Dutch Republic, and its northern environs contributed few settlers to New Netherland.

By 1673, when perhaps six thousand persons inhabited the colony, relatively few were Dutch. Nearly 40 percent came from High Germany—mostly from Aachen, Cleves, East Friesland, Westphalia, Bremen, Hamburg, and Oldenburg. From an early list of German immigrants to New Amsterdam and New York between 1630 and 1674, 125 of the 180 families can be traced from the Hanseatic cities or extreme northern Germany and not further south than Cologne, Braunschweig, and Berlin. The earliest recorded emigration among the Frieslanders—a cryptic petition cited by the chronicler Peter Sax in 1639–1640—probably refers to the migration via Amsterdam to North America. Danes and Norwegians were attracted to the colony, and European Jews also trickled into the colony's main town. Together, these European arrivals mingled with the dwindling native Americans and growing numbers of African-American slaves in contributing to the heterogeneity of the settlements.[4]

Before the English conquest, but more notably after, Dutch-speakers further diluted their culture by scattering widely. Thus, by 1663, Horekill, a Mennonite colony on the Delaware, numbered only forty-one Dutch Mennonites from Zwaanendael, under Pieter Cornelius Plockhoy's leadership. Jasper Danckaerts and Peter Sluyter, both radical Dutch pietist followers of

4. John O. Evjen, *Scandinavian Immigrants in New York, 1630–1674* (Minneapolis, Minn., 1916), 401–436; Oliver A. Rink, "The People of New Netherland: Notes on Non-English Immigration to New York in the Seventeenth Century," *N.Y. Hist.*, LXII (1981), 5–42; David Steven Cohen, "How Dutch Were the Dutch of New Netherland?" *N.Y. Hist.*, LXII (1981), 43–60; Elsa Godberson, "Die Annalen des Peter Sax: Bericht über die Arbeit mit Quellen zur Auswanderung im 17. Jahrhundert," in Paul G. Buchloh *et al.*, eds., *Die vergessene Deutschen: Schleswig-Holsteiner in Nordamerika* (Kiel, 1983), 137–155; John Michael Montias, *Artists and Artisans in Delft: A Socio-Economic Study of the Seventeenth Century* (Princeton, N.J., 1982). Despite some misgivings, I avoid treating European Jews as parts of the Dutch or German communities to which they, in many respects, clearly belonged. Enough evidence exists, however, of the transfer of old prejudices and animosities against them to prohibit such inclusion. The definitive study still remains Jacob R. Marcus, *The Colonial American Jew, 1492–1776*, 3 vols. (Detroit, Mich., 1970).

Jean de Labadie, secured Bohemia Manor on the Delaware from Ephrahim Hermann in 1683, but the experiment in communitarian farming never exceeded one hundred persons and by 1698 faltered, having attracted no migrants from the Netherlands, only displaced Dutch from New York.[5]

The diversity of the original New Netherland population, together with the scattered, isolated locations of later Dutch-speakers, effectively prevented creation of support networks linking the settlements to each other and back to the Netherlands. Settlements were virtual islands, interested only in the territory immediately surrounding them.[6] The New Jersey Dutch or those on the Delaware cared little about Manhattan's life or what went on in Schenectady or Albany. In 1741 the Swedish traveler Peter Kalm pointed out that in New Brunswick, New Jersey, a supposedly Dutch town, immigrants from Albany lived on one lane in utter isolation from the other Dutch "and seldom or never go amongst the other inhabitants."[7]

II

Leadership was also a long-standing problem among the Dutch. From the beginning of New Netherland, private merchant-traders were at odds with the Dutch West Indies Company. Private, successful merchant-traders, not initially a part of the vision of the West Indies Company for the colony, smuggled, traded in furs, and in 1639 finally got the company to abandon monopoly for regulation. Even as the Schuyler and Cuyler merchant families emerged into prominence in the 1660s, they married on the basis of religious disputes and business alliances brought from the Netherlands that divided rather than united the merchant cadre. Clerical leaders, too, failed to emerge as symbols of unity and concord. In the 1630s Walloons refused to attend the simple services conducted in a mill loft by Jonas Michaëlius. The liberal Amsterdam classis, which favored an episcopal governance, often supplied ministers to a population drawn from more orthodox parts of the United Provinces favoring a presbyterian polity. When Jasper Danckaerts

5. David S. Lovejoy, *Religious Enthusiasm in the New World: Heresy to Revolution* (Cambridge, Mass., 1985), 154–158.

6. On cultural persistence in the Albany area, see Donna Merwick, "Dutch Townsmen and Land Use: A Spatial Perspective on Seventeenth-Century Albany, New York," *WMQ*, 3d Ser., XXXVII (1980), 53–78. But Rink's judgment seems indisputable: the merchant and clerical leaders of the New Netherland colony remained isolated from the more general populace.

7. See Thomas E. Burke, *"The Extreemest Part of All": The Dutch Community of Schenectady, New York, 1661–1710* (forthcoming); Adolph B. Benson, ed., *Peter Kalm's Travel in North America: The English Version of 1770*, 2 vols. (New York, 1937), 121.

labeled such parties "Voetians" or "Cocceians," he identified these imported squabbles.[8]

In the late 1650s Governor Peter Stuyvesant attempted to cement a social network of patrons and officers for the colony, much like his contemporary in Virginia, Sir William Berkeley. Through this patronage network, the governor apparently intended to create a self-conscious governing cadre to whom he formally gave *burgerrecht* (city privileges). Composed of clergy, militia officers, and the members of the government appointed by him, the coalition never came together. The wealthier merchants and younger family migrants failed to share a common vision for the scattered Dutch communities stretching along the Hudson to the Delaware.[9]

This failure is nowhere better evident than in the manner of the English conquest. The dominies and merchants, seemingly possessing a large stake in Dutch culture, urged capitulation. Those living closest to the symbol of Dutch authority, Fort Amsterdam, persuaded Stuyvesant to surrender. There is reason to believe that young people of modest means might have resisted, if given a lead by their superiors. Some excoriated "those devilish traders who have so long salted us," and the West Indies Company itself praised those who had not been "moved by the flattering tongues of Preachers and others who were troubled about their private property, without regarding the interest of the State and Company." Nor did a "charter group" of self-conscious leaders emerge after the Dutch recaptured New York in 1673. Anthony Colve, the interim authority in the reconstituted New Netherland, spent much of his time settling conflicts among fractious communities. Poorer Dutch Lutherans in Albany later in the 1670s mocked their new English rulers, the clash between supposed leaders and commoners an inherited fragmentation now intensified by final English conquest.[10]

8. William David Voorhees, " 'In Behalf of the True Protestants Religion': The Glorious Revolution in New York" (Ph.D. diss., New York University, 1988), 55–56. Johannes Cocceius (1603–1669) is known mainly as the leading theoretician of federal, or covenant, theology; his supporters tended to be the urban, mercantile groups who supplied ministers to New Netherland through the Amsterdam classis. Gysbertus Voetius (1589–1676) represented the more orthodox, rural views of the regions from which many emigrants to New Netherland originated.

9. George L. Smith, *Religion and Trade in New Netherland: Dutch Origins and American Development* (Ithaca, N.Y., 1973), 142–157, 179–235; Gerald F. De Jong, *The Dutch in America, 1609–1974* (Boston, 1975), 15–27; Oliver A. Rink, *Holland on the Hudson: An Economic and Social History of Dutch New York* (Ithaca, N.Y., 1986), 94–138, 172–213.

10. Joyce Diane Goodfriend, " 'Too Great a Mixture of Nations': The Development of New York City Society in the Seventeenth Century" (Ph.D. diss., University of California, Los Angeles, 1975); John M. Murrin, "English Rights as Ethnic Aggression: The English Conquest, the Charter of Liberties of 1683, and Leisler's Rebellion in New York," in William Pencak and Conrad Edick Wright, eds., *Authority and Resistance in Early New York* (New York, 1988), 56–94; Randall H. Balmer, *A Perfect Babel of Confusion: Dutch Religion and English Culture in the*

The rift between merchants and clerics on the one hand and the commonality on the other surfaced even more dramatically during Jacob Leisler's Rebellion. Leisler's Rebellion in 1689 nonetheless seems to undercut a simple story of assimilation of the Dutch by the conquering English. The rebellion occurred within six years of the Naturalization Act of 1683 and the adoption of an English-style Charter of Liberties that underscored the determination of English leaders to complete the political and cultural transformation of New Netherland into New York. The failure of eminent Dutch merchants and clerics to protest these developments completed their estrangement from commoners. Bitter Leislerians complained that "most of the magistrates . . . were also elders and deacons and therefore heads of our church." Following Leisler's execution, his unrepentant followers "began to feel more bitter hatred against those who had instigated this murder," especially clerical leaders like Dominie Henricus Selyns who reciprocated their hostility. Attendance at Dutch Reformed churches plummeted during the 1690s in the aftermath of Leisler's execution. Ministerial salaries went unpaid. Voting no confidence in spiritual and secular leaders with their feet, large numbers of poorer Dutch farmers left the colony for New Jersey.[11]

Orthodox, conservative, liturgical Dutch Reformed leaders had long faced problems in building networks of support for their people. True, the number of people attending the Dutch Reformed church in New York City increased during the last third of the seventeenth century, so that by 1698 the congregation comprised 57 percent of Dutch adults in the city. True, the loyalty of Dutch women to the church was deep; they represented more than 60 percent of the communicants. Yet this was a church of the eminent: the elders and deacons were exclusively merchants or skilled artisans. Wealthy Dutch women married to English men brought their spouses into the Dutch church. Most members were of more than ten years' standing by the 1680s, and

---

Middle Colonies (New York, 1989), 3–7; and Thomas J. Archdeacon, *New York City, 1664–1710: Conquest and Change* (Ithaca, N.Y., 1976)—all present various analyses of these events. Quotes from E. B. O'Callaghan, *History of New Netherland; or, New York under the Dutch*, 2 vols. (New York, 1845–1848), II, 531; and *Documents Relative to the Colonial History of New York* . . . (Albany, 1853), II, 509; both cited in Balmer, *Perfect Babel*, 5, 6.

T. H. Breen suggests the term "charter group" (borrowed from Eric Wolf) in his essay, "Creative Adaptations: Peoples and Cultures," in Jack P. Greene and J. R. Pole, eds., *Colonial British America: Essays in the New History of the Early Modern Era* (Baltimore, 1984), 195–232. On Albany, see Donna Merwick, "Becoming English: Anglo-Dutch Conflict in the 1670s in Albany, New York," *N.Y. Hist.*, LXII (1981), 389–414.

11. Balmer, *Perfect Babel*, 34 (citing "Documents Relating to the Administration of Leisler," New-York Historical Society, *Collections*, I [New York, 1868], 402), 43, 55–64. As Balmer points out, Leisler was not poor, but most of the wealthier Dutch and the clergy opposed him.

newcomers from other towns like Albany, with an occasional newcomer from the Dutch West Indies or the Netherlands, were generally also merchants, silversmiths, or traders. Defections that began with the outmigration to New Jersey in the 1690s afflicted the town congregations in New York by the 1740s. In 1756 William Smith reported that Trinity Church, the seat of New York Anglicanism, was growing from "proselytes from the Dutch churches."[12] In contrast to the defectors of the 1690s who left to preserve their Dutch religion, the eminent who later abandoned the Reformed church were numbered among the economic and social elite of New York.

III

The thinness of Dutch high culture in North America had other sources. In the highly rural world of seventeenth-century America, the cosmopolitan, urban quality of Dutch culture could not survive transport beyond New Amsterdam. In urban New York, portraiture, silverware, and finely crafted furniture certainly flourished for a time among wealthy Dutch merchants. But, before long, Dutch high culture became indistinguishable from English. Mannerist portraiture, painted furniture, and mourning rings and seals reflected bonds that William and Mary, one of whom was chief magistrate and captain general in the United Provinces, enjoyed with their wealthy English and Dutch subjects alike. Colonial Dutch paintings reveal no particular Dutch use of color, background, or technique; rather, English mezzotint engravings were their models.[13]

On the other hand, Dutch vernacular culture, particularly evident in the domestic and religious spheres, architectural styles, dietary habits, and testamentary patterns, was quite vibrant until at least the middle of the eighteenth century. "The tie that binds: church and language," in one scholar's words, accurately described the core of surviving Dutch colonial identity. The defense of the Dutch language, particularly by women in the Reformed church, was critical to its maintenance, especially when support for Dutch schooling was curtailed at the conquest.[14] Dutch Bibles were present in

12. Joyce D. Goodfriend, "The Social Dimensions of Congregational Life in Colonial New York City," *WMQ*, 3d Ser., XLVI (1989), 252–278, esp. 267 (citing William Smith, Jr., *The History of the Province of New York*, ed. Michael Kammen, 2 vols. [Cambridge, Mass., 1972], I, 204).

13. A. W. Vliegenthart, *William and Mary and Their House* (New York, 1979); Ruth Piwonka, "Dutch Colonial Arts," in Eric Nooter and Patricia U. Bonomi, eds., *Colonial Dutch Studies: An Interdisciplinary Approach* (New York, 1988), 78–94, esp. 92, nn. 20, 21; Paul R. Huey, "The Archeology of Colonial New Netherlands," in *Colonial Dutch Studies*, 52–77, esp. 61–64.

14. De Jong, *The Dutch in America*, 87–108; and more extensively, by the same author, *The Dutch Reformed Church in the American Colonies* (Grand Rapids,

many late-seventeenth-century New York homes. As late as 1769, when a catalog of more than seven hundred "mostly German" books was offered for sale in Philadelphia, the seventy-one titles in Dutch consisted mainly of Bibles, hymnals, and pietist tracts. Secular titles were limited to the occasional atlas, a description of the "old and new East Indies," a city directory of Amsterdam.[15] But there was no Dutch press in North America, no newspaper circulating in that language, and by the 1760s only one Dutch almanac still published, by German or English printers.[16] The arrival of the Dutch pietist pastors between the 1690s and the 1730s, however, reinforced the sense that the spoken, formal language was tied to the church. In the 1720s, with the arrival of these preachers, controversialist literature pushed the total of items published in Dutch in British North America to perhaps five a year from 1725 to 1750, as opposed to the normal single issue of the almanac. Indeed, this connection was so pronounced that in the nineteenth century, when one Dutch-American returned to the Netherlands, no one could understand his dialect any longer except an old man who said that it reminded him of the archaic form of "church Dutch" that had fallen out of use since his youth.[17]

The domestic area of Dutch life increasingly became the focus of a separate Dutch culture that in small ways influenced the broader American culture. Foods like beets, endive, spinach, dill, parsley, and chervil were added by Dutch farmers to North American diets. The onion-potato-carrot stew *hutspot* and oil cakes (*olykoek*, *koekje*: cookies) enriched colonial cuisine. Dutch celebrations of Christmas, particularly the children's figure of Sinter Claes and the practice of putting out the wooden shoe by the door in anticipation of gifts, found imitators in North America from other cultures. The Dutch homes that spread these cultural practices also taught other colonials to speak of "stoops" (*stoep*) on their houses and to appreciate the

---

Mich., 1978); Howard G. Hageman, "The Dutch Battle for Higher Education in the Middle Colonies," and Gerald F. De Jong, "The Education and Training of Dutch Ministers," in Charles T. Gehring and Nancy Anne McClure Zeller, eds., *Education in New Netherland and the Middle Colonies: Papers of the Seventh Rensselaerswyck Seminar of the New Netherland Project* (Grand Rapids, Mich., 1984), 1–7, 9–16.

15. Heinrich Miller, *Catalogus von mehr als 700 meist deutschen Büchern . . .* (Philadelphia, 1769). Item 44, *De Nederlandsche Maandelyke Post-Ryder*, seems to be a duodecimo binding of old newspapers; apparently Miller had acquired someone's library for sale in offering these rather unusual items. I have checked them against current catalogs for the book fairs at Leipzig and Frankfurt; the books were not currently for sale.

16. Hendrick Edelman, *Dutch-American Bibliography, 1693–1794: A Descriptive Catalog of Dutch-Language Books, Pamphlets, and Almanacs Printed in America* (Nieuwkoop, 1974).

17. Van Cleaf Bachman *et al.*, " 'Het Poelmeisie': An Introduction to the Hudson Valley Dutch Dialect," *N.Y. Hist.*, LXI (1980), 161–185.

bulbous Dutch clay pipes exchanged in trade with native Americans from Long Island and Connecticut to the Mohawk Valley and with other Europeans as well.[18]

This domestically oriented culture was unquestionably a hybrid adaptation to North American conditions. If Peter Kalm's observations can be trusted, most rural Dutch were frugal eaters and contented themselves with *sapaan* every night for supper—a porridge of cornmeal in which, Kalm said, "a large hole is made in its center, into which milk is poured, and then one proceeds to help himself." German settlers from Swabia knew the identical dish as *Stöpper* or *brennts Mus*; their descendants would also adapt native American maize to the traditional dish.[19] Like Dutch barns, so-called Dutch houses, with their gambrel roofs and flared bell eaves, were in fact composite structures, reflecting many influences of Friesian and Danish origin. They were not simple transfers from the Netherlands.[20] From upstate New York, a painting hung in the Van Bergen home details house and barn with hay barracks in 1735, all reflecting this North American rural architecture one would not have found in the Netherlands. Black slaves, visiting Indians, and whites, presumably conversing in the dialect of the upper Hudson (itself an archaic form of Dutch by the mid-eighteenth century), complete the panorama.[21]

18. Richard J. Hooker, *Food and Drink in America: A History* (Indianapolis, Ind., 1981), 32–34; Peter O. Wacker, "The Dutch Culture Area in the Northeast, 1609–1800," *New Jersey History*, CIV (1986), 1–22. Linda Keller Brown and Kay Mussell, eds., *Ethnic and Regional Foodways in the United States: The Performance of Group Identity* (Knoxville, Tenn., 1984), introduction, iii–iv.

19. Alice P. Kenney and others suggested that Dutch popular culture underwent a revival in the early 19th century among interested Anglo-Americans who probably reinvented popular Dutch culture at about the same time that popular culture in Europe was being "rediscovered" by the Grimms and other middling folk. For the European pattern, see Peter Burke, *Popular Culture in Early Modern Europe* (New York, 1979). See Kenney, *Stubborn for Liberty: The Dutch in New York* (Syracuse, N.Y., 1975), 257–267; Benson, ed., *Peter Kalm's Travel*, 629.

20. On the varieties of Dutch barns and houses linking architecture to regional origins of the Dutch, see Peter O. Wacker, "Dutch Material Culture in New Jersey," *Journal of Popular Culture*, XI (1977–1978), 950–957; and "The Dutch Culture Area," *N.J. Hist.*, CIV (1986), 1–22. On Dutch barn building and its wider influence, see, for example, Peter O. Wacker, "Dutch Barns and Barracks in New Jersey (Abstract)," in Austin Fife *et al.*, eds., *Forms upon the Frontier: Folklife and Folk Arts in the United States* (Logan, Utah, 1969), 27.

21. Eric Nooter, "A Note on Sources and Future Directions," in Nooter and Bonomi, eds., *Colonial Dutch Studies*, 95–105, esp. 99. One modest example of the complex patterns of cultural interaction involving Dutch, German, British, and native Americans is provided by Conrad Weiser's journal. Born in Württemberg, raised in New York and Pennsylvania among both native Americans and the Dutch, Weiser's fluency in Dutch, English, and several native American tongues secured his role in Pennsylvania as cultural broker. On one of his trips he records giving a gift of a "wooden Dutch pipe" to an Indian friend. See "Conrad Weiser's Journal of a Tour of

The protection of family and hearth among the Dutch took a practical and serious form in property settlements. Dutch-Roman law provided that, unless a marriage contract had been entered into, a common property system prevailed, with the husband acting as the agent for his wife. Yet both partners held common property equally as well as all property acquired during the duration of marriage. Unlike English common law, Roman law provided for the woman's right to make a will jointly with her husband in disposing of both real and chattel property. The right to perpetuate this practice was guaranteed under the Articles of Capitulation of September 1664. Until the eighteenth century, the Dutch in New York continued to write mutual wills, and most gave the widow life use of the *boedel*, or estate. Moreover, Dutch women continued to use their maiden name in these documents until the early eighteenth century. Even when English practices crept in and husbands wrote wills by themselves, Dutch wives through the 1720s continued to receive the same rights of inheritance as women had who jointly prepared wills in the seventeenth century. The widow continued as before to be the administratrix of the property. Until the 1730s, wills generally gave half the estate to the widow, half to the children, in the event of a second marriage.

Unlike the English, who attempted to establish sons on the land and so excluded daughters from realty, Dutch rural testators until about 1770 either gave daughters land or stipulated that they be compensated in cash equaling the value of land given their brothers. The collapse of Dutch tendencies to provide widows with an equal proportion of the estate enjoyed by children occurred by the 1730s in urban New York; rural Dutch continued this practice for another generation. The most obvious question becomes, then, What accounts for the changed status of Dutch women and the rise of the children's interest and their capacity to inherit a larger estate upon the death of the father, and not at the mother's decease or remarriage?[22]

Economic and social developments provide clues to the gradual erosion of distinctive testamentary patterns. If the Dutch area around Acquackamonk and Totowa is any indication, the practice of equal partition began to pro-

---

the Ohio, August 11–October 2, 1748," in Reuben Gold Thwaites, ed., *Early Western Travels, 1748–1846* (New York, 1966), I, 43, n. 42.

22. David Evan Narrett, "Patterns of Inheritance in Colonial New York City, 1664–1775: A Study in the History of the Family" (Ph.D. diss., Cornell University, 1981); Narrett, "Dutch Customs of Inheritance, Women, and the Law in Colonial New York City," in Pencak and Wright, eds., *Authority and Resistance*, 27–55; less successfully, Linda Briggs Biemer, *Women and Property in Colonial New York: The Transition from Dutch to English Law, 1643–1727* (Ann Arbor, Mich., 1983); William John McLaughlin, "Dutch Rural New York: Community, Economy, and Family in Colonial Flatbush" (Ph.D. diss., Columbia University, 1981), 239–244; Firth Fabend, "The Yeoman Ideal: A Dutch Family in the Middle Colonies, 1660–1800" (Ph.D. diss., New York University, 1988); Wacker, "Dutch Culture Area," *N.J. Hist.*, CIV (1986), 11–13.

duce insufficient estate to sustain all heirs by the second decade of the eighteenth century. Concerned fathers naturally shifted control over diminishing resources to children earlier in their lives, even at the expense of widowed wives. Yet the continuation of control over half the estate exercised by rural Dutch women belies a simple economic explanation. Perhaps the rise of Dutch members of the urban bar in New York by the first decade of the eighteenth century is also significant. Dominie Boel's lawyer brother Tobias in New York was but one of a number of eminent Dutchmen to practice at this, one of the colonial bars where technical pleading and correct procedure were increasingly important. Successful Dutch lawyers penetrated the mysteries of the common law to demonstrate sufficiently their prosperous families' adaptation to the public British legal and political world.[23] With Dutch-speaking legal advisers who could intervene to protect at least some of their interests, Dutch urban women may have felt less threatened by the alien legal system than did their rural cousins. Increasingly, prominent Dutch families intermarried with the English and their legal advisers, further accelerating the decline in distinct Dutch testation customs.[24] It is not coincidental that the peculiar testamentary practices in urban New York began to falter in the same decade that the Dutch Reformed church bewailed the collapse of the language among younger people and noticed the first signs of drift away from the Dutch church by the elite in favor of the Anglican. In rural areas, the decline seems tied less to rational, intentional economic planning than to a withering away of a tradition that was also no longer sustained by the perpetuation of either a separate language or a separate religious culture.

This separate religious culture was closely bound up with a radical separatist ideology of Dutch pietism.[25] Not that all Dutch settlements were

23. Howard Harris, "Towns-People and Country People": The Acquackamonk Dutch and the Rise of Industry in Paterson, New Jersey," *N.J. Hist.*, CVI (1988), 23–52; Paul M. Hamlin, *Legal Education in Colonial New York* (New York, 1939), 134–155. Dutch attorneys (for example, Olaff S. Van Cortlandt) can be found in these lists as early as the late 17th century; by contrast, the earliest Germans (the Hoffmans), not before 1760, a date that corresponds well to the first German members of the bar in Pennsylvania—for details, see below. For a similar picture for New Jersey, see Don C. Skemer, "The *Institutio legalis* and Legal Education in New Jersey: 1783–1817," *N.J. Hist.*, XCVI (1978), 123–134.

24. Jon Butler, *The Huguenots in America: A Refugee People in New World Society* (Cambridge, Mass., 1983), 187–188.

25. Randall H. Balmer and A. G. Roeber, eds., *Continental Pietism in Colonial British North America: Documents and Interpretations* (forthcoming), surveys much of the literature; see also S. van der Linde, "Der reformierte 'Pietismus' in den Niederlanden," and J. Wallmann, "Labadismus und Pietismus: Die Einflüsse der niederländischen Pietismus auf die Entstehung des Pietismus in Deutschland," in J. van den Berg and J. P. van Dooren, eds., *Pietismus und Reveil: Referate der internationalen Tagung: Der Pietismus in den Niederlanden und seine internation-*

affected by this new religious sentiment. Rather, the Dutch farmers who fled into New Jersey after 1700 to escape political, social, and religious ostracism at the hands of a prosperous Dutch-English leadership found in separatist Labadist pietism a congenial religious sentiment and self-concept. This radical pietist tradition had its origins in Dutch Labadist attacks on ungodliness, interpreted to mean the rather laconic, tolerant style of Dutch Christianity that had accompanied the commercial success of the Republic. Such radicalism enjoyed relatively little success in the Netherlands; it had limited appeal in New York; it would characterize the Jersey Dutch.[26]

The arrival of Theodorus Jacobus Frelinghuysen in New Jersey in 1720 signaled a revival in Dutch Reformed Christianity heretofore unknown in North America. Born in 1692 into a Westphalian Calvinist pastor's family, Frelinghuysen studied at Hamm and Lingen. Ordained in 1715, Frelinghuysen arrived from Friesland to accept a call in 1719 from the Raritan Valley Dutch. His arrival was matched by the emergence in the same year in New York of a second pietist leader, the Lutheran tailor Johann Bernhard van Dieren, born in Königsberg, but probably of Dutch or Huguenot ancestry. Removing to Hackensack by 1725, van Dieren preached in Dutch and German to Lutherans and Reformed alike. These two leaders were joined in 1735 by the Swiss-born pietist leader Johan Hendricus Goetschius, who also preached in both continental languages. It was around these popular, charismatic figures that Dutch religious revivals centered for a generation before the English experienced the so-called First Great Awakening of the 1740s.[27]

Pietist groups gathered by these leaders worshiped informally, as had separatist Labadist groups on the Continent. Religious services in this version of Dutch pietism emphasized emotive hymnody in simple meter and a psalmody that eventually gave way to English hymns. The tendency toward spontaneous prayer and a minimum of ritual was intended to unsettle worship in the congregations that pietists found filled with insincerity and rote prayer.

Using a formal liturgy that employed traditional Genevan hymnody in

---

alen Beziehungen (Leiden, 1978), 102–117, 141–168; on the more radical strains of pietism among Dutch Lutherans, see, in the same volume, Casper C. G. Visser, "Die mystisch-pietistische Strömung in der niederländisch-lutherischen Kirche in der zweiten Hälfte des 17ten Jahrhunderts," 169–181.

26. Patricia U. Bonomi, *Under the Cope of Heaven: Religion, Society, and Politics in Colonial America* (New York, 1986), 95; Joyce D. Goodfriend, "The Historiography of the Dutch in Colonial America," in Nooter and Bonomi, eds., *Colonial Dutch Studies*, 6–32.

27. On Goetschius, see below; Douglas Jacobsen, "Johann Bernhard van Dieren: Peasant Preacher at Hackensack, New Jersey, 1724–40," *N.J. Hist.*, C (1982), 15–30; Charles H. Glatfelter, *Pastors and People: German Lutheran and Reformed Churches in the Pennsylvania Field, 1717–1793* (Breinigsville, Pa., 1980), 30, 46–47.

complex meter, the mainstream Dutch Reformed celebrated a high church Dutch liturgy of preaching and sacrament and observed a strict segregation of the sexes in their churches, with preferential seats going to married males, females, and church leaders. A small increase in church attendance occurred in some traditional Reformed churches in the 1720s. But the decade was marked more by a mixing of Dutch and English styles in architecture. Typically, the interior furniture, pulpit, altar, pews, and baptismal font of Dutch churches remained largely unchanged in style. But windows and exteriors that connected worshipers with the English world took on eighteenth-century British forms, with more double-hung sash windows. Fewer churches assumed the octagonal shape traceable to the rural Netherlands. The inclusion of English architectural forms in the very institution that had protected Dutch linguistic and religious distinctiveness accompanied the lament that many of the young were abandoning this semianglicized institution and its Dutch language for worship in Anglican churches, where architecture and language both spoke as one for the dominant culture.[28]

Against this genteel, anglicized New World apostasy, Frelinghuysen mounted an assault using the separatist Labadist radicalism of his youth. Upon his own personal and immediate judgment, he claimed, he could recognize "unregenerate" people wanting baptism or access to the Lord's Supper. The public embarrassment visited upon members barred from taking communion earned him their undying enmity. Pietist children were forbidden to learn the Lord's Prayer by heart, since only a "regenerate" and "awakened" person could say these words and mean them. Prosperous Dutch bristled when told that the saved undoubtedly were to be found almost wholly among the poor and outcast of society. Despite fierce assaults directed at him by clergy and laity in North America and the Netherlands, Frelinghuysen's congregants remained fiercely loyal to him. Frelinghuysen, Goetschius, and van Dieren reached for simple values, preached a biblical loyalty to kin and family, viewed the outside world with suspicion and contempt, and enjoyed, as a result, a devoted following. Gilbert Tennent's friendship for Frelinghuysen was matched by George Whitefield's public admiration for the revivals conducted by the Dutch radical.[29]

The appeal of these charismatic figures to Dutch women and the private sphere they defended against English incursions is suggested by the language

28. Howard G. Hageman, *Pulpit and Table: Some Chapters in the History of Worship in the Reformed Churches* (Richmond, Va., 1962); Adrian C. Leiby, *Dutch and Swedish Settlers of New Jersey* (Princeton, N.J., 1964), 81–85; Alice Kenney, "Religious Artifacts of the Dutch Colonial Period," *de Halve Maen*, LIII (1977–1978), 1–22.

29. Randall H. Balmer, "Dutch Religion in an English World: Political Upheaval and Ethnic Conflict in the Middle Colonies" (Ph.D. diss., Princeton University, 1985), 215–235, 241–244.

of their sermons. When Goetschius's sermon "The Unknown God" was reprinted by John Peter Zenger in New York in 1743, the pastor's introduction immediately presented his own image as the embattled son of a persecuted mother: "Woe is me, my mother, that thou hast borne me a man of strife and a man of contention to the whole earth." Goetschius peppered his text with references to the "daughter of my people," the anguish of women in childbirth, and threats to the "daughter of my people," whose children and sucklings begged in vain for corn and wine from their mothers. These harrowing images drawn from Lamentations and Jeremiah could not have failed to touch the beleaguered Dutch, at whose center Dutch women defended both home and altar. Goetschius urged them to be patient, resisting the wealthy and the hypocrite who thinks "he does God a favor when he oppresses the true believers and usurps God's inheritance." The imagery that tied threats to family and meager property was delivered in a fiery Dutch. Observers who found both message and medium harsh and unbending, Frelinghuysen chastised. Dutch was decisively preferable to English, he retorted, the language of the seductive tempter in the garden. Even Frelinghuysen's exclusion of unworthy, unregenerate Dutch worshipers from the Lord's table smacked of the defense of home and religion against those who had cast their lot with the larger worldly, profane society. Such people would only endanger the entire congregation of the saved by their behavior.[30]

Dominie Goetschius's ministry—a Swiss German-speaker finally ordained in Pennsylvania to minister among the Dutch by the German Reformed Peter Dorsius, the Labadist Frelinghuysen, and Presbyterian Gilbert Tennent—personified radical pietism's weakness as a system of cultural support. This was an international movement largely uninterested in ethnic, national, or cultural issues as such. By its very nature it was antagonistic to elaborate institutions and programs, and once the charismatic leadership of the prophetic first generation dissipated, the movement found affinities with English-speaking Presbyterians but failed to perpetuate uniquenesses of a Dutch religious culture.

The preservation of Dutch dialect within the walls of church and home, however, was already in trouble as the Dutch pietist renewal movement got underway, reinforced by the belated English awakening of the 1740s. The Dutch contributed to the common continental legacy of religious renewal that Scots and Irish shared with them, but even the creation of an indigenous North American clerical association dominated by the pietists, the Coetus ("assembly" or "uniting"), did not preserve the separate quality of Dutch

30. Randall H. Balmer, ed., "John Henry Goetschius and *The Unknown God*: Eighteenth-Century Pietism in the Middle Colonies," *Pennsylvania Magazine of History and Biography*, CXIII (1989), 575–608; William Demarest, trans., *Sermons by Theodorus Jacobus Frelinghuysen* (New York, 1856), 64–70.

culture for long. The classis at Amsterdam finally agreed, after much pietist lobbying from North America, to create this body in 1747.[31] This organization, coming into being when the Dutch language was already disappearing among younger worshipers, provided a clerical network of exchange and cooperation. But by 1753 "the Dutch spoken by ministers educated in the Netherlands could no longer be understood by the Dutch of the Middle Colonies," according to one contemporary observer. The "common barbarous Dutch spoken in our families" was wholly different from the "studied and ornamented Style of the Pulpit."[32] Preaching in the Dutch churches shifted finally to English, precisely a century after the political conquest of New Netherland. Dutch pietism was tamed, finding an institutional home in Queen's College in 1766, where its peculiarly Dutch qualities swiftly vanished. Van Dieren had dropped his ministry to become a prosperous miller by the 1740s; Goetschius also figured in the founding of Queen's and by the time of his death in 1774 was advertising his services as a tutor in the secular press.

The rural, religious, family-centered Dutch culture of the eighteenth century had enjoyed an extension on life partly because Dutch families perpetuated for a time culturally distinct notions about marital property and faith, at least until midcentury. Yet, lacking a systematic, institutionalized support for educating the young, bereft of the charismatic personalities of the pietist revivalists of the 1720s and 1730s, further isolated by more prosperous Dutch families who adapted to English legal ways, this rural culture too began to fade, though still evident in remote hamlets in New Jersey and New York in the early nineteenth century.[33] Despite earlier seventeenth-century differences in agricultural practices, by the mid-1700s no compelling economic or political grounds existed to perpetuate even a separate domestic culture upon a younger generation.[34]

31. Marilyn J. Westerkamp, *Triumph of the Laity: Scots-Irish Piety and the Great Awakening, 1625–1760* (New York, 1988), suggests the transfer of a Reformed sacramental piety to Scotland that reemerged in the colonies by the 1720s; for connections between Frelinghuysen, Tennent, and this tradition, see 161–176.

32. Balmer, *Perfect Babel*, 129.

33. Walter Christaller's central place theory is the basis for this analysis. For a reevaluation of his thesis, see K. S. Beavon, *Central Place Theory: A Reinterpretation* (White Plains, N.Y., 1977). James T. Lemon explains that one large center with two at a second level and more in larger hinterlands best describes a central place where "population and function reflect one another, as does the level of wealth. The real world does not neatly fit the theory, but it does provide a useful starting point and a model for comparison." Lemon, "Colonial America in the Eighteenth Century," in Robert D. Mitchell and Paul A. Groves, eds., *North America: The Historical Geography of a Changing Continent* (Totowa, N.J., 1987), 133.

34. Robert D. Mitchell, "The Colonial Origins of Anglo-America," and James T. Lemon, "Colonial America in the Eighteenth Century," in Mitchell and Groves, eds., *North America*, 93–146. For an attempt to suggest transferred agricultural practices

By the 1730s, local Dutchmen in rural New York and New Jersey were functioning as justices of the peace, and their homespun notions of rough justice fitted the domestic-religious sphere they cherished. But whether the Dutch actually understood the laws they were sworn to administer is unclear. Pastor Heinrich Melchior Mühlenberg met Dutch justices of the peace in New York befriended by his father-in-law Conrad Weiser. One of these Dutch justices, Mühlenberg wrote, "had not been very well versed in English law, and . . . lived rather remote from the higher and more learned authorities. Hence, when a quarrel was brought before him, he was not always able to help, and at times he could do nothing but advise both parties to go out in the courtyard and settle the matter with their fists. Whenever this happened, they had to become reconciled and go home in peace. This finally led to his resigning his office." Among the Hackensack Dutch, Mühlenberg reported, the older people were possessed of "a certain natural honesty and artlessness. They did not use documents, seals, signatures, bonds, and other such contracts. A man's word and handshake were his bond. . . . Like all other nationalities, they have a special love for their mother tongue."[35] By 1750, when Mühlenberg wrote, these Dutch in both New York and New Jersey preserved this mother tongue only among themselves at home. Those who had appeared to function in the public arena without comprehending English laws were vanishing from the scene. In their places, Dutch-speakers entered politics or the bar, even from rural New Jersey, working in the public arena in English for their own people and the Germans, who together may have composed one-quarter of New Jersey's population.[36]

The Revolutionary war in the Hackensack Valley proved to be a genuine civil war, pitting poorer Dutch and English settlers against rivals, reflecting bitter religious and cultural quarrels bequeathed to that area by the dis-

---

among New York Germans that tends instead to demonstrate New World techniques and habits, see Robert Kuhn McGregor, "Cultural Adaptation in Colonial New York: The Palatine Germans of the Mohawk Valley," *N.Y. Hist.*, LXIX (1988), 5–34; for the Dutch, see McLaughlin, "Dutch Rural New York"; Richard H. Amerman, "Dutch Life in Pre-Revolutionary Bergen County," New Jersey Historical Society, *Proceedings*, LXXVI (1958), 161–181; Reginald McMahon, "The Achter Col Colony on the Hackensack," *N.J. Hist.*, LXXXIX (1971), 221–240.

35. Patricia U. Bonomi, "Local Government in Colonial New York: A Base for Republicanism," in Jacob Judd and Irwin H. Polishook, eds., *Aspects of Early New York Society and Politics* (Tarrytown, N.Y., 1974), 29–50; Theodore G. Tappert and John W. Doberstein, eds., *The Journals of Henry Melchior Muhlenberg*, 3 vols. (Philadelphia, 1942–1958), I, 247–248, 310.

36. Michael C. Batinski, *The New Jersey Assembly, 1738–1775: The Making of a Legislative Community* (Lanham, Md., 1987), 33, 195–196, 209, 231, 264–265, on the Dutch and Huguenot leadership and the sole German (Hendrick Fisher) in the Assembly; see also Thomas L. Purvis, *Proprietors, Patronage, and Paper Money: Legislative Politics in New Jersey, 1703–1776* (New Brunswick, N.J., 1986), 20, 65–66.

placed radical pietist Dutch of the early 1700s. Dominie Goetschius had laid the groundwork for an ethic of resistance that Frelinghuysen also pioneered on the Raritan: both areas became virulently anti-British by the 1760s. The violent response of the Dutch in New Jersey to English political authority seems to have been linked to the intensity of religious renewal that did less to perpetuate an institutionalized form of Dutch life than it did to reawaken and draw upon a heritage of oppression and embattled self-definition that evoked memories of 1664, 1689, and the religious fervor of brave, embattled, charismatic pietist leaders.[37]

Significantly, the Dutch by the 1770s seemed little threatened by Anglo-American political culture. The Dutch had made that culture their own in great measure both at home and in church organizations. They supported the Revolution in proportion to their affinity for separatist religion and a willingness to make their own way, without oversight by or connection to Amsterdam's classis.[38]

That decision, however, worked for Dutch-Americans only when language, a peculiar domestic culture (reflected in property use and inheritance), and religious doctrine and practice watched over from Europe were no longer broadly valued within the Dutch community. The Dutch had long prospered in commerce, politics, and law. By the 1750s their religious and linguistic particularism had waned. Perhaps in rural areas, churches and homes still operated as cultural havens necessary for emotional sustenance. But the gradual disappearance of the language, the peculiar inheritance customs, and the religious identity provoked little comment from Dutch-American communities. Since more than half the Dutch-speakers on the British North American mainland lived in New York and another fifth in New Jersey's Bergen and Somerset counties, what had occurred there comprehended the experience of most Dutch in British North America. The remaining third—scattered along the Delaware in New Castle County, Delaware, in Pennsylvania, in Virginia, and in small groups from New York to Charleston and Savannah—had anglicized even faster.[39]

37. Adrian C. Leiby, *The Revolutionary War in the Hackensack Valley: The Jersey Dutch and the Neutral Ground, 1775–1783* (New Brunswick, N.J., 1962). See also Leiby, *The Early Dutch and Swedish Settlers of New Jersey* (Princeton, N.J., 1964).

38. Balmer, *Perfect Babel*, 144–152.

39. Rink, *Holland on the Hudson*, 117–138, 246–263; Lester J. Cappon *et al.*, eds., *Atlas of Early American History: The Revolutionary Era, 1760–1790* (Princeton, N.J., 1976), 24, 99; Hennig Cohen, "Index of Personal Names for the South Carolina Gazette, 1732–1738," typescript, Caroliniana Library, University of South Carolina. South Carolina Court of Common Pleas Journals, I–III, 1713–1715, 1754–1763, 1763–1769 (South Carolina Department of Archives and History, Columbia, S.C.) reveal the suits for recovery of debts owed the Dutch-American merchants; Martha Zierden *et al.*, comps., *A Survey of Economic Activity in Charleston, 1732–1770* (Charleston, S.C., 1982), for occupations and addresses of John Scher-

Yet the Dutch in North America were from the outset intertwined not only with the English-speakers who rapidly engulfed them but also with a larger continental group. The presence of German-speakers in New Netherland and the settlement by Dutch and German Mennonites of Germantown, Pennsylvania, in 1683 were instances where German-speakers, in the first instance, adjusted to the numerically larger Dutch and, in the latter, dominated the Pennsylvania community.[40] Even as the Dutch declined numerically in North America in the eighteenth century, Dutch merchants in Rotterdam correctly sensed new opportunities as they heard of the official charity of the burgomasters of the city. In early 1709 those officials voted 450 gulden to be distributed by Samuel de Back among the poor Palatines on their way to British North America.[41]

IV

The first phase of the German-speaking *Auswanderung*, or emigration, to North America lasted almost a hundred years, beginning in the early seventeenth century. A few German-speakers were among the 1607 Jamestown colonists; the 1618 pamphlet describing "Diversions that may be enjoyed by noble persons and others" in Virginia was aimed at the nobility and merchant classes, which did produce some early adventurers. By 1625 Peter Minuit helped survey the New Netherland colony and a year later wrested control of the colony away from the council. Minuit's probable Huguenot merchant background parallels that of Jacob Leisler, whose family fled to Basel and eventually to Frankfurt am Main. These German-speakers in North America were joined by men like Hans Kierstade, who left Magde-

---

merhorne, the Vanderhorst, Vander Dusen, and other merchants who established themselves firmly by the 1730s.

40. The spirited, sometimes acrimonious debates at the Krefeld Conference on the tricentennial of German migration to North America, October 1983, rehearsed again all the arguments for a "Dutch" or "German" character of early Germantown. The question is anachronistic, since the political and cultural boundaries between the Netherlands and the Reich territories were still porous. Both linguistically and culturally, the Germantown settlers were, amid Dutch Mennonites and with the exception of prominent persons such as the Rettenhuysens, either Quakers or Brethren of Low German or transplanted Swiss backgrounds from Saint Gall, Bern-Emmental, or other Swiss cantons who had settled in the Kraichgau, the Wetterau, and the lower Rhine since the 1640s. For examples of their writings and movements, see George Frederick Newman and Clyde Lester Groff, comps., *Letters from Our Palatine Ancestors, 1644–1689* (Hershey, Pa., 1984).

41. Dutch West Indies Co., Copies of Dutch Correspondence and Dutch Transcripts concerning German Emigration; 3 DWI Company 8, 1709 Extract uit de Resolutien end Dispositien van Burgemeesteren Reg., Historical Society of Pennsylvania, Philadelphia.

burg to practice physick and medicine in New Netherland. They were part of a constant trickle of largely unorganized individuals. Such well-to-do people financed their own way. Others relied upon charitable help for their journey, and the few German glassblowers at work in early Jamestown had arrived with the help of the Virginia Company.[42] From the family names and history of New Netherland, it would seem that these seventeenth-century migrants came from the North German territories and old Hansa cities as far east as Danzig and Königsberg.

This early migration pattern persisted in the aftermath of the Thirty Years' War, since its devastation depopulated the German southwest and destroyed that region's social and economic institutions, which were renewed only because of immigration by religious refugees from Switzerland. The removal of the Turkish threat after the siege of Vienna was lifted in 1683 threw open vast lands for colonization to the east and south. German migration out of the Palatinate, Baden, Württemberg, and smaller territories located along the Rhine tilted toward the Banat in Hungary or to Prussia's eastern territories, not toward England's distant colonies. Prussia bid aggressively for Dutch maritime artisans to transform Berlin into a major river nexus between east and west and for Calvinist Huguenots fleeing the Revocation of the Edict of Nantes in 1685. This new northern German power also eagerly sought Protestants from territories in the now-prospering southwest, regardless of confessional distinctions.[43] Prussian interest in German-speaking emigrants in North America came from its newly founded university at Halle.

The War of Palatine Succession (1688–1697), which saw Halle rise like a phoenix from Heidelberg's ashes (as a contemporary student hymn put it), was followed by another devastation of the Rhineland in the War of Spanish

42. *Was die Adelspersonen und andere in Virginia für Kurtzweil haben können* (Oppenheim, 1618); on Leisler, see Voorhees, " 'In Behalf of the True Protestants Religion,' " and "The European Ancestry of Jacob Leisler," *New York Genealogical and Biographical Record*, CXX (1989), 193–202; on Minuit and Kierstade, Evjen, *Scandinavian Immigrants*, 390–392.

43. Werner Hacker, *Auswanderungen aus Baden und dem Breisgau: Obere und mittlere rechtsseitige Oberrheinlande im 18. Jahrhundert archivalisch dokumentiert* (Stuttgart, 1980), 35–37, 93–132; Hans Georg Majer, "Die Türken-Gegner des Westens am Ende des 17. Jahrhunderts," in Hubert Glaser, ed., *Kurfürst Max Emmanuel: Bayern und Europa um 1700* (Munich, 1976), 362–372; Hacker, *Auswanderung aus Rheinpfalz und Saarland im 18. Jahrhundert* (Stuttgart, 1987), further documents the small percentage of German migration oriented overseas; of some 16,000 entries in this volume, only some 2,000 names can be conclusively identified with the *Amerikaauswanderung*. On Prussian policies and colonization, see, for example, Otto Kerschhofer, "Die Salzburger Emigration nach Preussisch-Litauen," *Aus Mitteilungen der Gesellschaft für salzburger Landeskunde*, CXVI (1976), 175–254.

Succession in 1709. These wars reoriented early German migration patterns decisively. Now, migration came mostly from the German southwest. Between 1683 and 1783, 500,000 German-speakers left the Reich, to settle not only in Hungary, Russia, and Spain but also in French overseas colonies. And perhaps 125,000 of that total chose British North America. For the Reformed of the German Rhineland among them, no experience remained more decisive than the repeated devastation of the Palatinate—in the Thirty Years' War, in 1688–1697, and finally in 1709. The destruction of 1709–1710 captured the imagination of the British as well as of the Palatines and transferred to North America both hostility and fear directed against France and Catholicism, and a positive assessment of British religious and political liberties. Queen Anne's succor of the 1709 refugees who were eventually sent on to New York helped to secure a long-term German–North American awareness that on the English colonial periphery their hereditary foe, the French, waited, in alliance with some of the native American tribes. In the 1730s, correspondents from the lower Rhineland darkly informed relatives in New York, "We . . . have little confidence in France, since they generally conspire with the Turks under the table, as everyone has known very well all along; and if France should get mixed up in it, then Germany will again be plunged into widespread unrest."[44]

The new southwest German migration of 1709 looked both backward in time to religiously motivated seventeenth-century migration by free church dissidents and forward to the more massive, economically driven movements by mainstream Lutherans and Reformed that followed in its wake. Scattered groups of transplanted Swiss in the Kraichgau southeast of Heidelberg and in the Palatinate at large who continued on to Britain's colonies were typically dispossessed or marginal handworkers, weavers, agricultural day laborers. Many were conscience-stricken perfectionists who reached for North America. Most religious radical groups succumbed within a generation to English-speaking cultures; others simply isolated themselves, as was the case with monks like Johannes Kelpius.[45]

These people had few ties to the public life of their former homelands, and their contacts with the dominant English-speaking culture in North America were marginal. Linguistic, political, and social conversations were held at bay by firm retention of various German dialects. On occasion, these groups were decidedly at odds with their neighbors, as was the case with those German Quakers and Mennonites who had signed the earliest known (1688)

44. F. J. Sypher, trans., "Voices in the Wilderness: Letters to Colonial New York from Germany (1726–1737)," *N.Y. Hist.*, LXVII (1986), 331–352, esp. 344.

45. Elizabeth W. Fisher, "'Prophesies and Revelations': German Cabbalists in Early Pennsylvania," *PMHB*, CIX (1985), 299–333; Julius Friedrich Sachse, *The German Pietists of Provincial Pennsylvania* (Philadelphia, 1895).

protest against slavery, or the Mennonites who engaged in peaceful relationships with native Americans.[46] Indeed, Amish, Mennonite, and Brethren leaders seemed to want little more from British North America than to be left alone; they were gratified to find their wishes largely granted.

The radical dissidents from Bern-Emmental, the Kraichgau, Palatinate, and lower Rhine had developed an understanding of God, humankind, and society that rejected a role for the prince or the republic in determining matters of conscience. They rejected infant baptism and denounced oath taking as satanic. Such frontal attacks on the very basis of the Swiss Confederation's existence as a compact bound together by solemn religious oath (*Eidgenossenschaft*) made them far more dangerous to contemporaries surrounded by the imperial Hapsburgs than later sympathizers have conceded.[47] Spurning as well the need for a learned hireling ministry and demanding absolute submission to the will of the community, the *Gemein*, they were hounded into migration as mercilessly by Reformed as by Catholic or Lutheran countrymen.

But the 1709 migration of German-speaking people to British territory also looked beyond this religiously motivated, small, and scattered migration of the seventeenth century. The 13,000 persons who left the Palatinate presented British authorities with an unprecedented crisis, since the impoverished refugees could not be adequately housed or transported to the colonies. Eventually, 2,344 settled in New York, and another 650 reached North Carolina to join the early Swiss settlements planted by Christoph von Graffenried. This migration was larger than any that preceded it and presaged the scale of renewed movement that began in the 1720s as more Dutch traders realized that what had worked among the Irish and Scots looking to emigrate to North America might work among the German-speakers too. By 1727, the large migration to Pennsylvania, which also trickled into German

46. For more typical German-Afro-American relations, see Betty Wood, *Slavery in Colonial Georgia, 1730–1775* (Athens, Ga., 1984), 59–73. Despite expressions of admiration for Moravian accomplishments among native Americans, neither Reformed nor Lutheran groups managed to mount significant missions among them; see, for example, Tappert and Doberstein, eds., *Journals of Muhlenberg*, I, 386–387.

47. Approximately 4,000 free church Swiss arrived in Pennsylvania, 1705–1756; about 800 Reformed Swiss settled at Purrysburg, South Carolina, and at least another 100 populated the Orangeburg area. An indeterminate number of Swiss Reformed were among the congregants of 16 German Reformed communities in Pennsylvania—perhaps 5,000 German-speaking Swiss in all. See Leo Schelbert, "Schweizer Auswanderung in das Gebiet der Vereinigten Staaten von Nordamerika" (forthcoming in Paul Hugger, ed., *Handbuch der schweizerischen Volkskunde*); Schelbert, *Swiss Migration to America: The Swiss Mennonites* (New York, 1980); Paul Wernle, *Der schweizerische Protestantismus im 18. Jahrhundert*, I (Tübingen, 1922), 111–356. "Swiss" here refers to German-speakers, regardless of origin in or outside one of the cantons, who were connected to the Swiss Brethren, the radicals who subscribed in 1527 to the Schleitheim Confession.

Lutheran and Reformed settlements in the piedmont of Virginia, included mystics and spiritualists represented by Pennsylvania's Schwenkfelder communities and the mixed settlement of Rosicrucians, Protestant monastics, and radical pietists who came to rest at Ephrata, northeast of Lancaster. But German-speaking migration was now primarily Lutheran, Reformed, and Moravian in composition. Lutherans alone by the 1770s would account for more than half of the German settlers in North America.[48]

The early arrivals in New York, Pennsylvania, and the Carolinas up to the 1720s had provoked only sporadic concern over their alien language and ways. The most noted example occurred when the immigrants' misunderstanding of their rights to property conflicted with their obligations to produce pitch and tar for Governor Robert Hunter in New York. Owing both to language barriers and to conflicting expectations on the part of both parties, some of the Palatines emigrated illegally to the Schoharie Valley between 1713 and 1719, fleeing from what looked to them like the hated forced labor of the German territories. Threats of legal action to hold them to contractual obligations propelled a further migration into Pennsylvania. Word of the Palatine difficulties in New York reached the Reich, and the royal colony never again played the significant role in shaping the culture of German-speakers it seemed to be destined for in 1709. But the incident was striking precisely for its oddity: German-speakers' relations with British political institutions were overwhelmingly positive, in no small part because so many of the settlers were religious and economic refugees.[49]

48. Horst Weigelt, *The Schwenkfelder in Silesia*, trans. Peter C. Erb (Pennsburg, Pa., 1985); Peter C. Erb, ed., *Schwenkfeld and Early Schwenkfelderism* (Pennsburg, Pa., 1986); on transconfessional support for Reformed and Lutheran groups, spurred in part by anxieties about more radical sectarians, see Eamon Duffy, "The Society of Promoting Christian Knowledge and Europe: The Background to the Founding of the Christentumgesellschaft," *Pietismus und Neuzeit*, VII (1981), 28–42; Geoffrey F. Nuttall, "Continental Pietism" in van den Berg and van Dooren, eds., *Pietismus und Reveil*, 207–236; Marthi Pritzker-Ehrlich, *Michael Schlatter von St. Gallen (1716–1790): Eine biographische Untersuchung zur schweizerischen Amerika-Auswanderung des 18. Jahrhunderts* (Zurich, 1981); the size and extent of German Lutheran contributions to North American congregations can be followed in Kurt Aland, ed., *Die Korrespondenz Heinrich Melchior Mühlenbergs: Aus der Anfangszeit des deutschen Luthertums in Nordamerika* (Berlin, 1986–); Tappert and Doberstein, eds., *Journals of Muhlenberg*, I, II. I have commented on one aspect of this pattern in "Germans, Property, and the First Great Awakening: Rehearsal for a Revolution?" in Winfried Herget and Karl Ortseifen, eds., *The Transit of Civilization from Europe to America: Festschrift in Honor of Hans Galinsky* (Tübingen, 1986), 165–184. Richard K. MacMaster, *Land, Piety, Peoplehood: The Establishment of Mennonite Communities in America, 1683–1790* (Scottsdale, Pa., 1985), 19–78, suggests that sustained support from the Netherlands or Switzerland was atypical for Mennonites; Amish migration seems to have been self-financed.

49. Peter Kalm confirmed the negative reports sent back by German-speakers; see Benson, ed., *Peter Kalm's Travel*, 142–143. For a standard version of this conflict, see

From 1727 until 1783, the second phase of German migration assumed impressive proportions. From surviving lists of arrivals that can be compared with local records in villages of origin, it appears that more than three-quarters were family members who traveled together, in groups of about four persons.[50]

In response to this movement, private entrepreneurs, the so-called Newlanders who plied the routes often free of charge, emerged as key figures in the trade and in the creative attempt to get cash-poor migrants passage to the colonies. Securing in North America a future purchaser for the price of passage, the Newlander helped invent the redemptioner contracts for the merchants whose credit they were extending. The small but successful German-speaking population already living in Pennsylvania provided the most natural market for "redeeming" the new arrivals. Quite humane and workable in its early stages, the system degenerated as the number of migrants swelled and as delays occurred in redeeming contracts, sometimes separating family members permanently and confining the newcomers to unsanitary ships swept periodically by "Dutch fever." At least 5 percent perished in the crossing; at least another 5 percent failed to survive the seasoning, a rate higher among small children. Despite these horrors, the majority of

---

Lawrence H. Leder, *Robert Livingston, 1654–1728, and the Politics of Colonial New York* (Chapel Hill, N.C., 1961), 211–226.

50. For the 4,300 migrants from the Rheinpfalz, Saarland, Baden, and Breisach, see Werner Hacker, *Auswanderung aus Rheinpfalz und Saarland*; Hacker, *Auswanderungen aus Baden und dem Breisgau*; the same pattern applies to the Kraichgau. The 500-plus emigrants documented are also overwhelmingly family members related to each other; see Hacker, *Kurpfälzische Auswanderer vom Unteren Neckar: Rechtsrheinische Gebiete der Kurpfalz* (Stuttgart, 1983); and Annette Kunselman Burgert, *Eighteenth Century Emigrants from German-speaking Lands to North America: The Northern Kraichgau* (Breinigsville, Pa., 1983). See also Farley Grubb, "German Immigration to Pennsylvania, 1709 to 1820," *Journal of Interdisciplinary History*, XX (1989–1990), 417–436, who presents convincing evidence that most German migration (in contrast to English) was in family groups before 1760, and that even for the more than half who entered some form of servitude, family bonds remained largely intact. On social mobility in the Rhineland, where stagnation in the countryside and some downward mobility because of population pressures characterized town life, see Jeffry M. Diefendorf, "Soziale Mobilität im Rheinland im 18. Jahrhundert," *Scripta Mercaturae*, XIX, nos. 1–2 (1985), 88–112. On social and legal background surrounding the migration, see Roeber, "The Origins and Transfer of German-American Concepts of Property and Inheritance," *Perspectives in American History*, n.s., III (1987), 115–171. Migration siphoned off about 20 percent of population increase. See Wolfgang von Hippel, *Auswanderung aus Südwestdeutschland: Studien zur württembergischen Auswanderung und Auswanderungspolitik im 18. und 19. Jahrhundert* (Stuttgart, 1984), 27–33. See also, for an example of how migration alleviated social tensions in one area, Robert Selig, *Räutige Schafe und geizige Hirten: Studien zur Auswanderung aus dem Hochstift Würzburg im 18. Jahrhundert und ihre Ursachen* (Würzburg, 1988), 85–195.

arrivals from the Reich in all the colonies from Nova Scotia to Georgia established themselves eventually as smallholders and artisans. A smaller handful emerged as genuinely wealthy and highly influential merchants and traders.[51]

Increasingly after 1763, single young men and families less well connected than those who were funneled into the Rotterdam-Philadelphia route began arriving in Baltimore, Charleston, Savannah, and other ports. From the end of the Seven Years' War to the Revolution this migration contributed another 25,000 Germans to the 100,000 previous arrivals. Periodic interruptions occurred for the entire period, caused by the efforts of authorities concerned about the loss of wealth and potentially valuable labor. As recruiting efforts spread, authorities in the Palatinate, Mainz, and Württemberg sought to stop the flow along the Rhine. Prussia, Hannover, and Saxony took steps to halt movement down the Elbe and to block a late-blooming role for Hamburg as a port of debarkation.[52]

51. Marianne S. Wokeck, "Promoters and Passengers: The German Immigrant Trade, 1683–1775," in Richard S. Dunn and Mary Maples Dunn, eds., *The World of William Penn* (Philadelphia, 1986), 259–278; Abbot Emerson Smith, *Colonists in Bondage: White Servitude and Convict Labor in America, 1607–1776* (Chapel Hill, N.C., 1947), 3–25, 50–52; David W. Galenson, *White Servitude in Colonial America: An Economic Analysis* (Cambridge, 1981), 13–15, 233; Hans-Jürgen Grabbe, "Das Ende des Redemptioner-Systems in den Vereinigten Staaten," *Amerikastudien / American Studies*, XXIX (1984), 277–296; Farley Grubb, "The Market Structure of Shipping German Immigrants to Colonial America," *PMHB*, CXI (1987), 27–48; Grubb, "The Incidence of Servitude in Trans-Atlantic Migration, 1771–1804," *Explorations in Economic History*, XXII (1985), 316–339; Grubb, "Redemptioner Immigration to Pennsylvania: Evidence on Contract Choice and Profitability," *Journal of Economic History*, XLVI (1986), 407–418.

52. This simplifies Lowell C. Bennion, "Flight from the Reich: A Geographic Exposition of Southwest German Migration, 1683–1815" (Ph.D. diss., Syracuse University, 1971); Marianne Sophia Wokeck, "A Tide of Alien Tongues: The Flow and Ebb of German Immigration to Pennsylvania, 1683–1776" (Ph.D. diss., Temple University, 1982); William I. Hull, *William Penn and the Dutch Quaker Migration to Pennsylvania* (Swarthmore, Pa., 1935); and Wokeck, "Harnessing the Lure of the 'Best Poor Man's Country': The Dynamics of German-speaking Immigration to British North America, 1683–1783," in Ida Altman and James Horn, eds., *To Make America: European Emigration in the Early Modern Period* (forthcoming). I wish to thank Dr. Wokeck for a copy of the manuscript and several important comments on the issue of migration in general. The migration of the first German and Dutch families from Krefeld to North America was part of an older, internal migration back and forth from the county of Mörs, with Hollanders settling in the Palatinate around Kriegsheim near Worms. See both Samuel Whitaker Pennypacker, *The Settlement of Germantown, Pennsylvania, and the Beginning of German Immigration to North America* (Lancaster, Pa., 1899); and Stephanie Grauman Wolf, *Urban Village: Population, Community, and Family Structure in Germantown, Pennsylvania, 1683–1800* (Princeton, N.J., 1976). On migration from the Nassau-Oranien district which confirms both the fact that most migrants were marginal propertyholders and documents the activities of recruiting agents, see Martina Sprengel, "Studien zur Nordamerikaauswanderung in der ersten Hälfte des 18. Jahrhunderts: Nassau-Oranien"

By 1768 an imperial edict from Joseph II forbade all emigration to lands not connected with the empire, a directive aimed squarely at the *Amerikaauswanderung*. Nonetheless, by 1773, transports to Baltimore and Philadelphia again numbered one thousand persons per year. By the time this repeated migration was interrupted in 1775, many British colonies had significant German-speaking populations. Pennsylvania had the highest proportion, for its population was about 33 percent German; in other regions, New York and New Jersey's combined population was 14 percent German-speaking; Maryland with Virginia's, 17 percent; and South Carolina with Georgia's, 9 percent. Nearly 10 percent of the total mainland British colonial population was now German-speaking. Small wonder the former Bostonian Benjamin Franklin fretted that the English were being "Dutched."[53]

V

This overview of German migration begins to assume its proper cultural dimensions, however, only in the context of the support networks that bound German-Americans to one another in various colonial settlements, and back to the Reich as well. Early migrants, largely from free church groups, were supported in their journeys by charitable groups such as the

(master's thesis, University of Cologne, 1984). Migration from northern Germany did not cease completely. Andreas Brink's dissertation (in progress) at the University of Hamburg examines the 17 ships departing from that port, 1748–1754, and finds at least some evidence that the older northern or Low German migrants continued to leave, though in much smaller numbers than from the territories further east and south. I wish to thank Mr. Brink and his adviser, Professor Günther Moltmann, for permission to summarize his work here. By choosing to emphasize confessional differences, I do not ignore more recent historiography that points to traditions of peasant rebellion, communalism, and chronic unrest in certain areas of the Reich. For a sample of this research, see Winfried Schultze, ed., *Aufstände, Revolten, Prozesse: Beiträge zu bäuerlichen Widerstandsbewegungen im frühneuzeitlichen Europa* (Stuttgart, 1983); and for a telling critique of Peter Blickle's hypotheses about communalism, peasant revolts, and constitutional developments in the Reich, Dietmar Willoweit, "Genossenschaftsprinzip und altständische Entscheidungsstrukturen in der frühneuzeitlichen Staatsentwicklung: Ein Diskussionsbeitrag," in Gerhard Dilcher and Bernhard Diestlekamp, eds., *Recht, Gericht, Genossenschaft, und Policey: Studien zu Grundbegriffen der germanistischen Rechtshistorie: Symposion für Adalbert Erler* (Frankfurt, 1987), 126–138.

53. Benjamin Franklin, "Observations concerning the Increase of Mankind," in Leonard W. Labaree *et al.*, eds., *The Papers of Benjamin Franklin*, IV (New Haven, Conn., 1961), 234. On the debate over population estimates and ethnic percentages, see Thomas L. Purvis, Donald H. Akenson, and Forrest McDonald and Ellen Shapiro McDonald, in "The Population of the United States, 1790: A Symposium," *WMQ*, 3d Ser., XLI (1984), 85–135.

London Yearly Meeting of the Quakers, the Mennonite Committee on Foreign Needs in Rotterdam, or Amish and Mennonite authorities in Switzerland. Calvinist Rhineland centers (Heidelberg and later other capitals) played no significant role in sustaining Reformed activities in the English-speaking world during the early migration.

By the 1720s, emigrants were aided in their journeys by elaborate networks of trade and communication, by aggressive recruiting and organizing efforts by independent agents, and, more rarely, by individual colonies themselves. Of no small importance to the approximately 125,000 German-speakers who eventually arrived in British North America between 1683 and 1783, traders and shippers on the Neckar-Rhine network, from Stuttgart-Canstaat and Ulm to Heilbronn, Mannheim, and Heidelberg on the Rhine, matched their Main River competitors on the route from Nürnberg to Würzburg, the imperial city of Frankfurt, and then Mainz.[54]

By the 1740s, Dutch traders transporting ever larger numbers of Germans, arriving at the mouth of the Rhine "on credit" to the British colonies, had fashioned a system of advertising and promotion through agents often based in Frankfurt that attracted British interest.

Rotterdam and Amsterdam merchants who competed for prospective German emigrants picked up arrivals from the Reich at the border until 1739, when the Netherlands required posting of bond to prevent German-speakers from remaining in the republic and becoming public charges. British merchants like John Hunt joined Dutch firms and German-speaking Newlanders in this recruitment and transport business by 1740. More unusual were the efforts of individual colonies like Nova Scotia, whose organizers commissioned John Dick to attract settlers; South Carolina used its agent Charles Garth for the same mission in the 1760s.[55]

Another network arose in the early eighteenth century paralleling the Dutch-German transport connection, adding support of incalculable importance to the German-speakers in North America. This network was built through the Lutheran chapel at the Court of St. James's in London first through Heinrich Wilhelm Ludolf, a member of the British Privy Council, and through preachers like Anton Wilhelm Böhme and, after 1723, Friedrich Michael Ziegenhagen. The Frankfurt diplomat and scholar Hiob Ludolf (and uncle of Heinrich Wilhelm Ludolf) had known both August Hermann

54. Hermann Aubin and Wolfgang Zorn, eds., *Handbuch der deutschen Wirtschafts- und Sozialgeschichte* (Stuttgart, 1971), I, 555–560.

55. Wokeck, "Harnessing the Lure," in Altman and Horn, eds., *To Make America*, 15–19; and Wokeck, *The Trade in Strangers: Transporting Germans and Irish to Colonial America: Precursors of Modern Atlantic Migrations* (forthcoming), chap. 5; Robert A. Selig, "Emigration, Fraud, Humanitarianism, and the Founding of Londonderry, South Carolina, 1763–1765," *Eighteenth-Century Studies*, XXIII (1989), 1–23 (I wish to thank Professor Selig for a prepublication copy of the paper).

Francke (the pietist leader at Halle) and the Frankfurt pietists. The Ludolfs encouraged through their contacts in London a Halle tie to the Society for the Propagation of Christian Knowledge recently founded by Dr. Thomas Bray. Francke and two associates were elected to membership, and they commissioned a pamphlet on settling in the New World. Their choice fell on the Reverend Daniel Falckner, a Lutheran pastor with mystical inclinations tying him to Johann Kelpius's early group of hermits, the Wissahickon Brethren who settled in Pennsylvania in 1700. Falckner produced the first practical guide for Germans contemplating removal to British North America. Published in 1702, Falckner's *Curieuse Nachricht von Pennsylvania* reflected both the fact that early migrants were free church radicals and the growing importance of Halle's political, financial, and diplomatic ties to London and the colonies. By the 1720s, as Halle's religious, linguistic, and scientific expeditions were penetrating Siberia, Ghana, Tehran, Tranquebar, and Brazil, interest also quickened about North America. Early patrons donated generously to establish a connection between Halle and the British colonies.[56]

The pietist renewal movement that began within German Lutheranism and shaped Halle's destiny shared characteristics with Reformed efforts that drew on independent sources in Swiss and Dutch theology. Moravians, too, participated in the pietist vision and the support networks that grew out of its institutionalized energies. Mainstream German Lutheran pietism pioneered by Phillip Jakob Spener and Francke constrained the exuberance of the mystical and separatist elements of pietism and gave it a powerful institutional and social thrust that reached beyond its center at Halle. International in their outlook, mainstream pietists aimed at renewing and uniting a dispirited Protestantism.[57]

The range of cultural reinforcement that Halle missionary efforts extended to German communities in North America was exceptionally broad. Direct monetary patronage and leadership were confined to the struggling Lutheran congregations in Georgia and the Pennsylvania mission field, in-

56. Halle representatives in London attempted to influence the kind of migrants and to maintain good relations with British patrons by issuing (from the pen of Anton Wilhelm Böhme) *Das verlangte, nicht erlangte Canaan* . . . (Frankfurt, 1711), an attack on the behavior of the Palatine migrants of 1709 and the false expectations raised by their leader Josua von Kocherthal, in his *Ausführlich und umständlicher Bericht von der berühmten Landschafft Carolina* . . . (Frankfurt, 1709). On Böhme, see R. Barry Lewis, "The Failure of the Anglican-Prussian Ecumenical Effort of 1710–1714," *Church History*, XLVII (1978), 381–399; and Arno Sames, *Anton Wilhelm Böhme, 1673–1722: Studien zum ökumenischen Denken und Handeln eines halleschen Pietisten* (Göttingen, 1990).

57. For a definitive overview of research on pietism, see Martin Schmidt, "Epochen der Pietismusforschung," in van den Berg and van Dooren, eds., *Pietismus und Reveil*, 22–79.

cluding groups from Hebron Valley, Virginia, to New York. But the pharmacopoeia, printed materials, orphanages, and tradition of preparatory and university-level education extended far and wide, beyond confessional bounds, and beyond the Caribbean and continental North America.[58] Swiss, German Reformed, and Dutch pietists came to Halle to study and write; the later Moravian leader Count Nicholas von Zinzendorf drew upon Halle for his visions of the organized Moravian towns. So did George Whitefield, who exchanged a lively correspondence with Halle as he schemed to establish an orphanage, complete with slaves, in Georgia. The Halle leadership disapproved, since bound labor would undercut their goals of training orphans to be literate and economically self-sufficient.[59]

By the 1730s, Anglicans like John Wesley and Whitefield envisioned broad cooperation in evangelism based on Halle's network and long association with the Society for the Propagation of Christian Knowledge. Halle's contact in Philadelphia, the former Silesian Daniel Weisiger, received shipments of books and gratis samples of Halle pamphlets for distribution and encouragement of education. When the Reformed South Carolina Swiss Johannes Tobler tried unsuccessfully to obtain some books from Hamburg, he turned to pastor Johann Martin Boltzius, who secured them from Halle. Cotton Mather and Jonathan Edwards read accounts of Halle's work in Latin books they had ordered from the Leipzig and Frankfurt book fairs, Mather describing in approving terms the warmth of God now glowing in the heart of Germany at "Hale." Halle's Lutheran missionary Heinrich Melchior Mühlenberg counseled all German pastors to brush up on their Latin before arriving in America, since English-speaking clerics knew no German but could converse in the international learned tongue about the treatises they had read outlining Halle's work and objectives.[60] Analyzing the costs and

58. For instance, see the philosophical studies of the first Ghana student at Halle, in Dorothea Siegmund-Schultze *et al.*, trans. and eds., *Antonius Guilielmus Amo Afer of Axim in Ghana: A Translation of His Works* (Halle, 1968); also Burchard Brentjes, "Daniel Gottlieb Messerschmidt—ein Absolvent der hallischen Universität und ein Entdecker Sibiriens (1720–1727)," *Acta Antigua Academiae Scientiarum Hungaricae*, XXXI (1985–1988), 101–169; A. Lehmann, *Es begann in Tranquebar: Die Geschichte der ersten evangelischen Kirche in Indien* (Berlin, 1956).

59. Karl Zehrer, "Die Beziehung zwischen dem hallischen Pietismus und dem frühen Methodismus," *Pietismus und Neuzeit*, II (1975), 43–56; Udo Sträter, "Pietismus und Sozialtätigkeit: Zur Frage nach der Wirkungsgeschichte des 'Waisenhauses' in Halle und des Frankfurter Armen-, Waisen-, und Arbeitshauses," *ibid.*, VIII (1982), 201–230.

60. Samuel Urlsperger, comp., *Detailed Reports on the Salzburger Immigrants . . .*, ed. and trans. George Fenwick Jones *et al.* (Athens, Ga., 1972–), XII, 5–6 (1748) (hereafter cited as *Detailed Reports*); Ernst Benz, "Ecumenical Relations between Boston Puritanism and German Pietism: Cotton Mather and August Hermann Francke," *Harvard Theological Review*, LIV (1961), 159–191; Aland, ed., *Korrespondenz Mühlenbergs*, I, 323 (1748).

advantages of sending missionaries and materials over Hamburg-Altona and London against sending through Rotterdam, Halle's financial analysts found the Hamburg-London connection better, as did German-speaking recipients like the Lancaster merchants who reported their preferences to Halle through Philadelphia contacts in 1775.[61]

Other German-speaking groups not so well connected to this network did not fare as well. The German Reformed had to rely upon Amsterdam and Switzerland for money and ministers and were permanently hampered in their bid for organizing church life. In Philadelphia they sent Jacob Reiff back to Europe in 1730 in an attempt to collect funds for the struggling congregation. The handful of German Reformed pastors who did finally arrive in Pennsylvania in the 1750s were from Herborn on the upper Rhine. But the patronage exercised by Amsterdam was more resented than appreciated and, in any event, continued to be disbursed via the historic Dutch contacts in New York, where the German Reformed were numerically weak. A vicious court battle between recently arrived pastors and wealthy lay

61. No published study documents adequately Halle's connections to the New World. My statements rest on examinations of advertisements of booksellers throughout Germany appearing in the Frankfurt *Ordentliche wochentliche Kayserl. Rechts-Post-Zeitung* for the years from 1740 to 1790; from the materials on donations and support for American missions in the Archiv der Franckeschen Stiftungen, Universitäts- und Landesbibliothek Sachsen-Anhalt, Halle, German Democratic Republic. Medicines, Halle drugs, and prescriptions can be studied in Mühlenberg's *Korrespondenz*, and see also the new edition of Christian Friedrich Richter, *Waisenhaus-Arzneien Leipzig, 1705*, 3 vols. (Leipzig, 1985), which should be considered alongside traditional works emphasizing folk medicine in Pennsylvania: for example, Thomas R. Brendle and Claude W. Unger, *Folk Medicine of the Pennsylvania Germans: The Non-Occult Cures* (New York, 1970); Andrew S. Berky, *Practitioner in Physick: A Biography of Abraham Wagner, 1717–1763* (Pennsburg, Pa., 1954). On the Moravian networks and accomplishments, see Jacob John Sessler, *Communal Pietism among Early American Moravians* (New York, 1933); Mabel Haller, *Early Moravian Education in Pennsylvania* (Nazareth, Pa., 1953); Gillian Lindt Gollin, *Moravians in Two Worlds: A Study of Changing Communities* (New York, 1967); William J. Murtagh, *Moravian Architecture and Town Planning: Bethlehem, Pennsylvania, and Other Eighteenth-Century American Settlements* (Chapel Hill, N.C., 1967); John R. Weinlick, "Moravianism in the American Colonies," in F. Ernest Stoeffler, ed., *Continental Pietism and Early American Christianity* (Grand Rapids, Mich., 1976), 123–163; Daniel B. Thorp, *The Moravian Community in North Carolina: Pluralism on the Southern Frontier* (Knoxville, Tenn., 1988); the literature and argument of Rudolf Dellsperger's essay "Kirchengemeinschaft und Gewissensfreiheit: Samuel Güldins Einspruch gegen Zinzendorfs Unionstätigkeit in Pennsylvania, 1742," *Pietismus und Neuzeit*, XI (1985), 40–58; and Beverly Prior Smaby, *The Transformation of Moravian Bethlehem: From Commercial Mission to Family Economy* (Philadelphia, 1988), 27–86. On Hamburg's role as distributing point, see Tappert and Doberstein, eds., *Journals of Muhlenberg*, for example, II, 534–536; for an example of a European bequest passing over Halle for Philadelphia via Hamburg, see Senatsprotokoll, CL VIII Lit C c Nr. 15, June 20, 1787, Staatsarchiv Hamburg.

leaders in the 1750s over charitable bequests, land issues, and variant traditions within Reformed theology hurt this church in Pennsylvania.[62] In the other colonies, Reformed settlers languished without pastoral or educational support except for what Johann Michael Böhme and Michael Schlatter could extend in the North, or what the Zublys, Giessendanners, and Theusses could manage in South Carolina and Georgia. Many Reformed Germans outside Pennsylvania rapidly adapted to English Presbyterianism and through this relatively simple adjustment anglicized probably more rapidly than any other German group. The German Reformed seemed to be traders, acquirers, entrepreneurs, and adjusters to the Anglo-American world, perhaps as much by choice as necessity.[63] German Calvinism was replanted in American soil largely by the Swiss and Dutch; English Presbyterianism, despite initial language barriers, could not have looked entirely novel. Only in Pennsylvania, where migration continued to reinforce their numbers, did the German Reformed enjoy leadership from clergy and Philadelphia merchants, who linked them to the broader network of numerically greater Lutherans.[64]

Until the early 1730s, Count Nicholas von Zinzendorf and his wife were among the major contributors to Halle's network building. They later broke with Halle's international and transdenominational orbit to construct a Moravian version of their own centered at the village of Herrnhut, but the Moravians also relied upon the London conduit to the North American colonies. After a failed experiment in Georgia, Zinzendorf decided by the 1740s upon Pennsylvania as a major base of operations, from where the Moravians developed both institutions and ideas that found expression in

62. The best modern assessment of these developments is Pritzker-Ehrlich, *Michael Schlatter*; see also William J. Hinke, *Ministers of the German Reformed Congregations in Pennsylvania and Other Colonies in the Eighteenth Century* (Lancaster, Pa., 1951); James Tanis, "Reformed Pietism in Colonial America," in Stoeffler, ed., *Continental Pietism*, 34–73.

63. On this pattern in general, see Eloise Hiebert Meneses, "Traders and Marginality in a Complex Social System," *Ethnology: An International Journal of Cultural and Social Anthropology*, XXVI (1987), 231–244; on the Philadelphia German-speaking merchants, see below.

64. For the literature, see Roeber, "Origins and Transfer," *Perspectives in Am. Hist.*, n.s., III (1987), 118–119. Yearly amounts of support given by Europeans to the North American Reformed are unknown, and Dutch or German records on the subject are exceedingly scarce. For an example of the tensions between German Reformed and Dutch patrons over money and language, see the exchange in Hugh Hastings, ed., *Ecclesiastical Records: State of New York*, VI (Albany, N.Y., 1905), 4036–4038, and for the successful attempt to secure a pastor from Heidelberg for New York German Reformed with an account of charitable contributions from Europe, 4038–4039 (1766). On the difficulty in reconstituting charitable contributions to Reformed congregations, see Aland, ed., *Korrespondenz Mühlenbergs*, II, 159, n. 81.

North Carolina by the 1750s. Zinzendorf, Spener's godson, educated at Halle, fascinated by Catholic organizations he encountered in Strassburg, originally envisioned a pan-Protestant union under which Lutheran, Calvinist, Moravian, and perhaps Anglican traditions could operate together. Ordained both as a Lutheran pastor and a Moravian bishop, Zinzendorf possessed both the financial means and the persuasive powers to establish communities at his estate that came to be known as "Herrnhut," a second center in the Wetterau, another in the Netherlands, and the American communities at Bethlehem, Pennsylvania, and Wachovia, North Carolina. Moravians in London sparked John Wesley's conversion experiences at Fetter Lane meetings and impressed George Whitefield, to the dismay of his Halle correspondents, who hoped to use Whitefield in their own network of support and who disapproved of the Moravian version of pietism. Securing legal recognition of the Moravian church as an "ancient apostolic Protestant Church" by Parliament, thereby removing the stigma of a dissenting conventicle from their meetings, Zinzendorf secured his followers access to Anglican patrons as well. Pulling members from Saxony and Silesia, the Moravians also penetrated Württemberg, where Zinzendorf had studied, and made converts in the Swabian villages, including the later bishop Johannes Ettwein of Freudenstadt and Matthäus Gottfried Hehl, a graduate of the university at Tübingen and eminent hymnist and preacher among the Moravians in Pennsylvania.

The mystical-radical side of German pietism, by contrast, had difficulty in creating support networks among its adherents, as had Dutch radical pietists. For example, Pennsylvania radicals came from some of the same widely disparate regions of the Reich as the Moravians, from the mountainous, impoverished regions of Saxony's Ore Mountains and Silesia and the lowlands weaving centers along the Rhine where Conrad Beissel and his Brethren affiliates around Schwarzenau in Wittgenstein originated. The mystic Paracelsus developed his thought at a remote monastery in Württemberg; Valentin Weigel, perhaps most responsible for propagating Paracelsus's forms of pantheistic theosophism, worked for most of his life as pastor in the village of Zschopau in the Ore Mountains of Saxony on the borders of Bohemia. Jacob Böhme studied Weigel in neighboring Lusatia. But the Pennsylvania Schwenkfelders, Rosicrucians, Philadelphians, Wissahickon Brethren, and other experimental groups who drew adherents from all these sources never matched the organizational genius of the Moravian connection, which, like Halle's, was anchored to the imperial capital in London.[65]

65. The best summary remains F. Ernest Stoeffler, "Mysticism in the German Devotional Literature of Colonial Pennsylvania," *Pennsylvania German Folklore Society*, XIV (1949), 1–181. See Sessler, *Communal Pietism*, 20–71; Gollin, *Moravians in Two Worlds*; and an important assessment by Carter Lindberg, *The Third Reformation? Charismatic Movements and the Lutheran Tradition* (Macon, Ga.,

Initially, perhaps, the various German-speaking groups who gathered at Ephrata, Pennsylvania, to form a loose community of pietists, mystics, Rosicrucians, and hermits may have envisioned a loose federation of religious experimental communities in North America. Few English-speakers understood the deep Gnostic roots, for instance, of Conrad Beissel, the most eminent leader of one of Ephrata's components. This former Reformed Rhinelander developed an alternative theology and the option of a style of life far removed from domesticity. His search for a male-female image of God perhaps helps explain his mesmerizing hold on many German women adherents. Pietist prophets like John Peter Miller, who represented another group at Ephrata, carried the medieval tradition of mysticism to this New World center. Miller conversed with English-speaking colonists only on rare occasions, usually on topics like printing, music, and manuscript illumination, which the community excelled in.[66] Suspicious of institutions, rejecting hierarchical relationships, and lacking connections abroad, this collection of radical groups pioneered impressive German-American printing, developed its own peculiar system of singing, and excelled in producing illuminated manuscripts inspired by European models. But internal upheavals in the 1740s that ended in the expulsion of more entrepreneurial-minded brethren wanting to expand Ephrata's trade with outsiders helped to doom the experiment and, with it, a Protestant German monastic network.

Yet, one of the master movers in the process of replanting German-speakers in American soil and developing supporting networks sprang from one of these separatist, radical traditions. The (temporary) Dunker Christopher Saur, among the entire "charter group" of Germans who put their stamp upon their people's later history, surely belongs in the first rank. Saur showed a shrewd awareness of how support and communication networks operated in the German-speaking world. In 1735, he wrote to the court chaplain Friedrich Michael Ziegenhagen in London and to the Halle pietist Gotthilf August Francke offering to report regularly on the conditions and behavior

---

1983), chaps. 2, 3, "Luther and the 'Spiritualists,'" and "'The Second Reformation'—Pietism," 55–178.

66. See Leo Schelbert, trans. and ed., "'A Modest Sketch of God's Work': John Peter Miller's Letter of 1743 about Ephrata's Spiritual Evolution," *Historic Schaefferstown Record*, XIX (1985), 1–16; and Wendy Everham, "The Recovery of the Feminine in an Early American Pietist Community: The Interpretive Challenge of the Theology of Conrad Beissel," MS, University of Illinois at Chicago. I am indebted to both Professor Schelbert and Ms. Everham for bringing these pieces to my attention; see also E. G. Alderfer, *The Ephrata Commune: An Early American Counterculture* (Pittsburgh, Pa., 1985); Schelbert, "From Reformed Preacher in the Palatinate to Pietist Monk in Pennsylvania: The Spiritual Path of Johann Peter Müller (1709–1796)," in Hans L. Trefousse, ed., *Germany and America: Essays on Problems of International Relations and Immigration* (New York, 1980), 139–150.

of Pennsylvania Lutherans. Their cool response deepened Saur's already independent, free church suspicions. Moved, perhaps because of his personal resentment at his wife's removal to Ephrata, he chose to make his living as a printer in 1738 and triggered far-reaching consequences within and beyond the bounds of Lutheran-Moravian-Reformed migration. The inveterate enemy of Lutherans and Anglicans, he secured his own printing press from Frankfurt and assaulted all proposals that hinted at closer English-German union in religious or political affairs in Pennsylvania. From his press streamed warnings, advice, offers to aid in reestablishing familial contacts within Pennsylvania, with other provinces, and back to the Reich. His readership crossed all sectarian lines, and his analysis of social, economic, and political questions boiled down to one simple lesson hammered home from 1739 until the Seven Years' War forced a reassessment before his death in 1758: Support the Quakers and avoid courts, lawyers, politics, and unnecessary involvement with English-speakers that might endanger our language, our families and customs, and our faith.[67]

By the late 1740s, the sheer size of the German migration, transatlantic monetary support, and the arrival of Lutheran and Reformed clerical leaders combined with Saur's printing press at Germantown to create a pattern of settlement that allowed Mühlenberg a decade later to inform a Leipzig correspondent that Philadelphia was truly the center of this new German world.[68] Philadelphia emerged as the American *Oberamt*, a district clearing center for German religious, political-legal, printing, and kinship networks that partially replicated the pattern of life in the German territories. All villages in the Reich were organized into *Ämter*, the district centers for legal, religious, and administrative as well as trade affairs. Within Philadelphia's

67. Stephen L. Longenecker, *The Christopher Sauers: Courageous Printers Who Defended Religious Freedom in Early America* (Elgin, Ill., 1981), 38–39; Alexander Waldenrath, "The Pennsylvania-Germans: Development of Their Printing and Their Newspress in the War for American Independence," in Gerhard K. Friesen and Walter Schatzberg, eds., *The German Contribution to the Building of the Americas: Studies in Honor of Karl J. R. Arndt* (Hanover, N.H., 1977), 47–74; Willi Paul Adams, "The Colonial German-Language Press and the American Revolution," in Bernard Bailyn and John B. Hench, eds., *The Press and the American Revolution* (Worcester, Mass., 1980), 154–161; Frank H. Sommer, "German Language Books, Periodicals, and Manuscripts," in Catherine E. Hutchins, ed., *Arts of the Pennsylvania Germans* (New York, 1983), 265–304. On early political awareness and the Germans, see Alan W. Tully, "Ethnicity, Religion and Politics in Early America," *PMHB*, CVII (1983), 491–536. On Saur's reassessment by 1755, see below.

68. Aland, ed., *Korrespondenz Mühlenbergs*, II, 85 (1753); for another, Swiss German, example in the late 1730s that measured both distance and culture from Philadelphia and pointed out the dependence of South Carolinian German-speakers on Pennsylvania wheat for breadmaking, see Leo Schelbert, ed., "On the Power of Pietism: A Documentary of the Thommens of Schaefferstown," *Historic Schaefferstown Record*, XVII (1983), 42–78, esp. 47, 49, 51.

orbit, secondary towns like York, Lancaster, Reading, Bethlehem, and Raritan provided agricultural markets and evolved into artisanal technology centers semi-independent of Philadelphia, but never in isolation from German affairs flowing through that clearinghouse.[69]

Subsequent migration and settlement extended the range of Philadelphia's influence into more rural areas like the Shenandoah Valley in Virginia and later into Frederick County, Maryland. Saur's almanacs, his newspaper, Mühlenberg's and the Reformed minister Michael Schlatter's travels and correspondence with clergy, lay merchants, and traders reached Stone Arabia on the Mohawk in New York, though the echoes of Philadelphia's influence were weak at such a distance. Apparently the older, pre-1727 settlements, such as the New York hamlets or the oldest Lutheran-Reformed community in Virginia at Germanna and Hebron Valley, rarely received news and support emanating from the Reich via London, Rotterdam, and eventually, Philadelphia. For the Hebron Valley and some New York Lutherans, the alienation of their high church orthodox pastors from the critical Halle support network explains in part the relatively weaker cultural development in those locales. For example, after a successful tour of the Hanseatic cities, Berlin, and Frankfurt, the Hebron Valley settlers gleaned a new pastor and an extensive library and proceeded to build a church and school in the piedmont in the late 1730s. Halle's patrons who knew of this group contributed financial support for a few years. But by the late 1740s, when the pastor secured on the trip to Europe, Samuel Klug, reportedly burned a barrel of pietist tracts Halle sent to him and the community, his congregation vanishes from Halle's records. He lamented later his isolation from the mainstream of news and financial support presided over by Mühlenberg at Philadelphia. Shenandoah Valley Mennonites, Reformed, and Lutherans were served by Pennsylvania itinerants only sporadically. These communities developed with irregular support from outside, but they were connected, younger settlements whose numbers swelled as immigrants passed through Lancaster on their way into Virginia and North Carolina.[70]

69. Jerome H. Wood, Jr., *Conestoga Crossroads: Lancaster, Pennsylvania, 1730–1790* (Harrisburg, Pa., 1979); Laura Becker, "Diversity and Its Significance in an Eighteenth-Century Pennsylvania Town," in Michael Zuckerman, ed., *Friends and Neighbors: Group Life in America's First Plural Society* (Philadelphia, 1982), 196–221.

70. Elizabeth Augusta Kessel, "Germans on the Maryland Frontier: A Social History of Frederick County, Maryland, 1730–1800" (Ph.D. diss., Rice University, 1981); for Virginia, John Walter Wayland, *The German Element of the Shenandoah Valley of Virginia* (Bridgewater, Va., 1964; orig. pub. 1905); Edward A. Chappell, "Acculturation in the Shenandoah Valley: Rhenish Houses of the Massanutten Settlement," American Philosophical Society, *Proceedings*, CXXIV (1980), 55–89; Robert D. Mitchell, *Commercialism and Frontier: Perspectives on the Early Shenandoah Valley* (Charlottesville, Va., 1977); on the Virginia Hebron settlement, Roeber, "Ori-

Mühlenberg had originally wanted the center of this German-American world elsewhere. Disgusted after a few years of labor in Pennsylvania, he had urged Halle and London supporters to help him establish a printing shop and bookstore in New York City and to tie the future of German Lutheranism squarely to that royal colony and the Anglican church. His thinking continued to reflect the older assumptions of Germans in London and in the Reich that the New York colony, also the former seat of Dutch Reformed efforts administered through Amsterdam, would be the focus of German-speaking culture in the British colonies. Thoroughly dismayed at the riot of religious and cultural traditions he found in neighboring Pennsylvania, Mühlenberg wanted to quit by 1750. He informed both his Halle superiors and the German pastors on the Savannah, where he had visited upon arriving in America in 1742, that he intended to retire to Ebenezer. This pietist refuge for exiled Salzburgers expelled by Archbishop Leopold Anton Eleutherius von Firmian in 1731 was supplied with pastors by Halle and enjoyed financial support from both British and German patrons. There, Mühlenberg sighed, where religious and political affairs were run in an organized manner by the pietist pastors, one avoided the chaos and fractious behavior he saw in Pennsylvania and New York. He could live out his days working at an honest trade. Instead, Mühlenberg gradually realized that Philadelphia was to be the new center of German life in a culturally diverse North America. In 1752, with some wry self-awareness and amusement, he admitted his own growing discomfort as a Pennsylvania German among New Yorkers who "are astonished when they see German dress, for some of the natives think that New York is the metropolis of the world and that all other regions are only suburbs of New York." Whatever his aspirations and exasperations about that royal colony, it failed to emerge as one of the central places for German-speakers during the eighteenth century.[71] Instead, contrary both to the initial pattern of migration into New York from 1709 to the 1720s, contrary to the expectation of Halle's directors, and despite an earlier

gins and Transfer," *Perspectives in Am. Hist.*, n.s., III (1987), 165–166. My conclusions also rest on analysis of surviving deeds, wills, and letters for the Virginia community as well as a survey in German archives of surviving attempts to collect inheritances, 1720–1800. Those involved in such attempts came from Philadelphia or its orbit, or from the Charleston-Orangeburg-Ebenezer connection. I have found no evidence for such contacts and communication for New England, North Carolina, Virginia, and, with surprisingly few exceptions, New York. For details, Roeber, "Origins and Transfer."

71. Aland, ed., *Korrespondenz Mühlenbergs*, I, 454–463; Tappert and Doberstein, eds., *Journals of Muhlenberg*, I, 343. On the break between recently arrived Germans and the older Dutch Lutherans over language and customs, see also Harry Julius Kreider, *Lutheranism in Colonial New York* (Ann Arbor, Mich., 1942), 53–64; Tappert and Doberstein, eds., *Journals of Muhlenberg*, I, 108, 287, 290; Aland, ed., *Korrespondenz Mühlenbergs*, I, 458.

Reformed and Lutheran tie in New York to the Dutch at Amsterdam, the center of the German-American world shifted firmly south.

Germans in almost all parts of North America by the 1750s affirmed Philadelphia's role as *Oberamt.* Ten years later, additional migration confirmed a similar regional role for Charleston among German-speakers on the continental southern periphery of British settlement. There, Swiss Reformed commercial leaders like Johannes Tobler and Jeremiah Theus had emerged by the 1730s as justices of the peace, traders with the Cherokee, and official translators of German for South Carolina, paralleling Conrad Weiser's role for Pennsylvania. The Swiss Reformed community at Purrysburg and Orangeburg in South Carolina kept in contact with the German Lutherans across the Savannah at Ebenezer. But much orbited around the town of Charleston, where trading was cheaper than at Savannah. A regular post service linked Charleston to the Theus's trading post at Monck's Corner, stopped at the Reformed congregation at Orangeburg, thence to take news on to Purrysburg and the Salzburg settlement before ending at the port of Savannah. An extensive German-speaking merchant and artisan culture sprang out of these initial Swiss and Reformed contacts, so that by the 1760s the settlement along the avenues and northwest road leading from Charleston into the upcountry was commonly referred to as "Dutchtown."

Charleston's role as a center for German-speaking cultural brokers who emerged from within this southern orbit could never come close to matching Philadelphia's, of course. Halle's ties with Ebenezer, Georgia, to cite but one reason, had developed in the 1730s, a generation earlier than the corresponding merchant network connecting Charleston to the Reich. By the 1740s, this settlement on the Savannah River, populated by Salzburgers and, increasingly, Württemberg Lutherans, successfully exported lumber to the West Indies and silk for reexport to Halle and ground grain for settlers from Augusta to the Georgia coast.[72] Nonetheless, eminent Charleston Lutherans like Michael Kaltheisen and the Henry Geiger and David Sailer families did emerge, along with a prosperous small group of German artisans in the town who owned plantations in the lowcountry and as far west as the Lexington district and at Saxe Gotha. These South Carolina leaders joined the earlier Swiss Reformed in cooperation with the Ebenezer, Georgia, justice of the peace Johannes Treutlen in prosecuting suits in the Charleston courts for German clients, some of whom owned property in both colonies. Many of these local worthies were cheerfully insouciant about their religious and

72. George Fenwick Jones, "The Salzburger Mills: Georgia's First Successful Enterprises," *Yearbook of German-American Studies*, XXIII (1988), 105–118; Renate Wilson, "Halle and Ebenezer: Pietism, Agriculture, and Commerce in Colonial Georgia" (Ph.D. diss., University of Maryland, 1988); Hermann Winde, "Die Frühgeschichte der lutherischen Kirche in Georgia" (Ph.D. diss., Halle / Saale, 1960), 41–55.

ethnic identities, contributing willy-nilly to German Reformed and Lutheran building projects but securing pews in Presbyterian and Anglican churches and plots in their burial yards. And like their counterparts in Philadelphia whose newspapers and almanacs they imported, read, and helped distribute, they also operated as dispensers of news, helped to recover inheritances and bequests from Germany, and operated as cultural interlocutors. They functioned in the political, legal, and social world on behalf of their remoter relatives in the backcountry or for humbler Charleston immigrants as well.[73]

Clerics, arriving in the lower South in larger numbers by the 1750s, recognized the advantage that networks would give to all German immigrants of the region. Here, as among the Dutch- and German-speakers to the north, the church operated as a center of cultural life among the Reformed and Lutherans. Johann Martin Boltzius, pastor to the Salzburgers, was as bewildered as Mühlenberg by the multiplicity of peoples and cultures of North America he encountered in the 1730s. But, like Mühlenberg, he early recognized the value and significance of a center for distributing information and knowledge among the Germans in America. Hence, his premature joy in discovering a "German Printer" who he thought would be kindly disposed toward the Ebenezer Lutherans. Boltzius could not have guessed at the complexity of Peter Timothy's New World evolution—a man of Huguenot background born in the Netherlands, transplanted as a boy to learn the printer's trade under Benjamin Franklin in Philadelphia and only recently arrived in Charleston. Fluent in Dutch, French, German, and English, Timothy and others like him had begun to create Charleston's role as *Amt* for a German region of influence that spread out over Orangeburg to include the six hundred Germans at Saxe Gotha on the Broad and Saluda in present-day Lexington County. That role was so successful that a German mercenary observed in 1780, "In Charleston one meets people of all nations of Europe . . . the Germans are resident here in large numbers, and they speak their

73. Florence Janson Sherriff, "The Saltzburgers and Purrysburg," South Carolina Historical Association, *Proceedings*, 1963 (Charleston, S.C., 1964), 12–22; Arlin Charles Migliazzo, "Ethnic Diversity on the Southern Frontier: A Social History of Purrysburgh, South Carolina, 1732–1792" (Ph.D. diss., University of Washington, 1982); Margaret Simons Middleton, *Jeremiah Theus, Colonial Artist of Charles Town* (Columbia, S.C., 1953), 45–61; Gilbert T. Voigt, "The German and German-Swiss Element in South Carolina, 1732–1752," *University of South Carolina Bulletin*, no. 13 (Columbia, S.C., 1922); Charles G. Cordle, ed., "The John Tobler Manuscripts: An Account of German-Swiss Emigrants in South Carolina, 1737," *Journal of Southern History*, V (1939), 83–97; Walter L. Robbins, ed. and trans., "John Tobler's Description of South Carolina (1753), (1754)," *South Carolina Historical Magazine*, LXXI (1970), 141–161, 257–265; and my reading of wills, deeds, and inventories, plus the court of common pleas records for the period 1730–1770. See also, for leading German artisans, the lists in Zierden *et al.*, comps., *Survey of Economic Activity in Charleston*, appendix; and see also Roeber, "Origins and Transfer," *Perspectives in Am. Hist.*, n.s., III (1987), 151, 157–158, 166–169.

mother tongue better than I have ever heard Germans speak in America." German-speaking colonists, not merely in Pennsylvania's orbit but on the British southern periphery too, had created by the 1760s a world that partially transcended provincial and international boundaries, built as it was upon a European network of communication and financial and kinship support.[74]

VI

As so many German-speakers arrived in North America between 1727 and the 1750s, their first concern was economic survival. Within the bounds set by that simple necessity, however, they also began to develop a culture composed of transferred European habits and those North American material elements that the German-speakers quickly seized and utilized for economic security. German settlements remained separate from the English, guarded by their language dialects. Still, minimal English was acquired rapidly in order to deal with outsiders in commerce. Beginning as servants, day laborers, redemptioners on farms in a subsistence economy, or modest shopkeepers, German-speakers began to prosper as they acquired their own land and commissions to produce for wealthier outside clients. At first aided by the occasional learned leader like Daniel Pastorius of Germantown, German-speakers more commonly relied on clergy and schoolteachers or successful traders and shopkeepers who emerged as intermediaries with the larger culture. At the same time, these leaders also helped to reinforce German cultural institutions, by contributing to churches and schools or running taverns that continued as in the Reich to be centers of information—all three German-American institutions that emerged by the 1730s. Over the next generation, until the outbreak of the Seven Years' War, German-Americans developed a culture whose domestic and religious spheres, separate from British-American life, can still be discerned in evidence from the middle and southern provinces of North America.

From the settlement of Germantown in 1683, German-speakers had been involved in the production of linens, paper, oil, and gristmills—some 100 around Philadelphia and another 350 in Lancaster and York by 1750. As early as 1701 a fair was organized at Germantown, which rapidly evolved as the distribution point of handicraft trade in Pennsylvania. Caspar Wistar's glass factory near Allowaystown, New Jersey, opened by 1739. Lieutenant

74. George Fenwick Jones, "John Martin Boltzius' Trip to Charleston, October 1742," *SCHM*, LXXXII (1981), 87–110; Hennig Cohen, "Four Letters from Peter Timothy, 1755, 1768, 1771," *SCHM*, LV (1954), 160–165; Jones, ed., "The 1770 Siege of Charleston as Experienced by a Hessian Officer," *SCHM*, LXXXVIII (1987), 22–23, 63–75, esp. 71.

Governor Alexander Spotswood brought ore miners from Siegen to Germanna in Virginia in 1714 in an effort to develop the region's economic potential and to serve as a barrier against potentially hostile native Americans. Although the venture failed, it pointed to later, successful ironworks at Tulpehocken, Pennsylvania, by midcentury. In Georgia and South Carolina, interest by the English in more exotic enterprises, such as silk and viticulture, stimulated primitive farming communities to greater efforts that would also receive endorsement by Halle leaders and other interested parties in the Reich.[75] German linens, the famous "Osnaburgs" (from Osnabrück), appeared. German-speaking colonists lived on the edge of British-American society in all these ventures.

Surviving almanacs, newspapers, and correspondence from before the Seven Years' War reveal economic and legal terms that never appear in German form, but are borrowed from the English exclusively. Thus, German-speakers early on spoke of "die Fairen" (fairs), loaning money "auf Intress" (instead of *Hypotheken* or *Zinsen*); "ein Band," a bond (instead of *Schuldverschreibung*); ein "Bill of Sääl"; "ein Accort." Legal terms were equally impossible, as were objects that reflected legal relationships. For example, from Nova Scotia to Georgia, Germans never used the word for "fence" (*Zaun*), but interlarded German with the borrowed term "ein Fenss" when discussing the problem of demarcating private property in disputes before courts. Other legal and political concepts were never translated into rough German equivalents. Instead, in letters these terms were left in their original English: "ein Freeholder," or "der Cort" (instead of German *Gericht*), or "ein Trusteeschaft." As pastor Mühlenberg explained, German-speakers like others in North America swarmed like bees into the public arena, retreating into their cultural hives for German dialect use in church and family matters.[76]

The first German-language work in North America was published in 1729 and was characteristically concerned with theological dispute, the topic that marked much of what was printed in German in North America for the next

75. See Carter Litchfield *et al.*, *The Bethlehem Oil Mill, 1745–1934: German Technology in Early Pennsylvania* (Kemblesville, Pa., 1984). For additional comments on paper mills, linen weaving, and gristmills, see John Joseph Stoudt, *Sunbonnets and Shoofly Pies: A Pennsylvania Dutch Cultural History* (New York, 1973). On German ironwork, see Henry C. Mercer, *The Bible in Iron: Pictured Stoves and Stoveplates of the Pennsylvania Germans . . .*, ed. Horace M. Mann and Joseph E. Sandford, 3d ed. (Doylestown, Pa., 1961). On economic development at Ebenezer that pitted communal experiments partly sustained by European benefactors against private enterprise, and the resulting tensions within the communities, see Winde, "Frühgeschichte der lutherischen Kirche," 47–67, 105–115. Our understanding of linen manufacture and distribution awaits the conclusions of Professor Dr. Jürgen Schlumbohm at the Max Planck Institut für Geschichte, Göttingen.

76. Aland, ed., *Korrespondenz Mühlenbergs*, I, 353–354.

generation. The German Reformed pastor George Michael Weiss wrote a pamphlet defending the role of orthodox Reformed pastors against the accusations of a group of radical perfectionists. Those critics, led by Mattäus Baumann, had settled at Oley, Pennsylvania, transplanting their trances and raptures that accompanied conversion at Lambsheim in the Palatinate.[77] In 1730, the Ephrata leader Beissel further stimulated this religious character of German printing by approaching Benjamin Franklin to print the collection of sacred songs known as the *Göttliche Liebes und Lobes Gethöne*. Two years later, Franklin attempted to expand beyond religious topics in German-American printing by issuing the *Philadelphische Zeitung*, and failed. Readers of German remained unconvinced that a newspaper about public affairs in German edited by an outsider was needed. Surely Franklin's grammatical errors did not help; more significant were the roman fonts he used. When Christopher Saur finally began publishing *Der hoch-deutsch pennsylvanische Geschichts-Schreiber* in 1739, the paper appeared in gothic Fraktur type he had secured from Frankfurt. It prospered. The creation of a hybrid German-American speech that was solidly German in domestic and religious affairs but full of borrowed terms in economic and legal matters developed sufficiently to become the topic of commentary in the almanacs and newspapers of the 1750s.[78]

The simultaneous engagement with a broader economic world and the creation of a separate cultural sphere is also evident in German-American use of home space, utensils, and consumption patterns. German-speakers initially transferred and retained from the German southwest a consistently spare home style. German homes were on the whole small, and separation of sleeping from the heated cooking, eating, and spinning space did not develop until after the 1760s. That same simplicity characterized early German-American houses as well, though more elaborate stone buildings and expanded numbers of rooms rapidly developed by the 1740s, somewhat later than contemporary homes of English-speakers of comparable wealth and occupation. The oldest form of German-American material artistic culture

77. Georg Michael Weiss, *Der in der americanischen Wildnusz . . . herum wandelte [sic] und verschiedentlich angefochtene Prediger* (Philadelphia, 1729). Baumann, who arrived from Lambsheim in 1714, had written a treatise in 1723 published in Germany, to which Weiss was responding.

78. For the technical discussion of this pattern, see Suzanne Romaine, *Pidgin and Creole Languages* (London, 1988), 206–210, 312–334. I have counted such words in immigrant letters, newspapers, and almanacs and am also indebted to Professor Hermann Wellenreuther for his sharing with me identical findings from his unpublished lecture "Pennsylvania, Germantown, und die Deutschen im achtzehnten Jahrhundert." For the Nova Scotia example, see Winthrop Pickard Bell, *The "Foreign Protestants" and the Settlement of Nova Scotia . . .* (Toronto, 1961), 584–585. Mühlenberg's thoughts on the subject are in Aland, ed., *Korrespondenz Mühlenbergs*, I, 353–354.

developed in these German-American houses. The stove plates of the 1720s represented the adaptation of the painted tiles of the European stove to cruder North American iron forms, thereby revolutionizing heating techniques, though only among the continentals. English women and their families continued to cook in their fireplaces. Not even Benjamin Franklin's attempt to adapt the stove to fit the English fireplace induced non-Germans to rethink their cooking and heating methods. The German-American diet in these homes consisted of little meat; rather, the German-speakers developed home vegetable cultivation in Pennsylvania and other settlements, a practice that was copied in some degree by outsiders. Inventories from these early settlements reveal sparse, culturally separate existences. For example, German-speakers exhibited a marked preference for small amounts of pewter and avoidance of English tinware in eating utensils; German-American stoneware and finer porcelain shows a marked preference for red, yellow, and green as the basic colors for use in the home, though not for goods made for English consumers. German shopkeepers found, too, that German women favored certain styles of bonnets and specific colors for clothes. Michael Hillegas complained to an English supplier that in contacting German shopkeepers he could not be rid of a large quantity of "the Calico; believe they might have gone off if instead of Green Ground they had been blew."[79]

Taverns run by arrivals from the Reich, such as the Moravians' Sun Inn at Bethlehem, introduced Britons to German-American domestic consumption with offerings uniquely German-American. Foods like *Pfannhaas* (the fried slices from a loaf composed of cornmeal and pork liver and lights flavored with marjoram and sage)—more broadly known as scrapple—were often served with maple syrup. Raisin pies and Dutch goose (the pig's stomach stuffed with sausage, potatoes, and kitchen-garden herbs) reflected the adaptation to North American bounty by thrifty cooks who also perpetuated dishes from the German southwest. The importance of supplying these

79. Scott T. Swank, "The Architectural Landscape," and "Proxemic Patterns," in Hutchins, ed., *Arts of the Pennsylvania Germans*, 20–34, 35–60; Hooker, *Food and Drink in America*, 68–69. On the use of space in German villages, I base my conclusions on a reading of some dozen travel accounts published in the late 18th century and on a vast secondary literature, among which see Werner Habicht, *Dorf und Bauernhaus im deutschsprachigen Lothringen und im Saarland* (Saarbrücken, 1980); Henrich Schneider, *Das Baugesicht in sechs Dörfern der Pfalz: Eine geographische Untersuchung zum Gestalt u. Funktionswandel der Gebäude unter dem Einfluss der wirtschaftlichen Entwicklung seit dem Anfang des 19. Jhts.* (Marburg, 1971); Erwin Huxhold, *Das Bürgerhaus zwischen Schwarzwald und Odenwald* (Tübingen, 1980). Quote from Letterbook of Michael Hillegas, 1757–1760, Am.0803, letter to P. Clopper, July 1757? (illegible), Historical Society of Pennsylvania.

public houses with the best provender received permanent status when the Farmer's Market at Lancaster was established in perpetuity by royal charter in 1742. As these taverns spread the variety of German foods among broader segments of Pennsylvania's population, partly to accommodate non-Germans, partly to overcome dialect differences in terminology, some of the tavern owners abandoned written names for their establishments and resorted to crude, hand-painted signs instead. Thus, both German- and English-speakers knew of the German tavern as the Brown Horse and not by the Palatine word *Gaul* or the Swabian *Ross*. Only in the written table of inns provided in the Saur almanac was the correct High German term *Braunes Pferd* given. [80]

Although German-American domestic life could be glimpsed by English-speakers who sometimes frequented their taverns, German-speakers tended to socialize separately. For instance, in Philadelphia, Lancaster, and Reading, they seem not only to have kept to their own taverns, but in urban centers they drank coffee almost exclusively, rejecting the new British-American rage for tea, teapots, services, and accoutrements. Perhaps reflecting the discovery of coffee in Vienna after the Turks retreated from Europe, the Germans favored the continental drink. Coffee drinking had spread northward, creating coffeehouses in Leipzig, Hamburg, and beyond, to London. In the British capital the Germans maintained their own, separate houses. Sumptuary laws had forbidden peasant consumption of coffee in the Reich, and authorities imposed regulations against itinerant peddlers and grinders, but to little avail. Pastor Mühlenberg received and sent letters via the Coffee House in Philadelphia, where coffee and chocolate were dispensed, but he frowned on the elaborate tea ceremony in which his daughter-in-law indulged. German-Americans in Pennsylvania produced tea services for the English; coffee pots in elaborate metalwork had been given as wedding presents for their own brides since the 1730s and continued to be until the Revolution. In the lower South, buttermilk, beer, and wine remained the social drinks of choice, except for coffee, which was known in Charleston and Ebenezer. When tea and taxation emerged as issues for the British-Americans in the 1760s, the connection between a domestic and a public issue was lost on indifferent German-Americans.[81]

80. Julius Friedrich Sachse, "The Wayside Inns on the Lancaster Roadside between Philadelphia and Lancaster," Pennsylvania German Society, *Proceedings and Addresses*, XXI (1912), 9.

81. See, for instance, Donald L. Fennimore, "Metalwork," in Hutchins, ed., *Arts of the Pennsylvania Germans*, 214–215; Arlene Palmer Schwing, "Pennsylvania German Earthenware," *ibid.*, 172–173, 178, 182–183; Hooker, *Food and Drink in America*, 91–92. On the British-American rage for tea, see T. H. Breen, "'Baubles of Britain': The American and Consumer Revolutions of the Eighteenth Century," *Past*

This domestic sphere of German-American life was graphically summed up for many in the hand-lettered and painted cultural form of gothic Fraktur marriage, death, and birth certificates, *Haussegen* (house blessings), furniture, and religious folk art. By the mid-1740s, these German-American art forms began to abound, especially in the Pennsylvania settlements.[82] Since the southern German communities developed more slowly and suffered from high mortality rates, the early Swiss and German Reformed seem not to have developed these art forms much before the Revolution. Yet interest in them was clearly shown when a Pennsylvania Fraktur artist made his way through the Carolinas in the 1790s. His work was appreciated and much patronized, though decorative arts had apparently been underdeveloped in most of the remote places until he traversed the region. This domestic hybrid form incorporated German elements such as the hex sign, usually including a six-pointed star, tulips, and hearts used to ward off evil, with the *Distelfink* (the bird of good fortune), which is actually the indigenous American Carolina parakeet that populated most of the eastern seaboard of North America in great flocks in the eighteenth century. Such creations, executed in the red-green-yellow colors that seem also to reflect an adaptation to American pigments, continued and deepened, beyond the German-American center of Pennsylvania. Though much has perished because of war, carelessness, and climate, instances remain of late-eighteenth-century German-American chairs and decorated chests along the Savannah, as in the Orangeburg and Lexington County areas. Linguistic, superstitious, and food and drink patterns peculiar to German backgrounds survived on this southern perimeter of North American German settlement until the early 1800s. In more isolated areas nearer to the Pennsylvania source such as Virginia's Shenandoah Valley, the residues were still visible until the Civil War.[83]

---

and Present, no. 119 (May 1988), 73–104, esp. 83–85. On the regulations in the Reich, see Hessisches Hauptstaatsarchiv Wiesbaden, Abt. 179 Nassau-Oranische Ämter, #11 Missbrauch des Kaffeetrinkens, Gedruckte Verordnung, v. 19, V. 82 [1767–1791].

82. Besides the essays contained in Hutchins, ed., *Arts of the Pennsylvania Germans*, see also Beatrice B. Garvan and Charles F. Hummel, *The Pennsylvania Germans: A Celebration of Their Arts, 1683–1850* (Philadelphia, 1982); C. Kurt Dewhurst *et al.*, eds., *Religious Folk Art in America: Reflections of Faith* (New York, 1983), 44–46, figs. 80–96. The editors fail to recognize in fig. 191 ("Portrait of a Clergyman") the famous motif of Luther with Bible and swan, a direct copy of a popular painting in German-speaking Europe. For its provenance there, see Martin Scharfe, *Evangelische Andachtsbilder* (Stuttgart, 1968), figs. 88–89.

83. John Biveus, Jr., "Fraktur in the South: An Itinerant Artist," *MESDA: Journal of Early Southern Decorative Arts*, I (1975), 1–23; Christian Kolbe and Brent Holcomb, "Fraktur in the 'Dutch Fork' Area of South Carolina," *ibid.*, V (1979), 36–51; Christopher L. Dolmetsch, *The German Press of the Shenandoah Valley* (Columbia, S.C., 1984). A survey of German material objects along the Savannah has been

Domestic life rested ultimately on secure property. Scottish, Irish, and English settlers all had access to Britain and the legal forms necessary to obtain inheritances and, thereby, property and its succession that would render them secure in the colonies. German-speakers also turned toward the recovery of property in their ancestral villages. As the German-speakers became more interested in these affairs, they naturally had to begin thinking about expanding their repertoire of English words and phrases as well, since recovery meant swearing out a power of attorney before a British-American notary. Such contacts had important consequences for their own view of themselves and the broader, public realm of North American life.

The inheritance of family property among German-Americans had been guaranteed by German principalities and cities in part because of the system of manumission dues imposed upon emigrants. Those dues were calculated upon the value of the real and movable property they held in the village or that would fall to them in the future. Emigrants were thus reminded that they would be future lawful heirs to familial property in the villages after they left. And they did not forget, once in America.[84]

Philadelphia and Charleston, distribution points for German culture within the British world, were also conduits through which the value of

---

undertaken; I am indebted to Mr. Dale Coombs of the Department of Archives and History, Atlanta, for sharing the results of his research with me. I also acknowledge the aid of Mr. Horace E. Harmon of the Lexington County Museum, Lexington, South Carolina, for interpretation of objects preserved there. Mr. Brent Holcomb helped in a tour of the Dutch Fork country. For details on other customs in the Dutch Fork and Lexington areas, see Edwin J. Scott, *Random Recollections of a Long Life, 1806–1876* (Columbia, 1884; rpt. 1980), 93–117; James Everett Kibler, Jr., *Fireside Tales: Stories of the Old Dutch Fork* (Columbia, S.C., 1984); O. B. Mayer, *The Dutch Fork . . .*, ed. James E. Kibler and Brent H. Holcomb (Columbia, S.C., 1982). Based on Holcomb's genealogical work and my own readings, I estimate that 60–70 percent of the German-speakers in South Carolina came through Charleston, not down the backcountry from Virginia, the migration that ended largely in "little Pennsylvania," present-day Cabarrus County, North Carolina. On the material culture of the North Carolina settlements, see Brad Rauschenberg, "A Study of Baroque- and Gothic-Style Gravestones in Davidson County, North Carolina," *MESDA*, I (1975), 24–50; on the difficulties in supplying religious support to the area, Robert M. Calhoon, "Lutheranism and Early Southern Culture," in George Anderson and Robert M. Calhoon, eds., *"A Truly Efficient School of Theology": The Lutheran Theological Southern Seminary in Historical Context, 1830–1980* (Columbia, S.C., 1981), 1–21.

84. No evidence documents that such a network or recovery system occurred among the Dutch. Similarly, for the French in the Illinois Country, although French inheritance customs were replicated, no transatlantic system for recovery ever developed. Peter Hay is investigating French customs in Quebec, where one might reasonably think such a system could have been instituted. For the Illinois Country, see Winstanley Briggs, "The Forgotten Colony: *Le Pays des Illinois*" (Ph.D. diss., University of Chicago, 1985).

property inherited from kin and family in the Old World could be collected and redistributed in North America. Beginning slowly in the 1740s and increasing steadily for another forty years, the recovery of these inheritances further guaranteed for clergy and merchants their role as cultural brokers. Most needed little encouragement, eager as they were to sustain their own professions or enterprises. These leaders simultaneously supported their own community standing and helped to develop German-speakers' comprehension of Anglo-American legal and political subtleties.

The recovery of inheritances tended to include many more people than the relatively few directly involved. Comparing the names of emigrants from a particular region with those making requests for recovery, a cautious guess can be made about the prevalence of this practice. That most attempts occurred between the 1740s and the 1770s suggests that members of the family groups that characterized migration before the Seven Years' War—those who had been at least marginal propertyholders before emigrating—were those who pursued recovery. Scattered instances occurred in South Carolina, but most claims, even from New York or New Jersey, went through Philadelphia. The Philadelphia printer and book trader Ernst Ludwig Baisch, for instance, made repeated trips back to the Reich in the twenty years before the Revolution, sometimes pursuing five or more recovery attempts for clients per trip. Surpassing his earlier successes, in 1773 he initiated fifteen separate claims. Sufficient numbers of the German-speaking population took advantage of the printed double-language powers of attorney that first appeared in Philadelphia in the 1750s to warrant Peter Müller's printing and advertising the forms in Saur's Almanac. As early as 1748 Basel authorities made it clear that only dual-language powers of attorney, notarized before a British-American official, would be accepted in their courts, a clear sign of the difficulties German-speaking authorities recognized in an alien legal system. Philadelphia, Lancaster, and Reading traders, operating as self-styled merchants (*Handelsmänner*), like Baisch, Peter Müller, Peter Ulrich, Jacob and Valentin Geiger, Georg Börstler, Zacharias Endress, and Mathias Gänsel, were in fact tavernkeepers, dry goods, beer, and wine traders, and shopkeepers who represented colonial clients in the Palatinate, Württemberg, Ulm, and other territories.[85] Their services were sought out

85. On the pivotal role of innkeepers in village culture, see Hermann Rebel, *Peasant Classes: The Bureaucratization of Property and Family Relations under Early Habsburg Absolutism, 1511–1626* (Princeton, N.J., 1983), 113–126; and for a case that dramatizes the innkeeper's role, Horst Peter Schamari, "Aspekte der Schiedsgerichtsbarkeit," in Bernhard Diestelkamp, ed., *Forschungen aus Akten des Reichskammergerichts* (Cologne, 1984), 115–139. My own prosopography of these individuals in the colonies reveals that they, too, were sons or relatives of innkeepers, traders, village mayors, and other persons involved in commerce and communication. Despite its overall brilliance, Thomas Doerflinger, *A Vigorous Spirit of Enterprise: Merchants and Economic Development in Revolutionary Philadelphia* (Chapel Hill,

by Germans from New York City, Albany, Raritan, Baltimore, and upstate New York to the subsidiary towns of Pennsylvania. Their counterparts in South Carolina like Michael Kaltheisen and Heinrich Geiger—who were acquainted with and sometimes related to the Philadelphians—did the same for their neighbors. But others, hangers-on, busybodies in German-language taverns, entrepreneurs, and speculators, got involved. Out of one such attempt in 1762 involving a transaction from a father to his daughter, more than twenty-three different people became entangled, contesting claims and complicating the transaction on both sides of the Atlantic. The printers Saur and Miller notified potential claimants to come to the offices of the printers to learn "something of advantage" to them.[86]

Such developments highlighted the urgent need to master the public systems of law and language among British neighbors in North America. Earlier, the protection of property became simpler in Pennsylvania after a 1759 Pennsylvania statute provided that those who had died without going through naturalization processes would not thereby endanger the rights of their heirs. Even before this the Plantation Act of 1740 (13 Geo. II c. 7) made foreign Protestants eligible for naturalization after seven years' residence. But the German-speakers seem to have ignored the English courts and legal details before the 1750s in all the provinces. Instead, they sought out clerics, schoolteachers, and traders to deal with familial and marital property difficulties and to serve as their interlocutors with the English political and legal world and their former villages as well.[87]

N.C., 1986), fails to penetrate the German merchant groups and their functions. The above summarizes my reconstruction of about 80 such persons and the networks they operated between 1745 and the Revolution (Roeber, "Palatines, Liberty, and Property: Cultural Transfer and the Creation of an American Republic in German Speaking North America, 1727–1776," chaps. 4, 6 [in progress]).

86. The above summarizes my work in progress on these networks; for the specific case cited, see A 213 Bü 9415g, Hauptstaatsarchiv Stuttgart, 1775–1776, recovery attempt for property of Jacob Geigle, sent from Lancaster over Philadelphia with Jacob Schaffner, general storekeeper (Krämer) in Lancaster. He in turn delegated power of attorney to Heinrich Hilzmann, trader at Essen in Westphalia, who then turned the case over to Jacob Geiger of Ittlingen in the Kraichgau, who also had relatives for whom he worked such cases in Charleston and in Philadelphia. On the newspaper ads for such cases, see "Notices by German Settlers in German Newspapers," Pennsylvania German Folklore Society, *Proceedings*, III (1938), 1–41.

87. James T. Mitchell and Henry Flanders, comps., *The Statutes at Large of Pennsylvania, from 1682 to 1801* (Harrisburg, Pa., 1896–1911), II, 29–31, 297–300. Later parliamentary action (13 Geo. III c. 25) eventually allowed naturalized citizens in the colonies to hold office. There is no evidence, however, that Germans in any of the colonies before the 1760s responded to newspaper requests to naturalize themselves. Pastor Mühlenberg noted wryly that 200 German Lutherans suddenly became interested on the eve of the Stamp Act's taking effect when instead of obtaining papers for "2 thalers . . . after the Stamp Act goes into effect it will probably cost £9 or £10" (Tappert and Doberstein, eds., *Journals of Muhlenberg*, II,

Through their interest in testation, German-speaking colonists began to reveal their growing understanding of the need to use Anglo-American legal means to preserve family property and its distribution. Where the Dutch in North America had relied upon will writing because of the Dutch-Roman law system, German villagers were accustomed to intestate customs that accomplished much the same goal as the Dutch system—equal distribution of property among all children. As in the Roman-Dutch law, the laws of the German southwest distinguished between what the woman and man brought into a marriage and recognized a limited right of disposal by women over their chattels. Unlike the Dutch system, however, the German private law did not concede women control over real property, even when it recognized the woman's right to make a will. Only in the case of a mutual testament made by a married couple dying without children could a woman jointly dispose of realty. The community property system in the German southwest actually penalized the widowed woman with no children by reducing her percentage of rights to surviving estates during her lifetime; the kinship group of her husband retained significant rights if he died childless. Widows with children, on the other hand, were granted lifelong occupancy of an estate, which even remarriage could not impair. The one-half rule applicable to the residue (*Nachlass*) of the estate went to widows with up to four children; if more children survived, the widow's part was cut to one-third; children were outfitted for weddings out of their portions of the estate, and that amount deducted from what a child could expect when the second parent died.[88]

In the British colonies, German-speakers gradually realized that, to avoid common law intestate procedures at variance with German private law customs, they would have to learn to write wills. Some left bequests to German-language churches and schools, another form of adaptation to English ways that also helped to sustain German-speaking culture and ratified voluntary, associational group identity. Early testation patterns among the German settlers in the colonies suggest initial retention of European traditions. In the oldest Virginia German Lutheran settlement of the 1720s, for

271). On the courts, see Laura L. Becker, "The People and the System: Legal Activities in a Colonial Pennsylvania Town," *PMHB*, CV (1981), 134–155; for Virginia and South Carolina, this reflects my own reading of common pleas and quarter sessions records; no court records survive for Effingham County, Georgia, for the period in question; for Lancaster County, Pennsylvania, I have surveyed the fragmentary common pleas appearance dockets with the same results; for Maryland, Kessel, "Germans on the Maryland Frontier," 292–297, where a modest use of the courts for debt recovery seems to have begun among German settlers after 1748, when a court was established in Frederick County.

88. For details, see Roeber, "Origins," *Perspectives in Am. Hist.*, n.s., III (1987), 155–168.

instance, daughters as well as sons were given land, and wives tended to be named as executrices, usually along with another German-speaking male neighbor, a practice that looks like the village practice of appointing a spokesman, the *Kriegsvogt*, for women and minors to appear for them before the court. The number of German-speakers who actually left wills for the period before the 1750s was small, and informal adjustments may have been agreed upon as these people tried to keep alive the intestacy customs of their former villages.[89] That they did so is attested to by the essays that appeared in Saur's Almanac beginning in 1751 that urged will writing upon fellow immigrants who would otherwise fall victim to Pennsylvania intestate law that bestowed a double portion upon an eldest son and appeared to punish the faithful German woman. She who had labored hard all her life, Saur pointed out, would find that in the end English law would grant her only a paltry right of dower over one-third of movables in most colonies. A majority of Frederick County, Maryland, German-speakers either deeded widows more than their thirds or gave exclusive control of the estate during life and made them sole executrices of the estate, or asked them to share that responsibility with a son. The responsible Christian German-American husband, Saur had concluded, must know how to write a will. Saur's admonitions may have had some effect; as late as the 1790s, German will makers in Bucks County tended to leave more generous provisions for widows than did English-speaking neighbors.[90]

The preservation of a somewhat separate sphere guarded by language, domestic customs, and property rights paralleled successful proselytizing by German pastors that contributed to a distinct cultural identity. German-language churches and schools, sustained by the migration patterns and the networks connecting these former continentals back to the Reich, provided visible cultural institutions to German-speakers. How many attended services who do not appear on church roles, we can only guess. But pastor Mühlenberg's journal entries suggest that German churches attracted many for reasons of sentiment and emotional sustenance. Not merely doctrine, but architecture, organ playing, singing, and hearing the native language may

89. Based upon my reading of all extant wills for the Virginia settlement in the Spotsylvania, Orange, and Culpeper county records; all surviving German-language wills for South Carolina, and those for Georgia. Pennsylvania's early settlers after 1683 may have used the Germantown court more than later arrivals. Philadelphia wills and the records of the Orphan's Court (1719–1776) suggest that German-speakers resorted only after 1745 to extensive probate of wills and to British-American officials to resolve conflicts resulting from wills and those dying intestate.

90. Christopher Saur, *Der hoch-deutsch amerikanische Calendar . . .* (Germantown, Pa., 1751); Kessel, "Germans on the Maryland Frontier," 158–159, 251–279; Carole Shammas, "Early American Women and Control over Capital," in Ronald Hoffman and Peter J. Albert, eds., *Women in the Age of the American Revolution* (Charlottesville, Va., 1989), 146.

have seduced many a German into the back pews who was otherwise not notably religious.

Mühlenberg noted one aspect of the religious culture and its alluring quality in some detail. The traditions of singing widely known in German village life had apparently declined among immigrants when the pastor reached Philadelphia in the 1740s. Yet by the 1760s, English divines like George Whitefield requested and were gratified to hear exquisite choral performances that Mühlenberg proudly said reminded him of the choirs of Dresden or of Johann Sebastian Bach's Leipzig, where he had been ordained. By the 1760s Saur reprinted Lutheran, Reformed, and Schwenkfelder hymnals after first issuing his own version of the Halle Bible, and both the production of instruments and distribution of hymnals improved the music emanating from North American churches wherever German settlements were most developed. Both the curious and the culture-starved flocked to hear the organ built at Heilbronn and then imported to Philadelphia for Saint Michael's Lutheran Church or to similar instruments at Germantown and Lancaster.[91] By 1759 Michael Hillegas could open a German music store in Philadelphia, and perhaps his store attracted both English- and German-speakers.[92] Although British admirers occasionally translated German hymnody, they found the polyphonic singing mystifying, and apparently German musical culture found little corresponding echo among English listeners.[93] Even more developed and sophisticated technology emerged

91. See Pastor Brunnholtz's letter to Halle authorities describing these events, March 3, 1752, IV, F 5, Archives, Franckesche Stiftung, Halle.

92. Letterbook of Michael Hillegas, Aug. 20, 1760, to William Peter Clopper, Historical Society of Pennsylvania, lists music ordered, apparently from British suppliers and not from Germany. The pieces are heavily Italian, include George Frederick Handel's *Water Music*, and show surprisingly little attention to German instrumental or choral compositions. Unfortunately, I find no lists of sales to ascertain who Hillegas's customers were.

93. Reformed, Lutheran, Schwenkfelder, and Moravian hymnals were printed between 1745 and 1765; 40 German editions of the Heidelberg Catechism were printed in Pennsylvania between 1755 and the 1840s. German Lutherans, according to Mühlenberg's letters and journals and from similar lists in Boltzius's accounts in the *Detailed Reports*, favored Paul Gerhardt's hymns. See also John Folkening, "The First Lutheran Hymnbook in America: Mühlenberg's *Erbauliche Liedersammlung*, 1786" (master's thesis, Concordia College, River Forest, Ill., 1972). For a sample of Gerhardt's work, see Heimo Reinitzer, ed., *Ich bin ein Gast auf Erden* (Berlin, 1986); the full version of his work is the *Geistliche Andachten* (Frankfurt an der Oder, 1666). Reformed Germans drew on sources from the German southwest, Switzerland, and Holland, showing a preference for such Reformed tunes as Joachim Neander's. Part of the uniformity among Lutheran hymn preferences stems from the decision of Halle to support the use of the Marburg Hymnal, a collection that did not reflect the peculiar regional hymnody for the areas of outmigration. I have found copies of this hymnal in inventories of estates in Württemberg, the Palatinate, and Nassau-Dillenberg, indicating that it was well known even before the migration. To this, Mühlenberg successfully added a liturgy, his *Agenda* of 1748 that overcame

among German-Moravian organ makers at Lititz, Pennsylvania, and in the awesome accomplishments of the Moravian trombone choirs. Complete performances of works by Bach's sons, for example, remained within these separate cultural preserves in North Carolina and at Bethlehem, Pennsylvania.[94]

A parallel tradition of folk songs also spread in rural German-language settlements. Deeply rooted in the European experience with want, fear, dread of failed crops, poverty, and death, the folk song tradition survived among a people living in the "best poor man's country," since most of the songs are tied to the rhythms of the agricultural year. Given a new measure of prosperity obvious in the German-American settlements at midcentury, these songs could now be accompanied by early instruments like the dulcimer, viola di gamba, and viola di bracchia, made by German-American craftsmen. The song texts reveal cultural origins in a bawdy sexuality coupled with a thoroughly pessimistic outlook about material prosperity. Perhaps they were preserved out of the emotional investments ordinary peasant farmers had in their traditional songs. Certainly their content and American experience bore only small resemblance to one another.

The songs reflected a cultural separateness. Both their message and medium conveyed emotional skepticism born of centuries of misfortune. Indeed, perhaps their perpetuation was a luxury—one that could be indulged in—now that their material good fortune, which German speakers marveled at again and again in describing their experiences in British North America, seemed secure.[95]

The same complexity, revealing both a separate, transferred cultural sphere but one that still could adapt to developments and contributions

---

regional liturgical differences, imposing a modified version of the Savoy Lutheran liturgy in London, another example of the significance of the German Lutheran connection to the imperial capital and its influence. See Tappert and Doberstein, eds., *Journals of Muhlenberg*, I, 193.

94. Tappert and Doberstein, eds., *Journals of Muhlenberg*, I, 85, 193, 297, II, 243, 441–442; for a similar pattern among the Salzburgers in Georgia, see *Detailed Reports*, VII, 9; Jones, *The Salzburger Saga* (Athens, Ga., 1984), 55; see also Henry Wilder Foote, *Three Centuries of American Hymnody* (Hamden, Conn., 1961), 124–142; Julius Friedrich Sachse, *The Music of the Ephrata Cloister* . . . (Lancaster, Pa., 1971 [orig. publ. 1903]); Stephen A. Marini, "Hymnody in the Religious Communal Societies of Early America," Russell P. Getz, "Music in the Ephrata Cloister," and Jeannine S. Ingram, "Music in American Moravian Communities: Transplanted Traditions in Indigenous Practices," in *Communal Societies: The Journal of the National Historic Communal Societies Association*, II (1982), 1–52.

95. Albert F. Buffington, *Pennsylvania German Folksongs* (Lancaster, Pa., 1974); see also Franzi Ascher-Nash, "The Astounding Heritage of Pennsylvania German Folksongs," in E. Allen McCormick, *Germans in America: Aspects of German-American Relations in the Nineteenth Century* (New York, 1983), 125–144.

from other sources, developed in the realm of cures, hexes, and faith healing. This aspect of domestic and religious culture dominated by German-American women brought a lively belief in witchcraft to their settlements. Traditional occult cures and talismans as well as a more general folk medicine flourished in the rural German-American settlements. Interlarded with these residues of Europe, indigenous American Indian lore and herb knowledge were eagerly sought out, even by clergymen like Boltzius in Georgia. To these transferred and acquired bodies of knowledge, Halle-trained physicians like Christian Ernst Thilo in Georgia or the medicines supplied by Halle and dispensed by Mühlenberg contributed cures based on the accepted scientific knowledge of German medicine. Other Pennsylvanians relied upon the Swiss treatise of Leonhart Fuchs for their herbal medicines.[96] Encountering new threats, especially rattlesnakes, some succumbed to folk superstition. Nearly killing one hapless settler by burying him naked in the Georgia clay to draw out the poison, they relented as wiser heads applied more appropriate medicinal remedies. Although the clergy often disapproved of the occult cures that prevailed in some homes, both in Pennsylvania and in southern settlements, recipes, or "useings," in rhymed verse prescribing incantations and the invocation of the Trinity over wounds found their way onto slips of paper carefully kept between pages of the Bible or sermon books.[97] The women who preserved these remedies also circulated as midwives in their settlements, and imported treatises on midwifery were eagerly sought from Halle and other German suppliers. Such transferred and adapted domestic remedies, combined with reluctance to part with money and a deep skepticism about the medical abilities of the English, kept German-speakers in Berks County steadfastly opposed to vaccination against smallpox. Dismissing the argument that one should be ready to submit to God's will in matters of disease, a German "by birth and education" pleaded: "Have not we the same regard and tenderness for our Children that other people have? or do we set a less value on our Lives or are our German Women less anxious about the preservation of their Beauty?"[98]

The capacity to sustain a transferred, medieval popular religious culture still conjuring, divining, and curing in the midst of rapid social, legal, and scientific change was not solely the preserve of German-speaking women, of

96. *Neue Kreüterbuch* . . . (Basel, 1543). Jena University–educated Lucas Raus relied on this source for his medical practice in York and Goshenhoppen. See Ronald Lieberman, *Keystone Ten: "Die Alte Zeite": German Americana and Classics of the Reformation* (Glen Rock, Pa., 1989), entry 388.

97. Brendle and Unger, *Folk Medicine of the Pennsylvania Germans*; *Detailed Reports*, V (1738), 14–15, IX (1742), 93–94, X–XI (1748), 65–66. For an example of the "useing," I am indebted to Brent Holcomb of Columbia, South Carolina, for alerting me to one found in the Epting family's papers in Pomaria, South Carolina.

98. Papers of Dr. Jonathan Potts, I, 1766–1776, letter 3 (sent to Henry Miller for publication in the *Pennsylvanische Staatsbote*), Historical Society of Pennsylvania.

course. The Revolutionary war veteran of Pennsylvania Peter Ensminger, fighting for "the famous English liberty," also made extensive marginal notes in his copy of a mystical alchemical work with no apparent sense of contradiction or tension. Similarly, transplanted German-speaking men and women devoured repeated editions of the medieval legend of Genevieve of Brabant. Her miraculous survival in the forest cave during an unjust exile was sustained by the roots of herbs; the milk of a doe sustained her son Schmerzenreich ("kingdom of sorrows"), a barely veiled reference to the many carvings of Christ as the Man of Sorrows (*Schmerzensmann*). The motifs of exile, the forest, a victimized, virtuous woman, and steadfast faith miraculously rewarded provided a many-layered text with which German-speakers in the colonies identified.[99]

Formal religion among the Lutheran, Reformed, and Moravian Germans emphasized education, as befitted traditions touched by German pietism's renewal principles. Both German Reformed and Seventh-Day Baptists opened schools in Pennsylvania in the 1730s, as did the Lutherans in Hebron Valley, Virginia, by the mid-1740s. Some forty German Lutheran churches had also built schools from Ebenezer in Georgia to Virginia and as far north as New York by the late 1750s. Christopher Dock, who had been teaching at Skippack, Pennsylvania, since 1714, wrote in 1750 his *Schulordnung*, one of the first theoretical treatises on pedagogy in North America, published in 1770 shortly before his death. Moravians had founded the first girls' school in 1746 two years after opening their Collegium Musicum for orchestral training at Bethlehem. By the early 1750s Moravians operated some thirteen schools in Pennsylvania alone. By the outbreak of the Seven Years' War, twenty-nine of the seventy-six Reformed congregations in that colony also included schools.

The first grammars and dictionaries produced in America or sent from Halle for use in these schools reveal the patterns of language acquisition that retained German universally in theological and domestic discourse but borrowed heavily in trade and, increasingly, legal and political matters.[100]

99. George von Welling, *Opus Magno-Cabbalisticum et Theosophicum* . . . (Homburg, 1735), entry 893 in Lieberman, *German Americana*; entries 400–402, *Eine schöne anmüthige und lesenswürdige History von der unschuldig-bedrängten heiligen Pfaltz Gräfin Genovesa* . . . (Philadelphia, 1762) (later editions include one in 1772 at Lancaster and a third in 1790). The most complete survey of German printed materials (which unfortunately misses even some of these catalog entries) is Karl J. R. Arndt *et al.*, eds., *The First Century of German Language Printing in the U.S.A.*, 2 vols. (Göttingen, 1989).

100. German demands for English dictionaries and for clarification of legal, economic, and political terms increased in the 1750s with the publication of Christopher Saur's *Eine nützliche Anweisung oder Beyhülfe vor die Teutschen um Englisch zu lernen* . . . (Germantown, Pa., 1751). Saur also offered Theodor Arnold's *Grammatica Anglicana Concentrata* . . . (Philadelphia, 1748), a Leipzig book he reprinted,

This pattern provoked commentary in essays widely disseminated in Saur's Almanac. The elder Saur's concern was in turn a product of worried English-speakers who grew alarmed at the successful creation of a German-American language that retained the European tongue while successfully borrowing in these areas of public life. The younger Christopher Saur, who succeeded his father in 1758, was an avid supporter of a Germantown school proposal of the early 1760s whose stated intent was to pursue just this avenue—to preserve German while providing mastery of English.[101]

The Society for Promoting Religious Knowledge and English Language among the German Emigrants in Pennsylvania reflected both the vigor of the hybrid German-American culture and the concern expressed by English-speakers to make clear in the English tongue the political importance of "Fear God and honor the King." To their annoyance, British supporters discovered that Lutheran and Reformed clerics intended to use the schools to promote the retention of formal, High German along with mastery of evangelical doctrine and English.[102] Founded because of Reformed pastor Mi-

---

and began a series of essays in *Der hoch-deutsche amerikanische Calendar* between 1748 and 1770 attempting to sort out these terminological boundaries and their meaning. Similarly, book lists kept in the financial records of expenditures to America by authorities at Halle suggest that in the 1750s and 1760s, demand for more English-German dictionaries grew and was recognized by the Lutheran pastors in the mission field. For some additional details, see Roeber, "Origins and Transfer," *Perspectives in Am. Hist.*, n.s., III (1987), 156–171; Frederick George Livingood, "Eighteenth Century Reformed Church Schools," Pennsylvania German Society, *Proceedings and Addresses*, XXXVIII (1930), 185–195.

101. Three languages were used by German-American immigrants—High German for church, dialect for daily use, English in contact with outsiders. The Palatine dialect dominated in most of Pennsylvania, although Swabian was more commonly heard in more western settlements, in Virginia's Hebron Valley settlement, and in much of South Carolina's backcountry settlements. It is true that "no two languages are ever sufficiently similar to be considered as representing the same social reality," but also that no one language ever creates just one culture, but instead incorporates several. See Harold R. Isaacs, *Idols of the Tribe: Group Identity and Political Change* (New York, 1975), 93–114, citing Edward Sapir, esp. 99. See also William F. Hanks, "Discourse Genres in a Theory of Practice," *American Ethnologist*, XIV (1987), 668–692; also Roeber, "In German Ways? Problems and Potentials of Eighteenth-Century German Social and Emigration History," *WMQ*, 3d Ser., XLIV (1987), 750–774, esp. 772, n. 37.

102. Michael Maurer, *Aufklärung und Anglophilie in Deutschland* (Göttingen, 1987); on German schoolmasters and education, Mabel Haller, *Early Moravian Education in Pennsylvania* (Nazareth, Pa., 1953); Livingood, "Eighteenth Century Reformed Church Schools," Pennsylvania German Society, *Proceedings and Addresses*, XXXVIII (1930), 185–195; for Lutheran pastors and schoolteachers, Glatfelter, *Pastors and People*. British literary penetration of German reading habits increased significantly in the 1700s, but as late as the 1720s English titles were almost unknown at the Frankfurt book fair. Inventories in the Palatinate, even for the aristocracy, reveal no awareness of English literature or culture. Leipzig, Hamburg,

chael Schlatter's reports to the Dutch synods, the schools enjoyed a network of supporters led by David Thompson, an English Reformed preacher at Amsterdam who translated Schlatter's appeal for dissemination among Scottish and Irish dissenters. Interest in making Germans into loyal Britons was stimulated, until the end of the Seven Years' War revealed both German-American loyalty and the great expense such schools entailed. At their height, eleven schools enrolled 750 students; three were destroyed during the war with France, and neither British, Dutch, nor German support from abroad could be had soon enough to underwrite them. Halle, although interested, was disbursing large amounts of money to bring two more preachers to America, and only later, after the schools' demise, obtained particularly large bequests that further sustained the American Lutheran congregations into the 1770s.[103]

Despite the collapse of these schools, the arrival in Philadelphia in 1770 of the Halle- and Leipzig-educated pastor Johann Christoph Kunze signaled the intention of German-Americans to support the founding of a seminary for young students, which opened three years later. The *Pennsylvanische Staatsbote* noted in August 1774 that the school's purpose, which a lottery was to help support, was intended "to raise youths in the mastery and purity of both the German and English languages."[104] The lesson that gradually began to dawn upon German-Americans as a result of these developments, however, was that they alone would be responsible for such undertakings and that charitable support from Britain or the Continent was increasingly insufficient for such ventures.

Halle, and Berlin, on the other hand, the areas that supplied pastors to North American Lutherans, were quite aware of England, hence Halle's pietist awareness of the new world settlers. See Friedrich Lübbecke, *Fünfhundert Jahre Buch und Druck in Frankfurt am Main* (Frankfurt, 1948), 83–88; Bernhard Fabian, "English Books and Their Eighteenth-Century German Readers," in Paul J. Korlin, ed., *The Widening Circle: Essays on the Circulation of Literature in Eighteenth-Century Europe* (Philadelphia, 1976), 119–196.

103. For a summary of the literature on the charity schools and the expectations of Mühlenberg, Schlatter, and the German supporters vis-à-vis the British patrons, see Aland, ed., *Korrespondenz Mühlenbergs*, II, 151, 158–159, 241–242, 304–305, 535–536. See, for the statistics, Samuel Edwin Weber, *The Charity School Movement in Colonial Pennsylvania* (Philadelphia, 1905), 44–51. My summary of the Halle financial affairs depends upon a reading of disbursements to the American mission fields in the archives of the Francke Foundation, IV F 4 and F 9, IV G 7–11, University of Halle.

104. Carl Frederick Haussmann, *Kunze's Seminarium and the Society for the Propagation of Christianity and Useful Knowledge among the Germans in America* (Philadelphia, 1917), 65. Kunze was later named professor of classics and German at the University of Pennsylvania before taking a similar post at Columbia after accepting a pastorate in New York City. See Edward Potts Cheyney, *History of the University of Pennsylvania, 1740–1940* (Philadelphia, 1940), 132–133.

The German-language churches by the 1750s became fields of contest, but language was not the issue. Instead, the influence, connections, and future ambitions of the emerging traders, merchants, and innkeepers forced a close examination of how these private associations should be governed and what instruments of English law might serve that purpose best. Conflicts exploded in Lutheran congregations in Raritan, New Jersey, Germantown, Lancaster, and Philadelphia over the control of money and pastors. Reformed parishes experienced similar fights nearly simultaneously. From Mühlenberg's correspondence, the Reformed pastor Michael Schlatter's letters, and cryptic entries in German church records, the struggle for dominance in these voluntary religious associations becomes evident.[105] Less a history of the laity's general progress, these quarrels reflect contests pitting poorer congregants and clerics in the German churches against "the lordship of the elders."[106]

By the 1750s, German Lutherans and Reformed alike realized that the public authorities of the British colonies took no interest in such internal struggles. Rather, it became apparent to the Lutherans of New York as early as 1757 that they had to protect the future of churches that had been constructed with funds given as charitable bequests from Europe or in testaments written by German-speakers in America. These institutions and the schools that often accompanied or even predated them were significant only to the group using the language, making the bequest, and worrying about new forms of governance. Pennsylvania Germans developed the same concerns at nearly the same time. So, too, somewhat belatedly, did the oldest Lutheran congregation in Virginia. By 1770, from Georgia to New York, colonial authorities were considering requests for formal incorporation made by various German-speaking congregations.

The responses varied in the royal colonies. Requests were denied in New York, but Lutherans in New Germantown and Bedminster, New Jersey, were granted charters. Mühlenberg believed that it was too late to do anything in

105. See Elizabeth Fisher Gray, "A God of Order: Power and Authority in the German Lutheran Congregations of Pennsylvania, 1723–1776" (Ph.D. diss., Harvard University, 1990); see also Thomas Müller, "Die evangelische Obrigkeitsproblematik bei Heinrich Melchior Mühlenberg: Der Aufbau der lutherischen Kirche in Pennsylvania" (master's thesis, University of Göttingen, 1988), on the same difficulties.

106. Dietmar Rothermund, *The Layman's Progress: Religious and Political Experience in Colonial Pennsylvania, 1740–1770* (Philadelphia, 1961); see also Martin E. Lodge, "The Crisis of the Churches in the Middle Colonies, 1720–1750," *PMHB*, XCV (1971), 202–228; John B. Frantz, "The Awakening of Religion among the German Settlers in the Middle Colonies," *WMQ*, 3d Ser., XXXIII (1976), 266–288; and my discussion of the events at St. Michael's in Philadelphia in "Germans, Property, and the First Great Awakening," in Herget and Ortseifen, eds., *Transit of Civilization*, 165–184. Rudolf Schomerus, *Die verfassungsrechtliche Entwicklung der lutherischen Kirche in Nordamerika von 1638 bis 1792* (Göttingen, 1965), "Die Herrschaft der Ältesten," 110–125.

Virginia, where Anglican controls were hardening. His intervention in a particularly nasty internal dispute in Georgia's Salzburger community revealed the new charter to be legally deficient. The Anglican church could claim the glebe land of the Jerusalem church, since the words "Evangelical Lutheran" had not been duly written into the document. Reformed and Lutheran congregations in South Carolina, even though sometimes designating themselves self-consciously as "High-German Protestants . . . a separate people," could not secure incorporated status there despite the existence of written constitutions that many of these groups drew up in the 1760s.[107]

The merchants who figured in these disputes moved almost simultaneously to establish their public identity in political and social forums. The founding of the German Society of Pennsylvania in 1764, followed two years later by the erection of the German Friendly Society in Charleston, ratified their continuing roles as cultural brokers. Quickly, however, interested non-Germans were also included in these societies. Simultaneously, that same leadership, the "charter group" that had been in place almost from the beginnings in the 1730s, arrived politically as well. Throughout the entire spectrum of colonies from New Jersey to Georgia, prominent German-speakers were elected in the 1760s to the provincial assemblies. These leaders rested secure within elaborate institutionalized frameworks that had perpetuated language, property customs, religious congregations, and schools while economic and, now, legal-political contact with British-Americans increased.[108]

A major reassessment of the German-Americans' own culture and its relationship to British-American public life occurred because of the Seven Years' War. Indeed, between this war against the Germans' old foe, the French, and a second—the Revolution—that severed the German-speaking

107. Roeber, "Germans, Property, and the First Great Awakening," in Herget and Ortseifen, eds., *Transit of Civilization*; for the other instances, see Tappert and Doberstein, eds., *Journals of Muhlenberg*, II, 359 (on New Jersey), 374–375 (on Virginia), 598–600 (on the Georgia dispute); First Consistory Book of the German Evangelical Lutheran Church of St. John the Baptist, Charleston, S.C., 20; Marion Chandler, "Church Incorporation in South Carolina under the Constitution of 1778" (master's thesis, University of South Carolina, 1969). Mühlenberg forwarded copies of the charters to Halle and also sent his superiors a copy of the only German-language legal handbook published in North America, David Henderson's *Des Landsmans Advocat*. My check in the library at Halle failed to turn up a copy, however. On the Henderson volume, see Roeber, "Origins and Transfer," *Perspectives in Am. Hist.*, n.s., III (1987), 115–116.

108. The Pennsylvania German Society rules open with an identification of the members as "we, his royal Majesty of Great Britain's German Subjects in Pennsylvania." See Oswald Seidensticker and Max Henrici, *Geschichte der deutschen Gesellschaft von Pennsylvanien, 1764–1917* (Philadelphia, 1917), 40; George J. Gongaware, *The History of the German Friendly Society of Charleston, South Carolina, 1766–1916* (Richmond, Va., 1935), 1–14.

tie to Britain and the Continent, the public culture of North America became the German-Americans' own. Appropriately, Christopher Saur signaled the change. Although suspicious of the motivations of wealthy English-speakers, Saur tolerated the creation of a militia in Pennsylvania in 1755. In explaining the need for both taxes and a military force to a readership previously disinclined to support either, Saur printed Franklin's defense of both as consonant with the British constitution and privileges and the fundamental law of Pennsylvania. Saur had bitterly attacked Conrad Weiser in 1741 when Weiser, as a justice, had written a circular letter to fellow German-speakers in defense of a tax for defense funds. The proprietary scheme was rejected. But the attitudes of the German-speakers toward the public realm had changed subtly in the meantime. Weiser had reminded the Germans that, if they possessed "any thing of temporal goods," they needed to adopt a united front. If the appeal to the "priviledges and liberties" extended to German-speakers exactly like those "a native Born English man can enjoy" did not persuade them, he ended in using the biblical image, "A house divided in itself cannot stand." But no genuine engagement with the political culture was contemplated. Rather, Weiser had encouraged the German-speakers to "trust" the English, who were more "jealous and Carefull of their Laws" than any other nation. But it was "their" laws, and not "our" laws, Weiser pointed to. Similarly, emigrant letters back to the Reich before the Seven Years' War referred consistently to the colonies as "ein freies Land," meaning, simply, little government and no taxation. What this description also suggested was an absence of obligation toward the land or its protection. But the concept of obligation and active involvement began to arise not only in Saur's toleration of the militia bill but in his comments on the New Jersey land rioters of the same year, many of whom were Germans, and in his interpretation of the war.[109]

The land riots in New Jersey in 1755 involved German-speakers who were normally law-abiding. But, as Saur noted, the rioters near the Union Iron Works in Hunterdon County believed that they had been granted lands that were now confiscated upon which they had already paid taxes. People who had traditionally been respectful of authority in the villages, Saur went on, were learning the right of resistance.[110]

109. Adams, "Colonial German-language Press," in Bailyn and Hench, eds., *Press*, 158–159; Arthur D. Graeff, *Conrad Weiser, Pennsylvania Peacemaker* (Allentown, Pa., 1945), 99–106; Weiser Correspondence, box 1, 20 Sept. 1741, Historical Society of Pennsylvania.

110. Arthur D. Graeff, *Relations between the Pennsylvania Germans and the British Authorities (1750–1776)* (Norristown, Pa., 1934), 52; Saur, April 1, 1755, *Pennsylvanische Berichte*. The British-American view was simply that ignorant recent arrivals, "the very scum of Germany," no longer religious immigrants, had no understanding of and no respect for the law. See Penn Manuscripts, Official Correspondence, VI, 1753–1754, no. 159, Historical Society of Pennsylvania.

The right of resistance against threats to property expanded by late 1755 to the need for military defense as the Seven Years' War threatened German-speakers in the backcountry of several provinces. Saur even suggested parallels to the Thirty Years' War in his Almanac offering of 1758, which commanded attention with a woodcut and treatise on monstrosities and strange births, apocalyptic signs associated with warfare. To make the connection between German and British interests clearer, he interrupted a popular series, his conversation between a "Newcomer" and a seasoned German-American, to print a firsthand account by an English observer of the terrible effects of the war in Germany itself.[111] From his initial days of publishing an almanac containing "various needful and edifying theological things, and also household remedies," Saur had evolved from independent critic of the Reformed and Lutheran clergy, the redemption system, and warfare of any sort into a sophisticated observer of British policies and Pennsylvania politics and the rapidly expanding German-speaking population. Still skeptical of the political motives of many Pennsylvanians, encouraged by exemptions from military service for conscientious objectors, hopeful for a resumption by peaceful means of good relations with native Americans, Saur no longer opposed political involvement and support for defense policies by German-Americans so vigorously as he had a decade before. Like Pastor Boltzius, who condemned as sinful the desire of many colonists to destroy the Indians, "the first and legitimate inhabitants and hence . . . the rightful owners of this land," Saur tolerated a militia on Pennsylvania's part of the Protestant European perimeter in North America. By 1761, his son offered patriotic German-Americans an expanded version of the life of Frederick the Great, Britain's ally in the war.[112]

In the South, a German regiment was formed by Peter Kalb to fight in South Carolina's Cherokee War in 1759, in defense of both German-language settlements and the common provincial political future under British rule. Just before the Georgia colony began its last quarter-century of existence as a royal province, the Salzburgers for the first time in 1748 secured a lay justice of the peace and constable, ending the Reverend Mr. Boltzius's practice of exercising both ecclesiastical and secular jurisdiction in the settlement. The later justice and Revolutionary leader Johannes Treutlen's gradual rise to political prominence in Georgia can be traced to this period of

111. Saur, *Der hoch-deutsche amerikanische Calendar*, 1758.

112. Donald F. Durnbaugh, ed., *The Brethren in Colonial America: A Sourcebook* . . . (Elgin, Ill., 1967); Durnbaugh, "Christopher Sauer, Pennsylvania-German Printer: His Youth in Germany and Later Relationships with Europe," *PMHB*, LXXXII (1958), 316–340; *Detailed Reports*, XII, 67 (1748); W. H. Dilworth, *Das Leben und herosiche Thaten des Königs von Preussen* . . . (Germantown, Pa., 1761). Dilworth's history is supplemented by Saur's compilation from other sources of additional heroic episodes.

upheaval, ten years after his arrival in the colony. Already in 1748 the potential need for a military defense of this fragile German-American outpost on the Spanish frontier had created rangers whose behavior did not always please pastor Boltzius but whose presence reminded all the settlers of their responsibilities to a British, Protestant world.[113]

A public political culture, the subject of considerable speculation and writing by later German theorists, can exist only under certain conditions. Rather than remaining passive and silent toward authority and institutions, German-speakers in British North America awoke to a new engagement with political culture because of the disruptions of war. The formation of a German-American regiment in New York by 1770 underscored the political engagement of a people whose alliance to the De Lanceys was confirmed by former New York City mayor Johannes Cruger's standing for election to the assembly.[114]

Not all German-speakers made this significant discovery at once, nor in all the British provinces at the same time. For instance, when concerned British officials tried to inform rural New York Germans of their imminent peril from Indian depredations, the Germans laughed, "slapping their hands upon their buttocks and asking, 'why should the Indians wish to harm us?' "[115] As late as 1775 both upstate New York and backcountry North Carolina Germans, because of their isolation from the networks of communication and support that had created the German-American world, seemed not to have assumed this public, political identity. At least Philadelphia publisher Henry Miller did not think so. Chastising these uninformed Germans, Miller suggested that they had retained far too long a familial, dependent, and obedient attitude toward British authorities like the baronial Sir William Johnson, regarded by local Germans as their "father-in-law," perhaps because of his first common-law wife, who had been a Palatine indentured servant. Rather, Miller argued, Philadelphia German-Americans and others in touch with them who understood the times had taken upon themselves the image of the armed landowner who, shouldering his musket, would defend his property against the pretended claims of those who meant to tax them into submission. The need to protect one's private—and not merely separate, that is,

113. June Clark Murtie, *Colonial Soldiers of the South, 1732–1771* (Baltimore, 1983), 883–896; *Detailed Reports*, IX, 107, 109, XI, 70 (1747).

114. Jürgen Habermas, *Der Strukturwandel der Öffentlichkeit* (Neuwied, 1962); Ernst Mannheim, *Aufklärung und öffentliche Meinung: Studien zur Soziologie der Öffentlichkeit im 18. Jht.* (Stuttgart, 1979); Walter Euchner, *Egoismus und Gemeinwohl: Studien zur Geschichte der bürgerlichen Philosophie* (Frankfurt, 1973); Adams, "Colonial German-language Press," in Bailyn and Hench, eds., *Press*, 171; K. G. Davies, ed., *Documents of the American Revolution, 1770–1783* (Shannon, 1972–1981), I, 29–30, III, CO 5/1102, fol. 49.

115. Cited in Graeff, *Relations between Germans and British Authorities*, 93.

German—rights from possible abuse by a public authority engaged in oppressive behavior could not have been clearer to Miller.[116]

Miller, who began publishing the highly political *Pennsylvanische Staatsbote* in 1762, first arrived in North America in 1741. His essays translated the new political jargon about taxation, representation, representative government, and the like, without comment and explanation, simply assuming that his readership knew what he meant. Perhaps he consciously directed himself to the politically aware leaders created by the recent war. Miller joined the ranks of the emerging generation of eminent traders, merchants, publicists, and farmers who all came of age in the midst of the creation of British German-America before the outbreak of the war in 1755. He, like Michael Hillegas (the later United States treasurer), Peter Müller, Christopher Ludwig (the Continental Army's baker), Heinrich Keppele of Pennsylvania, and Johannes Treutlen of Georgia, or the Sailers, Geigers, and Kaltheisens of South Carolina, inherited the mantle of secular leadership that fell from an older generation in the 1750s. Conrad Weiser, Conrad Beissel, Christopher Saur, Sr., pastor Boltzius, Zinzendorf, to name but a few of the most prominent earlier leaders, had all died by 1760.

By then, in every province with a significant German-speaking population, not only German justices of the peace but even the first German-speaking lawyers and provincial politicians began to make their appearance, reflecting an ability and willingness to take on the legal and political concepts and terminology of the dominant culture while firmly rooted in their own. While some enterprising English-speaking attorneys studied German to expand their clientele, Thomas Henderson compiled a handbook on the law, which Henry Miller translated for him into German, detailing English liberties and rights in the language of this subculture, which showed no signs of disappearing when the treatise was published in 1761. Moreover, they seemed confident that they were capable of engaging British-American public culture even as they debated, argued, questioned, and defended their own separate interests as a part of the larger society in which they lived.[117]

From the beginning of their association with "the famous English liberty,"

116. *Schreiben des evangelisch-lutherisch und reformierten Kirchenraths . . . an die teutschen Einwohner der Provinzen von New York und Nord-Carolina* (Philadelphia, 1775); on Johnson, Bernard Bailyn, *Voyagers to the West: A Passage in the Peopling of America on the Eve of the Revolution* (New York, 1986), 576–582. Although one can only guess on how many people read such offerings, Grubb, "German Immigration," *Jour. Interdisc. Hist.*, XX (1989–1990), 429, suggests a literacy rate of more than 80 percent for Pennsylvania's Germans by 1770.

117. Thomas Henderson, *Des Landsmans Advocat* . . . (Philadelphia, 1761); for more details, see Roeber, "Origins and Transfer," *Perspectives in Am. Hist.*, n.s., III (1987), 115–116; Adams, "The Colonial German-language Press," in Bailyn and Hench, eds., *Press*, 178–181.

German-speakers expressed overall satisfaction with North America, even in the face of redemptioner mortality, warfare with the French and native Americans, suspicion on the part of English neighbors, and difficulties encountered with novel linguistic, legal, and political systems. By the 1760s, as tensions began to build between Great Britain and the North American mainland colonies, German-Americans had to ask whether they could continue to enjoy the privileges, the *ständische Freiheiten* that had been assured them as "his Majesty's loyal German subjects in North America."

All colonials share a sense of exile and absence from a metropolitan center; all rest more or less secure with imported mixes of transferred and adapted cultural systems. But a political revolution forces linguistic, racial, local, and cultural differences to the background and demands a unity intolerant of the diversity acceptable in a colonial system.[118] How the German-Americans managed the crisis of the Revolution and the adjustment to the new public culture is beyond the scope of this essay.

We can, however, observe that German-American migration, systems of support, and retention of cultural traits in a separate realm that focused on language, home, and faith still differed from the Dutch experience as long as the colonial relationship to Great Britain lasted. Numbers and institutionalized support enabled a retention and adjustment of German-speakers' varied cultural traditions to North American conditions. Freed from hostility toward the dominant culture that had characterized a large part of Dutch-English colonial relations outside the ranks of the wealthy, the majority Lutheran and Reformed Germans embraced British North America, first on economic and material grounds, later appropriating its legal and political terms to fit both their own separate ends and their expanding role in the larger culture.

Even pastor Mühlenberg, not particularly enamored of free churches and Pennsylvania's tolerance of them when he arrived in 1742, changed his mind. Reporting to Halle, he noted in 1763 the common experience of the German Reformed in their struggle with the synod in Holland and the recent grumbling of German Lutherans who identified pastors and wealthy trustees with "the Yoke of the Hallensians." "They will have *Freedom*, American Freedom," he noted, "to elect and replace their preachers themselves." Yet, when asked why he would not abandon the proprietary government and ask for a royal charter when the king was obviously the ultimate authority, Mühlenberg voiced precisely the subtle shift away from a separate culture that Saur, Miller, and other German-speakers had developed over the previous decade.

118. John H. Elliott, "Colonial Identity in the Atlantic World," Michael Zuckerman, "Identity in British America: Unease in Eden," Anthony Pagden and Nicholas Canny, "Afterword: From Identity to Independence"—all in Canny and Pagden, eds., *Colonial Identity in the Atlantic World, 1500–1800* (Princeton, N.J., 1987), 3–13, 115–158, 267–278.

Coyly replying that he always stayed out of politics, the pastor confided in his own notes that he had begun to make the distinction between public political pronouncements and his right as a private citizen to exercise political judgment in concert with others. Mühlenberg and his people were, he said, "ready to sacrifice life and property" for the king. But the "priceless religious and civil privileges" given Pennsylvania long ago by Charles II were not to be lightly tossed aside. The German-Americans paid taxes as did English-speakers, and "are not bastards, but his Majesty's loyal subjects and naturalized children." A decade later, Mühlenberg reiterated his belief to a correspondent that the success of private associations and groups like his Lutherans benefited the public good. Rather than support the Lutheran wish to build on Wine Street, however, the Penns had refused the "Gift for a School and Parsonage [that] does rather encrease than hurt [their] Interest."[119] Private choices, public benefits, perhaps summed up the Germans' final assessment of what the "famous English liberties" had wrought in British North America.

What, then, was unique about German-American cultural values that made them any different from the anglicized Dutch or their English-speaking neighbors? That they aspired to material security and noninterference in religious and familial affairs seems clear. The "famous English liberties" enshrined in public, political institutions, they made their own in the terrors of the Seven Years' War. As a result of the Revolution, they learned that they could have liberties without Britain, and the private sphere without the German language. Perhaps, less happily, they also retained a tendency to retreat again from the public realm except when it directly threatened private interests. Carl Schurz would complain of this characteristic among German-Americans a century later.

This last point, in fact, seems most significant. Ironically, despite the defenses erected for language, home, and faith by Dutch pietists in New Jersey, the close relationships of eminent Dutch and English carried many not only into American commercial but into political and legal life as well, far beyond the bounds of the original Dutch cultural areas of New York and New Jersey. The numerically much stronger German-speakers, by contrast, although never encountering comparable difficulties, seized English liberties and the English language for commerce and minimal political activity and were content. To be sure, one of pastor Mühlenberg's sons, Frederick Augustus, became speaker of the House in the First Congress. John Peter Gabriel

119. Aland, ed., *Korrespondenz Mühlenbergs*, II, xxxiii; Tappert and Doberstein, eds., *Journals of Muhlenberg*, II, 191–192; Mühlenberg to Edmund Physick, March 10, 1776, PM 95, Lutheran Theological Seminary Archives.

distinguished himself as a general in the Revolution. But most identifiable German-Americans did not play a conspicuous role in the legal or political, that is, public, life of post-Revolutionary America, especially in proportion to their numbers and the richness of their culture. Despite pleas by some leaders among them to become more politically active on behalf of German interests, they were satisfied with farm, commerce, home, and faith—all areas increasingly thought of as private by the late eighteenth century.[120] An inherited skepticism about government and authority survived the dangers of both the Seven Years' War and the Revolution to allow German-speakers to understand republican government as primarily absence of government. Even a younger generation raised on stories of oppressive taxation, forced public labor, and arrogant princes retreated easily into private concerns in the absence of impending danger. The self-reliant, thrifty, religious, and withdrawn image of the Pennsylvania Dutch, the Shenandoah Valley Germans, and inhabitants of Little Pennsylvania in the backcountry of North Carolina survived well into the nineteenth century. The sense of public responsibility for liberties, never strongly rooted in the German past, apparently remained fragile in the new political order.[121] Perhaps the centrality of domestic ways in the German southwest villages that had been devastated by rising taxation, overpopulation, and warfare; the dominant Lutheran theological attitudes that counseled obedience to but a certain disengagement from the state; and the presence in North America of free church dissenters who had even more reason to be skeptical of government than Reformed or Lutheran settlers—all continued to work deep within the religious and domestic memory of German-speaking men and women in North America, long after direct ties to the Reich had vanished.

For Jefferson, such dedication to the home, to religious belief that he regarded as "private opinion," and to independence from government were prized attributes of a free people. Those virtues, couched in the peculiarities of speech, dress, and the hard labor rural European women performed, defined for him what was nearly, but not quite, "English" in North America.[122] Such attributes of continental settlers, he believed, contributed

120. Don Yoder, "The 'Dutchman' and the '*Deitschlenner*': The New World Confronts the Old," *Yearbook of German-American Studies*, XXIII (1988), 1–17, argues persuasively for the retention of a peculiar Americanized German "private" culture among the rural "Pennsylvania Dutch" and repeated, frustrated attempts by learned clergy, educators, and publicists to perpetuate a "German" culture in America after the Revolution.

121. For an examination of this problem in the context of the Fries Rebellion, see Roeber, "Citizens or Subjects? German-Lutherans and the Federal Constitution in Pennsylvania, 1789–1800," *Amerikastudien / American Studies*, XXXIV (1989), 49–68.

122. See, for example, Julian P. Boyd *et al.*, eds., *The Papers of Thomas Jefferson* (Princeton, N.J., 1950), XIII, 48 (and for epigraph).

to the new nation's strength and diversity. Jefferson's definition of whatever was not English was clearly too narrow, but he was perceptive on one significant point. The Dutch- and German-speakers had shared with English-speakers considerable common ground in religious, commercial, and political heritage that facilitated their exchanges with British North America. Both Dutch and German women preserved language, religious norms, and distinct domestic habits in the British colonial settlements, the more numerous German-speakers enjoying a longer retention of all three because of their extensive networks and leadership. When the British center vanished in 1783 and the Netherlands and the Reich became increasingly distant memories, Dutch- and German-speakers had already successfully adjusted to an English-speaking society and its laws that enabled each to be content, in slightly different ways, with the results. Whether liberty should be extended beyond the periphery of one's own cultural heritage to other peoples in North America who were still unfree, only a few Dutch- or German-speakers had debated. Despite this limitation, the Dutch and German exchanges with others in the British colonies contributed to a fascination with the private sphere that for many generations to come would mark the new core culture as peculiarly American.

MALDWYN A. JONES

The Scotch-Irish in British America

Lord Adam Gordon, the son of a Scottish Highland nobleman, while traveling through the colonies in the 1760s, described Winchester, Virginia, as being "inhabited by a spurious race of mortals known by the appelation of Scotch-Irish."[1] In denying the legitimacy of the term by which immigrants from Ulster of Scottish descent had become widely known in America, Lord Adam unwittingly initiated what has become a recurrent historical controversy. Even today, nearly three centuries after the term "Scotch-Irish" first became current, some historians still refuse to accept that it reflects historical reality, namely, that the Scots who had lived in Ulster before they came to America were culturally distinct both from the native Irish and from the inhabitants of Scotland.

Lord Adam's skepticism about the name was understandable. It was virtually unknown alike in his native Scotland and in Ulster itself, where the usual designation was—and is—"Ulster Scots." It had, in fact, been coined in America, and even there had been slow to catch on. When the first great wave of Ulster immigrants burst upon the colonies early in the eighteenth century, colonial officials referred to them variously as "Irish Presbyterians" or "Northern Irish," but in most cases simply as "Irish." The first known use of the term "Scotch-Irish" stems from Maryland's Eastern Shore in 1695. Thirty years later it was widely current in both Pennsylvania and Delaware, and by the 1760s it had spread to other areas where the Scotch-Irish were thickly settled, namely, western Maryland, the Shenandoah Valley of Virginia, and the backcountry of the Carolinas and Georgia.[2] Nonetheless, most of those who had occasion to refer to Ulster immigrants continued to use the designation "Irish" while the newcomers themselves, though occasionally irritated at being mistaken for Irish Catholics, generally accepted the name throughout the eighteenth century and, indeed, well into the nineteenth. It was only after the Irish famine immigration of the mid-nineteenth

1. Cited in Ian Charles Cargill Graham, *Colonists from Scotland: Emigration to North America, 1707–1783* (Ithaca, N.Y., 1956), 18.

2. James G. Leyburn, *The Scotch-Irish: A Social History* (Chapel Hill, N.C., 1962), appendix 1, 327–334.

century had sparked outbursts of nativist hostility to all things Irish that the descendants of eighteenth-century Ulster immigrants, looking for ways to dissociate themselves from newcomers they despised as "the serfs of Rome and Tammany Hall," began to insist on being called Scotch-Irish. This insistence culminated in the establishment in 1889 of the Scotch-Irish Society of America, whose aim was to "preserve the history and perpetuate the achievements of the Scotch-Irish race in America" and which over the next decade or so published a succession of works commemorating the Scotch-Irish record in uncritical and extravagant fashion.[3]

Scotch-Irish claims soon provoked a fierce assault from Irish-American authors. Whereas Lord Adam Gordon a century earlier had objected to the term "Scotch-Irish" on the ground that those it applied to were simply Scots, Irish-American controversialists claimed that eighteenth-century Ulster immigrants were in reality Irish in all respects save religion. Spokesmen for this point of view, such as the prolific and disputatious Michael J. O'Brien, claimed that a century of residence in Ulster and of intermarriage with the native Irish had transformed the Scottish element into Irishmen. However, O'Brien failed to persuade other scholars that he had a credible case. Indeed, historians generally have dismissed him as an ethnic chauvinist.[4]

During the past decade, however, a group of scholars writing from a standpoint radically different from O'Brien's have renewed his attack on the "Scotch-Irish myth." The debate began when Forrest and Ellen McDonald and Grady McWhiney advanced their provocative "Celtic interpretation" of Southern history, which holds that the cultural distinctiveness of the Old South arose from the fact that the colonies south of Pennsylvania were settled during the seventeenth and eighteenth centuries overwhelmingly by emigrants from the Celtic fringe of the British Isles.[5] The Celtic interpretation denies that the Scotch-Irish were culturally distinct, linking them instead

3. Scotch-Irish Society of America, *The Scotch-Irish in America . . .*, 10 vols. (1889–1901).

4. For O'Brien's position, see Michael J. O'Brien, "The 'Scotch-Irish' Myth," *Journal of the American Irish Historical Society*, XXIV (1925), 142–153; J. D. O'Connell, *The "Scotch-Irish" Delusion in America* (Washington, D.C., 1897); Joseph Smith, *The "Scotch-Irish" Shibboleth Analyzed and Rejected . . .* (Washington, D.C., 1898).

For the opposition, see James P. Rodechko, "Michael J. O'Brien: Irish-American Historian," *New-York Historical Society Quarterly*, LIV (1970), 173–192.

5. The principal formulations of this interpretation appear in Forrest McDonald and Grady McWhiney, "The Antebellum Southern Herdsman: A Reinterpretation," *Journal of Southern History*, XLI (1975), 147–166; McDonald and McWhiney, "The South from Self-Sufficiency to Peonage: An Interpretation," *American Historical Review*, LXXXV (1980), 1095–1118; Ellen Shapiro McDonald and Forrest McDonald, "The Ethnic Origins of the American People, 1790," *William and Mary Quarterly*, 3d Ser., XXXVII (1980), 179–199; Grady McWhiney, *Cracker Culture: Celtic Ways in the Old South* (Tuscaloosa, Ala., 1988).

to the Scottish, Irish, Welsh, and English Borderers as peoples sharing a common Pan-Celtic, nomadic, pastoral, and warlike culture.[6]

Revisionism has been carried several stages further in two articles by Leroy V. Eid, which, in effect, question virtually everything assumed to be true about the Scotch-Irish and their culture. As well as reviving O'Brien's claims for the native, Celtic Irish contribution to the peopling of colonial America, Eid asserted that the McDonalds-McWhiney Celtic thesis offers an essential insight into colonial culture; indeed, he avowed, "Any historical view that does not build on that Celtic orientation is simply myth-making."[7]

A comprehensive critique of the Celtic interpretation lies outside the scope of this essay, but the reasons why it has failed to win general acceptance may be briefly noted. Some critics flatly reject the McDonalds' basic premise that such diverse and often antagonistic peoples as the Scots, Irish, Scotch-Irish, Welsh, and English Borderers can be regarded as a single cultural group.[8] To hold otherwise, it is argued, ignores the varied histories of the so-called Celtic peoples and betrays an unfamiliarity with the work of British and Irish historians. Other critics dismiss the Celtic interpretation as a throwback to an era when simplistic and even racist assertions about ethnic characteristics were the norm. But the heaviest criticism has fallen upon the McDonalds' preferred methodology, the quantitative analysis of surnames. The McDonalds' estimates of the makeup of the colonial population are, it is alleged, seriously flawed because they exclude some distinctively Scottish and Scotch-Irish surnames (all patronymics prefixed by *Mac-* or *Mc-*, for example) and include as distinctively Scottish or Irish or Welsh surnames which were equally common in England. Moreover, in a study based on more comprehensive and precise research than that of the McDonalds' and which drastically reduces their estimates of the Scottish, Irish, and Welsh strains in the southern population in 1790, Thomas L. Purvis makes the telling point that "the extraordinarily high rate of internal migration within . . . [the British Isles] during the early modern period prevents any methodology premised upon nomenclatural frequencies from identifying regional origins with any

6. Forrest McDonald, "Prologue," in McWhiney, *Cracker Culture*, xl–xli.

7. Leroy V. Eid, "The Colonial Scotch-Irish: A View Accepted Too Readily," *Éire-Ireland: A Journal of Irish Studies*, XXI, no. 4 (Winter 1986), 81–105, esp. 97–104; Eid, "Irish, Scotch, and Scotch-Irish: A Reconsideration," *American Presbyterians*, LXIV (Winter 1986), 211–225 (quotation on 213–214).

8. The weightiest rebuttal is Rowland Berthoff, "Celtic Mist over the South," *Jour. So. Hist.*, LII (1986), 523–546. See also communications by Francis Jennings and Rowland Berthoff and reply by Forrest McDonald and Ellen Shapiro McDonald, *WMQ*, 3d Ser., XXXVII (1980), 700–703; Ned C. Landsman, *Scotland and Its First American Colony, 1683–1765* (Princeton, N.J., 1985); Thomas L. Purvis, "The European Ancestry of the United States Population, 1790," *WMQ*, 3d Ser., XLI (1984), 101.

assurance of accuracy."[9] These objections apart, Kerby Miller's authoritative study of Irish emigration, far from supporting O'Brien or the Celtic interpretation, reaffirms that, although Protestants constituted only one-fourth to one-third of the Irish population, they composed three-fourths of all transatlantic departures from Ireland between 1700 and 1776. Furthermore, Miller concludes, about 70 percent of the Protestant emigrants were Presbyterians.[10]

Even so, it may well be the case that the Ulster outflow was less uniformly Scottish and Presbyterian than has commonly been supposed.[11] Some of the emigrants were Anglo-Irish Episcopalians, descendants of the English settlers who, along with the Scots, had formed part of the Plantation of Ulster of James I. Others were the product of intermarriage. The claim that, unlike the Cromwellian settlers in Munster, the Ulster Scots rarely intermarried with the native Irish has recently been challenged with some success by Irish scholars. They have proved Michael J. O'Brien partly right in one particular by demonstrating that, although segregation had been the basic principle of the Plantation of Ulster, it had never been fully implemented and was soon abandoned. Many Irish Catholics remained in areas of Scottish settlement, and there was a considerable degree of intermingling and even some intermarriage, at least in the seventeenth century. But, contrary to what O'Brien claimed, the two cultures did not interact to the extent of losing their distinct characteristics and producing a new hybrid. Rather did they remain, as David N. Doyle has insisted, two separate and antagonistic communities.[12]

They were divided not only by religion but to a considerable extent also by language; while there was a remarkable spread of English both as a written and as a spoken language after the Treaty of Limerick (1691), Irish was still the tongue of the majority of the native population in the eighteenth century. The two societies also differed in economic circumstances, working habits, and leisure activities. By comparison with those of the Scotch-Irish, the farms of the native Irish were smaller and were located in the more mountainous and less fertile areas of the province. Moreover, the Scotch-Irish engaged in linen weaving as well as agriculture while the native Irish, as a County Londonderry rector would report in 1814, were averse to manufacturing, preferring "the less regular and certain, but to them, more interesting gain, which arises from the quick transition of property, and the frequent

9. Landsman, *Scotland*, appendix A, 264–274; Purvis, "European Ancestry," *WMQ*, 3d Ser., XLI (1984), 84–101 (quotation on 101).

10. Kerby A. Miller, *Emigrants and Exiles: Ireland and the Irish Exodus to North America* (Oxford, 1985), 137, 149–150.

11. David Noel Doyle, *Ireland, Irishmen, and Revolutionary America, 1760–1820* (Cork, 1981), 77–78.

12. *Ibid.*, 78.

fluctuations in the cattle trade."[13] And whereas Scotch-Irish Presbyterians spent their leisure mainly in horse racing, hunting, gambling, cockfighting, and other pastimes, Irish Catholics, while not strangers to any of these activities, focused their social life rather on celebrations of saints' days and visits to holy wells as well as on such popular amusements as roadside dancing.

It was thus understandable that Scotch-Irish immigrants, like those at Londonderry, New Hampshire, in 1720, should have been surprised and chagrined to find themselves "termed *Irish* people, when we so frequently ventured our all, for the British crown and liberties, against the Irish Papists."[14] There was more reason, however, for confusing the Scotch-Irish with the Scots. Not only were there similarities of language and speech, but ties of kinship and sentiment long bound the Scotch-Irish to their ancestral land. The proximity of Ulster to southwest Scotland—a mere thirteen miles of water separate the Antrim coast from the Mull of Kintyre—meant that there was little barrier to communication. Moreover, Scottish colonization of Ulster was not the work simply of the plantation decade (1608–1618) but extended intermittently over the best part of a century, with its climax being reached only between 1690 and 1697, when bad harvests and famine in Scotland set in motion an unprecedented movement. In other words, more Scots settled in Ulster outside the plantation period proper than were planted during it, so that the Scottish connection was constantly being renewed by fresh waves of settlement. Ulster's association with Scotland was further strengthened by the presence of a Scottish army in Ulster after the Irish rebellion of 1641 had placed the entire Plantation in jeopardy. Thus, in much the same way that Ulster's Anglo-Irish maintained strong cultural links with England, those of Scottish origin tended to look to Scotland. One evidence of this was the steady stream of Ulster medical students to Scottish universities, an expedient forced on them by the fact that admission to the only Irish university, Trinity College, Dublin, was, like Oxford and Cambridge, restricted to communicants of the established Episcopal church.[15]

But it was in religion that Scottish influences were chiefly manifest. The Presbyterianism of the Scotch-Irish derived from Scotland; indeed, its formal organization in the North of Ireland originated with the "Army Presbytery"

13. William Shaw Mason, ed., *A Statistical Account, or Parochial Survey of Ireland* . . . (Dublin, 1814), I, 340, quoted in S. J. Connolly, "Religion, Work Discipline, and Economic Attitudes: The Case of Ireland," in T. M. Devine and David Dickson, eds., *Ireland and Scotland, 1600–1850* (Edinburgh, 1983), 241.

14. Cited in Leyburn, *The Scotch-Irish*, 331.

15. A.T.Q. Stewart, *The Narrow Ground: Aspects of Ulster, 1609–1969* (London, 1977), 39, 84–86; T. W. Moody and W. E. Vaughan, eds., *Eighteenth-Century Ireland, 1691–1800* (Oxford, 1986), 440, vol. IV of T. W. Moody *et al.*, eds., *A New History of Ireland*; Philip S. Robinson, *The Plantation of Ulster: British Settlement in an Irish Landscape, 1600–1670* (Dublin, 1984), 193.

formed by chaplains who accompanied the Scottish army in 1641. Moreover, the system of church discipline and government adopted by the Synod of Ulster, when it came into existence in 1690, was avowedly modeled on that of the parent church. The arrival of fundamentalist Covenanters after their defeats in 1666 and 1679, and again after 1690 when the restored Presbyterian establishment in Scotland fell short of their wishes, reinforced Scottish influence. Throughout the eighteenth century, Scotch-Irish Presbyterianism continued to be deeply influenced by developments in the Scottish Kirk. A high proportion of Ulster Presbyterian ministers had been educated in Scottish universities, especially Glasgow and Edinburgh, and held licentiates from the Presbyterian Church of Scotland. The schismatic tendencies that characterized the Church of Scotland were just as much a feature of Ulster Presbyterianism. Controversies that arose out of peculiarly Scottish conditions and had no relevance to Ireland were nonetheless carried over to Ulster and in the process lost none of their vehemence. Accordingly, two breakaway Scottish communions, the Reformed church, which consisted of Covenanters who could not accept the Revolution settlement of 1689–1690, and the Secession church, born of protest against the reimposition of lay patronage in 1712, both found followings in Ulster.[16]

Yet Ulster Presbyterianism was not, or at least did not long remain, a mirror image of the Church of Scotland. It was significant that the bitterest and most divisive religious schism in eighteenth-century Ulster was not imported from Scotland, but was a doctrinal one of purely indigenous origin: namely, the nonsubscription controversy of 1720–1727.[17] This arose when a group of ministers known as the Belfast Society, though professing to believe in the doctrinal and liturgical standards of the Westminster Confession of 1645–1647, rejected subscription to it as a qualification for the ministry. The controversy marked an important stage in the evolution of a distinct brand of Ulster Presbyterianism; henceforth, the latitudinarian emphases of the nonsubscribers came increasingly to permeate the Synod of Ulster. By the middle of the eighteenth century the Ulster Presbyterian church had diverged in significant ways from the Church of Scotland and had defined its separate existence. The fundamental source of the divergence was that, under the terms of the 1690 Act of Settlement, Presbyterianism became the established state church in Scotland, whereas in Ireland the Episcopalian Church of Ireland enjoyed that status and Presbyterianism, notwithstanding the payment of the regium donum (the royal grant in support of ministers' stipends), remained an unestablished voluntary church dependent for its survival on the support of local parishes and presbyteries.

16. Stewart, *Narrow Ground*, 96–99; Moody and Vaughan, eds., *Eighteenth-Century Ireland*, 99.

17. Moody and Vaughan, eds., *Eighteenth-Century Ireland*, 97.

At the same time, there was a significant change in the origins of the clergy. Until the Williamite wars most Presbyterian ministers in Ulster had been Scots; but of the 175 who were ordained between 1691 and 1720, 129 were born in Ulster.[18]

For these reasons Ulster Presbyterianism remained unaffected by the Erastian tendencies, the strict hierarchical control, and the uniformity and dogmatism that came to characterize the eighteenth-century Church of Scotland. While retaining the ecclesiastical organization and theological emphases of the Church of Scotland, it was more flexible and tolerant of diversity, more responsive to lay preferences, more committed to pure Scripture than to man-made creeds. It laid stress on an educated and pious clergy but also on lay involvement, which, incidentally, gave the Presbyterian communion in Ulster its close-knit character. Above all, it was a religion with a distinctively evangelical flavor. The "Six Mile Water revival," which erupted in 1625 near the town of Antrim and later spread throughout Ulster and, indeed, Scotland, was the first of its kind recorded in the British Isles. It established a tradition whose core was the "ritualized experience of community conversion," that is, of prayer meetings and communion services lasting several days, conducted by inspired lay persons, attended by large congregations, and having an intense emotional flavor.[19] These, then, were the distinctive religious forms and practices that the Scotch-Irish carried to the American colonies and that were to bring them into revealing conflict with other groups of American Presbyterians with different preoccupations and emphases.

In other ways, too, it gradually became evident that an autonomous Ulster Scottish culture, distinct from that of Scotland as well as from that of the rest of Ireland, was emerging. In the course of the eighteenth century the northernmost part of Ireland came to stand apart linguistically from the rest of the British Isles. Although relatively little is known about the way Ulster Scots then spoke, there is contemporary evidence of the distinctiveness of their speech. In particular, they no longer spoke like Lowland Scots. The anglicizing influences that swept over Scotland in the eighteenth century were less powerfully felt in Ulster, which in consequence clung to older forms. "The Dissenters speak broad Scotch," a Maghera minister would report in 1814, "and are in the habit of using terms and expressions long since obsolete,

18. E. M. Johnston, "Problems Common to Both Protestant and Catholic Churches in Eighteenth-Century Ireland," in Oliver MacDonagh *et al.*, eds., *Irish Culture and Nationalism, 1750–1950*, 16; Alan Gailey, "The Scots Element in North Irish Popular Culture: Some Problems in the Interpretation of an Historical Acculturation," *Ethnologia Europaea* (Göttingen), VIII, no. 1 (1975), 9.

19. Marilyn Jeanne Westerkamp, "Triumph of the Laity: The Migration of Revivalism from Scotland and Ireland to the Middle Colonies, 1625–1760" (Ph.D. diss., University of Pennsylvania, 1984), 25.

even in Scotland."[20] More important still, perhaps, was the fact that the hostile environment in which they lived had had profound psychological effects. Constituting only one-third of the population of the province, the Presbyterians lived in scattered settlements protected by castles, bawns, and fortified houses but surrounded by the dispossessed and resentful native Irish, whom they despised. Small wonder, then, that the settlers developed a kind of siege mentality in the face of endemic brigandage, and still more when their fears were given reality by the 1641 rebellion and again by the siege of Londonderry in 1689, when Ulster Protestants, who had rallied to the cause of William III, held the forces of James II at bay for 105 days. Not that Irish Catholics were the only neighbors Presbyterians feared and disliked: they were also antagonistic to, and were in return greatly resented by, those whom the native Irish saw also as interlopers, namely, the Anglicans, or ascendancy Protestants.

There was, of course, a peculiar irony in the situation in which Presbyterians found themselves. Resented by the Catholic Irish, they shared with them many of the same disabilities; and, moreover, these were imposed by the very government that looked to settlers to maintain Ulster's Protestant character. The resulting discontent with British rule was long believed to have been the main reason for Scotch-Irish emigration. This interpretation was given wide currency by nineteenth-century Whig historians like James Anthony Froude and W. E. H. Lecky, who, in their anxiety to demonstrate that the despotism of George III had been the root cause of the American Revolution, were ready to believe that Scotch-Irish Presbyterians had been driven to emigrate by religious persecution and had seen the Revolution as an opportunity to pay off old scores against the British crown. As Froude put it, "The resentment which they carried with them continued to burn in their new homes; and in the War of Independence England had no fiercer enemies than the grandsons and great-grandsons of the Presbyterians who had held Ulster against Tyrconnell."[21]

Leaving aside for the moment the question of whether the Scotch-Irish in fact supported the Revolution with near unanimity, there is no doubt that Froude and Lecky as well as some much later historians greatly overstated both the severity of religious persecution and the role of religion in prompt-

20. J. C. Wells, *Accents of English*, II, *The British Isles* (Cambridge, 1982), 436–450; Alan Bliss, *Spoken English in Ireland, 1600–1740: Twenty-seven Representative Texts* (Dublin, 1979), 20n; Linde Connolly, "Spoken English in Ulster in the Eighteenth and Nineteenth Centuries," *Ulster Folklife*, XXVIII (1982), 33–39 (quoting Mason, *Statistical Account*, I, 592); G. B. Adams, "Emergence of Ulster as a Distinct Dialect Area," *Ulster Folklife*, IV (1958), 61–73.

21. James Anthony Froude, *The English in Ireland in the Eighteenth Century* (London, 1872), I, 392; William Edward Hartpole Lecky, *A History of Ireland in the Eighteenth Century*, 5 vols. (London, 1892), II, 160.

ing emigration.[22] It is true that Presbyterians, like all non-Anglicans, were subject to certain statutory disabilities. The Test Act of 1704, by requiring a sacramental test, debarred them from officeholding; they were liable for tithes to support the Anglican church as well as for vestry service; the validity of their marriages could be challenged in the ecclesiastical courts; sites for meetinghouses were sometimes denied them; they were forbidden to teach in schools and were excluded from universities. But except briefly after the Restoration and again for about twenty years after the Glorious Revolution, these disabilities were largely nominal. With the accession of George I in 1714 the harassment Presbyterians had endured since 1689–1690 came to an end, and payment of the regium donum, the royal grant in support of ministers' stipends begun in the reign of William III but suspended during the reign of Anne, was resumed, thus restoring what one historian has termed the "quasi-establishment of Presbyterianism alongside Episcopalianism."[23] Then in 1719 toleration was legally extended to Presbyterians, but this they had already enjoyed in practice for several years. In 1719 also Parliament passed the first of a long series of indemnity acts giving officeholders time to take the sacramental test, and in 1729 the lords justices of Ireland acknowledged that the remaining laws against Presbyterians were being enforced with laxity or not at all. Shortly afterward, prosecutions on account of marriages in Presbyterian churches ceased, and in 1738 such marriages were formally legalized, providing that the oath prescribed in the Toleration Act of 1718 was taken. Thus, by the time that large-scale emigration from Ulster to the colonies began, Presbyterians had come to enjoy a large measure of religious freedom.[24]

Admittedly, the first great wave of Ulster emigration, that of 1717–1718, was planned and organized by Presbyterian ministers. But the main spur to the movement was economic, not religious. At the root of the trouble lay an iniquitous land system, with its absentee landlords, rack rents, and short leases. The immediate cause of the exodus was the expiration of leases that had been granted on easy terms after the Williamite wars in order to attract settlers. Landlords now saw their opportunity to raise rents, and, as tithes rose proportionately, tenants faced substantial new burdens. Many Presbyterians, unwilling to compete with Catholics who were prepared to accept a lower standard of living in order to pay higher rents, preferred to try their luck in America. Ten years later, when an even heavier wave of emigration set in, the two Presbyterian ministers who reported on it to the government

22. Examples of excessive emphasis on religious factors are provided by Wayland F. Dunaway, *The Scotch-Irish of Colonial Pennsylvania* (Chapel Hill, N.C., 1944), 30–32; and Leyburn, *The Scotch-Irish*, 164–168.

23. David W. Miller, "Presbyterianism and 'Modernization' in Ulster," *Past and Present*, no. 80 (August 1978), 73.

24. Moody and Vaughan, eds., *Eighteenth-Century Ireland*, lii–liii, 101–102.

explicitly discounted the religious motive, pointing instead to economic factors: tithes, short leases, high rents, and, above all, the poverty and distress caused by three successive bad harvests.[25] Similarly, it was not the "peculiar discouragements" under which Presbyterians labored that explained the last and heaviest wave of emigration in the early 1770s, but the depression in the linen industry combined with an acute agrarian crisis.

This is not to say that Presbyterians did not chafe at their religious disabilities; however imperfectly enforced, they were still a badge of inferiority. There was also irritation and disappointment that the services they had rendered the Protestant cause in 1689–1690 had received so little recognition from William III, whose Irish land grants went instead to court favorites. The measure of toleration that followed closely upon the accession of the Hanoverians ensured that George I was far more popular among Presbyterians than William III had ever been. But a lingering resentment could nonetheless be discerned in the Loyal Address of the General Synod of Ulster to George I after the failure of the Jacobite rebellion of 1715. After thanking the king for the many blessings they had enjoyed since his "happy accession," the synod assured him that "in our severall stations, we shall be ever ready to venture our all in Your Majesty's service, notwithstanding the Discouragements and Incapacities under which some of us Lye and by which we are distinguished from your other Protestant Subjects."[26]

That the Scotch-Irish saw themselves as a separate people with their own independent sense of community is confirmed by their patterns of settlement. Often emigrating in groups whose members had known one another in Ulster and who in many cases were related, they showed a marked propensity to cluster in ethnically homogeneous settlements, many of which bore Ulster place-names: Londonderry in New Hampshire, Belfast and Bangor in Maine, Colerain in Massachusetts, Orange and Ulster counties in New York, Newry, Tyrone, and Donegal in the favorite colony of the Scotch-Irish, Pennsylvania. The segmentation that had characterized Ulster society was duplicated in the colonies, where Scotch-Irish and Catholic Irish moved in different worlds even when they were not geographically separated. And when the two did interact, it was the Catholic Irish, who were fewer, who tended to lose their identity. By contrast there was in places considerable intermingling between the Scotch-Irish and immigrants from Lowland Scotland.[27] Ulster merchants, like Waddell Cunningham of Belfast and New

25. Francis Iredell and Robert Craghead to the Lords Justices of Ireland, in W. T. Latimer, "Ulster Emigration to America," *Journal of the Royal Society of Antiquaries of Ireland*, XII (1903), 389–392.

26. J. G. Simms, *The Williamite Confiscation in Ireland, 1690–1703* (London, 1956), 82–95. Quote from *Records of the General Synod of Ulster, 1691–1820*, 3 vols. (Belfast, 1890–1898), II, 37–38.

27. Doyle, *Ireland and Revolutionary America*, 77; Landsman, *Scotland*, 8.

York, often settled in and established trading relationships with Scottish mercantile communities. Scottish-born pastors frequently ministered to Scotch-Irish congregations, the best-known being the Reverend Henry Pattillo, who became a delegate to the North Carolina Provincial Assembly in 1775. Scots and Ulstermen were often joined in the same synods and sometimes merged their identities in a common Presbyterianism. But there was less interaction than might have been supposed, since the two groups tended to settle in different regions. Whereas the Scots were widely scattered along the Atlantic seaboard, the Scotch-Irish were thickly concentrated in certain regions.

Scotch-Irish emigration was at first directed toward New England, where the first sizable contingents arrived in 1717–1718. Welcomed to begin with, they soon became unpopular when their religious leaders denounced Massachusetts Congregationalists for theological error, particularly in respect of modes of baptism. Thus, far from being absorbed into the Congregational church, as the Massachusetts clergy had hoped and expected, Scotch-Irish Presbyterians refused to hold communion with them. Religion was not, however, the only source of antipathy. Bostonians complained of the burden of pauperism the newcomers had brought, and feelings on that score ran so high that in 1729 a mob would not allow several vessels arriving from Belfast and Londonderry to land their passengers. New England hostility, the economic opportunities and religious freedom offered by Penn's colony, and the fact that Ulster's transatlantic shipping connections were largely with ports on the Delaware combined to divert almost the whole of the Scotch-Irish movement to Pennsylvania from 1725 onward. Settling first in the vicinity of Philadelphia, the Scotch-Irish advanced up the Delaware, then across the Susquehanna and in the 1730s fanned out widely through the Cumberland Valley. From this cradle of settlement they spread over the Alleghenies in strength to the vicinity of the future Pittsburgh, but from the 1740s the Scotch-Irish stream was deflected southwestward into western Maryland, the Shenandoah Valley of Virginia, and the piedmont regions of the Carolinas and Georgia. By the 1750s there was a chain of Scotch-Irish backcountry settlements along the entire seven-hundred-mile length of the Great Wagon Road that extended from Pennsylvania to Georgia. Some of the Carolina and Georgia settlements owed their existence, however, not to the diaspora from Pennsylvania, but to immigration direct from Ulster. While Ulster-born land speculators like Henry McCulloh and Arthur Dobbs planted Scotch-Irish colonies in backcountry North Carolina, officially assisted settlement schemes in South Carolina and Georgia established Scotch-Irish inland townships at Williamsburg on the Santee and Queensborough on the Great Ogeechee.[28]

28. Dunaway, *Scotch-Irish of Pennsylvania*; Leyburn, *Scotch-Irish*; R. J. Dickson,

Whether their Ulster background fitted the Scotch-Irish for life on the American frontier, as has often been claimed, is in fact doubtful. Some problems, it is true, were common to both Ulster and the American colonies: the sparseness of settlement, the difficulty of defining property boundaries, the presence of a hostile native population. But one should not make too much of these resemblances. The demographic and economic structure of the American colonies differed sharply from that of Ulster. America was much more isolated and lacked intimate contacts with a metropolitan country such as Ulster had with Scotland; there was no counterpart in America for the manorial courts that, among other things, had served to settle property disputes in Ulster; and the problems with the native population were dissimilar, because the Indians were an entirely unknown quantity, whereas the native Irish, however much disliked, had at least been known to the Scots for centuries.[29] Even so, the insecurity of existence in Ulster probably did something to fit the Scotch-Irish for the tasks they faced in America. Occupying land of which the indigenous inhabitants had been dispossessed and, moreover, excluded from political power by an entrenched oligarchy, they were well aware of the need for solidarity. The assertiveness, not to say aggressiveness, which many contemporaries saw as their distinguishing characteristic, may well have been the product of their precarious position in Ulster.

At all events, colonial officials concerned for the protection of exposed frontiers saw the Scotch-Irish as being specially qualified by their Ulster background to act as a shield against Indian attack. Thus, in 1720, the provincial secretary of Pennsylvania, James Logan, a Quaker who had himself been born in Ulster and was familiar with its history, explained why he had granted an extensive tract of land two years earlier to the Scotch-Irish in Chester County, where they had established the frontier township of Donegal. "At the time," he wrote, "we were apprehensive . . . from the Northern Indians. . . . I therefore thought it might be provident to plant a settlement of such men as those who formerly had so bravely defended Londonderry and Enniskillen as a frontier against any disturbance."[30] Similar reasoning may well explain the decision of the Massachusetts authorities in 1718 to send newly arrived Scotch-Irish immigrants to the frontier to establish settlements that soon extended in an arc from the colony's western borders to the coast

---

Ulster Emigration to Colonial America, 1718–1783 (London, 1966); E.R.R. Green, "Queensborough Township: Scotch-Irish Emigration and the Expansion of Georgia," *WMQ*, 3d Ser., XVII (1960), 183–199; Verner W. Crane, *The Southern Frontier, 1670–1732* (Philadelphia, 1929); Robert L. Meriwether, *The Expansion of South Carolina, 1729–1765* (Kingsport, Tenn., 1940), 17–28.

29. Doyle, *Ireland and Revolutionary America*, 79; Raymond Gillespie, *Colonial Ulster: The Settlement of East Ulster, 1600–1641* (Cork, 1985), 219–222.

30. Cited in Leyburn, *The Scotch-Irish*, 191.

of Maine. In South Carolina, too, after the colony had narrowly escaped destruction in the Yamasee war of 1715, and again after the Cherokee uprising of 1756, the authorities offered inducements to the Scotch-Irish, among other Protestant groups, to settle in the middle- and backcountry to act as a buffer against the Indians and their French and Spanish allies as well as to counterbalance the growing number of black slaves.

On the frontier the Scotch-Irish were, like other settlers, frequently victims of Indian depredations. A not untypical experience was that of the Scotch-Irish settlement in the Long Canes region of the Carolina backcountry in 1760. Forewarned of an impending Cherokee attack, some 250 settlers left their homes to seek safety in Augusta, Georgia. But the party was ambushed by 100 mounted Cherokee, and about 40, mostly women and children, were killed or captured. (One of those killed was the grandmother of John C. Calhoun, the preeminent spokesman for the South in the period preceding the Civil War.) Ten days later, another party of 23 Scotch-Irish women and children was also butchered by the Cherokee. Further north, too, the Scotch-Irish bore the brunt of Indian raids. They suffered heavily in 1753–1754, when the Shawnees and the Tuscaroras of the Shenandoah Valley descended on frontier settlements in Pennsylvania and Virginia to burn, pillage, and murder, and again during Pontiac's uprising in 1763, when 2,000 settlers were killed in Pennsylvania alone.

It would be wrong, however, to regard the Scotch-Irish necessarily as the passive victims of Indian savagery. The Indian outbreaks were, after all, but a reaction, all the more violent for being so long delayed, to long-continued pressure from land-hungry pioneers, of whom the Scotch-Irish were among the most importunate. In Pennsylvania continual Scotch-Irish incursions into Indian territory and blatant Scotch-Irish disregard for Indian rights and sensibilities produced a succession of dangerous incidents that threatened to undermine the pacific Indian policy of the ruling Quaker oligarchy. Eager to deal fairly with the Indians, Quaker officials repeatedly had to make amends to the Indians for Scotch-Irish misbehavior. But like frontiersmen generally, the Scotch-Irish felt no remorse about their rough treatment of the red men; they dismissed them as savages and heathens who were barring the way to the advance of civilization. Hence official complaints of Scotch-Irish encroachment upon Indian territory west of the Susquehanna were met with the retort that "it was against the laws of God and nature, that so much land should be idle, while so many Christians wanted it to labor on, and to raise their bread."[31]

In the set battles of the Seven Years' War, British regulars did most of the fighting, but it was chiefly the Scotch-Irish who repelled Indian border raids. Since the Quaker-dominated legislature in Philadelphia refused for reasons

31. *Ibid.*, 192–193.

of conscience to take steps to defend the frontier, the Scotch-Irish had to depend on their own exertions. The importance of their military contribution can hardly be exaggerated. In 1756 a Scotch-Irish force captured Kittaning on the Allegheny, one of the two chief Indian strongholds in Pennsylvania. The Scotch-Irish also furnished most of the Pennsylvania militia who helped British regulars capture Fort Duquesne, the key to the French defenses in the Ohio Valley. Then, during Pontiac's rising of 1763–1764, it was again the Scotch-Irish who offered the only effective resistance. But while there can be no doubting their courage and steadfastness when facing the horrors of Indian border warfare, it should not be forgotten that they were not averse to adopting the ruthless methods of their adversaries. They were guilty, for example, of the Conestoga massacre of 1763, when a group of young Scotch-Irishmen in Dauphin County, Pennsylvania, barbarously slaughtered twenty Conestoga Indians whom they suspected of having aided Indian marauders. Although no proof of Conestoga complicity was ever forthcoming, many Scotch-Irishmen, including some clergymen, clung to the view that the action had been justified.

The outrage simply confirmed the general view in Pennsylvania that the Scotch-Irish were a turbulent and lawless people. James Logan soon lost the good opinion he had initially had of them. Less than a decade after sanctioning the Chester County grant, he was complaining that "a settlement of five families from the North of Ireland gives me more trouble than fifty of any other people." What exasperated Logan, in addition to the fact that the Scotch-Irish were "hard neighbors to the Indians," was their "audacious and disorderly" habit of squatting on "any spot of vacant land they fancied," without bothering to acquire a legal title. Fiercely resisting attempts to expel them, the squatters justified their conduct with the statement: "The Proprietary and his agents had solicited for colonists and . . . they came accordingly." Logan seems to have repented of the encouragement he had offered, for he now expressed apprehensions that "it looks as if Ireland is to send all her inhabitants hither. . . . And the common fear is, that if they continue to come, they will make themselves proprietors of the province." Another source of concern for the proprietors of Pennsylvania was that the Scotch-Irish were constantly at odds with the Germans, who may have constituted an even larger proportion of the colony's population than the Scotch-Irish themselves. Their mutual antagonism produced so many disturbances, especially at election times, that in 1743 the Penns instructed their agents to sell no more land to Scotch-Irishmen in the predominantly German counties of Lancaster and York and to offer those already there generous terms to remove farther west to the Cumberland Valley.[32]

There is reason to believe, however, that the Scotch-Irish predilection for

32. *Ibid.*, 191–192.

settling in frontier regions may have been exaggerated, at least so far as the period after 1750 is concerned. Thomas L. Purvis's analysis of the 1790 census data for Pennsylvania shows, for example, that Scotch-Irish surnames were not unduly concentrated on the frontier: 46 percent were to be found in Philadelphia or the long-settled southeastern counties, and only 38 percent in the more western counties. Moreover, Sharon V. Salinger has concluded that most eighteenth-century Pennsylvania indentured servants, a large proportion of whom were Scotch-Irish, did not on gaining their freedom set up for themselves as farmers, as had been the case in the seventeenth century. Not only did those who had served their time in Philadelphia remain there, but many who had been indentured to rural owners gravitated to the city in search of work.[33] Until late in the colonial period many servants in Pennsylvania had been owned by artisans, and some freed bondsmen may have entered skilled trades themselves. But the likelihood is that most freed servants became wage laborers or, more especially in the case of women, domestic servants. Another group of Scotch-Irish urban-dwellers, perhaps never very numerous, were those who carved out successful careers for themselves in the professions and commerce. Among the most prominent were the bookseller Hugh Gaine, founder of the *New York Mercury*; the printer John Dunlap, publisher of the *Pennsylvania Packet*; the future secretary of war James McHenry, who studied medicine with Dr. Benjamin Rush; the Philadelphia merchants William Patterson and Blair McClenachan; and the surgeon William Irvine, who left his practice in Carlisle, Pennsylvania, to become a Revolutionary war brigadier general.[34] Even so, there is no reason to doubt that the great bulk of the Scotch-Irish settled in rural rather than in urban areas and that in every colony from New Hampshire to Georgia they were engaged mainly in agriculture.

Like immigrant farmers generally, the Scotch-Irish discovered that unfamiliar physical and economic environments necessitated a measure of adaptation and adjustment. Patterns of land use, for example, had to be modified to take account of the circumstance that in the colonies, in sharp contrast to Ulster, cultivable land was plentiful and cheap and labor scarce and expensive. Consequently, the intensive working of arable land that had prevailed in the homeland gave way to an extensive form of land utilization that permitted farmers to move crops from one tract of land to another, leave land fallow, and avoid labor-intensive jobs like manuring and draining. In the northern and middle colonies Scotch-Irish farmers had to learn to substitute Indian corn, rye, or wheat for oats and barley and to familiarize themselves

33. Thomas L. Purvis, "Patterns of Ethnic Settlement in Late Eighteenth-Century Pennsylvania," *Western Pennsylvania Historical Magazine*, LXX (1987), 107–122; Sharon V. Salinger, *"To Serve Well and Faithfully": Labor and Indentured Servants in Pennsylvania, 1682–1800* (Cambridge, 1987), 135–136.

34. Carl Bridenbaugh, *The Colonial Craftsman* (New York, 1950), 67.

with the cultivation of pumpkins, squash, and beans. In the Southern colonies, besides growing wheat, they broke with the past with new staples like tobacco and indigo and took advantage of year-round forage and milder winters to keep herds of cattle larger than they had known in Ireland. In heavily wooded areas, again traditional habits of animal husbandry had to be adapted to allow for the raising of hogs, which in Ireland were despised and rarely kept.[35]

Even so, there were striking continuities in farming patterns and practices. As in Ireland, the Scotch-Irish lived in scattered homesteads, preferred lightly timbered and well-drained rolling hillsides to the more fertile but wetter bottomlands, and, far from abandoning tillage for grazing (as Leroy V. Eid suggested), practiced a traditional grain-and-livestock agriculture that was largely subsistence-oriented. Farm implements—spades, hoes, mattocks, axes, flails, and wooden plows—were likewise similar to those used in Ireland.[36] The Scotch-Irish brought the Irish potato with them to New England, and both there and in the middle colonies introduced the combined farming-weaving economy based on flax growing and the spinning and weaving of fine linen cloth that had distinguished them from their Ulster neighbors. And just as part-time linen manufacture and the principle of partible inheritance (the division of property among all the children) had resulted in the subdivision of farms in Ulster, so it produced the same result in the colonies.[37] Finally, while the open field, or rundale, system, which remained the basis of agrarian organization in Ulster until about 1750, was never transferred to America, the communal obligations associated with it persisted in Scotch-Irish immigrant communities. Contrary to the view of those historians who have seen them as essentially individualistic, the Scotch-Irish, like frontiersmen generally, found that cooperation with neighbors was indispensable for defense against Indians, the accomplishment of essential pioneering tasks like barn raising, and the successful functioning of economic life.[38]

35. Ralph Stuart Wallace, "The Scotch-Irish of Provincial New Hampshire" (Ph.D. diss., University of New Hampshire, 1984), 316–317; Lewis Cecil Gray, *History of Agriculture in the Southern United States to 1860*, 2 vols. (New York, 1941), I, 119–120, 169, 232; Doyle, *Ireland and Revolutionary America*, 82–83.

36. E. Estyn Evans, "The Scotch-Irish: Their Cultural Adaptation and Heritage in the American Old West," in E.R.R. Green, ed., *Essays in Scotch-Irish History* (London, 1969), 80–81, 84–85; James T. Lemon, "The Agricultural Practices of National Groups in Eighteenth-Century Southeastern Pennsylvania," *Geographical Review*, LVI (1966), 477–496.

37. Wallace, "Scotch-Irish of New Hampshire," 319–321; Moody and Vaughan, eds., *Eighteenth-Century Ireland*, 248–249; K. Miller, *Emigrants and Exiles*, 36, 40–41.

38. D. McCourt, "The Decline of Rundale, 1750–1850," in Peter Roebuck, ed., *Plantation to Partition: Essays in Ulster History in Honour of J. L. McCracken* (Belfast, 1981), 118; Doyle, *Ireland and Revolutionary America*, 86.

Until recently scholars have been unimpressed by the Scotch-Irish record in colonial agriculture. They have tended to accept uncritically the contrasted pictures of German and Scotch-Irish farming practices drawn by contemporaries such as the Reverend Charles Woodmason and Dr. Benjamin Rush. According to such accounts the German settlers were not merely better judges of soil than the Scotch-Irish but were more skillful farmers, more concerned for the niceties of agriculture. In the German settlements, so this version goes, farmhouses were sturdy and weathertight and the landscape well kept, whereas the Scotch-Irish seemed to be content with primitive log cabins, floorless and often open to the sky, while their fields, like their clothing, bore an appearance of the slovenliness characteristic of eighteenth-century rural life in Ireland. The contrast, according to these contemporaries, was most marked in methods of clearing land. Whereas the Germans took the trouble before planting crops to fell trees and pull out stumps by the roots, the Scotch-Irish merely girdled the trees and planted crops between the stumps.[39]

These stereotypes have, however, been strongly challenged. David N. Doyle, for example, while conceding that there was much bad Scotch-Irish farming, argues that travelers like Woodmason and historians like Carl Bridenbaugh who have relied heavily upon their testimony may have been deceived by the admittedly slovenly appearance of Scotch-Irish farms. According to Doyle, the persistence of ingrained attitudes was fundamental.

> The traditional Ulster (and Irish) reluctance to display prosperity, lest it invite the rapacity of laird, landlord, merchant or tithe proctor; the Presbyterian injunctions against conspicuous ease; the money to be saved if a wife's [weaving] talents were still exploited long after grain surpluses could acquire imported Irish linens and English woollens, these and other factors inclined the Scotch-Irishman to maintain the threadbare appearance of subsistence farmer after he had passed that stage.[40]

Then, again, James T. Lemon's examination of Pennsylvania tax lists and estate inventories led him to the conclusion that there were no major differences in farming practice between the Germans and the Scotch-Irish. Similarly, A. C. Lord's study of pre-Revolutionary agriculture in Lancaster

39. For Woodmason's bigoted and lurid strictures on the "vile crew" of Scotch-Irish frontier dwellers he encountered, see Richard J. Hooker, ed., *The Carolina Backcountry on the Eve of the Revolution: The Journals and Other Writings of Charles Woodmason, Anglican Itinerant* (Chapel Hill, N.C., 1953). Rush's comments are to be found in L. H. Butterfield, ed., "Dr. Benjamin Rush's Journal of a Trip to Carlisle in 1784," *Pennsylvania Magazine of History and Biography*, LXXIV (1950), 450–451, 455.

40. Doyle, *Ireland and Revolutionary America*, 83–84.

County, Pennsylvania, concluded that the Scotch-Irish were no less industrious than the Germans. Indeed, the Scotch-Irish cleared more land and devoted more acreage to wheat, flax, and hemp than the Germans, who tended, by contrast, to concentrate on increasing the size of their cattle herds.[41]

Moreover, anthropologists, agronomists, and geographers have now demonstrated that what is known as "slash-and-burn" cultivation—the practice of clearing temporary fields in forests by chopping and firing the natural vegetation, planting crops for a brief time, and then letting the land revert to scrub forest—far from being primitive and wasteful, has been highly effective in many parts of the world and is a virtual necessity in heavily forested regions where labor is at a premium. For these reasons slash-and-burn techniques were common throughout the American colonies, and even after 1800, when intensive agriculture gradually ousted them, they persisted for decades in much of the South and even into our own day in the southern Appalachian highlands. The geographer John Fraser Hart has claimed that the Appalachian system of brush fallow can be traced back to the ancient Scottish outfield system of cultivation, whereby marginal land was briefly cropped before being allowed to revert to fallow pasture. According to Hart, the Scotch-Irish who emigrated to Pennsylvania in the early eighteenth century simply adapted their traditional outfield system to the local environment of extensive woodland.[42] Later studies have, however, painted a more complex picture. They point out that the Scotch-Irish had lived in relatively treeless areas and thus had little experience of forest fallowing. Hence it would appear that Appalachian slash-and-burn farming represented not simply a holdover from Scottish outfield cultivation but "a synthesis of native American, Scottish, and Irish agricultural techniques." Faced with the densely forested landscape of southeastern Pennsylvania, the Scotch-Irish adopted the agricultural techniques of the Delaware Indians, who had long practiced slash-and-burn cultivation and forest fallowing. But in cultivating the upland slopes, as the Delawares did not, the Scotch-Irish were also drawing on one of the characteristics of Scottish and Irish outfield cultivation.[43]

Logistical and environmental circumstances, then, and persistent conser-

41. Lemon, "Agricultural Practices," *Geog. Rev.*, LVI (1966), 467–496; Arthur C. Lord, "The Pre-Revolutionary Agriculture of Lancaster County, Pennsylvania," *Journal of the Lancaster County Historical Society*, LXXIX (1975), 23–42.

42. J. S. Otto and N. E. Anderson, "Slash-and-Burn Cultivation in the Highlands South: A Problem in Comparative Agricultural History," *Comparative Studies in Society and History*, XXIV (1982), 131–147; John Fraser Hart, "Land Rotation in Appalachia," *Geog. Rev.*, LXVII (1977), 148.

43. Otto and Anderson, "Slash-and-Burn Cultivation," *Comp. Studies in Soc. and Hist.*, XXIV (1982), 136–138.

vatism, rather than innate indolence or a lack of skill in husbandry, explained Scotch-Irish agricultural practices. Burning undergrowth and girdling trees required far less labor than felling forests and grubbing up stumps and, moreover, often produced better crop yields. Not surprisingly, therefore, when in the 1730s the Scotch-Irish began settling the backcountry of the southern colonies with its wooded, hilly terrain, they took with them the system of slash-and-burn farming that had proved so efficacious in Pennsylvania.

If Presbyterianism had been the most conspicuous element in Scotch-Irish identity in Ireland, it remained no less so in British America. Zealous in establishing churches and in attempting to secure learned clergy, the Scotch-Irish were determined to cling to their religious heritage and to reproduce in the New World the precise religious forms of the Old. The discovery that Presbyterianism, with its rigid insistence on a uniform and detailed church order, was fundamentally incompatible with New England Congregationalism was the inevitable consequence of such an attitude. The antipathy between Scotch-Irish Presbyterians and English-stock Congregationalists that developed in Massachusetts was duplicated in New Hampshire, where in 1771 the inhabitants of the Scotch-Irish settlement of Goffstown refused to accept a Congregationalist as minister, protesting that they were "Presbyterians by Proffession" who had vowed to "maintain the Doctrine, Discipline and Government of the Church of Scotland."[44] In these circumstances the Presbyterian church was the most effective Scotch-Irish institution, serving as the focus of community life in much the same way as in Ulster. On the frontier the church usually antedated civil authority, and both there and elsewhere the local kirk sessions, or religious courts, dealt not only with moral offenses like drunkenness, Sabbath breaking, lying, and adultery but also with property rights and public order. It was because the Presbyterian clergy were acknowledged to be secular as well as religious leaders that colonial officials, as in North Carolina in the 1760s, appealed to them to assist in regulating settlement and maintaining community peace.[45]

When Scotch-Irish immigrants began arriving in Pennsylvania in force about 1720, they found that organized Presbyterianism had preceded them. But although the Synod of Philadelphia, founded in 1706, owed its existence to the initiative of Ulster-born Francis Makemie, "the father of American Presbyterianism," and a group of ministers all but one of whom were from Ireland or Scotland, it had fallen under the domination of a New York faction that had evolved from New England Puritanism. Almost immediately the Scotch-Irish and the New Yorkers were at loggerheads. While they

44. Wallace, "Scotch-Irish of New Hampshire," 299–300.

45. Guy Soulliard Klett, *Presbyterians in Colonial Pennsylvania* (Philadelphia, 1937), 68, 257.

were agreed on the Calvinist interpretation of salvation, a common sacramental theology, and the need for personal piety, the two groups differed on various aspects of church government and policy, notably on the question of credal subscription. Whereas the New Yorkers were completely opposed to subscription to the Westminster Confession or, indeed, to any creed as a test of orthodoxy, many of the Scotch-Irish clergy insisted that it was central to their religious identity. Thus the nonsubscription controversy then convulsing Ulster was carried across the Atlantic, and by 1725 the Synod of Philadelphia was experiencing the same difficulties as the Ulster synods. But whereas in Ulster the outcome was schism, in America the contending factions were able to reach a compromise. Mainly because, in contrast to Ulster, the colonial laity did not get involved and also because an influential group of ministers led by William Tennent and his four sons refused to take sides, the Synod of 1729 found a solution by separating essential from inessential articles of faith and requiring subscription only to the former.[46]

But if the subscription controversy did not end in schism, the Great Awakening did. By the end of the 1730s the colonial Presbyterian church, which had greatly expanded its membership through heavy immigration and had assumed in consequence a heightened Scotch-Irish coloring, had suffered the fate of American churches generally in splitting over revivalism. The points at issue in the controversy, which culminated in the schism of 1741, when the prorevivalists left or were driven out of the "Old Side" Synod of Philadelphia, have always been plain enough, namely, the methods of the revivalists and the church's institutional structure. But historians have found it difficult to agree on or even identify the cultural background of the opposing parties. Leonard Trinterud's classic account of American Presbyterianism, *The Forming of an American Tradition*, detected a conservative, Old Side, Scotch-Irish party to which were opposed two groups that coalesced to form the Synod of New York in 1746. These were the New York Presbyterians and the "Log College" men, the latter being products of William Tennent, Sr., and his seminary at Neshaminy in Bucks County, Pennsylvania, and among the most enthusiastic proponents of the Great Awakening. But modern scholarship has found these categories unsatisfactory. Marilyn J. Westerkamp has argued, for example, that the concept of a conservative Scotch-Irish party ceases to be valid if the Log College men are classified according to their ethnic background, which was overwhelmingly Scotch-Irish, rather than as a separate category. Elizabeth Nybakken has suggested, on the other hand, that the division of opinion over revivalism arose from a distinction between Scottish New Side and Irish Old Side Presbyterians. But Nybakken concedes that the Scotch-Irish were to be found on both sides of the argument, and this is confirmed by Westerkamp's analysis, which reveals an

46. Westerkamp, "Triumph of the Laity," 289–299.

almost even split. She estimates that, of twenty-nine Scotch-Irish Presbyterian ministers who took a stand at the time of the 1741 schism, sixteen were Old Side and thirteen New Side, and that at the time of the 1758 reunion, the division stood at twelve to fifteen. Ned Landsman's explanation for this divergence is that it is related to the age of the Scotch-Irish settlements and their economic orientation. In the middle colonies, he suggests, revivalism derived its greatest support from the older Scotch-Irish congregations that were settled around 1720 and that had remained within Philadelphia's commercial orbit; the newer settlements in the Susquehanna Valley, on the other hand, were very little affected by the Great Awakening.[47] But this explanation, too, seems flawed, since the Scotch-Irish laity, wherever they were located, seem to have given overwhelming support to revivalism. Never having abandoned a revivalist tradition that stretched back to the Six Mile Water revival, they responded enthusiastically when such Log College men as the Tennents, Samuel Finley, and Samuel Blair restored inspirational preaching and personal conversion to the center of Presbyterian religious orthodoxy.

Given the strength of the revivalist tradition among the laity, the growing conservatism of Presbyterian church leadership after the reunification of 1758 made it likely that there would be defections to other churches that reached out more effectively to ordinary people and offered them a religion that was exciting, purifying, and personal. Between 1760 and the Revolution, indeed, many of the Scotch-Irish left the Presbyterian church to become Methodists or Baptists, for, although the Arminianism of these churches contradicted the Calvinist doctrine of predestination, their traditional rituals constituted a strong appeal.[48] The difficulty Presbyterianism experienced of filling pulpits with qualified and educated clergy, a requirement that the Methodists and Baptists were more disposed to waive, contributed further to the decline of Presbyterian membership. Only a few ministers accompanied their flocks from Ulster; the Irish and Scottish synods, to which the colonial church appealed for reinforcements, could offer only limited help; and the

47. Leonard J. Trinterud, *The Forming of an American Tradition: A Re-examination of Colonial Presbyterianism* (Philadelphia, 1949); Westerkamp, "Triumph of the Laity," 370–373; Elizabeth I. Nybakken, "New Light on the Old Side: Irish Influences on Colonial Presbyterianism," *Journal of American History*, LXVIII (1981–1982), 813–832; Landsman, *Scotland*, 242–243.

48. K. Miller, *Emigrants and Exiles*, 165. In places the drift away from Presbyterianism appears to have begun even earlier. Thus Hugh McAden, a Presbyterian minister who visited the Scotch-Irish settlements in the Carolinas in 1755, reported: "Many adhere to the Baptists that were before wavering, . . . [in addition to] several that professed themselves to be Presbyterians; so that very few at present join heartily for our ministers, and will in a little time, if God prevent not, be too weak either to call or supplicate for a faithful minister." William Henry Foote, *Sketches of North Carolina* . . . (New York, 1846), 160–167.

Log College and similar institutions could turn out only a handful of ministers. Hence many Scotch-Irish settlements, especially in remote frontier regions, were without church or minister for years on end and had to rely on occasional visits from itinerant preachers. Thus, if they did not join other churches, the neglected sheep tended to drift away from religion altogether.

It has generally been assumed that the Scotch-Irish had few aesthetic accomplishments. Their stern and character-building religion, it has been argued, did little to encourage and much to discourage devotion to aesthetic ideals and the cultivation of the graphic and plastic arts. Admittedly, since the immigrants were as a rule poor and humble, they had no very sophisticated tastes, and the precariousness of their existence both in Ulster and in the American colonies allowed little opportunity for artistic expression. Nonetheless, a study of Scotch-Irish gravestones in Adams County, Pennsylvania, by Theodore and Cynthia Corbett demonstrates that their material culture was not merely utilitarian. The outstanding characteristic of these stones is their baroque ornamentation, a style rarely found in eighteenth-century American cemeteries. In contrast to the carving on New England gravestones, which was flat and linear and aimed at abstract rather than realistic interpretation of objects, that on Scotch-Irish gravestones was done in raised, naturalistic fashion and used undulating surfaces to define space. And whereas New England burial stones generally featured coffins and gravediggers, reminders of the emphasis in New England popular theology on human mortality, their Scotch-Irish counterparts bore a more varied array of figures. These included coats of arms emblazoned with popular heraldic symbols such as stags' heads and leopards; a much-favored representation of martial prowess was a hand wielding a sword. Several stones bore figures of a traditional religious nature, such as winged cherubs and turtle doves, both representing the resurrected soul, but, according to the Corbetts, the tone even of these religious figures is "decorative and exuberantly secular." As is the case with stone-carving generally, the distinctive style and iconography of Scotch-Irish gravestones reflect the social and religious values of the community they served. But the fact that the stones were executed in so accomplished a fashion testifies to the possession of skills that could only have been learned in Europe and affords an example of the culture of the British Isles being carried direct and undiluted to the margin of Britain's American empire.[49]

An equally striking example of cultural transfer is afforded by a distinctive feature of Pennsylvania town planning. Many of the small towns established in Pennsylvania in the eighteenth century incorporated an elongated central

49. Theodore Graham Corbett and Cynthia Arps Corbett, "Europeans on the Frontier: Scotch-Irish Burial Stones in Pennsylvania," *Pennsylvania Folklife*, XXXII (1982–1983), 59–63.

square, uniformly known as "the Diamond," housing the market and other public buildings. In Europe the use of the term "diamond" in this sense is practically limited to Ulster and occurs in such Plantation towns in the west of the province as Stewartstown and Omagh, Magherafelt and Londonderry, Monaghan and Enniskillen and indicates centrally located groups of buildings that form a diamond-shaped figure. There seems no doubt that this feature of town planning was taken to Pennsylvania by the Scotch-Irish, and there is reason to believe that the central position of the courthouse in many trans-Appalachian towns founded before 1800 is also an indication of Scotch-Irish influence.[50]

Cultural borrowing rather than cultural transfer characterized the Scotch-Irish role in diffusing both the name and the constructional techniques of the log cabin throughout Pennsylvania and the trans-Appalachian West. In Ulster there were no dwellings of round or hewn logs, but after crossing the Atlantic the Scotch-Irish lost no time in imitating the style of house building used by their German and Swedish neighbors in Pennsylvania and Delaware. This was unsurprising, since the ground plan of the German log cabin was almost identical to that of the rectangular, single-storied farmhouses of mud and stone they had known in Ireland. The average internal dimensions of the Scotch-Irish log cabin were sixteen by twenty-two feet, virtually the same as in the traditional Ulster cottage. In both types of dwelling the open fireplace lay at the heart of the house, but whereas in Ireland the chimney was invariably built within the gable, in the American log cabin it was placed outside, possibly because of the fire risk. Another feature common to both was the provision of two opposite doors. Lacking the tradition of skilled craftsmanship in wood that the Germans and Swedes possessed, Scotch-Irish building could at first produce only crude versions of the prototype. Whereas German and Swedish log cabins were interlocked with skillfully executed notches to produce tight, flush corners, the crude corner notching of the Scotch-Irish meant that there were gaps between the logs that had to be chinked with mud, stones, or wood. However, the standard of craftsmanship improved as Scotch-Irish builders grew more experienced, and ethnic diversity in design and mode of construction gradually gave way to a uniform American product. As for its name, the Scotch-Irish appear to have been the first to use "cabin" to denote log houses rather than the Indian

50. E. Estyn Evans, "Cultural Relics of the Ulster-Scots in the Old West of the United States," *Ulster Folklife*, XI (1965), 33–38; G. B. Adams, "The Diamonds of Ulster and Pennsylvania," *Ulster Folk and Transport Museum Yearbook*, 1975–1976, 18–20; Alan Crozier, "The Scotch-Irish Influence on American English," *American Speech*, LIX (1984), 320–321; John W. Reps, *Town Planning in Frontier America* (Princeton, N.J., 1969), 20, 22; Frederic G. Cassidy, "Geographical Variation of English in the United States," in Richard W. Bailey and Manfred Görlach, eds., *English as a World Language* (Ann Arbor, Mich., 1982), 182–183.

wigwams of earlier American usage, and the first recorded use of the compound "log cabin" is by a Scotch-Irish author in 1770, referring to two dwellings in the "Irish Tract" of Botetourt County in the Shenandoah Valley of Virginia.[51]

While linguists are agreed that the Scotch-Irish greatly influenced American folk speech, they have found it difficult to determine the nature and extent of that influence. The difficulty is that many of the linguistic features common to Ulster and America were probably not attributable to the influence of one upon the other, but rather to the fact that certain features of Elizabethan speech that had died out in England survived independently in both Ulster and the colonies. (Examples of such archaisms are *deck* of cards and the use of *sick* for "ill.") But it is at least clear that in the colonies, as in Ireland, the speech of the Scotch-Irish was distinctive enough to identify them. When in 1749 John Hempstead of New London, Connecticut, visited a Scotch-Irish congregation in Cecil County, Maryland, he remarked that their "Tongues Run like mill clocks, and haveing an Irish brogue on their Tongue I could understand but little they said." Moreover, eighteenth-century newspaper advertisements for the return of runaway Scotch-Irish indentured servants, besides listing distinctive physical attributes, frequently asserted that from his or her dialect the fugitive "may be known to be a native of the north of Ireland."[52] In regions where the Scotch-Irish settled in strength, neighboring peoples tended to pick up their accents and speech patterns. Thus fugitive black slaves were occasionally said to speak "in the Scotch-Irish dialect." It seems likely, too, that the Pennsylvania Germans learned their English, or at least certain pronunciations, from their Scotch-Irish neighbors. At all events it is difficult on any other hypothesis to explain why Pennsylvania German speech included such archaic borrowings as *chaw* for *chew*, *ingine* for *engine* and such renderings as *bile* and *jine* for *boil* and *join*.[53]

But as Alan Crozier has pointed out, the case for Scotch-Irish influence on American speech rests, not on the spread of Ulster English forms to other

51. C. A. Weslager, *The Log Cabin in America: From Pioneer Days to the Present* (New Brunswick, N.J., 1969), 225–239; Evans, "The Scotch-Irish," in Green, ed., *Essays in Scotch-Irish History*, 78–80; Edward Lay, "European Antecedents of Seventeenth and Eighteenth Century Germanic and Scotch-Irish Architecture in America," *Pennsylvania Folklife*, XXXII (1982–1983), 2–43; Crozier, "Scotch-Irish Influence," *American Speech*, LIX (1984), 320.

52. Weslager, *Log Cabin*, 248–249, quoting notes and queries, *Maryland Historical Magazine*, XLIX (1954), 347; Crozier, "Scotch-Irish Influence," *American Speech*, LIX (1984), 317.

53. Carl Bridenbaugh, *Myths and Realities: Societies of the Colonial South* (Baton Rouge, La., 1952), 169; Carroll E. Reed, "English Archaisms in Pennsylvania German," American Dialect Society, *Publications*, XIX (1953), 3–7 (quoted in Crozier, "Scotch-Irish Influence," *American Speech*, LIX [1984], 317).

groups, but on the prevalence in certain regions of features common to Ulster and America but to nowhere else. Fortunately, the material on localized speech collected by the team of linguists led by Hans Kurath and published as the *Linguistic Atlas of the United States and Canada* strongly suggests, without perhaps conclusively proving, that certain features of Ulster English have had a lasting influence on speech patterns in certain parts of the United States.[54] One probable Scotch-Irish legacy is the retention of the postvocalic /r/ in such words as *barn*, *fear*, and *hours* in Kurath's Midland speech area (southern Pennsylvania, southern New Jersey, northern Maryland, the Southern Appalachians, and the trans-Appalachian West), which coincides broadly with the regions of Scotch-Irish settlement. In regions of concentrated English settlement (New England and the tidewater South) the postvocalic /r/ is generally absent because its loss was already far advanced in England when the colonization of English America began in the early seventeenth century. As in pronunciation, so in lexical characteristics American speech in the Midland area, and especially in western Pennsylvania, affords strong evidence of Scotch-Irish survivals. Among many examples one can cite *spouting* (for "gutter"), *bucket* (meaning "pail"), *bottom* ("low-lying land"), *piece* ("short distance"), *poke* ("a paper bag"), and *hull* ("to shell beans or fruit").[55]

The passion for learning, which constituted one of the leading characteristics of the Scotch-Irish, resulted in an extraordinary expansion of schools and colleges and a great increase in educational opportunities in the colonies. William Tennent's Log College, modeled on the dissenting academies of England and Ireland, inspired the founding of similar institutions, some of which, like Samuel Blair's at Fagg's Manor, eventually developed into true colleges, Tennent's Log College also prompted the founding—by Scotsmen rather than the Scotch-Irish—of the College of New Jersey (1746; the later Princeton), which served in turn as the model for Hampden-Sydney, founded in 1776 by Presbyterians in the Virginia piedmont, and Dickinson College (1783) at Carlisle, Pennsylvania, by the Scotch-Irish of the Cumberland Valley. More crucial in some ways was the work of Ulster-born Francis Alison (1705–1779), professor of moral philosophy at the College of Philadelphia and probably the greatest classical scholar in colonial America. Soon after emigrating to Pennsylvania in 1735, he started a school at New London, among whose alumni were Charles Thomson, secretary to the Continental Congress, and three other Scotch-Irish youths who were destined to

54. Crozier, "Scotch-Irish Influence," *American Speech*, LIX (1984), 310–311, 317.

55. *Ibid.*, 317–328; Cassidy, "Geographical Variation," in Bailey and Görlach, eds., *English as a World Language*, 182–183; Robert J. Gregg, "The Scotch-Irish Dialect Boundaries," in Martyn F. Wakelin, ed., *Patterns in the Folk Speech of the British Isles* (London, 1972), 109–110.

become signers of the Declaration of Independence: Thomas McKean, James Smith, and George Read. From Alison these future Revolutionary leaders learned not only the classics and natural and moral philosophy but also the Radical Whig political philosophy he himself had imbibed while studying with Francis Hutcheson in either Dublin or Glasgow.[56]

While the seeds of political awareness were thus being sown among some of the relatively privileged, the farmers, laborers, and craftsmen who made up the bulk of the Scotch-Irish population remained politically uninvolved, even apathetic. But the end of the Seven Years' War brought to the fore in two colonies issues that intimately concerned them. In Pennsylvania, Scotch-Irish frontiersmen had long resented the fact that the ruling Quaker oligarchy denied them the vote and adequate representation in the assembly and overtaxed them while failing to provide protection against Indian attacks. With Pontiac's uprising their anger boiled over, and the Conestoga massacre was followed in 1764 by the march of the Paxton Boys on Philadelphia to demand redress. In North Carolina, too, Scotch-Irish backcountry farmers took the lead in a struggle against eastern political oppression. Here, as in Ulster, Anglican exclusiveness was a source of grievance: tithes were burdensome, and it was not until 1766 that Presbyterian marriages were validated. But it was mainly to counter the tyranny of eastern officials and especially the extortion that accompanied the administration of justice that the Scotch-Irish joined the Regulator movement of 1768–1771. Though not a secret, oath-bound society like the Oakboys and Steelboys of contemporary Ulster, it resembled them in being an agrarian movement that relied chiefly on intimidation and violence.[57]

These ethnic and sectional conflicts help explain why the colonial Scotch-Irish, far from rallying unanimously to the patriot cause, were in fact sharply divided in their attitudes toward it. In Pennsylvania they overwhelmingly supported the Revolution. Taking advantage of the hesitations of the Quaker assembly, Scotch-Irish frontiersmen combined with eastern radicals to carry through a political revolution that at the same time placed the state decisively behind the drive for Independence and replaced the proprietary government with a radical and democratic one. Yet even in Pennsylvania the Scotch-Irish were not entirely united: Sir Henry Clinton succeeded during his occupation of Philadelphia in 1778 in raising a loyalist regiment consisting

56. Lawrence A. Cremin, *American Education: The Colonial Experience, 1607–1783* (New York, 1970), 325.

57. Brooke Hindle, "The March of the Paxton Boys," *WMQ*, 3d Ser., III (1946), 461–486; A. Roger Ekirch, *"Poor Carolina": Politics and Society in Colonial North Carolina, 1729–1776* (Chapel Hill, N.C., 1981); Marvin L. Michael Kay, "The North Carolina Regulation, 1766–1776: A Class Conflict," in Alfred F. Young, ed., *The American Revolution: Explorations in the History of American Radicalism* (DeKalb, Ill., 1976), 71–123.

of both Scotch-Irishmen and Irish Catholics.[58] But it was in the backcountry of the Carolinas that opinion was most deeply divided. In North Carolina, where the fight for Independence was led by their old tidewater oppressors, the Scotch-Irish were, if not actively loyalist, at least unsympathetic to the patriots. They remained unmoved even when the Continental Congress sent two Presbyterian ministers to persuade them of "the rectitude of the American side of the question" and to liken the American cause with that of "our forefathers who fought for liberty at Londonderry and Enniskillen in King James' time." But in the Waxhaws—the backcountry borderland between North and South Carolina—the British found the population "universally Irish and universally disaffected" while elsewhere in the South Carolina backcountry there were many Scotch-Irish loyalists, mostly recent immigrants who had received government land grants and feared to lose them if they joined the rebellion.[59]

Even where the Scotch-Irish strongly supported Independence, however, as in Pennsylvania, the liberal and humanitarian aspects of the Revolution seem to have had little appeal for them. Their own experience of religious and political prescription did not prevent them, once they and their allies had won control of the assembly, from imposing test acts and loyalty oaths of a stringency that even some whigs found objectionable or from reconstituting the Anglican-dominated College of Philadelphia as the Presbyterian-controlled, and hence ideologically acceptable, University of Pennsylvania. And while they may have acquiesced in 1776 in the extension of full civil and political rights to Pennsylvania Catholics, their part in the no-popery agitation that had greeted the Quebec Act two years earlier suggests that they were not fully committed to the ideal of religious freedom.[60] Still less did they favor any step smacking of racial equality. On meeting fierce resistance from the backcountry Scotch-Irish to his 1779 bill providing for the abolition of slavery, Dublin-born George Bryan, the first vice-president under the new Pennsylvania constitution, found it "irksome . . . that these few opposers of the bill should generally be members of the Presbyterian Churches, which are otherwise remarkable for their zeal, and for their exertions in the cause of freedom." Again, in 1783, it may well have been the Scotch-Irish

58. R. A. Ryerson, "Political Mobilization and the American Revolution: The Resistance Movement in Philadelphia, 1765–1776," *WMQ*, 3d Ser., XXXI (1974), 565–589.

59. E.R.R. Green, "The Scotch-Irish and the Coming of the Revolution in North Carolina," *Irish Historical Studies*, VII (1950–1951), 78–86; Jeffrey J. Crow, "Liberty Men and Loyalists: Disorders and Disaffection in the North Carolina Backcountry," in Ronald Hoffman *et al.*, eds., *An Uncivil War: The Southern Backcountry during the American Revolution* (Charlottesville, Va., 1985), 125–178.

60. Owen S. Ireland, "The Ethnic-Religious Dimension of Pennsylvania Politics, 1778–1779," *WMQ*, 3d Ser., XXX (1973), 423–449; Doyle, *Ireland and Revolutionary America*, 142; K. Miller, *Emigrants and Exiles*, 166.

who were referred to when it was reported that Philadelphia's "old Irish settlers," provoked when a free black bought two Irish indentured servants, threatened to kill him if he did not immediately free them on return of the purchase price and if the governor did not proclaim a law prohibiting free blacks from owning "slaves."[61]

It is tempting to conclude from the diversity of their responses to the imperial crisis that by 1776 the Scotch-Irish had become completely assimilated to their environment, with attitudes being shaped, not by cultural inheritance, but by local American circumstances. The large-scale abandonment of the Presbyterian faith that had long defined and warranted their separateness would seem to point to the same conclusion. Yet contemporaries, with the single exception of Lord Adam Gordon, were unanimous in accepting that the Scotch-Irish were a discrete group that retained much of their sense of cultural identity. A British general made the point explicitly when he remarked that "from their numbers . . . national customs were kept up amongst them and the pride of having sprung in the old country . . . prevented them from entirely assimilating with the Americans."[62] Admittedly, he was referring to immigrants who had only recently arrived in the colonies from Ulster, and his observations are not necessarily accurate about those who had come earlier and whose descendants had had two, three, or even four generations to become assimilated. Thus in the Scotch-Irish settlements in New Hampshire, founded in 1719, it was becoming increasingly difficult by the late eighteenth century to distinguish a Scotch-Irish farm from any other, though in Londonderry itself, the chief Scotch-Irish stronghold, there was still an inordinate number of flax fields, and, moreover, weddings remained traditionally boisterous affairs at which guns were fired and drunkenness was common. But as the Londonderry example suggests, location was as important as time of arrival. In Londonderry's satellite townships, where the Scotch-Irish were in a minority, they had been largely assimilated, even to the point of having joined Congregational churches.[63] A similar pattern prevailed in large towns like Philadelphia and Boston. But in central and western Pennsylvania and the backcountry South where they were heavily concentrated, the Scotch-Irish remained for the most part culturally distinctive. One reason for this was, like the contemporary influx from Germany but unlike that from Catholic Ireland, a large part of the Scotch-Irish movement consisted of families and included a substantial pro-

61. Arthur Zilversmit, *The First Emancipation: The Abolition of Slavery in the North* (Chicago, 1967), 125–131; Carl L. Baurmeister, *Revolution in America: Confidential Letters and Journals, 1776–1783 . . .*, trans. Bernard A. Uhlendorf (New Brunswick, N.J., 1957), 593.

62. K. G. Davies, ed., *Documents of the American Revolution, 1770–1783*, XV (Dublin, 1976), 227–229, quoted in Miller, *Emigrants and Exiles*, 164.

63. Wallace, "Scotch-Irish of New Hampshire," 306, 323–324, 360, 362.

portion of women. This made for marriage within ethnic and religious boundaries even where there was geographical intermingling. More significant, perhaps, was the fact that Scotch-Irish immigrants were bound together by a sustaining historical tradition. As Kerby Miller has convincingly argued, Scotch-Irish leaders persisted in seeing themselves and their flocks as part, not of the secularly motivated migration that it had been in reality, but of "a communal exodus compelled by religious and political oppression." To be sure, the character of Scotch-Irish immigration had changed over the six decades preceding the Revolution. Those arriving in the early 1770s were conspicuously poorer, less Scottish, more secular, and more liberal than the pioneers of 1717–1718, and they came from an Ulster transformed by a rapidly growing population and by economic and social change.[64] It is evident also that the diversity of the immigrants' American experiences tended to differentiate them. But they still remained a coherent and identifiable group, not least because of a shared belief that they were a chosen people whose successive tribulations were but the prelude to their ultimate deliverance from their enemies. Paradoxically, however, the very way in which Scotch-Irish leaders invoked their historical past in order to justify support for the Revolution served to undermine their claim to distinctiveness. By asserting an identity of moral and political aspirations with the patriots, by attempting, that is to say, to reconcile their dual loyalties by linking Scotch-Irish and American nationalism, they were abandoning their separateness and laying claim to being Americans.[65]

Even without the Revolution, however, it would have been increasingly difficult to remain insulated from the greater Anglo-American world. Indeed, it had already become so, as is evident when one considers the Scotch-Irish experience within the changing context of eighteenth-century cultural life in the colonies. The sixty years or so of large-scale Scotch-Irish immigration coincided broadly with the period that historians have now defined as one in which the various Anglo-American colonial communities became conscious of a shared cultural identity.[66] Thus, at a time when local customs and identities generally were being eroded, the Scotch-Irish could hardly hope, except briefly and in relatively isolated locations, to recreate familiar patterns of life. The experience of other eighteenth-century newcomers indicates the dominant trend: the Huguenots, for example, and even the Scots in

64. K. Miller, *Emigrants and Exiles*, 159–160; Doyle, *Ireland and Revolutionary America*, 56–57.

65. For similar attempts by 19th-century Irish-American nationalists, see Thomas N. Brown, *Irish-American Nationalism, 1870–1890* (Philadelphia, 1966), esp. 28–29.

66. T. H. Breen, "Creative Adaptations: Peoples and Cultures," in Jack P. Greene and J. R. Pole, eds., *Colonial British America: Essays in the New History of the Early Modern Era* (Baltimore, 1984), 215–217, 221–223.

remote Vermont could not—in the former case, did not want to—seal themselves off from Anglo-American influences and rapidly lost their ethnic distinctiveness.[67] The Scotch-Irish, it is true, had not experienced that fate at the time of the Revolution. Even constrained by their new environment, they had retained certain aspects of their Old World style of life. But despite their cultural continuities, the various borrowings, adaptations, and compromises they had been forced to make through interaction with their environments and with other groups signaled that a new cultural synthesis had emerged.

67. *Ibid.*, 223; Bernard Bailyn, "1776: A Year of Challenge—A World Transformed," *Journal of Law and Economics*, XIX (1976), 447.

MICHAEL CRATON

Reluctant Creoles
The Planters' World in the British West Indies

Their founders carried no Gods with them. On the contrary they go out into the wilderness of mere materialism, into territories where as yet there is nothing consecrated, nothing ideal. Where can their Gods be but at home?—J. R. Seeley, *The Expansion of England* (1883), quoted by Frank Wesley Pitman, *The Development of the British West Indies, 1700–1763* (1917)

Despite considerable interaction between the two colonial areas, the British West Indian colonies differed from those on the North American mainland in fundamental as well as subtle ways. As Seeley and Pitman recognized long ago, the primary and lasting motive for West Indian colonization was economic adventure: a symbolic quest for El Dorado, first in mining and looting the Spaniards, then, more prosaically, in plundering the soil by means of monocultural plantations. In North America, the profit motive, though never absent, was less central, often incidental. Only for some individuals and groups, and during the short period of the English Civil Wars, were Bermuda and the West Indian colonies places of religious and political refuge similar to the New England colonies.

For the most part small islands south of the Tropic of Cancer, the West Indian colonies were fragmented, disjointed, and dominated by the subtropical and maritime environment. Because of opposition from largely inimical natives and Spanish forerunners, the colonies were settled with difficulty and comparatively late in the phase of European incursion, with a concentration on islands that were manageably small, uninhabited, and of little value to the Spanish imperialists. Relations with the native Amerindians (particularly the problems of defense and diplomacy against the fierce and wily Caribs) showed some parallels with North American experience in the earliest years. But the struggle first against Spain and then the rival mercantilist powers of Holland and France presented more general and more severe problems than to the American mainland colonists—just as the priority of European rivals and their solutions to similar problems faced in the region exerted a greater influence on British West Indian colonies than on British colonies farther north.

Size as much as climate was a critical determinant for West Indian colonies. The differences between temperate mainland areas with well-defined seasons and tropical islands with high temperatures changing as little throughout the year as did the length of nights and days led to fundamental differences in the patterns of agriculture, society, human demography, and health. The central government of all colonies tended toward a common imperial pattern, but for mainland colonies, with their almost illimitable backwoods, the county was for the most part the most appropriate model for local government. For the West Indian islands, most of them no bigger than the comparatively small Virginia tidewater counties, however, the English-type parish was the more suitable local unit. Barbados, for example, with a superstructure of colonial government at least as large and complex as Virginia's, was divided into eleven parishes, averaging a mere fifteen square miles, or ten thousand acres. Only Jamaica of the island colonies was large enough to be subdivided into three counties, and this did not occur until the 1750s or ever mean as much as the parochial divisions.[1]

The predominant influence on the West Indies, and chief difference between the two spheres of British colonization, though, was economic: the all-embracing consequences of the "sugar revolution," which made the Caribbean settlements invaluable plantation colonies indissolubly linked to the British imperial economy as long as mercantilism lasted and sugar profits stayed high. Sugar monoculture had socioeconomic consequences unmatched even in the southern mainland colonies with their own plantations: a peculiarly intensive and degraded system of chattel bondage involving African and Afro-Caribbean slaves, and a privileged but beleaguered white minority—constantly under threat of pestilence, famine, earthquake, hurricane, war, or the insurrection of their slaves, and denuded of political and cultural leadership by the chronic absenteeism of its most fortunate members.

This essay attempts a brief socioeconomic and cultural analysis of the British West Indies during the slavery era and after, with a concentration on the structures, style of life, and world view of the dominant planter class. Viewed as a distinctive type of imperial periphery, this colonial sphere devel-

1. The sole purposes for the creation of Surrey, Middlesex, and Cornwall counties in Jamaica in 1758 seem to have been to concentrate the militia into three divisions and to allow the high court to go on assize. For the geography and ecological development of the West Indies, see Helmut Blume, *The Caribbean Islands*, trans. Johannes Maczewski and Ann Norton (London, 1974); David Watts, *The West Indies: Patterns of Development, Culture, and Environmental Change since 1492* (Cambridge, 1987).

oped, in sequence, its own core areas in Barbados, the Leeward Islands, and Jamaica, each with its shifting ecological peripheries as well as an internal cultural frontier represented by the interaction between a still-Europeanized white elite and a majority of African or Afro-Caribbean slaves. Overall, the essay attempts to assess whether white creole society was an idealized fiction created by plantocratic writers, a parody version of English society doomed to extinction, or a truly indigenous re-creation (largely unrecognized by its subjects) that bestowed a lasting legacy on the British West Indies.

I

Rather than a single expanding periphery, the development of the British West Indies during the slavery era (1609–1838) saw the creation of successive core areas based upon sugar plantations, each following a similar pattern of development but representing a distinctive stage and having its own special characteristics and its own expanding peripheral margins—with the process cut short only by the ending of slavery and the concomitant decline of British sugar plantations and of the plantocracy itself.

Bermuda, the anomalous coral island in the latitude of North Carolina, was the first English island "plantation." Yet the scarcely larger, equally uninhabited, evenly fertile island of Barbados was first to move from the production of tobacco and cotton on smallholdings with the labor of indentured whites to establish a sugar monoculture based on large estates and the labor of imported African slaves and, as an essential part of this process, to develop a settled ruling class of substantial planters. Never conquered by a foreign power, always retaining a sizable white population (including a good number of poor whites), and having more than two hundred years to develop before slavery ended, the island exhibited the most complete and sophisticated plantocratic system, including the highest proportion of resident planters. This led to a sense of identity that was almost nationalistic, expressed in a declaration of legislative independence prefiguring the American Declaration of 1776, issued as early as 1652.[2] Barbados had a slave population that was creolized, culturally as well as demographically, earlier than anywhere else in the British Caribbean.

Even while completing its own sugar revolution in the 1650s and 1660s,

2. "A Declaration of Lord Willoughby and the Legislature of the Island of Barbados against the British Parliament," quoted verbatim in Sir Robert Schomburgk, *The History of Barbados: Comprising a Geographical and Statistical Description of the Island, a Sketch of the Historical Events since the Settlement, and an Account of Its Geology and Natural Productions* (London, 1848), 706–708. See also N. Darnell Davis, *The Cavaliers and Roundheads of Barbados, 1650–1652 . . .* (Georgetown, British Guiana, 1887).

Barbados had sent out ambitious and aggressive planter magnates, displaced poorer whites, and surplus slaves to conquer (or reconquer), tame, and plant the Leewards, Jamaica, and South Carolina, and, with less success, the French possessions of Martinique and Guadeloupe, the "wild" islands of Saint Lucia, Grenada, and Tobago claimed by the French, and even a stretch of the Wild Coast of South America, Surinam—reluctantly given up to the Dutch in 1667. After this early, ebullient phase, however, Barbados stabilized and turned back inward to concentrate on its own internal development and plantocratic affairs.

In the Leewards, Saint Kitts was first settled even earlier than Barbados, followed, in sequence, by Nevis, Antigua, and Montserrat. But Antigua became the inner core and capital island of the group, a drier and rather less prosperous and populous economic, political, and social replica of Barbados. The development of Leeward Island sugar plantations and plantocracies was delayed and slowed by the attacks of Caribs and European rivals and only climaxed after the saturation of Barbados and the surrender of Surinam. But at the apogee of their slave sugar system in the early 1700s, the Leeward Islands and Islanders extended outward to their own regional periphery: to the marginal sugar island of Tortola, to other islands in the Virgin Islands group that never grew sugar, and to the equally marginal small islands of Barbuda and Anguilla.[3]

Twenty-seven times the size of Barbados and twelve times the area of all the Leeward Islands put together, Jamaica was not acquired until the Barbadian sugar revolution was almost complete and did not undergo its transformation into a major sugar producer until the process had long been completed in the Leewards. Moreover, mainly for topographical reasons but also because of competition, Jamaica never approached the level of sugar monoculture in Barbados or Antigua and had not even realized its full potential as a sugar producer before slavery ended. Ridged with mountains soaring over seven thousand feet, and divided by impenetrable karst limestone features, all densely forested, Jamaica had its own internal frontiers, inhabited by fierce maroons who inhibited the spread of plantations until 1740. The large coastal plains, interior valleys, and lower mountain slopes, however, were immensely fertile and productive.

Despite threats of slave rebellions and attacks from the French and Span-

3. For the early history and expansion of Barbados and the Leewards, see James A. Williamson, *The Caribbee Islands under the Proprietary Patents* (London, 1926); Vincent T. Harlow, *A History of Barbados, 1625–1685* (Oxford, 1926); Arthur P. Newton, *The European Nations in the West Indies, 1493–1688* (London, 1933); A. P. Thornton, *West-India Policy under the Restoration* (Oxford, 1956); Carl Bridenbaugh and Roberta Bridenbaugh, *No Peace beyond the Line: The English in the Caribbean* (New York, 1972); Richard S. Dunn, *Sugar and Slaves: The Rise of the Planter Class in the English West Indies, 1624–1713* (Chapel Hill, N.C., 1972).

Table 1. British West Indian Sugar Colonies

Measure	1670	1700	1730	1760	1775	1820	1833
BARBADOS, 1627. 166 sq. miles; 11 parishes (avg. size 9,658 acres)							
Population							
Whites (× 1,000)	21	16	15	16.5	18.5	15	13
Free coloreds (× 1,000)	a	a	a	a	.5	4	7
Slaves (× 1,000)	44	60	62	65	69	75	83
Proportion whites/ whites + slaves	32%	21%	20%	20%	22%	17%	14%
Sugar production (× 1,000 tons)	7.5	8.2	7.5	8.7	6.7	13	17.4
LEEWARD ISLANDS (Antigua, Montserrat, Saint Kitts, Nevis), 1625–1632. 370 sq. miles; 27 parishes (avg. size 8,770 acres)							
Population							
Whites (× 1,000)	9	7.5	10	8	7	5	4.5
Free coloreds (× 1,000)	a	a	a	a	1	5	8
Slaves (× 1,000)	10	24	51	70	83	68	60
Proportion whites/ whites + slaves	47%	24%	16%	10%	8%	7%	7%
Sugar production (× 1,000 tons)	2.0	6.8	20.3	20.8	19.1	17.0	16.7
JAMAICA, 1655. 4,411 sq. miles; 21 parishes (avg. size 135,271 acres; 3 counties)							
Population							
Whites (× 1,000)	8	7	8	17	19	20	15
Free coloreds (× 1,000)	a	a	1	3.5	4.5	10	35
Slaves (× 1,000)	9	40	100	160	193	305	310
Proportion whites/ whites + slaves	47%	15%	7%	10%	9%	6%	5%
Sugar production (× 1,000 tons)	.5	4.5	16.5	31.6	41.6	77.3	68.4

Table 1 (*continued*)

WINDWARD ISLANDS (Dominica, Grenada, Saint Vincent, Tobago), 1763. 672 sq. miles; 28 parishes (avg. size 15,630 acres)			
Population			
Whites (× 1,000)	7	3.7	2.3
Free coloreds (× 1,000)	2	9	12
Slaves (× 1,000)	64	85	74
Proportion whites/ whites + slaves	10%	5%	4%
Sugar production (× 1,000 tons)	11	28.3	31.8
TRINIDAD, 1763. 1,864 sq. miles; 44 quarters (avg. size 9,000 acres)			
Population			
Whites (× 1,000)		2.9	3.3
Free coloreds (× 1,000)		10	16.3
Slaves (× 1,000)		25	20.7
Proportion whites/ whites + slaves		10%	14%
Sugar production (× 1,000 tons)		8.8	14.7
BRITISH GUIANA (Berbice, Demerara, Essequibo), 1803. 83,000 sq. miles; 17 parishes (ca. 1,500 sq. miles; avg. size ca. 56,000 acres)			
Population			
Whites (× 1,000)		3.2	3.7
Free coloreds (× 1,000)		6	8
Slaves (× 1,000)		91	84
Proportion whites/ whites + slaves		3%	4%
Sugar production (× 1,000 tons)		46	54

Sources: Noel Deerr, *The History of Sugar*, 2 vols. (London, 1949–1950); Richard B. Sheridan, *Sugar and Slavery: An Economic History of the British West Indies, 1623–1775* (Barbados, 1974); Jerome S. Handler, *The Unappropriated People: Freedmen in the Slave Society of Barbados* (Baltimore, 1974); Gad J. Heuman, *Between Black and White: Race, Politics, and the Free Coloreds in Jamaica, 1792–1865* (Westwood, Conn., 1981); Barry W. Higman, *Slave Populations of the British Caribbean, 1807–1834* (Baltimore, 1984); David Watts, *The West Indies: Patterns of Development, Culture, and Environmental Change since 1492* (Cambridge, 1987).

[a] Insignificant numbers.

ish (especially during the Seven Years' War and American War of Independence), Jamaica by 1775 boasted seven hundred sugar plantations, each on the average two or three times the size of those in Barbados and the Leewards, and at least twice as many smaller estates growing other crops. Until the end of slavery this single island produced half of the total tonnage of British West Indian sugar, from the labor of half of all British West Indian slaves, possessing a plantocratic system commensurate in its relative size and absolute power. The governor of Jamaica was frequently a nobleman, more viceroy than governor, presiding over a mini-empire that encompassed not merely most of the small islands within two hundred miles and the logcutters' colony at Belize but, in practice, most of the Caribbean shore of Central America, from the Bay of Campeche to the San Juan River in Nicaragua.[4]

The power of Jamaica and the pretensions of its planters, however, did not go unchallenged. Despite the opposition of the Jamaica lobby, the British acquired four new plantation colonies in the Windward Islands at the Treaty of Paris in 1763: Dominica, Saint Vincent, Grenada, and Tobago. These were regarded as a potential extension of the sugar frontier by a new, uniquely aggressive generation of would-be planters (many of them Scots) and their mercantile backers. Progress was slowed, though, not just by opposition from the older colonies, but by the islands' mountainous terrain, the resistance of the Caribs and maroons in Saint Vincent and Dominica, and the fact that the established planters were mostly francophone Catholic smallholders, many of them colored, growing rival export crops such as coffee, cocoa, and spices. The dominance of the anglophone sugar planters seemed assured after 1783 (though Tobago temporarily was given up at the Treaty of Versailles), but it was once more threatened by the internal and external upheavals of the French Revolution and Napoleonic Wars and was by no means complete by the time the slave trade was ended in 1808.[5]

4. Edward Long, *The History of Jamaica* . . . , 3 vols. (London, 1774; rpt., 1970), I, 309–339; George Wilson Bridges, *The Annals of Jamaica*, 2 vols. (London, 1828), II, 118–155. For the early history of Jamaica, see also Charles Leslie, *A New and Exact Account of Jamaica* . . . (Edinburgh, 1739); W. J. Gardner, *A History of Jamaica* . . . (London, 1873); George Metcalf, *Royal Government and Political Conflict in Jamaica, 1729–1783* (London, 1965); Samuel J. Hurwitz and Edith F. Hurwitz, *Jamaica: A Historical Portrait* (London, 1971).

5. For the expansion into the Windward Islands following the Seven Years' War, see Bryan Edwards, *The History, Civil and Commercial, of the British Colonies in the West Indies*, 2 vols. (London, 1793); Frank Wesley Pitman, *The Development of the British West Indies, 1700–1763* (New Haven, Conn., 1917; rpt., 1967); Lowell Joseph Ragatz, *The Fall of the Planter Class in the British Caribbean, 1763–1833: A Study in Economic and Social History* (New York, 1928; rpt., 1971); Richard Pares, *War and Trade in the West Indies, 1739–1763* (Oxford, 1936).

Colored in this essay is used in the common West Indian sense to refer to persons of mixed African and European parentage or ancestry (cf. Spanish *mulato*). The word

Similar factors curtailed the development of the fifth and final wave of British plantocratic expansion, following the takeover of Saint Lucia from the French, Trinidad from the Spanish, and (potentially richest of all) three contiguous colonies in the Guianas from the Dutch, in the last French wars. Not only did the incoming British planters have to contend with different existing colonial institutions and settler populations (though they were congenial enough in the case of the Dutch) and the cutoff of the direct supply of slaves from Africa in 1805, but the creation of true plantocracies was hampered and the behavior of the planters toward their slaves was increasingly monitored as the result of these new colonies' being directly ruled by the crown rather than allowed self-legislation under the Old Representative System.[6] The huge hinterland of the British Guiana colonies and even the interior of the small islands of Trinidad and Saint Lucia remained undeveloped frontier zones long after slavery ended.

II

The initial English venturers to the Caribbean were a kind of Protestant conquistadores, a product both of the European Renaissance and of the Reformation. Their epitome was perhaps Sir Henry Colt, who in 1631, finding the rigors of planting in Saint Kitts little to his liking, opted instead to attack the Spaniards: "For rest we will nott, until we have doone some thinges worthy of ourselves, or dye in the attempt."[7] Fittingly, no more of Colt is heard thereafter. For the future belonged to those more earthbound planters whom he left behind in the infant colony of Saint Kitts. Such strenuous settlers, and the society of each successively successful island plantation, were profoundly influenced by two salient sequential changes: the formal institution of colonial government and the creation of a monocultural plantation economy dependent on the labor of African slaves. Together,

---

Negro is used, as in the 18th century, only for persons of unequivocally African stock. Elsewhere, the term *black* is used in the modern sense (as Americans traditionally used *colored*) to include all persons with recognizable or acknowledged African antecedents. *White* is used for those of unequivocally unmixed European ancestry.

6. For the takeover and development of Saint Lucia, Trinidad, and British Guiana, see Henry H. Breen, *St. Lucia: Historical, Statistical, and Descriptive* (London, 1844); Ragatz, *Fall of the Planter Class*; Raymond T. Smith, *British Guiana* (London, 1962); D. J. Murray, *The West Indies and the Development of Colonial Government, 1801–1834* (Oxford, 1965); Eric Williams, *From Columbus to Castro: The History of the Caribbean, 1492–1969* (London, 1970); Bridget Brereton, *A History of Modern Trinidad, 1783–1962* (London, 1981).

7. "The Voyage of Sir Henrye Colt Knight to the Ilands of the Antilles . . . ," in V. T. Harlow, ed., *Colonising Expeditions to the West Indies and Guiana, 1623–1667*, Hakluyt Society, 2d Ser., LVI (London, 1925), 54–102.

these changes compelled the emergence of a distinctive local type of white planter ruling class, a plantocracy.

Yet this evolutionary process itself was influenced by at least four models, ideals, or paradigms of social behavior originating in the mother country and its expanding periphery, commingling, conflicting, and fading before the imperatives of local politics and the harsh socioeconomic realities of the sugar plantation, but retaining traces everywhere and remaining strong on the ever-expanding colonial margins beyond the settled plantations. These paradigms were the maritime, the military, the aristocratic (or feudal-seigneurial), and the traditional household-familial.

England's colonization of tropical islands symbolically began with the hurricane wreck of Sir George Somers's ship *Sea Venture* on Bermuda in 1609, which occasioned Shakespeare's profound meditation on the nature of colonies and colonial societies in *The Tempest* (1611). As an avid reader of Renaissance authors who was personally acquainted with noble and gentlemanly would-be colonizers such as Southampton, Pembroke, Delaware, and Sir Dudley Digges, Shakespeare naturally described colonization as a fit pursuit for aristocratic adventurers. But it was also essentially a maritime activity. As Frank Kermode has pointed out, the key words in *The Tempest* include "nature," "noble," "vile," and "virtue." Yet the overwhelming element is the sea.

> The most remarkable changes are rung on the word "sea" and its compounds. The sea, the voyages it supports, and the wrecks it causes, are types of the action of grace and providence. Hence the "sea-change" and the "sea-sorrow." Hence the description of the sea as never surfeited, as incensed, as invulnerable, as apparently cruel, as revealing guilt, as a force which swallows but casts again, which threatens but is merciful.[8]

Just as Shakespeare's *Tempest* is not only a deeply Renaissance work but the quintessential product of English maritime activity and involvement on the eve of colonization, so English colonization in the Caribbean began and remained closely involved with the all-encompassing sea, with its language and metaphors and its societies of captains and crews. The first English venturers into the Caribbean were those whom the Spaniards called "Lutheran corsairs," such as Sir John Hawkins, Drake, Raleigh, or Robert Rich, earl of Warwick—the last of whom profitably combined privateering ventures against the Spaniards with the promotion of Puritan plantations in Bermuda and Providence Island at least partially worked by captured Negro

8. Frank Kermode, ed., *The Tempest*, by William Shakespeare, the Arden Shakespeare (London, 1954), lxxx.

slaves. The lineal descendants of the Elizabethan and Jacobean Seadogs were the Buccaneers, the greatest of whom, Henry Morgan, once peace was made with Spain, transferred his plunder into a Jamaican plantation named after his Welsh birthplace, was knighted by Charles II, and became moderately respectable as lieutenant governor of Jamaica and vice-admiralty judge—a significantly transitional figure.[9]

The sea remained the common Caribbean element, the essential medium of communication, a symbol of distance, isolation, and danger but also of escape. The sea not only linked the islands with the metropole, the cousin colonies of the North American seaboard, and the heartland-homeland of the African slaves but was also the means of communicating between Caribbean colonies, even, for lack of roads, between different parts of individual islands—with distances measured in time taken rather than nautical miles, because of the prevailing winds and currents and the vagaries of the weather. A high proportion of all West Indian plantations were within sight of the sea, and planters kept spyglasses on hand and a regular lookout and maintained a permanent weather eye. Colonial newspapers too were largely shipping gazettes, with even the sparse and delayed news of the outside world advertised as brought in by the latest-arriving vessel.

The southwestward-setting trade winds that brought provisions, slaves, news, and new white recruits and carried away plantation produce and home-returning whites also turned the sugarcane windmills—themselves often likened in Barbados and Antigua to ships dotted across a green sea of canes. The trade winds also brought rain and less welcome storms and, for four months each year, the dread threat of a tropical hurricane. In the early years of settlement in the Leeward Islands the equally dreaded Caribs came in by sea in their swift canoes (especially when the moon was full), and during the dozen imperial wars that punctuated the years between 1652 and 1815, a distant sail anxiously espied might variously betoken famine-averting succor, naval or military relief, the onset of an enemy blockade, or the descent of an invading army. For isolated coastal settlements as for legitimate traders sailing alone, pirates remained a peacetime hazard too, into the nineteenth century. A literally marginal category of desperadoes, pirates were a reproach to plantocratic notions of law and order: polyglot, multiracial, virtually classless groups of international outlaws, including runaway white bondsmen and black slaves, lurking from bases in the least developed,

9. Arthur Percival Newton, *The Colonising Activities of the English Puritans: The Last Phase of the Elizabethan Struggle with Spain* (New Haven, Conn., 1914); Kenneth R. Andrews, *The Spanish Caribbean: Trade and Plunder, 1530–1630* (New Haven, Conn., 1978); Ernest A. Cruikshank, *The Life of Sir Henry Morgan: With an Account of the English Settlement of the Island of Jamaica (1655–1688)* (Toronto, 1935).

most unproductive fringes of the Caribbean. Such marginal freemasonries, such undeveloped margins, were among the chosen destinations of those many fugitive bondsmen who took flight by sea.[10]

Not unnaturally, most West Indian planters, and their slaves, knew the sea almost as well as the land. Edward Long in 1774 listed some twenty-five words in common plantation parlance that had a maritime derivation.[11] It is highly likely that the gang system used on slave plantations had a maritime provenance. In Belize and Providence Island, and doubtless other places too, working gangs, or even any group of male slaves met together, were referred to as "crews." The slave name Boatswain, common throughout the West Indies, usually betokened, not a slave mariner, but a trusted slave gang leader. Similarly, at least one loyalist planter in the Bahamas referred to his slaves as "the people," the term used by seventeenth- and eighteenth-century captains for their crews. Conjuring up the surrounding element and the model of life on shipboard, with its watches and working parties under the command of "bo'suns," as well as more poignantly symbolizing a longing for the outside world in one of the most scattered, impoverished, and isolated colonies are the remarkably accurate drawings of sailing vessels still found scratched into the plaster of the ruins of plantation houses in the islands of the Bahamas.

The fading feudal tradition that a landholder and his retainers formed a local military unit, ultimately linked to the sovereign through a chain of command and fealty, was revived on this colonial periphery, given fresh impetus in the English Civil Wars, and retained in the form of the parish-based colonial militias. As much soldiers as sailors, Elizabethan Protestant hidalgos like Humphrey Gilbert, Drake, Raleigh, Thomas Gates, Thomas Dale, first in Ireland, then in North America, the Spanish Main, and the Caribbean, were eager to carve a new patrimony and carry the Word with the sword, wresting the land from its Catholic usurpers or its pagan inhabitants. Once settlements were actually made, moreover, the need for military defense remained as important as it had ever been on the fringes of the Roman Empire or the marches of Europe in the Middle Ages.

That doughty Lincolnshire warrior John Smith (whose title of Captain was surely amphibious and who had, significantly, fought and earned a coat of arms in Transylvania against the Turk) was a key figure in the earliest history of Virginia. His Caribbean equivalent was Captain Thomas Warner, the founder of Saint Kitts: Suffolk squire (and neighbor of John Winthrop),

10. Marcus Rediker, *Between the Devil and the Deep Blue Sea: Merchant Seamen, Pirates, and the Anglo-American Maritime World, 1700–1750* (New York, 1986).
11. Long, *History of Jamaica*, II, chap. 13, 319.

soldier, sailor, and settler, who was knighted for his loyalty, persistence, and success by James I. Like Raleigh and Drake as well as Smith himself, Warner saw the value of treating with friendly and useful Indians but an equal necessity of resorting to the sword to cut down unfriendly, "treacherous," or inconvenient natives. When Warner decided to slaughter his Carib ally Tigreman and his followers as they lay in their hammocks after a feast, John Hilton approvingly claimed that "he acted like a wise man and a soldier."[12] For more than thirty years thereafter, the English militias in the Leewards kept a nightly watch "in the trenches" against Carib attacks (doubled at times of full moon) and carried out periodic punitive raids on the neighboring Carib islands. The symbolic climax of this phase, though by no means its conclusion, was the personal combat in which Edward Warner, the English commander of the Antigua militia campaigning in Dominica, slew his own half-brother, Thomas "Indian" Warner (Sir Thomas's half-caste son), who on a visit to London had been rather casually appointed viceroy of Dominica by Charles II.[13]

The early militias of the Lesser Antilles took sides during the English Civil Wars, though they rarely, if ever, came to blows. With marginally more resolution, they sailed under their local commanders Lord Willoughby of Parham and the two Christopher Codringtons, father and son, to capture or recapture islands (and mainland Surinam) during the Anglo-Dutch and first Anglo-French wars. The most important military enterprise in the early years, however, was the amphibious operation involving discharged veterans of the Civil Wars and recruits from Barbados and the Leewards that led to the takeover of Jamaica by Admiral Penn and General Venables in 1655.[14] Though the original plan was far more grandiose and the local opposition in Jamaica was derisory—with the invading regiments settled in separate districts called "quarters" and the ordinary soldiers set to planting subsistence crops simply to avoid starvation—yet the surviving officers of the expeditionary force who remained as planters always referred to themselves as "the conquerors of Jamaica," thus legitimizing their landholding and ranks by right of conquest. In so doing, the founders of English Jamaica were at least instinctively expressing the political philosophy of the Royalist James Har-

12. John Smith, *The True Travels, Adventures, and Observations of Captaine John Smith* . . . (1630), in Philip L. Barbour, ed., *The Complete Works of Captain John Smith (1580–1631)* (Chapel Hill, N.C., 1986), III, 228–233; Egerton MSS 2395, 503–507, British Library, quoted in Williamson, *The Caribee Islands*, 23.

13. Aucher Warner, *Sir Thomas Warner, Pioneer of the West Indies* . . . (London, 1933); Vere Langford Oliver, *History of the Island of Antigua: One of the Leeward Caribbees* . . . , 3 vols. (London, 1894–1899).

14. Davis, *Cavaliers and Roundheads*; Harlow, *Barbados*; Harlow, *Christopher Codrington, 1668–1710* (Oxford, 1928); Newton, *European Nations*; S.A.G. Taylor, *The Western Design: An Account of Cromwell's Expedition to the Caribbean* (Kingston, Jamaica, 1965).

rington, whose *Oceana* was published within a year of the takeover of Jamaica: "As he [Hobbes] said of the law, that without this sword it is but paper, so he might have thought of this sword, that without an hand it is but cold iron. The hand which holdeth this sword is the militia of a nation."[15]

Even more than in the mainland colonies, in all British West Indian colonies the militia remained an essential part of the sociopolitical fabric. All free white males between the ages of sixteen and sixty were enrolled into regiments based on each parish, under the command of officers whose ranks were in almost exact proportion to their standing as landed proprietors. For much of the slavery period, the local planters were proudly known by their militia ranks. The founder of the Price fortune in Jamaica, for example, was first known simply as Lieutenant Francis Price, presumably from the rank he had held at the time of the conquest of 1655. But later, as a successful planter and member of the Assembly, he was promoted to captain and then major in the Saint John's militia regiment. His son Charles (1678–1730) was colonel and commander of the parochial regiment, and his grandson Sir Charles (1708–1772) was not only speaker of the Jamaican Assembly and a baronet but as a major general was the senior officer of the militia forces of one of Jamaica's three shires.[16]

At the apex of the colonial militia structure was the king's deputy, the governor, who was general and commander in chief of the local militia but also, in a remarkably high proportion of cases, a man with actual military experience. For the often beleaguered West Indian colonies the thesis of Stephen Saunders Webb that English colonies in America were essentially military outposts—an extension of models forged on the Scottish and Welsh borders and in Ireland—is truer than for the thirteen colonies.[17] But the military paradigm became weaker as the colonies became more securely established and defense and warfare more the concern of professional garrison troops and naval ships on station. The chief sociopolitical purpose of the militia, though, remained an important one: not the external military defense of the colony, but the function of an internal police force against rebellious white bondsmen, black slaves, and militant runaways. As Richard Ligon recognized as early as 1647, the parish-based militia of Barbados was the visible and audible instrument of plantocratic power: "They [the slaves]

15. James Harrington, *Oceana*, ed. S. B. Liljegren (Heidelberg, 1924), 16, quoted in Michael Craton and James Walvin, *A Jamaican Plantation: The History of Worthy Park, 1670–1970* (London, 1970), 18.

16. Craton and Walvin, *A Jamaican Plantation*, 26–94.

17. Stephen Saunders Webb, *The Governors-General: The English Army and the Definition of the Empire, 1569–1681* (Chapel Hill, N.C., 1979). But see also Webb's debate with Richard R. Johnson, Notes and Documents, *William and Mary Quarterly*, 3d Ser., XLIII (1986), 408–459; and Ian Steele, "Governors or Generals: A Note on Martial Law and the Revolution of 1689 in English America," *WMQ*, 3d Ser., XLVI (1989), 304–314.

are held in such awe and slavery, as they are fearful to appear in any daring act; and seeing the mustering of our men, and hearing their Gun-shot, (than which nothing is more terrible to them) their spirits are subjugated to so low a condition, as they dare not look up to any bold attempt."[18]

Militias continued to be mustered in times of war—first with white bondsmen, then colored and black freedmen, and finally even reliable slaves employed in subordinate roles under the pressures of need (though on the rare occasions they were used in campaigns the militias scarcely distinguished themselves). Even when summoned at times of threatened Carib attacks or slave uprisings or called upon to leave their native parishes to fight maroons (as in Jamaica in the 1730s), the white rank and file and even the officers were notoriously reluctant to serve. Colonial whites, moreover, were conspicuously unwilling to obey governors whose qualifications were too obviously based upon irrelevant military service or whose attitudes were too militaristic. The most extreme case of this was the occasion of 1710 when the whites of Antigua were so incensed with their governor, the Virginia-born Daniel Parke—allegedly appointed because he had been the officer who first brought the news of the victory of Blenheim to London in 1704—that they shot him and hacked his body to pieces on the steps of Government House. For the planters, however, the militia and their ranks within it remained vital components of the internal structure of law and order as long as slavery lasted.[19]

The first English colonies in the Americas were founded at a time when the Stuart kings were attempting to resuscitate quasi-feudal concepts of aristocracy, sociopolitical relations, and royal administration. Even more than in England itself, and completely contrary to New England, vestiges of such aristocratic and royalist structures, styles, and attitudes survived among the planter class of the British West Indies, despite the religious and political turmoil of the Civil Wars and the rising tide of bourgeois capitalism—almost certainly as a defensive response to the harsh realities of the West Indian climate, the plantation economy, and the fact that the overwhelming majority of the population consisted of African or Afro-Caribbean slaves.

The first English island colony, Bermuda, though ostensibly run by a chartered company for sixty-nine years, exhibited the initial tendency to provide colonies with marchland extensions of English institutions and pop-

18. Richard Ligon, *A True and Exact History of the Island of Barbados*, 2d ed. (London, 1673; rpt., 1970), 46.

19. Long, *History of Jamaica*, I, chap. 10, 123–155; Roger Norman Buckley, *Slaves in Red Coats: The British West India Regiments, 1795–1815* (New Haven, Conn., 1979); Dunn, *Sugar and Slaves*, 140–148; Webb, *Governors-General*, 123–124.

ulate them with tenants and bondsmen, on almost feudal lines. The planters were noblemen and privileged gentry granted strips of land from sea to sea across the narrow islands, which they either worked with landless bondsmen or (if, as was usual, they remained at home) on which they placed tenants who paid them rent in a share of crops. There was a political superstructure of governor, council, and elective assembly even before the crown assumed direct control in 1684, but the basic unit of local government and daily life was parochial. In 1616, Bermuda was divided into six "tribes" (a term of obscure derivation recognized by 1679 as being exactly synonymous with parishes), each with its church, glebe, and common land, its militia unit, and its local justices of the peace, elective vestry, and parochial officers drawn from the substantial landowners and long leasehold tenants.[20] Helped by the absence of an indigenous population and the presence of a remarkably large number of white settlers (more numerous than those in Virginia before 1625 and outnumbering the black inhabitants down to 1700), Bermuda by 1684, in the words of Henry C. Wilkinson, possessed all the English trappings of "counsellors, bailiffs, sheriffs, marshals, courts of law, grand juries, petty juries, justices of the peace, inquests, the militia system, trained bands, churchwardens, sidesmen, glebe, common land" while at the same time, like seventeenth- and eighteenth-century England, it was dominated by a class of local landed proprietors.[21]

Though the most common response of would-be colonizers, with or without titles of nobility or influence at court, was to seek a royal charter for a company, a more telling Stuart solution to the problem of authorizing and controlling new colonies was the granting of quasi-feudal proprietorships. Thus Barbados, the Leewards, and the other Caribbee Islands were granted (in patents that confusingly overlapped because of an ignorance of Caribbean geography) to two royal favorites, the earls of Carlisle and Pembroke, whose prerogatives were often in conflict with individuals and companies that had founded the actual settlements.[22] Significantly, the form of the first proprietary grants (including that of Carolina and the Bahamas to Sir Robert Heath in 1629) was that of a feudal tenancy in chief, subject to the ceremony of homage and the paying of a "peppercorn" rent, "after the manner of the County Palatine of Durham"—strongly suggesting the conception of such

20. "Q.: How many Parishes, Precincts, or Divisions are within your Corporation? Ans: Each Tribe is a distinct parish." Answers to queries from Council of Trade and Plantations, July 15, 1679, in J. H. Lefroy, *Memorials of the Discovery and Early Settlement of the Bermudas or Somers Islands, 1511–1687*, II (London, 1879; rpt., 1981), 430.

21. Henry C. Wilkinson, *The Adventurers of Bermuda: A History of the Island from Its Discovery*, 2d ed. (London, 1958), 123. For the early history of Bermuda, see also Lefroy, *Memorials*; Vernon A. Ives, ed., *The Rich Papers: Letters from Bermuda, 1615–1646 . . .* (Toronto, 1984).

22. Williamson, *The Caribbee Islands*.

colonies as borderlands, calling for the special delegation of prerogatives by the monarch and special ties and duties, including military service in return for land, imposed on all subfeudatories.

Equally significantly, later grants (such as the Carolina patent of 1663 and that adding the Bahamas in 1670) were made by the monarch "in free socage, after the custom of our manor of East Greenwich in the County of Kent." This indicated a far freer form of tenancy, in which land was held by the proprietors and their subtenants in permanent leasehold, subject only to its development and the payment of an annual quitrent, and able to be bought and sold and bequeathed hereditarily. Barbadian, Leeward Island, and Jamaican planters naturally wanted more—absolute freehold in their land—and were, indeed, in favor of royal over proprietary government to the degree that it would both facilitate access to undeveloped land and organize, regularize, and validate their tenures. The earliest tenures in Barbados (as in most new West Indian colonies) were of yeoman size and type, but the early development of freehold in real estate aided the consolidation of land into sugar plantations and the emergence of a sugar planter class in the later 1640s.

Elsewhere, quitrents and the nominal obligation to develop patented lands remained in place in most colonies a century after the crown assumed direct control. But, in general, the early establishment of freehold tenure and the ready availability of undeveloped crown land in new colonies to potential planters with political influence or financial means facilitated the creation and perpetuation of a native class of landed gentry even more tightly tied to the aristocratic system than were their English counterparts. The importance of tenure, possession, and inheritance also helps to explain why West Indian planters were so scrupulous and litigious when it came to matters of real estate and why, of all the structure of courts established on the English model, it was the colonial courts of chancery that were the best organized and busiest of all.

The biographies and family histories of successful West Indian planters illustrate both the disparate range of classes from which they sprang (and thus how West Indian plantations were a machine for creating wealth and aiding upward mobility) and the way in which they gravitated toward an aristocratic norm or ideal, derived from feudal culture, in their attitudes and behavior. At one end of the scale were the genuine aristocrats like the Codringtons, feudal magnates of Gloucestershire, whose ancestor had carried the royal standard at the battle of Poitiers (1356). Christopher Codrington the elder (1640–1698) built up one of the richest estates in Barbados during sugar's earliest and most profitable years, was a councillor at twenty-six and deputy governor at twenty-nine. Later, as governor-general of the Leewards he assembled the largest set of holdings in Antigua and acquired the entire island of Barbuda through his privileged access to the patenting process, though many of his lands lay undeveloped for years despite the requirements of the law. As military commander of the expedition that recaptured Saint Kitts in 1690, he even sought to augment his personal empire by taking over the best lands in the French section of the island, though this was thwarted by the terms of the Treaty of Ryswick (1697). The younger Christopher Codrington (1668–1710), brought up in England, an Oxford scholar and socialite, followed in his father's footsteps as colonial governor-general and military commander during Queen Anne's War (similarly capturing French Saint Kitts and invading Guadeloupe). The richest and most splendid of all early West Indian grandees, on his premature death in 1710 (three years before the Treaty of Utrecht gave the whole of Saint Kitts to the English) he bequeathed his magnificent library to his alma mater and left his two Barbadian plantations, with their slaves, to the Society for the Propagation of the Gospel for the establishment of a theological and medical college and a school for white Barbadian youths.[23]

The elegant Georgian buildings of Codrington College (completed between 1721 and 1738), now housing the theology faculty of the University of the West Indies, remain the most conspicuous relic of the golden, or aristocratic, phase of Barbadian sugar plantations. The two Christopher Codringtons, however, were quite exceptional in their aristocratic provenance, their lordly disdain for bourgeois convention, and their style of noblesse oblige. Rival planters complained that they bent the law to their own advantage—not just the restrictions on the allocation of crown lands, which all planters ignored as best they could, but also the Acts of Trade, which forbade commerce with the Dutch and French in nearby islands. For their part, the Codringtons tended to be dismissive of self-made planters and their legislative pretensions and were openly contemptuous of low-born landless whites. Conversely, though, like true aristocrats, they were able to leap the intervening classes and form bonds of mutual respect with at least some of their numerous African slaves. In an oft-quoted passage, Christopher Codrington the younger in 1701 recalled his father's special relationship with the Coromantees, whom most planters regarded as the most obdurate, troublesome, and rebellious of slaves:

> They are not only the best and most faithful of our slaves but are really all born Heroes. . . . There never was a raskal or coward of the nation, intrepid to the last degree, not a man of them but will stand to be cut to pieces without a sigh or groan, grateful and obedient to a kind master, but implacably revengeful when ill-treated. My Father, who had studied

23. Harlow, *Codrington*; J. Harry Bennett, Jr., *Bondsmen and Bishops: Slavery and Apprenticeship on the Codrington Plantations of Barbados, 1710–1838* (Berkeley, Calif., 1958).

the genius and temper of all kinds of negroes 45 years with a very nice observation, would say, Noe man deserved a Corramante that would not treat him like a Friend rather than a Slave.[24]

In many ways a more typical, perhaps even the quintessential, early West Indian planter was James Drax (1602–1675), one of the chief characters (if not heroes) of Richard Ligon's *History of Barbados* (1657). Drax had sailed with the first settlers under John Powell in 1627, an adventurer of obscure, probably yeoman background, with three hundred pounds sterling in company stock. Within a year he had cleared enough ground to grow and send a cargo of tobacco to England. With the proceeds he purchased forty white indentured servants, diversifying into cotton once the tobacco market failed with the help of Arawak Amerindians from the Orinoco. Around 1640, he visited Pernambuco to learn the techniques of sugar planting from the Portuguese and Dutch, forging valuable trading and credit links with Dutch and Sephardic Jewish merchants based in Amsterdam. Opting for the Dutch system of consolidated factory-based farming units rather than the Portuguese-Brazilian system of *senhors de engenho* and cane farming, sharecropping *lavradores*, Drax imported large numbers of slaves from 1644 and erected the first windmill in Barbados.[25]

Selfishly keeping his expertise from his neighbors as long as he could, James Drax, along with his kinsman William Hilliard, was one of the first two Barbadian sugar planters, and soon the richest. By 1647 he was writing that he would not transfer to England unless he could purchase an estate worth ten thousand pounds sterling a year. Though in principle approving the Royalist Governor Lord Willoughby's declaration of legislative independence in 1651 and opposed to the Navigation Act of the same year and the Anglo-Dutch War that followed it, Drax was identified as a Commonwealth supporter by his Cavalier rivals and fined eighty thousand pounds of sugar in

24. Codrington to Board of Trade and Plantations, December 30, 1701, CO 152/4, or Great Britain, Public Record Office, *Calendar of State Papers*, Colonial Series, *America and West Indies* (London, 1864) XIV/XIX, 1701, 1132.

25. Bridenbaugh and Bridenbaugh, *No Peace beyond the Line*, 36, 54–59, 78; Dunn, *Sugar and Slaves*, 62–67; Stuart B. Schwartz, *Sugar Plantations and the Formation of Brazilian Society, 1550–1835* (New York, 1985).

Barbados adopted what is sometimes called the Pernambuco System after the way the Dutch developed self-contained factory-plantation units in northeastern Brazil during their conquest. This differed from that system developed around Bahia, farther to the south, whereby the factory owners (*senhors de engenho*) grew only a proportion of the cane that their factory could process, obtaining the rest from the surrounding *lavrador* sharecroppers. The *lavradores* thus provided an intermediate class of dependent poor whites almost unknown in the British West Indies, serving both to augment the white militias and to provide some production elasticity when sugar prices were low and factory output was reduced.

1650. A colonel of militia and assemblyman before his temporary eclipse, he really came into his own with the Cromwellian ascendancy, becoming a councillor and commissioner of roads in 1653 and sent off with almost royal pomp on his first return to England (after twenty-seven years) in 1654. On a subsequent visit in 1658, he was knighted by Cromwell himself.[26]

Yet James Drax was an equivocal Puritan and in Barbados lived in almost baronial style. His plantation house, Drax Hall, though much altered, is one of the principal Barbadian monuments to the old plantocracy, and his splendid style of life and hospitality are exemplified by the fifty lines that Ligon takes mouthwateringly to describe the menu of a typical dinner at Drax Hall around 1647.[27] James Drax was also one of the first and most notable of upwardly mobile West Indian planter dynasts. He married the daughter of James Hay, first earl of Carlisle, by Lucy Percy, one of the ladies-in-waiting to Queen Henrietta Maria; and his own daughter, Frances, married the younger Christopher Codrington. Despite his Cromwellian knighthood, James Drax comfortably survived the Restoration, dividing his time between Barbados and England, where he was one of the prominent members of the prototype committee of West Indian merchants and planters that met informally at the Jamaica Coffee House in Saint Michael's Walk near the Exchange in London. His fortune continued to grow with the help of new interests in Jamaica, but, unlike his son-in-law, he was not a notable Barbadian benefactor. His son, Colonel Henry Drax, who died in Middlesex, England, in 1682, though, left two thousand pounds sterling in his will for the establishment of a "free school and college" in Bridgetown, Barbados.[28]

Richard Sheridan has shown how similar conditions led to the creation of a local aristocracy out of those who settled Antigua before 1680, with the Willoughbys and Codringtons illustrating fortunes transferred or extended from Barbados and families like the Martins and Tudways replicating the history of the Draxes from an Antiguan base.[29] But the way in which West Indian sugar plantations not only generated increasing wealth down to at least 1775 but also created a kind of native aristocracy, imitative of European patterns but uniquely West Indian, is epitomized in the history of the Price family, the Jamaican (as opposed to the absentee) phase of which climaxed in the career of the first St. Charles Price (1708–1772).

Despite the myths contributed to *Burke's Peerage* by a pious descendant,

26. Bridenbaugh and Bridenbaugh, *No Peace beyond the Line*, 137–139, 158–159.

27. Ligon, *Barbadoes*, 38–39.

28. Bridenbaugh and Bridenbaugh, *No Peace beyond the Line*, 137–139, 158–159.

29. R. B. Sheridan, "The Rise of a Colonial Gentry: A Case Study of Antigua, 1730–1775," *Economic History Review*, 2d Ser., XIII (1960–1961), 342–357.

the Welsh origins of the family were as obscure as Henry Morgan's, and probably not dissimilar—impoverished minor gentry. The founder of the Jamaican fortune, Francis, was possibly one of the few officers recruited by General Venables from among the less successful Barbadian smallholders in 1655. Within twenty years of the conquest of Jamaica, Francis Price had painstakingly graduated to the ownership of a 175-acre sugar plantation, worked by about thirty white servants and black slaves, in Guanaboa Vale, not far from the capital, Spanish Town, and the coast. Francis Price, though, also owned the 840 prime acres of Lluidas Vale in the undeveloped center of Jamaica, which his son Charles turned into the sugar estate called Worthy Park, one of the richest and longest-lived of all such Jamaica operations.[30]

From this nucleus, Charles's son and namesake, the third-generation head of the Jamaican Prices, became the greatest of all contemporary magnates, owning in his prime about twenty-six thousand acres and some thirteen hundred slaves, located in eleven of Jamaica's fifteen parishes. This bloated (indeed, overambitious) patrimony came partly from canny dynastic marriages and successful speculations during Jamaica's most expansive era but mainly through Charles Price's unashamed manipulation of the plantocratic spoils system, which rewarded political power with landed wealth in due proportion. Educated at Eton and Oxford, he returned to Jamaica in 1730 to forge a political alliance with the long-serving (and therefore proplanter) Governor Edward Trelawny (1738–1752), during the phase of expansion that followed the signing of peace with the Jamaican Maroons. Charles Price's power base was challenged by Edward Trelawny's successor, Admiral Charles Knowles, who formed a Tory, town, merchant, or progovernment faction and symbolically shifted Jamaica's capital from the planters' stronghold, Spanish Town, to the mercantile center, Kingston, thirteen miles away. Behaving much like English Whig landed magnates, with whom they enjoyed many useful connections, Charles Price, his cousin Rose Fuller (brother of the Jamaican agent in London), and Richard Beckford (the brother of Alderman William Beckford, the friend of William Pitt the elder) headed the country and planter clique that engineered the recall of Knowles and the triumphal retransfer of the Jamaican capital from Kingston to Spanish Town. A few years later this victory was reinforced by the defeat of Governor Edward Lyttelton over a question of the Assembly's privileges, his recall to England, and his replacement by Lieutenant Governor Roger Hope Elletson, a Jamaican native.

Thereafter, as Jamaica reached the peak of its sugar prosperity and importance after the Seven Years' War, Sir Charles Price (created a baronet during the regime of Governor Sir William Trelawny, Edward Trelawny's naval

30. Craton and Walvin, *A Jamaican Plantation*, 26–45.

cousin) was the most notable member of that fortunate elite that, while passing local legislation nakedly in its own interest, negotiated successfully for protective imperial sugar duties and naval protection while still indulging in Whiggish rhetoric and loyal addresses in support of the North Americans' stance against the Stamp Act and later imperial enactments and actions. For his leadership in this political juggling game, Sir Charles Price was grandly dubbed "The Patriot" by his fellow planters—an echo of the nickname that William Pitt had held while in opposition in England.[31]

Besides building up his personal landholdings, Sir Charles Price tried to ensure their development by promoting public acts to push roads into the Jamaican interior as well as a private act to build an aqueduct in Lluidas Vale that doubled the efficiency of Worthy Park and another to grant himself the monopoly of tolls between Spanish Town and the coast. With such widespread holdings, so many political interests, and a distaste for the sordid details of plantation management, he did not spend much time on any of his sugar estates, being almost an internal Jamaican absentee. The legislative and socializing season was spent at his grand house in Spanish Town (which occupied a whole city block) while the hot summer months were mainly passed at a mansion called the Decoy, two thousand feet up in the hills of Saint Mary parish. Though constructed entirely of wood, this country retreat, surrounded by a park in which grazed imported fallow deer, was the nearest Jamaican equivalent to an English country house. Edward Long in 1774 described it as being

> well finished, and has in front a very fine piece of water, which in winter is commonly stocked with wild-duck and teal. Behind it is a very elegant garden disposed in walks, which are shaded with the cocoanut, cabbage, and sand-box trees. The flower and kitchen-garden are filled with the most beautiful and useful variety which Europe, or this climate, produces. It is decorated, besides, with some pretty buildings; of which the principal is an octagonal saloon, richly ornamented on the inside with lustres, and mirrors empaneled. At the termination of another walk is a grand triumphal arch, from which the prospect extends over the fine cultivated vale of Bagnals quite to the Northside Sea. Clumps of graceful cabbage-trees are dispersed in different parts, to enliven the scene; and thousands of plantane and other fruit-trees occupy a vast tract, that environs this agreeable retreat, not many years ago a gloomy wilderness.[32]

31. *Ibid.*, 71–94; Long, *History of Jamaica*, I, 438; Pitman, *British West Indies*, 34; Metcalf, *Royal Government*, 86–198; T. R. Clayton, "Sophistry, Security, and Socio-Political Structures in the American Revolution; or, Why Jamaica Did Not Rebel," *Historical Journal*, XXIX (1986), 319–344.

32. Long, *History of Jamaica*, II, chap. 7, 76–78, quoted in Craton and Walvin, *A Jamaican Plantation*, 85.

At the Decoy, separated from all but his domestic slaves (and also in his last years insulated from the imminent collapse of his overblown empire), Sir Charles Price could well indulge the style and tastes of a grand seigneur. He kept a famous open house, especially to visitors from England, and according to the admiring Edward Long was a notable benefactor who pursued a lifelong interest in theology and Latin. His most famous act of noblesse oblige was to manumit each year on his birthday a slave whose behavior had been characterized by exceptional industry and fidelity.[33] When Sir Charles Price died, his virtues were extolled by his son (and successor as speaker of the Jamaican Assembly) on an ornate marble tombstone (erected at the Decoy but later transferred to the parish church at Spanish Town), fittingly, if incongruously, couched in the language of Livy.[34]

A fourth and final paradigm that pertained to the plantocratic lifestyle, congenially related to the ideal of a quasi-feudal aristocracy and bound to fade (as in England itself) under the influence of capitalistic materialism, was that of the patriarchal family household. As Peter Laslett above all others has shown, this notion was still so prevalent in all ranks of English society at the time the first colonies were founded in the Americas that one can talk of a homogeneous social system rather than a true class system (while stopping short of Laslett's own claim that it was a "one-class society").[35] From the sovereign downward, the titled nobility were grand patriarchs, with virtually

33. Long, *History of Jamaica*, I, chap. 5, 468, quoted in Michael Craton, *Sinews of Empire: A Short History of British Slavery* (London, 1974), 222–223. An even more remarkably self-centered (and familial) act of noblesse oblige was Governor and Lady Nugent's practice of giving their domestic slaves presents on their (the Nugents') wedding anniversary. Entry for Nov. 15, 1801, in Philip Wright, ed., *Lady Nugent's Journal of Her Residence in Jamaica from 1801 to 1805* (Kingston, Jamaica, 1966), 39.

34. Craton and Walvin, *A Jamaican Plantation*, 79, 91. In general, a study of planter memorials in British West Indian churches illustrates the extent, and the limitations, of plantocratic pretensions and style. Traditionally attracting the interest (as in Europe) mainly of antiquarians and genealogists, the memorials would also repay the attentions of sensitive demographers, semioticians, and iconographers. Often flamboyant in form, and inscribed in terms of poignant, now incongruous, grandiloquence, they differ from similar memorials in English parish churches mainly in showing a much higher incidence of infant mortality and widowhood, and a more complex and fractured pattern of dynasty building. Except for some of the earliest and most ingenuous examples, they are also conspicuously imported artifacts, either carved from Italian marble by transient artists or, in the grandest cases, ordered and shipped out from London studios. See, for example, Lesley Lewis, "English Commemorative Sculpture in Jamaica," *Jamaican Historical Review*, IX (1972), 1–24.

35. Peter Laslett, *The World We Have Lost* (London, 1965), 23–54. For the application of Laslett's ideas to the Barbados case, I am largely indebted to Gary A. Puckrein, *Little England: Plantation Society and Anglo-Barbadian Politics, 1627–1700* (New York, 1984).

no private family life, heads of great households consisting of servants of different ranks living in intimate proximity with each other. They exercised almost absolute authority and dispensed both justice and bounty. Even at the gentry and yeoman levels, households were not the close-knit nuclear family units that the Industrial Revolution made the norm, but larger functional groups of persons not necessarily related by blood. Domestic servitude was such a common feature of life that it was not necessarily demeaning (giving opportunities for upward and outward mobility through formal adoption or marriage), with young family members quite casually interchanged as servants from one patriarchal household to another of similar rank. Even in the commercial life of the towns, the system of apprenticeship widened the size and circumference of household units, with the master of the household and shop either tyrannical or kind, and the bound apprentices sleeping "under the counter"—just as rural servants traditionally slept in any available corner of the baronial hall.

Such a system of family households was naturally carried into the colonies, reinforced where the viability of the early settlements was determined by the need for medium-sized households with a good proportion of working hands, and tending to prevail wherever later plantations continued to approximate to English rural estates. This was particularly true of Barbados, where the first units were no larger than yeoman holdings (averaging 25 acres in 1640) and plantations never grew to an enormous size (an average of 125 acres in 1700). Colonel Henry Drax, James's son, for example, giving careful instructions to his plantation manager in the 1670s, wrote of "all the members of my family, black and white," and this letter was quoted in full in a best-selling manual of plantation management published by William Belgrove as late as 1755.[36] The purpose of patriarchal authority in the slave plantation context, and the limits of patriarchal benevolence, however, are clearly revealed when Henry Drax's instructions are read in their entirety. "You must never punish either to satisfy your own anger or passion," he wrote, but to use the punishment either to "reclaim the malefactor or to terrify others from committing the like fault." Punishments, moreover, were not confined to moral misdemeanors: indeed, were less concerned with strictly moral misdeeds than with industrial misbehavior and inefficiency. Head sugar boilers, for example, were to be especially monitored (since their efficiency had a crucial bearing on profitability) and upon their "neglect to be severely punished." And while Drax recognized that slaves often pillaged food crops to augment their diet and acknowledged that if slaves stole "for the belly, it is the more excusable," he added, "But if at any time they are taken stealing, sugar molasses or rum, which is our money and the final

36. William Belgrove, *A Treatise upon Husbandry or Planting* (Boston, 1755), 51; Puckrein, *Little England*, 79–80.

product of all our endeavours . . . they must be severely handled being no punishment too terrible on such an occasion as doth not deprive the party of either life or limb."[37]

Despite the example of the Portuguese *casa grande*, which the early Barbadian planters must have encountered, even admired, in Brazil, the idea of a cohesive extended family household was bound to fade under the conditions essential to the optimal operation of a sugar plantation. The sheer size of the population units in the labor-intensive Dutch or English system of sugar production made the concept of an all-embracing family household increasingly difficult to sustain. Further, a more naked capitalism reduced the laborer to a mere cog in an industrial machine, depersonalized, and soon a mere commodity to be bought and sold. And finally, the immense cultural differences between white European masters and black African slaves made the creation of a social rather than purely functional economic matrix virtually impossible. What sustained the Latin conception of the easygoing multiracial ambiance of the *casa grande* (in the Spanish and, to a certain extent, French Caribbean colonies as well as in Central and South America) was, not just a lower level or capitalistic exploitation, but a longer juridical and Christian tradition of socioeconomic integration. Roman law quite effectively integrated masters and slaves into a common socioeconomic system, and the marriage of canon and Roman civil law, which characterized the legal systems of the Catholic imperialists, actually reinforced the master-slave matrix by giving it a godly mandate. All this required was that the *bozal* (that is, pagan and uncivilized) African slave be Christianized as part of the civilizing process, that is, taught the proper dutiful behavior of the good Christian slave, while the slave's owner, in theory at least, was expected to play the part of a good Christian master and patriarch.

Just as the patriarchal household rested on biblical precedents, so Christian observance was an essential feature of the ideal quasi-feudal household. For English planters this was relatively easy to sustain when the majority of their laborers were white indentured servants accustomed to the parish-based society of rural England, but more difficult when the servants were Irish or Scottish Catholics, and almost impossible once the labor force consisted of much larger numbers of black African *bozales*. Indeed, most planters believed that, in order to maintain that all blacks were slaves and that all slaves were chattel, it was best to prevent all slaves and blacks from becoming Christians. Thus the first English colonial laws that defined slaves as chattel made an almost explicit distinction between "slaves" (that is, blacks) and "Christians" (meaning whites). This crucial divide was manifest

37. Henry Drax, "Instructions I would have observed by Mr. Richard Harwood in the management of my plantation," Rawlinson MSS, A 348, fol. 7, Bodleian Library, Oxford University, in Puckrein, *Little England*, 78–79.

in Henry Drax's instructions during the 1670s: "all the whites in the family [that is, plantation household]" being "called to hear morning and evening prayers" on pain of being denied their week's food ration, while the black slaves were presumably left to their own religious observances.[38]

The degree to which black slaves becoming Christian were any less slaves remained a plantocratic debating point as long as slavery lasted, running in delicate counterpoint to the argument (picked up, no doubt, from Catholic planters) that Christianizing one's slaves might have a useful socializing function.[39] The experimental crucible for these debates was, not the plantation as a whole, but the narrower ambit of the "great house," where the domestic slaves not only lived in familiar intimacy with their masters but were the most acculturated of plantation slaves. A significant irony was that in such great houses, with the black housekeepers, hordes of colored domestics, and their raging social and sexual intrigues, the resident owner-master was normally an observant Christian in reverse proportion to the degree he behaved like a patriarchal *senhor de engenho* in his *casa grande*. Thus, while elements of the traditional aristocratic family household were sustained, the realities of West Indian plantation life determined that these would either survive in a narrower context or a (literally) bastardized form or would become, as in England, part of "the world we have lost."

III

Barbados, its wild woods entirely supplanted by contiguous sugar plantations, with a network of good roads radiating from the capital, was the first colony to be called the "jewel in the British crown" (1667). Père Labat, visiting the island in 1700, was among the first to liken the whole island to a garden and praised the planters' riches, elegance, and taste, though at the same time he condemned the brutality of relations between masters and

38. *Ibid.*, 80–81.

39. One of the most cogent official statements about the relationship between Christianity and slavery was made by Sir John Heydon, governor of Bermuda, in a proclamation dated Nov. 13, 1669: "Masters and Servants are hereby advised, and in the kings name required to live in peace, mutuall love and respect to each other, Servants submitting to the condition wherein God hath placed them. And such Negroes as formerlie, or lately have bin baptized by severall Ministers, should not thereby think themselves free from their Masters and Owners, but rather, by the meanes of their Christian profession, obliged to a more strict bond of fidelity and service. And if all persons professing Christianity would be careful in the discharge of their duties, living in the feare of God, and in due obedience to his Maiestys Laws, complaints of this nature would be prevented, true religion, and civill conversation would be encouraged, the service of God would be esteemed the greatest freedome." Lefroy, *Memorials*, II, 293–294.

slaves. Either ignoring or dismissing such strictures, the planters themselves began to speak of Barbados as "the civilised island" or "Great Britain in miniature," boasting of a newspaper and printing press as early as 1731 and a whole range of clubs, societies, and "polite entertainments," including a theater and two bowling greens.[40]

The same process of cultivation and civilization, and the same degree of cultural pride on the part of the planters, was displayed in Antigua and the other Leeward Islands, if at a rather later stage and with rather less justification than in Barbados.[41] Yet by 1740 it was clear (as remained true till slavery ended in 1838) that Jamaica was the quintessential as well as the most valuable British sugar island. To understand most truly the planters' world of the British West Indies, we ought therefore to study the Jamaican plantocracy at the peak of Jamaica's importance on the eve of the American War of Independence, as seen and described by the Jamaican planters themselves—of whom the most important and self-revealing was Edward Long, author of the two-volume *History of Jamaica* (1774).[42]

Edward Long is usually quoted for his crude Negrophobia and is, conversely, characterized as an equally simplistic admirer of the planter class.

40. "God bless Barbados that fair jewell of your Majesty's crown" (Lord Francis Willoughby to Charles II, May 1666, quoted in Harlow, *Barbados*, 165); Neville Connell, "Father Labat's Visit to Barbadoes in 1700," *Journal of the Barbados Museum and Historical Society*, XXIV (1957), 164–171; Jack P. Greene, "Changing Identity in the British Caribbean: Barbados as a Case Study," in Nicholas Canny and Anthony Pagden, eds., *Colonial Identity in the Atlantic World, 1500–1800* (Princeton, N.J., 1987), 213–266.

41. Oliver, *History of Antigua*; Sheridan, "Colonial Gentry," *Econ. Hist. Rev.*, 2d Ser., XIII (1960–1961), 342–357; [Mrs. Flannigan], *Antigua and the Antiguans . . .*, 2 vols. (London, 1844); Vere Langford Oliver, ed., *Caribbeana: Being Miscellaneous Papers Relating to the History, Genealogy, Topography, and Antiquities of the British West Indies*, 6 vols. (London, 1909–1919); Elsa Goveia, *Slave Society in the British Leeward Islands at the End of the Eighteenth Century* (New Haven, Conn., 1965).

42. Edward Long (1734–1813), son and grandson of Jamaican planter-politicians, was born in Cornwall and educated at Bury Saint Edmunds, Liskeard, and the Inns of Court. On the death of his father in Jamaica in 1757, Long went out to manage the family estate, Longville in Clarendon parish. Married in 1758 to Mary Ballard, widowed daughter of Thomas Beckford, he became secretary to Lieutenant Governor Sir Henry Moore, his brother-in-law, and was appointed judge of the Vice-Admiralty Court—a lucrative sinecure, which he enjoyed, even as an absentee, until 1797. Leaving Jamaica ostensibly for health reasons in 1769, he never returned, combining the life of an affluent country gentleman, West Indian lobbyist, and litterateur. He died, before his West Indian fortune was seriously eroded, in the Sussex home of one of his sons-in-law, Lord Henry Howard, and was buried in Slindon churchyard.

Edward Long's *History of Jamaica* (1774), augmented by the notes he compiled for the never-published second edition (British Museum Add. MSS, 12, 404–412, 431), is by far the most important plantocratic account of Jamaica. But it can be compared with Charles Leslie, *A New History of Jamaica*, extensively quoted in Pitman, *British West Indies*, 23–26.

His paranoid denigration of the Negro is real enough, extending to an almost equal contempt for persons of mixed race. He also combines an extreme class-consciousness with racism in his condemnation of the lower-class white males' "base familiarity with the worst-disposed among the slaves" and the "gross affinity" of lower-class white females for Negro men "for reasons too delicate to mention."[43] But Long does far more than present a blind encomium of the planter class. Besides modifying the picture by presenting generally unfavorable descriptions of many other types and classes of local whites, he is critical of many aspects of the plantocratic style of life and severely condemns what he regards as the salient faults and deficiencies of the system—reserving his worst censures for the evils of absenteeism.

Edward Long, in fact, is almost schizophrenic: torn between wish-fulfillment and harsh reality, between patriotic praise for the class and island home that bore and bred him, and condemnation for those conditions that militated against the ideal. He is also something of a pre-Darwinian evolutionist, at his most enthusiastic almost suggesting that the best Jamaican planters belong to a separate subspecies of European man: English aristocrats made even more admirable by the new environment. "Their cheeks are remarkably high-boned, and the sockets of their eyes deeper than is commonly observed among the natives of England," he claims. "Their sight is keen and penetrating; which renders them excellent marksmen." Moreover, "the effect of climate is not only remarkable in the structure of their eyes, but likewise in the extraordinary freedom and suppleness of their joints, which enable them to move with ease, and give them a surprising agility, as well as gracefulness in dancing. Although descended from British ancestors, they are stamped with these characteristic deviations."[44]

Munificent patriarchs in the true aristocratic mold, creole Jamaican planters are said (against much of the evidence) to be generally "of quick apprehension, brave, good-natured, affable, generous, temperate, and sober . . . lovers of freedom . . . tender fathers, humane and indulgent masters; firm and sincere friends." Above all they are noted for their hospitality, keeping open house for their fellow whites, including transient strangers, whom they regale with a profusion of food and drink. "Fond of social enjoyments," he adds, "they affect gaiety and diversions, which in general are cards, billiards, backgammon, chess, horse-raising, hog-hunting, shooting, fishing, dancing, and music."[45]

The Jamaican planters' white womenfolk Long also praises with a kind of restrained gallantry. He shares with male members of his class in England the

43. Long, *History of Jamaica*, II, chap. 13, 266–350, III, chaps. 1–3, 351–475.
44. *Ibid.*, II, chap. 13, 261–262.
45. *Ibid.*, 262.

paternalistic condescension that regarded wives and daughters as a kind of elegant property, and he also exhibits the tendency common among gentlemen throughout plantation America to place their gentlewomen on a pedestal, isolated from the mundane or sordid concerns of daily life. This makes Edward Long a suitable target for modern feminists almost as much as for liberated blacks. But Long does write generously of the general good looks of Jamaican planter women, their cleanliness, their fidelity and chastity, their temperance and piety, their indulgence (to a fault) toward their children, and their accomplishments in needlework, music, dancing, and, perhaps surprisingly, horsemanship.[46]

Edward Long's model planter and his wife, however, are very much the cream of the dominant classes in Jamaica. Long's praises do not extend equally to the merchants and professionals (though many planters had mercantile connections, and lawyers and doctors were often planters too) and are withheld almost completely from "the lower order of white people," who "are, for the most part, composed of artificers, indented servants, and refugees." Though Long (unlike at least one earlier writer) denies that "the gaol-delivery of Newgate" had been "poured in upon this island," he admits that "it is an occasional asylum for many who have deserved the gallows." Many immigrants in the lower and middling ranks are "natives of Scotland and Ireland . . . come over to seek their fortunes." The best of the former are more adaptable, hard-working, and reliable, more skilled and generally better educated than the English, making the best craftsmen and overseers and providing most of the island's doctors. As planters, though, like all who had risen too fast up the social scale, the Scots tend to be the harshest and least gentlemanly, bringing the rest into disrepute. To the Irish, as Catholics with an almost alien tongue and culture, Edward Long shows that almost racist contempt predictable in one of his sound Anglican provenance, while his attitude toward the Sephardic Jews (a community vital to Jamaica's commerce that antedated the English occupation) is positively anti-Semitic.[47]

Edward Long criticizes even the most prominent planters for certain "foibles in their disposition," which include indolence, intemperance, and promiscuity—all attributable to the social as well as purely meteorological climate. Planters tend to be poor "oeconomists," for the tropical weather

46. *Ibid.*, 271, 280.

47. *Ibid.*, 289, 293–300. Long is here countering the scurrilous attacks on the white settlers of Barbados and Jamaica originated by Henry Whistler in 1655, relished and repeated in nearly all secondary accounts. "Extracts from Henry Whistler's Journal of the West India Expedition," in C. H. Firth, ed., *The Narrative of General Venables, with an Appendix of Papers Relating to the Expedition to the West Indies and the Conquest of Jamaica, 1654–1655* (London, 1900), appendix E, 144–169.

and too easy access to the trappings of power make them both lazy in business affairs and "too much addicted to expensive living, costly entertainments, dress, and equipage." Planters, who notoriously tend to overeat and overdrink, are also subject to hurricanelike fits of anger, which, though they soon subside "into a calm: yet they are not apt to forget or forgive substantial injuries. . . . They are fickle and desultory in their pursuits; though unshaken in their friendships."[48] Rather than attributing this intemperate behavior to intemperate consumption habits (which include the tendency to "swallow pepper without moderation") or to the effects of the slavery system and the uncertainty of plantation economics, Edward Long essays a remarkable psychological or psychosomatic explanation, based on the difference between the English and Jamaican climates. Climate affects the passions, just as the passions affect health. In Jamaica, "men are more *feelingly alive* to joy or inquietude" because "the nervous system is far more irritable than in a Northern climate." Jamaican whites, being "men of lively imaginations and great vivacity . . . are more liable than others to sudden and violent emotions of the mind, and their effects; such strong and sudden transports may actually throw them into acute diseases." Explosive emotions, though, rarely last long or strike deep. Far more dangerous, and sometimes mortal, are the effects of "the slow and durable passions." For Long, these include "solicitude, grief, stifled resentment, and vexation," but, above all, prolonged anxiety. "Anxiety," he concludes, "affects men in this country in proportion to their sensibility, and to its duration," hinting that, to his mind, Jamaican planters are either indifferent to fickle fortune or have little reason for concern.[49]

Yet Edward Long's own account undermines his meteorological determinism by showing how social and racial (if not economic) concerns contribute to what he regards as the planters' mental and social instability. Anxiety about slave uprisings is clear throughout the book, overshadowing the economic threats posed by the growing rift between England and the mainland colonies. Moreover, Long's distaste for Africans is clearly heightened not just by the danger of rebellion but by the way in which the propinquity of so many black female slaves contributes to the deplorable sexual promiscuity of the planters. "With a strong natural propensity to the other sex, they are not always the most chaste and faithful of husbands," he begins mildly enough. In earlier times (when white males greatly outnumbered white females) "the married men and bachlors used to carouze together almost every day at taverns; the spirit of gaming then prevailed to a great excess; and the name of a *family man* was held in the utmost derision." But even now, the formal marriage vow is treated very lightly, planters, whether they are married or

48. Long, *History of Jamaica*, II, 265.
49. *Ibid.*, 267, III, chap. 6, 542–543.

not, commonly keeping black or colored slave mistresses. "In a place where, by custom, so little restraint is laid on the passions," thunders Long in one of his most memorable passages, "many are the men, of every rank, quality, and degree here, who would much rather riot in these goatish embraces, than share the pure and lawful bliss derived from matrimonial, mutual love."[50]

Such behavior, says Long, produces not only "spurious offspring" and the dissipation of planter fortunes but also a greater number of spinster ladies than was usual in polite European society. Promiscuity was not an option for these supernumerary females—or, at least, its occurrence was unthinkable for white Jamaican males. All white creole ladies, though, according to Long, suffered from nonsexual intercourse with their slaves as well as from the habits of indolence that resulted from an overabundance of domestic servants. "Those, who have been bred up entirely in the sequestered country parts, and had no opportunity of forming themselves either by example or tuition, are truly to be pitied," writes Edward Long.

> We may see, in some of these places, a very fine young woman aukwardly dangling her arms with the air of a Negroe-servant, lolling almost the whole day upon beds or settees, her head muffled up with two or three handkerchiefs, her dress loose, and without stays. At noon, we find her employed in gobbling pepper-pot, seated on the floor, with her sable hand-maids around her. In the afternoon, she takes her *siesto* as usual; while two of these damsels refresh her face with the gentle breathings of the fan; and a third provokes the drowsy powers of Morpheus by delicious scratching on the sole of either foot. When she rouzes from slumber, her speech is whining, languid, and childish. When arrived at maturer years, the consciousness of her ignorance makes her abscond from the sight or conversation of every rational creature. Her ideas are narrowed to the ordinary subjects that pass before her, the business of the plantation, the tittle-tattle of the parish; the tricks, superstitions, diversions, and profligate discourses, of black servants, equally illiterate and unpolished.[51]

The most glaring deficiencies of plantocratic Jamaica for Edward Long are the weakness of the established church and the lack of good local schools for the children of the planters. His two chapters on these topics are among the

50. *Ibid.*, II, chap. 13, 281, 328. Edward Long must have been fairly exceptional for his class if during his 12 years in Jamaica he enjoyed nothing but connubial bliss. The practice of the majority is exemplified by Long's own paragon, Sir Charles Price, who was said by his political enemies to be one who "frequently Lyes with Black women" and who in his will manumitted "a Mulatto woman named Margaret residing at Rose Hall and her two Elder children," with a £10 annuity. Craton and Walvin, *A Jamaican Plantation*, 77, 94.

51. Long, *History of Jamaica*, II, chap. 13, 279.

most telling in his book. Since, according to Long, it had "always been a rule, in our West-India islands, to assimilate their religion, as well as laws, to those of the mother-country," he alleges a surely almost mythical parallelism between the history of religion in England and Jamaica. The Cromwellian divines accompanying the original expeditionary force were, by his account, "fanatical preachers; a sort of irregulars" who were soon superseded by "more orthodox divines" at the Restoration. The atmosphere was tolerant toward Catholicism and nonconformists alike under Charles II, but allegedly "popery became the favourite system in Jamaica" under the Catholic James II, coupled with a "spirit of persecution . . . against all non-conformists." However, the Glorious Revolution, according to Long, "happily expelled or subdued these superstititions, and gave the inhabitants, at one and the same time, the enjoyment of religious and civil liberty."[52]

The Anglican church was firmly established, though with the parish priests paid by legislated stipends, not tithes as in England, and with their functions defined and controlled by local statute. The governor in his role as viceroy was "supreme head of the provincial church," with the right to license, appoint, and suspend all clergymen. The claimed episcopal authority of the bishop of London, though, was hotly contested—or at least regarded as void. Could the bishop guarantee to send out good ministers "regularly trained at one of our English universities, and early versed in the knowledge of our religion," and were he able to control them once in Jamaica, his authority might be more acceptable. For while most Jamaican parsons were "worthy the public esteem and encouragement" and "would do honour to their profession in any part of England," there were some "who, in their moral conduct, would disgrace even the meanest of mankind." "Some labourers of the Lord's vineyard have at times been sent, who were much better qualified to be retailers of salt-fish, or boatswains to privateers, than ministers of the Gospel."[53]

Good local schools for white boys and girls depended on a numerous and sound local clergy as well as on the benevolence of individual planters and the support of plantocratic legislation. Despite Edward Long's praise for the Jamaican planters' testamentary generosity, none of these conditions existed sufficiently to provide an educational system in Jamaica approaching the level in New England, Virginia, or even Barbados. Between 1695 and 1770, seven schools had been established in various parts of Jamaica as the result of charitable bequests. According to Long, none had succeeded (though, curiously enough, at least four of these foundations still exist), largely because the planters preferred to send their children back to England for their

52. *Ibid.*, chap. 10, 234.
53. *Ibid.*, 234–240.

education. In the metropolis, he claimed, many acquired no more than mere literacy and a preference for London over Jamaica, and few boys returned to their "native country with any other acquisition than the art of swearing, drinking, dressing, gaming, and wenching."[54]

Instead, Edward Long made thoughtful and detailed proposals for a centrally located boarding school for Jamaican planters' sons (to be situated at Old Woman's Savanna in his own parish of Clarendon) and a "seminary" for their daughters. Planters' sons with the ability and means to enter the learned professions would still expect to go to Europe, but, for the majority destined to be planters in their turn, their education should be completed locally, and be both practical and relevant.

> The articles to be taught here should be restricted to reading, writing, arithmetic (including book-keeping), the Spanish and French languages, surveying, mechanics, together perhaps with such instructions in agriculture and botany as relate to the improvement of the vegetable productions of the island. The pupils might likewise be taught music, dancing, fencing, and the military manual exercise, to qualify them better for a course of life which requires agility and strength of body, and occasionally the use of arms.[55]

Long also suggested that "a certain number of white servants should be constantly kept, in proportion to the number of boarders, that the latter might not, by a too early familiarity and intercourse with the Negroes, adopt their vices and broken English." As for the girls,

> they require not the elements of Greek, Latin, or Hebrew; nor the precepts of the university, nor the theory of the sciences, mechanic arts, or learned professions. Reading, writing, arithmetic, needlework, dancing, and music, will, with the additional helps of their own genius, prepare them for becoming good wives and mothers. . . . The utility of a boarding-school for these girls, where their number might admit of employing the ablest teachers, where they might be weaned from the Negroe dialect, improved by emulation, and gradually habituated to a modest and polite behaviour, needs not, I think, any argument to prove it.[56]

Nonetheless, though some of his precepts may have filtered into the practice of the few good schools for white creoles—Manning's, Wolmer's, and Rusea's in Jamaica, Lodge (Codrington's) and Harrison's in Barbados—

54. *Ibid.*, chap. 12, 248.
55. *Ibid.*, chap. 12, 254.
56. *Ibid.*, 250.

Edward Long's educational arguments did not prevail. Unlike the mainland colonists, West Indian planters continued to depend upon the metropole for ordinary schooling for their sons, if not their daughters, as well as for university and professional education.

Edward Long's ideal planter was clearly a transplanted, and improved, English country gentleman, and Long deplored those local conditions that made such a type hard to realize. Yet, in the central paradox of his work, it was not local conditions in themselves that militated against the creation of a native gentry, but the continuing attractions of metropolitan society that led most planters to become absentees as soon, and for as long, as possible. For Edward Long and other planter-writers, as for modern commentators from Frank W. Pitman to Orlando Patterson, absenteeism was an overriding and cumulative evil that ensured that plantocratic society never became more than an incomplete imitation or a degraded version of English society.[57]

The nature and value of the triangle trade based on West Indian plantations as well as the continuous need for naval and military defense ensured that all linkages between colonies and metropole would be far stronger than for the thirteen colonies. But West Indian conditions also ensured that most West Indian planters saw their residence at the source of their wealth on the tropical periphery as, at best, a necessary evil. Like Shakespeare's Prospero in *The Tempest*, having endured their exile as best they could, they felt destined to return to enjoy a comfortable retirement in the land of their birth or roots. Life in an English country house set in a few acres of calm countryside was infinitely preferable to that on a West Indian sugar plantation, though it extend to thousands of acres of stunning landscape. This was true even for relatively calm and civilized Barbados and Antigua but applied with particular force to incompletely tamed, perhaps untamable, colonies like Jamaica, the Ceded Islands, Trinidad, and Guiana. As wonderfully conveyed in the first pages of Richard Hughes's novel *A High Wind in Jamaica*, beyond the tropical luxuriance and sloth-inducing almost seasonless and equinoctial climate lurked the constant threat of sudden danger: disease, drought, flood, hurricane, earthquake, foreign invasion, slave insurrection. And for white children there were the more subtle and insidious dangers of corruption by the slavery system and too close an association with Negro slaves.[58]

57. See, particularly, Pitman, *British West Indies*, 30–41; Ragatz, *Fall of the Planter Class*, 42–67; Orlando Patterson, *The Sociology of Slavery: An Analysis of the Origins, Development, and Structure of Negro Slave Society in Jamaica* (London, 1967), 26–51, 278.

58. Richard Hughes, *A High Wind in Jamaica* (London, 1931; Long, *History of Jamaica*, II, chap. 13, 254, 276–280. The interrelationship between slaves, children, masters, and parents in plantation slave societies, particularly the way that the role,

Edward Long reckoned in 1774 that three-quarters of the planters' children were sent to England for their education, of whom no more than two-thirds ever returned. Though partly the result of the prevailing primogeniture system (which gave younger sons and planters' sisters little incentive to return to the colonies) and having positive effects in providing valuable political and economic connections in the metropole, it represented a steady drain from the creole elite—a kind of unnatural selection in which, generally, the most successful left and the least successful stayed. Moreover, as time went on, to those successful plantation owners who spent all or most of their time in England was added a slowly rising tide of socioeconomic refugees, as declining sugar profits led to the bankruptcy of some plantations and the harsher exploitation of the rest.[59]

The most fortunate absentees were those who through ancient gentry or strong mercantile connections, by judicious dynastic marriage, or by the redeployment of their West Indian fortune were able, first, to keep an equal footing in England and the Caribbean and then, in due course, to escape their West Indian ties altogether. Yet an equal number never fitted the role of absentee—misfits in England and the islands alike, and even tortured in absence by a nostalgia as powerful as the longing that had drawn them "home." Codringtons, Draxes, Pinneys, Pennants, and Lascelleses fitted back comfortably into the classes from which they had sprung, their wealth and status reinforced by West Indian profits and lateral reinvestments.[60] But many more West Indian nabobs faced envy, ridicule, and social ostracism, with rejection often intensified by subsequent economic failure. The famous anecdote of the inquiry of George III about an absentee planter traversing the countryside near Weymouth in a style far grander than his own tells its own tale of the self-defeating need to flaunt new wealth.[61] Clare Taylor's article on the absentee Nathaniel Phillips of Saint Thomas, Jamaica; Sle-

---

status, and relationships of children changed once they became adults, remains a challenging topic. See, for example, Mark Golden, "The Effects of Slavery on Citizen Households and Children: Aeschylus, Aristophanes, and Athens," *Historical Reflections / Réflexions historiques*, XV (1988), 455–475.

59. Long, *History of Jamaica*, I, 438; Pitman, *British West Indies*, 34; Ragatz, *Fall of the Planter Class*, 286–457; Craton, *Sinews of Empire*, 243–247.

60. Such families are best traced through their genealogical bible, *Burke's . . . Peerage, Baronetage, and Knightage*, though it is almost axiomatic that inclusion precludes any mention of a West Indian slave plantation connection. In general, studies of West Indian absentees tend to be fragmented and skewed, if not piously evasive. Richard Pares's superb study of the Pinneys, *A West-India Fortune* (London, 1950), remains a pioneer without comparable successors, and a general study of West Indian absentees as a class remains a great social history yet to be written.

61. "Sugar, sugar, hey?—all *that* sugar? How are the duties, hey, Pitt, how are the duties?" Quoted in Richard Pares, *Merchants and Planters*, Economic History Review Supplements, no. 4 (Cambridge, 1970), 38.

bech, Pembrokeshire; and Portman Square, London, shows that some of the wealthiest absentees, particularly if they had emerged from mercantile ranks, spent most of their time in England, not in high society, but socializing with their fellow absentees.[62]

A few absentees overreached themselves into gross ostentation, lapsed into social deviation, or exhibited behavior bordering on madness. The most extreme case was that of William Beckford, homosexual author of the gothic extravaganza *Vathek*, who dissipated a million pounds of Alderman Beckford's Jamaican fortune on the folly of Fonthill Abbey. But even the Prices of Worthy Park, Jamaica, and Trengwainton, Cornwall, kept a pack of hounds and drove a quarter-mile to church by coach, and Sir Rose Price (1764–1835) signalized his absence from his five hundred slaves and the steady erosion of his West Indian income by a tyrannical paternalism toward his family, explosions of anger against encroaching neighbors, and tantrums in print directed against parliamentary abolitionists. Other absentees exhibited schizophrenia, awkwardly combining a philistine ostentation with self-effacement, as if proud of their wealth but ashamed of its source. That notorious family autocrat Edward Barrett, the father of Elizabeth Barrett Browning, for example, in the words of John Carey, was "proud and withdrawn . . . the house he built at Ledbury reflected both traits. A palatial Turkish affair bristling with minarets and ablaze inside with brasswork and crimson flock, it was stuck in a hollow so as to be invisible from the surrounding countryside. Its name, Hope End, perhaps referred to its owner's gloom over the impending abolition of slavery, which, he saw, would ruin sugar profits."[63]

An unjustly neglected study of the Barrett family and its fortune by Jeannette Marks (1938) suggests the deep ambivalence of the English Barretts toward Jamaica and a nostalgia for a style of life passed beyond recall. Margaret Forster, in her life of Elizabeth Barrett Browning, recounts the touching story of Edward Barrett, when shipped off to school in England at the age of seven, sending back to his mother in Jamaica as a keepsake a glove soaked in his tears. Karl Watson tells a similar tale of poignant homesickness for Barbados (an island in which, of course, absenteeism was much less an institution than in Jamaica) expressed in a letter from a young man at Oxford to his brother at Cambridge: "Torn from the arms of a fond and indulgent Parent," wrote John Pollard in 1772, "it seems dark and gloomy,

62. Clare Taylor, "The Journal of an Absentee Proprietor, Nathaniel Phillips of Slebech," *Journal of Caribbean History*, XVIII (1984), 67–82.

63. Alexander Boyd, *England's Wealthiest Son: A Study of William Beckford* (London, 1962); Brian Fothergill, *Beckford of Fonthill* (London, 1979); Craton and Walvin, *A Jamaican Plantation*, 184–207; John Carey, review of *Elizabeth Barrett Browning*, by Margaret Forster, *Sunday Times* (London), May 26, 1988, 1.

situated as I am amidst strangers and aliens."[64] At a deeper level yet, one might characterize Edward Long's impassioned plea for an idealized resident Jamaican plantocracy as the anguished nostalgia of an unwilling absentee. And what is one to make of the seemingly incongruous insertion in an ardently proslavery work by his fellow Jamaican plantocrat and absentee, Bryan Edwards, of a fervent "Ode to the Sable Venus," with an almost erotic illustration in the style of William Blake?[65]

IV

The sixty years between the outbreak of the American War of Independence and the ending of British slavery undoubtedly saw great changes in the West Indian planters' world. The tide of absenteeism that Edward Long deplored was not reversed, and later plantocratic writers like Bryan Edwards complained of the decline of profits under the pressure of rising costs and falling produce prices. At the same time, West Indian planters increasingly felt under siege from metropolitan economists and philanthropists who attacked both the system of protection for plantation products and the institution of slavery and gradually swayed a majority in the imperial Parliament. Taking the planters' complaints at their face value, many modern scholars have characterized the age, in the terms of Lowell Joseph Ragatz, as that of "the fall of the planter class in the British Caribbean."[66]

Later scholarship has projected a far more positive and creative image. Elsa Goveia has redefined "slave society" to include "the whole community based on slavery, including masters and freedmen as well as slaves," and Edward Brathwaite, in direct contradiction to the wholly negative analysis of Orlando Patterson, has convincingly stressed the way that the era between 1770 and 1820 saw the creation of an authentic "creole society," in which slaves and black freedmen participated along with the whites, albeit in special ways.[67] This creolization process—defined by Brathwaite as the

64. Jeannette Marks, *The Family of the Barrett: A Colonial Romance* (New York, 1938); Forster, *Elizabeth Barrett Browning*, 4–5; Karl Watson, *The Civilised Island: Barbados, A Social History, 1750–1816* (Barbados, 1979), 45–46.

65. Edwards, *West Indies* (1806 ed.), II, 218–221. David Brion Davis, *The Problem of Slavery in the Age of Revolution, 1770–1823* (Ithaca, N.Y., 1975), 194–195.

66. The "Decline Thesis" of Ragatz was most famously adopted by Eric Williams in *Capitalism and Slavery* (London, 1944; rpt., 1964), the analysis and criticism of which has been something of an academic industry in recent years. See, for example, Seymour Drescher, *Econocide: British Slavery in the Era of Abolition* (Pittsburgh, Pa., 1977); and "The Decline Thesis of British Slavery since Econocide," *Slavery and Abolition*, VII (1986), 3–24.

67. Goveia, *Slave Society in the British Leeward Islands*; Edward Brathwaite, *The Development of Creole Society in Jamaica, 1770–1820* (Oxford, 1971).

emergence of an indigenous "great tradition" through the melding of other "great traditions" (African as well as European) in the new environment—was one that plantocratic writers either deplored or failed to recognize, one that the abolitionist commentators opposed to them derided or condemned. It was, therefore, the later newcomers and nonplantocratic, nonabolitionist visitors to the West Indies who provided a truer picture than those men like Long and Bryan Edwards, James Ramsay and Thomas Coke with a deeper commitment and vested interests.[68]

Such relatively disinterested persons were the Jamaican governor's wife, Maria Nugent (1801–1805), the doctor accompanying a military expedition to the Lesser Antilles, George Pinckard (1805–1806), the new planter's wife in Saint Vincent and Trinidad, Mrs. A. C. Carmichael (1807–1823), and the absentee dilettante, gothic novelist (and friend of William Beckford), Matthew Gregory "Monk" Lewis (1815–1817).[69] These visitors sometimes pointed out, with contempt, distaste, or glee, the imitative and incomplete aspects of planter society. But they also depicted, if unconsciously, the existence of a distinctive creole style and identity, owing much to the environment and local conditions and a declining amount to metropolitan influences.

Lady Nugent and Dr. Pinckard, writing in wartime, gave good accounts of the British West Indies as military outposts. Officers of the garrisons and stationed naval vessels were welcome recruits to the provincial polite society of the colonial capitals—whose climactic winter season, with its round of dinners, parties, balls, militia parades, and official opening and closing of the Assembly both describe well. Public entertainments, such as the theater, were found no better or worse than—and little different from—those in an English provincial town. But such spectacles as the Christmas *Junkanoo*, where the whites were avid spectators to the masked carnival of the slaves, and the all-too-frequent funerals of prominent whites, in which the roles of participants and spectators were almost reversed, provided exotic variations.[70]

68. Long, *History of Jamaica*; Edwards, *West Indies*; James Ramsay, *An Essay on the Treatment and Conversion of African Slaves in the British Sugar Colonies* (London, 1784); Thomas Coke, *A History of the West Indies . . .*, 3 vols. (Liverpool, London, 1808–1811). For further plantocratic and abolitionist writings, see the indispensable bibliography by Lowell Joseph Ragatz, comp., *A Guide for the Study of British Caribbean History, 1763–1834, Including the Abolition and Emancipation Movements* (Washington, D.C., 1932).

69. Wright, ed., *Lady Nugent's Journal*; George Pinckard, *Notes on the West Indies . . .*, 3 vols. (London, 1806; rpt., 1970); [A. C.] Carmichael, *Domestic Manners and Social Condition of the White, Coloured, and Negro Population of the West Indies*, 2 vols. (London, 1833; rpt., 1970); Matthew Gregory Lewis, *Journal of a West India Proprietor, Kept during a Residence in the Island of Jamaica* (London, 1834).

70. Pinckard, *Notes*, I, 239–330; Wright, ed., *Nugent's Journal*, 31–53, 130–139, 182–190, 218–221.

Both Nugent and Pinckard had a good eye for the formal and domestic architecture and for the layout and appearance of towns and plantations in the different islands. Jamaica boasted the largest of the few towns of the British West Indies. Kingston (with thirty thousand people in 1800) was formally laid out on a gridiron pattern like a Spanish colonial city, and Spanish Town, the capital (with seventy-five hundred inhabitants), focused on a quite splendid and symbolic central square, with the Georgian porticoes of Government House and the facing Assembly building at right angles to the Supreme Court and Record Office—the latter fronted by a magnificent rotunda, under which stood a statue of Admiral George Rodney, Jamaica's naval savior in 1782, incongruously sporting a Roman toga. Bridgetown, Barbados, and most of the other colonial capitals, in contrast, were the chief commercial entrepôts, located on the southwestern leeward coasts of each island, with substantial stone warehouses fronting a combustible jumble of wooden houses and the official buildings of the colonial government, grown up with little if any formal planning.

Bridgetown's architecture, at least before the devastating fires of the eighteenth century, showed few concessions to tropical conditions, presenting in the fine panoramic painting by the Dutchman Samuel Copen (1695) the image of a transplanted Amsterdam or Bristol. Among Barbadian country houses there were also those that retained an imported aspect, such as the original three-storied Drax Hall, the elaborate parsonage planned for Saint John (1679), or the still surviving great house Nicholas Abbey, with its plastered stonework, gable ends, dormers, glazed windows, three stories, and four chimneys, forever like a small Jacobean manor house. By 1800, however, most town and country houses had been adapted to the local climate, style of life, and materials—creolized. The governor-general of Barbados still lives in the magnificent stone mansion, Fontabelle, originally built for the Royalist planter Henry Walrond (perhaps to a design by Richard Ligon).[71] But Monk Lewis described the standard Jamaican plantation great house when he described his own residence at Cornwall in Westmoreland parish:

> The houses here are generally built and arranged to one and the same model. My own is of wood, partly raised upon pillars; it consists of a single floor: a long gallery, called a piazza, terminated at each end by a square room, runs the whole length of the house. On each side of the piazza is a range of bed-rooms, and the porticoes of the two fronts form two more rooms, with balustrades, and flights of steps descending to the lawn. The whole house is virandoed with shifting Venetian blinds to admit air; except that one of the end rooms has sash-windows on account of the rains, which, when they arrive, are so heavy, and shift

71. Dunn, *Sugar and Slaves*, 287, 294–295.

> with the wind so suddenly from one side to the other, that all the blinds are obliged to be kept closed.[72]

A later visitor added a fuller description of the interior and furnishings of a typical Jamaican planter's house. The large central hall

> forms the principal sitting room; and, from its shape, admits the cooling breeze to sweep through it, whenever there is a breath of air. . . . This large and cool apartment is furnished with sofas, ottomans, tables, chairs, etc., not differing from ours; but there are no fire places, nor any carpet. Instead of the latter the floor is made of the most beautiful of the native woods, in the selection of which much taste is displayed, as also in the arrangement, so that the various colours of the wood may harmonise or contrast well with each other. Mahogany, green-heart, bread nut, and blood-heart are among the trees whose timber is employed for floors. Great hardness is an indispensable requisite in the wood used, and capability of receiving a high polish, which is given and maintained with great labour. Scarcely anything surprises an European more than to tread on floors as beautifully polished as the finest tables of our drawing rooms.[73]

Such a modest but elegant, commodious, and fitting wooden building was the rule, even if the complex of mill, factory, and even slave hospital that it overlooked were built of stone by imported masons in a grandiose Palladian Georgian style. Such a contrast is still to be seen at Good Hope, the centerpiece of John Tharp's small empire of seven contiguous sugar plantations in Trelawny parish.[74]

The elegance of plantation great houses depended, of course, very much on the time that the planter-owners spent in them and whether they were

72. Quoted in Brathwaite, *Creole Society*, 123.

73. Philip Gosse, *A Naturalist's Sojourn in Jamaica* (London, 1851), quoted *ibid.*, 124, 126.

74. Michael Craton, *Searching for the Invisible Man: Slaves and Plantation Life in Jamaica* (Cambridge, Mass., 1978), 6, 34; Barry Higman, *Jamaica Surveyed: Plantation Maps and Plans of the Eighteenth and Nineteenth Centuries* (Kingston, Jamaica, 1988). A general scholarly study of plantocratic architecture (as of material culture at large) remains to be written; the existing literature, largely aimed at the tourist industry, is mainly fragmented, antiquarian, and picturesque. Even the few general studies stress the local influences of European models. See, for example, Angus W. Acworth, *Treasure in the Caribbean: A First Study of Georgian Buildings in the British West Indies* (London, 1949); David Buisseret, *Historic Architecture of the Caribbean* (London, 1960); Florita Z. L. De Irizarry, *Architecture in the Caribbean / West Indies: A Bibliography* (Monticello, Ill., 1982). One imaginative exception, attempting to describe the creolization of West Indian architecture through the marriage of Palladian and other European styles with indigenous forms, especially the Amerindian *ajoupa* house, is John Newel Lewis, *Ajoupa: Architecture of the Caribbean, Trinidad's Heritage* (Trinidad, 1983).

married men with an active circle of local family and friends. Absentees' houses, or those owned by hardworking bachelor planters, were usually bare and dusty, surrounded by unkempt gardens, if not also overrun by disorderly slave domestics. Many resident owners, however, prided themselves on their furniture and tableware, their books and pictures, as well as their laden tables and well-stocked cellar, their well-trimmed lawns, burgeoning orchards and kitchen gardens, their carriages and horses—as much as their large retinue of liveried servants. As indexes of the commitment of Jamaican planters to an elegant residential life, Douglas Hall has pointed out the widespread cultivation of flowers and purely ornamental shrubs, and Barry Higman has found that the average area of land set aside for great houses and their surrounding (and insulating) gardens continued to grow until the 1780s and declined only from the last decade of the eighteenth century. Likewise, there was a steady increase in the trappings of polite society. Printing and the first newspaper in the British West Indies, the weekly *Jamaica Courant*, had been introduced as early as 1718, and by 1800 the newspapers aspired beyond mere gazettes. Spanish Town boasted its first permanent theater as early as 1776, and by that time there were circulating libraries, a literary society, and an Agricultural Society as well as social clubs for planters and other gentlemen in most of the towns—a great advance on the taverns that had been the planters' earlier meeting places. Yet Jamaican planter society, particularly when striving its hardest in Spanish Town during the Christmas season, continued to seem philistine and provincial, even to visitors from Barbados, Charleston, Philadelphia, or Boston, let alone London.[75]

Lady Nugent traversed Jamaica with her husband in almost Elizabethan state but for the most part found plantation social life as dull, and sometimes as "disgusting," as that in the colonial capital. Ill-mannered aristocrats, such as the bachelor ex-governor Lord Balcarres, and ostentatious nouveaux riches such as John Shand of Kellits (whose plantation buildings were notably grand and who had ten children by his black slave housekeeper) she found especially distasteful. But she did develop a grudging respect, even affection, for the greatest resident Jamaican magnate of the time, Simon Taylor, Sr. (1740–1813). Educated at Eton, he was (like John Shand and many other resident planters) unmarried, preferring to live "principally with overseers of estates and masters of merchant vessels" and distributing his sexual attentions between the slave mothers of the mulatto families he maintained on each of his many estates. Custos (that is, chief magistrate) of the parish of Saint Thomas-in-the-East and major general in the militia, this

75. Douglas G. Hall, *Planters, Farmers, and Gardeners in Eighteenth Century Jamaica* (Mona, 1988); Higman, *Jamaica Surveyed*, 231–242; Brathwaite, *Creole Society*, 105–150, 266–295.

grand patriarch, despite his "most extraordinary manner," was said to be "well informed and a warm friend to those he takes by the hand. He is also very hospitable and civilised occasionally, but is said to be most inveterate in his dislikes."[76]

Many later commentators echoed Edward Long in denigrating the indolence, inanity, and drawling accents of the planters' ladies and described with varying degrees of accuracy and malice the planters' accustomed heavy drinking and gourmandizing, their casual dress and manners, and their bucolic recreations. But it needed the sharp-eyed visitors who lived for extended periods close to the daily life of the plantations, such as Monk Lewis and Mrs. Carmichael, to sense the creole essence of these characteristics.

Far from being a drawling version of bad English (or in francophone or Dutch-speaking colonies, bad French or Dutch), the everyday language of West Indian whites was fast becoming a true creole language. Subtly different from island to island, or even between different districts, it was a parlance common to all classes and races and passed the dominant language through an African filter of structure, inflection, and accentuation and added vocabulary from the native peoples and other European languages as well as from the far more numerous African languages. The result was a wonderfully flexible and expressive lingua franca, associated with rich resources of wit and wisdom drawn from Africa and Europe, forever augmented by the comedy, tragedies, and contradictions of everyday West Indian life. The distillations of this verbal wealth were the "Negro Proverbs" that even a member of the Jamaican plantocracy like Frank Cundall could admire, recount, and adapt—though not always fully recognizing their social content: "Sleep hab no massa"; "Massa horse, massa grass"; "Neger tief half a bit, Bockra tief whole estate"; "When cockroach gib party, him no ax fowl"; "Fowl 'cratch up too much a dutty, him run de risk a findin' him gramma keleton"; "Ebry John Crow think him pickney white"; "Time longer dan rope."[77]

West Indian creole food and drink likewise mixed local with imported

76. Wright, ed., *Nugent's Journal*, 318–319.

77. Ian F. Hancock, "A Repertory of Pidgin and Creole Languages," in Albert Valdman, ed., *Pidgin and Creole Linguistics* (Bloomington, Ind., 1977), 362–391; Douglas Taylor, "The Origin of West Indian Creole Languages: Evidence from Grammatical Categories," *American Anthropologist*, n.s., LXV (1963), 800–814; R. B. Le Page and David De Camp, *Jamaican Creole: A Historical Introduction* (London, 1960); Frederic G. Cassidy, *Jamaica Talk: Three Hundred Years of the English Language in Jamaica* (London, 1961); Izett Anderson and Frank Cundall, eds., *Jamaica Proverbs and Sayings*, 3d ed. (Shannon, 1972; orig. publ. 1910); Martha Warren Beckwith, ed., *Jamaica Proverbs*, 2d ed. (New York, 1970; orig. publ. 1925).

ingredients and methods of preparation and consumption. Planters drank wine from Madeira and the Mediterranean and also imported Burton beer from England. But favorite beverages also included sangaree (that is, the Spanish sangria), made from imported wine and local sugar, citrus, and spices, and several kinds of toddy with partly African origins, as well as planters' punches concocted from rum and other purely local ingredients. The Lucullan planters' meals, which feature in nearly all travelers' accounts, may have given a prominent place to imported dainties and retained on the surface an English tone (roast beef being almost a sine qua non). But the majority of the dishes and their ingredients were not English and were locally produced: an infinite variety and number of permutations based upon native American as well as African, Asian, and European starches, meats, and fruits. The exotic fame of West Indian pineapples, turtles, and certain spices spread back across the Atlantic along with tobacco, sugar, rum, and cocoa, but visitors from Europe were introduced to innumerable new delights. Especially in Trinidad, Guiana, or Belize, as evidence that they were on the outer periphery and as a kind of passage rite, newcomers were also often proffered varieties of wild meat, including alligator, iguana, armadillo, agouti, or manicou.

Another notable creole crossover occurred in music and dance, for which West Indian whites and blacks shared a common enthusiasm. To a certain extent the music and dancing styles were truly syncretic, with Negro musicians performing on fiddles and trumpets as well as banjos and drums, for slave and white creole dances alike. But the way in which black slaves adapted European dancing modes such as the quadrille evinced less amazement than the manner in which even at their formal dances the white creoles performed with a fervor and grace that seemed practically African. "Even if the music of the violins were better than it is," wrote John Stewart of Jamaica in 1823, "it would be spoiled by the uncouth and deafening noise of the drums, which the negro musicians think indispensable, and which the dancers strangely continue to tolerate."[78]

The most absolute form of creole syncresis occurred, though, in sexual intercourse. All commentators touched on the subject of miscegenation, varying only in the degree of their delicacy and ignorance, and it was in fact, in the long run, a more potent shaping factor in West Indian society than planter absenteeism. Miscegenation and the consequent increase in the number of mulattoes, slave or free, varied in reverse proportion to the ratio of whites in each colonial population. Thus it was least in civilized Barbados, with its relatively high proportion of whites and, conversely, probably great-

78. J[ohn] Stewart, *A View of the Past and Present State of the Island of Jamaica* . . . (Edinburgh, 1823), 207.

est in a colony such as Belize, with very few whites, and among them a disproportionately high proportion of males. Yet even in Jamaica, the incidence of miscegenation was always high among all ranks of white males—a function of the whites' exercise of power relations, of the social value to black women of bearing lighter-colored children, and (as Edward Long argued) of the loose bonds of European conventions, as much as of disproportionate numbers. Whatever the causes, miscegenation (as well as the coupling of coloreds themselves) led to an exponential increase in the number and importance of Jamaican free coloreds (all free coloreds and blacks gaining full civil rights in 1830), from 6,000 in 1790 to 35,000 in 1838—at a time when the white population was actually falling from 20,000 to 15,000. In Barbados, on the other hand, the number of free coloreds rose only from 1,000 to 7,000 over the same period while the number of whites stayed more or less stable around 15,000—representing some 15 percent of the total population, compared with less than 5 percent in Jamaica.[79]

Almost as surprising and shocking as were creole ways in general to outside commentators were the ease and rapidity with which English newcomers assumed them. Mrs. Carmichael went so far as to claim that anyone who survived a single Trinidadian rainy season was immediately creolized.[80] The experience of the Jamaican newcomer and eventual planter Thomas Thistlewood (referred to elsewhere in this volume) would argue for a far slower and more traumatic transition—with the enthusiastic and licentious young overseer surviving horrific sieges of venereal disease as well as social and economic disappointments before settling down in relative quiet if not contentment as a small planter in later middle age, wedded for life in all but law to his remarkable black slave mistress Phibbah, mother of his mulatto only son. Perhaps in the Thistlewood case—which was almost certainly far more common in Jamaica than has previously been recognized—the best analogy was provided, unconsciously, by Monk Lewis. In discussing the virtues of importing British terriers to reduce the rat population of Jamaica, Lewis remarked, "Those from England were blinded by the sun, but their puppies adapt and impose their domination over the rat population." As Barbara Friesen has suggested: "The same is true of the British settlers themselves. They adapted to West Indian ways of life, yet had to preserve their dominance over the black population in order to survive."[81]

79. Barry Higman, *Slave Populations of the British Caribbean, 1807–1834* (Baltimore, 1984), 401–702; Jerome S. Handler, *The Unappropriated People: Freedmen in the Slave Society of Barbados* (Baltimore, 1974); Gad J. Heuman, *Between Black and White: Race, Politics, and the Free Coloreds in Jamaica, 1792–1865* (Westwood, Conn., 1981).

80. Carmichael, *Domestic Manners*, 315.

81. Douglas G. Hall, *In Miserable Slavery: Thomas Thistlewood in Jamaica,*

V

The world of the West Indian planters is now everywhere part of the past. Yet it did in many places survive the ending of formal slavery and has left remnants not only wherever sugar plantations have lasted. For the relative persistence of the world the planters made depended not solely on the institution of Negro slavery or even the existence of sugar and other plantations but on the extent to which the planters were able and willing, and had the time, to adapt to West Indian conditions and modify the institutions, attitudes, and behavior that they had brought with them, to create not only a resident creole ruling class but also an effective creole culture. In some respects and in some areas, especially where class relations have come to count for more than racial divisions, the legacies have run even deeper, to help shape the more democratic, diversified, multiracial West Indian societies of today, including the ways in which they continue to regard and relate to the original metropolitan homeland and its core culture.

At least two visitors from Victorian England, Philip Gosse in 1851 and Anthony Trollope in 1859, wrote of the Jamaican plantocracy as if it had survived slave emancipation almost intact. Perhaps, indeed, it was easier for a planter to assume a gentlemanly style now that he was no longer living cheek by jowl with his slaves. "He was, I may say still is," wrote Trollope of the typical Jamaican landowner,

> the prince of planters—the true aristocrat of the West Indies. . . . He has so many of the characteristics of an English country gentleman that he does not strike the Englishman as a strange being. He has his pedigree, and his family house, and his domain around him. He shoots and fishes, and some few years since, in the good days, he even kept a pack of hounds. He is in the commission of the peace, and as such has much to do. . . . In Jamaica . . . there is scope for a country gentleman. They have their counties and their parishes. . . . They have county society, local balls, and local race-meetings. They have local politics, local quarrels, and strong old-fashioned local friendships. In all these things one feels oneself to be much nearer to England in Jamaica than in any other of the West Indian islands.
>
> A better fellow cannot be found anywhere than a gentleman of Jamaica, or one with whom it is easier to live on pleasant terms. He is generally hospitable, affable and generous; easy to know and pleasant when

---

1750–1786 (Basingstoke, 1988); Lewis quoted in Brathwaite, *Creole Society*; Barbara Friesen, senior essay, University of Waterloo, April 1988.

known; not given much to deep erudition but capable of talking with ease on most subjects of conversation; fond of society, and of pleasure, if you choose to call it so; but not generally addicted to low pleasures. He is often witty, and has a sharp side to his tongue if occasion be given to use it. He is not generally, I think, a hard-working man.[82]

As recently as the 1970s, the authors of the tercentenary history of Worthy Park found the white owner-managers of the estate, though far harder-working, replicating much of the style of life and behavior and many of the attitudes of their eighteenth-century predecessors—though the last of the original owners, the Prices, had left more than a hundred years earlier and they themselves came from altogether humbler, technocratic stock.[83] Anthony Trollope, indeed, wrote his somewhat overblown praise of the planters just before the event that led to the Prices' final desertion, the loss by the Jamaican plantocracy of its self-legislating Assembly, which came in the wake of the most serious popular uprising since the last great slave rebellion of 1831. Broadly speaking, the first century after slave emancipation in 1838 belonged increasingly to the brown Jamaican middle class (descendants of that class of mulattoes, slave and free, that Edward Long had feared), as the subsequent half-century (since 1938) has belonged, progressively, to the black majority. Sugar collapsed to a nadir by 1900, and though it revived dramatically during and after World War II, it was produced by Cuban-style central factories (now almost all nationalized, and losing money), with half of the cane grown by small cane farmers, the majority of them little more than peasant cultivators. In this world, the old-style planters no longer have a place.[84]

Elsewhere, the world that the British West Indian planters made (or attempted to make) withered and disappeared even more rapidly and completely, for a variety of reasons. In some islands of the Lesser Antilles, failure of the sugar plantations was even more comprehensive than in Jamaica, resulting in, and accelerated by, an even greater exodus of whites. This is the world of Jean Rhys of Dominica, author, out of her own experiences, of the most haunting novel of plantocratic decline, nostalgia, and schizophrenic madness, *Wide Sargasso Sea*.[85] Perhaps the most extreme example of the decayed plantation colony is Antigua, once the second-ranked of sugar

82. Anthony Trollope, *The West Indies and the Spanish Main* (London, 1860; rpt., 1968), 94–98.

83. Craton and Walvin, *A Jamaican Plantation*, 259–285; Michael Craton, *Searching for the Invisible Man*, 332–336.

84. Clinton V. Black, *The Story of Jamaica*, 2d ed. (London, 1965), 171–214; Hurwitz and Hurwitz, *Jamaica*, 134–214.

85. Jean Rhys, *Wide Sargasso Sea* (London, 1966); and *Smile Please: An Unfinished Autobiography* (London, 1979); Francis Wyndham and Diana Melly, eds., *Jean Rhys: Letters, 1931–1966* (London, 1984).

colonies, which now neither grows sugar nor possesses a measurable native white population. The last plantation colonies acquired by the British, in contrast, have continued to produce sugar down to the present as independent countries. But their late acquisition, their crown colony status, and their more overtly capitalistic operations (with steam-powered central factories run by managers and technicians and often owned by merchant bankers or limited companies), coupled with the ex-slaves' preference for peasant farming or town life over plantation labor, determined that they would not develop a true plantocracy and that the plantation labor force would consist of a new ethnic ingredient, the indentured workers brought in from the Indian subcontinent between 1835 and 1917. Trinidad, with the richest ethnic and cultural mix of all, did diversify—at first mainly into cocoa, then to oil—and produced a modern, if fragile, economy and complex new class structure. But British Guiana (Guyana) always remained drastically underdeveloped as well as racially splintered—its huge interior an almost unexplored tropical wilderness into the twentieth century.[86]

Other British West Indian colonies were equally peripheral, or marginal, in different senses: the imperial appendixes or footnotes of the Turks and Caicos Islands, British Virgin Islands, and Cayman Islands; Belize, which graduated from cutting logwood to cutting mahogany, to near oblivion, embodiment of the tristes tropiques; and the Bahamas, where the failure of Loyalist cotton plantations between 1783 and 1820 merely punctuated the history of a colonial backwater with an episode that encapsulated the larger history of British West Indian plantations, played out at ten times the speed. In certain respects, however, the Bahamas, like Bermuda, differed from other marginal island colonies. A large white minority, shifting laterally from often shady maritime activities and failed plantations but continuing to monopolize the land, created a white mercantile oligarchy, which continued to dominate the black ex-slaves and persuaded the imperial authorities to permit the retention of the self-legislating and far from democratic Houses of Assembly. Most ironical of all, though the Bahamas became an independent nation in 1973, Bermuda, England's first overseas island colony, by a majority vote of its people, remains a British dependency 380 years after its foundation.[87]

86. Gregson Davis and Margo Davis, *Antigua Black: Portrait of an Island People* (San Francisco, 1973); Donald Wood, *Trinidad in Transition: The Years after Slavery* (London, 1964); Alan H. Adamson, *Sugar without Slaves: The Political Economy of British Guiana, 1838–1904* (New Haven, Conn., 1972).

87. The Turks and Caicos Islands, indeed, rate as yet little more than passing references in the histories of the Bahamas and Jamaica. For the other territories, see Isaac Dookhan, *A History of the British Virgin Islands* (Epping, 1975); Narda Dobson, *A History of Belize* (London, 1973); C. H. Grant, *The Making of Modern Belize: Politics, Society, and British Colonialism in Central America* (Cambridge, 1976); O. Nigel Bolland, *The Formation of a Colonial Society: Belize, from Conquest to Crown Colony* (Baltimore, 1977); Michael Craton, *A History of the Baha-*

The colonial history of Barbados was forty-three years shorter than Bermuda's (1627–1965), but this tiny modern nation remains the salient relic of the planters' world of the old British Empire. The longest-lived of the English sugar colonies, the one with the earliest and most complete sugar monoculture and the most homogeneous class of planters with the fewest absentees, Barbados had the most complete and efficient structure of courts, the best-organized parochial system, the most and best-educated parsons, and the best schools for whites. It was the first island to declare its legislative independence and never lost it, the planters asserting their right as Englishmen to self-legislation by setting up the first (and model) plantocratic code of socio-economic laws. With the largest community of poor as well as wealthy whites, Barbados also had the lowest rate of miscegenation as well as the most discriminating laws against the few free coloreds and blacks.

For their part, though, the Barbadian blacks were among the earliest and most completely creolized of British slaves, demographically self-sustaining before 1775 and virtually all island-born by 1800. Already by 1755, all the trumpeters and drummers in the militia were black slaves, one hundred in all. To the degree that the Barbadian slaves were Christians, their adherence was to the Anglican church (for long there was no other), which gave them respectability as well as the consolations of the Christian religion. In conjunction with the planters' strategy to reward only those most anglicized, while punishing African retentions, it also helped them achieve a respectable degree of literacy by 1838. Many commentators remarked that slaves in Barbados saw themselves as Barbadians first, Africans second; and even when, to the consternation of the complacent whites, they rose up in rebellion in 1816, they marched into hopeless battle under the captured flag of the Saint Philip parochial militia.[88]

After slavery ended, the Barbadian plantocracy continued its united front against social and economic dilution, resisting the extension of civil rights, retaining control over its workers by the monopoly of land and the control of legislation, and managing an almost absolute if unofficial veto on the alienation of plantation land to peasant settlers. Barbadian sugar production, thanks to control over wages and work conditions as well as canny if modest technical improvements, uniquely in the old sugar colonies actually in-

mas, 3d ed. (Waterloo, Ont., 1987); Colin A. Hughes, *Race and Politics in the Bahamas* (Saint Lucia, Queensland, 1981); Henry C. Wilkinson, *Bermuda in the Old Empire: A History of the Island . . . 1684–1784* (London, 1950); Wilkinson, *Bermuda from Sail to Steam: The History of the Island from 1784 to 1901*, 2 vols. (London, 1973); W. S. Zuill, *The Story of Bermuda and Her People* (London, 1973).

88. Higman, *Slave Populations of the British Caribbean*; Greene, "Barbados," in Canny and Pagden, eds., *Colonial Identity*, 258; Michael Craton, *Testing the Chains: Resistance to Slavery in the British West Indies* (Ithaca, N.Y., 1982), 254–266.

creased to a peak in the mid-nineteenth century. Even when sugar profits declined irreversibly after 1880, the Barbadian plantocracy continued its socioeconomic hegemony, shifting into commerce and even becoming to a limited but unique extent regional minicapitalists.[89]

Though continuing to be separated from the whites by a socioeconomic divide, the Barbadian blacks were better educated, healthier, and more uniformly faithful to the Anglican church than those of any other sugar colony. Proud of their island home, they were sometimes contemptuous of the blacks of other islands, a sentiment that was often countered with accusations of arrogance. For these reasons as well as for their general reliability, healthiness, and relatively good education, Barbadian blacks were often recruited as policemen for other colonies. The wearing of a British uniform undoubtedly helped their tendency to visualize England (however distant and mythical in their imaginations) as much their home as Africa—perhaps even more of a homeland than it had become to most Barbadian whites. Black Barbadian radicals such as the historian Hilary Beckles disparage the "lackey mentality" of such "Black Englishmen." It might be fairer, though, to say that in the distinctive creole culture of Barbados, with its long tradition of sophisticated race relations and its long colonial history, the ethnic stance of most black Barbadians represents a decision that, while black remains beautiful and Africa a proud parallel inheritance, to be even more English than the whites is to be a more authentic Barbadian.[90]

The Englishness of Barbados, with its statue of Nelson in Trafalgar Square, Bridgetown, its mild climate and quaint country lanes, is often noted by English visitors (and even more firmly underlined by the Barbados Tourist Board). And it has been an English game, cricket, that has most significantly cemented the Barbadian social matrix. Not developed in England itself before the eighteenth century, the game was brought in by visiting servicemen and young whites returning from school. At first, the cricket clubs were exclusively white, though blacks informally picked up the game through emulation, and in due course there were clubs for blacks of different social levels as well as for middle-class "browns." Initially, the teams representing Barbados were similarly drawn only from the white inhabitants, but blacks

89. Woodville K. Marshall *et al.*, "The Establishment of a Peasantry in Barbados, 1840–1920," in *Social Groups and Institutions in the History of the Caribbean*, Proceedings of the Sixth Annual Conference of Caribbean Historians, (Puerto Rico, 1975), 85–104; Cecilia A. Karch, "The Transportation and Commercial Revolution in the West Indies: Imperial Policy and Barbadian Response, 1870–1917," *Jour. Carib. Hist.*, XVIII, no. 2 (1983), 22–42; Bonham C. Richardson, *Panama Money in Barbados, 1900–1920* (Knoxville, Tenn., 1987), 31–52.

90. Margaret Prescod-Cisse, "Hilary Beckles: Another Voice to Be Heard," *New Bajan*, February 1989, 12–15.

forced their way into the teams on merit, earning respect for their demeanor as well as their skills.[91] Gradually, both local cricket and the Barbadian representative side became fully integrated, the last all-white clubs admitting black players and members in the 1960s and the Barbadian national team actually consisting entirely of blacks by the 1980s. Despite this remarkable racial transformation, the Barbadian game continues to be played (sometimes in contrast to other West Indian territories) in the most rigid English tradition, with the national team fervently supported by all Barbadians, white as well as black. Cricket in England (once purely a gentleman's pursuit, normally played in a country house setting) has long been quintessentially an intercounty game, and though the current Barbados team is more fit to take on the whole might of England than to compete at county level, the cricket connection as well as a general affinity to all things English may help to explain why many Barbadians refer affectionately to their island as Bimshire (shortened form, Bim). A more widespread appellation for Barbados, resonant of the process to which this essay and book are dedicated, though today usually used as a sort of wry disclaimer, is Little England.

91. C.L.R. James, *Beyond a Boundary* (London, 1963), 13–137; Hilary McD. Beckles, *A History of Barbados: From Amerindian Settlement to Nation-State* (Cambridge, 1989), 149–151; Brian Stoddart, "Cricket, Social Formation, and Cultural Continuity in Barbados: A Preliminary Ethnohistory," *Journal of Sport History*, XIV (1987), 317–340.

J. M. BUMSTED

The Cultural Landscape of Early Canada

At the beginning of the nineteenth century, British North America consisted of a heterogeneous collection of colonies with little in common administratively, culturally, or historically. The coherence of British North America had earlier been lost when the thirteen colonies separated into an independent United States, leaving the mother country with an assortment of marginal jurisdictions on the northern peripheries of its older empire. What was left to the British fell into roughly three groups.

First, there was Newfoundland, one of the oldest British colonies in North America and the only remaining part of British North America with a long tradition of British settlement. Singularly underdeveloped both administratively and constitutionally, Newfoundland lacked a year-round colonial government and a representative assembly; many considered it not a proper colony at all, for it was really a permanent fishing station located off the Grand Banks, administered by a governor and other officials who resided in Saint John's during the summer fishing season.

Second, there was a group of more or less settled colonies taken over gradually from the French in the course of the Anglo-French wars of the seventeenth and eighteenth centuries. In the Maritime region, from which the French Acadian population had ostensibly been removed in the 1750s, the colonies of Nova Scotia, Isle Saint John (after 1798 Prince Edward Island), Cape Breton Island, and New Brunswick had been repeopled with Americans (many of them Loyalist refugees from the United States) and new British immigrants. In the region the French had called Canada and the British (after 1763) called Quebec, two colonies had been created in 1791. Upper Canada was virtually uninhabited by Europeans before the arrival of the Loyalists. Lower Canada was peopled by a large French-Canadian population that had been given British political privileges and guaranteed significant elements of the culture that they had developed during 150 years of French colonial presence.

Thanks to Bill Godfrey, John Reid, Larry McCann, Phil Buckner, Wallace Brown, Robin Fisher, Graeme Wynn, John Kendle, and Barry Ferguson, who read and commented upon an earlier draft of this paper.

Third, in the west and north, a vast territory of millions of square miles stretching across the top of the continent from Labrador to British Columbia, the British claimed sovereignty but had established neither government nor settlement, preferring instead to allow the Hudson's Bay Company (which had a charter to administer the huge drainage basin of Hudson Bay) and other fur traders to manage as best they could.

Settlement everywhere tended to be in pockets or long, thin lines rather than as a broad and seamless whole.[1] The vast majority of inhabitants of European origin had been born neither in Britain nor in Europe; they were native North Americans whose ancestors' European culture (either French or British) had adapted to the North American environment. The largest single component of the population in British North America remained the original indigenous peoples, who were no longer an important force in the main areas of Europeanized settlement but who still retained considerable autonomy in the vast reaches of the north and west, where they were an integral part of the fur trade.[2]

The British colonial experience in what would become Canada is difficult to categorize. It was not simply one of white settlement pushing native peoples ruthlessly aside and rapidly establishing some cultural consonance between the official culture of political systems and the vernacular cultures or subcultures of the settlers.[3] Nor were the British in Canada merely imperial administrators, running (as in Asia and Africa) their political and commercial system superimposed on native cultures that were allowed to function virtually undisturbed. Although there were such elements in the British administration of Quebec between 1759 and 1791, the French-Canadians had been admitted to full political privilege (if they could effectively exercise it) by the Constitutional Act of 1791, which also had partitioned Quebec into two provinces. Finally, the early British experience in Canada was not one in which a creole elite dominated a subordinate, indigenous population within an imperial context, although the fur traders of the west and north were plainly moving in such a direction.

1. See R. Cole Harris, "Regionalism and the Canadian Archipelago," in Lawrence D. McCann, ed., *Heartland and Hinterland: A Geography of Canada*, 2d ed. (Toronto, 1987), 531–559.

2. For another view, see Cole Harris, "Presidential Address: The Pattern of Early Canada," *Canadian Geographer*, XXXI (1987), 290–298.

3. The term "culture," as Raymond Williams has rightly pointed out, is one of the two or three most complex ones in the English language. I use it here in its anthropological sense as meaning the constellation of beliefs, values, and behavioral practices that characterize a group or a people, and not in any of the senses that restrict the word particularly to intellectual, spiritual, artistic, or aesthetic activity. See Raymond Williams, "Culture," in Williams, *Keywords: A Vocabulary of Culture and Society* (London, 1976), 76–82; A. L. Kroeber and Clyde Kluckhohn, *Culture: A Critical Review of Concepts and Definitions* (New York, 1961).

What happened to the British—and to British culture—in Canada was both quite distinctive and quite complex. While on one level the official British culture of politics and commercial enterprise controlled the disparate colonies, no two jurisdictions had the same mix of population or posed the same problems of colonial administration. It was therefore impossible for the British to find a unified general strategy with which to relate their official culture of trade, law, religion, and government to the dissimilar vernacular cultures of the settlers—Newfoundland's problems were hardly Lower Canada's. Thus the British experience on the vernacular level addressed a series of relatively isolated emergent cultures, each with its own historic base and its own response to the North American experience, and the British authorities found it difficult to force a common official culture at the top to penetrate to the grass roots.[4] How the British had ended up in this position and what it meant for the Canadian cultural experience are the subjects of this essay.

Early French Settlement

Before 1749 and the founding of Halifax, the British had paid little attention to the northernmost colonies of their empire except as strategic wartime areas. We can thus begin with a survey of the cultural landscape of Canada on the eve of the new British initiative in Nova Scotia, focusing particularly on the existing French settlements and population. Although Great Britain and her colonists to the south did not often make the distinctions, the French presence in North America was not itself homogeneous. Indeed, it consisted of several different regions, each with its own sense of development and identity. The French empire in North America included most of the present-day Maritime Provinces (vaguely identified as Acadia); the major settlement colony along the banks of the Saint Lawrence River commonly called New France (although that term should properly be applied to French North America in general, apart from Louisiana, with the Saint Lawrence settlements called Canada); and a western hinterland, serving mainly as a source

4. I take the term "emergent culture" from Raymond Williams. See his "Base and Superstructure in Marxist Cultural Theory," *Studies on the Left*, no. 22 (1973), 3–16. Pioneering efforts at dealing with the problem of cultural complexity in Canadian development are to be found in Louis Hartz, *The Founding of New Societies: Studies in the History of the United States, Latin America, South Africa, Canada, and Australia* (New York, 1964); and the opening chapter of Gad Horowitz, *Canadian Labour in Politics* (Toronto, 1968), which criticizes and modifies the Hartz approach. Both these works fail to appreciate the extent of cultural complexity in the early period and tend not only to oversimplify but to see the cultures they identify as frozen "fragments" from Europe and America rather than as dynamic and emergent entities.

of furs, that stretched to the foothills of the Rockies and down the Mississippi River system to another settlement colony at Louisiana.

The Maritime region of Acadia was peopled by the descendants of French settlers of the first half of the seventeenth century and had been relatively neglected by the mother country.[5] Acadia was less an administrative or geographic unit than a demographic and linguistic region. Most of its early population came from a relatively small area of southwestern France, including the provinces of Vienne, Poitou, Aunis, and Saintonge, and spoke a particular southwestern dialect of French. This dialect was preserved relatively intact, and the population of Acadia did not adopt the official parlance (the King's French of the Paris region) as did their compatriots along the Saint Lawrence. Many may have been sufficiently bilingual to get on, at least commercially, in English. The importance of the family (*le clan*) as a social unit in Acadia and the absence of new immigration are emphasized by the fact that, as late as 1938, nearly 90 percent of the families of Acadia held only seventy-six surnames, and those patronymics went back well into the seventeenth century.[6]

After 1713, the Acadians were politically divided into two groups: those who remained in territory ceded to the British by the Treaty of Utrecht, and those who remained in or moved to French territory on Cape Breton Island or Isle Saint John. Cape Breton was dominated by the fortress of Louisbourg, about which more has been written than any other community in early Canada.[7] As inhabitants of a garrison town with a strong commercial orientation, the people of Louisbourg were hardly typical Acadians, but the seaport handled much trade in the region and might ultimately have become better integrated with its hinterland. Estimates of the size of the Acadian

5. The best general survey of early Acadia remains Andrew Hill Clark, *Acadia: The Geography of Early Nova Scotia to 1760* (Madison, Wis., 1968). For the 17th century, John G. Reid, *Acadia, Maine, and New Scotland: Marginal Colonies in the Seventeenth Century* (Toronto, 1981) is indispensable. For the "Acadian Fact" in Canadian history, consult Jean Daigle, ed., *The Acadians of the Maritimes: Thematic Studies* (Moncton, N.B., 1982).

6. On bilingualism, see R. Babitch, "The English of Acadians of the Seventeenth Century," *Atlantic Provinces Linguistic Association Papers* (1981), 96–115. On names, see Geneviève Massignon, *Les parlers français d'Acadie: enquête linguistique* (Paris, 1962), I, 31, 72.

7. Among the major recent works on Louisbourg are the following: Bona Arsenault, *Louisbourg, 1713–1758* (Quebec, 1971); Terence Allan Crowley, "Government and Interests: French Colonial Administration at Louisbourg, 1713–1758" (Ph.D. diss., Duke University, 1975); Olive Patricia Dickason, "Louisbourg and the Indians: A Study in Imperial Race Relations, 1713–1760," in *History and Archeologie / Histoire et archeologie*, VI (Ottawa, 1976), 3–206; Allan Greer, *The Soldiers of Isle Royale, 1720–45* (Ottawa, 1979); A.J.B. Johnston, *Religion in Life at Louisbourg, 1713–1758* (Kingston, 1984); Christopher Moore, *Louisbourg Portraits: Life in an Eighteenth-Century Garrison Town* (Toronto, 1982); Gilles Proulx, *Aubergistes et cabaretieirs de Louisbourg, 1713–1758* (Ottawa, 1972).

population in the late 1740s range from eleven thousand to nineteen thousand, with thirteen thousand perhaps the most acceptable figure.[8]

Acadian culture was a transplanted peasant culture, oriented around the family and the local community. Fundamentally farmers, the Acadians practiced meadowland cultivation on tidal marshland, often employing complex dikes to claim additional land from the sea. Raising livestock was the principal effort of Acadian farming, especially in newly settled districts. Perhaps the key feature of Acadian culture, particularly in British-controlled Nova Scotia, was a relative autonomy in respect to its putative political masters. Government had always sat lightly upon the Acadians, chiefly because the French had never regarded the region as one of major importance. After the cession of Nova Scotia to the British, the Acadians were until the 1750s allowed to administer themselves: their religious rights were guaranteed by Article XIV of the Treaty of Utrecht, and the British were powerless to intervene in property matters or local government (where the priests adjudicated most minor civil differences). A large part of the British frustration with the Acadians (eventually resulting in the deportations of the 1750s) was British inability to impose any aspects of British culture upon the Acadian population, which observed the ancient traditions and coütumes of France and of the Roman Catholic church, as modified by more than a century of local experience. This deliberate resistance to acculturation—culminating in Nova Scotia in oaths of allegiance—would characterize not only the Acadians but other cultural groups in Canada. At the same time that the Acadians remained outside Anglo-American culture, they also distanced themselves from French Canada and were never really thoroughly integrated into the larger French colonial experience.

The bulk of the French-speaking population of North America in 1749 was located on a thin line along the Saint Lawrence River, in the colony that most British North Americans called *Canada*. Many of that population of fifty-five thousand people were farmers, or habitants, as the French referred to them, who resided in a fairly continuous series of tiers, or *rangs*, of land, usually no more than two or three deep from the banks of the river, that stretched for 150 miles along the north shore of the Saint Lawrence and for nearly 200 miles along the south shore. Along this span of river were three towns, Quebec, Trois-Rivières, and Montreal, that among them contained more than twelve thousand people.[9]

The traditional picture of this Canada (established by the romantic American historian Francis Parkman) as a colony with an authoritarian govern-

8. Raymond Roy, "Le croissance démographique en Acadie de 1671 à 1763" (master's thesis, University of Montreal, 1975), 81.

9. See R. Cole Harris, ed., *Historical Atlas of Canada*, I, *From the Beginning to 1800* (Toronto, 1987), esp. plates 52–56.

ment and an undynamic economic and commercial system, inhabited mainly by cleric-ridden and docile peasant farmers, is no longer tenable. Although most scholars would still admit that the government of New France was basically centralized, authoritarian, and paternalistic, considerable doubt has been cast on the efficiency of the political system, on the absence of popular participation in it, and particularly on the question of its oppressiveness.[10] Plainly, the landholding system of the colony—the seigneurial system—did not *function* as a feudal carryover from the mother country. Equally plainly, there was much more entrepreneurial and commercial activity in eighteenth-century Canada than the familiar picture of a monopolistic economy centered on the fur trade could possibly allow. One of the major debates among Quebeçois historians in recent years has been the extent of economic growth in the colony, particularly in the years before the British conquest. Many scholars are convinced that a promising economic situation was cut off after 1760 by the new regime.[11]

As for Canada's religious condition, most specialists would allow that the colony was fervently Roman Catholic, but its religious beliefs did not translate into a cleric-dominated society, at least not before the arrival of the British conquerors.[12] Outside the towns, there simply were not enough parish priests to provide a regular influence. Even the reputed success of the French missionaries with the Indians, particularly in terms of acculturation to French values, has been strongly questioned. In place of a clerically dominated society, some historians have increasingly been emphasizing the extent to which Canada was dominated by the military.[13]

10. For the most recent synthesis of historical work on Canada in the first half of the eighteenth century, see Dale Miquelon, *New France, 1701–1744: A Supplement to Europe* (Toronto, 1987). A useful recent bibliographical essay is Cornelius J. Jaenen's "Canada during the French Régime," in D. A. Muise, ed., *A Reader's Guide to Canadian History*, I, *Beginnings to Confederation* (Toronto, 1982), 3–44. See also L. R. MacDonald, "France and New France: The Internal Contradictions," *Canadian Historical Review*, LII (1971), 121–143.

A good discussion of the issues, both historical and historiographical, is to be found in Yves F. Zoltvany, *The Government of New France: Royal, Clerical, or Class Rule?* (Scarborough, Ont., 1971).

11. On landholding, see Richard Colebrook Harris, *The Seigneurial System in Early Canada: A Geographical Study* (Madison, Wis., 1966). On commercial activity, see, for example, Dale Miquelon, *Dugard of Rouen: French Trade to Canada and the West Indies, 1729–1770* (Montreal, 1978); Cameron Nish, *Les bourgeois-gentilshommes de la Nouvelle-France, 1729–1748* (Montreal, 1968); J. F. Bosher, *The Canada Merchants, 1713–1763* (Oxford, 1987).

The debate on economic growth can be followed in Dale Miquelon, ed., *Society and Conquest: The Debate on the Bourgeoisie and Social Change in French Canada, 1700–1850* (Toronto, 1977).

12. Cornelius J. Jaenen, *The Role of the Church in New France* (Toronto, 1976).

13. On missionaries, see Cornelius J. Jaenen, *Friend and Foe: Aspects of French-Amerindian Cultural Contact in the Sixteenth and Seventeenth Centuries* (New York,

Comprehending the cultural world of early Canada, especially the nonofficial, vernacular culture, has been a difficult task for historians. The colony did not have a printing press before the arrival of the British, and much of its culture was oral rather than written.[14] It is now clear that, linguistically, the first years of the settlement of the Saint Lawrence colony saw the transplantation of a variety of French dialects and speech patterns. However, the importation after the royal takeover of the colony in 1663 of a large number of women from the Paris region contributed greatly to standardizing the language spoken in Canada, and while by the eighteenth century the French spoken there had some new vocabulary (mainly taken from the Indians) and a distinctive accent, the Canadians came to use Parisian French rather than any of the regional dialects or an Americanized one. Peter Kalm, a Swedish visitor who toured the northern English colonies and Canada in 1748 and 1749 and the only early observer to comment on both cultures from first hand, observed, "In Canada the ordinary man speaks a purer French than in any province in France, yea that in this respect it can vie with Paris itself."[15] In its Parisian-ness, Canada was linguistically quite distinct from Acadia.

Although New France was no feudal remnant or transplant from the Old World and shared much with British North America, its culture was distinct from that in the English-speaking colonies to the south. Some of the differences were obvious. New France (whether Canada or Acadia) spoke a different language, embraced a different religion, and employed a different set of political institutions and landholding patterns. Other distinctions were less apparent. According to Peter Kalm, the Canadians had better manners, seemed in general more intellectually alert, and had acculturated far more with the native peoples than had the English colonists.[16] At least in Canada, there was a military tradition within the population, particularly within the upper classes, that did not exist in the English colonies.

1976); James Axtell, *The Invasion Within: The Contest of Cultures in Colonial North America* (New York, 1985). On military dominance, see W. J. Eccles, "The Social, Economic, and Political Significance of the Military Establishment in New France," in Eccles, *Essays on New France* (Toronto, 1987), 110–124; G.F.G. Stanley, *New France: The Last Phase, 1744–1760* (Toronto, 1968).

14. For one attempt at an analysis of the vernacular culture, see Peter N. Moogk, " 'Thieving Buggers' and 'Stupid Sluts': Insults and Popular Culture in New France," *William and Mary Quarterly*, 3d Ser., XXXVI (1979), 524–547.

15. Philippe Barbaud, *Le choc des patois en Nouvelle-France: essai sur l'histoire de la francisation au Canada* (Sillery, Que., 1984); Mark M. Orkin, *Speaking Canadian French: An Informal Account of the French Language in Canada*, rev. ed. (Toronto, 1971); Adolph B. Benson, ed., *The America of 1750: Peter Kalm's Travels in North America*, 2 vols. (New York, 1966), II, 554.

16. Benson, ed., *Kalm's Travels*. On feudalism, see Roberta Hamilton, "Feudal Society and Colonization: A Critique and Reinterpretation of the Historiography of New France," *Canadian Papers in Rural History*, VI (1987), 17–136.

If career soldiering and the seigneurial system gave a more European cast to the Canadian elite, that same seigneurial system also meant that the Canadian habitant remained more a traditional peasant than did his colonial English counterpart. He was less market-oriented, less interested in land speculation, and relatively inelastic in his demands for consumer goods. Despite his extensive adaptation of Indian customs—in his attitudes toward gender roles and in his vulgar speech, for example—the Canadian retained European models and was quite conservative. The elite in Canada consciously aped the culture of the mother country, and the habitants adapted French folk tradition to the New World. But the habitant was no frontier capitalist; instead, he was rather more a backwoods French peasant.

Unlike the British colonies to the south, New France gained little from immigration. During its entire existence under the French, for example, Canada received only ten thousand immigrants, most of them before 1672. By the mid-eighteenth century, therefore, the culture of Canada had enjoyed nearly a century free of significant influence from European immigration. Such a hiatus to allow cultural consolidation was unusual in North America: it meant that Canadians were secure in their culture when they were forcibly added to the British Empire in 1763.

The thin ribbons of settlement along the Saint Lawrence constituted very little direct threat to the British Empire or the colonies of British North America. What did threaten the British was French expansion into the interior of the continent, particularly when the western thrust along the river systems appeared to be literally encircling and hemming in the American colonies. French expansion involved a relative handful of individuals, whose success depended, not on the extent to which the Indians had absorbed French values, but on the extent to which the Europeans had taken on Indian characteristics. Frenchmen had been living with the natives from the early days of colonization, and by the end of the seventeenth century a cadre of skilled *hivernants* had emerged as a distinctive group among the Canadian population. Perhaps as many as 20–25 percent of the able-bodied Canadian males were involved in the western trade at some point in their lives, usually in their younger years before settling down with a wife and family in some less peregrine occupation along the Saint Lawrence.[17] During much of the first half of the eighteenth century, official French policy attempted to restrain the adventurers from traveling ever further into the heart of the

17. Hubert Charbonneau *et al.*, "Le comportement démographique des voyageurs sous le régime français," *Histoire sociale / Social History*, XI (1978), 120–133. The classic early "hivernant" was Pierre Radisson, whose journals, or "voyages," are available in several editions. For the later "voyageurs," see Allan Greer, *Peasant, Lord, and Merchant: Rural Society in Three Quebec Parishes, 1740–1840* (Toronto, 1985).

continent in search of richer sources of furs, but attempted without much success. The French were forced to drop their territorial pretensions to the Hudson Bay drainage basin in 1713, but lines of trading posts (the Postes du Nord) were established after that date. These posts enabled the French fur traders to control most of the trade of the upper Mississippi and Missouri River basins and to explore west as far as the Rocky Mountains.

Although there were probably fewer than one thousand of these "woodrunners" or "bushlopers" (as the English called them) in the territory west and north of the Appalachians, they constituted a serious obstacle to British expansion. By stirring up competition among the Indians and by supplying them with arms, they threatened the settlements much farther east. Already these men had begun forming marital alliances with Indian women, from which would spring the mixed-blood peoples who would be so important in the Canadian west.[18] The culture of both the hivernants and, especially, of their progeny was quite unlike that of the settlements, where European values were mimicked and maintained. Both because the vast majority of mothers (rather than fathers) were Indian and because many Indian tribes were matrilineal, most mixed-bloods were raised as natives, not as Europeans. In the west, Indian ways dominated, and there was even the beginning of distinctive languages born of the merger of European with native tongues.

Early British Settlement

Since the founding of the Hudson's Bay Company in 1670, the British had managed to retain a toehold in the west, with a series of trading factories established at the bottom edge of Hudson Bay and James Bay. Unlike the French, however, British fur traders were not encouraged to winter with the Indians; they preferred to wait at their trading posts for native middlemen to bring the furs to them. The British posts did draw some Indians into their orbit as semidependents, and the Hudson's Bay Company was quite unable to enforce rules against liaisons with native women. Thus the Hudson's Bay Company posts, staffed mainly by Highland Scots and Orkneymen, began producing their own mixed-blood populations.[19] These people would even-

18. Marcel Giraud, *Les métis Canadien: son rôle dans l'histoire des provinces de l'Ouest* (Paris, 1945).

19. Sylvia Van Kirk, *"Many Tender Ties": Women in Fur-Trade Society in Western Canada, 1670–1870* (Winnipeg, 1980); Jennifer S. H. Brown, *Strangers in Blood: Fur Trade Company Families in Indian Country* (Vancouver, 1980).

The best study of the early British fur trade is in Arthur J. Ray and Donald B. Freeman, *"Give Us Good Measure": An Economic Analysis of Relations between the Indians and the Hudson's Bay Company before 1763* (Toronto, 1978), which sup-

tually develop into an English-speaking Protestant mixed-blood community, but in 1750 their lives were altered mainly through a decreased mobility and increased dependence on the traders.

The few score British fur traders on the Bay were, from the perspective of British colonial administrators, no less peripheral a population than the substantially larger number of British fishermen in Newfoundland. Neither group met any enthusiasm from Britain for the growth and expansion of their settlements. Newfoundland had been one of the earliest centers of English colonization activity in the first half of the seventeenth century, but most of the settlements founded under the auspices of the Newfoundland Company and other proprietors had failed badly, and attention had shifted farther south, to the mainland.[20] Many of the sites of the early ventures continued to be visited by summering fishermen sailing from England each year, but the permanent population was very small at the end of the seventeenth century, perhaps no more than one thousand to twelve hundred English and fewer than one thousand French. The latter would be removed from the island to Île Royale (Cape Breton) under the terms of the Treaty of Utrecht.

There is little evidence that the British government actively and persistently opposed settlement or set up legal obstacles to it. Instead, the government ignored Newfoundland development and thus allowed the fishing interests from the West Country of England to have their own way. As a result, the substantial growth in permanent residents on the island in the eighteenth century occurred quite independently of any government policy or supervision: thousands of fishermen (and a few women and children) simply chose to remain behind rather than return home with their vessels. Population grew rapidly, to thirty-five hundred by 1730 and to seventy-three hundred by the 1750s.[21] The proportion of permanent residents in the total summering population similarly increased, from 15 percent in the 1670s to 30 percent in the 1730s and to at least 50 percent by 1753.

The cultural background of the residents changed as well. In the seven-

---

plants in large measure Harold A. Innis's classic, *The Fur Trade in Canada: An Introduction to Canadian Economic History*, rev. ed. (Toronto, 1956) for this period. See also Arthur J. Ray and Conrad E. Heidenreich, *The Early Fur Trades: A Study in Cultural Interaction* (Toronto, 1976).

20. Gillian T. Cell, *English Enterprise in Newfoundland, 1577–1660* (Toronto, 1969); G. M. Story, ed., *Early European Settlement and Exploitation in Atlantic Canada: Selected Papers* (St. John's, Newf., 1982).

21. Keith Matthews, *Lectures on the History of Newfoundland, 1500–1830* (St. John's, Newf., 1973); C. Grant Head, *Eighteenth Century Newfoundland: A Geographer's Perspective* (Toronto, 1976); John J. Mannion, ed., *The Peopling of Newfoundland: Essays in Historical Geography* (St. John's, Newf., 1977).

teenth century, almost all residents were of English origin, chiefly from the West Country region of Cornwall, Devon, and Dorset. As late as 1732, 90 percent of the permanent population of Newfoundland was still English, but most of the increase in the eighteenth century came via fishermen from southern Ireland, through the increasing connections between Newfoundland and the Irish ports of Waterford and Cork. Thus, one census of wintering inhabitants in 1753 showed 2,683 Irish and 1,916 English. Pushed out of Ireland by famine and unemployment, the Irish were attracted to Newfoundland by cheap transportation and work prospects there. By 1750 Newfoundland had become a conduit for Irish Catholics to North America, and it remained so throughout the period before 1815. It had also begun to develop a deep schism within its population that was simultaneously ethnic, religious, and economic. The chief economic division was between those who owned boats and those who worked on the boats of others. Some westcountrymen were not boatowners, but virtually none of the Irishmen were.

Newfoundland also exhibited the biculturalism so common to these early settlements. A poem of the 1740s by Donnach Ruah MacConmera illustrates the point quite clearly. It was written in two languages, English and Irish, and assumed that the Irish audience was familiar with both tongues:

As I was walking one evening fair,
Agus mé go déanachma m-baile Sheagain
[*and I lately arrived in St. John's town*]
I met a gang of English blades
Agus iad da d-traohadh ag neart a namhaid;
[*and they being subdued by their enemies' strength*]
I boozed and drank both late and early,
With those courageous "men-of-war";
'S gur bhinne lion Sasanaigh ag ruith ar
'S gan do Ghaoidhil ann acht fior bheagan
[*And sweet it was for me to see English retreating*
And but few Irish there.]

That the vernacular cultures were largely oral doubtless has disguised the ubiquity of this bilingualism and biculturalism, still to be found among ethnic groups in Canada.[22] Despite the casual way in which it developed, Newfoundland constituted (before the founding of Halifax in 1749) the largest concentration of British north of the thirteen continental colonies.

22. Cyril Byrne, "Notes on Some Early Newfoundland Poems," in Ken MacKinnon, ed., *Atlantic Provinces Literature Colloquium Papers* (Saint John, N.B., 1977), 24–39.

The European population of the northern settlements of North America in the late 1740s, therefore, consisted of about seventy-five thousand French-speaking inhabitants and perhaps eight thousand English-speakers. In addition, of course, there were the Amerindians. The native peoples, decimated by centuries of disease and warfare, were no longer an important cultural influence in the Atlantic region or along the Saint Lawrence River. Only a few hundred Beothuks survived in Newfoundland, and would become extinct as a people in the early nineteenth century. In Nova Scotia, the Micmacs and Abenaki were also declining in numbers and importance.[23] The territory now known as Labrador and eastern Quebec was populated by small numbers of migratory hunters and was not highly desirable for settlement. In the central region of what is now Ontario and Quebec, the surviving natives had mainly been pushed back into the Canadian Shield (or Laurentian Highlands) or onto reserves.

Only from the Sault west and in the subarctic and Arctic north were natives still in control of their own destiny. Because of the relative slowness of European settlement in these areas, the continued importance of the fur trade, and the increasing liaisons between European fur traders and native women, the Indians of Canada would continue to be an important cultural factor until well into the nineteenth century.[24] Whatever the importance of the Indians in the development of the transplanted European cultures and the extent of their control over their own destiny, the natives unquestionably represented a series of separate and unassimilated cultures or subcultures extending across the northern part of the continent. Recognizing the presence of multiple cultures helps make it possible to integrate the native peoples into the historical development of Canada in a way not comprehensible to earlier generations of historians.

British Settlement before the Treaty of Paris

Between 1749 and 1763, British settlement policy for its northward territories was vacillating and uncertain. Through large expenditures of public

23. L.F.S. Upton, *Micmacs and Colonists: Indian-White Relations in the Maritimes, 1713–1867* (Vancouver, 1979); Kenneth M. Morrison, *The Embattled Northeast: The Elusive Ideal of Alliance in Abenaki-Euramerican Relations* (Berkeley, Calif., 1984). The best modern study of the native peoples and cultural contact is Bruce G. Trigger, *Natives and Newcomers: Canada's "Heroic Age" Reconsidered* (Kingston, 1985).

24. The best introduction to the Indians and the fur trade remains Arthur J. Ray, *Indians in the Fur Trade: Their Role as Trappers, Hunters, and Middlemen in the Lands Southwest of Hudson Bay, 1660–1870* (Toronto, 1974). But see also Charles A. Bishop, *The Northern Ojibwa and the Fur Trade: An Historical and Ecological Study* (Toronto, 1974).

funds, Halifax grew rapidly, but much of its population (3,082 when first counted in 1752) was military, and the few Britons in Nova Scotia outside Halifax were part of what was still a military occupation of foreign territory, whose power was so weak that the British authorities were unable to take a proper census of the Acadian population presumably under their control. Britain had recruited the Halifax settlers with promises of land and support, partly among soldiers and sailors recently dismissed from the nation's military services but also among London artisans. A listed 2,547 passengers left England with the first fleet of 1749. There were 1,174 heads of families on the ships arriving in that first wave, with 509 wives, 414 children, and 420 servants also on board. Fifty-one former naval officers and 452 common seamen joined 33 former army officers and 118 enlistees: 654 of the 1,174 family heads (56 percent) were ex-servicemen. More than 100 other occupations were given on the passenger lists. There were 161 farmers, 107 workers in the building trades, 19 shoemakers, 11 butchers, 11 tailors, 10 coopers, and men from dozens of London trades, including the luxury ones of peruke-maker, upholsterer, and buckle-maker. Within days of arrival, more than half of the 2,547 names had disappeared permanently from the Halifax record, probably to the New England colonies further south.[25]

Many of the disbanded soldiers were Irish and provided an Irish tinge to the Halifax population, subsequently enhanced by arrivals from Newfoundland and eventually by emigrants directly from Ireland itself. A number of New England merchants, many already active in the trade with Louisbourg, also appeared in Halifax, helping to establish the town as a northern subsidiary of Yankee trading patterns. Some of the Yankees came with the Louisbourg garrison and transferred to Halifax in the summer of 1749. By February 1750 there were more than seventy houses serving spiritous beverages, thus to some extent confirming Anglican missionary William Tutty's remark that the new settlers were "a set of profligate wretches, intemperance has destroyed many of the worst."[26]

Neither the disbanded servicemen nor the London artisans shipped to Halifax proved to be very satisfactory settlers, so more than 2,700 Germans and Swiss (many of the latter actually French Huguenots from Lorraine) were recruited for the garrison town and Nova Scotia in the early 1750s. Of those whose origins are identifiable, 1,327 came from the states of southwestern Germany, 233 from northern Germany, 316 from Switzerland, 433 from Montbéliard (a countship of French Protestants connected to the Aus-

25. Thomas Raddall, *Halifax: Warden of the North* (Toronto, 1948), 20–46 (see also R. Cole Harris, ed., *Historical Atlas of Canada*, I, plate 31); George T. Bates, "The Great Exodus of 1749; or, The Cornwallis Settlers Who Didn't," Nova Scotia Historical Society, *Collections*, XXXVIII (1973), 27–62.

26. Bates, "The Great Exodus of 1749," Nova Scotia Hist. Soc., *Colls.*, XXXVIII (1973), 27–62.

trian Empire but almost totally surrounded by French territory), and 76 from the Netherlands. For a variety of reasons, including the enormous costs of resettlement, the British government ceased its active recruitment of foreign Protestants in 1752 and never resumed it. The policy left behind only an emphasis on the settlement of foreign Protestants in the grants made to private proprietors, who were expected to carry the expenses of settlement in the northern provinces after Britain's one brief venture at it, and one community of foreign Protestants at Lunenburg, founded by transferring many of the Halifax settlers there between 1753 and 1755. The Nova Scotia authorities had always intended to settle these newcomers on agricultural lands mixed among the Acadians, but were unable to do so because of confusion over land titles. The emigrants, forced to survive in Halifax after their arrival, complained bitterly of costs and conditions in that town. Lunenburg's early history was tumultuous and complicated for many reasons, not the least of which was its population: not at all homogeneous, but drawn from many parts of Europe. Indeed, a brief armed rebellion occurred there late in 1753. However, the German majority did preserve something of its language and customs through the eighteenth century.[27]

In 1755 the British government in Halifax, ostensibly for security reasons, attempted a final solution to the thorny presence of the Acadians. The story of the expulsion of the Acadians from Nova Scotia is well known. What is worth noting here is that the Acadians after 1713 had expanded from their original base in the Minas Basin within territory controlled by the British and also moved into French-controlled areas.[28] The Acadian people obviously had more than sufficient resources for expansion and survival, and the expulsion of 1755 was hardly complete. A second, less-publicized expulsion occurred in 1758 as the British evacuated the French population of its newly conquered territory without waiting for a peace treaty. In many ways, the removals from Île Royale and Isle Saint John after the British capture of Louisbourg in 1758 were more disruptive to the Acadians than the 1755 expulsions that have drawn the most attention. Many of the people evacuated in 1758 were sent back to France, whence they would have great trouble returning to North America. Moreover, hundreds died on the transatlantic voyage to France, mainly when storms sank the transports carrying them.

27. Winthrop Pickard Bell, *The "Foreign Protestants" and the Settlement of Nova Scotia: The History of a Piece of Arrested British Colonial Policy in the Eighteenth Century* (Toronto, 1961).

28. See Bernard Pothier, "Acadian Emigration to Ile Royale after the Conquest of Acadia," *Histoire sociale / Social History*, no. 6 (November 1970), 116–131; and D. C. Harvey, *The French Regime in Prince Edward Island* (New Haven, Conn., 1926). A good selection of a vast literature on the expulsion was reprinted in Naomi E. S. Griffiths, ed., *The Acadian Deportation: Deliberate Perfidy or Cruel Necessity?* (Toronto, 1969).

In any event, "le grand dérangement," while producing extreme dislocation of and suffering by a people—whether innocent victims or misguided protagonists in imperial conflict—was hardly the total elimination of the Acadian population from the region. Indeed, one of the major stories of the post-1760 period is the gradual reestablishment of a substantial Acadian presence in parts of the Maritimes. On the eve of the deportation, there had been about ten thousand Acadians in Nova Scotia, a few hundred on Île Royale, and nearly three thousand on Isle Saint John. While six thousand were deported in 1755, mainly to the English colonies to the south, another six thousand were removed in 1758 (thirty-five hundred from Isle Saint John alone), and more than three thousand were sent back to Europe.[29] The British would not pursue such a draconian policy again.

The problems with the Halifax settlers and with the foreign Protestants, particularly in adjusting to North American conditions, led the government of Nova Scotia to seek another source for settlers when it moved the Acadians off their lands. New England, with its surplus population and close maritime ties to Nova Scotia, was an obvious alternative. The government's advertisements in October 1758 of the opening of Acadian land for settlement found a ready audience in the southern New England colonies, especially in eastern Connecticut, southern Rhode Island, and southeastern Massachusetts, where available land was in short supply. Transportation to new homes would be by water rather than overland, the land was already cleared and improved (so said the Nova Scotia government), and transportation costs and initial support in the new settlements would be paid for out of the public purse. More than eight thousand Yankee settlers were recruited and transported to Nova Scotia between 1759 and the termination of bounties in 1763.[30]

29. Robert G. LeBlanc, "The Acadian Migrations," *Canadian Geographical Journal*, LXXXI, no. 1 (July 1970), 10–19.

30. The best single study of this movement and its results remains John Bartlet Brebner, *The Neutral Yankees of Nova Scotia: A Marginal Colony during the Revolutionary Years* (New York, 1937). But Brebner's work is shaped by a particular thesis (that Acadians and Yankees in Nova Scotia shared a neutral response to events occurring outside the province), and although it heavily utilized available unpublished material, much new documentation has surfaced since it was researched in the mid-1930s. A new study of the Yankee migration is much needed. One suggestion of its shape, from the perspective of human geography and recent research, comes in Graeme Wynn, "A Province Too Much Dependent on New England," *Can. Geog.*, XXXI (1987), 98–113. Other useful works, written in the same period as Brebner's, are Katherine R. Williams, "Social Conditions in Nova Scotia, 1749–1783" (master's thesis, McGill University, 1936); and J. S. Martell, "Pre-Loyalist Settlements around Minas Basin" (master's thesis, Dalhousie University, 1933). More recent work includes E. C. Wright, *Planters and Pioneers: Nova Scotia, 1749–1775* (Windsor, N.S., 1978), largely a list of names; and Gordon Stewart and George Rawlyk, *A People Highly Favoured of God: The Nova Scotia Yankees and the American Revolution* (Toronto, 1972), another work molded by a strongly argued thesis.

The New England Yankees had a good deal of difficulty adjusting to Nova Scotia political institutions, laid down by a British government eager to avoid the sorts of problems it had faced in the southern American colonies and tending to be hostile to New England local government in church and state. The Yankees also had much trouble with their new lands, since the successful Acadians had depended upon diking out the seawater and New Englanders had little experience with such operations. But although the Yankees did not exactly prosper and there was the usual turnover of population, they did take root in the province, particularly in the fishing communities of the south coast and the farming communities of the Bay of Fundy–Minas Basin region. Given their origins in the parts of New England most heavily affected by the Great Awakening in the 1740s, it was not surprising that they had strong evangelical traditions within a framework of eighteenth-century New England Puritanism and would experience a religious revival of their own in the 1770s. Indeed, a Puritan-style evangelical pietism was probably the most distinctive feature of the Yankee culture transplanted to the Maritime region.[31]

After the Conquest of Canada

Circumstances and timing prevented the British authorities from ever molding such disparate cultures as French-Canadian and New England Yankee into a single whole in her northernmost colonies during the rest of the eighteenth century. Britain never had a viable or coherent settlement policy for the region, partly because she was continually reacting defensively to separatist movements from the thirteen colonies. The French-Canadians would eventually be outnumbered, but not before Britain found it necessary to accept their right to language, religion, and institutions (at least in what would become the province of Quebec). The Acadians returned to the Maritime region in large numbers, despite their supposed final removal. The Proclamation of 1763 failed to deflect many American colonists from the west into the north between 1763 and 1775. Although the British finally found in the persons of the Loyalists a sizable American population willing to resettle, it was not the population they had intended, and their resettlement was traumatic and expensive. Nor, despite some concerted efforts, did foreign Protestants flock to the northern region. And perhaps most significantly, those people in Britain who did emigrate to British North America,

31. See my *Henry Alline, 1748–1784* (Toronto, 1971); and for some contemporary reflections of the transplanted culture, Harold A. Innis *et al.*, eds., *Diary of Simeon Perkins*, 5 vols. (Toronto, 1948–1978). Also consult G. A. Rawlyk, *Ravished by the Spirit: Religious Revivals, Baptists, and Henry Alline* (Kingston, 1984).

particularly after the American colonies had won their independence, tended to come from the less culturally assimilated parts of the kingdom.

Great Britain was not culturally homogeneous in the eighteenth century. Ireland, Scotland, and Wales had not yet been fully integrated, and each of these regions, or countries, contained many people whose culture did not conform to the official culture of the kingdom. The departure of large numbers of culturally distinctive Britons for North America—often seeking not only prosperity but the preservation of their ways of life—and settling in ethnic nodes in the unpopulated wilderness of the northern colonies created a population whose non-English culture paralleled certain distinctive cultural traits among the incoming Loyalists. These realities combined with a fierce defensive strategy on the part of the French-Canadians as well as with the emergence of a mixed-blood society in the west to produce a North American empire distinguished by its extraordinary cultural complexity.

After the conquest of Canada, some American traders and merchants did move into the newly acquired territory. The merchants established themselves mainly in Montreal, always the center of the French fur trade, and some began to move into the western wilderness as wintering traders, replacing the French in this role. A few hundred additional Americans and disbanded British soldiers established themselves in the Saint John River valley in what is now New Brunswick, centering around Maugerville, and there were a handful of merchants at the mouth of the Saint John River near what would become the city of Saint John. Some of these Americans entered the timber business in the upper Richelieu Valley and obtained seigneuries in the region, and there was frequent movement between Quebec and the disputed territory that would eventually become Vermont.[32] American merchants also began to frequent Newfoundland, to supply the growing resident population with foodstuffs brought from the American colonies. By the 1770s Newfoundland was heavily dependent upon American suppliers, and the difficulties of trade during the Revolutionary period would greatly hamper its development. Where American arrivals came into conflict with a locally established population, as in Montreal and Quebec generally, cultural differences played a significant role in the politics. But the constantly growing crisis with Britain and the attractions of the transappalachian west prevented Americans from moving in significant numbers before 1775.

More important than American settlement in the interwar years of 1763–1775 was the exodus to North America of Britons themselves. Their immigration began in the late 1760s and really took hold in 1770, fueled by unfavorable economic conditions in the British Isles and the acquisition of large tracts of unsettled land by former soldiers and speculators in the newly

32. See, for example, Allan S. Everest, *Moses Hazen and the Canadian Refugees in the American Revolution* (Syracuse, N.Y., 1976).

acquired territories. Most of the emigrating Britons went to the better-established colonies to the south, where they would constitute a less Americanized population at the outbreak of rebellion; many would remigrate to the north as Loyalists. But there was a continued outpouring of Irish into Newfoundland, nearly doubling the resident population on that island, to fifteen thousand by 1775. And a major movement from Scotland, especially from the Highland region, often including Gaelic-speaking Roman Catholics, was building as well.[33]

The Maritime Provinces became the principal northern destination of the Highland Scots. The Isle Saint John, where a number of parties (including more than two hundred Roman Catholics) were brought by proprietors between 1770 and 1775, was particularly attractive.[34] A few parties also went to Quebec, to territory that later became part of Upper Canada. The Highlanders of this period came mainly from the more isolated western region of Scotland and adjacent islands, where Gaelic was still the common language and where Roman Catholicism survived and even flourished semi-clandestinely. They tended to emigrate not only in nuclear but in extended family groupings and to set sail together in chartered vessels straight to isolated destinations that allowed them to replicate their Old World communities in the New. Lowlanders were more attracted to Nova Scotia, and a beachhead of settlement was established on the northern coast of the colony around the Pictou region in 1774.[35] A number of Yorkshiremen also migrated to the Cumberland region of Nova Scotia in the mid-1770s, where they clashed politically and culturally with the established New England settlers. This transatlantic migration was not favored by the authorities in Britain, but it was only gaining momentum, at least to the northern areas, when the American rebellion effectively ended it for the duration of hostilities.[36]

Among the principal results of the increasing disagreements between Britain and her colonies in the 1760s and early 1770s were not only the relative absence of American migration to Quebec (where American settlers complained of political and legal disabilities in a province that the British hoped gradually to anglicize) but the abandonment in 1774 of the policy of assimilation in favor of an acceptance of many of the institutions and values of the

33. See J. M. Bumsted, *The People's Clearance: Highland Emigration to British North America, 1770–1815* (Edinburgh, 1982).

34. See J. M. Bumsted, *Land, Settlement, and Politics on Eighteenth-Century Prince Edward Island* (Kingston, 1987).

35. D. Campbell and R. A. MacLean, *Beyond the Atlantic Roar: A Study of the Nova Scotia Scots* (Toronto, 1974); Donald MacKay, *Scotland Farewell: The People of the Hector* (Toronto, 1980).

36. Bernard Bailyn, *Voyagers to the West: A Passage in the Peopling of America on the Eve of the Revolution* (New York, 1986), esp. 361–400.

French-Canadian majority. American spokesmen attacked the Quebec Act for its recognition of the Roman Catholic church in the province, but behind that action was an equally significant British acceptance of French civil law and the seigneurial system of land granting and land tenure. Canadian historians have long insisted that the Quebec Act was not directed against the Americans, but was intended to deal with the internal problems of a province with an overwhelmingly French population. But while the legislation was only coincidentally passed by Parliament at the same time as the Intolerable Acts, the Quebec Act was a tacit recognition of the failure of a policy of assimilation.[37] In that failure the political crisis to the south played its part.

Loyalists and Others

Ironically enough, the British acceptance of the dominant cultural and institutional values of the French-Canadian majority in Quebec came on the very eve of the disruption of the British Empire in North America that would result in a major migration north of American settlers. Americans began moving into Quebec and Nova Scotia from the beginning of open warfare between the colonies and Britain, although the political situation along the Saint Lawrence heartland of Quebec was complicated in 1775 and 1776 by the presence of invading American armies seeking to "liberate" the province. Most of the migrating refugees to Quebec avoided the Saint Lawrence, preferring instead more isolated territory in the Niagara peninsula and northwest of Lake Champlain. Although there was no overall settlement policy for Loyalist exiles until after the war had ended, the governments in Quebec and Nova Scotia did their best to accommodate the new arrivals, though finding, particularly in Nova Scotia, that the newcomers did not get on very well with the resident population. There was much jockeying for place and preferment in a rather limited environment, and the incoming Loyalists were persuaded that the existing population had not shown sufficient commitment to the crown.

The Loyalists present complex problems for the historian attempting to explain the development of Canadian settlement and Canadian society from the standpoint of cultural groups and incoming cultural values. Those problems are typical of the difficulties involved in unraveling cultural patterns in any transplantation situation in which the culture of neither the host society

37. Hilda Neatby, *Quebec: The Revolutionary Age, 1760–1791* (Toronto, 1966); and *The Quebec Act: Protest and Policy* (Scarborough, Ont., 1972). See also Gustave Lanctot, *Canada and the American Revolution*, trans. Margaret M. Cameron (Cambridge, Mass., 1967).

nor the incoming immigrants was fixed or has been well understood by later scholars. The traditional Canadian view that the Loyalists represented the cream of American society, "the choicest stock the colonies could boast," is no longer tenable. One now sees the Loyalists as a cross section of an American population that at the time of the rebellion included large numbers of blacks and native Indians.[38] A practical definition of "Loyalist" is difficult, but the larger problems of assessing the cultural impact of the newcomers are even more complicated.

In the first place, there is the problem of the military settlers. Contemporaries in the northern provinces clearly distinguished between Loyalist refugees (the civilian exiles) and those disbanded soldiers from the various units fighting in the British army who were in some cases mixed with the refugees on vessels evacuating the colonies. The soldiers were dealt with by the same officials under similar programs and were often recipients of land grants and subsidies within the colony where they were mustered out of their units. Since at the close of the war a substantial proportion of the British army was based in the northern provinces, many soldiers were able to take advantage of the government largess. No exact figures are available, but probably close to half of the total usually regarded as Loyalist settlers were actually disbanded soldiers. The British force was a polyglot mixture of Loyalists, German mercenaries, British regulars (often Highland Scots and Irish), and even men recruited in the northern colonies themselves; Newfoundland supplied men for a number of regiments, for example.[39] The question of the backgrounds of the disbanded soldiers has never been properly addressed by historians, but plainly many were not American colonials at all and therefore lacked the political commitment of the Loyalists. The Anglican clergyman Jacob Bailey, for example, characterized his neighbors in the Annapolis

38. James W. St. G. Walker, *The Black Loyalists: The Search for a Promised Land in Nova Scotia and Sierra Leone, 1783–1870* (Halifax, 1976); Barbara Graymont, *The Iroquois in the American Revolution* (Syracuse, N.Y., 1972). See also Esmond Wright, ed., *Red, White, and True Blue: The Loyalists in the Revolution* (New York, 1976). For a general historiographical discussion, see my *Understanding the Loyalists* (Sackville, N.B., 1986), 9–38. See also Wallace Brown and Hereward Senior, *Victorious in Defeat: The Loyalists in Canada* (Toronto, 1984). Also consult Wallace Brown, *The King's Friends: The Composition and Motives of the American Loyalist Claimants* (Providence, R.I., 1965); Neil MacKinnon, *This Unfriendly Soil: The Loyalist Experience in Nova Scotia, 1783–1791* (Kingston, 1986); Graeme Wynn, "A Region of Scattered Settlements and Bounded Possibilities: Northeastern America, 1775–1800," *Can. Geog.*, XXXI (1987), 319–338; Esther Clark Wright, *The Loyalists of New Brunswick* (Fredericton, N.B., 1955). There is no good general study of Upper Canadian Loyalism, but see Larry Turner, *Voyage of a Different Kind: The Associated Loyalists of Kingston and Adolphustown* (Belleville, Ont., 1984).

39. For the Loyalist component, see Robert S. Allen, ed., *The Loyal Americans: The Military Rôle of the Loyalist Provincial Corps and Their Settlement in British North America, 1775–1784* (Ottawa, 1983).

Valley as "a collection of all nations, kindreds, complexions and tongues assembled from every quarter of the globe and till lately equally strangers to me and each other."[40]

In the second place, there is the problem of the persistence of the new settlers in their allotted homes. Most historical discussion of Canadian Loyalists focuses on their arrival and initial resettlement rather than upon their subsequent dispersion. High rates of transiency are common to North American settlement, and very few Loyalists stayed where they originally settled. Shelburne, Nova Scotia, a town of more than ten thousand people at its height in the mid-1780s, was virtually a ghost town ten years later.[41] Nor was the situation much improved elsewhere. In Adolphustown, Upper Canada, one-quarter of the households turned over every two years. On the Isle Saint John, fewer than one-quarter of Loyalist land grantees were still on the island for the nominal census of 1798. In Wallace, Nova Scotia, two-fifths of the grantees never took up their lands, and another third were gone within two years.[42] No full-scale study of forward linkages has been done with this disappearing population, and so we do not know whether it remained within British North America or, as contemporaries claimed, returned to the United States when the dust had settled and subsidies ended.[43] Some evidence from the Maritimes suggests that disbanded soldiers, as opposed to refugee settlers, were most likely to move off their land grants, further complicating the problem of assessing their impact upon their new homeland. On the other hand, in Quebec, townships with a higher proportion of American-born were most transient, a fact perhaps suggesting both dissatisfaction with conditions and a willingness to return to the United States. Certainly the Loyalist officeholding elite tended to persist in influential positions, particularly in New Brunswick and Upper Canada. Perhaps they will turn out to be, as they were once held to be, the important figures.[44]

In the third place, assertions that the newly arriving American Loyalists represented a cross section of the American population beg the question in several ways. No scholar has systematically pursued William Nelson's observation (made a generation ago): that Loyalism was particularly attractive to ethnic and religious minority groups who found the tolerance of the British

40. Quoted in Wynn, "A Region of Scattered Settlements," *Can. Geog.*, XXXI (1987), 336n.

41. Marion Robertson, *King's Bounty: A History of Early Shelburne, Nova Scotia* (Halifax, 1983).

42. Darrell A. Norris, "Household and Transience in a Loyalist Township: The People of Adolphustown, 1784–1822," *Histoire sociale / Social History*, XIII (1980), 399–415; Bumsted, *Land, Settlement, and Politics*.

43. See MacKinnon, *This Unfriendly Soil*, 158–179.

44. For the New Brunswick elite, see Ann Gorman Condon, *The Envy of the American States: The Loyalist Dream for New Brunswick* (Fredericton, N.B., 1984).

Empire preferable to the aggressive national ethos of the new republic. Certainly there are suggestions that many of the most recent immigrants to the colonies, particularly among the Scots, were overrepresented among the Loyalist population.[45] Moreover, no studies of the cultural complexities of Revolutionary America are sufficiently detailed to enable us to measure the Loyalist population—if ever we have a detailed profile of it—against the American one.

In short, we do not know whether the Loyalist arrivals were predominantly Good Americans, Un-Americans, or Non-Americans. It is therefore difficult to ascertain the extent to which the Loyalist migration was responsible for importing or reinforcing American cultural values, particularly at the vernacular level. The best evidence for the Americanizing effect of the Loyalists comes in speech patterns and domestic housing style. So, despite a substantial and continued emigration from the British Isles, Maritimers would speak their English with an American pronunciation and cadence. Popular housing style also was American: simple frame houses, usually one and one-half stories covered with shingles, predominated and have become a popular visual symbol of the Maritime region. Only the odd wealthy immigrant built in brick or stone, while the occasional Loyalist squire imitated Georgian models, usually in wood.[46]

In Upper Canada, no one doubted the American influence of the early settlers. Traveler after traveler in that province commented upon how peopled the province was with former Americans. Again, the most apparent evidence was in speech. The Scotsman Patrick Campbell, on the Grand River in 1792, was answered by a man "in a twang peculiar to the New Englanders": "I viow niew you may depen I's just a-comin." When asked how far, the response was "I viow niew I guess I do'no,—I guess niew I do'no—I swear niew I guess it is three miles." A few years later another visitor reported the Americanized Upper Canadians "never seek to disguise their sentiments in public, but express themselves with as much freedom as you would do at the Theatre or Tontine Coffee-House."[47] The problem in Upper Canada was

45. William H. Nelson, *The American Tory* (Oxford, 1961), 91; Hazel C. Mathews, *The Mark of Honour* (Toronto, 1965).

46. Peter Ennals, "The Yankee Origins of Bluenose Vernacular Architecture," *American Review of Canadian Studies*, XII, no. 2 (Summer 1982), 5–21.

47. P[atrick] Campbell, *Travels in the Interior Inhabited Parts of North America in the Years 1791 and 1792*, ed. H. H. Langton (Toronto, 1937), 157; Christian Schultz, Jr., *Travels on an Inland Voyage . . . Performed in the Years 1807 and 1808 . . .* (New York, 1810), II, 55. In general, see Fred Landon, *Western Ontario and the American Frontier* (Toronto, 1941; rpt. ed., 1967); Wallace Brown, "First Impressions: Through Colonial Canada with Our Pioneer Tourists," *Beaver*, LXVIII, no. 2 (March 1988), 4–20.

that Americans were not necessarily Loyalists. American westward movement into British North America after 1783 was continual, and the "late Loyalists" have always posed a problem for Canadian historians. Although they may have been relatively apolitical, attracted mainly by cheap land, they nevertheless brought a good deal of cultural baggage with them.

The Loyalist resettlement has probably been given more credit than it deserves for reshaping development in British North America after the American Revolution, but it did help produce three new provinces (New Brunswick, 1784; Upper Canada, 1791; and Cape Breton, 1784) that would have official British or Anglo-British cultures, and it reinforced the British-American emphasis in three others (Nova Scotia, Quebec, and Isle Saint John / Prince Edward Island). Newfoundland was itself not much affected internally by Loyalism, although many former residents may have resettled elsewhere as disbanded soldiers. As for Quebec (or Lower Canada, so called after 1791), its vernacular culture was less monolithically French-Canadian after the Loyalist arrivals, but its official culture remained unable to adopt an Anglo stance despite Loyalist settlement. French Canada had been geographically limited, perhaps even isolated; but especially after the appearance of representative government in Lower Canada in 1791, it was unchastened and articulately emergent in its homeland.[48] The church and the seigneurs were both more important than ever before, and a professional class was growing to provide political leadership for the habitant.

Some Acadians had avoided the deportation, chiefly those in remote settlements and those able to escape to them. After the Treaty of Paris of 1763, British policy permitted Acadian resettlement, providing that oaths of allegiance were taken and that the population moved to designated places in small numbers. Throughout the Maritime region, Acadians gradually returned to farm and fish, usually in remote districts farthest from existing settlement and often on marginal land. The governments of the region made no attempt to assist them or fully accept them, but they were tolerated and left to create their own institutions apart from the remaining population. By 1803 a religious census showed nearly four thousand Acadians in Nova Scotia, nearly seven hundred in Prince Edward Island, and nearly four thousand in New Brunswick.[49] Left to fend for themselves, the Acadians developed both their own culture and eventually the institutions to support it.

48. Fernand Ouellet, *Economic and Social History of Quebec, 1760–1840* (Toronto, 1980).

49. Graeme Wynn, "Late Eighteenth-Century Agriculture on the Bay of Fundy Marshlands," *Acadiensis*, VIII, no. 2 (Spring 1979), 80–89; Edme Rameau de Saint-Père, *Une colonie féodale en Amérique: l'Acadie, 1604–1881*, 2 vols. (Paris, 1889), II, 255–266. See also William F. Ganong, "A Monograph of the Origins of Settlements in the Province of New Brunswick," Royal Society of Canada, *Transactions, Section 2, 1904*, esp. part 3, 109–180.

With a population doubling every twenty-five years (despite much emigration to the United States), the Acadians reentrenched themselves before the authorities turned their attention to this distinctive culture, so different from the officially acceptable ones in the region.

In what became Upper Canada and New Brunswick, the Loyalist infusion itself produced a quite complex cultural conflict. English (or British) elements often jostled with American varieties of "Loyal Whiggery," the latter supported by the continued largess of the British government to the Loyalists in the form of pensions. In these Loyalist provinces, not even the official culture was completely homogeneous, and it certainly displayed little consonance with the vernacular American culture of the typical settler, which tended to be far more concerned with practical political and economic matters than with ideology.[50] Official Loyalism exhibited a hostility to the United States probably not shared at the vernacular level as well as a general policy of noblesse oblige toward ethnic, religious, and racial minorities at variance with a perceived American pressure for civic conformity and national identity.[51]

A few non-American pockets were to be found in Loyalist settlements, such as the Glengarry district of Upper Canada settled by Scottish Highland refugees from upstate New York, most of them only a few years in America at the time of the Revolution. Highland Scots were also quite visible among the Carolina and Georgia Loyalists in the Maritimes.[52] Joining fellow Scots who had migrated directly to British North America before the war and joined by more compatriots after 1791, Highlander communities were strikingly distinctive, frequently Roman Catholic in religion, Gaelic-speaking in language, and transhumant livestock-producing in economy.

Even in those provinces where Loyalists did not predominate—such as the Isle Saint John, Nova Scotia, Cape Breton, and Newfoundland—other vernacular cultures of varying origins survived and flourished in isolated pockets of settlement. Local English and Irish cultures existed in the Newfound-

50. For "Loyal Whiggery," see William Allen Benton, *Whig-Loyalism: An Aspect of Political Ideology in the American Revolutionary Era* (Rutherford, N.J., 1969); and Janice Potter, *The Liberty We Seek: Loyalist Ideology in Colonial New York and Massachusetts* (Cambridge, Mass., 1983). For the pensions, consult Howard Temperley, "Frontierism, Capital, and the American Loyalists in Canada," *Journal of American Studies*, XIII (1979), 5–27. On the culture, see Jane Errington, *The Lion, the Eagle, and Upper Canada: A Developing Colonial Ideology* (Kingston, 1987); David Bell, *Early Loyalist Saint John: The Origin of New Brunswick Politics, 1783–1786* (Fredericton, N.B., 1983).

51. For example, Catherine L. Albanese, *Sons of the Fathers: The Civil Religion of the American Revolution* (Philadelphia, 1976).

52. Mathews, *The Mark of Honour*; Georgia Carole Watterson Troxler, "The Migration of Carolina and Georgia Loyalists to Nova Scotia and New Brunswick" (Ph.D. diss., University of North Carolina, 1974).

land outports, where English was spoken with Devon and Waterford accents (and still is) and traditional folk wisdom, tradition, and song from the Old Country were adapted to the new environment. German was spoken in the streets of Lunenburg and used in the town's schools and churches.

Later Immigration

With French-Canadian culture both altering and becoming more assertive; with Acadian culture replanting; with official British culture divided into Old World and Anglo-American wings, neither having a single focus; with "late Loyalists" moving in a steady stream northward, especially into Upper Canada; with vernacular cultures surviving in scattered settlement nodes—British North America entered still another period of British immigration beginning in the 1790s. In this movement, the Irish and the Highland Scots predominated and reinforced communities and districts where they had previously established cultural beachheads, often providing further complexities to the already complicated patchwork of vernacular cultures in the rural settlements and urban centers of what would become Canada.[53]

The new British immigration was greeted with no more enthusiasm by authorities in either the mother country or the colonies than earlier movements had been. Britain still wanted to retain laborers and potential soldiers, and colonies that had experienced great difficulties with Loyalist resettlement had no energy left for dealing with new arrivals. But Britain did little to prevent the exodus until 1803, when Parliament, to cut the flow, legislated better conditions on immigrant vessels sailing to North America, fully aware that subsequent higher fares meant fewer departures of the less affluent.[54]

Parliament was responding to a new type of immigration, not involving organization by local community leaders, but operated by individuals acting as immigrant contractors in the hopes of making a profit. This form of contracting became prevalent in the first years of the nineteenth century. The nascent timber trade was already providing vessels sailing to America without cargo, and after the closure of the Baltic in 1807 the upsurge in the timber trade with British North America provided increasing numbers of vessels that could carry immigrant passengers. Until well into the nineteenth century, the association between timbering and British immigration would be close. The vessels provided relatively cheap transport, sailed to places in British North America rather than in the United States, and dropped their passengers either in important timber ports or at important timbering re-

53. Helen I. Cowan, *British Emigration to British North America: The First Hundred Years*, rev. ed. (Toronto, 1961).

54. See my *People's Clearance*, 128–154.

gions (such as the Miramichi in northeastern New Brunswick), thus influencing the patterns of settlement.[55] Since little assisted passage was available before 1815, most of the immigrants of this period had some capital for their passage money, but many arrived in British North America without money to obtain land. They drifted to the cities and into the timbering regions and often settled in areas where landlords were looking for tenant farmers, such as Prince Edward Island. By 1815 the Irish were the majority population in Newfoundland and an important element in New Brunswick and in major port cities. As for the Highland Scots, by 1815 they had made Gaelic the third most common European language in British North America; it was particularly prevalent in Prince Edward Island, parts of Nova Scotia and Cape Breton, and eastern Upper Canada.

The new immigration further confirmed the tendency of the population of British North America to diverge from the officially supported Church of England, in the directions both of Protestant dissent and of Roman Catholicism. Unlike the thirteen colonies, where the Church of England had a dominant position in some places, Anglicanism in early British North America was outnumbered not simply by Protestant dissent but, more important, by Roman Catholics. Indeed, Catholics were in the overwhelming majority in Lower Canada, a majority in Newfoundland and Rupert's Land, and the largest single denomination in Cape Breton and Prince Edward Island by the end of the century. By the 1780s the British authorities had given up attempting to enforce positive proscriptions against Catholics in the various provinces, and also eliminated were the earlier exemptions of them from governors' instructions to allow religious liberty to all.

But official tolerance of Roman Catholicism, even the right to hold land, was not the same as full acceptance. The situation was complex. By the end of the eighteenth century, Catholics were enfranchised only in the Canadas (by the Constitutional Act of 1791) and in Nova Scotia (by a 1789 legislative enactment). New Brunswick withdrew Catholic enfranchisement after its first elections and did not restore it until 1810. Prince Edward Island did not allow Catholics to vote until 1830. Newfoundland, Cape Breton, and Rupert's Land had no popularly elected political bodies—in the first two colonies, partly because of the prevalence of Catholics. Moreover, until 1830 the Canadas alone allowed Catholics to sit in the bodies for which they could vote.[56] Catholic disabilities encouraged British North Americans of that

55. For the timber trade, consult Graeme Wynn, *Timber Colony: A Historical Geography of Early Nineteenth Century New Brunswick* (Toronto, 1981); A.R.M. Lower, *Great Britain's Woodyard: British America and the Timber Trade, 1763–1867* (Montreal, 1973).

56. John Garner, *The Franchise and Politics in British North America, 1755–1867* (Toronto, 1969), 131–145.

denomination to think of themselves as outsiders, and thus their communities were encouraged to operate as distinctive cultural units.

Few of the new immigrants made their way into the Canadas, Lower Canada remained dominantly French Canadian, and Upper Canada was largely American and ethnic Loyalist. The prevalence of Americans in Upper Canada bothered the British government and observers from the mother country. The earl of Selkirk, for example, a major proponent of immigration in the early years of the nineteenth century, brought a party of Highlanders into Upper Canada and advised his agent, "I would not have the people speak English, since to learn to speak English is to learn to be American."[57] Selkirk favored Irish and Highland Scottish immigration to Upper Canada as part of a general strategy of hemming in the American settlers with ethnic populations that spoke different languages and practiced different religions. On one occasion he argued, "A national settlement, speaking their original and favourite dialect will be equally attractive to the Irish as to the Highlanders; and it will be of use to preserve among the Settlers, those national customs and peculiarities, which are associated in their minds, with the traditions of the ancient greatness of their race." Selkirk insisted that, were the Canadian provinces divided into four or five districts, "each inhabited by Colonists of a different nation, keeping up their original peculiarities and all differing in language from their neighbours in the United States, the authority of Government would be placed on the most secure foundation." In such a scheme, it was critical to provide sufficient numbers "to preserve themselves from the contagion of American manners."[58] The War of 1812 did much to alleviate the political dangers for American residents in Upper Canada, since they were forced to choose sides, but it did not settle the problem of culture.

The earl of Selkirk became intimately, if inadvertently, involved in one of the most striking examples of an emergent culture, involving the mixed-bloods of the Red River region, which he attempted to settle with Highlanders and Irishmen beginning in 1811. The Red River Settlement was at the center of a complex trade war between the Hudson's Bay Company (which had granted Selkirk his land) and the North West Company. The latter assisted in stirring up the district's mixed-bloods, who constituted themselves "a New Nation" and even created a "halfbreed flag," about "4½ feet

57. See J. M. Bumsted, ed., *The Writings and Papers of Thomas Douglas, Fifth Earl of Selkirk*, I, *The Collected Writings of Lord Selkirk, 1799–1809* (Winnipeg, 1985).

58. Selkirk, Memorial on Irish Emigration transmitted to Lord Sidmouth, Nov. 19, 1806, Selkirk Papers at the Public Archives of Canada (hereafter SPPAC), 13875–13892; "Outlines of a Plan for the Settlement and Security of Canada 1805," SPPAC, 13919–13926.

square, red and in the middle a large figure of Eight horizontally of a different colour."[59] The ending of the fur trade war in 1821 with the merger of the two companies ended mixed-blood violence in the west for half a century. But the mixed-bloods, neither Indian nor European, constituted a major force in Rupert's Land (as the Hudson's Bay Company territory became called) throughout most of the nineteenth century. The refusal of the British government to assume direct responsibility for the territory claimed and administered by the Hudson's Bay Company ensured the absence of an official culture in which (as would be the case after 1870) the Métis could have only a limited role.

Many Canadians have always assumed that there were in Canada two historic cultures—the French and the English (or British)—and that assumption was elevated to the level of national policy in the 1960s. But the important points about the cultural landscape of early British North America are much more complex than a single concept of biculturalism would allow. In addition to the British and French-Canadian cultures, a variety of emergent vernacular cultures, most with French or British roots, flourished. Moreover, the authorities were unable to create a cultural hegemony in which the official British and the emergent cultures were made similar, if not identical.

The extent of cultural complexity in British North America around 1800 can hardly be overemphasized. Only the French in Lower Canada had a reasonably mature and well-developed culture, dominating throughout most of a province governed by men with an alternative set of cultural values and assumptions. But the French culture of Lower Canada was not the only French one to be found. In the Maritime region, the Acadians were redeveloping and reentrenching—after the expulsions—their own particular brand of North Americanized French peasant culture. And in the west, the Métis offered yet another French variant, in which European origins were subordinated to Indian ones. The Métis spoke French (or at least a fur trade dialect of it) and were Roman Catholics, but otherwise their culture was at least as different from Lower Canada's as Lower Canada's was from France itself. Moreover, the extent of miscegenation in British North America reflects the relative importance of its Indian population. Large portions of the territory on the continent claimed by the British had few European inhabitants beyond the male fur traders. As for the British, the only place their official culture could be found relatively intact was among the ruling elites in pro-

59. Peter Fidler, "A Narrative of the Re-establishment, Progress, and Total Destruction of the Colony in Red River 1816," SPPAC, 2509–2531. For early Red River in general, see the introduction to *The Collected Writings of Lord Selkirk*, II (forthcoming). See also Margaret A. MacLeod and W. L. Morton, *Cuthbert Grant of Grantown: Warden of the Plains of Red River* (Toronto, 1963).

vincial capitals and commercial centers. Even in colonies where the French did not predominate, outside the major urban areas American culture, mixtures of American and regional British, or isolated regional British culture (particularly Irish and Highland Scots) were strong, constantly adapting to their new situation.

Why were the British unable to create a cultural hegemony? The traditional explanation has been the existence of the French in Lower Canada, and certainly in the Canadas the French-Canadian presence was critical. But in the absence of national institutions, the French in Canada had little influence upon policy elsewhere in British North America. The only coordinating body for British policy was the Board of Trade, only gradually developing into the Colonial Office, and its outlook was both limited and reflexive.[60] Not until after Canadian Confederation in 1867 would the French-Canadians become a national factor.

More critical in limiting cultural hegemony was the absence of a common and unifying traumatic experience, such as the war of national liberation experienced by the American colonies. Unlike the United States, which also was ethnically complex, there was no powerful fusion force of a national revolution in British North America and no development of a pervasive national political and sociocultural ideology.[61] The provinces that would become Canada moved toward nationhood and dominion status in much the way that the American colonies would have done had there been no American Revolution. The process was gradual and piecemeal; and, while hardly free from ideologies, those that developed, such as "responsible government," were difficult to translate into cultural symbols and icons. Moreover, without a national framework and perspective, the importance of the individual culture such as that of French Canada remained geographically limited. The British governments in Newfoundland or Prince Edward Island, for example, had no need to take French Canada into account in formulating their policies.

Finally, the British seemed unable or unwilling to find ways to transmit and impose their official culture upon the divergent vernacular ones. In some places, they were even reluctant to establish proper governmental institutions, allowing the people of Newfoundland, Rupert's Land, and Acadian New Brunswick to work out their cultural existence almost totally unimpeded by an official British culture. Policy toward Roman Catholics was

60. Helen T. Manning, *British Colonial Government after the American Revolution, 1782–1820* (Hamden, Conn., 1966); Phillip A. Buckner, *The Transition to Responsible Government: British Policy in British North America, 1815–1850* (Westport, Conn., 1985).

61. For an outline of American cultural development and policy after the Revolution, see Ralph Ketcham, *From Colony to Country: The Revolution in American Thought, 1750–1820* (New York, 1974).

equally symptomatic. A failure to draw Catholics into the body politic encouraged isolation, but full acceptance of Catholicism was both slow and generated from the mother country itself. Public schooling was slow to develop, initially over the opposition of the British colonial governments that saw public schools as dangerous and expensive rather than as potential assimilating forces. In Quebec / Lower Canada, political considerations may have prevented the government from moving as fast or as far as it would have liked in furthering assimilation. But in most provinces, it was less a political weakness than an absence of political vision that was involved.

British North America in 1800 was a collection of relatively autonomous and culturally distinctive provinces with weak colonial administrations incapable of melding their various emergent cultures into a coherent whole. Whether or not such a situation was good or bad depends, in the final analysis, on one's perspective.

III

The Homeland Transformed

JACOB M. PRICE

Who Cared about the Colonies?

The Impact of the Thirteen Colonies on British Society and Politics, circa 1714–1775

From the settlement of Jamestown to the onset of the Revolution, the thirteen colonies were part of the English (later British) imperium, subject to the British crown and Parliament and to British laws and very much part of the British market system and the British religious-cultural world. A vast library exists purporting to explain what this connection meant for the thirteen colonies, but relatively little has been written to explain or explore what it meant for England and Scotland. This essay attempts a foray into, if not a full-scale exploration of, the latter question: the backward influence of the colonies on Britain.

In 1924 Jay Barrett Botsford published a well-received book (originally a Columbia thesis) entitled *English Society in the Eighteenth Century as Influenced from Overseas.*[1] Botsford cast his net rather wide: in addition to such obvious topics as trade and trading companies, missionary societies, and the like, he included the rise of port cities and urban civilization, the increased importance of the middle class, new urban patterns of consumption (particularly tea, coffee, sugar, and tobacco), new facilities for social intercourse (such as coffeehouses), and new scientific interests. Botsford's book is based heavily on travelers' accounts and literary texts and tends in a rather journalistic style to regard all phenomena as equally important. For him, too, "overseas" meant the whole world outside Europe, so that he can skip in one paragraph from America to Asia and back again. Botsford's work is interesting in conception, though I suspect that few dissertation students today would attempt to emulate either his world scope or methodology.

Here, I essay a much more limited investigation of the impact of the colonies on Britain, focusing on the concern in Britain for the thirteen colonies in the years between the accession of the House of Hanover in 1714

1. Jay Barrett Botsford, *English Society in the Eighteenth Century as Influenced from Overseas* (New York, 1924).

and the end of the old empire in 1775. I shall not pay too much attention to such epiphenomena as the consumption of snuff made from Virginia tobacco or of pudding made from Carolina rice, but shall instead be looking for evidence of the ability of the colonies to involve the interests and command the attention and concern of people in Britain, from the politically eminent to those in trade and to the nation at large.

Those on High

Lance Davis and Robert Huttenback have analyzed the costs and benefits of the Victorian and Edwardian empire. They demonstrate quite convincingly that, while the empire meant careers for some and opportunities for advantageous investment for others, fiscally it was disadvantageous for the United Kingdom as a whole, creating a significant burden for most British taxpayers, especially those unable to draw private benefit from the overseas dependencies.[2] However, this British Empire of 1857–1914 differed greatly from the thirteen colonies of 1714–1775. Before the Peace of Paris in 1763, the British government spent very little on the civil administration of its North American colonies, leaving responsibility for most expenses to local assemblies and local taxes. Even defense expenditures before 1755 were minimal—except in wartime. Although questions of colonial expenditures and taxation assumed the highest political importance from 1763 and although even earlier the expenses connected with the French wars of 1744–1748 and 1756–1763 were substantial, the negligible *peacetime* expenditures before 1763 meant that the British taxpayer qua taxpayer had little reason then to think much about the colonies. Moreover, because both expenditures and establishments in North America were normally so modest, there could not have been very many people in Britain who had experience in North America or anticipation of appointments there. Aside from the customs establishment and the governorships, there were only a scattering of positions in the North American colonies likely to attract any of the well-connected or the hungry in Britain.[3]

2. Lance E. Davis and Robert A. Huttenback, *Mammon and the Pursuit of Empire: The Political Economy of British Imperialism, 1860–1912* (Cambridge, 1986), esp. chaps. 8, 11.

3. On British expenditures in North America, see Julian Gwyn, "British Government Spending and the North American Colonies, 1740–1775," *Journal of Imperial and Commonwealth History*, VIII (1980), 74–84. On the military arrangements in the thirteen colonies before 1760, see John Shy, *Toward Lexington: The Role of the British Army in the Coming of the American Revolution* (Princeton, N.J., 1965), chap. 1; and Stanley McCrory Pargellis, *Lord Loudoun in North America* (New Haven, Conn., 1933), chaps. 1–4.

Some readers will wonder at this point whether the importance of colonial patronage is not being sloughed off too unthinkingly. They should reflect that its alleged importance is in good part a matter of perspective. For the student of the individual colony, royal or proprietary, patronage frequently emerges as a central problem in that colony's corporate history.[4] Politically active or involved colonists were, naturally, concerned about the naming of a governor, attorney general, naval officer, or customs collector. However, from the standpoint of London, such positions are just details in the grand schema of British patronage. One can get some idea of the relative weight of colonial offices in this schema by looking at some of the manuals of officeholders published circa 1750–1775. In those published in the 1750s or 1760s we find only 2 or 3 pages devoted to colonial posts (in volumes of 225–250 pages), though, with heightened interest, this rises to about 5 pages in the 1770s (in volumes of 250–300 pages). When we deduct from the totals all the pages in these books devoted to Parliament, baronets, dignitaries of the established church and universities, army and navy officers, lords lieutenant of counties and all places not in crown patronage (officers of municipalities, companies, charities, and so forth) and thus reduce our coverage to crown civil patronage only, we find the colonial posts still come to only 3–4 percent of this reduced total in the 1760s and about 6 percent in the 1770s. If we put back the higher offices in the armed forces and the church, the share of colonial posts shrinks even more. The duke of Newcastle and colleagues thus had reams of other patronage matters to fuss with, even after surrendering colonial patronage to the Board of Trade in 1752.[5]

There were, to be sure, people in Britain who had substantial politico-economic interests in America not dependent on royal office, starting with the owners of proprietary colonies. In the seventeenth century, persons of the greatest political importance had been included among those to whom the Carolinas and Jerseys were granted—persons as important as George

On the customs establishment, see Thomas C. Barrow, *Trade and Empire: The British Customs Service in Colonial America, 1660–1775* (Cambridge, Mass., 1967). On the general character of the pre-1763 administration, see James A. Henretta, *"Salutary Neglect": Colonial Administration under the Duke of Newcastle* (Princeton, N.J., 1972). On officeholding in the colonies, see Bruce C. Daniels, ed., *Power and Status: Officeholding in Colonial America* (Middletown, Conn., 1986).

4. For the patronage problem as seen from the perspective of the individual colony, see Stanley Nider Katz, *Newcastle's New York: Anglo-American Politics, 1732–1753* (Cambridge, Mass., 1968); Donnell MacClure Owings, *His Lordship's Patronage: Offices of Profit in Colonial Maryland*, Studies in Maryland History, no. 1 (Baltimore, 1953).

5. Based on a more detailed examination of *The Court and City Register* (1764, 1772); *The St. James Register; or, Royal Annual Kalendar* (1765); *The Court and City Kalendar* (1769); and *The Royal Kalendar* (1774). For the duke's role in colonial patronage before 1752, see Henretta, *"Salutary Neglect,"* esp. 306–318.

Monck, duke of Albemarle, Edward Hyde, earl of Clarendon, and Anthony Ashley Cooper, earl of Shaftesbury. However, this phase had more or less ended by the time of the surrender of the Carolinas in the 1720s. The remaining governing proprietors, the Penns in Pennsylvania and the lords Baltimore in Maryland, were, particularly after 1689, primarily concerned with retaining their proprietorships. (In fact, the lords Baltimore temporarily lost theirs from 1689 to 1715.) At least as limited and defensive were the aspirations of the nongoverning proprietors of the Jerseys and the Northern Neck of Virginia. Such restricted ambitions were appropriate to proprietors whose political importance gave them little expectation of being able to influence colonial policy more generally.[6]

A few apparent and temporary exceptions during the ascendancy of Robert Walpole and Henry Pelham (1721–1754) merely proved the rule in the long run. Charles Calvert, fifth Lord Baltimore, proprietor of Maryland, was an active parliamentary politician in the 1740s, attaching himself to the group around Frederick, Prince of Wales. That foray led nowhere, for both the prince and Lord Baltimore died in 1751.[7] A more important figure in the same circle about the prince was John Perceval, second earl of Egmont, son of one of the founders of the Georgia Society, of which he also was a trustee. In the 1760s Egmont was to hold the position of first lord of the Admiralty, among other places. However, the second earl's involvement in Georgia was quite minimal: he became a trustee only on the death of his father in 1748 and, in effect, joined only in time to help with the winding up. He was not otherwise meaningfully involved in American affairs.[8]

Among others who were politically important there is even less evidence of significant interest in the colonies. Curious Britons did visit the colonies from time to time, and some of them left travel accounts, but no member of the royal family or inner cabinet appears to have visited the thirteen colonies between 1714 and 1775. Nor did many other prominent people become involved as individuals in matters American in these years, except for the

6. Charles M. Andrews, *The Colonial Period of American History*, 4 vols. (New Haven, Conn., 1934–1938), II, chaps. 8–9, III, chaps. 5–7; J. M. Sosin, *English America and the Revolution of 1688: Royal Administration and the Structure of Provincial Government* (Lincoln, Nebr., 1982), chaps. 8, 12, 13; Sosin, *English America and Imperial Inconstancy: The Rise of Provincial Autonomy, 1696–1715* (Lincoln, Nebr., 1985), chaps. 6–8. There were, of course, partial exceptions, such as Paul Docminique, a Jersey proprietor and member of the Board of Trade, 1714–1735.

7. Romney Sedgwick, *The House of Commons, 1715–1754*, 2 vols., The History of Parliament (London, 1970), I, 518–519; John B. Owen, *The Rise of the Pelhams* (London, 1957).

8. Sedgwick, *House of Commons, 1715–1754*, II, 339–340; Owen, *Pelhams*, s.v. Perceval; Allen D. Candler, ed., *The Colonial Records of the State of Georgia*, I (Atlanta, 1904), 27–30. For key literature on the trustee period in Georgia, see Kenneth Coleman, *Colonial Georgia: A History* (New York, 1976).

aforementioned service by a few as trustees of Georgia before 1752 or the membership by a larger number in the Society for the Propagation of the Gospel in Foreign Parts. That most respectable organization was heavily clerical in membership, with only a few and very senior politicians moved to join.[9]

Within the home government, there were, of necessity, a handful of permanent or semipermanent officials who were paid to know something about the colonies: undersecretaries of state and functionaries at the Board of Trade. Most of this small set were quite knowledgeable about American affairs, and they generally knew how to get more information when they needed it, even if their channels of communication were, of necessity, limited. The most obvious, if somewhat suspect, of these channels were the London agents of the several colonies. In the generation before the Revolution, six of those representing the North American colonies were also, as we shall see, members of Parliament.[10] Earlier the agents had tended to be more obscure people, though men quite obscure to us may have had channels of influence whose extent we can scarcely guess at. For example, Peter Leheup, who was at various times agent for Virginia, Barbados, New Jersey, and New York, was a pluralist Treasury clerk and deputy to Horatio Walpole, auditor general of American revenues, to whom he was also connected by marriage. Leheup's influence extended to legislation.[11]

Undersecretaries, legal counsel, and senior clerks could only advise; they

9. For published accounts of British travelers in colonial America, see Thomas D. Clark *et al.*, eds., *Travels in the Old South: A Bibliography*, 3 vols. (Norman, Okla., 1956–1959), esp. vol. I; and Frank Freidel, ed., *Harvard Guide to American History*, rev. ed., 2 vols. (Cambridge, Mass., 1974), I, 139–141. Lord Adam Gordon, an army officer, member of Parliament, and son of the duke of Gordon, would appear to be the only (nonproprietary) visitor of the highest social status.

The membership lists of the Society can be found appended to the published annual commemoration sermons. In the outer cabinet, at least four first lords of the Admiralty—Wager, Anson, Saunders, and Hawke—had some experience of America while naval officers on sea duty, but only Anson and perhaps Hawke had any significant exposure to the society of the thirteen colonies.

10. Franklin B. Wickwire, *British Subministers and Colonial America, 1763–1783* (Princeton, N.J., 1966); Ella Lonn, *The Colonial Agents of the Southern Colonies* (Chapel Hill, N.C., 1945); Dame Lillian M[argery] Penson, *The Colonial Agents of the British West Indies: A Study in Colonial Administration in the Eighteenth Century* (London, 1924); Edward P. Lilly, "The Colonial Agents of New York and New Jersey" (Ph.D. diss., Catholic University of America, 1936). Cf. also Jack M. Sosin, *Agents and Merchants: British Colonial Policy and the Origins of the American Revolution* (Lincoln, Nebr., 1965), chap. 1; and Michael G. Kammen, *A Rope of Sand: The Colonial Agents, British Politics, and the American Revolution* (Ithaca, N.Y., 1968), esp. chap. 1.

11. On Leheup, see Jacob M. Price, "The Excise Affair Revisited: The Administrative and Colonial Dimensions of a Parliamentary Crisis," in Stephen B. Baxter, ed., *England's Rise to Greatness, 1660–1763* (Berkeley, Calif., 1983), 274–276.

did not make policy. Colonial agents could hope to influence policy only if they could reach people of policy-making responsibility either directly or via the undersecretaries and others at that level. The body that was formally charged with advising the crown on colonial affairs (via the Privy Council or the secretaries of state) was the Board of Trade. In its earliest days following its foundation in 1696, it was quite active both in administration and policy formation, but became progressively less energetic and influential in the eighteenth century. By the time of the Pelham ascendancy (1743–1762), membership was too frequently viewed as a sinecure. During the presidency of the second earl of Halifax (1749–1761), the board reasserted some—not total—control over patronage but did not otherwise change its character or effect real control over policy. For service on such a board, interest in or even knowledge of the colonies was desirable but hardly a prerequisite. Of the seventy-five men who served on the board between 1696 and 1775, only five had any conspicuous connection with the Americas: three with the West Indies only; one, Paul Docminique, with the Jerseys; and one, Martin Bladen, with both the West Indies and North America. Bladen, whose wife had inherited a sugar plantation on Nevis, was a director of the Royal African Company (1717–1726) and a prominent spokesman for the West India interest. His brother William Bladen (1670–1718) had in the 1690s emigrated to Maryland, where he became, inter alia, clerk to the provincial council (1698–1716), commissary general (1708–1718), secretary of the colony (1701–1718), and attorney general (1704–1718). William's son Thomas moved to England on his father's death and became a member of Parliament, but returned to Maryland for a time as deputy governor (1742–1746). However, one swallow doesn't make a spring, and one Bladen doesn't constitute an American interest on the Board of Trade.[12]

12. On Martin and Thomas Bladen, see Sedgwick, *House of Commons, 1715–1754*. On William Bladen, see *Dictionary of American Biography*; and Edward C. Papenfuse *et al.*, eds., *A Biographical Dictionary of the Maryland Legislature, 1635–1789*, 2 vols. (Baltimore, 1979, 1985), I, 136. Another rather insignificant member of the Board of Trade, William Sloper (1756–1761) was the son of an original Georgia trustee of the same name. For membership of the Board of Trade, see J. C. Sainty, *Officials of the Boards of Trade, 1660–1870*, Office-Holders in Modern Britain, III (London, 1974). See also Ian K. Steele, *Politics of Colonial Policy: The Board of Trade in Colonial Administration, 1696–1720* (Oxford, 1968); Oliver Morton Dickerson, *American Colonial Government, 1696–1765: A Study of the British Board of Trade* (New York, 1912); Arthur Herbert Basye, *The Lords Commissioners of Trade and Plantations: Commonly Known as the Board of Trade, 1748–1782* (New Haven, Conn., 1925), esp. 71–84, 220–232.

Others on the Board of Trade may have had different sorts of connections with the American colonies, even though they had neither experience nor property interests there. The sixth earl of Westmorland, first lord, 1719–1735, was the head of the aristocratic Fane family, a cadet branch of which resided near Bristol, where they had intermarried with local merchant families (with American trade connections), including the Swymmers and the Scropes (the family also of the secretary of the Treasury).

Paradoxically, the very thinness of American experience on the Board of Trade meant that any lone commissioner who did attend and read the papers—most noticeably Halifax or Charles Townshend—could quickly acquire the reputation of an expert and exert a disproportionate influence on his colleagues. Realistically, too, it meant that senior members of the board's staff and colonial governors trusted by this activist board minority could also have an influence on policy greater than their rank would suggest. However, here we are not concerned with how specific individuals influenced specific policy decisions, but, rather, with the relations of broader strata—within and without the political nation—to American questions.

Below the level of statesmen and significant placemen lay the several thousand knights of the shire and burgesses who between 1715 and 1775 sat in the House of Commons, the very heart of the political nation. We may usefully divide this corps into those serving in the relatively quiet years (from a North American perspective) down to the death of Pelham in 1754, and those entering Parliament only in the more turbulent ensuing generation. In the first period (1715–1754) there was at least one conspicuous group in the House of Commons associated with North America: the Georgia trustees. Approximately three-fourths of the colony's lay trustees between 1732 and 1752 (some 47 individuals) were members of either the British House of Commons (44) or House of Lords (3). However, only a handful—most noticeably, James Oglethorpe and Lord Egmont— were seriously involved in the affairs of the trust. For the rest this American activity was largely eleemosynary and passive.[13]

We can legitimately look for other and possibly more intense American interests in the House of Commons among three occupational groups: navy officers, army officers, and merchants.

Between 1715 and 1754, 54 naval officers served in the House of Commons. The naval war of 1739–1748 helped swell the number from an average of 12 in the parliaments of 1715–1741 to 20 in the parliaments of 1741–1754. It is difficult to ascertain readily the full details of the professional postings of naval officers, but the information on those elected to the Commons assembled by Romney Sedgwick suggests that at least 21 of the 54 served in the West Indies or Newfoundland but that only 2 had any noticeable experience of the thirteen colonies. Matthew Norris, of a naval family,

Such connections go far in explaining how Francis Fane of Bristol became counsel to the Board of Trade. The connections by blood and marriage between aristocratic and mercantile families are well known but have not been systematically studied. See also Alison G. Olson, "The Board of Trade and London-American Interest Groups in the Eighteenth Century," *Jour. Imperial and Commonwealth Hist.*, VIII (1980), 33–50.

13. Candler, *Records of Georgia*, I, 27–30; Sedgwick, *House of Commons, 1715–1754*.

was in New York long enough to marry a daughter of Lewis Morris of Morrisania, sometime governor of New Jersey. Sir Peter Warren was also in those waters long enough not only to marry a De Lancey but also to acquire substantial landholdings in New York and South Carolina.[14]

In part because the military was a less technical service preferred by the landed classes, army officers were more numerous (182) than naval officers in the House of Commons during 1715–1754. However, American experience was no more common. Of the 182, only 3 appear to have had experience in the thirteen colonies before 1755: James Oglethorpe and two governors of New York, James Montgomerie and the Honorable John West. A few others of this pre-1754 contingent served in the West Indies or in Canada, or later in the thirteen colonies during the Seven Years' War. However, the New York governors and those serving after 1755 saw North America after their years in the House of Commons. They thus had no American experience to draw upon while in Parliament. In effect, among the army officers in the House of Commons before 1755, only Oglethorpe could call on prior North American experience.[15]

In the same parliaments of 1715–1754, there were 169 merchants and 12 bankers. Inasmuch as merchants frequently traded to more than one area, one cannot be absolutely sure that one has classified them comprehensively. Even so, it is noteworthy that only 14 of the 169 can definitely be identified as trading to the thirteen colonies: 12 to Virginia and Maryland and 2 elsewhere.[16]

In the next generation, 1754–1776, the American connection in the House of Commons became much more conspicuous. America, it should be remembered, was not a constant. While the population of England and Wales was increasing by only 27 percent between 1701 and 1771 (from about 5.1 million to about 6.4 million), that of the thirteen colonies increased by something like 756 percent between 1700 and 1770, or from about 250,000 in 1700 to about 2.1 million in 1770 and 2.5 million in 1775. This much bigger satellite had a much stronger pull upon the tides of interest in the mother country, observable even in the House of Commons. In this last generation we find some new types there, such as the four or five members born in the thirteen colonies and six colonial agents: James Aber-

14. Sedgwick, *House of Commons, 1715–1754*, I, 144–145, 155, II, 299, 522–523; Julian Gwyn, *The Enterprising Admiral: The Personal Fortune of Admiral Sir Peter Warren* (Montreal, 1974).

15. Sedgwick, *House of Commons, 1715–1754*, I, 142–144.

16. *Ibid.*, 148–150, utilizing also my own file of merchants trading to America. Those with interests in Virginia and Maryland: Thomas Benson, Robert Bristow, Neil Buchanan, John Buck, John Burridge, Daniel Campbell, Sir William Daines, Abraham Elton the younger, Richard Gildart, Sir Thomas Johnson, Micajah Perry, Edward Tucker; elsewhere in North America: William Baker, John Sargent. Many of those interested in Virginia and Maryland also had interests in other colonies.

cromby (Virginia), Edmund Burke and John Sargent (New York), Charles Garth (South Carolina and Maryland), John Thomlinson and Barlow Trecothick (New Hampshire). We also begin to find for the first time a small group in the Commons who had American interests without any usual career or professional involvement.[17] More striking was the great new speculative interest in the North American lands either ceded by France and Spain in 1763 or newly secured for settlement. Dozens of members of Parliament, peers, and other prominent people applied for and received extensive land grants in East Florida, though only five members had actually secured such grants by settlement before 1776. Equally impressive was the large number—five great peers and seventeen members—who were persuaded to subscribe for shares in the Grand Ohio (or Walpole) Company, which was striving, circa 1768–1772, to obtain royal confirmation to their title to more than two million acres acquired from Indians by the Treaty of Fort Stanwix.[18] However, as in the earlier period, the overwhelming majority of

17. E. A. Wrigley and R. S. Schofield, *The Population History of England, 1541–1871: A Reconstruction* (Cambridge, Mass., 1981), 208–209; U.S. Bureau of the Census, *Historical Statistics of the United States: Colonial Times to 1970* (Washington, D.C., 1975), II, 1168; Sir Lewis Namier and John Brooke, *The House of Commons, 1754–1790*, 3 vols., The History of Parliament (London, 1964), I, 159–162.

Lauchlin Macleane (member of Parliament, 1768–1771) had been a civil and military surgeon in Pennsylvania (1756–1763). Among other American posts, Thomas Pownall (member, 1767–1780) had been governor of Massachusetts Bay (1757–1760). Denys Rolle (member, 1761–1774) had worked hard to attract settlers to his land grant in East Florida. All particulars on individual army and navy officers among the members can be found in Namier and Brooke, *House of Commons, 1754–1790*, II–III.

The subject of the American interest in the House of Commons on the eve of the Revolution has been dealt with most interestingly in Sir Lewis Namier, *England in the Age of the American Revolution*, 2d ed. (London, 1961), chap. 4. My compressed handling of the topic here covers a different block of years and is somewhat more quantitative.

18. The five members "who settled their land before 1776" were John Tucker, Peter Taylor, Admiral Sir Edward Hawke, Denys Rolle, and Henry Strachey. For the others, see Charles Loch Mowat, *East Florida as a British Province, 1763–1784*, University of California Publications in History, XXXIII (Berkeley, Calif., 1943), 58–61. Two other members, Lord Adam Gordon and Staats Long Morris, acquired large land grants in New York and Canada, respectively. See also Wilbur Henry Siebert, *Loyalists in East Florida, 1774 to 1785*, 2 vols., Publications of the Florida State Historical Society, 9 (Deland, Fla., 1929), II, 307–308, which shows that other important people had acquired land claims in Florida by 1783, including lords Arden, Brownlow, Loughborough, and Moira and members of Parliament Robert Barker and Jacob Wilkinson.

Of those subscribing for shares, the peers (all earls) were Hertford, lord chamberlain; Camden, lord chancellor; Rochford, secretary of state; Gower, lord president of the council; and Temple, head of the Grenville clan. The members of Parliament were Thomas Bradshaw, junior secretary of the Treasury; Sir George Colebrooke, bart.; General Henry Seymour Conway, secretary of state; Grey Cooper, secretary of the

members with American interests belonged to the three big occupational groups: navy officers, army officers, and merchants.

The Seven Years' War should have noticeably expanded the Western Hemisphere experience of many navy and army officers. In the case of the navy, however, the American experience of most naval members of Parliament was in the West Indies or as governors of Newfoundland or, in this war, in the Quebec campaign. The number of naval officers in the Commons with evident experience in the thirteen colonies proper rose from two in 1715–1754 to four in 1754–1776. The situation was rather different among army officers serving in the Commons during those same years, owing particularly to the extensive military operations on the North American frontiers. Thus, in place of one member with military experience in the colonies in the parliaments of 1715–1754, we find eleven in the ensuing generation of 1754–1776.[19]

This expanded army–American service element in the Commons was but one manifestation of the impact of the Seven Years' War on British public life. The period between the start of the war in 1755–1756 and the end of the American Revolutionary war is marked by the extreme prominence of government remittance and supply contractors in the House of Commons, where they all too obviously used their political influence to obtain bigger and better contracts for themselves. Their activities became so notorious that their eligibility to sit in the house was removed by Clerke's Act of 1782. In the generation 1754–1776 the House of Commons included 29 merchant members with some sort of connection with the thirteen colonies (compared with 14 during 1715–1754). Six of these were interested only in remittance

---

Treasury; Sir Matthew Fetherstonehaugh, bart.; George Grenville, former prime minister; Richard Jackson; Lauchlin Macleane; Thomas Pitt; Thomas Pownall; John Robinson, later junior secretary of the Treasury; John Sargent; William Strahan; Richard Walpole; Thomas Walpole; Robert Wood. Clarence Walworth Alvord, *The Mississippi Valley in British Politics*, 2 vols. (Cleveland, Ohio, 1917), II, 96–101, 127, 179n; Jack M. Sosin, *Whitehall and the Wilderness: The Middle West in British Colonial Policy, 1760–1775* (Lincoln, Nebr., 1961), chap. 8; J. A. Cannon, "Hon. Thomas Walpole," in Namier and Brooke, *History of Parliament, 1754–1790*, III, 598–602; Peter Marshall, "Lord Hillsborough, Samuel Wharton, and the Ohio Grant, 1769–1775," *English Historical Review*, LXXX (1965), 717–739.

19. Naval officers: Hon. George Clinton and Sir Charles Hardy, governors of New York; Lord William Campbell, governor of South Carolina; and Hon. Augustus Keppel, naval commander in chief in North America, 1754–1756.

Army officers: James Cuninghame, Sir Charles Davers (?), Simon Fraser, Francis Grant, James Grant, Hon. William Hervey, Hon. Robert Monckton (governor of New York, 1761–1765), Hon. Archibald Montgomerie, Staats Long Morris, James Murray, John Stanwix. Others, particularly Isaac Barré and William Howe, appear to have served in the Quebec campaign but not in the thirteen colonies.

or supply contracts and do not appear to have had other involvement in those colonies. The remaining 23 had more conventional, continuing interests in the colonies, including New England (5), Virginia and Maryland (5), South Carolina and Georgia (4), New York (2), New Jersey and Pennsylvania (1 each), and North America generally (5).[20]

Though the number of army officers and merchants with American interests or experience had increased markedly in the period 1754–1776, when compared with the previous period, persons with such interest or experience were still a tiny minority in the Commons, and few expected that many officers interested in promotion or merchants interested in contracts would take an independent line in debate—though some merchants without contracts did so most energetically. All in all, though, as Isaac Barré pointed out at the time, "there are very few [in the House of Commons] who know the circumstances of North America."[21]

Those in Trade

So much for Parliament. What about the political nation out-of-doors—that section of the British populace that participated in parliamentary elections, served on grand juries, or were members of bodies corporate of some dignity and weight? And the wider community beyond them? Did elements in either have much observable knowledge of or concern for the North American colonies? This is an almost impossible question to answer precisely. One could, perhaps, start by examining the thousands of names on petitions, but too many motives might be involved in signing a petition, including both

20. For the contractors during the American Revolutionary war, see Norman Baker, *Government and Contractors: The British Treasury and War Supplies, 1775–1783* (London, 1971), esp. chap. 9. Remittance and supply contracts: Sir George Colebrooke, James Colebrooke, Adam Drummond, Henry Drummond, Hon. Thomas Harley, and Arnold Nesbitt (Nesbitt was active in the West India trade).

Conventional interests: New England: John Henniker, John Huske, John Thomlinson, Chauncey Townsend, B. Trecothick; Maryland and Virginia: William Alexander, Anthony Bacon, Robert Bristow, Ellis Cunliffe, John Hardman; South Carolina and Georgia: Sir William Baker, Brice Fisher, Nicholas Linwood, Charles Ogilvie; New York: H. Cruger, Sir Samuel Fludyer; New Jersey: Henry Drummond; Pennsylvania: D. Moore; North America generally: G. R. Aufrere, P. Cust, G. Hayley, John Sargent, S. Touchet.

21. Namier and Brooke, *House of Commons, 1754–1790*, I, 161. For other expressions of similar opinions at the time, see Paul Langford, "The First Rockingham Ministry and the Repeal of the Stamp Act: The Role of the Commercial Lobby and Economic Pressures," in Walter H. Conser, Jr., *et al.*, eds., *Resistance, Politics, and the American Struggle for Independence, 1765–1775* (Boulder, Colo., 1986), 102–103.

political commitment and deference.[22] I think it preferable to start with a simpler and more neutral record of concern.

One such type of evidence not hitherto used can be found in the subscription lists printed in books. These vary in purpose and character. An expensive book with many plates depicting antiquities or flora and fauna might need advance subscriptions to help pay the costs of engraving the plates. Royal and noble names among the subscribers would, one might expect, give the book a definite éclat.[23] At the other extreme, a modest, utilitarian textbook of accounting would benefit from subscriptions from the proprietors of well-known private academies of bookkeeping. For our purposes the most useful are the extraordinarily long subscription lists included in the successive editions of John Wright's *American Negotiator* (1761–1765), a reference work on the varieties of coins and moneys of account used in the various American colonies.[24] Its three editions together contain the names of almost thirty-seven hundred people sufficiently interested in the American colonies to pay 2s. 6d. (about a day's pay for a junior clerk) for this information.

We do not know how Wright collected his subscriptions (probably through booksellers), but the contents of the successive lists suggest great ingenuity and application.[25] (No other known lists are remotely as long as his.) The fullest list, that in the first edition, consists almost entirely of names from London (1,998) and Bristol (185). In the second edition names were

22. For good use of the names on petitions, see James E. Bradley, *Popular Politics and the American Revolution in England: Petitions, the Crown, and Public Opinion* (Macon, Ga., 1986).

23. On subscription lists, cf. F.J.G. Robinson and P. J. Wallis, *Book Subscription Lists: A Revised Guide* (Newcastle upon Tyne, 1975). For an example of American interest, see Griffith Hughes, *The Natural History of Barbados* (London, 1750). The subscribers to this included the king of France; the Prince and Princess of Wales; the royal duke of Cumberland; 3 German princes; 9 English dukes; the archbishops of Canterbury, York, and Armagh; and the prime minister, Henry Pelham; and 33 persons from Virginia. By contrast, the subscribers to Patrick Browne, *The Civil and Natural History of Jamaica* (London, 1756), contained only 1 peer.

24. John Wright, *The American Negotiator; or, The Various Currencies of the British Colonies in America . . .*, 1st ed. (London, 1761), 2d ed. (London, 1763), 3d ed. (London, 1765). Numerous examples of accounting textbooks can be found in Robinson and Wallis, *Book Subscription Lists*. Particularly interesting are Thomas Harper, *The Accomptant's Companion . . .* (London, 1761); and Peter Hudson, *A New Introduction to Trade and Business . . .* (London, 1767). For a more advanced Scottish example, with subscriptions by eminent merchants, see William Stevenson, *Book-keeping by Double Entry . . .* (Edinburgh, 1762).

25. For the collection of subscriptions through provincial booksellers, see John Feather, *The Provincial Book Trade in Eighteenth-Century England* (Cambridge, 1985), 51–53; Marjorie Plant, *The English Book Trade: An Economic History of the Making and Sale of Books*, 3d ed. (London, 1974), 227–232.

added from southern England, the Liverpool-Manchester-Chester area, the London suburbs, and the maze of riverside hamlets and quarters along both sides of the Thames below London Bridge. The third edition noticeably adds names from Yorkshire and the east coast, northwest England, and southern Scotland. Residents of 144 different places in England and Scotland subscribed for copies, or 120 if we delete 24 Thames-side hamlets and quarters. With the exception of 3 subscribers from Dublin, there are no names from Ireland or Wales. We do find subscribers from all the coastal counties of England except Cornwall and Suffolk. Also unrepresented were 13 inland English counties embracing a great swath of territory from Hertfordshire and Bedfordshire in the Home Counties to the Welsh border and including all the Midlands except for the industrial towns of Birmingham, Coventry, and Nottingham.[26] The inland omitted areas were primarily agricultural. Their rural industries were not insignificant but, as we shall see, were unlikely to be in direct commercial communication with the North American colonies. In Scotland almost all the subscribers were located about Edinburgh in the Lothians or along the southwest coast between Glasgow and Dumfries.[27]

There are some rather odd features to the list of places. There were no subscribers from Oxford and only 1 from Cambridge, but there were a respectable number from Canterbury (22) and York (24) as well as from ten other English cathedral towns including the unexpected Rochester, Chichester, Salisbury, and Wells. Cathedral towns would, of course, have had booksellers, and the inclusion of such places suggests that in the south of England at least it was quite easy to subscribe.

The geographic distribution of subscriptions is summarized in Table 1, specifying places with more than 20 subscribers. The first thing that strikes one is that 62 percent of the subscriptions came from the greater London commercial (as distinct from fashionable) area. This is not unexpected when we reflect that Wright's book was published in London and subscriptions were undoubtedly easiest to procure there. Nor is it unexpected when we

26. The omission of Cornwall undoubtedly owes more to the organization of the book trade than to the lack of American awareness. The packet boats from New York terminated at Falmouth, where many vessels to and from America stopped for mail and instructions. Of Cornish ports with even minimal American trade circa 1750–1775, Falmouth and Truro had only one bookshop each. H. R. Plomer *et al.*, *A Dictionary of the Printers and Booksellers Who Were at Work in England, Scotland, and Ireland from 1726 to 1775* (Oxford, 1932), 4, 188.

The other omitted counties in England were Bedford, Bucks, Derby, Hereford, Herts, Huntingdon, Monmouth, Northampton, Oxford, Rutland, Shropshire, Stafford, and Worcester.

27. In Scotland, a few subscriptions were received from inland manufacturing centers including Paisley (6) and Kilmarnock (7).

remember that, at this time, from half to two-thirds of England's foreign trade was handled by the port of London.[28] The careful reader will also have noted that, of the 17 provincial centers responsible for 20 or more subscriptions each, a good number were ports trading to America: Bristol, Liverpool, Glasgow, Edinburgh-Leith, Lancaster, Portsmouth, Whitehaven, Hull, Poole, and Yarmouth. (Of the ports listed, only Chester and Preston then had no known direct trade with the American colonies.) If we add the subscriptions of the 10 ports just mentioned to those of the port of London, the share of ports trading to North America rises to more than 80 percent of subscriptions. The impressiveness of this share should not, however, lead us to disregard the remaining 20 percent of subscriptions that came from some 665 individuals in 105 other places, inland and coastal. These ranged from major manufacturing centers such as Manchester and Birmingham, with 60 and 48 subscriptions, to numerous minor places with only 1 or 2. Together they remind us both of the wide diffusion of interest in the American colonies and of the concentration or intensity of such interest in major marketing centers serving export industries.

The subscription lists to the three editions of John Wright's *American Negotiator* differ from most other such lists in a further important respect: they contain the occupations of most subscribers. Of the 3,694 subscribers, only 179 showed no occupation: of these, 10 were blank, the others being described only by a title of distinction (lord, baronet, knight, esquire, gentleman) or of an unpaid, honorific public office (mayor, provost, alderman) normally distinct from the holder's occupation. In addition to the 73 identified only as esquire, there were a substantial number of other esquires also described by an occupation (merchant, brewer, and so forth). These appear for the most part to have been businessmen who combined with their regular trades a distinguishing position, such as director of the Bank of England, the East India Company, an insurance company, or the like. We have classified these by their primary occupation (for example, merchant), as we have also done for knights and baronets for whom an occupation was given.

After deducting the 179 for whom we have no occupational information, we find the remaining 3,515 subscribers scattered among roughly 282 occupations. (Since many occupational descriptions overlap, the enumeration can be only approximate.) Given the function of Wright's book, it will not come as a surprise that 1,103 (31 percent) of the subscribers were merchants (Table 2). But what of the remaining 69 percent? We see that a prominent place was occupied by the mostly wholesale traders who supplied merchants with export goods on credit: such as warehousemen, woolen-drapers, linen-drapers, haberdashers, hosiers, mercers, ironmongers, and grocers. Even

28. Cf. Ralph Davis, "English Foreign Trade, 1660–1700," *Economic History Review*, 2d Ser., VII (1954–1955), 160.

Table 1. Places in Great Britain with Twenty or More Subscribers to John Wright's *American Negotiator*

Places	Number (Share) of Subscribers
Greater London	
London	2,106
Thames-side hamlets (24)[a]	163
Southwark	17
Total	2,286 (62.0%)
Major provincial subscription towns	
Bristol	193
Liverpool	181
Glasgow and Port Glasgow	78
Manchester	60
Edinburgh and Leith	55
Birmingham	48
Chester	44
Lancaster	38
Portsmouth	36
Preston	36
Whitehaven	33
Hull	27
Norwich	24
York	24
Poole	23
Yarmouth	22
Canterbury	22
Total	944 (25.6%)
Lesser places in England (89)	385 (10.4%)
Lesser places in Scotland (10)	71 (2.0%)
British total (144)	3,686 (100.0%)

Note: Table omits Dublin (3) and overseas (5), which would yield a worldwide total of 3,694.

[a] Places on north side of Thames from Tower to Blackwall and River Lea; on south side of Thames from Southwark's eastern boundary to River Pool, stopping short of Greenwich.

brewers and bakers belonged partly in this category, for they supplied beer and biscuit (hardtack) both as ship's stores and as export goods. Besides the major occupations (Table 2), there were among the subscribers more than 250 other callings both familiar and unfamiliar. For example, at Birmingham we find among them specialist makers of hinges, watch chains, spoons, awl blades, edge tools, and buckles. Dozens of more exotic specialties could be cited, suggesting at the very least the wide ramifications of American interest in eighteenth-century Britain.

The printed lists also contain evidence of further distribution beyond the 3,694 printed names. The lists in the second and third editions identify subscribers who ordered more than 1 copy: anywhere from 2 to 100 each. For example, the Board of Trade in 1764–1765 ordered 18 individual copies for named commissioners and senior clerks plus an unexplained bloc of 50 copies in the name of its secretary. (Some of these were perhaps to be distributed to colonial officials.) There were also multiple orders from ship captains and ship chandlers. The captains could have used theirs as gifts or as trading goods; the ship chandlers, all in the Thames-side hamlets, were obviously supplying customers in areas without bookstores. Most of the multiple copies, however, went to professional booksellers in London (24), the English provinces (48), and Scotland (34). The provincial and Scottish booksellers generally ordered from 6 to 12 copies each while those in London commonly took from 12 to 25, with one taking 100. These multiple-copy orders raise the total sales revealed by the second and third edition subscription lists by 80 percent (from 1,506 to 2,713). If the first edition list (which does not specify quantities) had had multiple sales in the same proportion, sales for the three editions together would have been in the vicinity of 6,650. However, adding the extra copies sold does not change the general picture of the market for Wright's book (Table 1), for the booksellers were distributed geographically much as were the ordinary subscribers.

Wright's subscription lists, it must be remembered, are not a census, but only a sample of persons interested in the colonies—but a very big sample. Other samples available are smaller and weaker in coverage than Wright's, but they confirm at least the outlines of the picture derivable from his lists: interest in the colonies widely diffused but disproportionately concentrated in the bigger ports and the important inland marketing centers for manufactures. One example arises from the difficulties British businessmen trading to America experienced after the Revolutionary war in attempting to collect their substantial prewar debts. In 1790–1791 a committee of these British creditors drew up a list of such debts still outstanding. Although the sums claimed were swollen by interest, some prewar debts had been paid since the peace; thus, the account does not represent the exact prewar weight of debt. Nor are the values shown likely to be proportionate to what the prewar debts totaled in 1776, for different centers employed different trading methods

Table 2. Occupations Furnishing Twenty-five or More Subscribers to Wright's *American Negotiator*

Occupation	Subscribers
Attorney-at-law	26
Baker	61
Bookseller	130
Brewer	42
Broker (every sort)	43
Captain (of merchant ships)	41
Cheesemonger	54
Coachmaker	33
Cooper	29
Distiller	55
Druggist	31
Goldsmith	30
Grocer	173
Haberdasher	54
Hosier	33
Ironmonger	57
Linen-draper	106
Mercer	49
Merchant	1,103
Oilman	53
Schoolmaster	49
Silversmith	35
Stationer	33
Sugar refiner	28
Tallow chandler	61
Warehouseman	32
Watchmaker	41
Weaver	37
Woolen-draper, draper	38

and organization and had different success in collecting their debts after the war. Glasgow, of course, was heavily involved in retail trade with planters in Maryland, Virginia, and North Carolina and had greater difficulty than other centers in realizing its claims. Even so, there is an air of familiarity about the geographic distribution of the 1790 claims (Table 3). All the major ports producing the most numerous subscriptions to Wright's book (Table 1) reappear here. (Although the list in Table 3 covers only ten places, those ten

Table 3. Unpaid American Commercial Debts (Including Interest) Claimed by British Creditors, February 1791

Place	Number of Claims	Value Claimed (Sterling)		
London	67	£2,324,652	11s.	8d.
Glasgow	96	£2,178,442	7	1
Liverpool	6	127,566	2	4
Bristol	4	104,583	12	10
Leeds	7	92,758	12	4
Chester	2	71,031	17	10
Greenock	2	34,501	7	10
Whitehaven	8	28,396	7	3
Kilmarnock	4	20,809	16	6
Workington	1	1,912	10	0
Total	197	£4,984,655	5s.	8d.

Source: PRO, PRO 30/8/343, fols. 167–169

accounted for 77 percent of the subscriptions for Wright's book received from 144 places in England and Scotland.)

Similarly consistent is the evidence from pro-American petitions to the House of Commons between 1766 and 1775. When the Rockingham administration decided to proceed with the repeal of the Stamp Act, Barlow Trecothick, member of Parliament for London, with ministerial encouragement, organized an influx of petitions from twenty-five trading towns depicting the commercial and industrial distress caused by the decline in exports to North America and asking for relief, that is, repeal. Among the twenty-five were sixteen major trading centers accounting for more than 80 percent of the subscribers to Wright's book. The nine other places, which do not appear in Wright's subscription lists, were mostly smaller manufacturing centers in the west, which most likely were not canvassed by or for Wright and which most probably did not have direct trading links with America even though the goods they manufactured found their way eventually to markets in the thirteen colonies.[29]

29. *Journal of the House of Commons* (London, 1801–), XXX, 462–465, 478–479, 484, 489, 499, 501, 503, 601–602, 611; R. C. Simmons and P.D.G. Thomas, eds., *Proceedings and Debates of the British Parliaments respecting North America, 1754–1783* (Millwood, White Plains, N.Y., 1982–), II, 95–97, 100–101, 103–104, 106–108, 115, 305 (omitting Nottingham and Worcester). See also P.D.G. Thomas, *British Politics and the Stamp Act Crisis: The First Phase of the American Revolution, 1763–1767* (Oxford, 1975), 187–190; Paul Langford, "The First Rockingham Ministry," in Conser *et al.*, eds., *Resistance, Politics*, 97–111; and John Money,

This lack of direct connection between some smaller manufacturing centers and their American markets can perhaps be better understood if we look at the marketing arrangements in the West Country woolen trade. Putting-out manufacturers and others in Somerset and Wiltshire (which included four of the eight omitted places alluded to above) commonly sent their cloth for sale to Blackwell Hall factors in London, who sold the same on commission to wholesale woolen-drapers; they in turn resold the cloth on long credit to export merchants who bought for their own speculative shipments or on commission for overseas correspondents. Similarly, in places like Birmingham and Wolverhampton there were few or no merchants who traded overseas. Instead, local factors acting for wholesale ironmongers in London and Bristol bought the nails and other hardware from small masters, paying them with cash obtained by selling short bills of exchange on their principals in London or Bristol. Those big ironmongers in turn sold to export merchants much as did the big drapers. The manufacturers and other traders in both the cloth and ironware manufacturing areas thus usually had no direct correspondence with the American colonies, though the factors with whom they dealt (and the wholesalers behind them) kept them informed about market conditions there and changing demand.[30]

Of comparable interest are the petitions to the House of Commons in early 1775 from trading centers complaining of the interruption of trade with the thirteen colonies and asking for relief—which in the context could mean only conciliation. By the beginning of the year the nonimportation in America had gone into effect, and news was arriving both of the deteriorating situation in Massachusetts and of the adoption by the Continental Congress of nonexportation. (In one striking case, this news soon doubled the

---

Experience and Identity: Birmingham and the West Midlands, 1760–1800 (Montreal, 1977), 161–166.

The 16 subscribing: London, Bristol, Liverpool, Halifax, Leeds, Lancaster, Manchester, Leicester, Bradford (?), Birmingham, Coventry, Chester, Taunton, Glasgow, Nottingham, and Sheffield.

The 9 not subscribing: Worcestershire: Stourbridge, Dudley, Worcester; Somerset: Frome, Minehead; Wiltshire: Chippenham, Melksham; Staffordshire: Wolverhampton; Oxfordshire: Witney. For the availability of bookstores, see Plomer *et al.*, *Dictionary of Printers*.

30. Cf. Jacob M. Price, *Capital and Credit in British Overseas Trade: The View from the Chesapeake, 1700–1776* (Cambridge, Mass., 1980), chap. 6; J. de L. Mann, *The Cloth Industry in the West of England from 1640 to 1880* (Oxford, 1971), 63–85; Jacob M. Price, ed., *Joshua Johnson's Letterbook, 1771–1774: Letters from a Merchant in London to His Partners in Maryland*, London Record Society, Publications, XV (London, 1979), xiii–xiv, nos. 35a, 41c, 47a. Some Birmingham firms traded to Europe but not to America; see Eric Robinson, "Boulton and Fothergill, 1762–1782, and the Birmingham Export of Hardware," *University of Birmingham Historical Journal*, VII (1959–1960), 60–79.

export price of tobacco in Britain.) If word of the disturbances in New England propelled the government toward further measures of repression, the commercial news from Congress stirred some merchants toward a new effort at conciliation, similar to that of 1766, but this time without the encouragement of the government. A petition from the merchants and traders of London was soon followed by sixteen comparable relief (conciliatory) petitions from eighteen places.[31] Although not everyone in the towns concerned agreed with the petitioning activity, in only three areas (Birmingham, Nottingham, and the West Riding) were there opposing loyalist petitions calling for the maintenance of British law. In Birmingham, the loyal petition appears to have reflected some local fear of the growth of iron and steel manufacturing in the northern colonies.[32] In other places, the petitioning of early 1775 still seems to have been commercial and relatively nonpartisan, after the mode of 1766. By contrast, the much more heavily solicited and canvassed petitioning in late 1775—after news had arrived of serious fighting in America and a state of rebellion had been proclaimed—was much more political and noncommercial, with both repressive (progovernment) and conciliatory (antigovernment) petitions coming from almost every significant commercial center. As political statements, the autumn petitions attracted many more signatures than those of the previous winter: for example, in London in October 1775, 941 for the loyal petition and 1,029–1,100

31. For general situation, see Ian R. Christie, "The British Ministers, Massachusetts, and the Continental Association, 1774–1775," in Conser *et al.*, eds., *Resistance, Politics*, 325–357; Paul Langford, "The British Business Community and the Later Nonimportation Movements, 1768–1776," in Conser *et al.*, eds., *Resistance, Politics*, 278–324; and Bradley, *Popular Politics*, chap. 1. For the jump in tobacco prices, see Jacob M. Price, *France and the Chesapeake: A History of the French Tobacco Monopoly, 1674–1791 . . .*, 2 vols. (Ann Arbor, Mich., 1973), I, 646–647, 676, II, 683.

The 18 places and their petitions include a combined petition from the Yorkshire woolen towns of Wakefield, Halifax, Bradford, and Huddersfield; 2 petitions from Bristol (1 from Society of Merchant Venturers, 1 from the traders); and individual petitions from Glasgow, Norwich, Dudley (Worcestershire), Birmingham, Manchester, Wolverhampton, Liverpool, Newcastle (Staffordshire), the pottery towns (Staffordshire), Leeds, Nottingham, Bridport (Dorset), and Whitehaven. In addition there were relief petitions from Belfast and Waterford in Ireland and a further London petition from the West India interest. *Journal of the House of Commons*, XXXV, 71–72, 74, 77–78, 80–83, 86–87, 89–92, 99, 108, 123–124, 139, 141, 171, 186; see also Simmons and Thomas, eds., *Proceedings and Debates*, V, 261–266, 287–328, 338–344, 405–406, 425–426, 517–519; and Bradley, *Popular Politics*, chap. 1.

32. Two conciliatory petitions from (1) Leeds and (2) Wakefield, Halifax, Bradford, and Huddersfield were balanced by two loyal petitions from (1) Leeds, Wakefield, Halifax, and Bradford and (2) Huddersfield. *Journal of the House of Commons*, XXXV, 89, 90, 124, 186. There are a few minor slips in the table in Bradley, *Popular Politics*, 22. For the complexities of the situation in Birmingham, see Money, *Experience and Identity*, 197–201.

for the conciliatory. Yet the increase in signatures does not imply any extension of the geographic area concerned with America. The winter 1775 petitions came from places accounting for 80 percent of the subscribers to Wright's handbook, whereas the petitions of the following October involved only 70 percent.[33]

Unlike those of 1766, the petitions of January–February 1775 were unwelcome to the government, which was determined not to be diverted by them. On January 19, Lord North had presented to the Commons 149 documents on the American situation preparing the way for later legislative action. These were immediately referred to a committee of the whole. When the London relief (or conciliatory) petition was presented on January 23, its supporters wanted it referred to the aforesaid committee of the whole on the American papers, but the government used its substantial majority to refer it instead to another, separate committee of the whole. As each additional relief petition was presented, it too was, after a division, referred to the committee considering the London petition.[34] Because the American merchants of London refused to testify before the latter committee, its meetings were continually postponed; the first committee (on the American papers) meanwhile proceeded expeditiously with the work that led to the legislation against the commerce, navigation, and fisheries of Massachusetts and other New England colonies.[35] Only after the Massachusetts Bay bill had passed its third reading in the house on March 8 did the other committee of the whole on the London and similar petitions meet and hear a few witnesses from the West Indian trade.[36]

As already noted, the petitions submitted by the merchants of London and the other commercial centers were all drafted along common lines similar to

33. Bradley, *Popular Politics*, chaps. 2, 3, esp. pp. 65, 67. Sainsbury has been able to identify 504 of the 1,100 signatories of an October 1775 pro-American petition to the king, though his categories are not helpful. He reports that they included only 7 company directors while contemporary loyal petitions included at least 50 such. This suggests the degree to which the petitioning had become politicized but is not in itself too surprising, since there were very few American merchants then among the directors of the major companies, circa 1775. John Sainsbury, "The Pro-Americans of London, 1769 to 1782," *William and Mary Quarterly*, 3d Ser., XXXV (1978), 447.

34. *Journal of the House of Commons*, XXXV, 71–124 passim (see n. 31, above).

35. The Commons did, however, receive two further petitions from the merchants and corporation of London against the Massachusetts Bay bill. These were considered when the Commons went into committee on that bill, at which time London witnesses against the bill were heard. *Journal of the House of Commons*, XXXV, 112, 129, 144, 151, 152, 163–164, 166, 182; Simmons and Thomas, eds., *Proceedings and Debates*, V, 322–323, 481–497, 501–503, 555–577.

36. *Journal of the House of Commons*, XXXV, 183, 197, 200, 202, 208, 232; Simmons and Thomas, eds., *Proceedings and Debates*, V, 534–536, 555–577, 581–583. The printed committee transactions in March were concerned mainly with effects upon the West Indies. It is not clear what other evidence was heard.

those used in the 1766 petitions. Each locality complained that its trade and manufactures were languishing because of the American nonimportation agreements and that serious unemployment threatened; it then prayed the house for relief. All constitutional or political argument was eschewed. Such tactics had been successful in 1766 but were not to work as well in 1775–1776, a situation forcing some of the petitioners to venture into more turbulent waters. When the merchants of London realized that their petition of January 23, 1775, would not be considered by the committee of the whole on the American papers, they submitted a second petition to the House of Commons on the twenty-sixth. This more radical document attacked the principle of dividing the American question between two committees—the principle that one could separate the American political problem from British-American trade. They insisted, on the contrary, "that the Connection be[tween] *Great Britain* and *America* originally was, and ought to be, of a commercial Kind, and that the Benefits derived therefrom, to the Mother Country are of the same Nature; . . . [so] that the fundamental Policy of those Laws of which they complain, and the Propriety of enforcing, relaxing, or amending the same, are Questions inseparably united with the Commerce between *Great Britain* and *America*; and consequently that the Consideration of the one cannot be entered on, without a full Discussion of the other."[37] This argument was not to impress George III or Lord North or the majority of the House of Commons in 1775.

Were the merchants of London engaging in the hyperbole of special pleading when they placed the commercial nexus at the heart of the whole imperial system? Such hyperbole came easily to them and to some historians of later centuries. But underneath the hyperbole lay at least one important truth: the American trades were extremely dynamic in an age when most branches of the British economy were relatively static. Precise measurement is impossible, but most scholarship now agrees that British (or English) national income per capita was either stagnant or increasing very slowly (about .3–.45 percent per annum) in the first two-thirds of the eighteenth century.[38] The most notable exception was foreign trade. For the political leadership the most important, or at least sensitive, aspect of foreign trade was traditionally the export market for home manufactures, so important for employment.

Very rough calculations suggest that as early as 1688 something like 33 percent of English national income could be ascribed to industry (including manufacturing, mining, and building) and commerce (including transportation). Another estimate, for 1770, ascribes to these two sectors 37 percent of

37. *Journal of the House of Commons*, XXXV, 80.

38. N.F.R. Crafts, *British Economic Growth during the Industrial Revolution* (Oxford, 1985), chap. 2, esp. p. 45.

national income. Much of this industrial and commercial activity was, of course, directed toward purely domestic demand. But exports were still impressive. Calculations by Nicholas Crafts show English exports rising between 1700 and 1760 from 24 percent to 35 percent of "gross industrial output."[39]

However measured, the export sector was the most dynamic sector of the English economy in the first three quarters of the eighteenth century. While total real output in England is estimated to have grown by 44 percent between 1700 and 1770, the product of the export industries grew by 156 percent; by contrast, purely home industries grew by only 14 percent and agricultural output by only 17 percent.[40] However, of particular relevance to our problem is the observation that, within the general pattern of dynamism, there were striking shifts of geographical direction. About 1700, more than 80 percent of English domestic exports went to the unprotected markets of Europe (exclusive of Ireland). By the early 1770s, the share of these markets had declined to only 40 percent. By contrast, the share of exports taken by the more protected markets of Ireland, the Americas, West Africa, and the East Indies had risen from less than 20 percent to 60 percent. Within this protected sphere, the share of North America had risen from 5.7 percent of all domestic exports at the beginning of the century to 25.3 percent in 1772–1773—even without counting the peak shipments of 1771 after the removal of most of the Townshend duties and the collapse of the nonimportation agreements. No other market for English exports had grown as much in those seven decades. (The addition of Scotland does not change the picture significantly.)[41]

39. Phyllis Deane and W. A. Cole, *British Economic Growth, 1688–1959: Trends and Structure*, University of Cambridge, Department of Applied Economics, Monograph no. 8 (Cambridge, 1962), 156; Crafts, *British Economic Growth during Industrial Revolution*, 132.

40. Deane and Cole, *British Economic Growth, 1688–1959*, 78.

41. *Ibid.*, 87; Ralph Davis, "English Foreign Trade, 1700–1774," *Econ. Hist. Rev.*, 2d Ser., XV (1962–1963), 302–303; B. R. Mitchell and Phyllis Deane, *Abstract of British Historical Statistics* (Cambridge, 1962), 312.

The addition of Scottish data to English data for 1772–1774 raises total imports by 9.2% and total exports by 9.7%; English data from Davis and Scottish data from Henry Hamilton, *An Economic History of Scotland in the Eighteenth Century* (Oxford, 1963), 414–415. However, when we add Scottish data to English for trade with the thirteen colonies, 1772–1774, we find that exports are raised by 10.2%, but *imports* are raised 38.3%! The difference is ascribable to the large transit trade in tobacco in Scotland. For Scottish trade with the thirteen colonies, see Jacob M. Price, "New Time Series for Scotland's and Britain's Trade with the Thirteen Colonies and States, 1740 to 1791," *WMQ*, 3d Ser., XXXII (1975), 318–321; for English trade with same, see U.S. Bureau of the Census, *Historical Statistics of the United States*, 1176–1177. (There is a typographical error in the column headings of series Z227–244 for Scotland, reversing the designations "imports" and "exports.")

If we add reexports to domestic exports, the change over the seven decades is not quite so striking: the European markets still took almost half of England's combined exports and reexports in the 1770s (instead of 40 percent for domestic exports alone) while the protected markets then took slightly more than half (instead of 60 percent). In other words the European market (in particular) for reexports was growing impressively down to 1776 even while the market there for English (or British) produce grew slowly or stagnated under the double burden of continental protectionism and sharp price competition.[42] Yet, the reexport of American produce to the Continent had a strategic implication that is often neglected. By the eighteenth century, almost all branches of British industry were dependent on imported raw materials to a greater or lesser degree. This was most noticeable in shipbuilding (where imports included masts, ship timbers, pitch, tar, and hemp and flax for sails, cables, and cordage), but it was true also of metallurgy (where a substantial proportion of the iron needed by British industry had to be imported) and textiles (where the same held true for raw and thrown silk, cotton, flax, and linen yarn). Even the woolen industry required significant imports of Irish wool and yarn. This dependence created payments problems for needed imports of raw materials, particularly from northern Europe. All English exports there (Russia, Scandinavia, and the Baltic littoral) covered only 19 percent of English imports thence. Of course, it wasn't necessary for individual trades to be balanced, since British earnings on exports to other areas in Europe, particularly Holland (the United Provinces) and Germany could be used to pay for imports from the Baltic via bills of exchange drawn on Hamburg or Amsterdam. Even so, combined English exports to northern Europe and northwestern Europe (Germany, Holland, Flanders, and France) covered only 62 percent of English imports from those areas. The difference was more than made up, though, by English reexports of overseas products, particularly calicoes and silks from the East Indies, coffee and dyestuffs from the West Indies, and tobacco and rice from North America. Reexports of the North American items (tobacco and rice) alone were enough to balance English trade with northern and northwestern Europe. These were, of course, not necessarily the richest imports from overseas. Sugar, in fact, was the most valuable import from any source and tea the most valuable from Asia, but both these commodities were consumed almost entirely in Britain and Ireland—or, in the case of tea, partly reexported to the American colo-

42. From 1756 to 1776, in Scotland reexports exceeded domestic exports in value by a considerable margin (Hamilton, *Economic History*, 414). For England in 1772–1774, reexports to the world were only 59% of domestic in value, but in those same years in the trade to northern Europe, northwestern Europe, Ireland, and the Channel Islands, reexports exceeded domestic exports in value. Davis, "Foreign Trade, 1700–1774," *Econ. Hist. Rev.*, 2d Ser., XV (1962–1963), 302–303.

Table 4. English and Scottish Exports (and Reexports) to the Thirteen Colonies

Measure	1699–1701	1772–1774
Population of colonies (estimated)	251,000 (1700)	2,320,000 (1773)
Annual English exports (official value)	£364,000	£2,561,000
Per head of colonial population	£1.45	£1.10
Annual English exports (current value)	£364,000	£2,682,000
Per head of colonial population	£1.45	£1.16
Annual British exports (official value)		£2,822,000
Per head of colonial population		£1.22
Annual British exports (current value)		£2,954,000
Per head of colonial population		£1.27

Sources: U.S. Bureau of the Census, *Historical Statistics of the United States: Colonial Times to 1970* (Washington, D.C., 1975), II, 116; Jacob M. Price, "New Time Series for Scotland's and Britain's Trade with the Thirteen Colonies and States, 1740 to 1791," *William and Mary Quarterly*, 3d Ser., XXXII, (1975) 325; John J. McCusker, "The Current Value of English Exports, 1697 to 1800," *WMQ*, 3d Ser., XXVIII (1971), 623–626.

nies—and thus did not provide significant reexports to the European continent.[43]

The fecundity of the North American population was the key to the dynamism of Britain's trade thither. Increased population meant an increased labor force to produce exports and an increased market for British and other foreign goods. The seven- or eightfold expansion of English (or later British) exports to those colonies between the periods 1699–1701 and 1772–1774 was based almost exclusively on the more than ninefold increase in the colonial population during the same decades. In fact, neither English nor British exports thither increased as much as colonial population, so there was actually a slight decline in exports per head of colonial population, whether calculated in official or current prices (Table 4).[44] But to contemporaries it was the growth in aggregate trade that impressed.

43. Davis, "Foreign Trade, 1700–1774," *Econ. Hist. Rev.*, 2d Ser., XV (1962–1963), 300–303. For the Irish yarn trade, see L. M. Cullen, *Anglo-Irish Trade, 1660–1800* (Manchester, 1968), 55. For the settling of English trade deficits with northern Europe by bills of exchange drawn on Amsterdam or Hamburg, see Jacob M. Price, "Multilateralism and / or Bilateralism: The Settlement of British Trade Balances with 'The North,' c. 1700," *Econ. Hist. Rev.*, 2d Ser., XIV (1961–1962), 254–274.

44. A somewhat different picture is evident in the data presented in John J. McCusker and Russell R. Menard, *The Economy of British America, 1607–1789* (Chapel Hill, N.C., 1985), 280. They show British exports to the thirteen colonies

From the perspective of the total British economy, the North American trades in the eighteenth century may now appear to have been of only moderate significance. Yet at the time they were of vital importance to many businessmen and should have impressed statesmen as worthy objects of concern on both their export and their import sides. We have just noted the rapid growth of the North American market, a particularly important vent for a number of British and Irish manufactures, particularly woolens, linens, and hardware.[45] Imports from both North America and the West Indies freed Britain from dependence on foreign suppliers (to the benefit of the trade balance); and, in the case of wheat, they could be helpful during crises of poor harvests, such as in fact occurred in the late 1760s and early 1770s.[46] Imports from North America, particularly tobacco and rice, also provided valuable reexports to areas of Europe with which Britain's trade would otherwise have been unbalanced and from which Britain obtained much-needed raw materials.

The impact of the burgeoning American trades was not felt evenly throughout Britain, not even among the ports. In the seventeenth century, when there were very few great merchants in the new American trades, numerous petty traders with bits of capital found it possible to enter the trades both to the West Indies and to North America. They traded from a wide range of ports, large and small. In the eighteenth century, the more substantial merchants, with access to easier credit, found it possible to expand their share of the trades. As a consequence, in the last quarter of the seventeenth century and throughout the eighteenth century, there was a gradual increase in firm size and a reduction in the number of firms in the principal branches of the American trades. The number of firms or individuals in the London tobacco import trade, for example, was reduced from 573 in 1676 to 56 in 1775 while the average annual importation per firm increased at least thirty-five-fold. At Glasgow, the average firm's annual im-

---

per head of colonial population increasing from £.90 in 1699–1704 to £1.20 in 1767–1774. Their figure for the earlier period is depressed by the inclusion of three war years, 1702–1704, when exports were artificially discouraged. The peace years 1699–1701 (also used by Ralph Davis) would appear to be less distorted.

45. The data given by McCusker and Menard, *British America*, 284, show that the American markets in 1770 took more than 50% of total English exports of wrought copper, wrought iron and nails, beaver hats, cordage, linen, printed cotton and linen, wrought silk, and "Spanish cloths." Their account is based on Elizabeth Boody Schumpeter, *English Overseas Trade Statistics, 1697–1808* (Oxford, 1960), 63–69. The year 1770, chosen by Schumpeter, probably underestimates the importance of the North American market, as some element of nonimportation was then being observed.

46. For the suspension of the corn laws to permit imports of colonial wheat, see Donald Grove Barnes, *A History of the English Corn Laws from 1660–1846* (New York, 1930; rpt., 1961), 31–32, 37–45.

portation in the 1770s was ten times as much as in the 1720s. In the sugar trade at Bristol, the number of importers was reduced by almost three-fourths between 1672 and 1789 while the average annual importation per firm increased about twenty-six-fold.[47]

At the same time, the number of ports involved in the American trades was significantly reduced. At the beginning of the century, London and Bristol had to share the English trades to America with a great range of havens, including the western ports of Whitehaven, Lancaster, Liverpool, Barnstaple, and Bideford; the south coast ports of Falmouth, Penryn, Fowey, Looe, Plymouth, Dartmouth, Exeter, Lyme Regis, Weymouth, Poole, Cowes, Portsmouth, and Dover; and the east coast ports of Hull and Newcastle. In Scotland, Glasgow (Port Glasgow and Greenock) in the first generation after the Union had to share part of the American trade with about thirty lesser ports, particularly Bo'ness, Dumfries, Kirkcaldy, and Montrose. By the generation of the American Revolution, however, the trade with North America and the West Indies had become concentrated in a much smaller group of ports: in effect, five key ports (London, Glasgow, Whitehaven, Liverpool, and Bristol) with minor shares (the equivalent of one or two ships a year) to a few other places (Lancaster, Hull, Penryn, Aberdeen, and Ayr). The three or four largest ports might easily dominate 80 or 90 percent of one of the American trades.[48]

This meant, of course, that traders in the smaller ports lost their close connections with and probably even their interest in the American colonies. They had, therefore, no pressing motive to petition in 1775, even if their ports were parliamentary boroughs. Among the places *not* petitioning then were the following ports and parliamentary boroughs, which had lost their North American trade entirely or seen it shrink radically since the beginning of the century: Fowey, Truro, Looe, Plymouth, Dartmouth, Barnstaple, Exeter, Lyme Regis, Weymouth, Portsmouth, and Dover. In such places, there likely were good local political reasons for not petitioning that reinforced the lack of economic interest. Several of them were for parliamentary elections considered in whole or in part Admiralty or Treasury boroughs (Plymouth,

47. Jacob M. Price and Paul G. E. Clemens, "A Revolution of Scale in Overseas Trade: British Firms in the Chesapeake Trade, 1675–1775," *Journal of Economic History*, XLVII (1987), 1–43.

48. *Ibid.*, 39–40. For data on lesser English ports, see PRO, T 1/278/30; T 1/345, fol. 5; T 38/363; T 64/276B/327; and PRO 30/8/297, fol. 150. For Scottish ports, see PRO, CO 390/5/13; T 1/139/29; T 1/282/23; T 1/329, fol. 128; T 36/13; BL Add. MS 8133B, fols. 366–367. A similar concentration had taken place in the English Newfoundland fishery, which earlier had attracted vessels from dozens of havens between Bristol and Southampton. By the 1760s, however, it had become concentrated in a smaller number of ports, particularly Bristol, Dartmouth, Teignmouth, Topsham, and Poole. Ralph Greenlee Lounsbury, *The British Fishery at Newfoundland, 1634–1763* (New Haven, Conn., 1934), 314.

Dartmouth, Portsmouth, Dover) while others were controlled by local families that most often preferred a proadministration stance (Fowey; Truro; Looe; Lyme Regis; and Weymouth and Melcombe Regis).[49]

Once the fighting started in America, there were very apparent *political* reasons for joining in prowar or antiwar petitions, whether or not one had connections of any sort with the colonies. Before the start of hostilities, however, when the political atmosphere was less tense, purely commercial concerns could express themselves more uninhibitedly.

Yet one would be wrong to assume that the commercial were the only concerns creating in such Britons interest in or even sympathy for the American colonies and colonists. There were also significant, long-established religious connections, particularly for the nonconformists, for whom so many of the colonists were simply "congregations of brethren beyond the seas." The keenness of such interests and the warmth of such sympathies showed themselves at the time of the American Revolution, when "most of the leaders of Old Dissent, Congregationalists and Baptists no less than rational Dissenters, supported their co-religionists on the other side of the Atlantic." Only John Wesley publicly supported the government uncompromisingly, even while privately hoping for conciliation and compromise.[50]

It does not necessarily follow, however, that these noteworthy religious connections were totally distinct from commercial links. The Church of England had, we know, formal connections with the colonial Anglican churches through the authority of the bishop of London and his commissaries in the colonies. Anglican missionary work in the colonies fell primarily to the Society for the Propagation of the Gospel in Foreign Parts, whose membership was heavily clerical. Relatively few politicians and businessmen—even merchants trading to North America—turn up among its members. Each dissenting denomination for its part had to design its own links with its brethren in North America. The nonconformists taken as a whole were more urban, hence more commercial, than the general English population.[51] Their

49. Namier and Brooke, *House of Commons, 1754–1790*, I, 227–228, 232–233, 241–242, 250–253, 257–258, 266–267, 272–273, 297–299, 445–446.

50. Namier, *England in the Age of the American Revolution*, 39; Michael R. Watts, *The Dissenters: From the Reformation to the French Revolution* (Oxford, 1978), 479–480. The attitudes of articulate, published dissenting leaders on the colonies after the start of hostilities are discussed in C. C. Bonwick, "English Dissenters and the American Revolution," in H. C. Allen and Roger Thompson, eds., *Contrast and Connection: Bicentennial Essays in Anglo-American History* (London, 1976), 88–112. Bonwick omits the Quakers, who, in any event, had little recourse to the self-publicizing activities of his "dissenters." See also Bernard Semmel, *The Methodist Revolution* (New York, 1973), 63–71; William T. Whitley, *A History of British Baptists* (London, 1923), 233–235, 238–239, 255–257.

51. Watts, *Dissenters*, 285. The membership lists of the Society were printed as appendixes to the annual commemoration sermon. The only merchants trading to North America noted in the lists for 1756 and 1766 were Thomas Harley (member

members were thus rather more likely than others to have private concerns in and correspondence with North America. Such private commercial links could facilitate noncommercial communication between coreligionists on both sides of the Atlantic.

The Society of Friends tended to have a higher proportion of merchants than other denominations and was probably the nonconformist group with the most continuous and intense links to America. The key central bodies for English Quakers were the London Yearly Meeting and the standing Meeting for Sufferings, which had a subcommittee for the American colonies. The latter included correspondents appointed to keep these London bodies in touch with Friends in different parts of the British Isles and the American colonies. A conspicuous, indeed a leading place among the correspondents was taken by prominent London merchants and others trading regularly to the colonies (see Table 5). In such cases, the Quakers' network of correspondence and the merchants' commercial networks substantially overlapped.[52]

The relations of the other nonconformist groups to America are more diffuse than those of the Quakers and harder to measure. Perhaps a good sample of them is to be found in the history of the missionary New England Company. Its membership was diverse geographically and socially and difficult to delineate exactly. Yet it is clear that merchants trading to America occupied a prominent place in its leadership in the eighteenth century, when it was an overwhelmingly nonconformist body. For many years a most prominent place in the company was occupied by the Ashurst family, merchants of London. Alderman Henry Ashurst (died 1680) was treasurer of the company (1659–1680); his son, Alderman Sir William Ashurst (died 1720), a director of the Bank of England, was also treasurer (1681–1696) and then became governor of the company (1696–1720), to be succeeded in turn as governor by his son Robert (1720–1726). Sir William Ashurst was particularly active as a merchant trading to Massachusetts and served the colony as agent.[53] A comparably prominent place in the company was after 1748

of Parliament), Stephen Theodore Janssen (member), John Thomlinson, Sr., John Thomlinson, Jr. (member), Chauncey Townsend (member), and Barlow Trecothick (member).

52. Many of these Quaker merchant-correspondents are discussed in Jacob M. Price, "The Great Quaker Business Families of Eighteenth-Century London: The Rise and Fall of a Sectarian Patriciate," in Richard S. Dunn and Mary Maples Dunn, eds., *The World of William Penn* (Philadelphia, 1986), 363–399. For a fuller discussion, see Anne Thomas Gary (afterwards Pannell), *The Political and Economic Relations of English and American Quakers, 1750–85* (D.Phil. thesis, Oxford, 1935).

53. William Kellaway, *The New England Company, 1649–1776: Missionary Society to the American Indians* (London, 1961), for both a general treatment of the society and for a list of its members and officers (in index). For Ashursts, see *ibid.*; J. R. Woodhead, *The Rulers of London, 1660–1689* . . . (London, 1965), 19; Bernard

Table 5. Prominent London Merchants and Others Serving as Correspondents with the North American Colonies for the Society of Friends, 1725–1775

Name	Occupation	Address	Colonies
Samuel Arnold	[merchant]	Gracechurch St.	South Carolina
Silvanus Bevan	apothecary	Lombard St.	New England
Timothy Bevan	apothecary	Lombard St.	New York
James Beesley	merchant	Paternoster Row	Maryland
John Bell	merchant	Lombard St.	North and South Carolina, Maryland
Elias Bland	merchant	Tower Hill	New England
John Bland	merchant	Lime St.	Virginia
James Collinson	mercer and merchant	Gracechurch St.	Maryland
Peter Collinson	mercer and merchant	Gracechurch St.	New York, Maryland
Philip Eliot	merchant	Bucklersbury	South Carolina
John Falconar	merchant	—	Maryland
Joseph Freame	goldsmith-banker	Lombard St.	North Carolina
John Gopsill	merchant	St. Saviours, Southwark	Maryland
Jacob Hagen	merchant	Mill St., Southwark	New York, Pennsylvania
John Hanbury	merchant	Tower St.	Virginia
Jeremiah Harman	merchant	St. Martin's Lane, Cannon St.	Maryland
John Hunt	merchant	Leadenhall St.	Pennsylvania, Maryland, Virginia, North Carolina
Thomas Hyam	merchant	Philpot Lane, Fenchurch St.	Virginia
John Midford	merchant	—	South Carolina
Daniel Mildred	merchant	Broad St. Buildings	New York, Pennsylvania
Richard Partridge	merchant	Water Lane, Tower St.	Pennsylvania, North and South Carolina
Thomas Plumstead	ironmonger	Gracechurch St.	Pennsylvania, New Jersey
John Roberts	merchant	Fenchurch St.	New England

Table 5 (*continued*)

Jonathan Scarth	merchant	Liberty of the Tower	Virginia
Peter Williams	warehouseman	Lombard St.	South Carolina

Source: Yearly Meeting Minutes, vols. VI–XIV, Friends House Library, London.

Note: The colonies shown are those for which each correspondent was responsible. He may have traded to other places as well. Where nonmerchants are shown, it is known or believed that they also traded abroad in merchant style. The list does not claim to be complete; only those readily identifiable have been included. Retailers and brewers in London have been excluded.

occupied by the Mauduit brothers and their firm Mauduit, Wright and Company. Jasper and Israel Mauduit, sons of a nonconformist minister, and Jasper's son-in-law, Thomas Wright, started as "warehousemen," or wholesalers, selling woolens to merchants exporting to America. They also had correspondents of their own in the colonies and in later years were described in the directories as merchants. Jasper (who died in 1772) was treasurer of the New England Company (1748–1765) and governor (1765–1772). Wright succeeded Jasper as treasurer (1765–1773), and Israel later became governor in 1787 just before his death.[54] On Jasper's death, his place as governor from 1772 to 1780 had been taken by William Bowden (died 1780), a director of the Bank of England and Virginia merchant. The leadership of the New England Company also had close links with the board of Deputies of the Protestant Dissenters, of which both Jasper Mauduit and William Bowden were chairmen, as was another member of the company, Nathaniel Polhill, a Southwark tobacco manufacturer and merchant and later banker.[55] There is no accessible information on all the callings of the ordinary members of the New England Company, but more than a dozen of them can be identified as merchants trading to the North American colo-

Bailyn, *The New England Merchants in the Seventeenth Century* (Cambridge, Mass., 1955), 183.

54. On the Mauduits and Wright, see Kellaway, *New England Company*, index; Price, ed., *Joshua Johnson's Letterbook*. Other examples of their dealings with the American trade can be found in the Norton cash-book, Virginia State Library, Richmond; and Robert Carter correspondence, Virginia Historical Society, Richmond.

55. Kellaway, *New England Company*, index. On Polhill, see Namier and Brooke, *House of Commons, 1754–1790*, III, 306; on Bowden, see W. Marston Acres, "Directors of the Bank of England," *Notes and Queries*, CLXXIX (1940), 116.

nies.[56] A smaller number of such American merchants can be identified as members of the Anglican Society for the Propagation of the Gospel in Foreign Parts, but I have found nothing to suggest that they were leaders in that clerically dominated society.[57]

Our evidence would therefore suggest a considerable overlap between the commercial networks linking the British and colonial economies and the less material networks linking at least dissenters in Britain and the thirteen colonies.

America and the British Nation

In the first part of this essay, we were concerned with the very limited experience of and interest in the American colonies among the ruling strata of Britain. In the second part we looked into the much greater concern with America among some limited sections of the population engaged in trade and manufactures. What about the British nation as a whole? This is a most difficult question. An assessment of the longer-term impact of the growing American colonies on Britain, circa 1700–1775, must include three important areas in which British society then was in varying degrees affected by the American connection: emigration, trade, and the military, civil, and fiscal burdens of empire.

Emigration

Between 1630 and 1700, it is estimated that 378,000 people left the British Isles (primarily England) for overseas. This was large enough to help cause a decline in total English population in the period 1650–1689. These high levels were interrupted during the wars of 1689–1713; and when emigration resumed in the next half-century, 1713–1763, it was to be at levels well below those of the seventeenth century. During this last span, emigration from England was partly balanced by immigration from Wales, Scotland, and Ireland, so that the net loss from emigration was not high enough to prevent the total population of England from rising along with that of Scotland and of Ireland.[58] This rise in population, associated with parallel

56. Trading to or connected with New England: Alexander Champion, John Lane, Thomas Lane; New York: Nathaniel Paice; Pennsylvania: Richard Neave; Virginia: Latham Arnold, Robert Bristow, Edward Hunt, Thomas Hunt, Sir Lyonel Lyde, bart., Nathaniel Polhill, Samuel Waterman. I am indebted to Mrs. Katherine Kellock for help on this point.

57. See n. 51, above.

58. Henry A. Gemery, "Emigration from the British Isles to the New World, 1630–1700: Inferences from Colonial Populations," *Research in Economic History*, V (1980), 179–231; Wrigley and Schofield, *Population History of England*, 185–187,

rises in other European countries, helps explain the higher prices for food and other agricultural products, which led gradually to higher rents throughout the British Isles. While larger and more efficient, progressive farmers could afford to pay these higher rents, tenants on very small holdings or on poorer lands could find the new rents more burdensome, particularly in parts of Ireland and Scotland where the new terms were part of a transition from customary (nonmarket) to market relationships.[59] The resulting difficulties are reported to have helped persuade some tenants to emigrate at a time when many artisans and others were pushed in the same direction by the higher cost of living. Between 1763 and 1775, emigration to North America took about 30,000 people from England, 40,000 from Scotland, and 55,000 from northern Ireland. Since the weight of the English emigration (less than 1 percent of the 1760 population) was much less than that of the Scottish and Irish (3 percent and 2.3 percent, respectively) and since emigrants were not evenly distributed among the population of any of the countries, the effects of the emigration would not have been uniformly felt. Abstractly, these departures should have reduced pressure on resources, thus improving real wages and reducing the upward trend of rents. But such tenuous benefits have left little trace in the records.[60] Instead, we find the complaints of landlords and employers at the loss of tenants and workers.

Trade and Manufactures

If British industry may have suffered a bit from the emigration of labor to America in the years immediately preceding the American Revolution, it benefited much more from the growth of population and markets in the thirteen colonies over the preceding century. As already noted, the seven- or eightfold expansion of English (later British) exports to those colonies be-

---

219–228; J. Potter, "The Growth of Population in America, 1700–1860," in D. V. Glass and D.E.C. Eversley, *Population in History: Essays in Historical Demography* (London, 1965), 642–646. Potter (p. 645) makes a rough guess of 350,000 for nonslave immigration to the United States, 1700–1790, from Europe as well as the British Isles. See also David W. Galenson, *White Servitude in Colonial America: An Economic Analysis* (Cambridge, 1981), 216–217. Gemery discusses the difficulties of estimating post-1700 American immigration in "European Emigration to North America, 1700–1820: Numbers and Quasi-Numbers," *Perspectives in American History*, n.s., I (1984), 283–342. For increases in Scottish and Irish population, see Mitchell and Deane, *Abstract of British Historical Statistics*, 5–6.

59. Jan de Vries, *The Economy of Europe in an Age of Crisis, 1600–1750* (Cambridge, 1976), 5; Deane and Cole, *British Economic Growth*, 91; J. D. Chambers and G. E. Mingay, *The Agricultural Revolution, 1750–1880* (New York, 1966), 109–112. On burden of rents, cf., for example, T. C. Smout, *A History of the Scottish People, 1560–1830* (New York, 1969), 340–351.

60. Bernard Bailyn, *Voyagers to the West: A Passage in the Peopling of America on the Eve of the Revolution* (New York, 1986), 24–66, esp. 26.

tween the periods 1699–1701 and 1772–1774 was based almost exclusively on the more than ninefold increase in the colonial population during the same decades. Since the increase in American population was greater than the increase in exports, there was a slight slippage in British exports per head of colonial population—caused most likely by the growth of some industries in the colonies. In Birmingham, at least, there was some uneasiness about possible dangers in the development of an American iron and steel industry. Most British merchants and manufacturers, however, were more than satisfied by North America's ever increasing importance as a major market for British manufactures down to the 1770s.

It can be argued that every landlord, farmer, manufacturing worker, and sailor benefited either directly or indirectly from the American market. However, in the world before Adam Smith, the benefits that were perceived tended to be only those that were direct and immediate. In this sense the benefits of the growing colonial market were not spread evenly over the British Isles. The most noticeable effects were to be perceived in the relatively few ports that dominated the American trades (particularly London, Glasgow, Liverpool, and Bristol). The shipbuilding trades did not benefit as much as might be expected, since the North American colonies themselves built about one-third of the vessels known to *Lloyd's Register* around 1770.[61] A much greater benefit was realized by the maritime supplies manufactures, which were relatively weak in the colonies: the making of sails, cable, cordage, and anchors. The industries that drew most orders and benefits from America tended to be concentrated in a few areas, particularly the West Riding of Yorkshire, South Lancashire / Cheshire, and Birmingham and the Black Country, though the luxury trades of London should not be forgotten (tailors, dressmakers, coachmakers, watchmakers).[62] We are familiar with all these places from the subscription lists to Wright's *American Negotiator*. But, even if we add in Nottingham, Norwich, and a few other places we have also met in Wright's lists and the petitions to Parliament, it remains evident that only very circumscribed areas of the country and occupational groups benefited much at first hand from the American connection.

61. Jacob M. Price, "A Note on the Value of Colonial Exports of Shipping," *Jour. Econ. Hist.*, XXXVI (1976), 704–724, esp. 713–716; Joseph A. Goldenberg, "An Analysis of Shipbuilding Sites in *Lloyd's Register* of 1776," *Mariner's Mirror*, LIX (1973), 419–436.

62. Though most types of English cloth undoubtedly found their way to North America, references to that from the West Riding are by far the most common in merchants' correspondence. In Ireland, the more limited benefits of the imperial connection were to a considerable degree concentrated in the linen manufacturing areas around Belfast and in the southern agricultural areas serving the Cork provisioning trade supplying victuals for both the West Indies plantations and vessels sailing to all distant overseas destinations.

However limited in number, the ports and inland towns that did benefit from American trade prospered substantially during the first three quarters of the eighteenth century. During those years, their population, like their trade, grew more rapidly than that of Britain as a whole. Their residents could see evidence of both: at Liverpool, for example, in the celebrated new docks and, with all the towns, in new residential and commercial streets, churches, and theaters. In the bustling ports of Glasgow, Liverpool, and Bristol, the North American, West Indian, and African merchants were the leaders of the public as well as of the commercial life of the towns, furnishing many of the mayors, provosts, town councillors, and other municipal dignitaries, not to mention a number of local members of Parliament.[63]

In the much greater world of London, where public finance, monopoly companies, and the older European trades were at least as important as the newer open American trades, the situation was more complex. Leaving aside the court, administrative, legal, and fashionable world of the West End and Westminster, we can detect within the City of London proper three distinct clusters of eminence: *municipal* (mayors, aldermen, and comparable officials), *national* (including directors of the great chartered companies, government contractors, members of Parliament for places outside the capital), and *unacknowledged* (those whose eminence lacked formal recognition). Retailers, it should be remembered, had to be freemen (citizens) in order to trade in London, but wholesalers and merchants did not. It is among the latter that we find most of our unacknowledged worthies.

Between the third quarter of the seventeenth and the third quarter of the eighteenth century, the businessman's City of London had in many respects continued its evolution from *Gemeinschaft* (community) to *Gesellschaft* (market society). In the former period, leading merchants were frequently as prominent in the communal life of the City as in its trade. By the latter this limited communitarianism was less evident, and we find in the directories a very noticeable population of foreigners, Catholics, Jews, Scotsmen, Irishmen, provincial English and Welsh, even Americans, who were for various reasons not "free of the City" but who still were important in its commercial life. Of probably the fifty richest men in the City in 1780, only 12 percent

63. For contemporary awareness of the importance of the American trades to the outports, see William Enfield, *An Essay towards the History of Liverpool* . . . , 2d ed. (London, 1774); John Gibson, *The History of Glasgow* . . . (Glasgow, 1777); Andrew Brown, *History of Glasgow* . . . , 2 vols. (Glasgow, 1795, 1797). See also T. M. Devine, *The Tobacco Lords: A Study of the Tobacco Merchants of Glasgow and Their Trading Activities, c. 1740–90* (Edinburgh, 1975); W. E. Minchinton, ed., *The Trade of Bristol in the Eighteenth Century*, Bristol Record Society's Publications, XX (Bristol, 1957); Minchinton, ed., *Politics and the Port of Bristol in the Eighteenth Century: The Petitions of the Society of Merchant Venturers, 1698–1803*, Bristol Record Society's Publications, XXIII (Bristol, 1963).

were municipal worthies and 34 percent national worthies while 54 percent belong to our category of unacknowledged eminence.[64]

This general pattern was repeated in the American trades. In the seventeenth century we find an impressive number of American traders among the aldermen and common councilmen of London, but they become much scarcer in those circles as the eighteenth century progresses, in part because firms in those trades become fewer and larger, in part because the municipal life of London becomes more inward-looking. Among the national worthies we find slightly more American traders, most noticeably among government contractors and on the boards of the London Assurance and the Bank of England. (Both had American traders as their governors circa 1750.)[65] But many of the leading American merchants on the eve of the Revolution were Quakers, Scots, or even Americans and were unlikely to attract formal recognition of any sort. (The election of William Lee as alderman was quite exceptional.) But those identities did not impede their business careers. Quaker merchants trading to America were founding partners before 1776 of the London predecessors of both Barclays and Lloyds banks. The Barclays entertained the royal family on official visits to the City, and those other great Quakers, John and Capel Hanbury, were known to and consulted by cabinet ministers.[66] Even so, American merchants did not loom as large in the great London of 1770 as did the tobacco lords in the smaller contemporary Glasgow, for in the capital they had to compete for luster with financiers and the grandees of the European and Asian trades.

Burdens of Empire

If the benefits of empire trade, no matter how large, were in fact enjoyed only by limited sections of the population, the same cannot be said of the costs of empire. At the beginning we noted that, unlike the Victorian empire of 1857–1914, the mercantilist Georgian empire through most of the eighteenth century involved the British taxpayer in no heavy peacetime administrative expenses. Yet there were heavy defense costs. The post-1689 British state was forged in the fires of war. Thus, in the peacetime year of 1737 almost 82 percent of central government expenditure went to defense and

64. PRO, T 47/8, Register of persons paying the tax on male servants, 1780. The 50 were those paying for 4 or more.

65. On continuity and inbreeding among London aldermanic families, see Nicholas Rogers, "Money, Land, and Lineage: The Big Bourgeoisie of Hanoverian London," *Social History*, IV (1979), 437–454. Cf. also Henry Horwitz, " 'The Mess of the Middle Class' Revisited: The Case of the Big Bourgeoisie of Augustan London," *Continuity and Change*, II (1987), 263–296. The governors were William Hunt, Bank of England; John Hyde II, London Assurance.

66. Cf. Price, "Great Quaker Business Families," in Dunn and Dunn, eds., *World of William Penn*, 363–399.

Table 6. British Government Expenditures, 1737, 1764

Expenditure	1737		1764	
Civil government	£ 930,000	(18.1%)	£ 1,137,000	(10.6%)
Defense				
Army	835,000		2,234,000	
Navy	933,000		2,150,000	
Ordnance	327,000		279,000	
Total	2,095,000	(40.8%)	4,663,000	(43.6%)
Debt charges	2,105,000	(41.0%)	4,887,000	(45.7%)
Total net expenditure	£5,129,000	(99.9%)	£10,686,000	(99.9%)

Source: B. R. Mitchell and Phyllis Deane, *Abstract of British Historical Statistics* (Cambridge, 1962), 390.

Note: All sums are rounded to the nearest thousand; deviations in totals are due to rounding in source.

debt charges, that is, the costs of past wars, going back to 1689 (Table 6). After the great conflicts of 1739–1763 total government expenditure almost doubled, with the share allotted to defense and debt charges rising to more than 89 percent in 1764.

This mounting volume of expenditure was of necessity balanced by a steadily mounting burden of taxation. Peter Mathias and Patrick O'Brien have punctured the comfortable myth that somehow constitutional Britain in the eighteenth century enjoyed levels of national taxation lower than those of arbitrary France. Their comparative work reveals that "on a per capita basis, in Britain taxes were more than double the level attained in France at the beginning of the century (1715–30), [and] remained at about twice the level of those in France for most of the rest of the period up to the Revolution." It is particularly noteworthy that the burden of taxation borne circa 1760–1775 was unprecedentedly high both per capita and as a percentage of national income—though much higher levels were to be reached later, particularly during the Napoleonic Wars.[67]

This mounting burden of taxation was a constant, if not always acknowledged, presence in British politics throughout the century. Through indirect taxes on beer, wine, gin, tobacco, tea, and such, the burden of taxation fell

67. Peter Mathias and Patrick O'Brien, "Taxation in Britain and France, 1715–1810: A Comparison of the Social and Economic Incidence of Taxes Collected for the Central Government," *Journal of European Economic History*, V (1976), 601–650, esp. 610–611; Mathias, "Taxation and Industrialization in Britain, 1700–1870," in Mathias, *The Transformation of England* (New York, 1979), 116–130. See also John Brewer, *The Sinews of Power: War, Money, and the English State, 1688–1783* (New York, 1989), esp. chap. 4.

upon the whole population, though the discretionary element in the consumption of such products made such taxes more acceptable to the puritanical streak in the British public mind. Direct taxes, particularly the land tax, were kept low in peacetime but allowed to rise in war, when they were felt as a particular burden by the landed classes. It was the irksomeness of this burden, when extended over many years, that helped create the political atmosphere and pressures that speeded the end of long wars in 1710–1713, 1760–1763, and 1780–1783. A significant, if not a major, part of the war expenditures of 1739–1763 was incurred on the American side of the Atlantic.[68] Whether expressed in debate or not, consciousness of fiscal burdens undoubtedly influenced the attitude toward the colonies of almost everyone in the British electorate, or political nation, who did not otherwise benefit from the American connection.

Those who did benefit, particularly businessmen, had, of course, a keener awareness of the importance and value of the American connection and of the need to maintain it. But how much could such persons influence what we now call the decision-making process? Such textbook tags as "commercial revolution," "industrial revolution," and "rise of the middle class" sometimes create the impression that the various middling classes had much more political weight than they in fact enjoyed through the greater part of the reigns of the four Georges. Commercial and industrial entrepreneurs and the like could not dictate policy. They could only try to influence decision making in one of four quite different ways: by participating in parliamentary politics, by negotiating or bargaining with those in authority, by quiet lobbying, and by open petitioning and related forms of legal public agitational activity.

Parliamentary Politics

The House of Commons after the Union with Scotland consisted of 558 members, including 405 burgesses representing English boroughs, 15 representing Scottish boroughs, and 12 sitting for Welsh boroughs, for a total borough representation of 432. Nevertheless, as is well known, most of the smaller boroughs had by the mid-eighteenth century fallen under the influence of individual borough patrons or the neighboring bigger landowners as a group, and they tended to elect as their members either local landed gentlemen or the friends, relations, and dependents of their patrons (including many of the noted army and navy officers). Businessmen in the smaller boroughs were seldom rich enough to bear the costs of campaigning and

68. Gwyn, "British Government Spending," *Jour. Imperial and Commonwealth Hist.*, VIII (1980), 74–84.

service in Parliament, though substantial merchants were more likely to be returned by larger boroughs and a few managed to buy their way in from particularly corrupt boroughs like Aylesbury. Even so, the number of merchants (including bankers and brewers) in the Commons was quite modest and was tending to decline through the first two-thirds of the eighteenth century. Thus the 73 merchants (and other businessmen) in Commons in the Parliament of 1715–1722 were reduced to only 51 in the Parliament of 1741–1747 but recovered to 64–68 in parliaments of 1754–1774. Most merchants in the Commons normally preferred to keep in the good graces of the government of the day, in part because they wanted to gain favors either for their constituencies or for themselves. (John Brooke reports that in the Parliament of 1754, 17 of them were government contractors, 27 in that of 1761, 14 in 1768, 14 in 1774, and 17 in 1780.) They were therefore very cautious and selective in choosing issues on which to take a conspicuous stand.[69]

Negotiating and Bargaining

If too few in numbers and too divided in interest to form a powerful battalion in the House of Commons, merchants and bankers as a class were not infrequently in a position to negotiate from strength with the government on particular issues. In wartime in particular the government most urgently needed to borrow money, to remit funds abroad, to purchase supplies, and to transport men and supplies overseas. For such services they, of necessity, had recourse to bankers, merchants, shipowners, and numerous specialists (from biscuit bakers to ropemakers to gunfounders). Under the pressure of war these people were usually in a position to obtain good terms for themselves. On large loans and refunding operations there could be important fringe benefits. Both the Bank of England and the South Sea Company were, for example, founded as part of such financial operations. To be sure, when charters came to be renewed, the government was often in a stronger position, particularly in peacetime, and could extract further loans and other services without necessarily making further concessions. However, even in wartime, there were limits to how much in the way of policy concessions even the biggest financiers could extract. The height of the hubris of the moneymen came in 1710, when a delegation of Bank of England directors led by Sir Gilbert Heathcote waited on Queen Anne and urged her not to dismiss Lord Treasurer Godolphin, lest the credit of the state suffer. The queen was polite, but Godolphin was dismissed a few weeks later. The

69. Sedgwick, *House of Commons, 1715–1754*, I, 155; Gerrit P. Judd IV, *Members of Parliament, 1734–1832* (New Haven, Conn., 1955), 89 (from Judd's "Net Total," I have deducted "Manufacturers and Nabobs" to get a category closer to Sedgwick's); Namier and Brooke, *House of Commons, 1754–1790*, I, 135–136.

directors had gone too far; their successors were to be more cautious. During the ministerial crisis of February 1746, the grands bourgeois did not take the initiative as in 1710, but some of the moneymen refused to commit themselves to continue their subscription to a pending government loan ("No Pelham, no money") and thus helped abort the formation of a Granville-Bath administration.[70]

Lobbying

A much more common way in which businessmen and others tried to influence policy was by rather deferential and quiet lobbying. This could be done in a more formal mode when members of Parliament, colonial agents, and individual merchants and other spokesmen for local corporations or interests appeared before the Board of Trade or the Treasury Board to argue the case of an interest or a policy.[71] Alternatively, such solicitation could take place in informal conversations with officers of state (particularly members of the Treasury Board or Board of Trade or secretaries of state) or lesser officials (undersecretaries of state or the secretaries and senior clerks at the Treasury or Board of Trade).[72] Such solicitation might even persuade the government to sponsor legislation desired by some local interest—such as the Walpolean measures permitting the exportation of Carolina rice to southern Europe or the importation of Iberian salt to New York.[73] Such successful solicitation, however, rarely involved fundamental government policy or important interests within Britain.

70. Sir Tresham Lever, *Godolphin: His Life and Times* (London, 1952), 238–240; Narcissus Luttrell, *A Brief Historical Relation of State Affairs . . .* (Oxford, 1857), VI, 594; Geoffrey Holmes, *British Politics in the Age of Anne* (London, 1967), 174; *Diary of the First Earl of Egmont (Viscount Percival)*, III, *1739–1747*, Manuscripts of the Earl of Egmont, Historical Manuscripts Commission (London, 1923), 315; earl of Ilchester [G.S.H. Fox-Strangways], *Henry Fox, First Lord Holland: His Family and Relations*, 2 vols. (London, 1920), I, 125; *Remarks on a Letter to Sir John Barnard . . .* (London, 1746), 11–12.

71. The printed minutes of the Board of Trade (to 1782) and the Treasury (to 1745) contain numerous examples of merchants' and colonial agents' appearing and speaking at meetings of those boards. For an example of how such a meeting was conducted, cf. Jacob M. Price, "Glasgow, the Tobacco Trade, and the Scottish Customs, 1707–1730: Some Commercial, Administrative, and Political Implications of the Union," *Scottish Historical Review*, LXIII (1984), 16–19.

72. It is more difficult to find records of these informal conversations. Some are referred to in the correspondence between Sir James Lowther, bart. (1673–1755), member of Parliament for Cumberland, and his agent at Whitehaven (Lonsdale Papers, Cumbria Record Office, The Castle, Carlisle), the correspondence between William Gooch, lieutenant governor of Virginia, and his brother (copies at Colonial Williamsburg Foundation, Williamsburg, Va.), and the printed correspondence of Benjamin Franklin and other colonials in London.

73. Cf. n. 8, above.

Public Agitation

When all else failed, special interests might be forced into the open and attempt by publishing, petitioning, letter writing, and other overt political activities to influence government policy at even the highest level. Such political noisemaking was likely to be successful, however, only when the interests involved were able to form alliances with other elements having the weight of numbers in the House of Commons. Some examples of this are well known. For the highest reasons of state policy Bolingbroke, when secretary of state, wished to conclude a commercial treaty with France in 1711–1713. He tried in negotiating the treaty to obtain commercial benefits for important sectoral interests in Britain, but failed conspicuously to protect the interests of the linen and silk manufactures or to obtain anything for the port interests trading to the sugar and tobacco colonies. He also failed to convince the great woolen interest (embracing landlords, graziers, manufacturers, and traders) that what they might gain from an enlarged French market would compensate them for what they were likely to lose from a diminished Portuguese market. The woolen, linen, and silk interests and the port-colonial interest allied themselves with the Whig minority in the Commons to defeat the commercial treaty in 1713.[74] Similarly, in 1733 the merchants, manufacturers, retailers, and other traders opposed to Walpole's excise scheme for the tobacco and wine revenues were able to persuade enough usual supporters of the government to abstain or join the opposition, to undermine Walpole's majority and persuade him to abandon his bill.[75] In both cases the numerical core of the opposition came from the continuing antiministerial element in the House of Commons—Whigs in 1713, Tories and antiministerial Whigs in 1733—but the relatively few extra votes that the commercial interests were able to influence enabled these parliamentary minorities to do what the merchants and their allies wanted them to do.

It is, therefore, not too difficult to deduce why the mercantile pro-American interest had such mixed results in the decade leading up to the American

74. For the part of the colonial trades in the history of the commercial treaty of Utrecht, see Price, *France and the Chesapeake*, I, 522–530; Geoffrey Holmes and Clyve Jones, "Trade, the Scots, and the Parliamentary Crisis of 1713," *Parliamentary History*, I (1982), 47–77, esp. 65; D. C. Coleman, "Politics and Economics in the Age of Anne: The Case of the Anglo-French Trade Treaty of 1713," in Coleman and A. H. John, eds., *Trade, Government, and Economics in Pre-Industrial England* (London, 1976), 187–213.

75. Paul Langford, *The Excise Crisis: Society and Politics in the Age of Walpole* (Oxford, 1975); Price, "The Excise Affair Revisited," in Baxter, ed., *England's Rise to Greatness*, 257–321.

Revolution.[76] In 1766, when allied with the big battalions of the Rockingham ministry, they were able to help persuade the same Parliament that had passed the Stamp Act to repeal it. But, in January–March 1775, when allied with the much weaker parliamentary opposition, they were unable to accomplish anything.

Matters that came before Parliament can, on reflection, be divided between the politics of regime and the politics of interest—local, sectoral, and special. Most of Parliament's time might be devoted to questions of interest, but statesmen (or would-be statesmen) could never forget the primacy of questions of regime on which compromise was almost impossible. Since most peacetime colonial questions that came before ministry and Parliament between 1660 and 1760 involved compromisable matters of interest, they did not stir disruptive passions. However, when the debates over the Stamp Act raised a fundamental question of regime—to wit, the authority of Parliament—metropolitan-colonial relations entered a more dangerous phase. The politics of interest did not disappear. As late as 1772 the land speculator interest could help manipulate the fall of Hillsborough. But, less than a year later, in drafting and defending the Tea Act of 1773, the ministers consciously rejected the possibility of compromise and intruded into the bill "political reasons . . . of such weight, and strength," that is, of regime, as would ultimately provoke armed resistance.[77] At this level of principle, the American interest within Britain was politically impotent.

To conclude, then, Who in Georgian Britain cared about the colonies? A lot of people did, though they were very unevenly distributed geographically and socially and quite diverse in their approach to American questions. In the political sphere the better-organized of these interests, particularly the port merchants and the exporting manufacturers, could influence the minutiae of legislation much more successfully than they could questions of regime or the main lines of government policy. To affect the latter they needed strong allies in the House of Commons. These they had in 1713, 1733, and 1766, but not in 1775, not even before the start of fighting, even less so afterwards.

76. For the political role of the merchants, cf. Jack M. Sosin, *Agents and Merchants: British Colonial Policy and the Origins of the American Revolution, 1763–1775* (Lincoln, Nebr., 1965); Alison G. Olson, "The London Mercantile Lobby and the Coming of the American Revolution," *Journal of American History*, LXIX (1982–1983), 21–41.

77. Cf. the exchange between Dowdeswell and North, in Benjamin Woods Labaree, *The Boston Tea Party* (Oxford, 1964), 70–73.

INDEX

NOTES ON CONTRIBUTORS

Bernard Bailyn is Adams University Professor at Harvard University and the author of *Voyagers to the West: A Passage in the Peopling of America on the Eve of the Revolution* and *The Peopling of British North America: An Introduction.*

J. M. Bumsted is Professor of History at St. John's College of the University of Manitoba and the author of *Land, Settlement, and Politics in Eighteenth-Century Prince Edward Island* and *The People's Clearance: Highland Emigration to British North America, 1770–1815.*

Nicholas Canny is Professor of Modern History at University College, Galway, and the author of *The Elizabethan Conquest of Ireland: A Pattern Established, 1565–1576* and *Kingdom and Colony: Ireland in the Atlantic World, 1560–1800.*

Michael Craton is Professor of History at the University of Waterloo (Ontario) and the author of *Testing the Chains: Resistance to Slavery in the British West Indies* and *Searching for the Invisible Man: Slaves and Plantation Life in Jamaica.*

Maldwyn Jones is Commonwealth Fund Professor of American History Emeritus at the University of London and author of *The Limits of Liberty: American History, 1607–1980* and *American Immigration.*

James H. Merrell is Associate Professor of History at Vassar College and the author of *The Indians' New World: Catawbas and Their Neighbors from European Contact through the Era of Removal* and coeditor (with Daniel K. Richter) of *Beyond the Covenant Chain: The Iroquois and Their Neighbors in Indian North America, 1600–1800.*

Philip D. Morgan is Associate Professor of History at Florida State University and coeditor (with Lois Green Carr and Jean B. Russo) of *Colonial Chesapeake Society.*

Jacob M. Price is Professor Emeritus of History at the University of Michigan and the author of *France and the Chesapeake: A History of the French Tobacco Monopoly, 1674–1791, and of Its Relationship to the British and American Tobacco Trades* and *Capital and Credit in British Overseas Trade: The View from the Chesapeake, 1700–1776.*

Eric Richards is Professor of History at the Flinders University of South Australia and the author of *A History of the Highland Clearances* and (with Monica Clough) *Cromartie: Highland Life, 1650–1914.*

A. G. Roeber is Associate Professor of History at the University of Illinois at Chicago and the author of *Faithful Magistrates and Republican Lawyers: Creators of Virginia Legal Culture, 1680–1810.*